PENGUIN BOOKS

WORDSWORTH: A LIFE

'Juliet Barker has written a detailed, rich and tactful biography of huge value and interest. She has delved deep [and] convinces on every page'
Philip Hensher, *Observer*

'Without doubt the most substantial biography of Wordsworth that has yet appeared . . . In terms of sheer scholarship, it is difficult to imagine it being surpassed' *The Times Literary Supplement*

'Uniquely readable, benefiting from the thoroughness of Barker's research . . . her accomplished, invigorating and accessible book marks an important stage in the recovery of Wordsworth' *Sunday Times*

'Extraordinarily dense and intense . . . Juliet Barker's scholarship is astounding . . . Immaculate' *Daily Telegraph*

'A long-overdue reappraisal of the poet, his life and his influence . . . Its research and scholarship is undeniable. So too is the clarity of Barker's writing which is full of warmth for her subject. She personalizes the man who, to many, is just a poet, no matter how great his reputation . . . After this work Wordsworth's memory and his life will no longer wander lonely' *Daily Post* (Wales)

'A minutely detailed account, told with a cool detachment and precision that announces scholarship and a loving care. No simplifying here. A book that brings Wordsworth and his poetry much closer to his readers' *Irish Independent*

ABOUT THE AUTHOR

Juliet Barker is internationally recognized for her ability to combine ground-breaking scholarly research with a highly readable and accessible style. Best known for her prizewinning and bestselling book *The Brontës* (1994), which was widely acclaimed as setting a new standard in literary biography, she is also author of *The Brontës: A Life in Letters*, *The Brontës: Selected Poems* and *Charlotte Brontë: Juvenilia 1829–35*, as well as two books on medieval tournaments, *The Tournament in England c. 1100–1400* and *Tournaments: Jousts, Chivalry and Pageant in the Middle Ages*. Born in Yorkshire, she was educated at Bradford Girls' Grammar School and St Anne's College, Oxford, where she obtained a doctorate in medieval history. From 1983 to 1989 she was the curator and librarian of the Brontë Parsonage Museum. She has, for many years, been a frequent contributor to national and international television and radio as a historian and literary biographer and has lectured as far afield as the United States and New Zealand. In 1999 she was one of the youngest-ever recipients of an Honorary Doctorate of Letters, awarded by the University of Bradford in recognition of her outstanding contribution to literary biography, and in 2001 she was elected a Fellow of the Royal Society of Literature. She is married, with two children, and lives in the South Pennines.

Wordsworth

A Life

JULIET BARKER

PENGUIN BOOKS

PENGUIN BOOKS

Published by the Penguin Group
Penguin Books Ltd, 80 Strand London WC2R 0RL, England
Penguin Putnam Inc., 375 Hudson Street, New York, New York 10014, USA
Penguin Books Australia Ltd, Ringwood, Victoria, Australia
Penguin Books Canada Ltd, 10 Alcorn Avenue, Toronto, Ontario, Canada M4V 3B2
Penguin Books India (P) Ltd, 11 Community Centre,
Panchsheel Park, New Delhi – 110 017, India
Penguin Books (NZ) Ltd, Cnr Rosedale and Airborne Roads,
Albany, Auckland, New Zealand
Penguin Books (South Africa) (Pty) Ltd, 24 Sturdee Avenue,
Rosebank 2196, South Africa

Penguin Books Ltd, Registered Offices: 80 Strand, London WC2R 0RL, England

First published by Viking 2000
This abridged edition published in Penguin Books 2001

1

This paperback edition abridged by Kati Nicholl

Set in Monotype Janson
Typeset by Rowland Phototypesetting Ltd,
Bury St Edmunds, Suffolk
Printed in England by Clays Ltd, St Ives plc

For my parents,
Richard and Judith Bateson,
with gratitude
for a lifetime's support and encouragement

Contents

Contents

List of Illustrations

Plate Sections

Chapter Head Illustrations

Illustration Acknowledgements

The author and publishers are grateful to the following for permission to reproduce illustrations:

Plate Sections

1, 41, John Garbutt; 2 from John Marsh & John Garbutt, *Wordsworth's Lakeland: Britain in Old Photographs* (Stroud, Sutton Publishing, 1997); 3, 25, John Marsh; 4, 7, 8, 9, 32, Abbot Hall Art Gallery, Kendal, Cumbria, UK/Bridgeman Art Library, London, London; 5, Cornell University Library, USA; 6, 10, 14, 15, 19, 20, 22, 24, 27, 31, 35, 38, 39, 40, The Wordsworth Trust, Grasmere; 11, 13, 26, 36, 37, National Portrait Gallery; 12, Dorset County Council; 16, Pierpont Morgan Library/Art Resource, NY; 17 from Martin, *In the Footprints of Charles Lamb, 1891*; 18, e.t. archive; 21, 30, from Frances Blanshard, *Portraits of Wordsworth* (London, George Allen & Unwin, 1959); 23, University of Bristol; 28, Master and Fellows of Trinity College, Cambridge; 29 from The Masquerier Album (HCR VIII) Trustees of Dr Williams's Library, London; 33, Trustees of Rydal Mount; 34 from *The Letters of William and Dorothy Wordsworth: The Later Years: Part IV, 1840–1853*, edited by Ernest de Selincourt, revised by Alan G. Hill (Oxford, Clarendon Press, 1988).

Chapter Heads

1, John Garbutt; 13, Trustees of Hawkshead Grammar School; 26, 410, St John's College, Cambridge; 52, 79, 101, 122, 191, 215, 256, 276, 293, 312, 349, 382, 396, 477, The Wordsworth Trust; 145, 446, Mary Evans Picture Library; 171, 332, National Portrait Gallery; 236, 463, Abbot Hall Art Gallery, Kendal, Cumbria, UK/Bridgeman Art Library; 367, Birmingham Museum and Art Gallery; 427, Paul Betz; 494, Trustees of Rydal Mount; 512, Cornell University, USA; 525, John Marsh.

Wordsworth Family Tree

*After his mother's death in 1792, Christopher Cookson adopted her family name of Crackanthorpe, which descended to his children.

William Cookson = Dorothy Crackanthorpe
1711–87 | 1719–92

John = **Ann** Christopher Crackanthorpe = Charlotte Cust Rev. William = Dorothy Cowper
1741–83 | 1747–78 [Crackanthorpe]* 1745–99 | 1756–1843 1754–1820 | b.1754

William   Sarah
1790–1888   1794–1845

Mary = Rev. J. Fisher Christopher   William   George   Anna   Elizabeth = Rev. Wᵐ
b. 1790 | 1788–1832 1791–1834 1792–1866 1793–1848 1796–1804 b. 1797   Fisher

Emmeline (Emmie)
1825–64

John   Rev. **Christopher** = Priscilla Lloyd
1772–1805 1774–1846 | 1781–1815

John   Charles   Chris
1805–39 1806–92 1807–85

Catherine   **Willy** = Fanny Graham
1808–12 1810–83 | 1820–88

Mary Louisa   William   Reginald   Gordon
1849–1926 1851 1852–1919 1860–1935

Charles   Edward
1839–1913 1841–5

John Hutchinson = Mary
1736–85   1744–83

William = Ann Cowper
1746–1809

John
1748–59

John (Jack) = (1) Jane Wilkinson
1768–1833   (2) Elizabeth Sleigh

Henry
1769–1839

Mary = William Wordsworth
1770–1859

see Wordsworth
Family Tree

Margaret
1772–96

Thomas = Mary Monkhouse*
1773–1849

Elizabeth
d. 1827

Jane
d. 1827

George [Sutton]†
b. 1801

Ann
d. 1883

Charles
b. 1805

Henry
1807–50

Lucy

William
d.1890

Thomas
1815–1903

Mary Monkhouse
1817–37

George
1818–76

Hutchinson/Monkhouse Family Tree

*Mary Monkhouse married her first cousin Thomas Hutchinson.
†On inheriting maternal family estates, George Hutchinson took the surname of Sutton.

John Monkhouse = Margaret Richardson
1713–96 | 1717–88

'Aunt' Elizabeth   Thomas   Henry   George = Mary Hall
1750–1828   1751–87   1754–81   1756–1802 | 1760–90

Isabella Addison = **John**   **Tom** = Jane Horrocks   Joe   **Mary***
1784–1807 1782–1866   1783–1825 d. 1834   1785–1822   1787–1858

Mary Elizabeth   George
1821–1900

Betsy   **Joanna**   William
1776–1832   1780–1843   1783–5

Sara   **George** = Margaret Roberts
1775–1835   1778–1864 | 1793–1869

2 sons
7 daus.

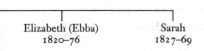

Elizabeth (Ebba)   Sarah
1820–76   1827–69

Wordsworth's
Lakeland

0   5   10 miles
0   5   10   15 km

Acknowledgements

Over the years it has taken to complete a work of this scale, I have naturally incurred many debts. I am especially grateful to Marcus Ackroyd, who trawled the French archives on my behalf, discovering new material on Annette Vallon and guiding me through the complexities of Revolutionary politics with quiet authority. Jeff Cowton of the Wordsworth Trust at Dove Cottage, Grasmere, was unfailingly helpful and cheerful, despite my taking up semi-permanent residence in the library; I could not have got through such a volume of material without his aid and that of his band of willing helpers. Les and Chris Johnson-Senior kindly provided me with a second home at How Foot, Grasmere, at much personal inconvenience to themselves. Peter and Marion Elkington, the curators of Rydal Mount, also went out of their way to make me feel welcome; through their kindness I have enjoyed the privilege of meeting many charming members of the Wordsworth family. Edward Cumming generously allowed me to read and quote from the unpublished manuscript of his book, *The Wreck of the English East Indiaman, Earl of Abergavenny, Weymouth Bay, 1805*, and gave me the benefit of his technical expertise. The munificence of Paul Betz, who volunteered material from his private collections, deserves especial mention and gratitude. John Taylor, of the Bridge Bookshop, Grasmere, was an invaluable, efficient and friendly supplier of books, old and new, on the Wordsworth circle, but without access to the resources of the Brotherton Library at the University of Leeds this book could not have been written.

I would like to thank all those who allowed me to follow the Wordsworth trail on to private land, or even into their own homes, among them Joyce Cracknell of Sockburn Home Farm, the Misses Gatheral of Sockburn Hall, the Hunt family of Allan Bank, Grasmere, and the Rev. Bob and Celia Wilkinson of the Rectory, Grasmere. I am also grateful to all those who answered my queries: in particular, Michael Ball, Head of the Department of Printed Books, National Army Museum; Barbara and the staff of the Cumbria Record Office, Carlisle; Dr Sidney Chapman, to whose exhibition at The Penrith Museum, Robinson's School, Penrith, I also owe much information about that town; Stewart Eastwood of the King's Own Border Regiment Museum, Carlisle; Chris Evans of Brompton-by-Sawdon; Elspeth Griffiths, Librarian of Sedbergh School; Michael J. Harrison of Gallows Hill, Brompton; Ken Reeves of the Kington Museum, Herefordshire; Michael Richardson, Librarian of the Special Collections at the University of Bristol; Roger Sims of the Manx Museum, Douglas, Isle of Man; John Spedding of Mirehouse, Keswick; Malcolm Underwood, Archivist, St John's College, Cambridge; John West of Hawkshead Grammar School, who also drew my attention to the previously unpublished drawing reproduced at the head of Chapter 2; Harvey Wilkinson of the Abbot Hall Art Gallery and Museum, Kendal; and Derrick Woolf, curator of

Coleridge's Cottage, Nether Stowey, Somerset, who kindly allowed me to visit out-of-hours.

Formal acknowledgement for permission to quote from manuscript material in their collections is due to the Archives Départementales of Loir-et-Cher, Blois; Archives Départementales of Loiret, Orléans; Archives Nationales, Paris; Carlisle Public Library, Cumbria; Cumbria Record Office, Carlisle; Dr Williams's Library, London; Pierpont Morgan Library, New York; Special Collections at the University of Bristol; Trustees of Hawkshead Grammar School, Cumbria; Trustees of Rydal Mount, Cumbria; Trustees of St John's College, Cambridge; West Yorkshire Archive Service at Calderdale, Halifax; Wordsworth Trust.

I have been fortunate in having the redoubtable Eleo Gordon as my editor. She and the team at Penguin have always been supportive and interested and I am truly grateful. Andrew Lownie has been an exemplary agent and I am indebted to him for his unstinting efforts on my behalf. Special thanks are also due to Stephen Gill, whose biography *William Wordsworth: A Life* (Oxford University Press, 1989) is a model of its kind; it first stirred my interest in the man and has been an unfailing source of reference ever since. Finally, I would like to thank all the long-suffering members of my family who have been forced to share their lives with the Wordsworths throughout the years this book has been in preparation. My brother, Tim Bateson, has repeatedly, if wearily, rescued me from the consequences of my own incompetence at word-processing. My husband, James, and children, Edward and Sophie, have all become reluctant experts, having given up their holidays and weekends to follow in the Wordsworths' (and Hutchinsons' and Monkhouses') footsteps. Though the children have complained unceasingly about this, we have all appreciated the excuse to acquire a more intimate knowledge of the Lakes. As my parents have not had this consolation, and yet have avidly read every chapter of this book as it was written, I think it only fair to dedicate *Wordsworth: A Life* to them.

1. *The Child is Father of the Man*

On a dark, stormy day in December 1783, a thirteen-year-old boy scrambled to the top of a rocky outcrop near the Lakeland village of Hawkshead. From this vantage point, half-sheltered by a dry-stone wall, and with only a sheep and a hawthorn tree for company, he sat on the damp grass, straining to see through the mist that intermittently shifted to reveal the woods and plain below. It was the eve of the Christmas holidays and William Wordsworth was waiting for the first sight of the horses that were coming to bring him home from school. Not knowing which of the two roads they might take and afraid to miss them, he stubbornly maintained his post through the storm, watching so intently that his eyes swam with tears at the effort. It was an experience he would never forget:

> . . . the wind and sleety rain
> And all the business of the elements,
> The single sheep, and the one blasted tree,
> And the bleak music of that old stone wall,
> The noise of wood and water, and the mist
> Which on the line of each of those two roads
> Advanced in such indisputable shapes –
>
> *Prelude (1799), i, 361–7*

The turmoil of the scene, so perfectly mirroring that of his own mind, the symbolism of the two roads and, most of all, the intensity of his longing to be home, would come back to haunt him. For the child waiting so anxiously was unaware that this would be the last time he would return to the home he was about to lose for ever. The whole course of his life was about to be changed and, with it, the history of English literature.

The Wordsworth family home lay in the small Cumberland market town of Cockermouth, some thirty miles away from Hawkshead. William Wilberforce, visiting the town in 1779, had dismissed it as 'consisting chiefly of one very large wide street.' A more favourably disposed visitor, William Hutchinson, declared 'the situation ... beautiful, in a country well cultivated, on the banks of two fine rivers'. He admired the picturesque ruins of the medieval castle on an eminence above the town and the 'pleasantly diversified' nature of the countryside. He wondered at the preference of the people of fortune for building their elegant houses on the short steep street leading up to the castle, but he had no hesitation in stating that 'the whole place bears the countenance of opulence'.

Standing not only at the confluence of the Derwent and Cocker rivers, but also on the main east-west route from Penrith to the prosperous ports of Workington and Whitehaven on the Atlantic coast, Cockermouth was ideally placed for the manufacture and distribution of goods. There were weekly markets and a fort-nightly cattle fair, held in the street which had attracted Wilberforce's attention. It was here, in the largest and most imposing house in the town, that the Wordsworth family lived. Set slightly back from the street, with a large garden running down to the Derwent at the rear, it was an elegant Georgian building, to all appearances the residence of a wealthy and influential gentleman.

Unfortunately for the Wordsworths, appearances were deceptive. The house, like Cockermouth itself, belonged to Sir James Lowther. Indeed, it might be said that the Wordsworths also belonged to him, for William's father, John, like his father and cousin before him, was law agent to Lowther. Their family fortunes had been, and were to be, dependent on the grace and favour of the Lowthers throughout William's lifetime and beyond. It was, therefore, doubly unfortunate for the Words-worths that this particular Lowther was notorious for his ruthlessness in the pursuit of power and riches. 'Wicked Jimmy', as he was known to his beleaguered tenants, had acquired a stranglehold on public appointments and local government in Westmorland and Cumberland and his officials, including the Members of Parlia-ment, were expected to put their master's interest before all others. Any show of independence met with dismissal and persecution.

On 5 February 1766, John Wordsworth married seventeen-year-old Ann Cookson, the only daughter of a wealthy Penrith mercer, and the newlyweds set off to begin their married life at Cockermouth. Like a dutiful wife, Ann applied herself to child-bearing and rearing. Her first son, Richard, arrived on 19 August 1768. He was followed by William, born on 7 April 1770 and Dorothy on Christmas Day, 1771, John, on 4 December 1772 and, finally, Christopher, on 9 June 1774.

William's memories of Cockermouth were uniformly happy ones. His family were together, the household, taking its tone from John Wordsworth, a cheerful one, and the children close enough in age to be natural playmates. Their favourite playground was the high terrace at the end of the garden, overlooking the fast-flowing waters of the Derwent. Only a low wall separated the two; covered with closely-clipped privet and roses, it made the perfect hiding place for birds, who built their nests in its most inaccessible depths. The river itself was a constant companion whose ceaseless music

> composed my thoughts
> To more than infant softness, giving me
> Among the fretful dwellings of mankind
> A knowledge, a dim earnest, of the calm
> Which nature breathes among the fields and groves.
>
> *Prelude (1799), i, 11–15*

At four years old, William would make 'one long bathing of a summer's day', alternately basking in the sun and plunging into the silent pools beneath the castle;

> or, when crag and hill,
> The woods, and distant Skiddaw's lofty height,
> Were bronzed with a deep radiance, stood alone
> Beneath the sky as if I had been born
> On Indian plains and from my mother's hut
> Had run abroad in wantonness to sport,
> A naked savage in the thunder-shower.
>
> *Prelude (1805), i, 294–300*

The banks of this 'fairest of all rivers' were an endless source of delight and, sixty years later, William could still vividly recall his boyish pleasure in collecting pebbles and gathering the wild flowers that grew there. There were also, of course, the more robust pleasures of boyhood: running races with his brothers, fishing, birds' nesting, exploring the hills, valleys and length of the river.

This was in marked contrast to Penrith, where Ann Wordsworth and her children spent much of this period. The Cookson household was nothing like the happy home at Cockermouth. The Cookson grandparents were elderly and their sons, Christopher and William, were already twenty-eight and nineteen. Both sons were unmarried.

According to the young Wordsworths, the atmosphere was one of relentless disapproval. There was certainly no condoning of the sort of carefree roaming about the countryside that characterized the Wordsworth home at Cockermouth: punishment for misdemeanours was swift and hard and there appears to have been much preaching about the perils of sin. One of William's earliest memories, as a child of four, was of lying awake at night, quaking under the bedclothes, 'in sharp conflict of spirit' at the idea that a good God permitted evil in His world. Not, one would have thought, a subject which would have naturally occurred to a four year old.

A spirited, adventurous boy, William's instinctive response was to rebel, thus incurring punishment which only made him more defiant. This led to a frightening escapade. Not yet six years old, William was learning to ride and, in company with his grandfather's servant James, made his way up the Beacon, the massive hill behind Penrith. Beacon Hill was then a bleak and treeless common, pock-marked with dozens of small, unfenced stone quarries.

The young Wordsworths had all suffered at the hands of the Cookson servants, who treated them with an insolence bordering on contempt. James was the worst offender and loathed by his young charges. William took the first opportunity to escape from his tormentor but bravado soon gave way to panic as he realized that he was lost. Afraid to ride on alone, he dismounted and, leading his horse, wandered into one of the quarries, only to realize that he had stumbled across the site of a notorious murder. The spot, marked by a stone carved with the murdered man's initials, was made even more ghastly by the knowledge that it was also the site of the gallows on which the murderer himself had been hung. To the terrified child, the long green ridge of turf appeared like a grave. He turned and ran. Regaining the summit, the first thing he saw was the strange juxtaposition of the beacon, a pool of water and a girl with a pitcher of water on her head struggling to walk against the wind.

> It was in truth
> An ordinary sight, but I should need
> Colours and words that are unknown to man
> To paint the visionary dreariness
> Which, while I looked all round for my lost guide,
> Did at that time invest the naked pool,
> The beacon on the lonely eminence,
> The woman and her garments vexed and tossed
> By the strong wind.
>
> *Prelude (1799), i, 319–27*

It was one of those recurring moments, a Wordsworthian 'spot of time', arising out of deep emotions, and fixed for ever in memory by the natural scene in which they had occurred.

William's mother was obviously troubled by her rebellious son, telling an intimate friend (but not William himself), that he was the only one of her five children about whose future life she was anxious: he would be remarkable, she pronounced, for either good or evil. 'The cause of this was, that I was of a stiff, moody, and violent temper; so much so that I remember going once into the attics of my grandfather's house at Penrith, upon some indignity having been put upon me, with an intention of destroying myself with one of the foils which I knew was kept there. I took the foil in hand, but my heart failed.'

William and his siblings may not have enjoyed staying with their grandparents, but Penrith itself had much to offer them. It was considerably larger than Cockermouth, with some 4,000 inhabitants. The visible symbol of the town's wealth was St Andrew's, a massive building of almost cathedral-like proportions. Within the quiet precincts of this church was the Dame School, attended by the Wordsworths and their friends, the Hutchinsons, one of whom, Mary, was to be William's future wife. Housed in a higgledy-piggledy sixteenth-century building, the school was run by an elderly lady, Ann Birkhead, 'a remarkable personage', who had taught three generations of the upper classes of Penrith. 'Tho' no bad teacher,' she 'was indifferent to method.' One of her most eccentric 'methods' was to allow her young pupils, the oldest of whom were only eight years old, to use Joseph Addison's periodical, *The Spectator,* as a reading book. Rather more endearingly, she was a passionate follower of all the old local customs. May Day in particular was a high festival. The children gathered flowers from all the gardens and wove them into garlands; the girls were required to bring their dolls in on May morning and seat them amidst the garlands, which were then hung from the school windows.

It was also customary to go out on Saints' days into the fields around Penrith to garland the springs and drink their waters. This practice, one can well imagine, would appeal to the young Wordsworth children. Certainly, as they grew older, they were more adventurous in exploring the neighbourhood. Brougham Castle, a vast medieval stronghold, was barely a stone's throw from the town. Only a few miles away across the hills were the strange legacies of an older world: megaliths and stone circles, such as Long Meg and her Daughters at Little Salkeld. Slightly further, but still only a pleasant day's excursion from Penrith, were the romantic riverside walks, literally blasted out of the rocks in the grounds of his house, The Nunnery, by Christopher Aglionby. And, of course, dominating all, was Penrith Beacon, from which the blue-black mountains of the Lakes could be seen.

The same mountains could also be seen from Cockermouth, and William would later say that he owed much to his birthplace and its neighbourhood. 'They did not a little in making whatever of a Poet I may be.'

Equally important was the influence of his sister, Dorothy. Only eighteen months younger than William, she shared his sensitivity to nature and his passionate love for it. What she had uniquely, however, was a sensibility so remarkable that it became a byword in the family. Though Dorothy would join in her brothers' play, she was always happier observing than being actively involved. She would chase butterflies, but drew the line at capturing them, or, as they did, killing the white ones 'because they were Frenchmen'.

> A very hunter did I rush
> Upon the prey: – with leaps and springs
> I followed on from brake to bush;
> But she, God love her! feared to brush
> The dust from off its wings.
> *To a Butterfly, ll.14–18*

Similarly, though Dorothy would accompany William to the low terrace wall at the bottom of their garden to see the sparrow's nest, with its clutch of bright blue eggs, she would look, but not touch.

> She looked at it and seemed to fear it;
> Dreading, though wishing, to be near it:
> Such heart was in her, being then
> A little Prattler among men.

It says something of William's own sensitivity that, even as a boy, he recognized and respected this quality in his sister. As a man, he came to realize that she had fundamentally changed his view of the world.

> She gave me eyes, she gave me ears;
> And humble cares, and delicate fears;
> A heart, the fountain of sweet tears;
> And love, and thought, and joy.
> *The Sparrow's Nest, ll.11–14, 17–20*

Had they remained together, the course of both their lives might have been very different. At the very least, Dorothy's love for her brother might never have acquired the somewhat desperate quality of their later years.

A parting was at hand, however. Ann Wordsworth had consumption and she died at Penrith, aged only thirty, on 8 March 1778. Her eldest child was nine, the youngest only three; William himself was not quite eight years old. Extraordinary as it may seem, Ann's final resting-place was never marked by any sort of memorial and, though clearly much-loved, she remains a shadowy figure. 'Blessed be her memory!' Dorothy would write, adding the more prosaic, but equally unenlightening, 'From her I know I received much good that I can trace back to her.' William was a little more forthcoming, describing her as his

> . . . honoured mother, she who was the heart
> And hinge of all our learnings and our loves;

He prefaced his eulogy with a curious comment: he had no wish to disturb the sanctity of her memory 'With any thought that looks at others' blame'. In the light of what follows, it is clear he was thinking of his Cookson grandparents and comparing them unfavourably to his mother. Her chief virtue was a serene faith that God would provide and that her children, left to His care and the natural instincts of innocent childhood, would grow in wisdom and strength.

> This was her creed, and therefore she was pure
> From feverish dread of error and mishap
> And evil (overweeningly so called)
> Was not puffed up by false unnatural hopes,
> Nor selfish with unnecessary cares,
> Nor with impatience from the season asked
> More than its timely produce – rather loved

The hours for what they are, than from regard
Glanced on their promises in restless pride.
Such was she; not from faculties more strong
Than others have, but from the times perhaps
And spot in which she lived, and through a grace
Of modest meekness, simple-mindedness,
A heart that found benignity and hope,
Being itself benign.

Prelude (1805), v, 257–90

The unspoken implication of this passage was that his grandparents were all the things his mother was not.

Ann's death placed John Wordsworth in a difficult position. What was he to do with his five motherless children? Not only was he a very busy man, but also he was often absent from home overnight and the Cooksons probably made it clear that they did not want any responsibility or additional trouble. So John did the only thing he could: he did his best and muddled through. Richard and William would return with him to Cockermouth, where they were already attending the local grammar school. John, aged five, and Christopher, aged three, are more likely to have remained at Penrith, where they were old enough to attend Ann Birkhead's Dame School, though too young for Cockermouth Grammar. Dorothy, only six years old, could not remain in a house full of males, so it was decided that she would go to live with her mother's cousin, Elizabeth Threlkeld, in Halifax, over seventy miles away. Having just lost her mother, she was now to lose her father and brothers as well. Ever after, she would regard the two events as the single great catastrophe of her life.

However cruel the decision may have seemed at the time, even Dorothy soon came to realize that she could not have found a better home. Elizabeth was already responsible for her five orphaned nieces and nephews and no greater tribute to her could be paid than Dorothy's simple statement: 'the loss of a Mother can only be made up by such a friend as my Dear Aunt'. 'Aunt' Threlkeld favoured a relaxed and loving regime for her adopted family. The family had many friends and a wide circle of acquaintance in Halifax, into which Dorothy was quickly absorbed and the friendships she made at this period would last for life.

While Dorothy settled into a new life in Halifax, her brothers remained at home in Cockermouth. In an effort to make them more comfortable, their father had taken on two new servants, Betty, and Sally Lowthian. Sally, who became nurse to the younger boys, was devoted to her charges and long afterwards William made it a point of honour to call upon her when visiting Cockermouth. He was not to enjoy her full-time attentions for long because he was about to be sent away to school.

Hawkshead Grammar School was a charitable foundation. Under its aptly-named master, James Peake, it was at the height of its reputation. There were over ninety pupils, a high proportion of whom went on to secure places at Cambridge. This was partly due to the excellence of the teaching in mathematics and partly to a seventeenth-century patron who had left £250 to St John's College to fund closed scholarships available only to boys from Hawkshead and Kendal Grammar Schools.

Richard and William went to Hawkshead in May 1779, a few weeks after William's ninth birthday. Most of the boys boarded with the master, but the Wordsworths were to lodge privately with the Tysons, a childless couple in their sixties. Hugh was a master joiner; his wife, Ann, had kept a small grocery and draper's shop for twenty years before taking in boarders. They lived in the centre of the village in a squat, low and angular cottage tucked away down a narrow alley. It might have been expected that William would be appalled at his new home: he was not; he revelled in it. A tiny artisan's cottage it might be, but it represented freedom from constraint and, in the motherly figure of Ann Tyson, emotional refuge. She allowed them the freedom to roam wherever and whenever they liked outside school hours and it was a freedom that William was to use to the full.

Hawkshead lies in the Vale of Esthwaite in the heart of the beautiful scenery which drives a wedge from the south of the Lakes into the centre of the mountains. Tucked away, high up in the hills between the great lakes of Windermere and Coniston, it has a hidden, secret, quality about it which even the ravages of tourism have been unable to destroy. After a steep climb up from the ferry at Bowness-on-Windermere (which operated even in William's day), and over the lip of the hill, the vale is unexpected, a pastoral bowl set among wooded hillsides. The valley is tiny but open and almost filled with Esthwaite Water. Lacking a mountain setting to reflect, it is not the prettiest of the lakes, but the bays and little peninsulas of its western banks give it a peculiar charm. At its northern end is Hawkshead.

Little cottages and inns jostle for elbow room in the alleyways and tiny court-yards, entered under archways leading off Market Square and the main street. In the struggle for extra room and light, some houses have a gallery along the upper storey. The whole village is built of the distinctive blue-grey Lakeland stone, much of which has been whitewashed. Dominating all is the low, squat church which perches on top of the churchyard's high grassy knoll in the centre. From this vantage point, the Vale of Esthwaite can be seen in its entirety and, on a rare clear day, the range of grey, green and russet mountains looming in the distance, so vast and alien to the immediate landscape that they appear unreal.

Just inside the churchyard, at the foot of the hill, stands Hawkshead Grammar School, a small, two-storey building, little more than a cottage. It must have been crammed to the rafters with almost a hundred pupils. In the Wordsworths' day there was a single large rectangular schoolroom. At one end, on a dais and next to the huge fireplace, stood the master's desk; at the other, and as far away from the warmth of the fire as it was possible to get, was the desk of the usher, his humble assistant. The boys sat on benches between them and along the walls, their desks a single simple ledge with a rest for pencils and books at the bottom end and a hole for an inkwell at the top. 'W. WORDSWORTH' is neatly inscribed into the wood of the desk nearest the door, where, for five years, he shared the hard bench with his friend, John Spedding. Outside was the little schoolyard, its grass worn down by the feet of the schoolboys as they ran about or played with quoits, marbles and balls. A corner was designated, in schoolboy parlance, 'the pissing corner'.

Between 25 March and 29 September, the school day began between 6 and 6.30 a.m. and ended at 5 p.m., with a break from 11 a.m. till 1 p.m.; in winter it began an hour later and ended an hour earlier, with a break from 11 a.m. till 12.30 p.m.

Clever and interested, William made an apt pupil. He was also very happy, 'chiefly because I was left at liberty, then and in the vacations, to read whatever books I liked.' He had a passion for fairy tales, his particular favourites being tales of Jack the Giant-killer, Robin Hood and St George, though he quickly progressed to more adult adventure fiction, such as *Don Quixote* and *Gil Blas*, and the novels of Fielding and Swift. He also adored *The Arabian Nights*. William remained a stout defender of such reading all his life; it might not be 'improving literature' of the type favoured by moralists, but it fostered the imagination.

> The child whose love is here, at least does reap
> One precious gain — that he forgets himself.
> *Prelude (1805), v, 368–9*

Unusually, for a boy of his age, William was equally drawn to more mundane stories about the everyday lives of the ordinary people around him and Ann Tyson had a fund of such tales. Born and brought up in Hawkshead, she knew everything about everyone there. She had also been in domestic service with the family of George Knott, who had a house in Scotland at Bunawe, on Loch Etive, where Ann would accompany them on visits. Visiting the area in 1803, William and Dorothy found themselves 'among familiar fireside names', the places of which Ann Tyson 'used to tell tales half as long as an ancient romance.' One such dramatic tale, that of a Lakeland shepherd and his son searching the mountains above Brothers Water for a lost sheep, is retold in *The Prelude* and credited to Ann, 'my household dame'.

In itself it was nothing: father and son search fruitlessly for sheep; son remembers sheep usually return to the place where they had grazed as lambs; son finds sheep but is stranded on rock in middle of brook; father rescues son. It was in the telling that it found its resonances and clearly, as William pauses in the midst of the story to repeat Ann's words verbatim, she had a poetic grasp of language which could hold her boyish audience spell-bound. Significantly, too, this passage is also the one which interrupts the action to relate the local tradition.

> 'For take note',
> Said here my grey-haired dame, 'that though the storm
> Drive one of these poor creatures miles and miles,
> If he can crawl he will return again
> To his own hills, the spots where when a lamb
> He learnt to pasture at his mother's side.'
> *Prelude (1805), viii, 253–8*

Such tales were to be the raw material of the later poet; as a boy, listening entranced by Ann Tyson's fireside, they wove a magic as potent as that of *The Arabian Nights*.

As William grew older, he grew more adventurous, ranging further afield in his expeditions. There were plenty of schoolfriends to encourage him, most from a similar background to the young Wordsworths. They were the sons of professional men or small landowners and were intended for the law, the Church, the army, the navy or the East India Company. Whatever the origins of his schoolfriends, and however rosy the tinted spectacles with which he looked back, William was always at pains to point out that they were all ordinary schoolboys, 'a noisy crew' and

> A race of real children, not too wise,
> Too learned, or too good, but wanton, fresh,
> And bandied up and down by love and hate;
> Fierce, moody, patient, venturous, modest, shy,
> Mad at their sports like withered leaves in winds;
>
> *Prelude (1805), v, 436–40*

All the Hawkshead schoolboys were 'impassioned nutters', gathering the hazel-nuts which grew in such profusion in the coppices along Esthwaite Water. The lake itself was one of the few which was home to trout, so fishing was a popular pursuit – and a good way of supplementing the 'frugal, Sabine fair' of Ann Tyson's dinner table. When they were not wreaking havoc on the fish population, the boys were after fowl. In the spring, they plundered birds' nests, challenging each other to dare the dangerous climb down the crags. William felt that stealing eggs was a mean and inglorious thing to do, but he could not resist the thrill of the climb and the sheer exultation of success against the odds.

> Oh! when I have hung
> Above the raven's nest, by knots of grass
> And half-inch fissures in the slippery rock
> But ill sustained, and almost (so it seemed)
> Suspended by the blast that blew amain,
> Shouldering the naked crag, oh, at that time
> While on the perilous ridge I hung alone,
> With what strange utterance did the loud dry wind
> Blow through my ear! the sky seemed not a sky
> Of earth – and with what motion moved the clouds!
>
> *Prelude (1850), i, 330–39*

In the autumn, when the frosts came, it was the turn of the woodcock, and William would spend half the night ranging over the fells alone to set his traps.

Best of all, when winter came and the shallower lakes froze over, there was ice-skating, a sport at which William excelled and which remained a lifelong passion. As an old man, he was observed skating on White Moss Tarn, at Grasmere, one hand tucked into his shirt front, the other into his waist band; his foot caught on a stone and he fell with a crash that starred the ice. Despite the assault on his dignity, he had the good grace to accept the accident cheerfully, merely sitting up and remarking to a watching child, 'Eh boy, that was a bad fall, wasn't it?'

The schoolboy William and his friends would chase each other across the ice, pretending to be huntsmen after the fox or hare, and hallooing so loudly that 'the precipices rang aloud'. Sometimes he would retire from the throng to pursue the reflection of a star, gleaming on the ice before him, and, at others, for the sheer giddy physical excitement of it, he would give himself up to the wind and race round and round the frozen lake till the whole world was spinning, then bring himself up short:

> yet still the solitary cliffs
> Wheeled by me – even as if the earth had rolled
> With visible motion her diurnal round!
>
> *Prelude (1805), i, 484–6*

On the rare evenings when it was raining too hard or the frost was too keen for the boys to go out, they would gather round Ann Tyson's cottage fire and while away the hours by playing loo or whist.

What makes William's memories of his Hawkshead schooldays, as recounted in *The Prelude*, so extraordinary and compelling is not just the simple beauty of the poetry but also the contrast between the frenzy of youthful activity and the silent stillness of the setting. Whether scurrying between his snares or playing noisy fireside games of cards, yet still hearing the echoes of splitting ice falling into the lake outside, the natural world impinged upon him.

> I held unconscious intercourse with beauty
> Old as creation, drinking in a pure
> Organic pleasure from the silver wreaths
> Of curling mist, or from the level plain
> Of waters coloured by impending clouds.
>
> *Prelude (1850), i, 562–6*

Often these experiences would be almost revelatory, coming at moments when he was entirely self-absorbed. This is captured to perfection in *There was a boy*, a poem describing how he had loved to stand on the lake shore at dawn or dusk and blow 'mimic hootings to the silent owls' through his cupped hands.

> And they would shout
> Across the watery vale, and shout again,
> Responsive to his call, – with quivering peals

And long halloos, and screams, and echoes loud
Redoubled and redoubled; concourse wild
Of jocund din! And, when there came a pause
Of silence such as baffled his best skill:
Then, sometimes, in that silence, while he hung
Listening, a gentle shock of mild surprise
Has carried far into his heart the voice
Of mountain-torrents; or the visible scene
Would enter unawares into his mind
With all its solemn imagery, its rocks,
Its woods, and that uncertain heaven received
Into the bosom of the steady lake.

This 'shock of mild surprise' as William describes it, arose from his suddenly becoming aware of his surroundings. 'I was often unable to think of external things as having external existence', he would later explain of this period in his life, '& I communed with all that I saw as something not apart from but inherent in my own immaterial nature. Many times while going to school have I grasped at a wall or tree to recall myself from this abyss of idealism to the reality.'

He also struggled with the concept of death. 'Nothing was more difficult for me in childhood than to admit the notion of death as a state applicable to my own being ... but it was not so much from animal vivacity that my difficulty came as from a sense of the indomitableness of the spirit within me.' He was about to learn, from bitter experience, that indomitableness of spirit was not enough to ward off death.

On 6 October 1783, William's father rode from Cockermouth to Haverigg to conduct inquests on two bodies which had been washed ashore on the coast. After completing the inquests, John set off home and, in threading the mountain tracks over Cold Fell, lost his way. He spent the whole night wandering on the mountains, exposed to the wind and rain.

The outcome was predictable. At Hawkshead, the end of term was approaching and William was in an agony of anticipation. Unable to wait at his lodgings, he ran out across the fields to the vantage point from which he could catch the first glimpse of the horses coming to take him and his brothers home. He probably already knew that his father was seriously ill; by the time the boys reached Cockermouth, John Wordsworth was on his deathbed. Ten days later, on 30 December 1783, only a month after his forty-second birthday, he died. Richard, William and John followed his coffin through the wind and snow to the churchyard at Cockermouth and, numb with cold and grief, stood by the side of his grave whilst he was buried. The next day, they left their beloved birthplace and were taken to their new home, their grandparents' house at Penrith.

2. A Poor, Devoted Crew

John Wordsworth's death left his children destitute. They had no parents, no home and, because he left no will (which seems remarkably careless for a lawyer), no money.

The children's two uncles, Richard Wordsworth of Whitehaven, and Christopher Crackanthorpe Cookson, obtained Letters of Administration which allowed them to administer John's estate for the benefit of his children. This was no light undertaking – many of John's clients took advantage to avoid paying for the work he had done on their behalf. By far and away the biggest single debt, just over £4,625 (the equivalent of £250,000 today), was owed by Sir James Lowther who used every means to avoid payment. The litigation would drag on for decades and the young Wordsworths were forced into a state of dependence on, and indebtedness to, their relatives.

By 5 May 1784 the fine house in Cockermouth had been stripped and its contents put up for auction, raising £260, in addition to the £40 made by selling John's gold watch, rings, silver coffee pot, wines and, oddly in this context, his cow. The key to the house was formally returned to Sir James's agent on 24 May. Ironically, this was the same day that Sir James was rewarded for giving William Pitt his first seat in Parliament by being created Earl of Lonsdale.

There was a steady trickle of receipts from various debtors. Additionally, there were the rents and income from John's properties, including his Sockbridge estate, giving enough to provide for the children's immediate needs and a small nest-egg to start them up in their future careers. Payment of the Lowther debt meant the difference between being obliged to work for a living and gentlemanly independence – but what no one could foresee was that the cost of pursuing the Lowther debt would totally unbalance the equation.

Much has been made of the fact that the Wordsworths supposedly ended up in debt to their guardians. When final accounts were drawn up, in 1812–13, Uncle Richard was indeed owed over £400, most of it for William's education. At the same time, Uncle Christopher Cookson actually owed almost £1,000 to his nephews and niece, which he had borrowed from their father's estate. From the very beginning, the guardians did very nicely out of their responsibilities. Every expense, no matter how small, from washing the children's clothes to the provision of schoolbooks, was duly noted and paid back from the estate. This was quite right and proper. But there were payments which seem at least questionable, such as the several sums, including one of over seventy-one pounds 'towards housekeeping', advanced to Uncle Christopher. Most dubious of all was the £930 lent in 1787 to Uncle Richard's son, Richard Wordsworth of Branthwaite, the lawyer who actually administered the estate. The interest was only paid once and, ultimately, the loan was set off against Richard's expenses in pursuing the Lowther debt, so the capital was never repaid either. The Richard Wordsworths also acquired the contents of John's library. This was only discovered when Dorothy made enquiries about her father's family Bible and it was found in Cousin Richard's collection.

In December 1785 Richard Wordsworth left school to take up residence and articles with Cousin Richard Wordsworth of Branthwaite. As the eldest son, he had probably always been intended for the legal profession and, at seventeen, he was chosen by his guardians to take up the responsibility of pursuing the Lowther debt. It was a struggle that would last almost as long as his entire legal career.

Having successfully launched Richard, his guardians now turned their attention to William. As a second son, he had a number of options, the most obvious being the Church. To become a clergyman, William would have to go to University so it was absolutely vital that he win one of the free scholarships attached to Hawkshead Grammar School. Whatever William's opinion of the Church as a career (and having no vocation was not a bar to success), going to University would allow him to put off the awkward moment when he would have to make choices.

The Reverend James Peake had resigned as master in June 1781. For little more than a year his place was filled by twenty-three-year-old Edward Christian who would later become the Wordsworths' advocate in the Lowther suit, though he is better known to posterity as the older brother of Fletcher Christian, of *Mutiny on the Bounty* fame. Christian was succeeded by the Reverend William Taylor, who would have a profound influence in forming and developing William's tastes and became the 'honoured teacher of my youth'. Taylor taught the usual curriculum of Latin, Greek and Arithmetic, but he had a passion for English literature and, in particular, poetry. His favourites were from what is known as the 'graveyard school', immensely popular eighteenth-century poets, such as Gray, Chatterton, Collins, Beattie, Young and Thomson, whose work was driven by an affectation of melancholy and musings on the grave.

William would later call Chatterton 'the marvellous Boy, The sleepless Soul that perished in his pride', and he retained a fondness for Collins and Thomson.

Gray, however, went down in his estimation more than any of the poets he admired
in his youth. 'He wrote English Verses, as he and other Eton school-boys wrote
Latin', was William's scathing comment in 1816, 'filching a phrase now from one
author, and now from another.' This was a mature judgement from an established
and confident poet – the impressionable schoolboy, having lost both his parents,
was naturally inclined to identify with the morbid preoccupations of Taylor's
favourite poets. He also saw nothing wrong in doing exactly as Gray had done, his
earliest efforts at poetry being highly self-conscious imitations of, and borrowings
from, the graveyard school.

This was probably inevitable, because it was exactly what the Classical curriculum trained its students to do. The study of Latin and Greek did not mean only
translating classic authors into English but also the reverse; passages of prose and
poetry by English writers had to be rendered into Latin or Greek in the style of
one of the ancients, which meant 'filching phrases' as well as imitating construction
and vocabulary. It was a system which encouraged facility at the expense of
originality. English poetry had been forced into the straitjacket of an alien language
and metre and William Wordsworth would be the one to set it free.

As a schoolboy he had no such ambitions. Under Taylor's instruction,

> My ears began to open to the charm
> Of words in tuneful order, found them sweet
> For *their own sakes* – a passion and a power
> *Prelude (1805), v, 577–9*

With his friend, John Fleming of Rayrigg, he would get up at dawn and wander
round Esthwaite Water, 'repeating favourite verses with one voice' or learning new
ones. Twenty years later, William remembered the rapture of these moments and
could only regret that the poems which had never failed to entrance him then,
should now be 'Dead in my eyes as is a theatre Fresh emptied of spectators'. He
still understood quite clearly what had been the appeal of their overwrought
sentiments and high-flown language:

> That wish for something loftier, more adorned,
> Than is the common aspect, daily garb,
> Of human life.
> *Prelude (1805), v, 599–601*

Not content with merely providing his pupils with poetry to learn, Taylor set
them verses to write, and William was one of the boys chosen in 1785 to write a
celebratory poem for the bicentenary of the foundation of Hawkshead Grammar
School. In an excess of enthusiasm, he composed one hundred and twelve lines of
precocious, scholarly verses which 'were but a tame imitation of Pope's versification,
and a little in his style'. Nevertheless, they were widely admired.

Perhaps it was the public success of this exercise which persuaded William that he could and should write verses 'from the impulse of my own mind.' His first effort was *The Vale of Esthwaite*, 'a long poem running upon my own adventures, and the scenery of the country in which I was brought up.' That was how William remembered it, though an unkind (but accurate) modern scholar has pointed out that the twenty-five pages written at Hawkshead contain a dead starling, a dead dog, a dead wife, two dead girls, three dead boys, a ghost, a grisly phantom, a band of druids bent on human sacrifice, a sobbing owl, some ghosts of 'murtherers', a tall thin spectre, and two visions of William brooding over his own grave. And this ignored the clanking chains, haunted castle and iron coffer marked with blood. One wonders how the poor boy survived such excitements.

Despite its Gothic terrors, *The Vale of Esthwaite* contained some glimmerings of the poet William would later become: the first account of his waiting for the horses coming to take him home, for instance, and some lovely lines descriptive of Lakeland scenery, including the earliest version of the last stanza of his poem addressed to his 'dear native regions', which would always stand first in William's collected editions of his poetry.

> As Phoebus, when he sinks to rest
> Far on the mountains in the west,
> While all the vale is dark between
> Ungilded by his golden sheen,
> A lingering lustre softly throws
> On the dear hills where first he rose.
>   *The Vale of Esthwaite, ll.519–24*

William's great schoolboy triumph was to get one of his poems published. It was called *Sonnet on Seeing Miss Helen Maria Williams Weep at a Tale of Distress*. Miss Helen Maria Williams was personally unknown to William. She was a poetical Barbara Cartland, admired for her cloyingly romantic lyrics, whose first volume of *Poems* was published in 1786. William's dire sonnet was an apt response: quivering with emotion and full of 'dear delicious pain'. It was sent off to the *European Magazine* in London and, astonishingly, found favour, appearing in the issue of March 1787 under the pseudonym 'Axiologus', William's Greek translation of his own surname. The decision to hide behind an assumed name was a convention and did not imply any wish to distance himself from the sonnet. Nevertheless, it was the first and last time the lines were to be published in William's lifetime, since they were the antithesis of everything he came to believe was important in poetry.

Less than four years into his mastership, Taylor fell seriously ill and died, aged 32, on 12 June 1786. His successor, the Reverend Thomas Bowman, was only twenty-five and believed it was of 'infinite consequence' for young people to have 'access to a variety of useful books'. He would later modestly suggest that he had done far more for William by lending him books than by his teaching. His most famous pupil had done 'well enough' under him at both Classics and Mathematics. 'But it was books he wanted,' Bowman's son remembered, 'all sorts of books; Tours and Travels, which my father was partial to, and Histories and Biographies, which were also favourites with him; and Poetry – that goes without saying.'

William acknowledged his gratitude to Bowman for lending him volumes of poetry which otherwise might not have fallen into his hands, naming specifically Langhorne's poems, Beattie's *Minstrel* and Percy's *Reliques of Ancient English Poetry*. These, with the poems of Cowper and Burns, were to be critically important to William's development as a poet and they shared important characteristics which are revealing about both William and Bowman. All, apart from Cowper, came from a northern tradition of writing and were the antithesis of the urbane, satirical schools of Pope, Dryden and Swift. They composed ballads in the vernacular and wrote about the lives of ordinary people. According to William, John Langhorne's *The Country Justice* was 'the first Poem, unless Shenstone's Schoolmistress can be excepted, that fairly brought the Muse into the Company of common life'. When Burns died, he would write:

> I mourned with thousands, but as one
> More deeply grieved, for He was gone
> Whose light I hailed when first it shone,
>   And showed my youth
> How Verse may build a princely throne
>   On humble truth.
>   *At the Grave of Burns, 1803, ll.31–6*

By introducing William to these contemporary poets, Bowman opened his pupil's eyes to new possibilities and helped him another step up on his way to becoming a poet.

In response to his reading, William's appreciation of the beauties of Nature had taken a more contemplative turn. Now he sought solitude in order to become one with the landscape and to experience what he would later call 'the instincts of immortality'.

>   For I would walk alone
> In storm and tempest, or in starlight nights
> Beneath the quiet heavens, and at that time
> Have felt whate'er there is of power in sound
> To breathe an elevated mood, by form
> Or image unprofaned. And I would stand
> Beneath some rock, listening to sounds that are
> The ghostly language of the ancient earth,
> Or make their dim abode in distant winds.
> Thence did I drink the visionary power.
> I deem not profitless those fleeting moods
> Of shadowy exultation; not for this
> That they are kindred to our purer mind

And intellectual life, but that the soul –
Remembering how she felt, but what she felt
Remembering not – retains an obscure sense
Of possible sublimity, to which
With growing faculties she doth aspire . . .

Prelude (1805), ii, 321–38

Despite his increasingly intellectual interests, William still delighted in the challenge of physical activity. With his schoolfriends, he would range far beyond the Vale of Esthwaite. Lake Windermere was a frequent destination in summer. The boys would race along its length in rowing boats and then enjoy a quiet picnic on one of its three islands; 'And I was taught to feel (perhaps too much) The self-sufficing power of solitude.'

In *The Prelude,* William would claim that it was due to 'nature and her overflowing soul' that, by the age of seventeen, 'all my thoughts were steeped in feeling' and would assign his wakening interest in the human condition to the French Revolution. This was true, as far as it went, but it did not go far enough.

It is self-evident from the number of his later poems drawing on people he had met at Hawkshead, that William was an interested observer, even as a schoolboy. The use of question and reply as a means of telling the story in these poems is partially a literary device, but it also suggests that he was unafraid to interrogate even total strangers. The old Cumberland beggar, sitting on a mounting block in the sun to eat the scraps given him on his round of the village, and involuntarily scattering the crumbs for the birds with 'palsied hand', was acutely observed 'with great benefit to my own heart when I was a child –'. The two thieves, Old Daniel and his three-year-old grandson, wandering through the streets and pilfering whatever came their way, yet tolerated and even pitied by their victims, who knew that Old Daniel's mind had gone and that his daughter would always reimburse them, were also described 'from the life as I was in the habit of observing when a boy at Hawkshead school'. The figure of the Wanderer was a composite one, but he identified one of the two main models as the packman who occasionally resided at Hawkshead, 'with whom I had frequent conversations upon what had befallen him & what he had observed upon his wandering life, &, as was natural, we took much to each other'.

William's liking for itinerants was strongly influenced by what he called his own 'passion' for '*wandering*'. He made the rather startling claim that 'had I been born in a class which would have deprived me of what is called a liberal education, it is not unlikely that, being strong in body, I should have taken to a way of life such as that in which my Pedlar passed the greater part of his days.'

William's preferred choice of company and his love of rambling at strange hours of the day and night were not calculated to appeal to his strait-laced Cookson relations. He was different; he was wild; he lacked the right sort of ambition. The summer holidays at Penrith became increasingly tense. He kept out of the Cooksons' way as much as possible, making lengthy excursions to The Nunnery Walks or to Ullswater.

One such expedition ended in a typical Wordsworthian 'spot of time'. Rambling out alone one moonlit evening from the inn at Patterdale, at the westernmost extremity of Ullswater, he came across a boat hidden in a rocky cave under a willow tree. In an 'act of stealth and troubled pleasure', he 'borrowed' the boat and set out to row across the lake, taking his bearings by fixing his eyes on the ridge of the sheer rockface of Stybarrow Crag. Suddenly and unexpectedly, from behind the Crag, loomed the vast naked summit of Glenridding Dodd 'As if with voluntary power instinct'. The further out he rowed, the greater it became, dwarfing the crag completely.

> And, growing still in stature, the huge cliff
> Rose up between me and the stars, and still,
> With measured motion, like a living thing
> Strode after me.
>
> *Prelude (1805), i, 409–12*

Overwhelmed, William turned the boat round and, with 'trembling hands' rowed back to the shore. For days afterwards, his thoughts and dreams were haunted by 'huge and mighty forms that do not live Like living men'. No doubt the Cooksons would have had much to say about their nephew's theft of the boat and nocturnal ramblings.

Christmases were usually spent more cheerfully at Whitehaven with Uncle Richard Wordsworth, who had nine children of his own. One son, John, was already a Captain in the East India Company and in a position to assist other members of the family. The choice fell on John, William's quiet and painfully shy younger brother. 'Our poor John was called a dunce because, poor Boy, he loved his own solitary dreamings, wanderings with his fishing rod, or social boyish sports, better than his master's tasks', Dorothy wrote. Other than his self-sufficiency, he seems an unlikely candidate for the notorious brutalities of a career at sea. Nevertheless, beggars could not be choosers. John willingly accepted his cousin's offer and would be taken out of school as soon as he reached fifteen, in December 1787.

The summer of 1787, however, had to be spent at Penrith – and there was a reason to look forward to the visit. Dorothy had come to live with her grandparents and, for the first time since the death of their mother, just over nine years before, the Wordsworth children would be together again.

Dorothy seemed to William like 'a gift then first bestowed'. She had been a child of six when they had parted and was now a young lady of fourteen and a half. Writing to Jane Pollard, her closest Halifax friend, Dorothy could not resist singing her brothers' praises.

I can bear the ill nature of all my relations, for the affection of my brothers consoles me in all my Griefs ... They are just the boys I could wish them, they are so affectionate and so kind to me as makes me love them more and more every day. William and Christopher are very clever boys – at least so they appear in the partial eyes of a Sister. No doubt I am partial and see virtues in them that by everybody else will pass unnoticed. John, (who is to be the sailor,) has a most excellent heart, he is not so bright as either Wm or Christopher but he has very good common sense and is well calculated for the profession he has chosen. Richard (the oldest) I have seen, he is equally affectionate and good, but is far from being as clever as William, but I have no doubts of his succeeding in his business for he is very diligent and far from being dull, he only spent a night with us.

Dorothy's insistence on the affection of her brothers is indicative of the depth of her own emotional need. 'Many a time have William, J, C, and myself shed tears together,' she told Jane, 'tears of the bitterest sorrow, we all of us, each day, feel more sensibly the loss we sustained when we were deprived of our parents'. What made this sense of a lost past almost unbearable, was the humiliation of the present.

Each day do we receive fresh insults, you will wonder of what sort; believe me of the most mortifying kind; the insults of servants who are every one of them so insolent to us as makes the kitchen as well as the parlour quite insupportable. James has even gone so far as to tell us that we had nobody to depend upon but my Grandfather, for that our fortunes were but very small, and my Brothers can not even get a pair of shoes cleaned without James's telling them they require as much waiting upon as any *Gentlemen*, nor can I get a thing done for myself without absolutely entreating it as a favour.

The children discussed their prospects at length. If Sir James did not pay, then they reckoned they would have £600 apiece. The self-effacing John was already offering to make sacrifices. 'John poor fellow! says that he shall have occasion for very little, two hundred pounds will be enough to fit him out, and he should wish William to have the rest for his education, as he has a wish to be a Lawyer if his health will permit, and it will be very expensive.'

Dorothy hoped that William might be permitted to stay at Penrith until October, but Uncle Christopher put his foot down. 'You may guess how much I was mortified and vexed at his being obliged to go away. I absolutely dislike my Uncle Kit who never speaks a pleasant word to one, and behaves to my Brother William in a particularly ungenerous manner'. 'Never, till I came to Penrith, did I feel the loss I sustained when I was deprived of a Father', Dorothy told Jane after her brothers had left.

One would imagine that a Grandm[other] would feel for her grandchild all the tenderness of a mother particularly when that Grandchild had no other parent, but there is so little of tenderness in her manner or of anything affectionate, that while I am in her house I cannot at all consider myself as at home, I feel like a stranger. You cannot think how gravely and silently I sit with her and my Gr[and]f[athe]r, you would scarcely know me ...

The Cowper household offered Dorothy a refuge and she often took advantage of it. The Reverend John Cowper was vicar of Penrith and his wife, Mary, was distantly related to the Wordsworths. His daughter, another Dorothy, was engaged to Uncle William Cookson. It was at the Cowpers' that Dorothy renewed her friendship with Mary Hutchinson, also an orphan, and Dorothy later recalled how 'Mary & her Sister Margaret, and I used to steal out to each other's houses, and when we had had our talk over the kitchen fire, to delay the moment of parting paced up one street and down another by moon or starlight.' Mary, too, recalled those early days of friendship with great affection: Dorothy 'was then as henceforth my chosen Companion; thro' life she continued to be.'

The two girls must have made an odd contrast. Dorothy, small and thin, her brown hair worn in light curls, frizzed and turned under at the ends, and so determined to remain 'as Girlish as possible' that she refused to wear high-heeled shoes. Excitable, hyper-sensitive, romantic and passionate, she seemed constitutionally restless in both mind and body; even her eyes were 'wild and startling, and hurried in their motion'. Mary, thin too, but tall, with pale, clear skin, dark hair and dark eyes with, apparently, a pronounced squint in one of them. Observers were virtually unanimous in declaring her plain, in the conventional sense, but were forced to admit that she exercised 'all the practical power and fascination of beauty, through the mere compensatory charms of sweetness all but angelic, of simplicity, the most entire, womanly self-respect, and purity of heart speaking through all her looks, acts and movements.'

When Dorothy introduced her to William in the summer vacation of 1787, he was instantly bowled over.

> She was a Phantom of delight
> When first she gleamed upon my sight;
> A lovely Apparition, sent
> To be a moment's ornament;
> Her eyes as stars of Twilight fair;
> Like Twilight's, too, her dusky hair;
> But all things else about her drawn
> From May-time and the cheerful Dawn;
> A dancing Shape, an Image gay,
> To haunt, to startle, and way-lay.
>
> *She was a Phantom of delight, ll.1–10*

Mary soon joined the brother and sister on their walks over the crags and exposed pools of Penrith Beacon. She lent a sympathizing ear to their tales of woe, shared their passion for the beauties of the landscape and, with her serene and sunny temperament, provided the perfect foil for their more highly charged ones. For William, this was 'a blessed time of early love' and Mary

> . . . breathed
> A gladness o'er that season, then to me
> By her exulting outside look of youth
> And placid under-countenance first endeared –
>
> *Prelude (1805), vi, 233–6*

The exact period of this 'early love' is impossible to date, but it is most likely to have begun during William's visit in July and August – a burgeoning love affair just before William was about to go off to college might have been the reason why Uncle Christopher despatched him back to Hawkshead so quickly. If not, then it probably began in October, when William returned to Penrith without his brothers. William's second visit was intended for the last-minute preparations before he set off for Cambridge. It should have been brief, since term began on 10 October, but it dragged on for three weeks.

William had made his farewells at Hawkshead. All school-leavers going on to Cambridge were encouraged to present a book to the school library and William was no exception. With two other lodgers at Ann Tyson's, his friend and fellow poet Robert Greenwood and Thomas Gawthrop, and another boy, John Millar, he presented the second edition of John Gillies's *The History of Ancient Greece, its Colonies, and Conquests from the Earliest Accounts till the Division of the Macedonian Empire in the East. Including the History of Literature, Philosophy, and the Fine Arts.* Just published in 1787, the book was as weighty as its title, running to four volumes. The same group also jointly presented another book newly published that year, John Hoole's two-volume translation from Torquato Tasso, *Jerusalem Delivered; An Heroic Poem.*

William set off for Cambridge in a state of high excitement. He had won the coveted sizar's place, which entitled him to pay reduced fees to both university and college and to take free dinners and suppers in hall. Ann Tyson and Dorothy had prepared a wardrobe of new clothes to match his new status. He was in the first flush of love and he was ambitious for academic success. His eagerness to go can only have been increased by the frustration of having to hang around in Penrith for a full two weeks after the usual date of the return to Cambridge. The suspicion is unavoidable that Uncle Christopher was being difficult about the travel arrangements again. It was not until 20 October that Uncle Christopher finally gave him £15 10s (which he charged to John Wordsworth's estate), enabling him to leave Penrith by the London coach. Before he left, he went to the book-club, and secured a copy of one of his own favourites, Burns's *Poems*, for his sister.

William's travelling companion was his cousin, John Myers, who was also going up to St John's College as a sizar. John had been at Sedbergh, and he was three years older than William. The journey itself must have been an exciting one for a seventeen-year-old boy who had never left his native Lakes before, and it took several days. On the way, they stopped for three or four days at York, where John's newly wed sister Mary, and her husband, Captain Robinson, lived in Micklegate. Captain Robinson was thirty years older than his wife and obviously thought it incumbent upon him to address some words of paternal advice to his young relations. 'I hope, William, you intend to take a good degree', he lectured. 'I will either be Senior Wrangler or nothing', was the determined reply.

On 30 October William and his cousin caught their first glimpse of Cambridge on the horizon. In his imagination, William had probably thought that it would be bathed in celestial light. Instead, it was a dull, cloudy morning, with not a single shaft of sunlight to accentuate the soaring pinnacles and towers of the breathtakingly

beautiful city. It was the vast, ethereal grandeur of King's College Chapel that first
caught his eye, rising out of the dark groves and dull fens like some mythic palace.
Magical though this must have seemed, it was William's first sight of a student,
wearing his gown and tasselled cap, which really impressed him.

> He passed – nor was I master of my eyes
> Till he was left a hundred yards behind.
> The place, as we approached, seemed more and more
> To have an eddy's force, and sucked us in
> More eagerly at every step we took.
>
> *Prelude (1805), iii, 8–12*

Passing beneath the castle and over Magdalene Bridge, they finally alighted. And,
like the schoolboy he had once been, he had to touch the walls and trees to convince
himself that it was true: 'I was the dreamer, they the dream!'

Built in 1511 in mellow red brick, St John's was far and away the largest college
in the university. Though William was now admitted to the prestigious ranks of
university men, he soon found out that, as a sizar, he was the lowest of the low. His
rooms turned out to be 'a nook obscure' and noisy. They were immediately over
the college kitchens, where the 'shrill notes Of sharp command and scolding' were
intermixed with the general hum of activity; to make matters worse, they were
also close to Trinity's 'loquacious clock', which chimed every quarter of an hour
throughout the day and night, and to its chapel, with its pealing organ. One
consolation was that, if he pushed his bed against the wall and stood on it, he could
see only a few yards away the statue of his hero Isaac Newton,

> with his prism and silent face,
> The marble index of a mind for ever
> Voyaging through strange seas of Thought, alone.
>
> *Prelude (1850), iii, 61–3*

The boy who had been absorbed in reading Newton's *Opticks* in his headmaster's
study now found himself literally in the shadow of the great man, whose works
were the basis of and underpinned Cambridge teaching. With hindsight, it seems
significant that William had to make such an effort to see what was actually so close.

William spent his first few days wandering round Cambridge in a daze.

> I roamed
> Delighted through the motley spectacle:
> Gowns, grave or gaudy, doctors, students, streets,
> Lamps, gateways, flocks of churches, courts and towers –
> Strange transformation for a mountain youth,
> A northern villager.
>
> *Prelude (1805), iii, 28–33*

There were many former Hawkshead schoolboys in Cambridge and, in this world of strangers, every familiar face seemed like that of a friend. There was John Fleming from Rayrigg, on Windermere, the 'Friend of my soul!' with whom William had walked round Esthwaite Water reciting verses, who was beginning his third year at St John's. Among the boys now entering their second year were William Penny, also a Johnian, Edward Birkett, at Christ's, and Fletcher Raincock, at Pembroke. These 'poor simple schoolboys, now hung round With honour and importance' were swift to offer the novice William the benefit of their wisdom and experience. The first thing he ought to do was to change his appearance, for the cut and make of his clothes marked him out as an uncouth northerner and therefore an object of amusement to the sophisticated gentlemen of the university. He was dispatched to buy something more appropriate to his standing and the Cambridge tailors were happy to offer him credit.

> To myself I seemed
> A man of business and expense, and went
> From shop to shop about my own affairs,
> To tutors or to tailors as befell,
> From street to street with loose and careless heart.
> . . . As if by word
> Of magic or some fairy's power, at once
> Behold me rich in moneys and attired
> In splendid clothes, with hose of silk, and hair
> Glittering like rimy trees when frost is keen –
> My lordly dressing-gown, I pass it by,
> With other signs of manhood which supplied
> The lack of beard!
>
> *Prelude (1805), iii, 23–7, 34–40*

Now that William also looked the part of a Cambridge gentleman, with his fashionable clothes and newly powdered hair, he was ready to embark on his academic career in earnest.

His hopes and spirits were high. After all, he had been one of the brightest boys at Hawkshead and knew more mathematics than most of the public-school boys, which would give him a head start on his peers. And, thanks to his Uncle William Cookson, a fellow at St John's who had been Fifth Wrangler, he had every prospect of obtaining a fellowship himself on graduation. The college statutes did not allow more than two men from the same county to hold fellowships at the same time and these had to be vacated on marriage. Uncle William intended to marry Dorothy Cowper as soon as he found a living lucrative enough to allow him to resign his fellowship and support a wife; when this happened, William had every chance of stepping into the vacancy. A fellowship was the inevitable stepping stone to preferment in the Church, not least because the college had the right to appoint to a large number of livings and schoolmasterships and always filled these with

Johnians. If William was serious in his expressed intention of going into the law, then the income from a fellowship would tide him over the years of reading for the bar at one of the Inns of Court. Should he need a helping hand, his former headmaster, Edward Christian, was now a lecturer in law at St John's and would soon become the University Professor of Common Law.

William had every prospect of a successful career at Cambridge: and succeed he did. Despite his late arrival he managed to impress his tutor, Edward Frewen (another friend of Uncle William), sufficiently to be awarded a Foundress Scholarship, worth between £23 and £26 a year, and two small exhibitions. St John's, unlike the other colleges, set examinations for its students twice yearly, so that it could keep track of potential wranglers. In December 1787, William completed a flawless first term by winning a place in the first class. On 17 December he signed the matriculation register and was formally admitted to the University of Cambridge. Everything was going according to plan and, back in Penrith, his Cookson relatives must have heaved a sigh of relief. William's future seemed set fair.

3. *Squandered Abroad*

Where William spent his first Cambridge vacation is a mystery. Given his recent successes, he might have felt justified in going to Whitehaven or Penrith to receive the family congratulations, but the cost of the journey was probably prohibitive. His brothers John and Christopher were at Whitehaven for the Christmas holidays. Dorothy had been 'fully expected' but had not been allowed to go, so she remained, miserable and resentful, at Penrith. Her birthday, Christmas Day, which she now claimed had never been a joyous occasion since her childhood at Cockermouth, was even more depressing, for, on or about 19 December 1787, her grandfather Cookson died; he was buried in St Andrew's Church, Penrith, on 22 December. 'At first it was a great shock to us all,' Dorothy confided in her friend Jane, 'the suddenness of it was very terrifying, but I am now quite thankful that he did not linger any longer, for, poor man! he has for these two years been a burthen to himself and [his] friends'. Though his death signalled a dispersal of the household, for the moment 'poor Dolly', as she called herself, continued to live with her grandmother and uncles.

William, far away from such traumas, had probably spent the brief month of his vacation in Cambridge, though the proximity of London may have tempted him to a visit. He certainly planned to go there for the equally short Easter vacation of 1788, because, in a letter he wrote ostensibly to inform his distant relative 'Jack' Robinson, who lived at Sion Hill, of his success in the December examinations, he asked for permission to pay a visit. Robinson's reply left him in no doubt that such distractions from his studies would not be countenanced. 'I was favoured with your Letter', Robinson wrote.

Believe me that I shall be truly glad to see you here, at all times, but my earnest recommendation to you is to stick close to College for the first two or three years; a little excursion now and then may be allowed, and in some of those I hope we may see you here. It will give me great pleasure to hear you go out high in your year, and I cannot by words alone express to you the satisfaction I shall feel in hearing you go out Senior Wrangler, strive for that, and establish a reputation at College which will go with you, and serve you thro' Life. To find this will give me much heartfelt Joy, for I most truly wish you well ...

After Christmas, the freshmen at St John's began to study the Roman historian Tacitus' *De Moribus Germanorum* and mathematics, which meant the study of algebra and the first three books of Euclid. It should have been an easy syllabus for William, especially as he had two full terms before the next college examinations in June. Instead, it proved fatal. In common with the other bright boys at Hawkshead, he had already studied all except the fifth of the first six books of Euclid and learned both simple and quadratic equations in algebra. 'This was for me unlucky,' William would later realize, 'because I had a full twelve-month's start of the freshmen of my year, and accordingly got into rather an idle way.' The Tacitus, too, should not have presented any problems; the Latin was not difficult and the subject, a eulogy on the simple manners and way of life of the German tribes, should have interested him. Over-confident in his own ability and knowledge, William obviously thought he did not need to make any great effort with his set books. Instead, he read nothing but 'classic authors according to my fancy, and Italian poetry'. The consequences became all too clear in the June examinations: he had slipped from the first into the second class. With application, it would not have been impossible for William to have regained the first class; unfortunately, his pride had taken a drubbing. It was bad enough to be in the second class but he had only just scraped that place. The men immediately below him in the order of merit had all been consigned to the third class.

For some young men, such a drop in status would have been a challenge to reverse the trend, but for William, who had always had a streak of obstinacy and defiance, it simply meant that the system was wrong and should therefore be ignored. 'Some Persons decline to sit for University honours from pride fed by erroneous notions respecting the construction put upon what is called a low honour', he wrote in 1816, when he was older and wiser.

If they cannot obtain a high one they had rather have none, imagining that if they do not contend at all people will give them credit for ability to have succeeded, whereas if their names are found not high in the list, then it is to be presumed, from their having been there at all, that they have done their utmost, and may fairly be regarded as industrious and well-meaning dunces.

In 1788, William thought he had better things to do with his time. Though he is usually considered to be a silent, solitary figure by those who know him only from his poetry, William himself knew better. 'I only cleave to solitude', he wrote in *The Prelude,*

> In lonesome places. If a throng was near,
> That way I leaned by nature, for my heart
> Was social and loved idleness and joy.
>   ... Companionships,
> Friendships, acquaintances, were welcome all;
> We sauntered, played, we rioted, we talked
> Unprofitable talk at morning hours,
> Drifted about along the streets and walks,
> Read lazily in lazy books, went forth
> To gallop through the country in blind zeal
> Of senseless horsemanship, or on the breast
> Of Cam sailed boisterously, and let the stars
> Come out, perhaps, without one quiet thought.
>
> *Prelude (1805), iii, 233–6, 249–58*

It is a picture any undergraduate of any generation will recognize immediately, but William was particularly unsuited to the rigours of academic study after the freedom of Hawkshead. He found the curriculum stultifyingly boring; even so, he could not remain untouched by Cambridge's golden past.

> I could not print
> Ground where the grass had yielded to the steps
> Of generations of illustrious men,
> Unmoved. I could not always lightly pass
> Through the same gateways, sleep where they had slept,
> Wake where they had waked, range that enclosure old,
> That garden of great intellects, undisturbed.
>
> *Prelude (1805), iii, 261–7*

There were so many Cambridge associations with great men of the past that it was impossible to ignore them. William could ride out to Trumpington, for instance, on the outskirts of the town, with a copy of Chaucer's *Canterbury Tales* in his pocket. Then, *in situ*, by the 'pleasant mills' he could read *The Reeve's Tale*, laughing at the bawdy exploits of the two clerks revenging themselves on the miller of Trumpington. Two of his favourite poets, Edmund Spenser and John Milton, had both been Cambridge men. Edward Birkett, William's friend from Hawkshead, actually had the very rooms at Christ's College which had once been occupied by Milton. This was, of course, an excuse for celebration and, on William's first visit to this hallowed spot, he joined in the party with enthusiasm, drinking toasts to Milton's memory 'till my brain reeled'. It was not until he heard the bell ringing that he realized he would be late for evening chapel, a punishable offence. He ran through the streets, 'ostrich-like' (a wonderful self-description for the gawky, long-legged boy), arriving after the bell had stopped and the organ had begun to play. A crowd of townsmen stood at the back of the chapel, not being permitted to enter because they were not members of the university. Still on a high with the drink and the knowledge that he too, like Milton, belonged to that élite, William ostentatiously flung his gown over his shoulder and 'clove in pride through the inferior throng'. Remembering this moment, in later years, he would feel only shame for 'the weakness of that hour' and his own 'unworthy vanity'.

William's first year at Cambridge 'in submissive idleness ... rolled pleasingly away', but the long weeks of the summer vacation loomed and he knew he would have to go home and face the music. It is hardly surprising that he was in no hurry to get there, choosing instead to make a leisurely progress northwards through Derbyshire and the Peak District. Arriving at Ashbourne on the evening of Sunday 8 June, he hired a horse and made a short excursion to see Dovedale, a small, pretty valley at the southernmost tip of the Peak District. In doing this he was consciously following in the tradition of those seekers after the picturesque, William Gilpin, Thomas Gray and Thomas West, whose works had been so familiar to him at Hawkshead. Like them, he jotted down his impressions, striving to re-create the scene in terms of perspective as if describing a picture.

Dovedale is a very narrow valley somewhat better than a mile in length, broken into five or six distinct parts, so that the views it affords are necessarily upon a small scale. The first scene that strikes you upon descending into the valley, is the River Dove fringed with sedge, and spotted with a variety of small tufts of Grass hurrying between two hills ... The scene was pleasing – the sun was just sinking behind the hill on the left – which was dark while his beams cast a faint golden tinge upon the side of the other. The River in that part which was streamy had a glittering splendor which was pleasingly chastized, by the blue tint of intervening pieces of calm water; the fringe of sedge and the number of small islands, with which it is variegated. The view is terminated by a number of rocks scattered upon the side of one of the hills of a form perfectly spiral –

The vocabulary is pure picturesque (though only William could describe a river as 'streamy'), but there is an effort and self-awareness about the description and, indeed, the whole excursion which bears out William's own claims in *The Prelude* that he was already conscious of a vocation to be a poet. He was certainly trying hard.

Rather than go to either Penrith or Whitehaven, William chose to head straight for Hawkshead. By the time he reached Windermere, he could not control his excitement. He bounded down the hill to the ferry at Bowness in exultant mood, hailed the old ferryman on the opposite shore by shouting his name, and was relieved to find he had not been forgotten. It was the first of many happy reunions. Ann Tyson, 'my old dame, so motherly and good', gave him a rapturous, if tearful, welcome, unable to restrain her admiration at his improvement in appearance. Filled with 'a parent's pride' in her boy, she insisted on taking him round the village and showing him off to all her neighbours. William was more than willing to go with her; it was an opportunity to display the fancy new clothes and powdered hair that marked him out as a gentleman instead of the schoolboy he had been when he left. His newly assumed airs and graces did not last long, however, and he reverted to schoolboy behaviour.

He could not resist hailing every familiar face he saw, interchanging 'unceremonious greetings', sometimes across the length of half a field. He rushed round the house and garden, ecstatic to discover that nothing had changed and that he would, once again, sleep in his old bed. Even the rough terrier, who had been the companion of his schoolboy walks, was still there. His youngest brother, Christopher, was probably there too, though, unlike the dog, he did not merit a mention in *The Prelude*.

William's return to Hawkshead for this summer vacation was almost like his reunion with Dorothy the previous year. There was a sense of rediscovery so strong that it seemed like having his eyes opened for the first time.

> When first I made
> Once more the circuit of our little lake,
> If ever happiness hath lodged with man
> That day consummate happiness was mine,
> ... Gently did my soul
> Put off her veil, and self-transmuted stood
> Naked as in the presence of her God.
> As on I walked, a comfort seemed to touch
> A heart that had not been disconsolate;
> Strength came where weakness was not known to be,
> At least not felt; and restoration came
> Like an intruder knocking at the door
> Of unacknowledged weariness.
>
> *Prelude (1805), iv, 127–30, 140–48*

The landscape may have been unchanged, but the people he had known and taken for granted since childhood were not. There were vacant places on the benches where the old men used to sun themselves, babies were now toddlers and some of the village girls had suddenly grown up to be rather pretty.

Apart from his admiration for Mary Hutchinson, this reference in *The Prelude* is the first indication that William had begun to take an interest in the opposite sex. It is perhaps surprising that this occurs in the vacation, rather than at Cambridge, which had an unenviable reputation as a hotbed of sin and iniquity. There were no female members of the university and senior members had to resign their fellowships in order to marry. Feminine company therefore came from the lower ranks of society, college servants, the daughters of innkeepers and tradesmen in the town, actresses at the playhouses, and there was only one reason any gentleman of the university would wish to seek out women of this type.

Though exaggerated by the satirical writers of the day, whoring was common-place. Among William's contemporaries, both Samuel Taylor Coleridge and Thomas de Quincey are known to have done so. William's slightly younger friend Raisley Calvert was so disgusted by the 'excessive Drunkeness' and 'Whoring' when he came up to Cambridge in February 1793 that he abandoned university altogether after only a week. The only memorable incident William recalled from his first journey to Cambridge in 1787 was 'for the first time in my life' seeing a prostitute in the 'pride of public vice' and hearing her blaspheme. His reaction was a mixture of shock, disgust (he shuddered) and distress. There is no reason to suppose he sought a closer acquaintance then or at Cambridge. Indeed, he tells us specifically that he never participated in 'dissolute pleasure . . . and only now and then observed' it.

Returning to Hawkshead, however, he was more than willing to impress and be impressed by the female sex. The 'Frank-hearted maids of rocky Cumberland' were far more attractive than the painted ladies of Cambridge, and their boisterous, but innocent, society had much more to recommend it. William would later feel that he should have given up his vacation to solitude and study but, aged eighteen, social pleasures proved more exciting.

> a swarm
> Of heady thoughts jostling each other, gauds
> And feast and dance and public revelry
> And sports and games (less pleasing in themselves,
> Than as they were a badge glossy and fresh
> Of manliness and freedom), these did now
> Seduce me . . .
>
> *Prelude (1805), iv, 272–8*

He began a 'vague heartless chase Of trivial pleasures', which was quite natural to his years, but would later come to seem a mere waste of time. First and foremost of these was undoubtedly the fairly recent innovation of a regatta on Windermere which was usually held in August. Yacht races and rowing competitions on the lake were followed by hunts, picnics, balls and parties at the Ferry Inn and in the houses of the local grandees on the lakeside. William was a participant in some of the sports and he certainly attended the balls. He had always loved dancing, but this summer vacation was probably the first opportunity he had to exploit his passion to the full. One ball lasted till dawn the following day.

> I had passed
> The night in dancing, gaiety, and mirth,
> With din of instruments and shuffling feet
> And glancing forms and tapers glittering
> And unaimed prattle flying up and down,
> Spirits upon the stretch, and here and there
> Slight shocks of young love-liking interspersed
> That mounted up like joy into the head
> And tingled through the veins.
>
> *Prelude (1805), iv, 319–27*

As he walked the two miles back to Colthouse, over Claife Heights, William watched the dawn break over the mountains. Revelling in the beauty of the landscape, the silence and the serenity, his heart was filled to the brim with thoughts and feelings he could not then articulate. Later, however, he remembered this moment of such emotional intensity that he came to see it as a turning point in his career as a poet, a symbolic rejection of social frivolity and acceptance of the eternal truths of nature. Like the heroes of antiquity, he did not seek to be a dedicated spirit, but passively accepted the role that was thrust upon him.

> I made no vows, but vows
> Were then made for me: bond unknown to me
> Was given that I should be, else sinning greatly,
> A dedicated spirit.
>
> *Prelude (1805), iv, 341–4*

Exhausted after another long evening of frenetic regatta entertainment, he enjoyed a similar moment as he walked home, late at night, along the silent public road. Drinking in the stillness of the starry night, he felt a 'restoration like the calm of sleep, But sweeter far'. This time, however, his musings were rudely interrupted when, round a corner, he suddenly came across a man of almost spectral appearance, gaunt, thin and seemingly of preternatural height, leaning against a milestone perfectly still. The shock of seeing this unexpected apparition, groaning quietly in the moonlight, was compounded for William because his imagination invested it with all the horrors of the graveyard school of poetry, to which he was still deeply attached. It took some courage (and some time) to approach the man, but his story proved real enough. He was a soldier who had been dismissed from the army on his return from service in the tropics, ten days previously, and he was making his way home. William offered to take him to a labourer's cottage nearby where he knew the man would receive food and lodging for the night. As they slowly made their way, William questioned the man intently about his experience of battle, hardship and pestilence. If he had hoped to hear blood-stirring tales of derring-do, he was mistaken; the man's replies were uttered in a tone of indifference, 'as of one Remembering the importance of his theme But feeling it no longer'. As he left the old soldier at the cottage, William begged him not to linger on the public roads in future, but to ask for assistance. He received an implicit reproof in return: 'My trust is in the God of Heaven, And in the eye of him that passes me!' It was the first of many memorable chance encounters with itinerants whose stories William would later immortalize in verse.

Looking back on this summer, it seemed to William as if there had been a new contagion in the air at Hawkshead, one that was

> Unknown among these haunts in former days.
> The very garments that I wore appeared
> To prey upon my strength, and stopped the course
> And quiet stream of self-forgetfulness.
>
> *Prelude (1805), iv, 291–4*

This was very much the view of the later poet of *The Prelude*, however, and at the time, he had no regrets at all. The later poet also exaggerated the 'vague heartless chase Of trivial pleasures' during this vacation, for it is clear from other sources that William had not entirely given up either his reading or his studies. He was still in regular contact with his old headmaster, Thomas Bowman, who allowed him to borrow books throughout all his college vacations.

Through Bowman, or possibly Mr Bowstead, the writing master at the school, who was one of Ann Tyson's lodgers in 1788, William was reintroduced to Charles Farish, a former pupil who had returned to Hawkshead as first assistant. Farish had overlapped with William at both Hawkshead and Cambridge, where his last year at Queens' College coincided with William's first at St John's. It is not unlikely that they had encountered each other at Cambridge, but the meeting during this summer vacation was an opportunity to pool experiences and ideas about writing poetry. Farish introduced him to the work of his brother, John Bernard Farish, who had been a pupil at Carlisle Grammar School and St Bees, before going up to Cambridge, where he died not long after taking his degree in 1778. As a sixteen-year-old schoolboy, in 1770 (the year William was born), John Farish had written two versions of a poem he called *The Heath*, one in the style of Spenser, the other in that of Shakespeare. They described the body of a murderer hanging on a gallows on a lonely heath, with a raven flying round, and the appearance of the ghost of the victim opening his shroud to reveal the fatal wound. This macabre but virtuoso effort impressed William immensely. He borrowed the images for his poem *Guilt and Sorrow*, which he began to write in 1791, acknowledging his debt to the two Farishes in a footnote. He also attempted to do something similar himself, composing lines describing a woman crossing a heath in alternative Spenserian and Shakespearian stanzas.

William, however, could not avoid paying duty visits to his guardian uncles, especially if he wished to see his sister and brothers. He seems to have been in Penrith on 21 June, when his Uncle Christopher gave him £36 8s 6d in cash, a sum possibly designed to see him through the vacation. With Dorothy and her friend Mary Hutchinson, he again explored his favourite walks around Penrith, or sat in the ruins of Brougham Castle, dreaming of an earlier poet associated with that place, Sir Philip Sidney.

None of them yet knew it, but this second summer together would also be the last they would share for many a year, for the Cookson and Hutchinson households were both about to break up. The death of William and Dorothy's grandfather had given his older son the financial independence he needed to marry and, on 27 August 1788, Uncle Christopher finally led Miss Charlotte Cust to the altar. At about the same time Uncle William had at last received his long-awaited promotion to a college living at Forncett, in Norfolk, resigned his fellowship and, on 17 October, was married to his faithful Dorothy Cowper. William missed the first wedding as he was at Whitehaven, where his brother John, newly returned from his first voyage across the Atlantic, was staying briefly with Uncle Richard Wordsworth, before setting out again for Jamaica.

It is possible, however, that William attended the second wedding, for the day after the marriage Uncle Christopher gave him some small sums in cash, indicating he was there in person. Another good reason for being in Penrith on the wedding day was to pay a final visit to his sister, who was about to leave the town for good. Uncle William and his fiancée had decided to offer Dorothy a home with them at Forncett. 'My happiness was very unexpected', Dorothy gushed to Jane Pollard, '. . . when my Uncle told me I was almost mad with joy; I cried and laughed alternately'. On the wedding morning, she attended the bridal couple to church and, with William Monkhouse, Mary Hutchinson's uncle, who was also brother-in-law of the bride, signed the register. There was, no doubt, a tearful parting between Dorothy and Mary.

Straight after the breakfast, the newlyweds and Dorothy set off for Newcastle. Dorothy had never expected to leave Penrith while her grandmother was still alive and she was wild with excitement. After a very agreeable fortnight at Newcastle, they set off for Norwich and their route naturally went through Cambridge, where William had already returned to college. For once, Dorothy seems to have paid more attention to a place than to her brother.

the buildings, added to the pleasure of seeing my Brother very well and in excellent spirits delighted me exceedingly; I could scarcely help imagining myself in a different country when I was walking in the college courts and groves; it looked so odd to see smart powdered heads with black caps like helmets, only that they have a square piece of wood at the top, and gowns, something like those that clergymen wear; but, I assure you, (though a description of the dress may sound very strange) it is exceedingly becoming.

After only a day in Cambridge, Dorothy was whisked off to Norwich. It was an auspicious moment to enter the town, which was deep in the throes of a double celebration, Guy Fawkes Night and the Centenary of the Glorious Revolution of 1688. The whole town was illuminated and the bells of all its many churches were ringing. To Dorothy, blossoming in the warmth of her uncle and aunt's affection, the general mood of exhilaration was the perfect expression of her own feelings. Nothing could disappoint her. Forncett, to which they made a day trip a couple of days later, proved to be 'a little village entirely inhabited by farmers, who seem very decent kind of people'; the house was very comfortable but would soon be excellent and the gardens were charming. 'I intend to be a great gardener', Dorothy announced proudly, 'and promise myself much pleasure in taking care of the poultry of which we are to have great abundance.' They were busy making plans to celebrate Dorothy's birthday and, after many consultations, decided that roast beef and plum pudding was the best Christmas Dinner. The comparison with the misery of the previous Christmas was unavoidable. 'I have now nothing left to wish for on my own account,' Dorothy acknowledged gratefully.

At Cambridge, William was equally blithe. He had come to an important decision which would have far-reaching implications for his future. As a result of his poor showing in the college's summer examinations and his increasing distaste for the sterility and restrictiveness of the university syllabus, he had decided that he 'wished to be a lodger in that house Of letters, and no more'. In other words, he would abandon all hope of becoming Senior Wrangler or, indeed, winning any honours, do only the minimum of set work required to prevent his being sent down and use the unrivalled facilities of the university to pursue a course of independent study. He was well aware that this decision was 'An act of disobedience towards them Who loved me, proud rebellion and unkind'; in retrospect it also seemed an act of cowardice which gave 'treacherous sanction' to his over-love of freedom and indolence.

William was by no means unusual in his rejection of a formal university career. Robert Southey, William's contemporary and predecessor as Poet Laureate, wrote to offer words of wisdom and experience to a young friend who went up to Pembroke College in 1811.

Do not be solicitous about taking a high degree, or about college honours of any kind. Many a man has killed himself at Cambridge by overworking for mathematical honours; recollect how few the persons are who after they have spent their years in severe study at this branch of science, ever make any use of it afterwards. Your wiser plan should be to look on to that state of life in which you wish and expect to be placed, and to lay in such knowledge as will then turn to account.

Of the forty-two freshmen, including William, who entered St John's in October 1787, almost a quarter had already dropped out before the end of the first year; by June of the second year, only twenty-one, half the original number, were still in contention. By the following December, William had joined the ranks of non-reading men. Robert Southey followed a similar route at Oxford, which was then the only other university in England. The course there did not have the mathematical element which alienated so many Cambridge undergraduates, but both universities faced the same problems of moral laxity, academic absenteeism (most professors never lectured and college tutors, when they were there, had to lecture to up to eighty undergraduates at a time) and an appointments and honours system bedevilled by corruption. Southey was not only intellectually gifted but also fanatically hard-working by any standards, yet it was his own tutor who advised him to drop out: 'Mr Southey, you won't learn any thing by my lectures, Sir', he was told, 'so, if you have any studies of your own, you had better pursue them.' Southey eventually left Oxford without even attempting to take his degree.

William hated the compulsory twice-daily attendance at chapel, which he felt was simply a hollow mockery of genuine piety. He objected to the examinations 'when the man was weighed As in the balance!' (and, in William's own case, found wanting), because they promoted all the deeper passions, excessive hopes, envy, jealousy, pride, shame and ambition. He had nothing but contempt for the entire academic system and its petty struggle for 'spurious fame and short-lived praise', attacking it in *The Prelude* with uncharacteristic bitterness.

> And here was labour, his own bond-slave; hope,
> That never sets the pains against the prize; . . .
> Honour misplaced, and dignity astray;
> Feuds, factions, flatteries, enmity, and guile;
> *Prelude (1805), iii, 630–31, 635–6*

Underpinning all these criticisms, though never explicitly mentioned, was William's own status as a university man. Like Dorothy, he had always been sensitive to personal slights, perceived or otherwise: as we have seen, when only a child at Penrith he had been ready to kill himself when 'some indignity' had been imposed upon him. And there is a very telling phrase in his description of being late for chapel after the drinking party at Christ's; running through the crowd of townsmen, he ostentatiously shouldered his gown which was both 'gloried in and yet despised'. It is a throwaway line (William actually discarded it when he prepared *The Prelude* for posthumous publication) but it goes to the heart of William's disenchantment with Cambridge. His gown was the public symbol to the outside world of his membership of that élite band, the gentlemen of the university; to the gentlemen of the university it marked him out as the lowest of the low.

At that time there were three ranks of Cambridge undergraduates: fellow commoners, who were noblemen and plutocrats; pensioners (by far the largest class), who were younger sons of the aristocracy, the gentry and professional classes; and then there were the sizars, bright boys who could not afford the fees, but were expected to bring honour to their colleges by doing well in the examinations. William's closest friends among the Hawkshead boys already at Cambridge when he arrived, John Fleming, Edward Birkett and Fletcher Raincock, were all pensioners. William not only had less money than them in any case, but he had to wear a different and distinctive gown so that he was instantly identifiable; he got the worst rooms in the college, as he had already discovered, and for his dinners and suppers he had to make do with whatever was left over from the fellows' table. Until only the year before he went up, sizars had been compelled to act as waiters at the fellows' table, where the undergraduate fellow commoners also dined.

Not surprisingly, many sizars chafed under these humiliations. Charles Lamb blamed Samuel Taylor Coleridge's sensitivity to his status for his bizarre decision to flee Cambridge and volunteer for the army under the delicious pseudonym, Silas Tomkyn Comberbache: he was, according to Lamb, 'ill-capable of enduring the slights poor sizars are sometimes subject to in our seats of learning'. More than fifty years later, when conditions were much improved, Bulwer Lytton could still depict the sizar's lot as one of bitter degradation. 'Do you know what a sizar is? In pride he is a gentleman – in knowledge he is a scholar – and he crawls about, amidst gentlemen and scholars, with the livery of a pauper on his back!' Because they were so humiliatingly marked out, the pressure upon sizars to prove themselves by doing well academically was immense. Many of them were dependent on scholarships and exhibitions which could be, and were, withdrawn from those who failed to perform.

William's decision to abandon any pursuit of academic honours did not mean that he gave up reading and studying altogether. Quite the contrary, in fact. In *The Prelude*, he tells us that he now abandoned the gay round of parties, invitations and social pastimes of the previous year.

> I lived henceforth
> More to myself, read more, reflected more,
> Felt more, and settled daily into habits
> More promising.
>
> *Prelude (1805), vi, 22–5*

Over the course of the next two winters, he 'devoured, Tasted or skimmed, or studiously perused' many books, but without any set plan in mind, other than the growing conviction that he wanted to be a poet. It is clear from his examination records, for instance, that he did not completely sever himself from the university syllabus but carefully selected only those subjects which interested him. In December 1788, the set texts were the first six books of Euclid, Thomas Rutherforth's *Institutes of Natural Law* and Sophocles' *Oedipus at Colonus*, in the original Greek. Which of these texts he read (or remembered, in the case of Euclid), is not known, but his report indicated that he 'did not go thro' the whole of the examination & yet had considerable merit'. The following June, the men of William's year were examined in mechanics, the twenty-first book of Livy's *History of Rome* and Locke's *Essay on Human Understanding*. William took only part of the examination and, as a result, was unclassed, though he distinguished himself in the classics. It seems likely that he simply studied the Livy and completely omitted the mechanics.

In place of the prescribed course of study, William decided to employ his time more productively in learning Italian. His first step was to secure a private tutor and, by great good luck, one of the most famous Italian teachers of the day happened to live and teach in Cambridge. Agostino Isola, a refugee from Italy, had taught a number of eminent people, including the Prime Minister, William Pitt, and the poet Thomas Gray. He had also published in 1786 a translation of Tasso's *Jerusalem Delivered*, one of the books (though not the actual edition) William had given to Hawkshead Grammar School. Isola and his new pupil hit it off immediately. 'As I took to these studies with much interest,' William later recalled, 'he was proud of the progress I made. Under his correction I translated the Vision of Mirza, and two or three other papers of the Spectator, into Italian.'

With Isola he also studied Italian poetry, for which he retained a lifelong affection, reading Tasso and Dante and translating Ariosto's *Orlando Furioso* and Michelangelo's sonnets. The sheer musicality of the language appealed to his poetic ear, though he later became convinced that 'an easy and mellifluous language was apt to tempt, by its facility, into negligence, and to lead the poet to substitute music for thought', whereas in struggling with words in the 'rugged language' of English 'one was led to give birth to and dwell upon thoughts'.

William obviously flourished under Isola's guidance and it is interesting to see

that, studying a subject he liked, for a teacher he admired, he fell victim to the
prevailing competitive spirit at Cambridge for the first and only time. 'I never felt
emulation with another man but once,' he told a friend when he was an old man,

and that was accompanied by envy. This once was in the study of Italian, which I entered
on at College with [blank]. I never engaged in the proper studies of the university, so that
in these I had no temptation to envy anyone; but I remember with pain that I *had* envious
feelings when my fellow student in Italian got before me. I was his superior in many
departments of mind, but he was the better Italian scholar, and I envied him. The annoyance
this gave me made me very thankful that as a boy I never experienced it.

Isola also taught Spanish, and William may well have studied this language with
him. Though Spanish poetry never attracted him as much as Italian, he had loved
Cervantes' *Don Quixote* since childhood, and always admired what he called the
'imagination' of the Spanish. Dorothy notes him reading in it extensively in a letter
to Jane Pollard which, unusually, contains implicit criticism of her brother. Had
he been like Uncle William, he could have secured a fellowship, a nice living and
a parsonage in the country, where Dorothy could live without any sense of being
the dependent relative. 'William you may have heard lost the chance, indeed the
certainty of a fellowship', she wrote ruefully,

by not combating his inclinations, he gave way to his natural dislike of studies so dry as
many parts of the mathematics, consequently could not succeed at Cambridge. He reads
Italian, Spanish, French, Greek and Latin, and English, but never opens a mathematical
book ... William has a great attachment to poetry ... which is not the most likely thing to
produce his advancement in the world; his pleasures are chiefly of the imagination, he is
never so happy as when in a beautiful country. Do not think from what I have said that he
reads not [at] all, for he does read a great deal and not only poetry and those languages he
is acquainted with but history &c &c.

William's study of the romance languages was a deliberate attempt to gain access
to some of the greatest poets of the past in their original tongue. It is clear from his
percipient criticisms that he was also studying carefully the form and structure of
the poetry, as well as the actual content, and the thoughts and feelings which had
given rise to it. In English literature, too, the scale, if not the scope, of his reading
expanded. He remained as enthusiastic as he had been when a schoolboy about the
melancholics: Young, Collins and Gray were still his favourite poets. However, his
appreciation of Milton, Shakespeare and Spenser increased as he read more deeply
in their work.

His early love of Roman and Greek literature remained undimmed by his new
enthusiasms. Throughout this period, he translated his favourite poets for his own
personal pleasure. Interestingly, the ones which preoccupied him most are the ones
which his great hero Milton drew on most heavily. We therefore find William
translating Virgil's *Georgics*, for which he had an immediate and natural sympathy.

Virgil, like William, had a rural upbringing and believed passionately in the virtues of a simple country life. His purpose in writing the *Georgics* was to revive a love of the land and agricultural pursuits in an urban age, not just from a sentimental attachment to the beauty of nature but from a deep conviction that country life was inherently more simple, pure and moral. It was the very same theory that would underpin all William's own poetry. Horace, another Roman poet of the first century BC, was far more sophisticated and urbane, but some of his lyrical poetry was exquisite; in his *Odes*, which William translated, he too celebrated the joys of retiring to the tranquillity of his country villa. Horace, unlike Virgil, had just the right tinge of melancholy, inspired by a sense of the brevity and futility of life, which appealed to William. The extent of William's indebtedness to classical literature in forming both his ideas and his poetical style has never been fully appreciated. It also accounts for the charges of paganism and pantheism levelled against him in later years which he struggled to deny, without, it has to be said, much success.

While he was studying poets of other lands and generations, William tells us that it was at this time he began to think that 'I might leave Some monument behind me which pure hearts Should reverence.' *An Evening Walk*, under which title the poem would be published in January 1793, drew heavily on verses William had written as a schoolboy, but began to take shape as an independent effort during his first summer vacation in Hawkshead. He worked on it at intervals, finishing it off in 1789, probably during his second summer vacation. The final version was 378 lines long. 'There is not an image in it which I have not observed', William later stated, adding that he even remembered the time and place he noticed most of them. He drew particular attention to two lines describing the effect of fading sunlight on an oak tree. 'This is feebly & imperfectly exprest', he admitted,

but I recollect distinctly the very spot where this first struck me. It was in the way between Hawkshead and Ambleside, and gave me extreme pleasure. The moment was important in my poetical history; for I date from it my consciousness of the infinite variety of natural appearances which had been unnoticed by the poets of any age or country, so far as I was acquainted with them: and I made a resolution to supply in some degree the deficiency. I could not have been at that time above 14 years of age.

Most of *An Evening Walk* was indeed both feebly and imperfectly expressed, but it did fulfil William's declared intention of describing the 'infinite variety of natural appearances' in rather a clever way. The poet's walk through the Lakes begins in the hazy heat of noon and ends in the light of a clear, bright moon, allowing him to note the progression of subtle effects caused by the changing light on the landscape and its inhabitants. Like *The Vale of Esthwaite*, William's earlier long poem, *An Evening Walk* 'filched' extensively from his favourite melancholic authors, Collins, Thomson, Charlotte Smith and Beattie, but his newer interests also left their mark in a phrase lifted out of Tasso and lengthy borrowings from both Milton and Horace. The poem was typical of the poetic conventions of the day in subject and in style. The allusions to, and quotations from, the work of other poets, which seem like mere plagiarism today, were then regarded as a sort of dazzling display, a game in which the poet could show off his erudition and the reader could test his own skill by identifying them.

For the moment, however, the poem remained unpublished and its author's budding talents went unrecognized outside the small circle of his friends. This was still composed largely of Hawkshead boys but, significantly, nearly all those William called 'my *intimate* associates' at Cambridge were among the academic élite. John Fleming, the 'Friend of my soul!', with whom he had recited verses round Esthwaite Lake, was Fifth Wrangler in 1789; Fletcher Raincock, Fleming's brother, was Second Wrangler in 1790. The following year, which was William's own graduation year, Robert Greenwood, with whom he had sent verses to the *European Magazine*, was Sixth Wrangler. Thomas Middleton, a future literary editor (of the *Country Spectator* and the *British Critic*) and Bishop of Calcutta, belonged to a brilliant circle of undergraduates who graduated in 1790. In William's own year at St John's, however, only one new friend was a high flier: William Terrot was eighth Senior Optime, effectively twenty-ninth in the order of merit in the final examinations. His two closest friends, his cousin John Myers and a jovial Welshman, Robert Jones, had careers as undistinguished as that of their friend. Taken as a whole, however, William's group of friends were intelligent, academically inclined and comparatively sedate, suggesting that his own interests were still predominantly intellectual.

It is, therefore, a measure of how far William was determined to distance himself from the pursuit of academic honours that he refused to compete even in those areas of university life where he might well have been successful. There were a number of annual prizes for poetry, for instance, which would have been an ideal opportunity to show off his skills and prove to his relatives that he was making some effort. Even more of a missed opportunity, at least in his Uncle William's eyes, was his blank refusal to write a set of verses when the Master of St John's, Dr Chevallier, died in March 1789.

According to the custom of that time, his body, after being placed in the coffin, was removed to the hall of the college, and the pall, spread over the coffin, was stuck over by copies of verses, English or Latin, the composition of the students of St John's. My uncle seemed mortified when upon inquiry he learnt that none of these verses were from my pen, 'because,' said he, 'it would have been a fair opportunity for distinguishing yourself.' I did not, however, regret that I had been silent on this occasion, as I felt no interest in the deceased person, with whom I had had no intercourse, and whom I had never seen but during his walks in the college grounds.

In William's proud refusal to bow to convention or to seek advancement by judicious flattery, not to mention his haughtily dismissive tone, we get a rare first-hand glimpse of the stubborn and rebellious nature which was the despair of his Cookson relatives.

Uncle William had the opportunity to express his mortification in person. As the summer term of William's second year at Cambridge closed, he decided not to go north immediately, but to pay a visit to Forncett where he had to explain to his uncle not only his failure to write verses for Dr Chevallier but also his having been unplaced in the June examinations. How long he stayed at Forncett is unclear but Dorothy was doubtless thrilled to show him her room, 'one of the pleasantest in the house', the garden and the beautiful views. Most likely, too, Dorothy would have introduced him to her pet robins, which, through regular feeding, she had made so tame that they would hop about the room where she was sitting.

When William left Norfolk, he went back to Hawkshead, where he spent a total of nine weeks this summer, boarding once again with Ann Tyson. This would be his last chance to stay with his 'grey-haired dame', for Ann was now seventy-six years old and had decided that she could no longer take boarders. William's love for her was only increased by absence; he saw her again with 'new delight'.

> Her smooth domestic life –
> Affectionate without uneasiness –
> Her talk, her business, pleased me; and no less
> Her clear though shallow stream of piety
> That ran on sabbath days a fresher course.
> With thoughts unfelt till now I saw her read
> Her bible on the Sunday afternoons,
> And loved the book when she had dropped asleep
> And made of it a pillow for her head.
>
> *Prelude* (1805), iv, 213–21

There seems to have been no visit to Penrith this summer. He had little incentive to go there now. Not only had Dorothy left, but also Mary Hutchinson. With her youngest brother, George, she had gone to make her home with their brother, Tom, on a farm at Sockburn-on-Tees, near Darlington, in County Durham. Instead, William visited his more congenial Wordsworth relations at Whitehaven and, with little else to distract him, spent the summer making forays further afield, exploring the Yorkshire Dales and the more obscure and wilder parts of the Lakes. On 16 October he returned to Penrith to catch the coach southwards and paid a fleeting duty visit to the Cooksons. 'Your Bro[the]r Wm called here on Friday last in his road to Cambridge', Uncle Christopher wrote to Richard, adding with a degree of asperity which reflects his frustration with his errant nephew, 'he looks very well, I should have been happy if he had favour'd me with more of his Company, but I'm afraid I'm out of his good graces'.

Richard, unlike William, was very much in his uncle's good graces. He not only accepted all his uncle's advice willingly but actually appeared grateful for it. The contrast between his behaviour and that of his brother could not have been more marked. Since the beginning of 1789, Richard had been living in London and working in the offices of his cousin's London attorneys, Parkin & Lambert, at

Gray's Inn. He was there specifically to keep an eye on the pursuit of the claim against Sir James Lowther which had, once again, ground to a halt. Uncle Christopher was still managing Richard's estate at Sockbridge, though not very competently. Richard, however, remained humbly grateful. He had just celebrated his twenty-first birthday and was legally of age to enter the estate in his own right, but, while he remained indefinitely in London, he had no one else to whom he could delegate the management.

William, the ingrate, meanwhile, was blithely compounding his sins at Cambridge by failing even to attempt the December examinations of 1789, the only occasion he failed to do so. In mitigation, it should be pointed out that only twenty men in William's year actually entered for any part of it and eighteen, including William, boycotted it altogether.

Now that his brother Richard was settled in London, it was easier and cheaper for William to spend time there. He almost certainly passed most of the Christmas vacation of 1789–90 in town, not least because this was a last opportunity to see their brother John before he set sail on his first voyage for the East India Company. John was now a relatively experienced sailor, with voyages to Barbados, Jamaica and America under his belt. Uncle Richard Wordsworth's second son, another John, had just been appointed captain of one of the largest ships in the Company's service, the *Earl of Abergavenny*, which was about to make its maiden voyage to India and China. Captain Wordsworth immediately offered his cousin a place on board as a midshipman and, since his return from America, John had been busy in London making his preparations, sparing only time for a brief visit, with Richard, to Dorothy at Forncett. They hurried back for the start of the new law term, whereupon Richard discovered that some of the vital papers were at Branthwaite, causing yet another long delay and earning himself a stern rebuke from Uncle Christopher. There was also some sharp criticism of William: 'I am sorry to say that I think your Bro[the]r Wm very extravagant he has had near £300 since he went to Cambridge w[hi]ch I think is a very shameful sum for him to spend, considering his expectations.' It was not a remark calculated to ease tensions between the two. Indeed, the sting of 'considering his expectations' was just the sort of comment to irritate and infuriate his nephew – and, of course, to make him even more determined to pursue his own course. Bearing in mind these undercurrents, Uncle Christopher's remark at the end of the same letter, that their grandmother 'Desires her Love in the warmest manner both to you and John', seems very pointed in its omission of William's name.

At the beginning of January 1790, John went to Gravesend to join his ship; the *Earl of Abergavenny* left its moorings on 17 January and sailed for Bombay and Canton on the 30th. It would be eighteen months before John set foot in London again, but he wrote in 'excellent spirits' to his sister before they set sail and again, on 21 February, to Richard, to reassure him that he was 'perfectly contented & happy'. The constant reiteration of these sentiments throughout John's sailing career cannot fail to instil some doubt as to their truth. Was he really happy? Or was he merely putting on a brave face for his loved ones?

Dorothy, at Forncett, and Christopher, at Hawkshead, were genuinely content. 'I have every reason my dear Jane to be satisfied with my present situation', Dorothy assured her friend. 'I have two kind Friends with whom I live in that retirement, which before I enjoyed I knew I should relish. I have leisure to read; work; walk and do what I please in short I have every cause to be contented and happy.'

The previous summer Dorothy had set up a little Sunday school to teach the local girls reading, spelling, prayers, hymns and catechisms; those who lived nearby came again every Wednesday and Saturday evening. The intention was that this would form the basis of a permanent school, employing a mistress who would teach the girls spinning and knitting during the week and, with Dorothy's assistance, reading on Sundays. Uncle William Cookson's old friend, William Wilberforce, who was now an MP and had already begun his parliamentary campaign against slavery, spent the Christmas holidays of 1789–90 with them and showed his approval of Dorothy's schemes by promising her ten guineas a year to distribute 'in what manner I think best to the poor', she proudly informed Jane, adding, 'I believe him to be one of the best of men'. Before he left, he presented her with a couple of Evangelical tracts and suggested she read the New Testament with Doddridge's exposition, the book to which he attributed his own conversion. Jane Pollard immediately heard wedding bells for her old friend. Uncertain whether she was simply being teased, Dorothy felt it necessary to reject the suggestion with due solemnity. 'My heart is perfectly disengaged', she purred, 'no man I have seen has appeared to regard me with any degree of partiality, nor has any one gained my affections . . . believe me, *if ever I do* form an attachment it shall not long be a secret from you.' In any case, she added, rather spoiling her protestations of indifference, 'Mr W. would, were he ever to marry, look for a Lady possessed of many more accomplishments than I can boast'. Hastening to prevent similar wild speculations about the seal on her last letter, which had also attracted Jane's attention, she explained, rather more crisply, that it was a gift from 'a Penrith F[riend] Mary Hutchinson'.

Dorothy was full of hope for her youngest brother, Christopher, who was still at school at Hawkshead and showing every sign of having a promising future. He was already planning to go to Cambridge but his ambitions, unlike William's, were much more in line with what his relations and guardians expected of him. His uncles considered him not only an excellent scholar but also, more crucially, 'a most amiable youth'. Dorothy, too, sang his praises in the same way she had once sung those of William. She also thought him 'rather handsome; at least, there is some thing very interesting in his countenance'.

William, on the other hand, was no longer immune from criticism. 'I am very anxious about him just now,' Dorothy confided in Jane, 'as he will shortly have to provide for himself: next year he takes his degree; when he will go into orders I do not know, nor how he will employ himself'. She added the slightly desperate, 'he must, when he is three and twenty either go into orders or take pupils'. Dorothy had begun to realize that her dreams of replicating her uncle's household idyll in a country parsonage shared with William were fast becoming unrealistic. Christopher might be a safer bet, but he was not her preferred choice of companion among her brothers.

William seemed set on a course which was not only at odds with every prospect of future success but even defied common sense. It is true that in June 1790 he made a partial return to the fold, taking (and doing well in) an examination in three of Juvenal's *Satires*, but he again ignored the greater part of the syllabus. Worse still, with his crucial university examinations looming, he decided to take a holiday abroad.

It was, as William later boasted rather proudly in *The Prelude*, a deliberate act of defiance: 'An open slight Of college cares and study was the scheme'. Though he declared that it was not 'entertained without concern for those To whom my worldly interests were dear', at the time he took great care to ensure that none of his family knew about it. Not even Dorothy was allowed to share the secret, probably because he knew she would give way to that 'feverish dread of error and mishap' which he found so irritating and claustrophobic. It was perhaps as well that he did not, for she shared in the general disapproval: 'had he acquainted me with his scheme before its execution I should (as many of his other friends did) have looked upon it as mad and impracticable.'

The grand plan was that William, together with his college friend Robert Jones, would make a pedestrian tour of the Alps. This would be a herculean feat, for the journey would take them some 3,000 miles in less than three months. As if this was not a sufficient challenge in itself, the route presented enormous dangers. They would not only be walking and climbing some of the most inaccessible and perilous mountains in Europe but the easiest part of their journey, in terms of terrain, lay through France, a country which was still in considerable turmoil after a revolution not yet a year old. The French royal family were virtual prisoners in the Tuileries, the volatile citizens' army paraded daily in Paris and at least four provinces were in a state of virtual anarchy. Massive preparations were taking place throughout the entire country to celebrate the first anniversary of the Fall of the Bastille; 14 July 1790 had been declared a national holiday, the *Fête de la Fédération*, on which every French man and woman, from the king downwards, was to swear an oath of allegiance to the new constitution. Though these ceremonies were to take place in towns and villages throughout France, thousands of provincial delegates were travelling to Paris to witness the king taking his oath. In the first flush of enthusiasm for the dramatic birth of a democratic nation, large numbers of English men and women flocked to see these events for themselves and to take part in what they clearly recognized as history in the making. William and Jones could hardly have chosen a more exciting time to travel to France.

But Switzerland, not France, was their destination. Their route was determined by authorities on the picturesque, most notably Thomas Gray and William Coxe, and it would take them in a fairly direct line down the eastern side of France from Calais to Lyons, where they would branch off eastwards into the French Alps to see the monastery of the Grande Chartreuse and Mont Blanc, before entering Switzerland and reaching the Italian Lakes, which they would explore exhaustively.

Foolhardy though the scheme seemed, William was not so reckless as to attempt it alone. In choosing Robert Jones as his companion, he could not have found a more congenial fellow traveller. Jones was, like William, the second son of an attorney and destined for the Church. His family home, Plas-yn-Llan, was at Llangynhafal, in Denbighshire, and the two young men shared a mutual passion for poetry, mountains and walking, which explains not only their friendship but also their plan for the pedestrian tour. What is perhaps more extraordinary is the fact that their friendship survived the tour. Some years later, William wrote a poem celebrating his friend's eccentricities:

> I marvel how Nature could ever find space
> For so many strange contrasts in one human face; . . .
>
> This picture from nature may seem to depart,
> Yet the Man would at once run away with your heart;
> And I for five centuries right gladly would be
> Such an odd, such a kind happy creature as he.
> *A Character, ll.1–2, 17–20*

Perhaps fortunately for his friend, William did not identify the subject of his portrayal, but, in January 1793, when he published the poem, *Descriptive Sketches*, which was the result of the tour, he prefixed it with a touching public dedication to Jones.

In inscribing this little work to you, I consult my heart. You know well how great is the difference between two companions lolling in a post-chaise, and two travellers plodding slowly along the road, side by side, each with his little knapsack of necessaries on his shoulders. How much more of heart between the two latter!

The intrepid pair left Cambridge early in July 1790; they had about £20 each and were equipped with identical lightweight coats (for ease of walking), oak staffs and small bundles of 'needments' which, to the amusement of observers abroad, they carried, peasant-fashion, on their heads. They hurried through London, deliberately avoiding any contact with Richard Wordsworth.

They arrived in Calais on the eve of the *Fête de la Fédération*. Most Englishmen would have made the effort to arrive earlier so that they could get to Paris for this unique occasion. The fact that William and Jones failed to do so speaks volumes for their lack of interest in contemporary politics. They could not ignore the celebrations in Calais, however, for at eleven-thirty on the morning of 14 July, all the bells in the town rang out, guns were fired and, under the guidance of the mayor, in a public ceremony that was repeated at the same time throughout the kingdom, the populace took the oath of allegiance. William and Jones were undeniably present and actually deferred starting out on the first leg of their pedestrian tour till the afternoon so that they could see it, but, astonishingly, William made no mention of it in his letters home or in the *Descriptive Sketches*. Even when he came to write *The Prelude*, which contains some of the most famous and enduring images of revolutionary France ever written in English, his attitude seems remarkably subdued and the references almost incidental. This is easily explained by the fact that, at the time, he was simply not interested. Poetry, not politics, was his passion. 'I looked upon these things', he wrote apologetically in *The Prelude*,

> As from a distance (heard, and saw, and felt,
> Was touched, but with no intimate concern)

Writing in 1804, however, he had a different perspective. He was then highly politicized. And, with the advantage of hindsight, he realized the importance of the events he had witnessed. He had first set foot on French soil at a time 'when Europe was rejoiced' and 'France standing on the top of golden hours'.

> it was our lot
> To land at Calais on the very eve
> Of that great federal day; and there we saw,
> In a mean city and among a few,
> How bright a face is worn when joy of one
> Is joy of tens of millions. Southward thence
> We took our way, direct through hamlets, towns,
> Gaudy with relics of that festival,
> Flowers left to wither on triumphal arcs,
> And window-garlands . . .
> Among sequestered villages we walked
> And found benevolence and blessedness
> Spread like a fragrance everywhere, like spring
> That leaves no corner of the land untouched.
>   *Prelude (1805), vi, 694–6, 355–64, 367–70*

These lines bear the unmistakable marks of having been written many years after the events they describe; beautiful though they may be, they lack immediacy, intimacy or any sense of personal involvement. Which, of course, was exactly how he felt in 1790.

In *The Prelude*, William noted, again merely in passing, that everywhere on their journey they saw dances of liberty, held in the open air to celebrate the *Fête de la Fédération* and lasting far into the night. When they joined a boat at Chalon to travel down the Saône, they found it full of southern delegates returning from the festivities in Paris.

> In this blithe company
> We landed, took with them our evening meal,
> Guests welcome almost as the angels were
> To Abraham of old. The supper done,
> With flowing cups elate and happy thoughts
> We rose at signal given, and formed a ring
> And hand in hand danced round and round the board.
> All hearts were open, every tongue was loud
> With amity and glee. We bore a name
> Honoured in France, the name of Englishmen,
> And hospitably did they give us hail
> As their forerunners in a glorious course –
> And round and round the board they danced again!
>
> *Prelude (1805), vi, 401–13*

What is particularly interesting about these impressions of France in 1790 is that they were only to emerge as distinct and important in retrospect. At the time, they did not even merit notice. Writing to his sister from Switzerland in September 1790, while he was still on his walking tour, William's only reflection on the French was that he found them much less imposing than the Swiss but their politeness, even in the lowest ranks of society, so engaging that he could only attribute it to real benevolence.

During the time which was near a month which we were in France, we had not once to complain of the smallest deficiency in civility in any person, much less of any positive rudeness. We had also perpetual occasion to observe that chearfulness and sprightliness for which the French have always been remarkable. But I must remind you that we crossed it at the time when the whole nation was mad with joy, in consequence of the revolution. It was a most interesting period to be in France, and we had many delightful scenes where the interest of the picture was owing solely to this cause.

The flatness of this description is startling: it is even more startling and revelatory when laid side by side with other parts of the same letter describing the landscapes of Switzerland and the Italian Lakes. 'My Spirits have been kept in a perpetual hurry of delight by the almost uninterrupted succession of sublime and beautiful objects which have passed before my eyes during the course of the last month,' he wrote. Despite his determination to keep his description of their route to an absolute minimum, so as not to exhaust his supply of paper, he found it impossible to check his enthusiasm or his pen. Significantly, it was one of the lakes, Como, which sparked a digression as unstoppable as it was characteristically Wordsworthian. Having explained that the banks of many of the Italian and Swiss lakes are too steep to take roads, he described walking for thirty miles along a lakeside footpath between two villages.

We entered upon this path about noon, and owing to the steepness of the banks, were soon unmolested by the sun, which illuminated the woods rocks and villages of the opposite shore. The lake is narrow and the shadows of the mountains were early thrown across it. It was beautiful to watch them travelling up the sides of the hills for several hours, to remark one half of a village covered with shade, and the other bright with the strongest sunshine. It was with regret that we passed every turn of this charming path, where every new picture was purchased by the loss of another which we would never have been tired of gazing at. The shores of the lake consist of steeps covered with large sweeping woods of chestnut spotted with villages, some clinging from the summits of the advancing rocks, and others hiding themselves within their recesses. Nor was the surface of the lake less interesting than its shores; part of it glowing with the richest green and gold the reflexion of the illuminated woods and part shaded with a soft blue tint. The picture was still further diversified by the number of sails which stole lazily by us, as we paused in the woods above them. After all this we had the moon. It was impossible not to contrast that repose that complacency of Spirit, produced by these lovely scenes, with the sensations I had experienced two or three days before, in passing the Alps. At the lake of Como my mind ran thro a thousand dreams of happiness which might be enjoyed upon its banks, if heightened by conversation and the exercise of the social affections.

Even at the age of twenty, William instinctively recognized that his own happiness was to be found in the solitude of a lakeland landscape, with the all-important proviso that his retreat should not be a hermitage.

The tour passed in a kaleidoscopic whirl of images: the 'awful solitude' of La Grande Chartreuse, where they spent the night in the monastery, which had not yet been desecrated by the Revolutionaries; the glaciers of the 'wondrous' vale of Chamonix, where 'winter like a tamèd lion walks, Descending from the mountain to make sport Among the cottages by beds of flowers'; most memorable of all, crossing the Alps by the Simplon Pass. In attempting to describe this to Dorothy, William was literally rendered wordless. 'The impressions of three hours of our walk among the Alps will never be effaced' was all he could say.

It would take him nearly fifteen years to find the words because, in 1790, he was still bound hand and foot by the metaphorical shackles of picturesque vocabulary. His is a textbook case of the dangers of using guidebooks: he saw what they saw and as they saw it. As he struggled to articulate his impressions for Dorothy, he inevitably fell back on the romantic conventions of his guides. 'Among the more awful scenes of the Alps,' he wrote, 'I had not a thought of man, or a single created being; my whole soul was turned to him who produced the terrible majesty before me.' While this was probably a genuine reaction, it was also a parroting of Thomas Gray's famous *dictum* on the Alps: 'Not a precipice, not a torrent, not a cliff, but is pregnant with religion and poetry. There are certain scenes that would awe an atheist into belief without the help of other argument.'

As the mature poet of *The Prelude*, however, William could express what are still recognizably the same sentiments in a profoundly new and unique way: he had found his own voice because he had released his imagination and learned to invest the scene with his own personal experience. Crossing the Alps thus became the poetic climax of the sixth book of *The Prelude*, because it was a climactic moment, spiritually and emotionally, for William.

This was how he described it. He and Jones had joined a guided party crossing the Simplon but, because they lingered too long over their lunch, were accidentally left behind. In attempting to follow, they took the wrong path, veering off up the mountainside instead of following the stony bed of the stream. They thought something was wrong when they did not overtake the rest of their party, but it was not until they met a peasant who pointed out the right route that the terrible realization dawned. The moment which they had anticipated so eagerly – which was indeed the main reason for the tour – had passed unnoticed. They had crossed the Alps without knowing it.

Thoroughly disappointed, they were forced to retrace their steps down the mountain to regain their road, which, for several hours, lay through a narrow chasm, the Ravine of Gondo.

> The immeasurable height
> Of woods decaying, never to be decayed,
> The stationary blasts of waterfalls,
> And everywhere along the hollow rent
> Winds thwarting winds, bewildered and forlorn,
> The torrents shooting from the clear blue sky,
> The rocks that muttered close upon our ears,
> Black drizzling crags that spoke by the wayside
> As if a voice were in them, the sick sight
> And giddy prospect of the raving stream,
> The unfettered clouds and region of the heavens,
> Tumult and peace, the darkness and the light –
> Were all like workings of one mind, the features
> Of the same face, blossoms upon one tree,
> Characters of the great apocalypse,
> The types and symbols of eternity,
> Of first, and last, and midst, and without end.
>
> *Prelude (1805), vi, 556–72*

Such an authoritative and resonant description was beyond the powers of the twenty-year-old boy walking the Alps and assailed on every side by overpowering images of grandeur. Even then, however, he was acutely aware that this whole experience would be of immense importance to him and he consciously tried to fix it in his memory. 'Ten thousand times in the course of this tour have I regretted the inability of my memory to retain a more strong impression of the beautiful forms before me,' he wrote wistfully to Dorothy,

and again and again in quitting a fortunate station have I returned to it with the most eager avidity, with the hope of bearing away a more lively picture. At this moment when many of these landscapes are floating before my mind, I feel a high [enjoyment] in reflecting that perhaps scarce a day of my life will pass [in] which I shall not derive some happiness from these images.

These were prophetic words. Not only would he return to these scenes in his imagination and his poetry for years to come but, thirty years later, in 1820, he would return in person to retrace his route and to attempt to re-create the experience.

Having dedicated two-thirds of their three-month tour to exploring Switzerland, William and Jones were now forced to draw it to a close. No doubt they were running out of money, though William had boasted to Dorothy that, between 14 July and 6 September, they had spent only £12 between them. More importantly, the new term at Cambridge would begin during the second week of October and they would have to get back to fulfil their residency requirements if they were to take their degrees. In a final gesture of bravado, they decided to buy a boat and sail down the Rhine from Basel to Cologne. 'The confidence of Youth [was] our only Art', William would later recall, 'And Hope gay Pilot of the bold design.' Youth and Hope were fortunately sufficient to keep them from harm and they arrived safely in Cologne, recovered their funds by selling the boat and set off on foot again to complete their journey home through Brabant.

Their tour had taken them through France, northern Italy, Switzerland, Germany and what is now Belgium. They had enjoyed uniform good health and become so inured to walking that they seemed incapable of fatigue; it was William's proud boast that they had several times walked thirteen leagues (almost forty miles) over the most mountainous parts of Switzerland without any more weariness than if they had been walking for an hour in a grove at Cambridge. This was undoubtedly an exaggeration, but thirty years later Robert Jones would recall, 'We were early risers in 1790 and generally walked 12 or 15 miles before breakfast and after feasting on the morning Landscape how we afterwards feasted on our Dejeuner of whatever the house might afford!'

There had been some disappointments in addition to failing to recognize that they had crossed the Alps. Neither the summit of Mont Blanc nor the famed Falls of Schaffhausen lived up to its reputation as the height of sublimity, but William was the first to admit that he had been unrealistic in his expectations. Like all travellers, they had suffered some misadventures, or 'little disasters' as William called them. They had been misled by the chimes of the village clock at Gravedona into rising in the middle of the night, instead of at dawn, and so had to spend a miserable night in the open, stung by insects and fearful of the unfamiliar noises emanating from the woods. They had become separated and lost their way in a torrential downpour during one of those terrifyingly dramatic thunderstorms for which the Italian Lakes are notorious. William had almost been swept away when he crossed a rapidly rising river to view the magnificent waterfall at the head of the valley of Lauterbrunnen. Far from depressing them, these mishaps had simply added to the pair's resolution and spirits. They had survived to tell the tale.

And what a tale it was! William's spirits were so high he even fondly imagined that, on his return to England, he would be welcomed with open arms at Forncett – even though it meant deferring his return to university till 10 November, a month after term had officially begun (this in his final term before his degree examinations). 'You will remember me affectionately to my Uncle and Aunt', he blithely informed Dorothy, adding a hope so forlorn it could not have convinced even himself: ' – as he was acquainted with my having given up all thoughts of a fellowship, he may perhaps not be so much displeased at this journey. I should be sorry if I have offended him by it.'

If William had persuaded himself that this was the case, he was soon to be disillusioned. His plea to visit Forncett received short shrift and, by the middle of October, he was back in Cambridge. He had triumphantly fulfilled his declared intention of offering 'An open slight Of college cares and study'. Now he would have to face the consequence.

4. A Vital Interest

The first thing William had to do on his return to Cambridge in October 1790 was to sort out his financial affairs. Uncle Richard, whatever he may have thought of his errant nephew, still sent him his autumn remittance on 19 October; at only £30, however, instead of the usual £35, it is tempting to see the reduction as a practical expression of disapproval. Perhaps that was why, when it came to paying five guineas he owed for his wine bills, William turned instead to his brother Richard in London. There would be no point in appealing to the generosity of his guardians for such an extravagance.

What use William made of this, his last full term at university, is unrecorded. There were no college examinations in December, as the undergraduates were supposed to be studying for their final university examinations. These would be held at the beginning of January. It was perhaps with this in mind that Uncle William revoked his ban on his nephew visiting Forncett. At least if William spent the Christmas vacation there, his family could be sure he had not concocted another madcap scheme and gone gallivanting off to London or the Continent again. It was also an opportunity to ensure that he did some work.

To Dorothy's great joy, therefore, William was invited to Forncett for the vacation. For the first time since their childhood they would spend her birthday, Christmas Day, together. If Uncle William did insist on some work from his nephew, he had also the sense to allow William and Dorothy to spend some leisure time alone. The weather was 'uncommonly mild', according to Dorothy; 'we used to walk every morning about two hours, and every evening we went into the garden at four or half past four and used to pace backwards and forwards 'till six'. As they wandered along the gravel path, arm in arm, in the gloom of the winter evenings, they had 'long, long conversations', which were only interrupted by the unwelcome summons of the tea-bell. They talked not just about the past and

William's travels on the Continent, but also about the future. Whatever doubts William may have had about the direction his life would take, Dorothy had still only that one object before her eyes: to live with him in a little cottage in the country, with a neatly furnished parlour, and a garden filled with roses and honeysuckle. It was to be '*our own*', but not exclusively, for even while building these cottages in the air, her happiness would only be complete if Jane Pollard, 'my earliest female Friend', could also live with them. Two and a half years later, having not seen William in the interval and with her cottage no nearer in reality than it had ever been, Dorothy would dwell forlornly on this visit and the happiness it had brought her: 'he is so amiable, so good, so fond of his Sister! Oh Jane the last time we were together he won my Affect[ion] to a Degree which I cannot describe.' Unable to stem her panegyric, she added,

I am willing to allow that half the virtues with which I fancy him endowed are the creation of my Love, but surely I may be excused! he was never tired of comforting his sister, he never left her in anger, he always met her with joy, he preferred her society to every other pleasure, or rather when we were so happy as to be within each other's reach he had no pleasure when we were compelled to be divided.

These seem curiously negative attributes to have been so valued by Dorothy; viewed dispassionately, they would seem to be little more than acts of common politeness. The fact that she read so much into her brother's patience and kindness towards her is an indication of her own depth of insecurity and desperate longing for affection. It says much for William, as a man and as a brother, that he responded in such a kindly manner to her emotional dependency, which was a burden and a responsibility he would never lay aside.

William returned to Cambridge in time to sit his examinations on 17 January. Defiant and insouciant to the end, he apparently chose to spend the previous week reading a novel. Like most of William's acts of youthful rebellion, it was not all it seemed. The novel was Samuel Richardson's *Clarissa Harlowe*, an overpoweringly dull exposition of 'the Distresses that may attend Misconduct both of Parents and Children in relation to Marriage', in seven ponderous volumes. It says little for the quality of the Cambridge system at this time that William passed his examination and, on 21 January 1791, was awarded the degree of Bachelor of Arts.

Much has been made of the financial cost of William's Cambridge education, not least because, in retrospect, it seems to have been unproductive. After all, it did not set him on the road to a successful establishment career, as his family had so fondly hoped when he went there. Uncle Christopher's complaints about his extravagance seem entirely justified when set beside William's own portrayal of himself in *The Prelude* as idle and careless. As we have seen, however, it is clear from other sources that *The Prelude* greatly exaggerates William's indolence at Cambridge; and there can be no doubt that his experiences (including the extracurricular ones of the vacations), his reading and friendships, laid the ground for much of his own future success.

Just how extravagant was he? From all the available evidence, it would seem that William was spending just under £100 a year, the maximum he could claim from his father's estate. This was a huge amount of money, especially at a time when a sizar's annual college expenses were officially reckoned to be only £15, excluding tuition fees. Patrick Brontë, father of the famous novelists, who from 1802 to 1806 was also a sizar at St John's, was a model example. His college bills amounted to between £12 and £15 a year. 'He came over from [Ireland], with 10£ in his pocket,' wrote Henry Kirke White, an admiring fellow sizar, 'and has no friends, or any income or emolument whatever, except what he receives for his Sizarship; yet he does support himself, and that, too, very genteelly.' The difference between Patrick Brontë and William Wordsworth was that Patrick came from a humble Irish tenant-farming background, was used to poverty, had no prospect of any income at all, except what he could earn by his own efforts, and, as an Evangelical, was personally committed to entering the Church. He was also much older (twenty-five to William's seventeen on entering college) and more self-disciplined. Nevertheless, even Patrick could not survive on the income from his sizarship and his exhibitions. Less than eighteen months after entering college, he had to appeal for assistance, and was given £20 a year by no less a person than the ubiquitous William Wilberforce.

John Jebb, who spent more than twenty years in Cambridge academic circles, was more realistic in assessing a sizar's expenses in 1775 at between £40 and £60 a year, without scholarships and exhibitions. William had incurred considerable expenses, not just in pursuing his social life but also in private tuition. Lessons with Isola cannot have been cheap.

Comparisons with other contemporaries also suggest that William's expenditure was not immoderate. Samuel Taylor Coleridge, who went up to Jesus College in 1791, managed to find himself £150 in debt after only two years at the university, even though he held two college awards worth £70 annually and a scholarship from Christ's Hospital. In the light of such examples, which were by no means unusual, William's own expenditure seems quite frugal and does not justify the opprobrium sometimes heaped upon him.

William's great dilemma now was what to do with himself. In the time-honoured fashion of undecided graduates everywhere, he decided to play for time. He allowed his family to assume that he would go into the Church; as he could not be ordained until he was twenty-three, this would give him two more years of freedom. He had no wish to return to his grandmother or Uncle Christopher at Penrith; his 'old dame', Ann Tyson, could no longer provide him with a home at Hawkshead; and Forncett would have stifled him. He chose therefore to go to London.

Quite what he intended to do there is not clear. Possibly, like Raisley Calvert, he simply thought he could live more to his satisfaction 'in every respect' in London than in Cambridge and at half the cost. This was not immediately apparent, however, as on 28 January 1791 Uncle Richard had to send him £60, almost double the usual remittance. Coming a mere seven days after William had received his degree, this unexpected generosity might have seemed like a pat on the back or, more likely, an expression of relief that he had actually got his BA. (Neither Coleridge nor Southey did.) More pragmatically, it was intended to pay off all his Cambridge debts before he left for London.

For the next four months, William apparently lived quietly in London. The account he gives in *The Prelude* is a composite picture of different visits made over the next twelve years, and it is impossible to disentangle what actually belongs to this period. Many of the most striking incidents and events can be dated with certainty to later visits, particularly that of 1802, when Charles Lamb accompanied him and Dorothy. Lamb was also indirectly responsible for one of the liveliest passages, which seems to capture perfectly the bewildered first impressions of a country visitor:

> the Babel din;
> The endless stream of men, and moving things . . .
> The wealth, the bustle and the eagerness,
> The glittering chariots with their pampered steeds,
> Stalls, barrows, porters; midway in the street
> The scavenger, who begs with hat in hand;
> The labouring hackney-coaches, the rash speed
> Of coaches travelling far whirled on with horn
> Loud blowing . . .
> Shop after shop, with symbols, blazoned names,
> And all the tradesman's honours overhead –
>
> *Prelude (1805), vii, 157–8, 161–7, 174–5*

Even this description is a paraphrase of a letter Lamb wrote to William in 1801, defending his love of city life against 'the mountaineers', as he called his poetical friends in the Lakes.

If *The Prelude* is confusing, the only surviving letter William wrote at this period is downright mysterious. He was writing to William Mathews, a friend from Pembroke College, who had taken up a temporary teaching post in Leicestershire. On 17 June 1791 William apologized for neglecting to write for so long; two months previously, he explained, he had taken up his pen with the intention of beginning a letter but had been interrupted. He was then in London and too busy to write, but, just as he offered no explanation of who or what had interrupted him, so he offered only the most enigmatic description of his preoccupations. 'I quitted London about three weeks ago,' was the only fact he now volunteered,

where my time passed in a strange manner; sometimes whirled about by the vortex of its *strenua inertia*, and sometimes thrown by the eddy into a corner of the stream, where I lay in almost motionless indolence. Think not however that I had not many very pleasant hours; a man must be unfortunate indeed who resides four months in Town without some of his time being disposed of in such a manner, as he would forget with reluctance.

The obscurity of William's meaning in this passage has led to great speculation as to what he was doing and what he was trying to hide. The general consensus appears to be that this spring of 1791 was the period of his initiation into radical politics. It was certainly a time when it was difficult to escape the radical agenda, which had been given new impetus in Britain by the successful, and hitherto comparatively peaceful, French Revolution. The London Revolution Society and the Society for Constitutional Information were both flourishing and eloquent in their demands for parliamentary reform and religious equality. The French Revolution had also provoked a war of words in pamphlet form. Edmund Burke's famously prescient denunciation of the inevitable bloody consequences of the fall of the Bastille, *Reflections on the Revolution in France*, had been published in 1790. It was answered in March 1791 (while William was in London) by Thomas Paine's equally passionate defence, *The Rights of Man*, and by James Mackintosh's *Vindiciae Gallicae*. As William himself would be in France before the end of the year, it is tempting to see his decision to go there as the result of his being drawn into the vortex of radical politics during the four months he spent in London. Attractive though this idea may seem, there is little evidence to support it. The rather more boring conclusion appears far more likely: that he spent the time as a tourist. His mysterious letter to Mathews therefore becomes merely an attempt to avoid seeming provincial to his friend, who was himself the son of a London bookseller, rather than a deliberate covering up of more sinister activities.

The only indisputable fact is that William paid a visit to 'Aunt' Threlkeld. Now in her mid-forties and having seen all her young charges safely through to adulthood and independence, Elizabeth had finally felt free to accept William Rawson, a Halifax mill-owner and banker. As part of the customary round of bridal visits, they had travelled down to London.

One can guess that it was the new Mrs Rawson who introduced William to Samuel Nicholson of Cateaton Street, Holborn. Nicholson was a haberdashery wholesaler who had, for many years, been the main supplier of her shop in Halifax. Like her, he was a Unitarian, but, more importantly for William, he was also a radical. He had been an early member of the Society for Constitutional Information, which campaigned for annual parliaments, full male suffrage and political rights for dissenters. He may not have been so active by 1791, nevertheless, he still had connections with radical and dissenting circles which were to become important to William in the future. Possibly during this spring of 1791, or, more likely, in 1793–4, Nicholson took pity on William 'at a time when I had not many acquaintances in London, [and he] used often to invite me to dine with him on Sundays'. On several of these occasions, William took the opportunity to go with his host to the famous dissenting house in Old Jewry to hear 'an able & eloquent man' preach. This was Joseph Fawcett, hailed by William Godwin as 'the first man [he] had ever known of great originality in thinking', and by William Hazlitt as 'one of the most enthusiastic admirers of the French Revolution'. Our William, however, was not particularly impressed by Fawcett's preaching. 'He published a Poem on War, [*The Art of War*, 1795] w[hic]h had a good deal of merit & made me think more about him than I should otherwise have done', he told Isabella Fenwick many years later. He also informed her that, in creating the disillusioned and misogynistic figure of the Solitary in *The Excursion*, published in 1816, he had drawn on Fawcett as one of his main models.

It is impossible to compile a chronology or an itinerary for William at this period. We do not even know where he lived. If *The Prelude* is to be believed, William spent most of his four months wandering round the capital, like any typical provincial tourist. He visited the great historic and national monuments; he walked in London's celebrated pleasure gardens at Vauxhall, in Lambeth, and Ranelagh, in Chelsea, where there were fireworks, balls and masquerades. He went to the theatre, a lifelong passion, and probably attended one of the last performances at the old theatre in Drury Lane, which Richard Brinsley Sheridan had decided to close on 4 June, transferring the company and its star, Dora Jordan, to the Haymarket, while he rebuilt Drury Lane on a grand scale. Mrs Jordan was famous for her fine legs, which she displayed at every opportunity by playing gender-swapping roles, from Shakespeare to modern farce. She was about to become infamous for leaving her then partner, Richard Ford, son of the co-owner of Drury Lane and father of her three children, in favour of the Duke of Clarence. Both she and Ford would play curious cameo roles in William's later history.

Much of the time, William claimed in *The Prelude*, he simply spent wandering the streets, just observing the crowds in what was, even then, a remarkably cosmopolitan city. He was, he said,

> At ease from all ambition personal,
> Frugal as there was need, and though self-willed,
> Yet temperate and reserved, and wholly free
> From dangerous passions.
>
> *Prelude (1805), vii, 69–72*

The most 'dangerous passions' of that time were those of radical politics, which were impossible to ignore. He read, 'eagerly Sometimes, the master pamphlets of the day', but he lacked that 'vital interest' which would later transform his political perceptions and commitment. He also went to listen to parliamentary debates. There he saw and heard the Earl of Lonsdale's former protégé, William Pitt the Younger, who had been Prime Minister since 1783. He was thrilled to see peers, such as Bedford, Gloucester and Salisbury, not just because of what they were saying, but because they were the living incarnations of lineages whose exploits were celebrated by Shakespeare. He listened avidly to the flesh-and-blood orators of his own time: Edmund Burke, still a lone voice crying out, like Cassandra, against the 'radical and intrinsic' evils of the French Revolution which must inevitably lead to bloodshed; Charles James Fox, stout defender of the new French constitution as 'the most stupendous and glorious edifice of liberty, which had been erected ... in any time or country'; and William Wilberforce, making his 'most impassioned and emphatic' but shamefully doomed appeals to end slavery in the

British colonies. The eloquence of such renowned speakers on such vital issues won William's admiration, but it could not hold his attention for long.

> Words follow words, sense seems to follow sense –
> What memory and what logic! – till the strain,
> Transcendant, superhuman as it is,
> Grows tedious even in a young man's ear.
>
> *Prelude (1805), vii, 539–42*

By the middle of May, William's enthusiasm for 'the Babel din' of London was growing thin. More importantly, his money was running out. He decided to visit his worthy friend Robert Jones, who was biding his time until eligible for ordination at his family home in north Wales. To disapproving uncles, this could be presented as an economy: there were, after all, no theatres, pleasure grounds or shops in rural Denbighshire. It could also be seen as a staging post on his return journey to Cumberland. Dorothy cannot have been alone in assuming that he was on his way there. The arguments must have been reasonably convincing, for Uncle Richard duly dispatched £20 on 19 May.

William arrived at Plas-yn-Llan in holiday mood. He had no intention of doing any serious work and travelling light gave him the excuse to leave almost all his books behind. He passed his time in a 'very agreeable manner'. The Jones family lived in the 'house by the church' in a glorious situation, halfway between Denbigh and Ruthin and high on the Clwydian range of mountains, with a seemingly endless prospect over the wide, fertile valley below. 'I often hear from my brother William who is now in Wales', Dorothy wrote to Jane on 26 June with more than a hint of envy,

where I think he seems so happy that it is probable he will remain there all the summer, or a great part of it: Who would not be happy enjoying the company of three young ladies in the Vale of Clewyd and without a rival? His friend Jones is a charming young man, and has *five sisters*, three of whom are at home at present, then there are mountains, rivers, woods and rocks, whose charms without any other inducement would be sufficient to tempt William to continue amongst them as long as possible.

Regardless of the inducements which may have been offered by Jones's sisters, the great object of William's visit was to plan a second pedestrian tour with their brother. This time they would explore the northern counties of Wales. Their tour would last a maximum of six weeks, between June and August, and, just as they had done the year before, they went guidebook in hand. This time they used Thomas Pennant's *A Tour in Wales* and the climax of their tour, as of his, was to be a nocturnal ascent of Snowdon to watch the dawn break from the summit.

Writing to William Mathews on 3 August 1791, immediately after his return, he dismissed the tour in less than half a sentence: 'we visited [the] greatest part of North Wales, without having any reason to complain of disappointed expectations'.

How different from his irrepressibly enthusiastic response to the Alps! There was, however, one experience which left an enduring impression on William's mind. His ascent of Snowdon came to assume almost mythical status for him, in much the same way as crossing the Alps the previous summer. Again, there was a palpable sense of expectation and excitement as they set out from Beddgelert on a close, warm night, wreathed with that 'dripping mist' which is a Welsh speciality. Collecting their guide, a shepherd who lived at the foot of the mountain, they began their climb. 'Hemmed round on every side with fog and damp', they could see nothing and, as the path became steeper and rockier, they were obliged to concentrate on where they put their feet.

> With forehead bent
> Earthward, as if in opposition set
> Against an enemy, I panted up
> With eager pace, and no less eager thoughts.

Suddenly William, who was at the head of the party, found himself unexpectedly bathed in light. Looking up, he discovered that he had emerged from the mist.

> The moon stood naked in the heavens at height
> Immense above my head, and on the shore
> I found myself of a huge sea of mist,
> Which meek and silent rested at my feet.
> A hundred hills their dusky backs upheaved
> All over this still ocean; and beyond,
> Far, far beyond, the vapours shot themselves
> In headlands, tongues, and promontory shapes,
> Into the sea – the real sea, that seemed
> To dwindle and give up its majesty,
> Usurped upon as far as sight could reach.
>
> *Prelude (1805), xiii, 29–32, 41–51*

It was this moment of unexpected revelation which inspired the only incident from the walking tour of Wales to be included in *The Prelude*. The sunrise, which was the real purpose of their ascent of Snowdon, was forgotten.

Returning to Plas-yn-Llan after their tour, William showed a marked disinclination to uproot himself and make his expected journey to Cumberland. This is surprising, if only because the suit against Lord Lonsdale was due to come before the Carlisle Assizes in August 1791 and there was the best possibility yet of a settlement, if not a decisive judgement against the Earl. But in the run up to the Assizes, difficulties multiplied. The Administrators had to serve a subpoena not only on their own supposedly friendly witness, 'Jack' Robinson, to force him to attend and give evidence, but also on the Earl's steward, Mr Arnott, who proved as evasive as his master.

On 29 August, poor Richard wrote to his Grandmother Cookson from Carlisle to tell her that it was expected that the case would come before the Assizes the next day. As Counsel, they had retained Edward Christian, now Professor of Common Law at Cambridge. Robinson had arrived the previous night and spent the next morning closeted with the Earl. Quite what Robinson was up to is unclear, but his role in the whole affair was becoming increasingly opaque. Despite being the only living witness to John Wordsworth's appointment as agent in his own stead, he had no wish to antagonize Lord Lonsdale and had consistently refused to give evidence against him unless formally subpoenaed to do so. Now that he was legally obliged to give his evidence, he succeeded in avoiding doing this in open court by persuading both parties to accept a settlement. It may be unfair to Robinson, but it does seem odd that he could not have done this before and that he brokered an agreement only at the moment when Lonsdale faced actual defeat. Both parties consented that the disputed accounts between Lonsdale and John Wordsworth's Administrators should be referred to an independent arbitrator for a binding judgement. The suggestion was accepted only on condition that Lonsdale admitted that the terms of John Wordsworth's appointment were that he 'was to be paid for all Law Business as other Gent[le]m[en] of the Profession were paid' or provide documentary evidence to substantiate otherwise. The court approved an award of damages in the region of £5,000 to John Wordsworth's estate, but referred the final figure to an arbitrator, Mr Burrow, who was appointed on Robinson's recommendation. Yet, less than a month later, when questioned by Richard, Robinson claimed to know nothing at all about the gentleman. It was unquestionably an ominous sign. And before the end of the year, the Administrators were beginning not only to suspect that Burrow was 'too much under the influence of his Lordship' but also to question openly his integrity. They were right to do so: Burrow was soon to be rewarded for his role in the affair by being presented to one of Lonsdale's pocket boroughs. It was possibly a sadistic little joke on the Earl's part that the borough in question was Cockermouth.

Out of his depth among such experienced practitioners of deceit, Richard had decided to stay on in London. Only days before the case came up at Carlisle, he transferred his articles from his cousin to Messrs Parkin and Lambert of Gray's Inn.

The Carlisle Assizes had been an opportunity for a meeting of the extended Wordsworth clan, and it was no doubt in response to urgent requests by William's uncles that Robinson decided to see what could be done about their errant nephew. William's Welsh idyll was interrupted by a summons from Robinson. The incumbent of Harwich, Uncle William Cookson's brother-in-law the Reverend William Cowper, 'from <u>expensive</u> habits, & other causes of improvident, & irregular conduct', had been obliged to flee his creditors and settle in Holland. The living, which was effectively in Robinson's gift, was not legally vacant, but as Cowper could no longer officiate, there was a desperate need for a curate to take his place. This post Robinson now offered to William. Even had he been in a position to accept (which he was not, being still too young to qualify for ordination), William was being offered a poisoned chalice. As curate, he could never enjoy the full benefits of the very rich living, which belonged of right to the incumbent; even if Cowper resigned or died, there was no guarantee that his curate would succeed him in office. What Robinson was seeking was someone to do all his protégé's work without the reward. Fortunately for William, he had the perfect excuse: at twenty-one, he was still almost eighteen months short of the requisite age for ordination.

Rather than simply write to reject Robinson's offer, he decided to return to London to plead his excuses in person. At this important juncture in his career, he wrote a letter to his friend William Mathews which is extraordinarily self-revelatory of both his current attitude and his intentions. There can be no question of his sincerity. Mathews was in the depths of despair about his own prospects, and William himself was distressed beyond measure that his friend's letter had been delayed, preventing him from offering comfort sooner. Mathews was unable to reconcile himself to the tedium of his schoolmaster post or to the prospect of returning to a home that was riven by religious factionalism. He proposed to William that they should take an extended tour abroad together. Tempting though the idea must have seemed, William had both the personal strength of mind and sufficient appreciation of his friend's character to resist. He set out his reasons in an impressively cogent and thoughtful letter which would probably have given his own guardians a pleasant surprise. 'I take it for granted that you are not likely to continue long in your present employment,' he wrote,

but when you leave it how you can put into execution the plan you speak of I cannot perceive. It is impossible you can ever have your father's consent to a scheme which to a parent at least, if not to every one else, must appear wild even to insanity ... I do not think you could ever be happy while you were conscious that you were a cause of such sorrow to your parents, as they must undoubtedly be oppressed with; when all that they will know of you is that you are wandering about the world, without perhaps a house to your head. I cannot deny that were I so situated, as to be without relations to whom I were accountable for my actions, I should perhaps prefer your idea to your present situation, or to vegetating on a paltry curacy. Yet still there is another objection which would have influence upon me which is this. I should not be able to reconcile to my ideas of right, the thought of wandering about a country, without a certainty of being able to maintain myself, without being indebted for my existence to those charities of which the acceptance might rob people not half so able to support themselves as myself. It is evident there are a thousand ways in which a person of your education might get his bread, as a recompence for his labour, and while that continues to be the case, for my own part I confess I should be unwilling to accept it on any other conditions. I see many charms in the idea of travelling, much to be enjoyed and much to be learnt, so many that were we in possession of perhaps even less than an hundred a year apiece, which would amply obviate the objection I have just made, and without any relations to whom we were accountable, I would set out with you this moment with all my heart, not entertaining a doubt but that by some means or other we should be soon able to secure ourselves that independence you so ardently pant after, and what is more with minds furnished with such a store of ideas as would enable us to enjoy it. But this is not the case; therefore, for my own part, I resign the idea. I would wish you to do the same. What then is to be done? Hope and Industry are to be your watchwords, and I warrant you their influence will secure you the victory.

This letter was written from Cambridge, where William had returned after visiting Robinson at Sion Hill in London. While he might have hated the thought of 'vegetating on a paltry curacy', William had made up his mind that this was to be his fate. His Uncle William Cookson had suggested that he should embark on a study of Oriental literature. It was a typically astute idea, taking account of his nephew's evident preference for languages and holding out the prospect to him of distinguishing himself as a man of letters in a field which was not incompatible with a career in the Church. An additional advantage, at least in his uncle's eyes, was that the difficulty of obtaining books and tuition would effectively tie William to Cambridge for the foreseeable future.

Unfortunately for everyone concerned, the plan went badly wrong. It made sense for William to begin his course of study with the start of the new term. Instead, towards the end of the month, William took himself off to London. He had some excuse in that it was an opportunity to see his brother John, who had returned to England after an absence of eighteen months. He was now 'a very tall handsome man' who, like his brothers, had acquired a taste for independence. Uncle Christopher was soon complaining that John had not written to either his grandmother or himself, which he considered 'a very great peice [*sic*] of Ingratitude'.

John's presence alone cannot explain William's decision to go to London. It seems to have been an attempt to put some space between himself and his Uncle William, while they argued about how he was to spend the remaining time before he was of age to be ordained. William was not exactly entranced at the prospect of studying Hebrew and Aramaic. His own wish was to be allowed to go to France, with the object of polishing up his French, so that he could qualify as a travelling companion to a gentleman.

For a month, there was some hard bargaining between uncle and nephew, but eventually they came to a compromise. William would be allowed to go to France for the winter but there were two important provisos. He would have to begin his study of Oriental languages as soon as he returned and he was to live in 'some retired Place' in France. Having secured the consent of the one uncle who was not his legal guardian, William persuaded his brother to act as his intermediary with the others. Richard duly wrote a propitiatory letter to Uncle Richard, stressing that William had been 'advised' to spend some time in France before taking orders, that the experience would be 'less expensive and more improving' than being obliged to remain in England and, as a masterstroke, that the £40 he was now requesting would support him till next summer. Uncle Richard responded with admirable promptness, dispatching the full amount within three days.

Events moved swiftly. Orléans, some eighty miles south and slightly west of Paris, was settled on as a suitably 'retired Place'. A medium-sized town on the

Loire, with a population of something more than 30,000, it had the reputation of being a sleepy backwater. Temporary accommodation had been arranged at Les Trois Empereurs, the best hotel in the city. By 22 November, William was at Brighton, waiting for a passage across the Channel and thwarted by the weather. For five long days he was left kicking his heels, 'which time must have past in a manner extremely disagreeable, if I had not bethought me of introducing myself to Mrs Charlotte Smith'. This was a stroke of genius, for Charlotte Smith was not only a poetess whose works he had long admired (and imitated) but also a distant relative by marriage. 'She received me in the politest manner, and shewed me every possible civility', William reported with delight to Richard. Flattered by her young admirer's enthusiasm for her poetry, Mrs Smith allowed him to read and copy some of her work in progress. She also gave him important letters of introduction to friends in Paris and Orléans, including one to Helen Maria Williams, the poetess to whom William had addressed his first published sonnet, who had been living in France since July and in Orléans since October. The introduction was to have significant repercussions, for she, like all her French contacts, was an enthusiast for the Revolution. Inadvertently, therefore, William had acquired a set of introductions to people within the most politically active and extreme revolutionary circles.

William crossed the Channel on the night of Saturday 26 November and arrived in Paris the following Wednesday. It was now almost two and a half years since the Fall of the Bastille and Paris was still in a volatile state. With hindsight, it is obvious that there were signs, in the months before William's arrival, that extremism was increasing and mob violence was becoming more likely. At the time, however, this was not apparent, even to the most acute observers. There had been a few alarms, not least in June, when the royal family's abortive attempt to escape had ended ignominiously in their recapture at Varennes. This had played into the hands of the republicans, including Thomas Paine, who was just one of many English radicals residing in the city. They now began to demand that Louis XVI should be dethroned and a republic set up in place of the mixed constitution which was then under discussion. Only two days after the annual *Fête de la Fédération*, a republican manifesto was read out at the 'altar of the country' in the Champ de Mars. Two spectators, hiding under the altar in order to get a better view, were seized by the crowd and brutally murdered as suspected counter-revolutionaries. The National Guard, called out to disperse the mob, fired on them, resulting in the deaths of some eighteen citizens. Alarmed at what was rapidly exaggerated into a massacre, the dominant party, the Jacobins, withdrew their support for the republican manifesto and things calmed down. The new constitution, which retained the king's right of veto, was approved by the National Assembly in September and the revolution seemed to have come to a suitably moderate and legitimate conclusion.

William therefore arrived in Paris to find the city comparatively quiet. He had only four days to spend before going on to Orléans, and he confined himself to visiting the main sights. For the second time this year, he was a tourist in a capital city, hastily notching off 'each spot of old and recent fame'.

Like most Englishmen visiting Paris at this time, he also attended the new National Assembly and the Jacobin Club in the Rue St Jacques, and was unimpressed by their disorderly proceedings. In their 'clamorous halls'

> I saw the revolutionary power
> Toss like a ship at anchor, rocked by storms;
>
> *Prelude (1805), ix, 48–9*

Though he could probably have found someone to endorse his application to visit these places, simply because he was English, Charlotte Smith's introductions enabled him to obtain the necessary passes speedily. The member who introduced him to the National Assembly would, William anticipated, be a useful contact on his return to Paris. He wandered round the Palais Royal, which was to remain one of his lifelong favourite haunts in Paris, and, joining the crowds which thronged the arcades, was mesmerized by the sight of coffee-shop politicians in heated argument amidst the taverns, brothels, gaming-houses and shops:

> I stared, and listened with a stranger's ears
> To hawkers and haranguers (hubbub wild!)
> And hissing factionalists with ardent eyes,
> In knots, or pairs, or single – ant-like swarms
> Of builders and subverters, every face
> That hope or apprehension could put on –
> Joy, anger and vexation, in the midst
> Of gaiety and dissolute idleness.
>
> *Prelude (1805), ix, 55–62*

The atmosphere was electrifying, its animation enhanced for William by the fact that his French was not yet good enough to follow all the arguments. 'The whole city is split into parties,' declared another English visitor at this time,

and, at the corner of every principal street, the glaring letters of some inflammatory handbill invite the eye. All the coffee-houses are crowded with pretended politicians, who, according to their various prejudices, vent the noxious torrents of their fury; and groups of hirelings, half intoxicated, are everywhere bawling out their national airs.

For William, the contrast between these noisy scenes of politics in action with the almost melancholy scene at the deserted Bastille became symbolic of the distance between the petty factionalism into which the revolution had descended and the great unifying cause in which it had begun. He sat among the ruins, where 'silent zephyrs sported with the dust', and 'in the guise Of an enthusiast' pocketed a stone to keep as a relic. It was an appropriate gesture, but it was an empty one. William 'in honest truth' was 'Affecting more emotion than I felt'. He was, he admitted, more genuinely moved by the celebrated painting by Charles Le Brun of Louis XIV's mistress Louise de la Vallière as the penitent Mary Magdalen than by anything else he saw in Paris at this time. Writing this section of *The Prelude* in 1804, he felt obliged to apologize for what then seemed his youthful 'indifference ... strange'.

> I was unprepared
> With needful knowledge, had abruptly passed
> Into a theatre of which the stage
> Was busy with an action far advanced.
>   ... At that time,
> Moreover, the first storm was overblown,
> And the strong hand of outward violence
> Locked up in quiet.
>
> *Prelude, (1805), ix, 92–5, 108–11*

On 5 December William left Paris, arriving at his ultimate destination the following day.

Orléans, a city with a venerable history, lies in the midst of a seemingly unending plain on a curve in the Loire. Surrounded on three sides by a medieval defensive ditch and city wall, fortified with towers at regular intervals, on the fourth it was protected by the broad waters of the river. The wharves and quays along the river frontage were the key to the city's economic success: they gave mercantile access to the Atlantic and the French colonies in the Caribbean. Sugar refining and cotton manufacture were the main industries dependent on this trade, which brought the region immense wealth. For centuries Orléans had been second only to Paris, enjoying royal protection and patronage, which was reflected in the large number of churches and convents crammed within its walls. It was also an outstanding intellectual centre. In early medieval times civil law and Greek were both taught there, even when banned in Paris, and one of its most famous scholars, Pope Clement V, founded its renowned university in 1306. It also had an equally prestigious medical school and an Académie Royale des Sciences. A monument to Joan of Arc, the 'Maid of Orléans', just off the main central square, commemorated her divinely inspired raising of the English siege of the city in 1429. Much of the medieval city, with its brick and timber houses, survived the siege and the depredations of the sixteenth-century Wars of Religion, but the fourth-century cathedral, where Carolingian and Capetian kings had been crowned, was blown up by Protestants and did not. Substantial rebuilding, funded by colonial wealth, began in the seventeenth century and continued well into the eighteenth: a magnificent nine-arched bridge over the Loire led to the grandly rebuilt Place du Martroy, in the heart of the city, and a vast Gothic-style cathedral. It was this cathedral, dedicated to the Sainte Croix, which, literally and metaphorically, dominated the whole city. Its great nave and towers soared above the surrounding buildings and, even today, are still visible for miles across the outlying plains. Orléans was devoted to throne and altar, and, as the revolution descended into extremism, became a centre of counter-revolutionary activity.

Even at this period, English visitors with radical political views found the city disappointing. Helen Maria Williams, the poetess, had dismissed the city as 'confined, illiberal, and disagreeable', a sure sign that its political conservatism, rather than the place, had disagreed with her. William, however, was blissfully unaware of Orléans's lack of political credibility. 'I have every prospect of liking this place extremely well–', he wrote enthusiastically to Richard; 'the country thou' flat is pleasant and abounds in agreeable walks, particularly by the side of the Loire, which is a very magnificent river.' He had quickly found lodgings which were both handsome and cheap: a first-floor apartment over the arcades on the finest street in town, the newly built Rue Royale, which ran directly from the bridge over the Loire to the Place du Martroy. For this, his landlord charged him thirty livres a month, which was just less than £1. His board, which excluded breakfast, cost him an additional fifty livres a month. In an effort to be frugal, William had turned down alternative lodgings which he had liked 'extremely', because they were too expensive. He had even managed to negotiate a sliding-scale reduction in rent to only twenty-four livres and ten sous if he stayed eight months – an early indication that he was already considering the possibility of a longer stay in France than had originally been agreed.

William's landlord, Jean Henri Gellet-Duvivier, a widower with three small children, was a silk merchant by profession. Although he is usually depicted as a rabid anti-revolutionary, this is not borne out by the evidence. It is true he was executed on 13 July 1793 for his part in an attack, four months earlier, on Léonard Bourdon, the Orléans deputy to the National Convention, but this was not quite the anti-revolutionary gesture it has been blown up to appear. Gellet-Duvivier, in common with most of the inhabitants of Orléans, was not always implacably opposed to the political developments that had taken place. He had, for instance, paid 100 livres as his *contribution patriotique*, a once-and-for-all voluntary tax assessed at a quarter of personal income decreed by the National Assembly on 6 October 1789. While the 'voluntary' nature of the tax might be queried, given the political pressures to conform, his children were also among the '*Citoyens Patriotes*' who offered their jewellery '*à la Nation*' the following December: eight- and six-year-old Pauline and Julie each offered a pair of gold earrings, and five-year-old Augustin, a pair of silver buttons.

Nevertheless, among Gellet-Duvivier's other lodgers were a young gentleman from Paris and several cavalry officers who had been stationed in the city since September. This latter group of men were certainly reactionary: they had been stoned on entering Orléans because their band had refused to play the revolutionary anthem *Ça ira*. It was perhaps his acquaintance with them which led William to the somewhat naïve judgement that 'almost all the people of any opulen[ce are] aristocrates and all the others democrates', adding, 'I had imagined that there were some people of wealth and circumstance favorers of the revolution, but here there is not one to be found.'

William's greatest disappointment at Orléans was to find that his introduction to Helen Maria Williams was useless; she had already left the city before he arrived. He made the acquaintance of another fellow countryman, the Sheffield manufacturer Thomas Foxlow, who had set up a cotton mill in Orléans. Through Foxlow, whose business had been funded by the Duc d'Orléans and was dependent on the slave labour of the French colonies, William expected to mix in 'the best society this place affords'. Naturally, Foxlow's associates were mainly aristocratic and anti-Jacobin (the Jacobins were calling for the abolition of slavery), though they could not risk blazoning their sympathies abroad. All political discussion was studiously avoided and William passed the time attending their parties and card games, for all the world as though no revolution had taken place.

In *The Prelude*, William says that he soon grew bored of this society and gradually withdrew into the noisier world of the revolutionary patriots. This is only partly the truth. His main reason for withdrawing from this society – and indeed from Orléans itself – was that he had fallen head over heels in love. Marie Anne Vallon, or Annette, as she was always known, was the sixth and last child of Jean Léonard Vallon, a third-generation surgeon from Blois, who had died some years earlier. Both Annette's older brothers, Jean and Charles, had followed in his footsteps and were employed at the same hospital, the Hôtel-Dieu, a charitable institution where nuns provided nursing care for the indigent sick. Their mother had remarried and their stepfather, M. Vergez, was yet another Blésois surgeon. Annette's third brother, Paul, had broken the family tradition and was a lawyer who lived and worked as a notary clerk in Orléans.

Why, how, where or even when William and Annette first met is a matter for conjecture, as is the progress of much of their affair. Any information not lost by chance, or deliberately destroyed by William and his widow, was suppressed by his grandson, Gordon Wordsworth. Yet the liaison was of crucial importance in almost every aspect of William's life and its repercussions were still being felt decades later. It is therefore deeply frustrating that we know so little about this momentous relationship.

We can surmise that the pair met in Orléans. William's sudden and unexpected removal to Blois can be explained only by his desire to follow Annette home; he had no other reason to go. It is most likely that they met through either Paul or their mutual friends the Dufours family. The attraction must have been instant and overwhelmingly physical, for the one indisputable fact is that within weeks of their first meeting Annette was pregnant with their daughter, Caroline.

Dorothy's description of William at this time is all we have to indicate what drew Annette to the young Englishman. Dorothy described William's character as 'ardent' and 'highly touched'. In her eyes, he possessed, to an eminent degree, steadiness and sincerity in his attachments, but also what she curiously calls

a sort of violence of Affection if I may so Term it which demonstrates itself every moment of the Day when the Objects of his affection are present with him, in a thousand almost imperceptible attentions to their wishes, in a sort of restless watchfulness which I know not how to describe, a Tenderness that never sleeps, and at the same Time such a Delicacy of Manners as I have observed in few Men.

Even this partial witness, however, could not persuade herself that her brother was handsome, 'his person is not in his favour ...' she admitted. 'He is ... certainly rather plain than otherwise, has an extremely thoughtful countenance, but when he speaks it is often lighted up with a smile which *I* think very pleasing'.

Of Annette, we know even less. She had been born at Blois on 22 June 1766 and she was a Roman Catholic. Given her family background, she was probably already conservative in her politics when she first met William, but it was not until the royalist rebellion in the Vendée that she became an active counter-revolutionary. Her only surviving portrait does not indicate that she possessed any great beauty: slight of figure, she had a mass of long curly hair, a long nose and dark eyes, her best feature, under delicately arched brows.

What she lacked in conventional beauty, Annette more than made up for in personality. Guillemin de Savigny described her as having been inculcated from childhood with the best principles and being always prepared to put the interests of others before her own. She had, he said, a great deal of sensibility, a very lively and very wild imagination and rare strength of character. In addition to her natural vivacity, ardour and gaiety, she had the frankness and freedom of manners which were typically French, but totally alien to young women of her class in England. Even so ingrained a puritan as Robert Southey found French women irresistible. They had 'something of Aspasia [a famous Greek courtesan] about them', he wrote, and were 'certainly more sensual than our country women' but also 'more intellectual'. This was, one would have thought, just the combination to capture an ardent young poet's eye and heart. Certainly, if William was as naïve sexually as he was politically, he would not have been difficult to seduce. Annette was a very determined young woman; at twenty-five, she was also four years older than her lover. Though it is dangerous to draw conclusions from differences in age alone, it would be natural to assume that this would have its effect on the balance of their relationship, particularly in its early days. Nor can one ignore the fact that Annette's older unmarried sister, Françoise, also gave birth to an illegitimate child, a son, whom she did not acknowledge as hers for twenty years. If nothing else, this suggests that the Vallons had a much more relaxed view of female morality than was customary in a comparable English family at the time.

Only one of Annette's letters to William survives out of all their long and frequent correspondence, together with two to Dorothy. All three were preserved accidentally; two of them never reached their destination but were held back by the French censor who, ironically, proved less efficient than the Wordsworth family in eradicating all evidence of the clandestine affair. Not a single letter to Annette, from either William or Dorothy, has seen the light of day.

Annette's letter to William, written on 20 March 1793, almost six months after they parted, is revelatory: her passion fairly sizzles on the page as, in a flood of ill-spelt and ill-written words, she assures him of her undying devotion. She is inconsolable not to have heard from him for eleven days; if her letters arrived as quickly as her thoughts she would not be troubled with painful fears; William is the best beloved of men, the tenderest of men. 'Come, my lover, my husband', she urges him,

receive the tender kisses of your wife, your daughter[.] she is so pretty this poor little one
... she resembles you more and more each day [–] I believe I hold you in my arms[.] her
little heart often beats against mine[;] I believe I feel that of her father ... always love your
little girl and your Annette who kisses you a thousand times on the mouth on the eyes and
[on] my little one that I love always[,] that I entrust to your safe-keeping [and then?] to
God, I will write on Sunday. Adieu I love you for life[.]

While not doubting the genuine nature of Annette's feelings for William, both this
letter and, perhaps even more so, the one she wrote the same day to Dorothy are
an eloquent form of emotional blackmail. Having been left, quite literally, holding
the baby when William returned to England, Annette was understandably terrified
that she had lost him for ever. Even if he had every intention of returning to marry
her, their two countries were now at war. She was in an impossible position. 'I
would be more comforted if we were married,' she wrote to him, 'but also I see it
is almost impossible for you to expose yourself to [the danger]. If we have war you
would perhaps be taken prisoner.'

A year earlier, however, in March 1792, neither of them had any forebodings
about their future. They seem to have given themselves up to the passion of the
moment and, when Annette's visit to Orléans came to an end, William followed her
to Blois. How he explained this change of residence to his family at home is not
known; no doubt he did not give the true reason, but at least he could claim that Blois
was also a 'retired Place'. In fact, it was an altogether smaller and quieter town than
Orléans. Lying some thirty miles downstream on the Loire, it had been the stronghold
of the powerful Comtes de Blois (who included the English king Stephen among
their number) since early medieval times, but from the end of the fourteenth century
it became a royal residence. The wonderfully eclectic château, a vast monument to
the aspirations if not architectural taste of generations of builders, was the scene of
the grisly murder of Henri de Guise in the sixteenth century. With only 12,000
inhabitants, clustered beneath the brooding presence of the château, the town
enjoyed an influence out of all proportion to its size. It had given the events of 1789 a
cautious welcome and its famous 'constitutional' bishop, Henri Grégoire, who was
elected president of the National Convention in November 1792, managed to retain
his power and influence in national politics throughout the worst excesses of the
revolution. Here was a supreme example of one of those 'people of wealth and
circumstance' who were 'favorers of the revolution', whom William had so signally
failed to find in Orléans. It was in Blois that his political education would begin.

Writing to Mathews on 19 May, William was as cheerful and sanguine as ever
as he made his excuses for not replying earlier. 'Since my arrival day after day and
week after week has stole[n] insensibly over my head with inconceivable rapidity',
he explained, without even hinting that he had acquired a French mistress. Unaware
that Annette was pregnant, he was busy laying plans for his own future career. The
world of literature still beckoned and he wrote with his usual robustness to
encourage Mathews, who, having just lost his schoolmastering post, was more than
usually inclined to depression and defeatism.

You have still the hope that we may be connected in some method of obtaining an Independence. I assure you I wish it as much as yourself. Nothing but resolution is necessary. The field of Letters is very extensive, and it is astonishing if we cannot find some little corner, which with a little tillage will produce us enough for the necessities, nay even the comforts, of life.

Urging Mathews to use his enforced residence in London as an opportunity to look around for some literary project they could start together, William made the startling announcement that it was now his intention to take orders in the approaching winter or spring. This new determination was the result of pressure from Uncle William. Fearing the worst from his nephew's reluctance to return to England, Uncle William, who had recently been appointed a Canon of Windsor, had offered to make him his own curate at Forncett. It was an offer that could not be refused.

In this letter, the first he had written Mathews since leaving Orléans, William gives the first indications that his political opinions were beginning to change. It is not so much what he actually said, but the way he said it. 'You have the happiness of being born in a free country,' he lectured Mathews, as if repeating a lesson given to himself,

where every road is open, where talents and industry are more liberally rewarded than amongst any other nation of the Universe. You will naturally expect that writing from a country agitated by the storms of a revolution, my Letter should not be confined merely to us and our friends. But the truth is that in London you have perhaps a better opportunity of being informed of the general concerns of france, than in a petty provincial town in the heart of the kingd[om] itself. The annals of the department are all with which I have a better opportunity of being acquainted than you, provided you feel sufficient interest in informing yourself.

Nevertheless, William knew all about the recent rout of the French 'patriot' army by the Austrians, their 'ignominious flight' and their brutal murder of their own commander at Lille. 'The horrors excited by the relation of the events . . . is [*sic*] general', he assured Mathews. 'Not but that there are men who felt a gloomy satisfaction from a measure which seemed to put the patriot army out of a possibility of success.' Such a comment shows a totally new political awareness. It is enforced by the subsequent analysis, which is almost messianic in its language.

The approaching summer will undoubtedly decide the fate of France. It is almost evident that the patriot army, however numerous, will be unable [to] withstand the superior discipline of their enemies. But suppose that the German army is at the gates of Paris, what will be the consequence? It will be impossible to make any material alteration in the constitution, impossible to reinstate the clergy in its antient guilty splendor, impossible to give an existence to the *noblesse* similar to that it before enjoyed, impossible to add much to the authority of the King: Yet there are in France some [?millions] – I speak without exaggeration – who expect that this will take place.

This is such a different voice (and one with strong Gallic inflections) that the conclusion is inescapable: it was not William's own. If not his own, then whose? Certainly not Annette's. Possibly Bishop Grégoire's, since he was resident in Blois for twelve months from September 1791, though William did not yet espouse his more extreme brand of republicanism. The voice is almost certainly that of Michel Beaupuy, a captain in the 32nd Bassigny regiment stationed at Blois, whom William identifies in *The Prelude* as his political mentor and credits with awakening his social conscience.

The portrait William draws of his friend is an extraordinarily romantic one, which (quite deliberately) owes more to Chaucer's 'verray, parfit, gentil knight' than to reality, for Beaupuy was the perfect example of an aristocrat who was also a fervent supporter of the principles of the revolution.

> Man he loved
> As man, and to the mean and the obscure,
> And all the homely in their homely works,
> Transferred a courtesy which had no air
> Of condescension, but did rather seem
> A passion and a gallantry, like that
> Which he, a soldier, in his idler day
> Had paid to women.
>
> *Prelude (1805), ix, 313–20*

The fifth son of an aristocratic family from the Périgord to enter the army, Beaupuy had been actively involved in revolutionary politics since 1789. Now thirty-seven, he had become increasingly hardline and extreme in his views. The defeats suffered by the patriot army were of the deepest interest to him as it was simply a matter of time till his own regiment was sent to the front. Nevertheless, it was Beaupuy's idealism that proved so inspirational to his young protégé – and, indeed, to others. His obituary described him as the personification of 'the religious spirit of the Revolution' and the 'Nestor and Achilles of our army'. The latter description was particularly significant; Achilles was the pre-eminent Greek champion in battle, but Nestor was the aged statesman who counselled moderation in the quarrels of the leaders.

William spent many hours with Beaupuy, walking along the Loire and in the vast medieval forests surrounding Blois, which were (and still are) dotted with late-medieval châteaux and hunting lodges. There could be no more obvious and spectacular reminder of the wealth and power of the *ancien régime*. The poet in William responded to the physical beauty: this was the incarnation of the Arthurian world of Spenser, Ariosto and Tasso, haunt of damsels in distress and jousting knights. The nascent democrat saw them as symbols of a corrupt and profligate system of government.

Against this emotive backdrop, William and Beaupuy discussed abstract ideas about the end and best forms of civil government, the nature of man and his capacity for both good and evil. Drawing on a mutual background of classical history, they painted for themselves the misery of royal courts,

> ... where the man who is of soul
> The meanest thrives the most, where dignity,
> True personal dignity, abideth not –

and then compared this with the democratic spirit that had brought about the greatness of Greece and Rome. It was this spirit, they agreed, that had inspired the citizens of France.

> Elate we looked
> Upon their virtues, saw in rudest men
> Self-sacrifice the firmest, generous love
> And continence of mind, and sense of right
> Uppermost in the midst of fiercest strife.
>
> *Prelude (1805), ix, 354–6, 392–6*

For the first time, William began to understand the idealism and commitment that had brought about the revolution. More importantly, he began to be enthused. Such discussions at Cambridge, or later in his native Lakes, were always an intellectual interest, sometimes even a passionate one. Now, in the literal and metaphorical heart of revolutionary France, William found the 'vital interest' which would change his life. This was no longer a purely academic argument but a personal crusade.

One particular image came to symbolize the object of the revolution for William. Significantly, it was pointed out to him by Beaupuy. In itself it was a commonplace sight, and one which William must have seen time and again in both France and England. On one of their walks in the aristocratic playground of the forests of Blois, they came across 'a hunger-bitten girl' creeping along a lane. Attached by a cord to her arm was a heifer which, having no other means of providing for its sustenance, she allowed to graze on the wayside. Instead of idly tending the beast, the girl was busy knitting. At the sight, an agitated Beaupuy cried, ''Tis against *that* Which we are fighting!' For a man of William's natural empathy, it was an irresistible challenge.

> I with him believed
> Devoutly that a spirit was abroad
> Which could not be withstood; that poverty,
> At least like this, would in a little time
> Be found no more; that we should see the earth
> Unthwarted in her wish to recompense
> The industrious and the lowly child of toil
>
> *Prelude (1805), ix, 520–26*

If that meant abolishing the monarchy and establishing a republic, then so be it.

On 27 July 1792, Beaupuy's regiment left Blois to defend the French frontier on the Rhine. William never saw him again. A misleading report in the *Moniteur* of December 1793 led him to believe that Beaupuy had been killed, ironically fighting a civil war against royalist rebels in the Vendée. In fact, though seriously wounded, he survived, became a general, and died fighting for France against the Austrians in October 1796. For William, believing his friend had died for his cause rather than his country, the conversations with Beaupuy assumed a greater poignancy and importance. The man had lived and died for what he believed in; what sacrifice would he have expected of William?

Events in France were taking a dangerous turn in the summer of 1792. The disastrous prosecution of the war against Austria had inflamed republican sentiment, not least because the French émigrés, both aristocrats and clergy, were openly supporting the Austrians. A mob attacked the Tuileries in June, and only the personal bravery of the King prevented the seizure and massacre of his family. When, on the eve of the *Fête de la Fédération,* the National Assembly declared that the country was in danger, thousands of men throughout France volunteered for service in the army. The Duke of Brunswick's ill-conceived *Manifesto*, written by émigrés with the implied sanction of Louis XVI, was published in Paris on 28 July. Threatening vengeance on Paris if any harm came to the King, it simply fanned the flames of republicanism. On 10 August the situation exploded. In a carefully orchestrated campaign, an armed mob of citizens, supported by the National Guard, marched on the Tuileries. The royal family escaped by taking refuge in the National Assembly, but hundreds of their loyal Swiss Guard were butchered in scenes of incredible barbarity. The practical deposition of Louis XVI would soon be followed by the formal abolition of the monarchy, proposed in the National Convention by no less a person than Henri Grégoire, the Constitutional Bishop of Blois.

'William is still in France, and I begin to wish he was in England', Dorothy wrote gloomily to Jane. Though he had assured her he was 'perfectly safe', she could not help worrying. Her only reassurance was that she was expecting him to be back in London by August. Little did she know that her brother's return would again be delayed and that he was actively seeking out the very dangers she most feared.

Since living in Blois, William had almost certainly attended the meetings of Les Amis de la Constitution, the provincial branches of the Jacobin Club in Paris. He may have been one of two Englishmen refused membership, but permitted to attend meetings, in February 1792. Alternatively, he may have attended under the aegis of Beaupuy. Undoubtedly, however, he was familiar with its proceedings. Henri Grégoire had been elected president of Les Amis at Blois the previous November and he had a decisive influence on the political tenor of the meetings. By the summer of 1792 these were becoming markedly more republican. On the *Fête de la Fédération*, Grégoire gave a stirring speech to the society in which he predicted a golden future, not just for France but also for its neighbours.

Soon we shall witness the liberation of all humankind. Everything confirms that the coming revolution will set all of Europe free, and prove a consolation for the whole human race. Liberty has been fettered to thrones for far too long! She will burst those irons and chains and as she extends her influence beyond our horizons, will inaugurate the federation of all mankind!

If this was a missionary statement, then William was ripe to receive it. Though he had always had confidence in his own power to earn a living, the actual necessity had been forced on him by the arbitrary whim of the Earl of Lonsdale who was typical of the aristocrats condemned by Grégoire for jeering at the sufferings of the people and yet being protected by the laws of the land. He watched the departing army volunteers leaving Blois to defend their country and the revolution against a foreign enemy and the forces of reaction and they seemed to him 'arguments from Heaven' that the cause was just. The example of Grégoire proved that it was possible to be both a radical and a clergyman, which was just as well, if William were to fulfil all expectations of him on his return home.

His thoughts were now turning that way. In August he wrote to Richard, asking for £20 to be sent to him, presumably to fund his journey home. There were difficulties in sending the money, because Blois was not a commercial centre which could readily exchange bank bills. On 3 September, when he again wrote to Richard, William was still in Blois. He anticipated staying there until the money came through, but he expected to be in London some time in October and hoped to find a bed for a few weeks in Richard's lodgings.

Despite these firm plans, and the necessity of waiting for his money to come through as arranged, William apparently left Blois immediately and unexpectedly. On the basis of his statement, repeated quite positively over fifty years later, in 1847 and again in 1849, that he was in Orléans when the September Massacres were committed in Paris, it has been assumed that William was in Orléans by the 6th of the month. This seems unlikely: he was demonstrably still in Blois when they began, on 2 September, and the following day when he wrote to Richard, dating his letter from the town. The money could not have come through in less than three days (the post took at least five days and then he would have to wait for a reply) and, having left for Orléans, he is unlikely to have wished to return to Blois to pick up his funds.

The only possible explanation which might have justified a precipitate departure from Blois was the discovery of Annette's pregnancy. This cannot have been news to William. Even if his sexual relationship with Annette was restricted to a single encounter (which does not seem likely), she was anxious to marry him and knew he intended to return to England, so had every reason for telling him as soon as she was certain herself. She was now six months pregnant and her condition would soon be obvious even to the most casual observer. It was therefore decided that she should go back to Orléans, probably to the Dufours household, and remain there until her baby was born. William decided to follow her.

Where he stayed on his return to Orléans is not known, just as it remains a mystery whether he had lived in lodgings or with the Vallons in Blois. Other than to settle his affairs with Annette, it is not even clear why he should have gone to Orléans at all, yet he lingered there well into October. He might not have been there when the September Massacres took place, and up to 1,400 priests, nuns and monks, who refused to take the civil oath, were dragged from prison and brutally massacred by the Parisian mob. He might not have been there on 4 September, when fifty-three political prisoners from Orléans were butchered in the streets of Versailles on their way to Paris. But he was probably in Orléans in the middle of September, when there were bread riots, in which fourteen people were killed and martial law was declared in the city.

On 21 September, while William was in Orléans, Henri Grégoire proposed the abolition of the monarchy to the National Convention. 'Morally speaking, kings have always been a grotesque freak', he declared to unanimous applause. 'The history of monarchy has been the martyrdom of entire nations'. The process of formally declaring France a republic had begun. These events, and the fact that William knew at least one of the main instigators of them, were surely as good as any to persuade him to be in Paris. That he remained in Orléans can only be testimony to the strength of his attachment to Annette.

French historians are not alone in bemoaning William's infuriating failure to record life in Orléans at such a momentous time, to which one might add the equally maddening silence on Annette. There are just two things we know for certain: that he walked extensively along the banks of the Loire, as he had done all year, and explored again his favourite walks southwards along the Loiret towards Orléans-La Source; and that he was writing poetry. Far from being love poems, he was working on a Continental version of his *Evening Walk*. *Descriptive Sketches* was an account, in much the same form as his earlier poem, of his pedestrian tour through France and Switzerland with Robert Jones in 1790.

William had been working on the poem (when his love affair and political interests permitted) throughout the year. By the time he left Blois, he was already planning to publish it on his return to England. The dramatic turn of events while he was in Orléans, however, inspired him to add a coda to *Descriptive Sketches* which is completely out of tune with the rest of what is, quite literally, a pedestrian poem. It is a rallying call to liberty, a song of praise to the French Revolution, a battle hymn of the republic.

> – Though Liberty shall soon, indignant, raise
> Red on his hills his beacon's comet blaze;
> Bid from on high his lonely cannon sound,
> And on ten thousand hearths his shout rebound;
> His larum-bell from village-tower to tower
> Swing on the astounded ear its dull undying roar:
> Yet, yet rejoice, though Pride's perverted ire
> Rouse Hell's own aid, and wrap thy hills in fire.
> Lo! from the innocuous flames, a lovely birth!

> With its own Virtues springs another earth:
> Nature, as in her prime, her virgin reign
> Begins, and Love and Truth compose her train:
> *Descriptive Sketches (1793), ll.774–85*

These were brave and defiant words, particularly after the September Massacres and the declaration of the republic, which alienated a large body of public opinion in France. What William had no notion of, as yet, was just how far out of step he was with public opinion in England.

Before he left France, William made arrangements to ensure that his name appeared on the birth certificate as the father, and for André Augustin Dufours to represent him at the baby's baptism. This was not simply a moral commitment, but a legal one, which would enable his child to claim maintenance from him in the future. That he was prepared to go so far and yet not marry Annette seems odd. All the obstacles which had stood in the way of their marrying before they consummated their relationship still remained in force and could never be removed. Annette was a Roman Catholic and he an Anglican: if he still intended to enter the Church, a Catholic wife was an insuperable impediment to ordination and promotion. She was French and he was English: if he was to earn a living, in the Church or otherwise, then he was more likely to be successful in England, where he had contacts and family connections.

If he truly intended to marry Annette, as she clearly expected and the frequency of his own letters to her after his departure implies, then there was nothing to be gained by delay. William may have hoped that he might persuade his uncles to approve the match and a change of career, but there is no reason why he should have been more successful in person than by letter. He may, of course, have attempted to do so in letters which have been lost; his uncles may even have forbidden the match. But William faced no greater difficulty in persuading them to accept his wife and child than his intended wife and child. He was of age to marry without their consent and in the civil wedding ceremony, available in France since the revolution, he had the perfect means to overcome the problems caused by difference in religion.

There was an additional obstacle to their union. Their affair had always been one of the heart, based on physical attraction. Intellectual sympathies, which were so vitally important to William, were simply not in the picture. Never once does Annette mention William's poetry in her letters, and where they had a common interest, politics, their views were daily becoming more opposed. As William became more radical in his views, Annette became more reactionary. It is pure speculation but, in the circumstances, a justifiable suspicion that William had private reservations about the relationship which prevented him taking the step that would make them partners for life.

For whatever reason, William and Annette did not marry. To save face, and to enable her to keep her daughter, Annette called herself variously 'William Wordsworth Vallon', the '*f[emme]* William' and the '*veuve* Williams'. As late as 1816, her own family still believed that she had married the English poet and Annette was begging him not to endanger their daughter's prospects of inheriting from her uncles by revealing that they were not. If William had balked at deceiving his own family by a secret marriage, he was later forced into colluding with Annette's deception that one had taken place.

William set off for Paris with the manuscript of *Descriptive Sketches* in his pocket. He had always intended to return for an extended visit, but the city in October and November of 1792 was very different from that of a year earlier. Shocked by the September Massacres, many of the English residents, including Lord Gower, the British ambassador, had left. Other visitors were deterred from coming altogether.

William was either oblivious or heedless. He arrived in Paris 'inflamed with hope' and set about seeing the sights again. This time he was in for a real shock, for what he saw was not some dignified re-creation of ancient Rome but the aftermath of mob violence. He saw the battle-scarred Tuileries, the Temple, where the royal family were now genuine prisoners, and the fire-blackened Carrousel, where the bodies of the Swiss Guard had been piled high and burnt. These were sights to shake his confidence in 'the lovely birth' of a republic, bringing love, truth and justice in its train. Nor was it much comfort the following morning to find the street hawkers in the Palais Royal bawling 'Denunciation of the crimes Of Maximilian Robespierre'. The pamphlets they were selling reported Jean-Baptiste Louvet's dramatic accusation in the National Convention the previous day. Robespierre, supremely arrogant as ever, had demanded that anyone who thought he was aiming at dictatorship should say so; in the silence that followed, Louvet had walked alone to face him and coolly said, '*Robespierre, c'est moi qui t'accuse.*'

William clearly admired Louvet's courage; whether he supported or even understood his attack on Robespierre at the time is another matter. Among the other pamphlets being hawked in the Palais Royal were a large number devoted to transcripts of the trial of Charles I of England and demands for the prosecution of Louis XVI. Henri Grégoire, elected president of the National Convention on 15 November, was one of those demanding that the King should answer for his crimes against the people. Robespierre, with his insistence that the King must die 'because the nation must live', was simply the most eloquent and ruthless of the anti-monarchists, among whose numbers one William Wordsworth must certainly be counted. He may have attended the meetings of the National Convention as the rowdy and ill-tempered debates raged; we simply do not know. Through Beaupuy and Grégoire, and possibly through Les Amis de la Constitution, he would have had introductions to any number of political figures in Paris. He later said he had met Jacques Pierre Brissot and Jean-Antoine Gorsas, both of whom were deputies, the former a Girondin, the latter a journalist and apologist for the September Massacres; both were to be executed only twelve months later, in October 1793.

Even to a newcomer like William, who was uncomfortably aware that he was out of his depth, it was clear that the revolution was in danger, not just from émigrés and counter-revolutionaries, but also from demagogues and factionalists in the National Convention and from the volatile mob outside it. He even considered offering his services to the republic.

An insignificant stranger and obscure
Mean as I was, and little graced with powers
Of eloquence even in my native speech,
And all unfit for tumult and intrigue,
Yet would I willingly have taken up
A service at this time for cause so great,
However dangerous.

Prelude (1805), x, 130–36

There has been much speculation as to what role William envisaged for himself, but the only practical one open to him was that of a political pamphleteer. This might have allowed him to influence the course of events and, as he well knew by the time he came to write *The Prelude*, had he been successful, he would undoubtedly have endangered his own life. In the Terror, journalists were as likely to be executed as politicians. This was only true, however, if he remained in France.

In England it was still possible for him to play an influential role as a political writer. On 19 November, while William was in Paris, the National Convention enacted a decree that the French Nation 'will offer *fraternité* and assistance to all peoples who wish to recover their liberty'. It was a provocative declaration of intent, made deliberately more so by being translated and printed into different languages. Here, then, was a way in which William could take up service in the cause: he could carry the revolutionary message back to England.

By early December he was back in London, lodging with his brother Richard in Staple Inn. On 15 December 1792, far away in Orléans, Annette gave birth to their daughter. She was christened the same day, in the Cathedral of St Croix, her absent father being represented by André Augustin Dufours. It somehow seems symbolic of the whole unhappy affair that no one knew how to spell William's surname and his daughter entered life inauspiciously named 'Anne-Caroline Wordswodsth'.

5. A Patriot of the World

William's first priority on returning to England was to get his poem published, but *Descriptive Sketches* alone was a very meagre foundation on which to present himself to the world as a poet. Hurriedly scouting around for something to add to it, he settled on *An Evening Walk*. Despite being written so long ago, it needed little revision, but he did add a discordant and significant digression: a description of a poor woman, her two children clasped in her arms, found frozen to death on Stainmore, near Penrith, earlier in the year. Beaupuy's lessons on the human face of poverty and suffering had not been forgotten.

William found a publisher almost immediately in Joseph Johnson of St Paul's Churchyard. Johnson was famous not only as the publisher of the poet William Cowper but also as a leading London radical. He was a member of the Society for Constitutional Information and Thomas Paine, William Godwin and Mary Wollstonecraft had all met at his house. As a Unitarian, he moved in the same circles as both Samuel Nicholson and Joseph Fawcett. William may have met him during his previous visit to London; if not, his recent return from France and new radical credentials would have assured him of attention.

On 29 January 1793 two large but very thin volumes, bound in cheap brown-paper wrappers, were published. They both boasted the snappy titles so beloved by eighteenth-century poets: *An Evening Walk. An Epistle; In Verse. Addressed to a Young Lady, from the Lakes of the North of England* and *Descriptive Sketches. In Verse. Taken during a Pedestrian Tour in the Italian, Grison, Swiss, and Savoyard Alps*. At least no disgruntled purchaser could pretend he had not known what he was getting. And both books proudly proclaimed that they were by 'W. Wordsworth, B.A. Of St John's, Cambridge'. In an endearing confession to his friend Mathews, William later admitted that he had 'huddled up' these two little works and sent them out in such an imperfect state by way of an apology for his Cambridge career: 'as I had done nothing by which to distinguish myself at the university, I thought these little things might shew that I could do something. They have been treated with unmerited contempt by some of the periodical publications, and others have spoken in higher terms of them than they deserve.'

The reviews (and there were not many) were, indeed, unkind. The *Critical Review* praised *An Evening Walk* for its 'new and picturesque imagery ... which would not disgrace our best descriptive poets', but crushed *Descriptive Sketches* beneath the heel of its contempt.

The wild, romantic scenes of Switzerland have not yet been celebrated by an English poet; and its uncultivated beauties, which of themselves inspire the most sublime and poetical ideas ... seem to have been surveyed by few of the poetic race ... Mr Wordsworth has caught few sparks from these glowing scenes. His lines are often harsh and prosaic; his images ill-chosen, and his descriptions feeble and insipid.

The *Monthly Review* was, if anything, more contemptuous in ridiculing his imagery. 'How often shall we in vain advise those, who are so delighted with their own thoughts that they cannot forbear from putting them into rhyme, to examine those thoughts till they themselves understand them? No man will ever be a poet, till his mind is sufficiently powerful to sustain labour.'

If William had hoped for indulgence from his family, he was swiftly disillusioned. Even Dorothy, the 'Young Lady' to whom *An Evening Walk* was dedicated, had cutting criticisms. She and Christopher, now in his first year at Trinity College, Cambridge, had amused themselves in the Christmas vacation at Forncett by 'analysing every Line' and preparing 'a very bulky Criticism', which they intended to send William as soon as Christopher's Cambridge friends had added their two penn'orth. Though William remained Dorothy's favourite, Christopher was now 'one of the dearest of my Brothers'. Among his Cambridge friends, with whom he would soon found a literary society, was Samuel Taylor Coleridge, who would hail *Descriptive Sketches* as announcing 'the emergence of an original poetic genius above the literary horizon'. Coleridge possessed greater powers of perception than most critics (as well as having the useful gift of hindsight in this instance), but he would be one of William's earliest and most vociferous champions.

Dorothy was less enthusiastic and transparently offended that her brother had not seen fit to show her his poems before publishing them. 'The Scenes which he describes have been viewed with a Poet's eye and are pourtrayed with a Poet's pencil;' she declared with crisp authority,

and the Poems contain many Passages exquisitely beautiful, but they also contain many Faults, the chief of which are Obscurity, and a too frequent use of some particular expressions and uncommon words for instance *moveless*, which he applies in a sense if not new, at least different from its ordinary one ... I regret exceedingly that he did not submit the works to the Inspection of some Friend before their Publication, and he also joins with me in this Regret. Their Faults are such as a young Poet was most likely to fall into and least likely to discover, and what the Suggestions of a Friend would easily have made him see and at once correct.

William was well aware of the justice of the criticisms. 'They are juvenile productions, inflated and obscure', he wrote in 1801, 'but they contain many new images, and vigorous lines'. He regarded them chiefly as having curiosity value, evidence of how much his opinions on poetry had changed in the intervening years.

The poor sales of William's two books meant that he now had to look elsewhere for funds. Two small family bequests came at this opportune moment. His Penrith grandmother, Mrs Cookson, died on 11 June 1792. On inheriting the Crackanthorpe estate eighteen months earlier, she had generously promised to give £500 to each of her sons and a similar sum to be divided among her late daughter's children. Her sons had been given their share almost immediately, but only two of the dutiful grandchildren, Dorothy, the invaluable companion, housekeeper and nursemaid to a fast-growing band of baby Cooksons at Forncett, and John, struggling to raise the capital to invest in his next voyage to China, received their £100 each in the spring of 1792. Uncle Christopher, who inherited the estate, made no attempt to fulfil his mother's wishes. Uncle William, on the other hand, offered to rectify the imbalance by personally giving his niece and nephews £150, so that his share should be no larger than theirs. All that they got from Uncle Christopher, almost a year after their grandmother's death, was £166 13s 4d, their third share of a bequest from their great-grandfather, made before they were born, which was legally their due. It is, incidentally, a reflection on the remarkable closeness and trust between the young Wordsworths that they always regarded these sums as a family pot and never queried its distribution among themselves.

Any hope that they might still win back their own family inheritance had now vanished. The case had ground to a complete halt and the Carlisle judgement against 'the Devil's likeness', as Uncle Christopher now termed the Earl, was effectively unenforceable: the Administrators could no longer afford to pursue the case in the courts and 'Wicked Jimmy' had won by default.

Living with Richard in the winter of 1792–3, William no doubt had it thoroughly drummed into him that he must accept the necessity of earning his own living. It was not something William wished to hear, which accounts, in part, for the coolness that now arose between him and his brother. Richard, who had been hard at work as a lawyer since he was seventeen, and had dutifully forfeited a life of leisure on the Sockbridge estate so that he could pursue the family claim, had little patience with his wayward brother. William's radical politics, not to mention the revelation of his mistress and child in France, can have done little to endear him to Richard. The atmosphere in the lodgings they shared with their mutual friend Joshua Wilkinson from Cockermouth must have become increasingly tense over the coming months.

Events had moved swiftly since William left France. On 21 January 1793 Louis XVI was guillotined in Paris. Having only recently returned from the city himself,

William was more prepared than most for this latest act of violence; he considered it an absolute necessity for the survival and progress of the revolution. In this, he was out of step with the majority of English public opinion. In the general shock and revulsion, even those who had previously welcomed the French Revolution and argued for political and religious reform in England now backtracked furiously. Most notable among these was Richard Watson, Bishop of Llandaff, a former Professor of Divinity at Cambridge, who now lived on a grand estate on the shores of Lake Windermere. On 30 January, in an attempt to calm 'the perturbation which has been lately excited, and which still subsists in the minds of the lower classes of the community', he published a sermon he had given some years before, which preached the doctrine of divine will as the reason and justification for poverty. This was the usual response of establishment clergymen to fear of popular unrest; it made any attempt to overturn the preordained ranks of society an act of rebellion against God. To this he added a hastily compiled *Appendix*, protesting at the recent trend of violent events in France, culminating in the execution of the King, and extolling the virtues of the British Constitution.

It was an obscure and rather ordinary publication which, in most circumstances, would not have merited any notice at all. In language and attitude it was oddly unprovocative, but what roused William to blazing indignation was the fact that its author had previously been renowned for his liberal views: 'While, with a servility which has prejudiced many people against religion itself, the ministers of the church of England have appeared as writers upon public measures only to be the advocates of slavery civil and religious, your Lordship stood almost alone as the defender of truth and political charity.' Watson was now a political apostate and his defection might have serious consequences for the progress of reform in Britain.

Even this might not have tempted William to put pen to paper had it not been for the single event which was to shake him to the core. Two days after the publication of the *Appendix to a Sermon*, France declared war on England. It was not unexpected, but its effect on William was cataclysmic.

> No shock
> Given to my moral nature had I known
> Down to that very moment – neither lapse
> Nor turn of sentiment that might be named
> A revolution, save at this one time.
>
> *Prelude (1805), x, 233–7*

William's natural and passionate love of his own country was now at odds with his equally passionate belief in the righteousness of the enemy's cause. By joining the alliance against France, Pitt's government had ranged itself alongside the powers of despotism against the defenders of democracy. Now, more than ever, there was need of someone to take up service 'for cause so great', and William did so with a violence which did more credit to the ardour of his principles than to the persuasiveness of his arguments.

Just as he had done when publishing his poems, he set out his credentials in the title, *A Letter to the Bishop of L[l]andaff on the extraordinary avowal of his Political Principles contained in the Appendix to his late Sermon*. Lest there should be any doubt about his own political affiliations, he nailed his colours firmly to the mast: *by a Republican*. In bold, vigorous prose he launched his attack on the Bishop of Llandaff by comparing him to Henri Grégoire, the Constitutional Bishop of Blois.

At a period big with the fate of the human race, I am sorry that you attach so much importance to the personal sufferings of the late royal martyr and that an anxiety for the issue of the present convulsions should not have prevented you from joining in the idle cry of modish lamentation which has resounded from the court to the cottage ... A bishop, a man of philosophy and humanity as distinguished as your Lordship, declared at the opening of the national convention, and twenty-five millions of men were convinced of the truth of the assertion, that there was not a citizen on the tenth of august who, if he could have dragged before the eyes of Louis the corse of one of his murdered brothers, might not have exclaimed to him, Tyran, voilà ton ouvrage. Think of this and you will not want consolation under any depression your spirits may feel at the contrast exhibited by Louis on the most splendid throne of the universe, and Louis alone in the tower of the Temple or on the scaffold.

Using the arguments of Jean-Jacques Rousseau's *Du Contrat Social* and Thomas Paine's *The Rights of Man*, William demolished the case for monarchy, aristocracy and primogeniture. Virtue cannot be inherited, was his basic premise, nor can its continuance be guaranteed: 'a man's past services are no sufficient security for his future character'. Power corrupts and the office of king is inherently beyond the virtue of any man; the only sensible way of restraining a legislator is to appoint him for a limited period, since the knowledge that tomorrow he will be a private citizen again, and subject to the laws he has enacted, will restrain him from oppressive measures. A republic, based on universal suffrage, proscription of heredi-tary authority and the abolition of statutes limiting wages, is the only form of government which truly represents the general will.

In prosecuting his arguments William demonstrated an unexpected turn for the pithy phrase and incendiary political slogan: 'Government is, at best, but a necessary evil'; 'Is your lordship to be told that acquiescence is not choice, and that obedience is not freedom?'; 'You have aimed an arrow at liberty and philosophy, the eyes of the human race'. William's own experiences added particular venom to some of his criticisms. 'I congratulate your lordship upon your enthusiastic fondness for the judicial proceedings of this country', he remarked with the heavy irony of one who had spent futile years trying to regain his inheritance in the Lonsdale suit. 'I am happy to find you have passed through life without having your fleece torn from your back in the thorny labyrinth of litigation.' Looking forward to the establishment of a republic in Britain, and a resolution of inequality in wealth, he expresses the hope that 'the miseries entailed upon the marriage of those who are not rich will no longer tempt the bulk of mankind to fly to that promiscuous intercourse to which they are impelled by the instincts of nature, and the dreadful satisfaction of escaping the prospect of infants, sad fruit of such intercourse, whom they are unable to support'. William could not have written this so soon after his separation from Annette and the birth of their illegitimate child without having himself and them in mind.

The most surprising element of his *Letter to the Bishop of L[l]andaff* is not so much his overt (not to say flaunted) republicanism, but his defence of the violence of the French Revolution. In doing so, he fell back on his usual catch-all explanation, which was its own justification: it was part of a natural cycle.

The coercive power is of necessity so strong in all the old governments that a people could not but at first make an abuse of that liberty which a legitimate republic supposes. The animal just released from its stall will exhaust the overflow of its spirits in a round of wanton vagaries, but it will soon return to itself and enjoy its freedom in moderate and regular delight.

He also put forward the dangerous argument so beloved of all revolutionaries: the end justifies the means. 'A time of revolution is not the season of true Liberty', he argued. 'Political virtues are developed at the expence of moral ones.' Compassion must be repressed when traitors are to be punished. Only afterwards can one afford to be more benign. Like all good revolutionaries, he also looked to education to solve the problems created in the wake of violent overthrow of government.

It is the province of education to rectify the erroneous notions which a habit of oppression, and even of resistance, may have created, and to soften this ferocity of character proceeding from a necessary suspension of the mild and social virtues: it belongs to her to create a race of men who, truly free, will look upon their fathers as only enfranchised.

What William did to such great effect in this essay is harness emotion and reason. Every line thrills with the sincerity of youthful idealism and passionate conviction. The result is powerful, eloquent and authoritative. If nothing else, *A Letter to the Bishop of L[l]andaff* is convincing evidence that William's heart was in politics, not poetry.

Had it been published in this spring of 1793, William would undoubtedly have been arrested, tried and found guilty of seditious libel. Even as he was writing his pamphlet, the newspapers were full of reports of trials and convictions for sedition, so he cannot have been unaware of the dangers. The sole surviving manuscript is unfinished, which suggests that William himself may have begun to have doubts about the wisdom of publication. It was not just the personal risk involved, but the fact that, once again, the pace of events in France had outstripped him. By early April, France was in a state of civil war, somewhat undermining his claims for the moral superiority of republican government. William's hesitation would have been increased by the advice of his friends. His publisher, Joseph Johnson, for instance, had shied away from Thomas Paine. After printing a few copies of the first part of *The Rights of Man,* he had taken fright and transferred the work to another publisher. *A Letter to the Bishop of L[l]andaff,* particularly after the outbreak of war with France, was an equally risky prospect. William's brother Richard would also have counselled caution. To publish a rabid republican tract now would be to play into the hands of the Earl of Lonsdale and prejudice still further the Wordsworth claim. Nor was it likely to impress their uncles. Richard might be prepared to overlook the offensive implications of William's tirades against 'the unnatural monster primogeniture', but Uncle Christopher, newly enriched by his inheritance of Newbiggin Hall and the Crackanthorpe estate, and Uncle William, royal protégé and Canon of Windsor, would be incandescent at his attacks on aristocracy, monarchy and the Church.

Even though William decided to suppress his pamphlet, matters were coming to a head between him and his uncles. On 7 April William would be twenty-three, so he could no longer hide behind the excuse that he was under-age to take orders. Confrontation was inevitable.

William could have taken the easy option. Uncle William knew nothing about either his revolutionary politics or his French mistress and illegitimate child. If William chose to keep silence, he could seek ordination and his future would be secure. He would have the certainty of a lifelong, comfortable and undemanding provision for himself in the Church. He would have leisure to pursue his vocation as a poet, without being dependent on precarious literary earnings. He could offer his sister the home she longed for in England and his mistress and child the financial support they needed in France. Though marriage with Annette would be out of the question, he could make amends by adopting Caroline: dependent female relatives of indeterminate status were so commonplace in England that he could bring her to live with him without provoking scandal. The same benefits were still open to him if he confessed all to his uncle. The war with France now gave him the ideal opportunity to renounce his republicanism, his mistress and his illegitimate child as 'juvenile errors'.

To his eternal credit, William stood firm by his principles. He could not be a hypocrite: he was debarred from ordination by his republicanism, which would prevent him swearing allegiance to the King, and by any thought of wishing to marry Annette. It was not the most sensible of decisions from a material point of view and the result was not unexpected. Uncle William refused to have anything more to do with him. And he was not welcome at Forncett.

The person most affected by this ban was not William, but Dorothy, whose loyalties were to be tested to the limits. William had always been her prime object of devotion, but she also sincerely loved and respected her uncle and aunt. They had been unremittingly kind and generous to her since rescuing her from Penrith, and, consequently, had been responsible for subtle changes in her opinions which distanced her far more effectively from her brother than physical separation. She was, for instance, 'charmed' with Windsor, where she had spent three months in the late summer of 1792. Thanks to Uncle William's appointment as a canon there, they had grace-and-favour apartments in the cloisters of St George's Chapel and were in daily contact with the royal family. She was equally enchanted with the royals themselves, fancying herself 'treading upon Fairy-Ground' when she walked on the castle terrace with them. She had never seen such a handsome family; it was impossible to see them informally at Windsor and not love them. Regaling her friend with anecdotes and repeating herself in her excitement, Dorothy artlessly revealed her royalist sympathies. The King had played with the Cookson children,

who though not acquainted with the new-fangled Doctrine of Liberty and Equality, thought a King's Stick as fair Game as any other man's, and that princesses were not better than mere Cousin Dollys . . . I am too much of an aristocrate or what you please to call me, not to reverence him because he is a Monarch more than I should were he a private Gentleman, and not to see with Pleasure his Daughters treated with more Respect than ordinary People.

These opinions, not to mention her contemptuously flippant use of revolutionary terminology, would be anathema to her republican brother, raising the question of just how much he confided in her at this time. Although he was writing to her 'regularly' from London, Dorothy was still looking forward 'with full confidence' to the happiness of receiving Jane Pollard 'in my little Parsonage' as late as the middle of February 1793, blissfully unaware that her 'charming' dream was nothing but a chimera. Within weeks, if not days, however, Dorothy not only knew all about Annette but was actually in correspondence with her.

It was typical of Dorothy that she should respond so immediately and emotionally to the other woman's plight. She literally wept for Annette. So much so that the deserted mistress found herself having to comfort the sister. 'Your last letter gave me such a powerful feeling', Annette replied,

in every line I saw the sensibility of your spirit and that interest, so touching, you take in my sorrows, they are great my dear sister, I confess, but do not increase them, by distressing yourself too much[.] the idea that I am making you miserable is bitter to me, and that it is I who disturbs your rest, who makes your tears flow. Calm yourself o my dear sister[,] my friend[,] I have great need of this assurance so that I do not become more harassed. I wish I could offer you consolations but alas, I cannot[;] I have to find them from you. I find some relief in the assurance of your friendship and in the inviolability of my dear William's feelings . . . it is on the breast of friendship that the unfortunate find comfort[;] it is on that of my sister that I love to lean, but if you are moved by my fate, I share just as much in your annoyances, you do not have anyone in whom you can freely confide the painful state of your heart and you are forced to stifle the tears your sensibility causes [-] o my dear sister, how miserable I am to know how you have been, tell me[.] never no never can I ever make up to you all that you have suffered for me.

The two women were soon making common cause. Dorothy confided in Annette her dreams of the little cottage in the country (which could no longer be a parsonage), and willingly offered to share it with William's wife and child. Annette responded by filling in the picture: how happy they would all be when they were reunited! 'And you', she asked William,

do you long for that day as ardently as your Annette[?] when you will be surrounded by your sister your wife your daughter who will live only for you[,] we will have only one feeling only one heart only one soul and all will be offered to my dear Williams – our days will slip by quietly [-] I will at last enjoy the peace I can only feel near you and in telling you that I love you with my own *living voice*.

Reading these letters 200 years after they were written is an uncomfortable experience. At a cursory level they appear to be those of a simple artless girl 'who not only loves but knows herself beloved'. For the romantically inclined, she is the model mistress, passively refraining from blame, reproach and selfish self-pity, while dashing off a heartfelt declaration of undying passion. It does not, however, require much penetration to see that, beneath the surface, there is a subtle subtext which I have already described as emotional blackmail. The impression is unavoidable that Annette was beginning to doubt whether William would return to marry her, and that she cleverly and deliberately applied pressure on the most vulnerable feelings of both William and his sister. She astutely appealed to William's paternal responsibilities and his fraternal affection, telling him that their daughter was growing daily more like him, that she would be happier if they were married and praising his sister to the skies for her empathy with Annette's own plight. 'The earth could not produce two like her[.] she does honour to her sex. I truly want my Caroline to resemble her. How I have wept my dear Williams what heart [she has] what soul, how deeply she shares in the sorrows that overwhelm me but how distressed I am to see that she is so tortured because of us'. To underline the fact that she and Dorothy also now loved each other as sisters, Annette does not fail to mention Dorothy's enthusiasm in speaking of the little cottage, '*notre petit menage*', which they would all share one day. The pressure on William to fulfil his obligation to marry was being discreetly but relentlessly applied.

The letter to Dorothy herself was equally subtle. Annette was very careful to ensure that Dorothy should not feel excluded by their relationship. She looked forward to the day when William would be surrounded by sister, wife and daughter (in that order) and she hoped Caroline would know only love for her father, her aunt and her mother (in that order). 'My dear sister, you will be her second mother,' she assured Dorothy, 'and I am convinced that you will take great care to turn her into your second self.'

In Dorothy, as Annette well knew, she would have a loyal and ardent advocate close to William. Her unerring instinct for addressing herself to the most vulnerable points in the Wordsworths' characters reveals her to be far more percipient and a better tactician than she is usually portrayed. And it says much for her persuasive skills that, although she never did marry William, she managed to achieve her aims without him: family, friends and neighbours were soon taught to accept her as Mme Williams. Annette would need all her powers of tact and diplomacy in the coming months and years. Ironically, at the very time William was at his most fiery, inditing his republican tract, Annette was being drawn into an actively counter-revolutionary role.

The romantic imagination which so easily takes over when writing on the revolution tempts one to portray Annette, Orczy-fashion, as a glamorous female Scarlet Pimpernel, risking her own life to save émigrés and non-juring priests from the guillotine. It is therefore salutary to be reminded that, though the guillotine stood in the Place de la Liberté in Blois throughout the course of the revolution, it was never used. This is not to say that Annette did not take risks, but the true extent of her activities is difficult to assess. The evidence can hardly be regarded as impartial: reports from surveillance committees and spies, on the one hand, and, on the other, royalist petitions for a pension as a reward for services rendered. What is interesting is that, though they come from different ends of the political spectrum, they are both agreed on two points: Annette was actively involved in counter-revolution and it was her diplomatic skills which made her so formidable. On 31 January 1801 the Minister of Justice gave an order to search her house for incriminating papers and arrest her if she was implicated in plots against the state. As she was not arrested, we can only assume she was tipped off by her friends in high places. The *préfet* of the Loir-et-Cher department in 1804 noted that the Vallon sisters had 'always' loved and served the royalists but he singled out Annette: '*La femme* Williams, notably, is known as *une intriguante decidée*', he declared. The police commission in Blois hastened to assure him that suspects were not meeting at her house, but the *préfet* himself was not convinced.

The fullest and most interesting accounts of her activities in the 1790s, and beyond, come from two references provided in 1818 to substantiate her claims that she deserved a civil-list pension. Guillemin de Savigny, who had known her since childhood, declared that, like her parents, she had always been devoted to God and the Bourbons. She had scoured both town and country to find refuges for priests who had refused to take the civil oath and devoted herself to saving the lives of royalists. She had herself hidden M. Delaporte, the aged intendant of Roussillon and Lorraine, when he was denounced to the Revolutionary Tribunal, and she had got the Comte Dufort, M. de Montlivaut and others out of prison. In 1795–6, proscribed émigrés returning to France were sent to her for a safe haven at Blois; in 1799–1800 the royal armies of the Vendée and Brittany had relied on her for a supply of recruits. The *maire* of Blois added his own glowing reference.

In the time of proscription, her house was the refuge and rendezvous of honest men and especially of those who were in communication with the Vendée; born with an enterprising character, she undertook different missions and, amongst others, to treat with the merchants of this town for provisions for the royal army.

How did Annette get away with it? Guillemin de Savigny has a startling revelation.

She took it on herself to win the friendship of the accomplices of the ferocities of the [National] Convention who were at the head of the odious club at Blois [Les Amis de la Constitution] and the infamous revolutionary committees of that town and she knew how to soften them in favour of all the unfortunates that she knew.

The conclusion is inescapable that Annette used the connections she had made through her revolutionary English lover to further the counter-revolutionary cause. It was perhaps fortunate that William, whose fiery republicanism had taken him beyond even the notorious Thomas Paine, was unaware of what she was doing.

William was still trying to find a means of earning money. Writing had failed, he had rejected ordination, the war with France had deprived him of his preferred option of becoming a travelling companion to a wealthy gentleman touring the Continent. So he fell back on the usual options open to impoverished Cambridge graduates. He would become a private tutor or he would take pupils. Fortunately, at this juncture, another opportunity offered. One of his old schoolfriends from Hawkshead, William Calvert, had inherited a considerable fortune and an estate on Lake Bassenthwaite on the death of his father. He was therefore a man of independent means and leisure. Calvert decided he would like to make a tour of the West of England and Wales and invited William to accompany him, offering to pay all his travelling expenses; the trip would last till October, but William was free to leave whenever he wished, should a better opportunity arise. It was the perfect arrangement for William: he could indulge his wanderlust without incurring any cost or risking the loss of a permanent situation.

An added advantage was that, having got as far as North Wales, William could comparatively easily and cheaply make the journey up to Halifax, where, since the spring, he had had a standing invitation to visit Mrs Rawson (the former 'Aunt' Threlkeld). Dorothy, who had spent the last few years dreaming of just such a visit herself, had finally obtained permission from the Cooksons to pass the winter in Halifax. This was something of an achievement, as she had become indispensable to the household at Forncett, where she was 'head nurse, housekeeper, [and] tutoress of the little ones or rather superintendent of the nursery'. Brother and sister had not met for over two and a half years; they planned to meet in Halifax, without Uncle William's prior knowledge, in case he withdrew his permission for Dorothy's trip.

Dorothy was beside herself with joy. She was about to be reunited with her favourite brother and Jane, 'the Friend of my Childhood, the companion of my pleasures "when Life reared laughing up her morning Sun". Oh Jane! with what Transport shall I embrace you! My dear Friend we shall live over again those Days, and we shall anticipate future joys, domestic felicity, Peace and retirement, when you visit me and find me united to my dear William.' To give Jane 'a faint idea' of her brother's affection for her and his desire to see her, she proudly copied out some passages from William's recent letters. 'Oh my dear, dear sister with what transport shall I again meet you,' he had written, 'with what rapture shall I again wear out the day in your sight. I assure you so eager is my desire to see you that all obstacles vanish. I see you in a moment running or rather flying to my arms.'

William and Calvert began their tour in leisurely fashion by spending a month on the Isle of Wight. For William it was an experience filled with contradiction. He loved that 'delightful island', particularly the walks along the seashore and in the woods, but the tranquillity of the natural scene was at odds with William's own emotional turmoil and the human activity in the Solent between the island and Portsmouth. The Royal Navy was assembling at Spithead in preparation for the war against France. Every evening, the stillness of the island was shattered by the thundering of the sunset cannon:

> at the sound
> The star of life appears to set in blood,
> And ocean shudders in offended mood,
> Deepening with moral gloom his angry flood.
> *[At the Isle of Wight. 1793], ll.16–19*

There could hardly have been a more ominous daily reminder to William of his divided loyalties. For him, this gallant fleet, which could not fail to be an inspiring sight of itself, was 'doomed' upon an 'unworthy service', by 'The unhappy counsel of a few weak men'. When they eventually left the island, William was filled with 'melancholy forebodings'.

The struggle which was beginning, and which many thought would be brought to a speedy close by the irresistible arms of Great Britain being added to those of the allies, I was assured in my own mind would be of long continuance, and productive of distress and misery beyond all possible calculation. This conviction was pressed upon me by having been a witness, during a long residence in revolutionary France, of the spirit which prevailed in that country.

In his *Letter to the Bishop of L[l]andaff*, William had already attacked the war as an 'infatuation which is now giving up to the sword so large a portion of the poor and consigning the rest to the more slow and more painful consumption of want'. Watching the fleet gathering at Spithead, he saw the first signs that this was indeed happening. Many of the sailors had been forcibly conscripted into service, regardless of family or other commitments. The press gangs were out in all the Channel ports and, further inland, the recruiting sergeants were offering the king's shilling to any able-bodied man willing to accept it. Many were driven to do so by desperation, being unable to provide for themselves or their families in any other way. William, like his later friend Tom Poole, could not see this unmoved. 'I consider every Briton who loses his life in the war as much murdered as the King of France,' Poole wrote, 'and every one who approves the war, as signing the death-warrant of each soldier or sailor that falls.'

As William and Calvert made their way towards Salisbury, Calvert's horse suddenly went out of control. Capering about the road, it dragged them into a ditch and smashed their vehicle beyond repair. William was anxious to continue and was quite willing to go on foot, but he could not keep pace with Calvert on horseback. The two friends therefore decided to part, Calvert riding back home on a more direct northern route and William keeping to their original plan of making a detour through Wales. He had five guineas, advanced to him by Richard before he left London, which would be sufficient to finance a pedestrian tour.

For two or three days William wandered alone over Salisbury Plain. It was a period of intense introspection, heightened by the bleak aspect of a landscape which seemed like a metaphor for his own aimlessness. He roamed

> There on the pastoral downs without a track
> To guide me, or along the bare white roads
> Lengthening in solitude their dreary line
> *Prelude (1805), xii, 316–18*

Fifty years later, he would declare, 'My ramble over many parts of Salisbury plain . . . left upon my mind imaginative impressions the force of wh[ich] I have felt to this day.' What he found so memorable was not just the emptiness of the swelling hills, but the contrasting profusion of relics of ancient British civilization: white horses carved into the red earth, hill-forts, standing stones and stone circles. Gigantic in size and mysterious in origin and purpose, they were literally monuments to a lost past, when supposedly uncivilized men had worked with unity of purpose on a grand design. William could not help but contrast the strength, simplicity and grandeur of these images with the feverish, petty, selfish interests of the modern world. They led him 'unavoidably to compare what we know or guess of those remote times with certain aspects of modern society, and with calamities, principally those consequent upon war, to which, more than other classes of men, the poor are subject'.

At Stonehenge, despite the solemnity of his surroundings, he was overcome with heat and fatigue and fell asleep in the stone circle. As he later remarked ironically to a friend, in such a place he ought to have been visited by the muse in his slumbers, but he was not. Nevertheless, landscape, antiquities and political conviction were all drawing together in his mind to produce a poem, *The Female Vagrant*, the object of which was, in part, 'to expose the vices of the penal law and the calamities of war as they affect individuals'. Informed by personal experience, inspired by compassion and articulated by rage, he had found a voice at last.

The Female Vagrant told the story of the accidental meeting of two wanderers seeking shelter during a stormy night on Salisbury Plain. The woman explained how she came to be alone and destitute: her father had been evicted from his cottage in the Lakes by an acquisitive neighbour, she had married her childhood sweetheart but the advent of war had ruined them and, in a last desperate attempt to support her and their three children, he had volunteered for the army. Within a year, she was the sole survivor, having lost husband and children to sword and plague. This tale of human suffering is sandwiched between two powerful pieces of political invective. The introduction argued Rousseau's principle that the life of a savage, however hard, was better than that of modern man, because there were no distinctions in wealth or power to exacerbate suffering by comparison. The closing lines were a revolutionary rallying call, urging the 'Heroes of Truth' to 'uptear Th'Oppressor's dungeon from its deepest base', wield the Herculean mace of Reason over the towers of Pride and drag 'foul Error's monster race' from darkness into the light which would kill it. The poem was as violently radical and just as unpublishable in the current political climate as *A Letter to the Bishop of L[l]andaff.*

Having crossed Salisbury Plain, William made his way through Bath to Bristol, then, crossing the Severn estuary by ferry, he landed at Chepstow and made his way northward up the River Wye. In doing so, he was consciously following in a literary and artistic tradition; indeed, that it is why he had decided to take that route. William Gilpin's *Observations on the River Wye*, first published in 1782, had become the bible of a generation of poets, artists and writers. Samuel Rogers had followed in Gilpin's footsteps and kept a journal of his tour in the summer of 1791; the next year, J. M. W. Turner, making the first of five tours in Wales, painted Chepstow Castle, Tintern Abbey and Llanthony Priory. At the time William produced a few fragmentary verses, expressing suitably republican sentiments, but far more importantly, the tour laid the seeds for future poems. Incidents and images which then impressed themselves on his mind would be mulled over in future years and subtly infused with his own imaginative colouring. At Goodrich Castle, for instance, he met a pretty little girl, about eight years of age, who insisted she was one of seven children, even though two of her siblings were dead. Her refusal to accept that she was now one of only five led William to write *We are Seven* several years later, as a graphic illustration of the inability of children to grasp the notion of death. Walking between Builth Wells and Hay-on-Wye, he fell in with a 'wild rover' who told him many 'strange stories'; his 'countenance, gait and figure' would later supply those of Peter Bell. Most famously of all, however, the landscape a few miles upstream above Tintern Abbey would furnish calming images, 'beauteous forms' of peace and tranquillity, to bring solace to a troubled mind.

> ... how oft –
> In darkness and amid the many shapes
> Of joyless daylight; when the fretful stir
> Unprofitable, and the fever of the world,
> Have hung upon the beatings of my heart –
> How oft, in spirit, have I turned to thee,
> O sylvan Wye! thou wanderer through the woods,
> How often has my spirit turned to thee!
>
> *Tintern Abbey, ll.50–57*

In *Tintern Abbey*, written when revisiting the Wye valley five years later, William gives a wonderful description of his younger self, which perfectly captures his mood on this tour: his joy in his own physical prowess, his rapture at the beauty of the landscape and, more disquietingly, his sense that he was taking refuge in nature as a flight from his problems, rather than as an answer to them. The natural beauties of the Wye bewitched his physical senses; it did not, as yet, offer him a philosophy for coming to terms with the human condition. He describes how, 'like a roe',

> I bounded o'er the mountains, by the sides
> Of the deep rivers, and the lonely streams,
> Wherever nature led: more like a man
> Flying from something he dreads, than one
> Who sought the thing he loved. For nature then
> (The coarser pleasures of my boyish days,
> And their glad animal movements all gone by)
> To me was all in all, – I cannot paint
> What then I was. The sounding cataract
> Haunted me like a passion: the tall rock,
> The mountain, and the deep and gloomy wood,
> Their colours and their forms, were then to me
> An appetite; a feeling and a love,
> That had no need of a remoter charm,
> By thought supplied, nor any interest
> Unborrowed from the eye.
>
> *Tintern Abbey, ll. 68–83*

How far William travelled up the meandering course of the Wye is not known, but by 30 August he was 'quietly sitting down in the Vale of Clwyd', awaiting his sister's arrival at Halifax. Dorothy herself was in a fever of anxiety and anticipation, waiting for the arrangements for her visit to be finalized. 'Oh count, count the Days, my Love', she urged Jane, 'till Christmas how slowly does each day move! and yet three months and Christmas will not be here. Three months! – long, long months I measure them with a Lover's scale, three months of Expectation are three Ages!'

While Dorothy fretted in Norfolk, William appears to have sat out the interval till Christmas at Plas-yn-Llan. Four months was a long period for someone as constitutionally restless as William to 'quietly sit down' in Clwyd, but, until he reappears at Whitehaven on 26 December, his existence is totally uncharted. This has given biographers ample scope for varying degrees of wild speculation, based on a single, much-quoted passage in Thomas Carlyle's *Reminiscences*.

He had been in France in the earlier or secondary stage of the Revolution; had witnessed the struggle of *Girondins* and *Mountain*, in particular the execution of Gorsas, 'the first *Deputy* sent to the Scaffold;' and testified strongly to the ominous feeling which that event produced in everybody, and of which he himself still seemed to retain something: 'Where will it *end*, when you have set an example in *this* kind?' I knew well about Gorsas; but had found, in my readings, no trace of the public emotion his death excited; and perceived now that Wordsworth might be taken as a true supplement to my Books, on this small point.

It seems inconceivable that Carlyle could be wrong. There was no one more likely to understand the references and the background than the great historian and author of *The French Revolution*. And he had the information direct from William himself. On these two premises alone, few have dared to challenge Carlyle's statement.

Yet if Carlyle was right, some time between the end of August and the beginning of October William left North Wales, returned to the south coast, caught a boat to France and made his way to Paris. There, on 7 October, he was in the crowd and witnessed as Antoine Gorsas, a journalist of the Girondin party, was executed by the guillotine. He then scuttled back to England and the safety of his Wordsworth relatives in Cumberland, in time for a jolly Christmas reunion with his sister. This presupposes so many insuperable difficulties that it defies belief. Where did he get the money to finance his journey and bribe a ship's captain to take him to France? How did he land at one of the French Channel ports, or travel to Paris without a French government passport or papers? How did he avoid the bands of armed royalist rebels and revolutionary guards roaming the countryside of Normandy? Or, for that matter, if he landed further east near Dunkirk, the triumphant French armies who had just trounced the English at the battle of Hondschoote on 8 September? How did he evade capture or arrest, given that, on 17 September, the National Convention had ordered the arrest of all foreign nationals from countries at war with France? How did he alone escape imprisonment in Paris, when such renowned English revolutionaries as Helen Maria Williams, her lover J. H. Stone and even the father of the revolution, Thomas Paine himself, were in detention?

Viewed in such a light, William's return to France at this time would have been not just foolhardy but suicidal. Moreover, there is no reason, logical or otherwise, why he should have wished to go back. It is unlikely that the man who balked at publishing his *Letter to the Bishop of L[l]andaff* in England would have believed he had any contribution to make by throwing in his lot with any of the factions in France; if nothing else, such a quixotic gesture would have destroyed any chance he ever had of providing that cottage for his sister or, indeed, his mistress and child.

Had he really been in Paris to witness the first public execution of a deputy to the National Convention, he would surely have recorded it in *The Prelude*. It would have been too significant an event, and too dramatically moving a moment, when Gorsas, in his final words from the scaffold, commended his wife and children to the pity of the republic, for anyone, much less a poet, to ignore. Nor could he have been unaware of the agitation in Paris which would lead, a week later, to Marie Antoinette being put on trial for her life and her execution on 16 October. It is worth noticing also that while William's poetry is littered with references to hangings, the scaffold and the rope, even to the point of obsession, there is nothing to indicate in any of his writings that he ever saw an execution by guillotine.

The inescapable conclusion is the boring, unglamorous one. Carlyle was simply mistaken. He was recalling a conversation which had taken place at least twenty-five years previously, with a man remembering events of almost fifty years before that. Carlyle did not think the conversation worth recording at the time: it does not appear in either his contemporary letters or his book *The French Revolution*. We can only conjecture that William talked about being present in Paris at the end of 1792, but, when the conversation moved on to Gorsas, Carlyle assumed that William had been a literal witness of events which he had only read about in the newspapers.

The likeliest scenario is that, in the autumn of 1793, William remained at Plas-yn-Llan for as long as he was welcome, writing his earliest version of *The Female Vagrant*, then moved on to visit his Wordsworth relations in Cumberland. His decision to visit them seems to have been a diplomatic one, a case of building much-needed bridges with the side of the family that had always been less judgemental and more kindly disposed than the Cooksons. Uncle Richard had consistently forwarded funds whenever requested to do so, and William had obviously got on well with his cousin Captain John Wordsworth when they met in London. He could hardly be in the north and not visit them, unless he deliberately wished to cause offence.

By the middle of February, however, William was settled at the Rawsons' house at Millbank, just outside Halifax, and reunited with his sister for the first time in over three years. His radicalism must have come as a profound shock to Dorothy, but whatever reservations she may have had, she loved her brother too much not to enter into this passion as fully as she had his others. As they explored the beautiful Ryburn valley, with its tumbling wooded hillsides and vista of moorland beyond, he must have talked to her at length about France, his conversion to the republican cause, Annette and his unseen daughter and, perhaps most of all, his plans for the future. He could not continue 'doing nothing' for ever.

Brother and sister decided that they wished to be alone together. Having spent literally years longing for at least a six-month visit to Halifax, Dorothy now packed her bags after only half that time. At the beginning of April, she set off by coach with William for what turned out to be a very leisurely trip to Whitehaven.

At Kendal, they dismounted and walked the eighteen miles to Grasmere. It was a journey which would be forever etched in Dorothy's memory as her first introduction to the Lakes and the beginning of her 'pilgrimage' with William. They paused at a public house at Staveley to fortify themselves before tackling the mountains by drinking a basin of milk. Dorothy washed her feet in the brook and, on William's advice, put on a pair of silk stockings to prevent her shoes chafing. They walked the length of Windermere, stopping again to rest and refresh themselves by a little stream feeding into the lake at Lowwood. By the time they wound their way under the craggy heights of Nab Scar and Loughrigg Fell, the sun was just setting and pouring a rich yellow light on the still waters of Rydal and Grasmere, in which the islands were reflected. They spent the night at Grasmere, before walking the next fifteen miles over Dunmail Raise and beneath the shadow of Helvellyn, to the far side of Keswick. The obliging William Calvert was in London and had offered to let them lodge at his house, Windy Brow, until his return. Dorothy was in ecstasies at her own wonderful prowess in walking, at the delightful manners of Calvert's caretaker tenants ('the most honest cleanly sensible people I ever saw in their rank of life') and, above all, the situation of the farmhouse itself. Standing at the top of a very steep bank rising 'nearly perpendicular' from the River Greta below, it looked out towards the little town of Keswick, over which towered the wooded steeps and silvery, rocky summit of Friar's Crag. About 100 yards above the house was a natural terrace along Latrigg Fell, the mountain under which Windy Brow sheltered, commanding a view of the whole Vale of Keswick. It was impossible, Dorothy declared, to describe the grandeur of this view over 'the vale of Elysium, as Mr Grey calls it', with Derwentwater lying in the lap of huge mountains to the south-west, the ribbon of Bassenthwaite to the north and Skiddaw's massive bosomy heights towering above the fields and cottages of the vale between. She had intended to stay for only a few days with William before travelling on to Whitehaven, but she could not tear herself away. A fortnight later, she had given up all thought of an early departure and was planning to stay for another month.

This blissful existence was rudely interrupted by a stinging letter of rebuke from Uncle Christopher's wife. Dorothy's conduct was disgraceful, her reputation in tatters. Not content with rambling about the countryside on foot, Dorothy was now living in lodgings at vast expense and, worse still, without any respectable guardian of her morals. To this shrill censure, Dorothy replied with admirable dignity and restraint. 'I am much obliged to you for the frankness with which you have expressed your sentiments upon my conduct', she wrote, 'and am at the same time extremely sorry that you should think it so severely to be condemned.' The walk from Kendal had given her pleasure and saved her thirty shillings. Her expenses were negligible, since they drank no tea, had bread and milk for breakfast and supper, and potatoes 'from choice' as their main dish at dinner. She considered 'the character and virtues of my brother' as 'sufficient protection' (one can imagine the explosion at Newbiggin Hall on reading this) but, in any case, 'I am convinced that there is no place in the world in which a good and virtuous young woman would be more likely to continue good and virtuous than under the roof of these honest, worthy, uncorrupted people'. As proof that her reputation had not suffered, she made pointed reference to the friendly attentions she had received from several of her brothers' friends and Mrs Spedding, mother of his old schoolfriend John, in particular, from whose house she had only just returned after a visit of three days and to whom she had promised further visits. Reiterating this at the close of her letter, Dorothy politely but implicitly snubbed her aunt: if Mrs Spedding of Armathwaite Hall chose to invite Miss Wordsworth into her house, who was Mrs Crackanthorpe to complain of ruined reputations and unprotected situation? Finally, Dorothy informed her aunt, she intended to remain a few weeks longer at Windy Brow to cultivate these new acquaintances and, above all, enjoy the society of her brother.

I am now twenty two years of age and such have been the circumstances of my life that I may be said to have enjoyed his company only for a *very few* months. An opportunity now presents itself of obtaining this satisfaction, an opportunity which I could not see pass from me without unspeakable pain. Besides I not only derive much pleasure but much improvement from my brother's society. I have regained all the knowledge I had of the French language some years ago, and have added considerably to it, and I have now begun reading Italian, of which I expect to have soon gained a sufficient knowledge to receive much entertainment and advantage from it.

Dorothy's intellectual hunger was a pleasant stimulus to William's own appetite for books and poetry. He wrote to Richard, asking him to forward to Keswick the Italian grammar and editions of Tasso and Ariosto he had left in his care after leaving Cambridge. Mindful of Dorothy's earlier criticisms and prompted by her presence, he began a thorough revision of *An Evening Walk* and *Descriptive Sketches*. In the case of *An Evening Walk*, this was a virtual rewriting, containing important additions which suggest that he was beginning to evolve his philosophy of 'seeing into the Life of things'. The sensitive heart, he now wrote, 'sees not any line where being ends' and 'Sees sense . . . Tremble obscure in fountain, rock and shade'; the unity and harmony of the natural world, of which man is an indivisible part, bear witness to man's potential for good and inspire 'Entire affection for all human kind'. Reviews of both poems were still appearing and William was hopeful that Johnson might be persuaded to publish a new edition. If he could be certain of earning some money by it, he intended to offer Johnson his Salisbury Plain poem, written the previous summer and now, neatly copied up by Dorothy, ready for the press. He even found time to write a new poem, an inscription for a seat by the pathway leading up to Windy Brow.

William's new-found creativity and sense of purpose obviously owed much to Dorothy's presence but it had far-reaching consequences. Calvert's younger brother, Raisley, was one of the people who paid 'the friendliest attentions' to William and Dorothy. He was a remarkable young man, not yet twenty-one years of age, who had much in common with William. He had been disenchanted with Cambridge, leaving before he had even matriculated, had a passion for travel and was a talented amateur sculptor. He was also in very delicate health and his chances of earning lasting fame were decidedly slim. It was perhaps for this reason that he now decided to offer William a share in his income. It is usually accepted that Raisley saw William's potential as a poet and wanted to free him from the necessity of earning his own living so that he could dedicate himself to writing poetry. This is undeniably true, but it cannot be the whole story. In acknowledging his debt to Raisley, William always couched his gratitude in specific terms. Just after the offer had been made, for instance, William declared, 'he is . . . ready to support me in a situation wherein I feel I can be of some little service to my fellowmen'. In 1805, it is still the same story: 'the act was done entirely from a confidence on his part that I had powers and attainments which might be of use to mankind'. Next to nothing is known about Raisley Calvert, but the implication of comments such as these is that he shared William's radical political beliefs.

Politics, more than poetry, were still uppermost in William's mind. In his *Letter to the Bishop of L[l]andaff* he had recognized that education was the key to bringing about change. Since then, he had read one of the most influential books of the day, William Godwin's *Enquiry Concerning Political Justice and its Influence on Morals and Happiness*. To account for the phenomenal impact of this book, not just on William but on a whole generation of young intellectuals and radicals, one has to realize that he offered them hope. The idealists who, in the name of republicanism, had welcomed the French Revolution, advocated the execution of the King and defended the massacre of counter-revolutionaries, found it increasingly difficult to justify the indiscriminate slaughter which resulted from warring factional interest. In the Terror that followed the fall of the Girondins and rise of Robespierre, literally thousands were executed: in Paris alone, 2,600 went to the guillotine, over 1,500 of them in the two months of June and July 1794. As William himself tellingly put it, the conservative cry now went up, 'Behold the harvest which we reap From popular government and equality!' In the light of Godwin's arguments, the violence could be explained as the result of centuries of ignorance and repression. It was necessary to educate in order to bring about a social and cultural revolution. Man is, he argued, essentially a being whose actions are determined by reason. Once he has been rationally persuaded, it is impossible for him to act unreasonably. Reason teaches benevolence and, in a rational society, all institutions and laws would be unnecessary. It was a seductive philosophy, not least because it offered disillusioned revolutionaries an alternative to violence as a method of achieving change. They could become evangelists for education and reason.

William was actively searching out a way of putting these ideas into practice at the very time Raisley Calvert offered him a share of his income. 'It seems to me', he wrote to his friend Mathews at the beginning of June 1794,

that a writer who has the welfare of mankind at heart should call forth his best exertions to convince the people that they can only be preserved from a convulsion [i.e. violent revolution] by oeconomy in the administration of the public purse and a gradual and constant reform of those abuses which, if left to themselves, may grow to such a height as to render, even a revolution desirable. There is a further duty incumbent upon every enlightened friend of mankind; he should let slip no opportunity of explaining and enforcing those general principles of the social order which are applicable to all times and to all places; he should diffuse by every method a knowledge of those rules of political justice, from which the farther any government deviates the more effectually must it defeat the object for which government was ordained. A knowledge of these rules cannot but lead to good; they include an entire preservative from despotism, they will guide the hand of reform, and if a revolution must afflict us, they alone can mitigate its horrors and establish freedom with tranquillity.

The best way of spreading this knowledge and educating the public was to set up a newspaper or journal. William would publish a monthly miscellany, together with Mathews, and one of the latter's friends. At the very outset, William set out his creed: 'You know perhaps already that I am of that odious class of men called democrats', he wrote proudly to Mathews, 'and of that class I shall for ever continue.' In a work of the kind they were planning, it would be impossible 'not to inculcate principles of government and forms of social order', so his fellow writers needed to know what they were letting themselves in for. This was not an idle remark: only a few days before he wrote this letter, three prominent members of the London Corresponding Society, Thomas Hardy, John Horne Tooke and John Thelwall, had been arrested and charged with high treason. The same risk attended anyone planning to write for a radical journal.

William could not afford to help finance the setting up of their publication or to live in London, so he could not assist with the editing. Instead, he offered to contribute essays on morals and politics and 'critical remarks' upon the arts, which he defined as poetry, painting and gardening. (The last might seem an odd subject, but William was a passionate landscape gardener all his life, believing it to be an art determined by the same principles as poetry.) 'I should principally wish our attention to be fixed upon life and manners,' he thundered, 'and to make our publication a vehicle of sound and exalted Morality.'

Ironically, the very day William wrote this outspoken declaration of his principles, his lawyer brother, Richard, wrote from London to warn him that the cornerstone of the English constitution, the Habeas Corpus Act, had been suspended. It would now be possible to be arrested on suspicion of fomenting political dissent and to be held indefinitely without charge. 'Tell me', Richard added suspiciously, perhaps having caught wind of the publication scheme, 'how you mean to dispose of yourself this summer.'

By the time William got this letter he was in Whitehaven, where he had at last accomplished the plan agreed at Halifax of escorting his sister to her Wordsworth relatives. There was an unpleasant surprise waiting for them at Branthwaite, the little village between Cockermouth and Whitehaven where their cousin Richard the attorney lived. His father, their guardian, Uncle Richard, was staying there and he was so seriously ill that he was not expected to live. In fact, he lingered till the middle of June, dying on the 16th, aged sixty-one.

The illness and death of Uncle Richard added even greater urgency to the need for a grand sort-out of the family finances. Cousin Richard drummed this into Dorothy, who wrote in a state of alarm to her brother Richard, forcefully demanding that he should make a speedy settlement of their affairs. He should harry Uncle Christopher to draw up his accounts; he must consult with those 'most able to advise' him; he should go to the House of Lords; he should go to Lord Lonsdale himself. At least 'you might *gain something*'. Dorothy's frustration was understandable, but Richard was clearly offended at this implicit criticism of his handling of the case. 'There is one circumstance which I will mention to you at this time', he replied with stiff dignity, '– I might have retired into the Country & I had almost said enjoyed the sweets of retirement & domestick life if I had only considered my own Interest.'

Dorothy spent the summer making a round of all her Cumberland cousins. Whenever he had the opportunity, William rejoined her from Keswick, where

Raisley Calvert was displaying all the classic signs of tuberculosis, alternately enjoying bouts of good health and spirits, followed by periods of extreme weakness and depression. In the light of Calvert's offer to share his income with him, William felt obliged to be there when required. This had become more necessary, because William Calvert had volunteered as an officer in the Duke of Norfolk's militia and been posted to Tynemouth in Northumberland. The very act of enlisting, even in a volunteer militia, suggests that William Calvert's political sympathies were at odds with those of his friend and his brother. That the friendship survived to the end of their lives, and into the next generation, says much for the strength of their personal affection.

Whether in Cumberland or in Keswick, William's mind was full of just one thing, his plans for the new journal. It should be called the *Philanthropist*, he suggested; each issue should begin with the topic of general politics, incorporating a commentary which would 'forcibly illustrate the tendency of particular doctrines of government'; then there should be essays on morals and manners, social and political institutions, all highly educational, followed by a blend of instruction and amusement in the form of biographies representing 'the advancement of the human mind in moral knowledge' and essays on taste and criticism. The potential readership, William believed, would be found among university students, dissenters and the Irish. This last suggestion had come from Mathews, but was taken up with alacrity by William, who even offered to go personally to Dublin to find an agent to disseminate the magazine. It was an astonishing plan and, had it been put into practice, one which would have been regarded as *prima facie* evidence of treasonable activity by the government.

William had backtracked a little from his previous incendiary declaration that he was a democrat by hastily explaining to Mathews, 'I recoil from the bare idea of a revolution', but he remained defiant and explicit in his condemnation of monarchical and aristocratical institutions, 'however modified'. He attacked the government for its brutal suppression of free speech. 'Freedom of inquiry is all that I wish for; let nothing be deemed too sacred for investigation; rather than restrain the liberty of the press I would suffer the most atrocious doctrines to be recommended: let the field be open and unencumbered, and truth must be victorious.' He denounced the conduct of foreign and domestic policy over the previous two years as driving the country into inevitable rebellion. There was only one thing that could save the country from the coming revolution: 'the undaunted efforts of good men in propagating with unremitting activity those doctrines which long and severe meditation has taught them are essential to the welfare of mankind'. William had no doubt that he was one of those good men. Whether his efforts would be undaunted remained to be seen.

6. Benighted Heart and Mind

In August 1794 William crossed the broad expanse of the River Leven estuary which divides the Furness peninsula from Grange-over-Sands. It was a bright sunny day, with glorious views of the mountains to the north and the great sweep of Morecambe Bay to the south. William was in serene mood: he was on his way back to his sister and cousins at Rampside, the tiny fishing village tucked into a fold of the southern extremity of the Furness peninsula, from an excursion that morning to Cartmel Priory. Wandering in the churchyard under its grey towers, he had accidentally come across the grave of his old schoolmaster William Taylor, whose love of poetry had been an inspiration to him as a boy. As he made for the rocky outcrop of Piel Island, with its little ruined chapel, the notoriously treacherous sands of the bay were thronged with guided columns of people on foot, on horseback and in carts and wagons, hastening across before the tide swept back in. Casually hailing one of the travellers, he asked if there was any news and received a thunderbolt in reply: Robespierre, the man of blood who had unleashed the Terror on France, was dead.

> Great was my glee of spirit, great my joy
> In vengeance, and eternal justice, thus
> Made manifest. 'Come now, ye golden times',
> Said I, forth-breathing on those open sands
> A hymn of triumph, 'as the morning comes
> Out of the bosom of the night, come ye!
> Thus far our trust is verified: behold,
> They who with clumsy desperation brought
> Rivers of blood, and preached that nothing else
> Could cleanse the Augean stable, by the might

Of their own helper have been swept away!
Their madness is declared and visible –
Elsewhere will safety now be sought, and earth
March firmly towards righteousness and peace.'
                                        Prelude (1805), x, 539–52

It was an elation which could not survive for long. True, Robespierre's execution effectively ended the Terror, but it did not end either the war with England and her allies or the internal factional struggles in the new republic. And in October the French armies became aggressors, invading and conquering their peaceable neighbours in the Low Countries. William, like most apologists for the French Revolution, would find himself once again trapped in the cycle of hope followed by disillusionment.

William spent about a month at Rampside, before returning to Windy Brow at the end of September, much later than he expected. He found Raisley Calvert 'worse than when I left Keswick, but a good deal better than he had been some weeks before'. Another winter in England would kill him, so Calvert had decided to go to Portugal, where the warm, dry climate offered at least a hope of recovery. William, seeing how fragile Raisley was, may have suspected that the scheme would come to nothing, but did not want to alarm or dishearten his dying friend by saying so. Instead, he decided to play along. If Raisley was determined to go, the obvious person to accompany him was William, who was at leisure to do so and knew Spanish, if not Portuguese. The problem was that William could not fund such a journey himself and Raisley, who was still under-age and living on an allowance, could not afford to pay for a companion. The obvious person to whom they should appeal was William Calvert, but an already awkward situation was rendered many times more delicate by Raisley's second decision. Knowing that he might never return from Portugal, he had determined to make his will. His intention was to leave everything to his brother, with a legacy to William of £600. 'He would leave me this sum', William told his own brother, 'to set me above want and to enable me to pursue my literary views or any other views with greater success or with a consciousness that if these should fail me I would have something at last to turn to.' It was an incredibly generous offer and one that was beset with problems, the most pressing of which was how to tell William Calvert.

William insisted that this should be done immediately and wrote the difficult letter to his friend. His discomfort is evident in his abruptness. He broke the news about Raisley's health first, and asked about the possibility of Calvert paying for him to go. 'This I think, if possible, you ought to do. You see I speak to you as a friend. But then perhaps your present expenses may render it difficult. Would it not exalt you in your own esteem to retrench a little for so excellent a purpose?' He then informed him of Raisley's intention with regard to the will. 'It is at my request that this information is communicated to you, and I have no doubt but that you will do both him and myself the justice to hear this mark of his approbation of me without your good opinion of either of us being at all diminished by it.' He ended with an appeal that 'it would be much the best' if Calvert could come over himself to discuss the matters face to face.

Calvert responded promptly and generously. Eight days after agonizing over this letter, William and Raisley set off together for Lisbon. They did not get far. They had completed only the first leg of their journey, as far as Penrith, when Raisley realized that he could go no further and returned to Keswick. Frustrated in their intention to consult Richard and other lawyers in London, it now became necessary to execute the will locally. The biggest problem, as William had pointed out to Raisley, was that the young Wordsworths owed their recently deceased Uncle Richard something in the region of £460. Raisley was concerned that the legacy he intended to form a nest-egg for William's future should not be seized upon in payment of this debt. He therefore stipulated that William's brother Richard should personally enter into a legally binding agreement that the legacy would not be used for that purpose and that, if a claim should be made by Uncle Richard's estate, Richard himself would pay the sum. In an agitated letter, William sought to persuade Richard to agree to the arrangement and offered repeated assurances that, if ever he was worth more than the £600 of the legacy, he would immediately repay the debt to their uncle.

Richard replied with irritating coolness. He had 'always most sincerely had my Sisters, yours & my younger Brothers Interest at Heart although I have not been fond of making professions which It could not be my intention to carry into effect'. He would 'readily' enter into the agreement and sent his sincere good wishes to 'Mr R. Calvert', but he could not resist a little amused irony at his and William's expense. 'I hope he will live to enjoy his Fortune. I suppose he has maturely weighed the matter and taken into consideration the claims of his Brother to keep any provision he may make for you alone.' For almost another two weeks, the fate of the legacy hung in the balance. William chafed, torn between fear of losing the money which would make him independent and reluctance to harass his would-be benefactor for purely selfish reasons. Raisley dithered over whether to save a guinea and a half by not employing a lawyer from Penrith, but in the end he decided he could afford to be profligate. On 23 October 1794 he employed Mr Lough to draw up his will and he increased the legacy to £900. A codicil, added the same day, directed William to use the money to purchase annuities for himself and (which probably explains the increase in the amount) to lay out 'such part and so much of the said £900 as to him shall seem meet for the use and benefit of his Sister Dorothy Wordsworth'. William Calvert was to be his brother's sole executor. Even now, as Richard had pointed out, William could not be sure of his legacy; if Raisley died before his twenty-first birthday in November, his brother could challenge and overturn the will on the grounds that it had been made by a minor.

Raisley did survive, lingering painfully and distressingly into the New Year. Some time before Christmas, they removed to Penrith and on 9 January 1795 Raisley Calvert died. It would be almost a decade before William considered that he had at last earned his patron's trust and felt able to write and dedicate a sonnet *To the Memory of Raisley Calvert*.

> . . . if in freedom I have loved the truth;
> If there be aught of pure, or good, or great,
> In my past verse; or shall be, in the lays
> Of higher mood, which now I meditate; –
> It gladdens me, O worthy, short-lived, Youth!
> To think how much of this will be thy praise.

Cooped up in the sickroom for months on end, William had had plenty of time to consider his future. The grand scheme for the *Philanthropist* had come to nothing, thwarted by the impossibility of funding publication. William remained undaunted. If he could not publish a monthly miscellany himself, he would work for someone else who could. Mathews had already come to a similar conclusion and had accepted a post as parliamentary reporter on a new 'democratical' paper, the *Telegraph*, whose first issue was published on 30 December 1794. He now offered to help William find a similar post. William instead proffered his services as a translator of French, Italian and Spanish gazettes. He was also prepared to write essays upon general politics and occasional commentaries on government measures, but only for an opposition newspaper. Cheered by the recent acquittal and release of Hardy, Horne Tooke and Thelwall, a sign that the British Constitution was not entirely rotten, William longed to be in the thick of things. 'I begin to wish much to be in town', he had written to Mathews early in November;

cataracts and mountains, are good occasional society, but they will not do for constant companions; besides I have not even much of their conversation, and still less of that of my books as I am so much with my sick friend, and he cannot bear the fatigue of being read to. Nothing indeed but a sense of duty could detain me here under the present circumstances. This is a country for poetry it is true; but the muse is not to be won but by the sacrifice of time, and time I have not to spare.

William could not leave the north without paying one last visit to his sister, who was now staying with their mother's cousins the Griffith family at Newcastle. She did not want to return to the domestic slavery of Forncett; the opportunities she had enjoyed over the last year of getting to know her brother (and his opinions) had made her aware that she could no longer be a compatible member of that household. Uncle Christopher's Newbiggin Hall could not be contemplated. She even seems to have avoided paying her duty visit there, for the Misses Griffith had to broker a meeting between uncle and niece. To her great surprise Dorothy found Uncle Christopher was not the monster she believed him to be: 'I never saw a man so agitated in my life as he was at our meeting', she told Jane later. He had been kind and affectionate in manner and had made her a handsome present of ten guineas before they parted. Bemused, Dorothy could only attribute his faults to the influence of that 'proud and selfish woman', his wife, the former Miss Cust.

Dorothy was temporarily saved from her dilemma by a timely invitation from Mary Hutchinson who, for the last six years, had been living Dorothy's own dream, keeping house for her brother. Tom had taken over his great-uncle's farm at Sockburn, in County Durham and was providing a home not just for Mary, but for their sisters, Margaret and Sarah, and youngest brother George. He was, Dorothy noted enviously, 'a very amiable young man, uncommonly fond of his sisters, and in short, every thing that they can desire'.

The Hutchinsons did indeed seem blessed. A close-knit and happy family, they lived in the large, elegant, red-brick house which their great-uncle had built, in a loop of the River Tees so pronounced that it almost made an island. It is, in fact, the last bastion of County Durham, for the river marks the boundary with Yorkshire. Accessible only over a narrow neck of land, Sockburn Farm still stands, its great sash windows facing out, over a small ha-ha, to lush flat meadows where Tom grazed his sheep. On every side there is the great circular sweep of the river, flowing broad and slow, round the edge of the property; beyond it rise the steep wooded banks of the opposite shore, enclosing Sockburn in an embrace which seems to protect it from the world outside. To add to its many charms, which completely seduced the Wordsworths and Coleridge, immediately in front of the house stand the grey stones marking the legendary spot where, in the year 1001, Sir John Conyers slew the local dragon, the Sockburn Worm, with his mighty falchion. Close by stands the Conyers family home, a remarkable seventeenth-century fantasy of gables and mullions, immured in woodland like Sleeping Beauty's castle, and, between the hall and the farm, what are now the picturesque ruins of All Saints' Church, where Sir John's effigy lies carved in stone, his feet resting on the slaughtered Worm.

'When shall I have the felicity of welcoming you my earliest friend to such a home?' Dorothy asked Jane mournfully. 'Would not you my dearest Jane be delighted beyond expression to be my guest? but these are airy dreams.' The reason why these were still airy dreams, instead of solid realities, was now living in London. Here, for the first time in two years, William had the opportunity to see his brother John, who had returned from China on 20 September 1794. John's ship, the *Earl of Abergavenny*, was in the process of being purchased by the government for the navy; its replacement, a heavier vessel, was to be built in Northfleet in Kent and would not be ready for service until 1796. John, not being able to afford to remain idle, accepted promotion to fourth mate on another East Indiaman, and sailed from London on 22 April. His new ship, the *Osterley*, was bound for Macao in south China, but would call at the Cape of Good Hope to land an English expeditionary force to help hold the Cape against the French. John had therefore become an involuntary part of the British war effort of which his brother so strongly disapproved.

Great as his pleasure must have been at this brief reunion with John, William's main objective in coming to London was to see Mathews and immerse himself in radical politics. By the beginning of March he had taken up residence in lodgings at 15 Chalton Street, Somers Town. It was a significant address and deliberately chosen, for, literally a few doors away, at number 25, lived William Godwin, author of *An Enquiry Concerning Political Justice*. The two men first met on 27 February, at

the London house of William Frend, the Cambridge fellow who had been expelled
from the university in 1793 for his radical views. This was another significant contact.
The same was true of almost the entire circle gathered in Frend's house that
evening. Among them were George Dyer, the Unitarian, who had been a close
friend of William Taylor, William's schoolmaster at Hawkshead; James Losh from
Carlisle, an older brother of a boy who had lodged with William at Ann Tyson's;
John Tweddell, the brilliant classicist of Trinity College, who had graduated the
year before William; and Thomas Holcroft, the writer who had so narrowly escaped
execution in the previous autumn's treason trials and had reviewed (patronizingly
and unkindly) *Descriptive Sketches* and *An Evening Walk* for the *Monthly Review* in 1793.

In this group of radicals, William felt instantly at home. Nor was he afraid to
argue with the Philosopher himself. Many years later, when he was a rather pathetic
figure, rejected and even laughed at by most of the young men whom he had once
enthused, Godwin claimed, 'I had the honour, in the talk of one evening, to convert
Wordsworth from the doctrine of self-love to that of benevolence – ask him.' (By
the doctrine of self-love, Godwin meant the belief that self-interest determines all
human actions.) William's writings reveal that he had been a convert since the
previous summer, but Godwin's book, not his conversation, deserved the credit.
Nevertheless, William was so impressed by this first meeting that he called on
Godwin the following day and thereafter the two men visited each other regularly
throughout the summer. William's circle of acquaintance among Godwin's disciples
now expanded rapidly.

The most important of these was Basil Montagu, an illegitimate son of the
Fourth Earl of Sandwich, with whom William had immediate empathy. They were
the same age, shared the same politics and had been to the same university. In 1791,
shortly after his twenty-first birthday, Montagu had married against his father's
wishes; the Earl never spoke to him again. On 27 December 1792, only twelve days
after Caroline Wordsworth was born in Orléans, Montagu's wife gave birth to a
son, young Basil. A few days later, she died. Montagu was left with the difficult
task of bringing up the boy unaided, while struggling to earn a living. By a curious
coincidence, which must have struck William with peculiar force when he learned
it, this child, so close in age to his own unseen daughter, was also called Caroline,
after his mother. When William met Montagu, father and two-year-old son were
living together in chambers in Lincoln's Inn. It was not an appropriate place to
bring up a child, especially as Montagu was given to bouts of excessive drinking
and wild behaviour. William not only made friends with the father but also took
the forlorn little boy under his wing. Montagu later paid tribute to his influence
on them both.

By an accident I became acquainted with Wm Wordsworth. We spent some months together.
He saw me, with great industry, perplexed and misled by passions wild & strong. In the
wreck of my happiness he saw the probable ruin of my infant. He unremittingly, and to me
imperceptibly, endeavoured to eradicate my faults, & to encourage my good dispositions. I
consider my having met Wm Wordsworth the most fortunate event of my life.

There could hardly have been a more practical expression of Godwinian benevolence and it resulted in a lifelong friendship.

Through Montagu, William was introduced to Francis Wrangham, a Yorkshireman, who would also become a friend for life. Wrangham was curate at the parish church of Cobham in Surrey and shared pupils with Montagu; he also had literary ambitions and, with William, embarked on a joint project, an imitation of the hard-hitting political satires of the Roman poet Juvenal. It probably began as an impromptu bit of fun, a scurrilous lampoon of the monarchy and aristocracy, but soon developed a momentum of its own. Of its very nature, it is full of topical references which are now obscure and humour which requires explanation to appreciate. What is still apparent, even for the modern reader, is the venom with which it was written. In lines not paralleled in the Juvenal original, William and Wrangham employed their punning wit in pouring scorn on aristocratic titles.

> Heavens! who sees majesty in George's face?
> Or looks at Norfolk and can dream of grace?
> What has this blessed earth to do with shame?
> If excellence was ever Eden's name?
> Must honour still to Lonsdale's tail be bound?

The swipe at Lonsdale must have given William personal satisfaction, but the satire was also a republican manifesto. In what he claimed was 'A single word on Kings and Sons of Kings', but was in fact several dozen lines, he offered the rational argument against hereditary power.

> – Were Kings a free born work – a people's choice,
> Would More or Henry boast the general voice?
> What fool, besotted as we are by names,
> Could pause between a Raleigh and a James?
> *[Imitation of Juvenal – Satire VIII], ll.9–13, 100–104*

Though ten guineas was offered for the work, plus half the profits should a second edition be required, the satire seems to have been left incomplete. The two friends ran out of steam and other work intervened. As far as William was concerned, an opportunity had also arisen which could not be ignored.

Montagu and Wrangham had, between them, been tutoring two young men, John and Azariah Pinney. They were the twenty-two- and twenty-year-old sons of John Praetor Pinney, a wealthy Bristol merchant, who was a partner in the Bristol West Indies Trading Company. Despite the fact that their fortune was founded on the back of the slave trade, the Pinneys were a liberal family. In an indefensible business, their father had sought to provide better conditions than many other plantation owners. His slaves never went without food, were allowed to own their own goats, pigs and poultry and, as Pinney pointed out in the argument always used by slavers, enjoyed better living standards than the free poor on the island of Nevis. His son, John, however, to whom he had given the Nevis plantations as a twenty-first birthday present, was 'a rabid Whig' and was very much part of the radical Godwinian circle centred on both London and Bristol. Azariah was as active as, if not more so than, his brother.

The elder Pinney had built a country house in Dorset during the American War of Independence; the war threatened his sugar interests and the house was intended as a refuge in the event of financial ruin. Having no use for the place himself, Pinney presented the property to his oldest son, expecting that he would either use it or derive an income from letting it out. This house, Racedown Lodge, John now offered to William, fully furnished and rent-free; the sole condition was that John was to be allowed, on occasion and only if convenient, to spend a few weeks there himself, paying for his own bed and board.

Had there been no other incentive, William would have accepted with alacrity. Living in London was expensive and he had been unable to find a position on a newspaper. The imitation of Juvenal remained unfinished and unpublished; if he had attempted to find a publisher for his Salisbury Plain poem, *The Female Vagrant*, he had failed. His one small success was the appearance on 21 August in the *Morning Chronicle* of a poem, *The Birth of Love*. It was not even an original composition, but a translation, made some time between 1792 and 1794, from the French allegorical poem *L'Education de l'Amour*. A deeply contrived piece, even in the original, it had little to recommend it except that it probably earned William an urgently needed guinea or two.

This had now become critical, for, as yet, William had received nothing from Raisley Calvert's estate. The £900 legacy could not be handed over instantly, because it had been loaned out in order to pay Raisley an annual income of £100. Unravelling this would take time, and it is a credit to William Calvert that the first payment of £250 was made in September, with an additional £50 the following month. Investing the money to get the best return, and on sufficient security, would cause William and Richard considerable anxiety over the next few months, but they anticipated the same 9 per cent interest rate that Calvert had enjoyed.

Even when all the legacy was paid, however, there would be only £100 a year to share between William and Dorothy. The offer of Racedown Lodge, rent-free, made all the difference. It also enabled William to offer a home not only to his sister but also to little Basil Caroline Montagu. There was a certain poetic justice in the fact that Montagu now asked William himself to take care of the child, offering him £50 a year for Basil's board, provided that Dorothy agreed to accompany them to Racedown. Indeed, the coming together of the offer of Racedown and the care of young Basil suggests that this was a concerted plan, and that John Pinney's generosity was as much a favour to Montagu, his tutor (to whom he had already made several loans), as to William.

About the third week in August, William left London for Great George Street, Bristol, where he had an invitation to await the arrival of Dorothy from Halifax and little Basil Montagu, both of whom were expected within a few days. In the end, however, Dorothy did not arrive until 22 September, allowing William to pass the time in the way he liked best. The weather was delightful and he was at liberty to walk where he pleased. He found the Pinneys an amiable family 'in all its branches' and 'my time slipped insensibly away'.

William took advantage of his residence in Bristol to cultivate his fellow radicals. Bristol had long been notorious as a centre of dissent, both political and religious. Earlier in the year, two fiery young democrats had leapt on to the centre of the stage with a series of public lectures. Robert Southey was almost twenty-one; his friend, Samuel Taylor Coleridge, two years older. The previous summer they had both abandoned potentially brilliant academic careers at Oxford and Cambridge respectively in order to put their republican ideals into practice by founding an ideal society, under a scheme which they called Pantisocracy. Twelve good men and true, with twelve ladies of similar principles, were to embark for America and found a self-governing and self-sufficient colony of philosophers on the Susquehanna River. 'When Coleridge and I are sawing down a tree we shall discuss metaphysics;' Southey had boasted, 'criticise poetry when hunting a buffalo, and write sonnets whilst following the plough.' Everything that could be said about the practicality of the scheme can be summed up by their choice of location, which was dictated chiefly by its pretty name. Surprisingly, they had convinced a number of friends to accompany them, including Edith and Sarah Fricker, who were to be their brides. Unsurprisingly, the whole idea foundered even before these New Age pilgrims set sail.

Southey and Coleridge had also collaborated on a three-act drama, *The Fall of Robespierre*, published in 1794. Characteristically, though Southey had written two-thirds of the play, Coleridge managed to claim all the credit by putting his name alone on the title-page. Their plans in February 1795 to write and publish a monthly journal, the *Provincial Magazine*, had fallen through for the same reasons as William's and Mathews's for the *Philanthropist*. Instead, in the spring of 1795, each had given a series of public lectures, Southey's ostensibly on historical subjects, Coleridge's on political ones, but all designed to promote the radical agenda. Both were lucky to escape prosecution, particularly when Coleridge's lectures were published in December as *Conciones ad Populum*. Coleridge would later backtrack furiously, defying his worst enemy to produce evidence that he had ever shown 'the least bias to Irreligion, Immorality, or Jacobinianism' in his writings. Southey was more honest. If Coleridge was not a Jacobin in 1795, he wrote, 'I wonder who the Devil was. I am sure I was.'

William already knew both men, as they knew him, by reputation. He knew of Southey through Mathews, and of Coleridge through published reports of his lectures and through his own brother. Christopher Wordsworth had been a founder member, with Coleridge, of the literary society at Cambridge at which William's own poems had been so eagerly discussed. 'Coleridge was at Bristol part of the time I was there', William later told Mathews. 'I saw but little of him. I wished indeed to have seen more – his talent appears to me very great. I met with Southey also, his manners pleased me exceedingly and I have every reason to think very highly of his powers of mind.'

Quite where they met is a mystery. An intimate friend of the Wordsworths and Coleridge asserted in 1810 that they had met at a political debating society, 'where on one occasion Wordsworth spoke with so much force & eloquence that Coleridge was captivated by it & sought to know Him'. William himself said, in old age, that he had met both Coleridge and Southey 'in a lodging in Bristol'. Whichever it was, there was no indication at the time that the latent spark between William and Coleridge would soon ignite into a fire of friendship and creativity. Coleridge was preoccupied with his own problems and on the brink of a breach with Southey over his increasing reluctance to honour his obligation to marry Sarah Fricker. Southey, genuinely anxious to marry his beloved Edith Fricker, was under pressure from his guardian uncle to abandon his radical principles, go to Portugal and become a clergyman.

The three young men shared an instant attraction. William and Southey read their most recent poems to each other and Southey suggested two additional lines for William's *Imitation of Juvenal*. William listened admiringly to some of Southey's epic poem *Joan of Arc*, which was about to be published. Southey probably introduced William to his own publisher, Joseph Cottle, an enterprising young man of William's own age, who had the good fortune and perspicacity to publish Southey, Coleridge and, later, William himself. It is likely that it was Cottle who offered William ten guineas for the satire if he and Wrangham could complete it. Most dramatically of all, William may have now read his Salisbury Plain poem to Coleridge, provoking a reaction which the latter would recall vividly more than twenty years later. 'I was in my twenty-fourth year, when I had the happiness of knowing Mr Wordsworth personally,' Coleridge would write in his *Biographia Literaria*, 'and while memory lasts, I shall hardly forget the sudden effect produced on my mind, by his recitation'. Coleridge was so impressed that he urged William to publish it as it stood. William was reluctant, feeling that he had not made the most of the different elements in the story, but this encouragement inspired him to make so many alterations and additions over the next couple of months that 'it may be looked on almost as another work'.

The friendships were to be important and long-lasting; in the case of Coleridge, it was to be of profound significance on both a personal and literary level. For the moment, however, they parted, Coleridge to go to his future patron, Tom Poole, at Nether Stowey, Southey to resume residence in his native Bath, and William to Dorset. Dorothy arrived late on the evening of 22 September: 'I like her manner and appearance extremely,' Eliza Pinney reported to her father, 'she is very animated and unaffected –'. Four days later, William and Dorothy set off in a chaise for the fifty-mile drive down through Somerset and over the Dorset Downs to Racedown Lodge. It was almost midnight on 26 September when they arrived at their destination.

Perhaps this was just as well, for they were spared the disappointment of their first sight of the ugly and forbidding exterior of what was to be their home for the next two years. Built of dark-red brick, Racedown stands on a bend in a narrow winding country lane, under the lee of a deceptively steep hill. Despite having three storeys and an unusually high-pitched grey slate roof, the house still appears squat and solid, an illusion fostered by the fact that it is sandwiched between two vast blocks of chimneys at each end. The frontage is uncompromisingly symmetrical, a sash window each side of the door, three similar ones above and another row of three smaller ones on the top floor, but there are not sufficient windows, and they are not big enough, to offset the blank expanse of brickwork. It is irredeemably a manufacturer's house, and uncomfortably out of place in the soft, undulating landscape of the Downs.

Waking up the next morning, however, the Wordsworths would instantly see the best Racedown had to offer: long-distance views down the steeply shelving, narrow valley of the little River Synderford (a grand name for what is no more than a stream), over sinuous wooded hills and a lovely pastoral landscape, towards the Vale of Taunton Deane. Even better, when they scrambled up the hillside behind the house, they found themselves in the grassy bowl of the Iron Age fortress on top of Pilsdon Pen, at 909 feet the highest hill in Dorset, with magnificent views in every direction. They could see not only far into Somerset but, facing southwards, the glorious sweep of coastline from Torbay in the west to Weymouth in the east, with the Isle of Portland rising from the sea and clearly visible on the skyline beyond. Closer to home, looking over the rounded contours of gentle hills patched with woodland, broom, orchards and ploughed fields, and across the flat plain of the Vale of Marshwood, the land rises again into the distinctive contours of the cliffs at Lyme Regis, some ten or twelve miles away.

It is a landscape that invites one to explore on foot, and it is no coincidence that one of William's first priorities (second only to having his books sent on from Montagu's) was to order six pairs of shoes from his London cobbler. Four of these were to be William's own early version of the walking boot, made to his design and consisting 'of the very strongest kind double soles and upper leathers'. When he accidentally left a pair behind in London, some years later, Charles Lamb, who was commissioned to forward them, was vastly amused by these 'strange thick-hoofed shoes', declaring mischievously that they were 'very much admired at in London'.

William was irresistibly drawn to the ocean. He often walked over the hills to Lyme Regis, delighting in hearing the murmur of the sea three miles before it was visible, though he also experienced its horrors when he watched the huge West Indies fleet setting out 'in all its glory', only to be wrecked in storms off the treacherous Chesil Beach. He also made regular forays to Crewkerne, which lay about the same distance away in the opposite direction. This big, bustling market town was the nearest source of all supplies and the collection point for all the incoming and outgoing mail in the district. As Dorothy admitted, it was fortunate that William was so good a walker, for otherwise they would have been greatly inconvenienced by their isolation.

Dorothy was in ecstasies, at last living out her dream and playing 'house' for real. It was almost two months before she could tear herself away to write to her friend Jane Pollard, who had recently married the enterprising and soon-to-be fabulously rich John Marshall, a cotton and flax manufacturer in Leeds. Dorothy was not in the least bit jealous, even though she knew her own household could not compare with that of Jane. It had not cost the Wordsworths ten shillings to fit out Racedown, for everything was in perfect readiness. They had two parlours, one a formal dining room with a best Axminster carpet, the other, smaller one being both a breakfast room and a library. On the shelves were 470 books, mainly early-eighteenth-century legal tomes, classical texts and commentaries, and histories, with a fair sprinkling of French and Italian works and, oddly out of place in an otherwise heavyweight collection, Henry Fielding's novel *Joseph Andrews* and Jonathan Swift's satire *A Tale of a Tub*. It comes as no surprise to learn that this latter room was their favourite, being 'the prettiest little room that can be; with very neat furniture, a large book[case?] on each side of the fire, a marble chimney piece, bath stove, and an oil cloth for the floor'. Upstairs, there were four 'excellent' bedrooms on the first floor, and a further four, also described as 'excellent', on the top storey; in addition to all the usual offices, including two outside 'Necessaries', there were a wash house, a brew house, a coach house and stabling for four horses.

A month after their arrival, they managed to acquire a servant, Peggy Marsh, 'one of the nicest girls I ever saw', and a woman who came in once a month (for 9d a day) to do the washing. All the best linen, silver and glassware was locked away in an attic room, but the Wordsworths were more than adequately supplied, and could borrow from this store by arrangement. The manager, or caretaker, of the house and its extensive grounds, which included a fruit and vegetable garden, and a 'pleasure ground', with flowers, shrubs, fountains and statuary, was Joseph Gill. A cousin of the Pinneys, he had formerly managed their Nevis estates but, having acquired at least one of the island vices, alcoholism, he had proved financially incompetent and been hauled back to England in disgrace. Apart from Gill, there were no close neighbours. The nearest villages were Blackdown, where some unsociable Pinney relatives lived, and, in the opposite direction, Birdsmoorgate; neither was much more than a cluster of two or three knapped flint and thatched cottages.

While William walked the Downs, investigated the library at Racedown and worked hard on his revision of the Salisbury Plain poem, Dorothy devoted herself to the care of young Basil Caroline Montagu. He was now almost three years old, 'a charming boy, [who] affords us perpetual entertainment. Do not suppose from this that we make him our perpetual play-thing', Dorothy told Jane, 'far otherwise, I think that is one of the modes of treatment most likely to ruin a child's temper and character.' However, William's hopes of being entrusted with the education of one of the younger Pinneys, a thirteen-year-old boy, were dashed. This was a severe blow, for Wrangham had earned £200 a year for tutoring one of his older brothers.

Dorothy was convinced that little Basil flourished under her care. 'He is quite metamorphosed from a shivering half starved plant, to a lusty, blooming fearless boy', she wrote proudly to Jane after six months. When he first came, he was 'perpetually disposed to cry', a combination, they believed, of his petted upbringing and feeble physique. To rid him of this irritating habit, they devised a plan:

w[e] used to tell him that if he chose to cry he must go into a certain room where he cannot be heard, and *stay* till he chose to be quiet, because the noise was unpleasant to us; at first his visits were very long, but he alway[s] came out again perfectly good-humoured. He found that this mode was never departed from, and when he felt the fretful disposition coming on he would say, 'Aunt, I think I am going to cry' and retire till the fit was over. He has now entirely conquered the disposition.

They had no predetermined system of punishments, except that they tried, as far as possible, to make them the consequences of misdoing. When, aged four, he failed to get up when called two mornings in a row, the second time he found everyone too busy to help him dress, so he was obliged to go back to bed till four in the afternoon. Modern child psychologists might beat their breasts over this treatment of such a young child, but at least it was more enlightened than the whipping he would have received in most turn-of-the-century households. Plain victuals 'cooked tolerably well' by the willing Peggy Marsh and plenty of fresh air effected an equally remarkable physical change 'He dreads neither cold nor rain. He has played frequently an hour or two without appearing sensible that the rain was pouring down upon him or the wind blowing about him.' Apart from teaching him his alphabet, they made no effort to instil 'book-learning' into him. 'We teach him nothing at present but what he learns from the evidence of his senses', Dorothy told Jane.

He has an insatiable curiosity which we are always careful to satisfy to the best of our ability. It is directed to everything he sees, the sky, the fields, trees, shrubs, corn, the making of tools, carts, &c &c &c ... Our grand study has been to make him *happy* in which we have not been altogether disappointed; he is certainly the most contented child I ever saw; the least disposed to be fretful.

William was altogether more sceptical about his progress. 'Basil is quite well *quant au physique*', he told Wrangham, '*mais pour le moral il-y-a bien à craindre.* Among other things he lies like a little devil.' What is more, William was quite right. Many years later, Basil's despairing father would feel obliged to write an account of his son to contradict all his lies. The one that had upset Montagu more than anything else was Basil's calumniation of the Wordsworths after he had left their care.

Basil had, day after day, vilified Wordsworth: he had stated, that when living with his Sister they had treated him with such cruelty that he was constantly employed in the most menial occupations: and, but for the pity of the poor Villagers, who privately supplied him with such pittance as they could ill share, he should have been starved. I had reason to suspect other calumnies.

There is no reason to believe these claims of deliberately inflicted cruelty. Basil told similar lies about harsh treatment meted out to him by his father, stepmother, uncle and another family friend with whom he lived for a time. He deeply resented being shunted off by his father to a succession of relatives and his lies were an understandable but clumsy attempt to secure sympathy by a deeply unhappy young man.

The education given to Basil may have been determined by the philosophy of Rousseau, but it owed more to William's memories of his own happy childhood. In re-creating those conditions for the boy, however, one essential ingredient was missing: the companionship of other children. His complaints about being hungry may also have been true. The war had brought an escalation of prices. Meat could not be had for under 6d, and William himself would ruefully confess, 'I have lately been living upon air and the essence of carrots cabbages turnips and other esculent vegetables, not excluding parsely [*sic*] the produce of my garden'. Tea (the Wordsworths drank fine Souchong, bought in Bristol at 4s a measure) and sugar were their only luxuries, and these were rapidly becoming unaffordable. This frugal diet was hardly an appropriate one for a growing boy, but it was one shared without distinction by the adults.

The Wordsworths' simple lifestyle was a personal preference, but major economies were also forced upon them by their lack of income. Montagu was not exactly prompt in paying the annual £50 for his son and by January 1796 they had received only £500 out of the £900 due from Calvert's legacy. Of this £300 had been lent to Montagu 'in a sort of irregularly secured annuity', for which they received 10 per cent interest, and the remainder to Montagu's friend, Charles Douglas, a barrister and cousin of the future Marquess of Queensbury, on a promissory note at the same rate of interest. This was all well and good; the slightly higher than average interest represented the higher risk to which the capital was exposed by not having more formally secured loans. Even if the interest was paid regularly and in full (which it was not), the Wordsworths had only £50 a year to support themselves, with a further £50 for Basil. It was nothing like the joint income of 'at least 170 or 180£ per annum' they had anticipated.

There were other problems, beside money. The greatest of these, especially for William, was isolation. Dorothy had hoped that having their own home would enable them to offer their brothers John and Christopher 'a place to draw to', so that they could meet more often and as a family. This did not happen. John was on the *Osterley* in the Far East and, even before the ship reached its final harbour in February 1797, he had transferred to another East Indiaman, the *Duke of Montrose*, and set sail for India. Christopher had graduated from Trinity College, Cambridge, in January 1796 as Tenth Wrangler and had now set his heart on entering the Church and becoming a fellow of his college. A jaunt to Racedown was therefore out of the question. It was, quite simply, too out of the way for visits to be made conveniently.

The frustration of being out of the heart of events and cut off from all political discussion began to gnaw at William. He could not afford a London newspaper and the only paper he saw regularly, and that probably borrowed from Joseph Gill or the Pinneys of Blackdown, was the provincial weekly paper, the *Weekly Entertainer*. Letters were a poor substitute for people, especially as the post was erratic. Those that did arrive were full of gloomy news. At the end of October, the King's carriage was attacked en route for the opening of Parliament by a crowd chanting, 'No Pitt, no war, Bread, Bread'; the King himself narrowly missed injury from a stone which smashed through his window. The government's reaction was to introduce the Convention Bill, popularly known as the 'gagging acts', extending the definition of treason to include speaking or writing anything critical of the British Constitution (an offence of which William was frequently guilty), and prohibiting more than fifty people meeting together in public without the prior permission of local magistrates. The two acts met with fierce opposition, not least in Bristol, where Azariah Pinney reported that Coleridge had played a leading role in attempting to add an amendment to a public address congratulating the King on his escape. When this failed, Coleridge had helped organize a petition protesting against the acts and, at a second public meeting, had moved its presentation to Parliament. Azariah thought this petition and the others like it flooding into Parliament were in themselves a hopeful sign, but if they were ignored,

I dread the consequences – the murmurs of the people will for a time be suppressed by the military forces but whenever circumstances shall favour resistance, their complaints will burst forth with the whirlwind's fury – I have not yet heard one argument that I have even thought plausible in fav[ou]r of the Convention bill: all I can learn from its supporters and advocates, is, that the Times justify the measure. Pray let me know what you think of it, but I can almost anticipate your sentiments.

Despite liberal protest throughout the kingdom, the acts were passed by a compliant and fearful Parliament, but not all radicals could be silenced. Coleridge leapt to the challenge by launching a new periodical, the *Watchman*. William, entombed at Racedown, could only admire such activity from afar. 'Best comp[li-men]ts to Coleridge,' he wrote wistfully to Cottle in the New Year, 'and say I wish much to hear from him.'

Throughout the autumn of 1795 and the following spring, there is a distinct sense of disillusionment and depression in William's letters. Clearly he felt excluded from what was going on elsewhere and paralysed by his own inaction. Writing to Mathews, for instance, he began with an apology for writing at all, 'not that I feel myself able to say anything which is likely to be particularly interesting'. He assured his friend that he and Dorothy were 'both as happy as people can be who live in perfect solitude'. The importance of this statement is always overlooked, because it is misread. William is not saying that they *were* perfectly happy, only that they were 'as happy as people *can be* who live in perfect solitude'. The qualification is underlined by what follows. 'We do not see a soul. Now and then we meet a miserable peasant in the road or an accidental traveller. The country people here are wretchedly poor; ignorant and overwhelmed with every vice that usually attends ignorance in that class, viz – lying and picking and stealing.'

At least one letter from Annette arrived not long after the Wordsworths' removal to Racedown; all we know about its contents is that Annette mentioned having dispatched half a dozen letters to William, 'none of which he has received'. While England remained at war with France, there was no possibility of a return to Blois or Orléans, and the unresolved problem of Annette and Caroline was yet another shadow on William's life.

The Pinney brothers were a life-line at this time. They sent or brought books, and at Christmas, when they stayed a week, they brought a gift from Joseph Cottle, who had just brought out Robert Southey's epic poem *Joan of Arc*. Southey himself was in Portugal, forcibly extracted from Bristol politics by his concerned guardian uncle. Defiant to the last, he had secretly married Edith Fricker before sailing and set in motion the publication of the poem, whose radical subtext was immediately obvious to reviewers. William studied it eagerly, but was disappointed: how could he read about the 'maid of Orléans' without being reminded of Annette? Though there were some passages of 'first-rate excellence', he thought that, on the whole, it was of 'very inferior execution'. Southey's preface declared that he had 'run a race with the press'; the whole twelve books had been written in six weeks, and, on its improved plan of ten books, it had been virtually recomposed during printing. To William, who was mortifyingly slow in composition, worse in revising, and was still labouring over his Salisbury Plain poem more than two and a half years after he had begun it, this seemed like both boasting and treating the reader with contempt.

Over the months at Racedown, William had virtually recomposed his Salisbury Plain poem. William had transformed the role of the wanderer, to whom the female vagrant had told her own story, by giving him a life-history too. He was now a fellow victim of the war, a sailor from Portland, who had returned from war service only to be press-ganged into the navy again. This was a common enough fate: the same thing had already happened to Henry Hutchinson, Mary's sailor brother, and would soon happen to him again. William's fictional sailor, fleeced of his earnings by fraud and desperate to provide for his starving family, murdered and robbed a traveller on the plain, then fled when suspected, becoming a homeless vagrant. The full consequences of his crime were brought forcibly home at the end of the poem. The sailor accidentally came across another solitary outcast, a dying woman, who turned out to be his wife. She had been driven from her home by the parish overseers, who suspected her husband was the murderer. Having begged her forgiveness, the sailor gave himself up to the authorities and was hanged. The poem ends with the grim image of his corpse hanging from the gibbet in an iron cage as a salutary warning to passers-by. But there is an unexpected twist in the final stanza which is far more shocking and memorable. The moral is lost on the passers-by, who care nothing for the sailor's fate.

> They left him hung on high in iron case,
> And dissolute men, unthinking and untaught,
> Planted their festive booths beneath his face;
> And to that spot, which idle thousands sought,
> Women and children were by fathers brought . . .
>
> *Adventures on Salisbury Plain, ll.820–24*

It is perhaps the bleakest and most pessimistic ending to any of William's poems. It offers neither hope nor consolation; indeed, by suggesting that casual indifference is the basis of human nature, rather than rational benevolence, it undermines the Godwinian premise of the poem that the suffering individuals are the victims of government injustice. William's belief in the essential benevolence of humanity had been severely shaken, not just by the savagery of the warring factions in France but also, perhaps, by a closer acquaintance with those wretchedly poor, ignorant and vicious, miserable peasants of Dorset with their 'lying and picking and stealing'.

The arrival in February of John Pinney, closely followed by his brother, proved a welcome diversion. 'While we were with him he relaxed the rigour of his philosophic nerves so much as to go a Coursing several times,' Azariah wrote in high glee to James Tobin, 'and I assure you did not eat the unfortunate Hares with less relish because he heard them heave their death groans, and saw their Eyes directed towards Heaven with that glare of vacant sadness which belongs to the expiring creature – for his usual Appetite shewed itself at the dining Table'. Dorothy was captivated by John, as well she might be. He was two and twenty, with a 'charming countenance' and 'the sweetest temper I ever observed'. Azariah, destined to be a merchant in the family firm, was naturally less attractive. He was merely 'much more pleasing in manners than the generality of young men'. Azariah's opinion of Dorothy was equally unenthusiastic. 'Miss Wordsworth has undoubted claim to good humour, but does not possess, in my opinion, that je ne sais quoi, so necessary to sweeten the sour draught of human misfortune and smooth the [rough?] road of this Life's Passage –'. The two young men entered fully into life at Racedown, on fine days walking with Dorothy and William, or riding out, hunting, coursing and even cleaving wood. In the evenings they would join the Wordsworths by the fireside, reading and conversing on politics and literature.

When they left, on 6 March, Azariah took with him an invitation to Racedown for James Tobin (with William's caveat that he should not expect anything more than 'democratic' fare) and a copy of the Salisbury Plain poem, which he was commissioned to take to Bristol and deliver to Cottle, with a request that Coleridge might look it over before publication. It was almost three weeks before William heard from Azariah, and then it was a letter that brought mixed tidings. Coleridge had gone through it with considerable attention, interleaving it with blank sheets of paper on which to write his observations, and had pronounced it 'a very fine Poem'. Indeed, Coleridge even went so far as to assure William that publishing it would cost him nothing. The expenses could be taken out of the profits and the rest would go to William himself. Not only that, but he recommended printing 500 copies, instead of the 250 William had suggested. This was a typically Coleridgean reaction: extravagant, wildly enthusiastic and, since it was dependent on the cooler judgement of a publisher, unsustainable. Nevertheless, it was just the sort of response William needed at that time. If a poet, critic and radical with Coleridge's impeccable credentials was so impressed by his work, then perhaps this was a valid way he could contribute to the cause.

With nothing else to do, William returned to his books, reading industriously 'if reading can ever deserve the name of industry'. 'As to writing', he added, 'it is out of the question.' The few pieces William wrote at this time were mechanical: short alternative treatments of sections of the Salisbury Plain poem in blank verse and in Spenserian stanzas, for instance, and a dire *Argument for Suicide*. More interesting, though not for its quality, was an *Address to the Ocean*, an imitation of Ossian inspired by, and quoting as its first line, a poem by Coleridge, *The Complaint of Ninathona*, which had first appeared in *Poems on Various Subjects*, published in April 1796. William's acknowledged borrowing was simply returning the compliment, for in the same volume Coleridge had included *Lines Written at Shurton Bars*, which quoted a phrase from William's *An Evening Walk*. In a note to his poem, Coleridge had added a characteristically generous assessment of William as 'a Poet, whose versification is occasionally harsh and his diction too frequently obscure; but whom I deem unrivalled among the writers of the present day in manly sentiment, novel imagery, and vivid colouring'. William's decision to publish his *Address to the Ocean*, acknowledging his own debt to 'Mr Coleridge', in their local newspaper, the *Weekly Entertainer*, on 21 November 1796, must surely be seen as an attempt to express his gratitude publicly.

By the end of May, Coleridge had sent the manuscript of the Salisbury Plain poem to London, even though Joseph Cottle had expressed keen interest in publishing it in Bristol. Whether this was simply so that Charles Lamb, Coleridge's old schoolfriend, fellow poet and most trusted critic, could read it or the intention was to obtain a London publisher is not clear. Lamb 'hurried thro' [the poem] not without delight', but, in what was perhaps a diplomatic move, declared himself too ill to return the manuscript to William in person. William and Lamb may have met for the first time, however, because on 1 June William had left Racedown and returned to London.

Since their removal to Racedown it had become evident that William needed more than rural solitude and reading to inspire him to write. The mental stimulation of like minds was a necessity. One of the first things he did on his arrival was to go with one of the Pinney brothers to call on Godwin. They met several more times during the five weeks William remained in London, on each occasion as part of the group of Godwinian disciples centred round the Pinneys. These included not only Basil Montagu (who had still not been to visit his son at Racedown) but James and John Tobin, the sons of Mr Pinney's partner in the Bristol West Indies Trading Company. James was three years older than William, John the same age. They both had literary aspirations but James had a degenerative eye condition which had already reduced him to virtual blindness, so it was John, an attorney by profession, who carried the standard as an aspiring dramatist. Robert Allen, an army surgeon who was about to be posted to Portugal, was a schoolfriend of Coleridge and Lamb, university friend and fellow Pantisocrat of Robert Southey, and a journalist. John Stoddart was a barrister at Lincoln's Inn, like Montagu, but also a journalist, who published translations of Schiller's works this year, 1796, and again in 1798, as well as a translation from the French, in 1797, of *An Account of the Committee of Public Safety*.

In this small, closely knit world, William could talk, theorize and dispute to his heart's content. If nothing else, this period in London seems to have settled his own view on the impracticality of Godwin's ideas. By the time William returned to Racedown, he was a man revitalized and determined to expose 'the dangerous use which may be made of reason when a man has committed a great crime'.

He embarked on a poem, now known as *Fragment of a 'Gothic' Tale*, describing a blind old sailor being led over chasms and up precipices towards a ruined castle, where his guide, having lodged him in the shelter of a dungeon, attempts to murder him for his little store of savings. This proved too simplistic to convey all the subtleties of motive and reasoning William had in mind. Instead, in a bold change of tack, he decided to write a play, or blank-verse drama, in which he could give each character a distinctive history and voice, allowing for greater interplay between them. *The Borderers* incorporated many strands of the Salisbury Plain poem, which William had now decided to withdraw from publication. Again we have wanderers walking over an empty, hostile landscape and an underlying theme of crime, guilt and retribution. Instead of coincidental meetings as the means of discovering the histories of the characters, however, there is a carefully structured plot, centred on the malevolent figure of Rivers, the incarnation of Godwinian thought, who drives the action forward. The play was set in the Middle Ages on the borders of Scotland and England. Mortimer is the popular leader of a band of outlaws, a sort of Robin Hood figure, protecting the defenceless and dispensing justice in a lawless land. Rivers, seeing in Mortimer a reflection of his own youthful self, is determined to subvert him. He decides to do this in the same way as he himself has been subverted, by causing Mortimer to put to death a man who, to all appearances and rational argument, is guilty of heinous crimes, but is, in fact, innocent. Rivers has reasoned himself into justifying his own crime and, in a remarkable anticipation of late-twentieth-century chaos theory, has argued himself out of feeling remorse:

> Remorse,
> It cannot live with thought, think on, think on,
> And it will die. – What? in this universe,
> Where the least things controul the greatest, where
> The faintest breath that breathes can move a world –
> What, feel remorse where if a cat had sneezed,
> A leaf had fallen, the thing had never been
> Whose very shadow gnaws us to the vitals?
>
> *The Borderers, iii, v, 81–8*

Mortimer, unable to kill with his own hand, leaves Herbert, a blind old man, to die, alone and exposed to the elements, on a deserted moor. Rivers exultingly reveals Herbert's innocence and argues that, by passing through this initiation, he and Mortimer are now brothers bound 'by links of adamant':

> To day you have thrown off a tyranny
> That lives but by the torpid acquiescence
> Of moralists and saints and lawgivers.
> You have obeyed the only law that wisdom
> Can ever recognize: the immediate law
> Flashed from the light of circumstances
> Upon an independent intellect . . .
>
> *The Borderers, iii, v, 26–33*

Mortimer, however, appalled by what he has done, rejects both Rivers's philosophy and his offer of companionship, and condemns himself to the exile of Cain: 'No prayers, no tears, but hear my doom in silence!' he tells his men.

> I will go forth a wanderer on the earth,
> A shadowy thing, and as I wander on
> No human ear shall ever hear my voice,
> No human dwelling ever give me food
> Or sleep or rest, and all the uncertain way
> Shall be as darkness to me, as a waste
> Unnamed by man! and I will wander on
> Living by mere intensity of thought,
> A thing by pain and thought compelled to live,
> Yet loathing life, till heaven in mercy strike me
> With blank forgetfulness – that I may die.
>
> *The Borderers, v, iii, 264–75*

Always powerful, alternately shocking and moving, *The Borderers* was a triumph of the sort that could not be foreseen in William's earlier work. It is still derivative, in the sense that the characters, passions, imagery and even the scenery owe much to Shakespeare: the influence of Lear, Hamlet and Iago is obvious, and there are deliberate echoes of, and borrowings from, *Macbeth, Julius Caesar, Hamlet* and *Othello*. What makes the play uniquely William's is his analysis of motivation and the influence of landscape. In his lonely wanderings, for instance, Rivers has perceived 'What mighty objects do impress their forms To build up this our intellectual being'. Mortimer, too, is prevented from murdering Herbert in the ruined castle when, like the boy William in the dungeon of Cockermouth Castle, he looked up and, through a crevice, beholds a star twinkling over his head.

William was so enthralled by his creation, that he wrote a preface, dissecting minutely Rivers's character and his motives for committing what might appear a motiveless crime. It is an explicitly moral and didactic reading, accepting Godwin's insistence on benevolent intention as the foundation of all virtue, but rejecting his basic premise that reason teaches benevolence. Mortimer is persuaded by rational means that Herbert is guilty and, having been persuaded, cannot do anything but follow the logic and execute justice. The fact that Herbert is innocent and that

Rivers has used 'perverted reasoning' to justify his own 'perverted instincts' strikes at the heart of Godwin's philosophy. William later claimed that he wrote this essay 'to preserve in my distinct remembrance what I had observed of transition in character & the reflections I had been led to make during the time I was a witness of the changes through which the French Revolution passed'.

It was undoubtedly true that William had witnessed the growth of extremism in France and had seen many former liberals perverted by fanaticism, fear of failure, even political expediency. He had himself been an apologist for the September Massacres and the execution of Louis XVI, believing then that the end justified the means. The Terror and France's aggressive wars against her neighbouring states had led him increasingly to question his own judgement and his hitherto unwavering support for the revolution. Reading Louvet, Madame Roland and Helen Maria Williams with his sister at Racedown had forced him to re-evaluate his own perceptions of what had happened, both to him and to France. Godwin had offered him a welcome light to help him out of the darkness.

> . . . What delight! –
> How glorious! – in self-knowledge and self-rule
> To look through all the frailties of the world
> And, with a resolute mastery shaking off
> The accidents of nature, time and place,
> That make up the weak being of the past,
> Build social freedom on its only basis,
> The freedom of the individual mind,
> Which (to the blind restraint of general laws
> Superior) magisterially adopts
> One guide, the light of circumstances, flashed
> Upon an independent intellect.
>
> *Prelude (1805), x, 818–29*

It was no accident that in these lines from *The Prelude* William quoted Rivers's own words from *The Borderers*. Godwin's 'One Guide' had led Mortimer fatally astray. For William, it was a light that flared, flickered and then went out. By adopting Godwin's microscopic system of philosophic analysis and demanding, as he did, formal proof for every point, William had succeeded only in confusing himself.

In *The Borderers* he resolved his own attitude towards Godwin and freed himself from the intellectual paralysis which had held him in its thrall for so long. Rationalism, he realized, provided 'a sophism for every crime'. It was a decisive step forward. *The Borderers* offered liberation of another kind, less grand in scale, but equally significant in William's evolution as a poet. By reverting to Shakespeare as a model, he had thrown off the shackles of the Spenserian stanza and the eighteenth-century affectation of melancholy. He had discovered the power of blank verse.

7. A Sett of Violent Democrats

Towards the end of November a new guest came to Racedown, the first of all those invited by the Wordsworths to accept their invitation. Mary Hutchinson arrived from Sockburn, after a long and arduous coach journey via York, London and Crewkerne. She was escorted by her sailor brother, Henry, who had just returned from a tour of duty in the Caribbean only to find his leave cut short by a summons to Plymouth. By great good luck, Racedown lay on the route to Plymouth. Mary had long wanted to see her friends again and was glad of an excuse to leave Sockburn for a while, after the death of her 'Sister-Companion', Margaret, in the summer.

Mary's visit was to prove a momentous one because it laid the foundations for what was to become a lifelong companionship. Dorothy was 'very happy in her society'; Mary was 'one of the best girls in the world and we are as happy as human beings can be'. William did not declare his thoughts at the time, but later revealed how much Mary came to mean to him during this visit. In 'She was a Phantom of delight', he reveals that the girl who had seemed 'a lovely Apparition' to him at Penrith had grown 'upon nearer view' into 'A Spirit, yet a Woman too!' In *The Prelude*, he gave a subtle assessment of Mary's other attractions, which makes it quite clear why her presence made such an impact at this juncture in his life. It also explains why and how she became his sheet anchor. Like both the Wordsworths, she loved nature, but not with the intense craving for new sights and experiences, the emotional intensity, which afflicted William and Dorothy. And she was serenely content.

> Her eye was not the mistress of her heart;
> Far less did rules prescribed by passive taste,
> Or barren intermeddling subtleties,

Perplex her mind; but, wise as women are
When genial circumstance hath favoured them,
She welcomed what was given, and craved no more;
Whate'er the scene presented to her view,
That was the best, to that she was attuned
By her benign simplicity of life,
And through a perfect happiness of soul,
          ... God delights
In such a being; for her common thoughts
Are piety, her life is gratitude.

Prelude (1850), xii, 153–62, 171–3

What is fascinating about this description of Mary is that the quality which William most admired in her, 'she welcomed what was given, and craved no more', is such a contrast with Dorothy's famous sensibility. It is also a quality that was shared by two of the other most important women in his life: his mother, Ann, who was 'pure From feverish dread of error and mishap' and his old dame, Ann Tyson, who was 'affectionate without uneasiness'. Annette, from what little we know of her from her letters, would appear to have been more like Dorothy, which raises an interesting question: what would have happened to William had he married her rather than Mary? Now, as they renewed their acquaintance after so many years of change and turmoil, his burgeoning love for Mary, and her quiet presence in the house, and his life, was a steadying influence.

By the end of February 1797 the first draft of *The Borderers* was almost finished and it was as if the pent-up tide of William's poetic creativity had suddenly been released. Flushed with new-found confidence, the poems poured from him. They have two striking features in common: they are nearly all in blank verse, like *The Borderers*, and they are all concerned with the poor. Most of them describe people and incidents William encountered on his daily walks round Racedown, like the woman and her five children unable to afford to buy bread and obliged to watch the baker's cart drive past their wretched hut, denied not just bread but also 'the common food of hope'. The sight and the woman's bitter comment, 'that waggon does not care for us', were a powerful reminder of the bread riots William had witnessed in France and a warning of the likely outcome of such poverty in England.

The peasants and itinerants of Dorset, whom William had dismissed on his arrival at Racedown as 'lying and picking and stealing', were now an object of increasing interest and sympathy. Even in old age, William's predilection for walking along the highway, rather than randomly over the hills, would be a subject of local comment. In *The Prelude*, he explained his preference. 'I love a public road', he wrote, because the sight of it disappearing over the horizon had seemed to him, since childhood, like a guide into eternity, or at least to things unknown. The unknown it now led him to was his fellow traveller along the roads of Dorset.

> ... I began to enquire,
> To watch and question those I met, and held
> Familiar talk with them, the lonely roads
> Were schools to me in which I daily read
> With most delight the passions of mankind,
> There saw into the depth of human souls –
> Souls that appear to have no depth at all
> To vulgar eyes.
>
> *Prelude (1805), xii, 161–8*

What he learned was that 'books mislead us': they were written by, and for, those with wealth and education, therefore they ignored the vast majority of mankind. The best measure of human nature, he argued, was to strip our hearts naked and look outwards, 't[owards me]n who lead the simplest lives most according to nature men who [h]ave never known false refinements, wayward and artificial desires, false criti[ci]sms, effeminate habits of thinking and feeling, or who, having known [t]hese things, have outgrown them'.

The men and women he met on the public roads of Dorset were 'obscure and lowly', but from them he learned 'truths Replete with honour', the simple virtues of courage, endurance, love, compassion and faith. They proved to him that the world was not rotten to the core, but that the glory of humanity was its capacity to rise above self and suffering. He put this idea forward forcibly in one of his best poems to date, the haunting *Lines Left upon a Seat in a Yew-tree*, describing the character of the man who built the seat within the yew-tree bower. He had been a youth of 'No common soul ... A favoured Being' but, feeling neglected by a world which did not owe him the living he expected, he turned from it, 'And with the food of pride sustained his soul In solitude'. In drawing the moral, William explicitly attacked the egotism at the centre of Godwinism:

> Stranger! henceforth be warned; and know that pride,
> Howe'er disguised in its own majesty,
> Is littleness; that he who feels contempt
> For any living thing, hath faculties
> Which he has never used; that thought with him
> Is in its infancy. The man whose eye
> Is ever on himself doth look on one,
> The least of Nature's works
>
> *Lines Left upon a Seat in a Yew-tree, ll.50–57*

William himself now chose to look outward, to the unsung individuals who formed the mass of humanity, and he appointed himself their champion. His theme, he declared, would be 'No other than the very heart of man'. It was a bold decision, and one which would bring ridicule upon him from those (the vast majority of the reading public) who believed that pedlars and waggoners were not fit subjects for poetry. At the somewhat late age of almost twenty-eight, William had at last found his vocation in life.

With Mary as a willing secretary, making fair copies and transcribing his work, William rapidly completed *The Borderers* and embarked on a major new project, *The Ruined Cottage*, which would embody his new philosophy. Unable to find employment to support his starving family, Robert cannot bear to witness their suffering, absconds, enlists as a soldier and leaves his bounty money to buy bread for his children. Margaret, his 'wife and widow', waits anxiously for his return. Her eldest child is sent to work on a distant farm, her baby, having caught from her 'the trick of grief . . . sighed amongst its playthings', drooped and died. After nine long years of fruitless waiting, Margaret herself dies, and her once cherished home falls into neglect and decay. It was a deeply affecting story, rendered more so because William presented it through the medium of a pedlar who has known the family for years and witnessed all the changes of fortune. In this earliest version it is a simple tale, simply told, but it had, as William quickly realized, the potential to become something much more. Revising it would occupy him for many years to come, but, as with *The Borderers*, the intense effort of working on a grand project sparked off a number of shorter poems.

The sense that he was at last *doing* something transformed William. Writing to Jane on 19 March 1797, Dorothy declared him 'as chearful as any body can be; perhaps you may not think it but he is the life of the whole house'. A few days earlier, while the whole household was still in bed, Basil Montagu had called unexpectedly on his first visit to his son at Racedown. Dorothy was 'excessively pleased' with him, echoing her brother Christopher's judgement that he was 'one of the pleasantest men I ever saw, and so amiable, and so good that every body who knows him must love him'. Montagu was on his way to Bristol and William jumped at the chance of accompanying him. Though Dorothy still had Mary for company, she wrote gloomily, 'you cannot imagine how dull we feel and what a vacuum his loss has occasioned'. They occupied themselves in making shirts for William and Richard.

William spent about a fortnight in Bristol with Montagu. It was an important foray from Racedown, not least because it was an opportunity for renewing old friendships and making new ones. They paid several visits to James Losh, brother of William's old schoolfriend and fellow lodger at Ann Tyson's. Losh had been in Paris during the revolution and become an active radical in London, where, like Montagu, he was a barrister at Lincoln's Inn and a member of Godwin's circle. Regarding Milton as 'one of the most illustrious friends of civil and religious liberty', he had provocatively published an edition of his *Areopagitica* in 1791, and, most recently, he had himself translated and published Henri Benjamin Constant's *Observations on the strength of the present government in France*. Overworked and, like many other English radicals, depressed by the course of the French Revolution, he had succumbed to pulmonary tuberculosis (and possibly a nervous breakdown) and was now living at Bath. Despite his ill-health, he was an active member of the Bristol radical circle, and was well known to both Southey and Coleridge.

Losh had been in almost monthly correspondence with William since the previous summer and, the day after William set off for Bristol, had dispatched him a large parcel of books. Its contents were telling: Coleridge's printed version of his Bristol lectures on politics, *Conciones ad Populum* and his *Ode on the Departing Year*, Edmund Burke's *Letters on a Regicide Peace* and *Letter to the Duke of Portland*; Thomas Erskine's *View of the Causes and Consequences of the Present War* (Erskine had defended Paine, Hardy and Horne Tooke in the 1794 treason trials); *Evidences of Revealed Religion*, a collection of sermons against atheism, by Coleridge's Unitarian friend John Prior Estlin; and the March to December 1796 issues of the *Monthly Magazine*. A second parcel was sent off soon after William's return to Racedown.

Montagu and Losh accompanied William to supper with John Wedgwood, son of the pottery magnate. The fact that Wedgwood was the elder brother of Coleridge's soon-to-be patrons, Tom and Josiah, and, indeed, the company all the Wedgwoods kept suggest the possibility that this was meant to be a potentially useful contact. Before he left Bristol at the end of March, William also called on Joseph Cottle. Resisting persuasion to publish his Salisbury Plain poem, William did, however, contribute his *Written on the Thames near Richmond*, a new revision of a poem he had written at Cambridge, to Cottle's personal Commonplace Book.

Returning to Racedown, he could not resist the temptation to make a detour and pay a visit to Coleridge, who, disillusioned with politicians and politics alike, had retired to contemplative treason in rural Somerset. Since 31 December 1796 he had lived with his wife and baby son at Nether Stowey, a pretty village west of Bristol, under the lee of the Quantock Hills. His patron, Thomas Poole, a wealthy tanner from the village, with radical sympathies and intellectual interests, had provided Coleridge with a tiny cottage in Lime Street. Their gardens interlinked, enabling Coleridge to avail himself of Poole's library and study whenever the cramped quarters of his own cottage became too much for him. Like Wordsworth, he could now boast, 'I raise potatoes & all manner of vegetables; have an Orchard; & shall raise Corn with the spade enough for my family.' Unlike Wordsworth, Coleridge had neither interest in nor aptitude for his garden.

It was not a good time for a visit. Coleridge was miserable and depressed, but William's 'conversation, &c' had the effect of rousing Coleridge 'somewhat'. They consoled themselves for their own lack of productivity by attacking the prolific (and increasingly successful) Southey. William uttered the obviously heartfelt complaint that Southey wrote '*too much at his ease* – that he seldom "feels his burthened breast Heaving beneath th' incumbent Deity"'. Coleridge added the equally jealous observation that Southey would 'make literature more *profitable to him* from the fluency with which he writes, and the facility with which he pleases himself'.

They then discussed their own projects. By an extraordinary coincidence, Richard Brinsley Sheridan had just approached Coleridge and asked him to write a tragedy for his new Drury Lane theatre. Shortly before William's visit, Coleridge had sketched out a plan, 'romantic & wild & somewhat terrible'. Having reviewed a number of Gothic novels over the last few months, he declared himself surfeited with 'dungeons, and old castles, & solitary Houses by the Sea Side, & Caverns, & Woods, & extraordinary characters, & all the tribe of Horror & Mystery', but this did not stop him using exactly the same scenario in his own tragedy, *Osorio*. The fact that he had embarked on his first drama and William had just completed his was an additional bond between the two young men.

Before William left Nether Stowey, Coleridge introduced him to the remarkable Tom Poole, a man who was 'never happy till he has introduced politicks' into the conversation, and whose robust republican views were the despair of his establishment cousins. Naturally, he and William found much in common. Poole was a fund of true stories about the rural poor. Walking with William and Coleridge out of the village, up to the top of an eminence overlooking Bin Combe and the Severn estuary, they came to a place named Walford's Gibbet. As a boy, Poole had known the man who was executed there; with the two poets hanging on his every word, he told them the dramatic and poignant tale. John Walford, a charcoal burner, had been prevented from marrying the woman of his choice by her mother. He had drifted into drunkenness and promiscuity, made a local idiot girl pregnant, been forced to marry her and, in a fit of self-loathing and disgust, killed her. On the gallows, he had an agonized reconciliation with the girl he loved, admitted his guilt and died expressing his remorse. Recognizing this as perfect material for William's poetry, he and Coleridge both begged Poole to write the story down.

William returned to Racedown at the beginning of April, full of enthusiasm. He set to work immediately and began to revise and adapt *The Borderers* for the stage. He had intended the tragedy to be read, rather than performed, but Coleridge had offered to forward it to Sheridan on his behalf and he could not pass up such an opportunity. An irritated letter from Richard brought him down to earth again. Richard reproached him for not writing to their brother John, who, having failed to get a place on the new *Earl of Abergavenny*, was now stuck in the Downs, with a mutinous crew on a leaky ship, the *Duke of Montrose*, awaiting a passage to India. More seriously, he took William severely to task over his financial arrangements. He demanded a clear statement of how his affairs stood with Montagu and Douglas, told him it was 'absolutely necessary' that he should keep records of the accounts and, having pointed out his own expenditure on William's behalf, asked, 'How am I to be repaid these and other sums?' It was a fair question, to which William had no answer: 'you should have been repaid immediately if I had not been disappointed in my settlements with Calvert,' he pleaded, 'which has reduced my income much lower than I had reason to expect. If it were all properly settled my expenses would fall within my receipts.'

To make matters worse, their cousin Robinson Wordsworth was about to be married and had therefore requested repayment of £250 from the Wordsworths' debt to his father. 'We are pestered with letters from every quarter upon this subject', Dorothy wrote miserably. Even Losh had reported hearing rumours in Cumberland that William had 'used his Uncle's children very ill' by not repaying the debt. They all looked to Richard to sort something out, preferably by extracting some of the money owed them by their Uncle Christopher. It was easier said than done. 'All these things are very unpleasant,' Dorothy admitted, 'besides their claims are so just that it is' (throwing Richard's own phrase back in his face) 'absolutely necessary that something must be done'. Just to remind Richard of their impoverished state she finished her letter with a tart request. 'Pray take care of your old cloaths. They will be of great use at Racedown.' Over a month later, William was writing with increased exasperation because he had not heard from Richard. 'What *is* to be done in this business? I cannot express my anxiety to see it brought to some sort of conclusion.' No conclusion, however, was reached.

One of the coldest springs Dorothy could remember brought the whole household down with colds and coughs. By the end of May, however, the country had 'burst into beauty' and they had all recovered. A parting was now at hand. Mary Hutchinson's six-month visit to Racedown had come to an end. On 5 June she set off for London, carrying with her a letter to Richard and some of the shirts she and Dorothy had made for him: 'If you are at home when she calls you will walk out with her', Dorothy ordered, 'and shew her the bridges and any thing you may have time for. Perhaps you may be able to go to St Pauls ... Somerset Terrace or Temple gardens would be a good place.'

Thirteen years later, seeing the Malvern Hills again, William was reminded of Mary's departure from Racedown, and was filled with anguish and regret.

I looked at them with a trembling which I cannot describe when I thought that *you* had not seen them, but *might* have seen, if you had but taken the road through Bristol when you left Racedown; in which case I should certainly have accompanied you as far as Bristol; or further, perhaps: and then I thought, that you would not have taken the coach at Bristol, but that you would have walked on Northwards with me at your side, till unable to part from each other we might have come in sight of those hills ... and ... I fancied that we should have seen so deeply into each others hearts, and been so fondly locked in each others arms, that we should have braved the worst and parted no more. Under that tree, I thought as I passed along we might have rested, of that stream might have drank, in that thicket we might have hidden ourselves from the sun, and from the eyes of the passenger; and thus did I feed on the thought of bliss that might have been, which would have [been] intolerable from the force of regret had I not felt the happiness which waits me when I see you again.

As Mary left, Coleridge literally leapt into their lives. 'We have both a distinct remembrance of his arrival –', William would recall almost fifty years later, 'he did not keep to the high road, but leapt over a gate and bounded down the pathless field, by which he cut off an angle. We both retain the liveliest possible image of his appearance at that moment.' Coleridge was in high excitement. Despite his scorn at Southey's speed in writing, he had completed two and a half acts of the tragedy which two months earlier had been only sketched in outline. The host having the honours, William first read his new poem, *The Ruined Cottage*, then, after tea, Coleridge read what he had written of *Osorio*. The next morning, William read *The Borderers*. It was a cataclysmic experience for them all. 'Wordsworth, who is a strict & almost severe critic, thinks *very* highly of [my Tragedy] – which gives me great hopes', Coleridge wrote proudly to his friends, adding a typically generous, but awed, tribute to William:

I speak with heart-felt sincerity & (I think) unblinded judgement, when I tell you, that I feel myself a *little man by his* side; & yet do not think myself the less man, than I formerly thought myself. – His Drama is absolutely wonderful. You know, I do not commonly speak in such abrupt & unmingled phrases – & therefore will the more readily believe me. – There are in the piece those *profound* touches of the human heart, which I find three or four times in 'The Robbers' of Schiller, & often in Shakespere – but in Wordsworth there are no *inequalities*. T. Poole's opinion of Wordsworth is – that he is the greatest Man, he ever knew – I coincide.

Dorothy, always predisposed towards people who admired her brother, was, quite simply, bowled over by Coleridge. Though she had never before shown any inclination to describe people in anything other than a few conventional phrases, she suddenly launched into a detailed description on Mary's behalf.

You had a great loss in not seeing Coleridge. He is a wonderful man. His conversation teems with soul, mind, and spirit. Then he is so benevolent, so good tempered and cheerful, and, like William, interests himself so much about every little trifle. At first I thought him very plain, that is, for about three minutes: he is pale and thin, has a wide mouth, thick lips, and not very good teeth, longish loose-growing half-curling rough black hair. But if you hear him speak for five minutes you think no more of them. His eye is large and full, not dark but grey; such an eye as would receive from a heavy soul the dullest expression; but it speaks every emotion of his animated mind; it has more of the 'poet's eye in a fine frenzy rolling' than I ever witnessed. He has fine dark eyebrows, and an overhanging forehead.

The feelings were mutual. Dorothy and Coleridge were in instant sympathy.

She is a woman indeed! – in mind, I mean, & heart – for her person is such, that if you expected to see a pretty woman, you would think her ordinary – if you expected to find an ordinary woman, you would think her pretty! – But her manners are simple, ardent, impressive –.

> In every motion her most innocent soul
> Outbeams so brightly, that who saw would say,
> Guilt was a thing impossible in her. –

Her information various – her eye watchful in minutest observation of nature – and her taste a perfect electrometer – it bends, protrudes, and draws in, at subtlest beauties & most recondite faults.

A visit of a few days turned into one of several weeks. Coleridge persuaded a willing Dorothy to copy out the last section of *The Ruined Cottage* for his friend John Estlin and worked hard on completing his own tragedy. At the end of the month, he reluctantly tore himself away, arriving back home on the evening of 28 June. A day or two later he returned over forty miles of 'execrable road' in a cart borrowed from Tom Poole, collected William and Dorothy, and bore them off in triumph to Nether Stowey. They would not return to Racedown.

Dorothy was in ecstasies. 'There is everything here', she enthused, 'sea, woods wild as fancy ever painted, brooks clear and pebbly as in Cumberland, villages so romantic.' There was also, of course, Coleridge. And Mrs Coleridge, struggling to cope on straitened finances, in a cramped cottage, with not only her husband and ten-month-old baby, but also an influx of visitors. For, not content with inviting the Wordsworths, Coleridge had also invited Charles Lamb, whose place on departure was immediately taken by the radical lecturer and poet John Thelwall. There was a certain poetical justice in that, on the second day after the Wordsworths' arrival, Sarah spilt a pan of boiling milk on her husband's foot, confining him to the house and preventing him accompanying his guests on their walks.

The Wordsworths evidently found Lamb a congenial companion, for this was the beginning of a lifelong friendship with this shy, charming, witty man. They had much in common. Lamb worked as a clerk in the East India House, so he knew their brother John and their cousin Captain John Wordsworth. He was unmarried and devoted to his sister, Mary, in circumstances which did him great honour. The previous September, on what Lamb would always call 'the day of *horrors*', she had murdered their mother in a temporary fit of insanity and been confined to an asylum. In an extraordinarily delicate gesture, Lamb had publicly dedicated the poems he had contributed to Coleridge's recent volume to Mary, 'The author's best friend and sister'. Though he always affected to despise the country, he was quite capable of appreciating its beauties; 'besides', William would later point out, 'Lamb had too kindly and sympathetic a nature to detest anything'.

Lamb stayed only a week at Nether Stowey but for him it was a restorative period. On his return to London, he begged Coleridge to send him a copy of William's *Lines Left upon a Seat in a Yew-tree.* 'I have some scattered sentences ever floating on my memory, teasing me that I cannot remember more of it.'

To Lamb's innocent inquiry, 'Are Wordsworth and his sister gone yet?' there was a resounding denial. 'I have *settled them* –', Coleridge declared triumphantly. 'By a combination of curious circumstances a gentleman's seat, with a park & woods, elegantly and completely *furnished* – with 9 *lodging rooms*, three parlours & Hall – in a most beautiful & romantic situation by the sea side – 4 miles from Stowey – this we have got for Wordsworth at the rent of 23£ *a year, taxes included!!*' It was indeed a startling coup. William and Dorothy, 'in a wander by ourselves,' shortly after their arrival, had found 'a sequestered waterfall in a dell formed by steep hills covered with full-grown timber trees'. A few days later, they returned and 'pryed into the recesses of our little brook, but without any more fixed thoughts upon it than some dreams of happiness in a little cottage, and passing wishes that such a place might be found out'. The Wordsworths had fortuitously wandered on to the Alfoxton estate, which belonged to the ancient family of St Albyn. The house, which had recently been inherited by a minor, was empty. William and

Coleridge immediately applied to Poole and affairs moved with bewildering speed. Poole promptly drew up a lease in his own hand, witnessed it and offered to stand guarantor for the rent. On 14 July 1797 William therefore became the official tenant of Alfoxton House and Park and Dorothy, scarcely able to believe their luck, informed Mary that they were now 'in a large mansion, in a large park, with seventy head of deer around us'.

Alfoxton was, and is, a lovely house in an exquisite situation. Built on classical lines in 1710, it is elegant and simple, two storeys high, with large gabled attic windows set into the roof. The frontage, facing into the hills, is dominated by a central pedimented portico containing three large sash windows on the first storey and a single round ornamental window above. The ground level at the front of the house has been raised, but when the Wordsworths lived there a short flight of steps led up to the central door. The approach remains the same: a narrow, twisting, steeply embanked lane, winding for rather more than a mile up from the little village of Holford, through the gloom of acres of ancient oak woodland and groves of huge hollies, until it opens out into a pastoral landscape. The house lies above, snuggled into the hillside, with woods behind and above; it looks out on a panoramic view over gentle rolling hills, meadows and woods down to the grey streak of the Bristol Channel, with the hazy blue coastline of South Wales rising beyond. Wild deer are everywhere: casually strolling through the grounds, or gazing with unfazed contempt when caught in the dazzle of headlights. When they cannot be seen, they can be heard, coughing or lowing menacingly in the bushes and bracken. For these are not the tiny roe deer native to the Lakes, but the huge red deer of the Quantocks, which can be as big as cattle.

From the house there are walks of infinite variety and delight. Down through the woods of Holford Glen, where the very air takes on the hues of the dense leaves and moss and becomes bathed in greenish light, and, following the course of the river, through the downs to the shelving rocks and beaches of East Quantoxhead. Or, preferably, up the barely noticeable ascent of a narrow combe, where the stream is gradually reduced to a trickle, or a flash of water in a self-dug ditch, and the trees thin out until there is only an occasional stunted thorn or holly, bent into foetal position by the prevailing wind. A final scramble, almost on hands and knees, over the final bulwark of the combe head cannot prepare you for the surprise beyond. Suddenly, without notice, a huge vista of empty moorland opens out in every direction, riven with plunging valleys and scored by ancient pathways; the coastal plain below is scattered with villages and church steeples. On the coast itself, the dominant features are clearly visible: the stone arm of Watchet harbour, braced against wind and tide, the frowning grey towers of Court House, on the coast at East Quantoxhead, and the brutally minimalist boxes of Hinckley Point nuclear power station, which, fortunately for them, the Wordsworths did not have to see.

Alfoxton had all this to offer (apart from the power station, naturally), and the society of Coleridge, a mere four miles away, at Nether Stowey. This last was, as Dorothy admitted, the principal inducement for their move. At Alfoxton they could have all the benefits of Racedown, without the drawback of its isolation. Bristol was close enough for comparatively effortless visiting and Coleridge himself was a magnet, drawing others to him besides the Wordsworths. The first of these visitors, arriving soon after Lamb left, was Citizen John Thelwall, a prominent and notorious radical. Trained as a lawyer, he had successfully bridged the gap between middle- and working-class protest, had been tried for his life, and acquitted twice, on charges of sedition and high treason, and was probably the most hated and feared of all radicals. Dogged by government spies and hounded by magistrates, who encouraged riots at his lectures and physical violence against him personally, he had finally decided to move from London and retire from politics.

Finding Coleridge not at home, Thelwall followed him to Alfoxton, where he also became the Wordsworths' guest. 'He really was a man of extraordinary talent,' William would later write, and there were 'delightful' rambles through the woods and to the Alfoxton waterfall, where the three poet-philosophers sat together on the turf on the brink of the stream 'in the most beautiful part of the most beautiful glen of Alfoxden'. 'This is a place to reconcile one to all the jarrings and conflicts of the wide world,' exclaimed Coleridge. 'Nay', said Thelwall, 'to make one forget them altogether.' Coleridge remembered the same conversation, but with rather a different twist, believing he had said it was a place to make one forget *treason*, to which Thelwall had replied that it was 'a place to make a man forget there is any necessity for treason'. Though undoubtedly a better story, it sounds suspiciously like one of Coleridge's improved versions of events.

Flushed with his recent success in securing Alfoxton for the Wordsworths, Coleridge now offered to find Thelwall and his family a suitable residence in the area. It was a big mistake. Thelwall's presence had already sent a *frisson* through the neighbourhood. The reaction of Tom Poole's stuffy cousin Charlotte was typical. 'We are shocked to hear that Mr Thelwall has spent some time at Stowey this week with Mr Coleridge, and consequently with Tom Poole. Alfoxton house is taken by one of the fraternity ... To what are we coming?' It was a question William could well have asked himself, for out of his hospitality to Thelwall arose a most bizarre incident: what Coleridge gleefully called the 'Spy Nozy' affair.

It all began with servant gossip. Charles Mogg, who had been employed at Alfoxton by the recently deceased Rev. St Albyn, came back to visit his former friends. In the course of a conversation with Thomas Jones, who lived at the farm house, they naturally discussed the new tenants. Jones proffered the information 'that some French people had got possession of the Mansion House and that they were washing and Mending their Cloaths all Sunday'. Jones, like the good patriot and Christian that he was, 'did not like It', and intended to leave. Scenting a nice juicy scandal, Mogg called on the St Albyns' former huntsman, Christopher Trickie, who lived with his wife at the ancient Dog Pound, just outside the gates of Alfoxton Park. The Trickies were even more forthcoming. They told Mogg that

the French people had taken the plan of their House, and that They had also taken the plan of all the places round that part of the Country, that a Brook runs in the front of Trickie's

House and the French people inquired of Trickie wether the Brook was Navigable to the Sea, and upon being informd by Trickie that It was not, they were afterward seen examining the Brook quite down to the Sea. That Mrs Trickie confirmd every thing her Husband had said. Mogg spoke to several other persons inhabitants of that Neighbourhood, who all told him, They thought these French people very suspicious persons, and that They were doing no good there. And that was the general opinion of that part of the Country. The French people kept no Servant, but they were Visited by a number of persons, and were frequently out upon the heights most part of the night.

Returning home to Hungerford, Mogg could not resist making a detour via Bath, to pass on what he had learned to another former servant of Alfoxton. In the best tradition of Chinese whispers, she duly reported all this to her new employer, Dr Daniel Lysons, who took it upon himself to inform the Duke of Portland, the minister in charge of the Home Office and, consequently, of both national security and espionage. Dr Lysons sent two letters, on 8 and 11 August, the latter adding even more juicy details. Not only were the new tenants Frenchmen but, even more sinisterly,

the man of the House has no wife with him, but only a woman who passes for his Sister – The man has Camp Stools, which he & his visitors carry with them when they go about the country upon their nocturnal or diurnal expeditions, & have also a Portfolio in which they enter their observations, which they have been heard to say were almost finished – They have been heard to say they should be rewarded for them, & were very attentive to the River near them . . . These people may *possibly* be under Agents to some principal at Bristol –

Even before this second letter was dispatched, James Walsh, an experienced government agent, was on his way to Alfoxton, charged with investigating the story. This extraordinarily swift response is explicable only in terms of recent events. In February 1797 three French frigates and a lugger had appeared off the north Devon coast near Ilfracombe. They scuttled several merchant ships and attempted to destroy shipping in the harbour before disappearing. This shock attack not unnaturally 'greatly agitated the Minds of all Ranks' and the local militia were called out. When the ships reappeared several days later, it was off the Pembrokeshire coast. They landed a small force of 1,200 Frenchmen, under the command of an American veteran, Colonel William Tate, which, two days later, surrendered to the local militia. Colonel Tate's orders were seized and it was discovered that the invasion of Wales was a fallback position: his prime objective had been to execute a *coup de main* on Bristol, 'which is the second city in England for riches and commerce; the destruction of Bristol is of the very last importance, and every possible effort should be made to accomplish it'.

The Wordsworths were known to have Bristol connections; they were believed to have come from Devon. Their behaviour was suspicious: their night walks over the Quantocks, notebook in hand, and their interest in charting the brook from Alfoxton to the coast near Kilve could only have a sinister appearance to local minds. They had arrived suddenly, did not employ servants and had no obvious possessions; their visitors were all strangers to Alfoxton. William had a strange north-country accent, read French books and talked endlessly about French politics. On learning of their inquiries about the brook, the Home Office at once ordered Walsh to leave Hungerford, where he had been interviewing Mogg, and found him 'by no means the most intelligent Man in the World'.

You will immediately proceed to Alfoxton or it's neighbourhood yourself, taking care on your arrival so to conduct yourself as to give no cause of suspicion to the Inhabitants of the Mansion house there – you will narrowly watch their proceedings ... you will of course ascertain if you can the names of the persons, & will add their descriptions – & above all you will be careful not to give them any cause of alarm, that if necessary they may be found on the spot.

It was a measure of how seriously the threat was taken that £20 – the equivalent of almost the entire annual rent of Alfoxton – was sent to Walsh to enable him to pursue his inquiries. He took up his headquarters at the Globe Inn at Stowey on 15 August and found himself immediately on the case. A Mr Woodhouse asked the landlord 'If he had seen any of those Rascalls from Alfoxton' and if Thelwall had gone. Walsh asked if they meant the famous Thelwall and, when they affirmed it was, needed no further inquiry to know what he had on his hands. For the last five years, he had followed Thelwall, reporting on his activities and lectures to the Home Office and, on at least one occasion, arresting him. 'I think this will turn out no French Affair', he wrote to the permanent under-secretary, 'but a mischiefuous gang of disaffected Englishmen.' His unwitting informants agreed. 'They are not French', was their opinion. 'But they are people that will do as much harm, as All the French can do . . .' Walsh ended his report with a significant bit of news. 'I have just procured the Name of the person who took the House. His name is *Wordsworth* a Name I think known to Mr Ford.'

That evening, Walsh went up to Alfoxton and interrogated Jones, who confirmed all that he had said to Mogg. No doubt flattered by the stir he had caused, he added a few more interesting titbits. On 23 July, shortly after their arrival, the Wordsworths had thrown a dinner party at which Thelwall had been present. Poole's mother had provided a fore-quarter of lamb, as fourteen people were expected to sit down to dinner and Poole himself was urged to hurry over by eleven o'clock in the morning, so that 'we may have Wordsworth's Tragedy read under the Trees'. Apart from Poole, Thelwall, the Wordsworths and the Coleridges, the identity of the other guests remains a mystery, though they were probably members of Poole's circle at Nether Stowey. As the Wordsworths still had no servant, Jones had been brought in to help with waiting on the table. After dinner, 'a little Stout Man with dark cropt Hair', who wore a white hat and glasses, had got up and talked 'so loud and was in such a Passion that Jones was frightened and did not like to go near them since'. This was, of course, Thelwall.

Jones also reported that William had lately been to Racedown and brought back a 'very Chatty' woman servant, the redoubtable Peggy Marsh, who had proudly informed Jones that 'Her Master was a Phylosopher'. William had also brought back little Basil and their personal possessions. John Perkins, the Pinney agent at Crewkerne, obviously suspected that the Wordsworths had done a moonlight flit and wrote in high excitement to the elder Pinney. No doubt he was disappointed to be reassured that, 'as Mr Wordsworth wrote to my Son and advised him of his intention of leaving Race-down, I have no doubt but he has left every thing in a proper state'. The arrival at Alfoxton on 14 August of Basil Montagu and Azariah Pinney was probably prompted by news of the Wordsworths' removal from Racedown.

By 16 August, only the day after arriving in the area, Walsh had convinced himself that the government had nothing to fear from the tenants of Alfoxton. He was clearly more troubled by what he found in Nether Stowey. Poole he described as 'a most Violent Member of the Corresponding Society' who had set up 'what He stiles *The Poor Mans Club*', with himself at the head of it: 'I am told that there are 150 poor Men belonging to this Club, and that Mr Poole has the intire command of every one of them', was his sinister analysis of poor Poole's efforts at practical philanthropy.

Coleridge dined out on the 'Spy Nozy' affair for years. William would simply dismiss the whole episode, declaring that the proceedings which inspired the investigation were 'such as the world at large would have thought ludicrously harmless'. Biographers have been divided into those who regard it as a hilarious case of mistaken identity and those who read into it every possible shade of sinister meaning. As usual, the truth would seem to lie between the two. There are unanswered questions. Walsh had shadowed Thelwall for years, for instance, yet it came as a surprise to him to find him at Nether Stowey and Alfoxton. Still more extraordinary is that Wordsworth's name should already have been known to both Walsh and his master, Ford.

One can only speculate on how, or why, Ford knew the Wordsworth name. There are two possibilities. William may have come to the attention of government agents while moving in radical circles in London, though this seems unlikely, given that they seem to have been unaware of such stridently active public figures as Coleridge and Poole. The most probable reason is the most mundane, but it is supported by the phrasing of Walsh's report. The personal identity of John Thelwall is unmistakable and needs no elucidation: he is '*Thelwall*' and 'the famous Thelwall'. William's personal identity, on the other hand, is not; it is the Wordsworth *surname* which is likely to be known to Ford. 'His name is *Wordsworth* a Name I think known to Mr Ford.' There were at least three reasons why Ford would know the Wordsworth surname. Captain John Wordsworth was a public figure in London, not just because of his East India Company connections but also because he moved in the same circles as Robinson and the latter's father-in-law, the Earl of Abergavenny. His brother, Robinson Wordsworth, had just been appointed Collector of Customs at Harwich under the aegis of 'Jack' Robinson. Finally, and most tellingly, because Ford was a lawyer and Bow Street magistrate, as well as a prominent member of London society, he could not have been unaware of the Wordsworth name in connection with the notorious Lonsdale suit.

It may even have been that personal enmities played their part. Eight years afterwards, in August 1805, Lord Somerville declared he was sure that Southey (his rival for a disputed inheritance) and William 'were still Jacobins at heart', and claimed that he had been 'instrumental in having us looked after in Somersetshire'. Southey immediately understood this to mean the 'spy who was sent down to Stowey to look after Coleridge and Wordsworth'.

Whatever the reasons prompting Walsh's commission, the most obvious one – that the initial reports suggested genuine fears that French agents might be preparing for another invasion – should not be underestimated. Walsh may have got drunk and revealed his mission, but not before he had satisfied himself that there was nothing to be feared. He departed as swiftly as he came. The consequences of his visit could not be so easily removed. 'The Aristocrats seem determined to persecute, *even Wordsworth*', Coleridge reported despairingly to Thelwall. Rumours about her tenant's alleged activities had reached the ears of Mrs St Albyn and William received notice to quit as soon as his lease expired in June 1798.

Within two months of taking up residence at Alfoxton, therefore, the Words- worths were already under notice to quit. In less than a year they would have to find an alternative home, though for the present they remained in undisturbed possession. Thelwall was less fortunate. Not for the first or last time, Coleridge had to retract a rashly made promise. It was simply impossible for Thelwall to settle near them.

Like all occupiers of large houses, William and Dorothy found that their supposed solitude was interrupted by a constant flow of guests. In the middle of September, they were visited by Coleridge's young friend and lodger Charles Lloyd, who was anxious to hear the remaining acts of *The Borderers*. He found William 'ill & incapable of reading it', so was reluctantly persuaded to stay for a few days because the Wedgwoods were due to arrive for a short visit.

The Wedgwoods' visit was quite extraordinary, for they came with a purpose. John Wedgwood, with whom William had dined earlier in the year at Bristol, in company with James Losh, wanted to introduce his younger brother, Tom, who had just moved into the area in order to receive treatment at Dr Beddoes's Pneumatic Institution. Tom Wedgwood was a committed philanthropist and Godwinian. Anxious to do his part for the furtherance of mankind, he had determined to devote a portion of his wealth to the education of a genius. One might wonder how he intended to identify a baby with such potential, but he had no such doubts. He believed, with Godwin, that there was no such thing as innate ability and that the source of all depravity was 'an erroneous and vicious education'.

Wedgwood had come up with a scheme. The child was to be protected from contact with bad example and from sensory overload by never being allowed to go out of doors or leave its apartment. The nursery was to be painted grey, with only a couple of vivid coloured objects to excite its senses of sight and touch. It was to be surrounded by hard objects to continually 'irritate [its] palms' (a peculiarly Godwinian notion, lifted straight out of *Political Justice*). All this sensory deprivation was to be enforced by a superintendent, who was to ensure that the child connected all its chief pleasures with rational objects and acquired a habit of 'earnest thought'. Godwin himself had doubted the practicality of finding a preceptor sufficiently qualified to teach such a system; and even if such a paragon could be found, 'who will consent to the profanation of employing him in cultivating the mind of a boy, when he should be instructing the world?' Wedgwood's solution was that of the politician: he would establish a committee of philosophers, composed of himself, Godwin, Dr Beddoes, Holcroft and Horne Tooke, to devise the plan, and employ one or two superintendents to carry it into practice. For his superintendents, he told Godwin, 'the only persons that I know of as at all likely for this purpose, are Wordsworth and Coleridge'. He had qualms about Coleridge, as being 'too much a poet and religionist to suit our views', but of William he had no doubt: 'from what I hear of him, he has only to be convinced that this is the most promising mode of benefiting society, to engage him to come forward with alacrity'.

William evidently disabused Tom Wedgwood pretty quickly. He quite agreed that an equable temper in dealing with children was an advantage, and might even agree with Dorothy that little Basil's solitary upbringing had prevented him learning habits of selfishness from other children. But there was not a chance that the writer of *The Prelude* could support the idea of shutting a child indoors and cutting him off from nature. Indeed, in a passage in that poem, contrasting his own upbringing among a race of 'real children', William launched into a startling polemic against this same Godwinian plan for educating a genius. The result would be not a child but a grotesque 'dwarf man ... The noontide shadow of a man complete'.

> He sifts, he weighs,
> Takes nothing upon trust: his teachers stare,
> The country people pray for God's good grace
> And tremble at his deep experiments ...
>
> Now this is hollow – 'tis a life of lies
> From the beginning, and in lies must end.
> Forth bring him to the air of common sense ...
>
> *Prelude (1805), v, 337–40, 350–52*

On the fifth day of the visit, the Wedgwood brothers agreed that the time had passed 'like lightning', but Tom's failure to persuade William rankled. Meeting Coleridge a few months later, Tom would express only 'a very indifferent opinion of his friend Wordsworth'. The full implications of this would not become clear until the following January, when Tom and his brother Josiah, prompted by Poole, offered a generous cash annuity to Coleridge but not to William.

Early in November William, Dorothy and Coleridge walked westwards along the coast to Lynmouth, just over the Somerset border in Devon. From Porlock, a village of tiny cottages crammed into narrow streets, lying on the edge of a vast flat foreshore, they took the coast road up a vertiginous wooded gorge and over the dizzying pinnacles of the highest cliffs in England, before beginning the dramatic plunge of the descent into Lynmouth. Two rivers meet at Lynmouth at the bottom of a cleft in a rocky gorge, just before they empty into the sea, the noise of waterfalls and sea combining in uproar. Here they stayed the night to recuperate before the climb up what Southey, visiting a year later, aptly describes as 'a road of serpentining perpendicularity' to the object of their tour, the remarkable Valley of Rocks. Running parallel to the coast, this narrow, streamless valley cowers under ramparts of bare rock, 'the very bones and skeleton of the earth', as Southey described them, 'rock reclining upon rock, stone piled upon stone, a huge and terrific mass'. Much beloved, then as now, by those of Gothic sensibilities, the desolation of the Valley of Rocks has inspired many an artist, and our poets were no exception. It was, they decided, the perfect setting for a description of the wanderings of Cain. Coleridge threw down a challenge: they would each write a canto, and whoever finished first would write the final one; the whole project was to be completed that night. It was a foregone conclusion. Thirty years later, Coleridge would still smile at the recollection.

Methinks I see his grand and noble countenance as at the moment when having despatched my own portion of the task at full finger-speed, I hastened to him with my manuscript – that look of humorous despondency fixed on his almost blank sheet of paper, and then its silent mock-piteous admission of failure struggling with the sense of the exceeding ridiculousness of the whole scheme – which broke up in a laugh: and the Ancient Mariner was written instead.

While Coleridge may have confused this walk with others, the two men occupied at least one pedestrian expedition towards Watchet in 'laying the plan of a ballad, to be published with some pieces of William's'. Their object was purely financial. The poems were to be published in the *New Monthly Magazine* and, from the profits, they hoped to finance another short excursion. The original idea for *The Ancient Mariner* had come from Poole's friend John Cruikshank, who had dreamt of a skeleton ship with figures in it. As they walked, they discussed the motivation and evolution of the plot. Once again, it was to be a joint effort, but this time there would be no artificial time limit. Even so, Coleridge was very much the dominant partner, inventing most of the story, though William's contributions were of central importance. Typically, for instance, he suggested that the Mariner should have committed some crime which brought about his spectral persecution. Having recently read a similar story in George Shelvocke's *A Voyage Round the World by the Way of the Great South Sea*, William also suggested that killing an albatross should be the Mariner's crime and that revenge should be sought by the tutelary spirits of the South Seas. Finally, he also put forward the idea of the dead men being reanimated to navigate the ship.

If some of the most crucial elements of the story came from William, the writing was almost exclusively Coleridge's. In the end, William contributed a mere ten or a dozen lines.

As we endeavoured to proceed conjointly (I speak of the same evening) our respective manners proved so widely different that it would have been quite presumptuous in me to do anything but separate from an undertaking upon which I could only have been a clog . . . The Ancient Mariner grew & grew till it became too important for our first object which was limited to our expectation of five pounds, and we began to talk of a volume . . .

And in this casual, almost accidental way, was born *Lyrical Ballads.* Nothing more came of the plan for some time. It was not even clear what William's contribution would be. Should he offer his Salisbury Plain poem, for instance, or perhaps *The Ruined Cottage?* The whole idea had to be shelved for a while, however, when the real possibility emerged that *Osorio* and *The Borderers* might both be staged in London.

Coleridge had transmitted his play to Sheridan at Drury Lane, through his friend and fellow poet William Lisle Bowles, on 16 October. Shortly afterwards he procured an introduction for *The Borderers* to Thomas Harris of the Covent Garden theatre. At the beginning of December, Sheridan rejected *Osorio,* but Harris held out such hopes that a few alterations might make *The Borderers* feasible that William and Dorothy dropped everything and went straight to London.

For the first week or so, William was kept fully occupied in rewriting and Dorothy in copying. The final draft was then presented and, while they waited for the verdict, they dreamt of all the possibilities a successful stage run might bring them. One of these schemes was a walking tour through Wales and Yorkshire into Cumberland. As their Halifax cousin Elizabeth Threlkeld tartly commented, 'This would *by many* be thought rather a *wildish* scheme, but by them it was thought very practicable'.

All these pleasant dreams were shattered when *The Borderers* was rejected. William was disappointed, but bore his rejection philosophically; the problem was not his play, but 'the deprav'd State of the Stage at present'. This may sound like sour grapes, but it was, in fact, quite true. Bowdlerized versions of Shakespeare and watered-down versions of Restoration comedy were staple fare, and the main performance of an evening was usually followed by a farce or even a pantomime. One could hardly imagine a psychological thriller like *The Borderers* taking London by storm; nor can one imagine William accepting non-authorial interference in his work. 'William is not determined whether he shall publish it or no,' Elizabeth Threlkeld reported to Halifax, where everyone was agog with curiosity at this latest enterprise by the family black sheep.

Before they left London, William and Dorothy paid a number of important visits. Southey, having determined to read for the bar, had been admitted to Gray's Inn at the beginning of the year and was now a resident in London. The Wordsworths dined with him three times and called there once or twice. Dorothy's opinion of him was decidedly cool, indeed almost frosty. The reason for this becomes clear in her description of him as 'a young man of rigidly virtuous habits and . . . I believe, exemplary in the discharge of all Domestic Duties', for she was merely parroting Coleridge. Only Coleridge could turn domestic virtues into a matter for blame. Despite being (and probably because they were) brothers-in-law, Coleridge had never fully forgiven Southey. As his own marriage fell apart, he would unjustly blame Southey for forcing him into it, and make increasingly spiteful remarks about the Southeys' own wedded bliss.

The possibility of publishing *The Borderers* rather than putting it on stage seems to have led the Wordsworths to go from London to Bristol. They stayed over Christmas and the New Year, probably with Cottle and his parents, returning to Alfoxton on the evening of 3 January 1798. A few days later they had to say goodbye to Coleridge, whose desperation at his financial affairs had prompted him to consider entering the Unitarian ministry. To see whether he was equipped for such a life, he had offered to act as a locum at Shrewsbury. For good or ill, his ministry was cut short by the offer of an unconditional annuity for life of £150 from Josiah and Tom Wedgwood. 'I accepted it on the presumption that I had talents, honesty, & propensities to perseverant effort', Coleridge informed William, with what would later come to seem painful irony. It would also enable him to stay near the Wordsworths, wherever they went when their lease ran out in June.

In Coleridge's absence, Dorothy felt the need to capture something of this beautiful place on paper. On 20 January 1798 she began to write a daily journal. It was to become a lifelong, if irregular, habit and a useful tool for her brother. So much of his poetry was reliant on memory for its inspiration that her contemporaneous records of people and places were an invaluable *aide-mémoire* for details that might otherwise have been forgotten. Veering wildly from staccato lists of deeds and visitors to lyrical descriptions of landscapes and the tenderly observed minutiae of nature, Dorothy's journals have indisputably established her as a literary figure in her own right. The argument over how much she contributed to William's (and indeed Coleridge's) poetry is less easily settled, and it continues to rage. Was she simply William's amanuensis, tirelessly jotting down his observations? Or was she herself a poet, denied a voice by a misogynist age and selflessly feeding lines and images to her brother?

The most important point is that William was not a poet who composed in solitude, or on paper. Throughout his entire life, his preferred method of composition was to walk and talk. According to *The Prelude* he had done this as a schoolboy at Hawkshead; and one of the most abiding impressions he left on the country folk in the Lakes was his habit of 'mumbling to hissel' along t'roads'. One of the Wordsworths' former servants gave a more explicit description: 'Mr Wordsworth went bumming and booing about, and she, Miss Dorothy, kept close behint him, and she picked up the bits as he let 'em fall, and tak' 'em down, and put 'em on paper for him.' For all the contrived quaintness of the dialect, this is a significant observation which goes a long way towards explaining the coincidence of vocabulary and imagery in William's poetry and Dorothy's journals. Dorothy's letters also reveal that she had a curious habit of unconsciously repeating words and phrases taken from her correspondents. Again, this has a bearing on her journal, as it reflects her ability to absorb and adopt the language of others, and explains Coleridge's description of her as 'a perfect electrometer'.

And there is a major difference between the early and late journals which also sheds light on this question. The early ones, coinciding with William's most prolific years, have been extensively published and therefore trawled for evidence to support the argument that William simply turned Dorothy's prose into poetry. The later ones, particularly those of 1824–35, have not, and their significance remains unappreciated. For the clear impression of these journals is that they were of purely personal interest and written for Dorothy's eye alone. They are a brusquely efficient record of daily life and the descriptive passages, which are such a feature of the early journals, are few and far between. It is true that, by this time, William was no longer in full creative flow, but he was still writing poetry, some of it as good as it had ever been. He was, however, no longer Dorothy's constant companion. Clearly, then, he was not totally dependent on the journals for his poetry.

On the other hand, William ceaselessly and publicly reiterated his debt to Dorothy, and there was no more obvious indication of the fact that 'she gave me eyes, she gave me ears' than her early journals. Their natural empathy makes it impossible to separate out what may or may not have been contributed by Dorothy: their reactions were the same and they drew on, and assimilated, each other's responses, so that these became indivisible. The difference between them, which is readily apparent in Dorothy's surviving poetry, was that her powers were purely observational; William was the poet because he had the ability to look beyond the stimulus of the physical senses and 'see into the Life of things'.

In addition to rhapsodic descriptions (and many a laconic 'an uninteresting evening'), the journal bears witness to the intimacy between the Wordsworths and Coleridge. Every few days they called on each other or walked together, regardless of the weather. Poole was frequently included, accepting and extending hospitality to them all. On one memorable occasion, he took his protégés to call on his disapproving relations at Marshmill. He begged his cousin Penelope to sing an aria for them from *Judas Maccabeus*, 'Come, ever smiling Liberty!', but she persistently selected another song. 'I *could* not sing it', she told her daughter years later. 'I knew what they meant with *their* liberty.'

The one person who was consistently excluded from this charmed circle was Sarah Coleridge. Dorothy had conceived an aversion to her from the start, believing her to be an unworthy wife and helpmeet for the wonderful poet. The unavoidable suspicion is that her dislike and contempt sprang from jealousy: Dorothy could not be Coleridge's wife so she disliked the woman who was. For Sarah, it was particularly mortifying that Coleridge was equally besotted with William's 'exquisite sister'. With one small child already and another due in May, it became increasingly difficult for her to join in the walks, visits and excursions which were such an important part of the friendship. An already tense relationship between the women was driven to breaking point by what must have seemed like calculated provocation to Sarah, in her heavily pregnant state.

Often it would happen that the walking party returned drenched with rain; in which case [Dorothy], with a laughing gaiety, and evidently unconscious of any liberty that she was taking . . . would run up to Mrs Coleridge's wardrobe, array herself, without leave asked, in Mrs Coleridge's dresses, and make herself merry with her own unceremoniousness and Mrs Coleridge's gravity.

It was an ominous indication of the state of affairs that, if Sarah expressed any resentment, Coleridge slapped her down for being narrow-minded.

Since returning from London and Bristol in the New Year, William had returned to *The Ruined Cottage*, determined to give it added depth and poignancy by developing the character of the Pedlar who tells Margaret's story. Instead of relating the bare facts, he would become a philosopher and draw out a moral from the tale. Coleridge's influence here was crucial, for the Pedlar became an embodiment of his philosophy of the 'One Life', which recognized the natural harmony and unity of the universe: ''tis God Diffused through all, that doth make all one whole'. By the beginning of March, the poem had grown to 900 lines in length, of which the Pedlar's character made 'a very, certainly the *most*, considerable part of the poem'. He was now a Cumbrian who, despite his lack of schooling and lowly trade, possessed 'no vulgar mind'.

> He was a chosen son:
> To him was given an ear which deeply felt
> The voice of Nature in the obscure wind,
> The sounding mountain and the running stream.
> To every natural form, rock, fruit, and flower,
> He gave a moral life; he saw them feel
> Or linked them to some feeling.

It was no coincidence that many of the lines now written for *The Ruined Cottage* would, the following year, be taken from the Pedlar, transferred to *The Prelude* and acknowledged as autobiographical. By the simple act of making the Pedlar a Cumbrian, William had finally tapped into the mainspring of his poetic power. 'His faculties seem to expand every day,' Dorothy wrote proudly to Mary Hutchinson, 'he composes with much more facility than he did, as to the *mechanism* of poetry, and his ideas flow faster than he can express them.'

This revolution in William's writing habits was also prompted, in part, by the sense that he now had a mission in life. Dorothy had always encouraged him to believe he should be a poet, whatever the financial penalties or his impotent despair at the course of public events. Even through his darkest days at Racedown, when 'in search of knowledge desperate I was benighted heart and mind', she had,

Maintained for me a saving intercourse
With my true self . . .
She, in the midst of all, preserved me still
A poet, made me seek beneath that name
My office upon earth.
            Prelude (1805), xii, 20–21, x, 914–15, 918–20

The months of almost daily contact with Coleridge at Alfoxton had stiffened William's resolve. That a man of Coleridge's dazzling intellectual gifts should be unstinting in his praise for William's work was an affirmation of its worth. Now Coleridge, in a gesture which was in itself a recognition of William's superior talents, handed over to William his own most cherished scheme: the idea of a great philosophic poem. 'I should not think of devoting less than 20 years to an Epic Poem', Coleridge had boldly declared to Cottle in April 1797, only a year previously, but before his friendship with William had blossomed.

Ten to collect materials and warm my mind with universal science. I would be a tolerable Mathematician, I would thoroughly know Mechanics, Hydrostatics, Optics, and Astronomy, Botany, Metallurgy, Fossilism, Chemistry, Geology, Anatomy, Medicine – then the *mind of man* – then the *minds of men* – in all Travels, Voyages and Histories. So I would spend ten years – the next five to the composition of the poem – and the five last to the correction of it.

William responded enthusiastically, though cynics might think it was hardly an act of friendship to pass on such a grandiose scheme, especially as Coleridge was, in Hazlitt's deliciously apt phrase 'a past master of the prospectus'.

In taking on Coleridge's idea of writing an epic poem, William accepted his premise that it would be 'of considerable utility'. He also accepted Lamb's considered judgement that nothing short of an epic poem 'can satisfy the vast capacity of true poetic genius. Having one great End to direct all your poetical faculties to, & on which to lay out your hopes, your ambition, will shew to what you are equal.' Writing to James Tobin to explain his project at the beginning of March, William was able to announce that he had already written 1,300 lines (he did *not* mention that this included *The Ruined Cottage*, which would be subsumed into the new poem), and that his object was 'to give pictures of Nature, Man, and Society. Indeed', he added with Coleridgean grandeur, 'I know not any thing which will not come within the scope of my plan . . . the work of composition is carved out for me, for at least a year and a half to come.' William even had a title for his poem, *The Recluse or views of Nature, Man, and Society.*

Coleridge was cock-a-hoop at William's decision to embark on this grand undertaking, and extravagant in his praise for what he had already written. 'The Giant Wordsworth – God love him! – even when I speak in the terms of admiration due to his intellect, I fear lest tho[se] terms should keep out of sight the amiableness of his manners – he has written near 1200 lines of a blank verse, superior, I hesitate not to aver, to any thing in our language which any way resembles it.' Even Poole, who was not given to hyperbole, gave grudging approbation, thinking it 'as likely to benefit mankind much more than any thing, Wordsworth has yet written'.

There was only one obstacle in William's path: if he was to write a work on such a scale, he needed to have mastery of all the subjects he covered. Friends were asked to perform 'an essential service' and forward books. Cottle was asked to borrow John Wedgwood's copy of Erasmus Darwin's *Zoönomia* and Tobin to send any books of travels, 'as without much of such reading my present labours cannot be brought to a conclusion'.

Ironically, his labours on *The Recluse* would never be brought to a conclusion. He would commit decades of his life to the project; it would entrance him and frustrate him, lead to periods of intense creativity and bring him to a complete standstill. Ultimately, it would become the bitterest disappointment of his whole poetic career, for he felt he had failed where it mattered most. This was odd, for, viewed with detachment, *The Recluse* was, like all Coleridge's other grandiose schemes, totally impractical. It was impossible for any one person ever to reach the point where he had sufficient knowledge to be able to expound a totally comprehensive philosophy to the world at large. Coleridge himself would suffocate in the attempt, unable to write because he was always in search of more complete knowledge. The confidence with which William set out his object, 'to give pictures of Nature, Man, and Society', obscured the fact that there never was a coherent plan on which it would proceed. As one scholar has so tellingly put it, it was the announcement of 'an ambition, not a poem'.

8. The Giant Wordsworth

'It is decided that we quit Allfoxden – The house is lett', Dorothy wrote to Mary Hutchinson on 5 March 1798. Any cherished hopes that they might be allowed to stay, after all, had been crushed. Mrs St Albyn had proved obdurate and Poole's friends from Nether Stowey, the Cruikshanks, would take over the lease at midsummer. If the Wordsworths could raise sufficient money they still hoped to make their projected walking tour through Wales and the north of England, taking in a visit to Mary at Sockburn. If not, they would have to return to Racedown.

Less than a week later, there was a dramatic change in their plans. On 11 March William wrote in great excitement to the newly married James Losh.

We have a delightful scheme in agitation, which is rendered still more delightful by a probability which I cannot exclude from my mind that you may be induced to join in the party. We have come to a resolution, Coleridge, Mrs Coleridge, my Sister and myself of going into Germany, where we purpose to pass the two ensuing years in order to acquire the German language, and to furnish ourselves with a tolerable stock of information in natural science. Our plan is to settle if possible in a village near a university, in a pleasant, and, if we can a mountainous, country; it will be desirable that this place should be as near as may be to Hamburg on account of the expense of travelling. What do you say to this?

It was, of course, a Coleridgean idea, and bore all his hallmarks: the educational scheme, and the 'little colony' of like-minded spirits, which he had been attempting to establish ever since dreaming up Pantisocracy with Southey. French aggression had made much of Europe inaccessible to English travellers, but the choice of Germany was not dictated solely by the constraints of Continental travel. Coleridge had been studying German daily in recent months and was already flirting with the German metaphysicians who would eventually tie his mind in knots.

Switzerland, which would probably have been William's preferred alternative, was out of the question, for the French had invaded this ancient bastion of independence only a few weeks earlier. Despite continued resistance from some of the more inaccessible cantons, Swiss liberties were abolished and a 'Helvetic Republic' would be proclaimed on 29 March. More than any other action committed by the French republic, it was this which alienated liberal, and even radical, feeling in Britain. William was not alone in reluctantly coming to the unpalatable conclusion that the standard of liberty had now passed from the French to the British.

The decision to go to Germany was easy: how to pay for it was another matter. Coleridge had his annuity from the Wedgwoods, but the Wordsworths were in more dire straits than usual. Montagu had abruptly left the legal profession the previous November and could not afford to pay his interest on the £400 he held on loan from Calvert's legacy; worse still, he was unable to pay the allowance for his son. The Wordsworths were therefore doubly straitened and having to support young Basil themselves. Their total joint expenditure of the previous year, 1797, had been a mere £110 – not far off the sum William had spent annually on himself as a student at Cambridge. Even so, for some time past the Wordsworths had reluctantly been forced to rely on small sums loaned to them by Poole and Cottle.

William's poetry was his only marketable commodity. Despite his recently expressed reluctance to go into print, 'a thing which I dread as much as death itself', within days of agreeing to accompany Coleridge to Germany, he had made an approach to Cottle.

What *could* you conveniently *& prudently*, and what *would* you, give for

1 Our two Tragedies – with small prefaces containing an analysis of our principal characters . . . To be delivered to you within a week of the date of your answer to this letter – & the money, which you offer, to be payed to us at the end of four months . . .

2 Wordsworth's Salisbury Plain & Tale of a Woman . . . with a few others which he will add . . . to be delivered to you within 3 weeks of the date of your answer – & the money to be payed, as before . . .

Coleridge, writing this letter on William's behalf, was evidently uncomfortable and begged Cottle to treat the matter 'merely as a bookseller' and not as a friend. William himself was determined to hold out for the thirty guineas he thought he needed to finance the trip to Germany; Cottle had first refusal, but if he could not offer so much, then William would approach other publishers. Cottle expressed interest in the volume of poems, so William set to work.

'You will be pleased to hear that I have gone on very rapidly adding to my stock of poetry', William wrote to Cottle on 12 April. 'Do come and let me read it to you, under the old trees in the park.' William was not exaggerating. Of the nineteen poems he eventually contributed to *Lyrical Ballads*, virtually all were new compositions, written in a period of remarkable creativity, between November 1797 and July 1798. What is even more extraordinary is that eleven of them were composed between

March and May 1798, and by the time *Lyrical Ballads* went to press William had almost enough poems in hand to furnish a second volume. For a man who had spent literally years toiling over *An Evening Walk* and *Descriptive Sketches*, not to mention the still-unpublished Salisbury Plain poem and *The Borderers*, this was some achievement.

The poems William wrote in this period are among his most striking and original. Viewed as a body of work, they divide neatly into two: those which fulfil William's wish to give a sympathetic voice to the plight of the poor and those which are purely autobiographical. Rather more than half fall into the former category and these are the most radical in style, content and vocabulary. Several drew on real-life anecdotes. A Holford farmer, denied poor relief and obliged to sell off his flock, one by one, to feed his large family, was immortalized in *The Last of the Flock*. Christopher Trickie, the one-eyed former huntsman to the St Albyns, who lived on the common just outside the gates of Alfoxton, inspired *Simon Lee*. The contrast of his former strength and vigour with his feeble and impoverished old age was pathetically illustrated in a single incident. William had come across him one day tottering beneath the weight of a mattock as he tried to uproot a stump of rotten wood and, being young and healthy, had severed the root with a single blow. Trickie's tearful but profuse thanks led William to a reflective conclusion.

> – I've heard of hearts unkind, kind deeds
> With coldness still returning.
> Alas! the gratitude of men
> Has ofter left me mourning.

(One wonders whether William would have been quite so sympathetic, or helpful, had he known of Trickie's role in the spying episode.) *The Idiot Boy* was composed 'almost extempore; not a word, I believe being corrected, though one stanza was omitted', in the woods of Alfoxton. 'I never wrote anything with so much glee', William would later admit, adding that the tale had been wrought up out of the idiot boy's words, reported to him by Poole, 'The cocks did crow & the sun did shine so cold'.

Madness, in less genial form, was represented by two powerful poems, *The Mad Mother* and *The Thorn*. *The Mad Mother* owed its origin to Coleridge's friend Mrs Estlin, who had observed the woman and her baby in Bristol. The story of *The Thorn* William devised himself, after noticing for the first time, on a stormy day, a thorn bush on a Quantock ridge which he had passed many times before. From this small beginning rose the moving tale of the woman who is daily seen at the thorn bush, repeatedly crying, 'oh misery! Oh woe is me!'; a small mossy hummock between the thorn and a pond (which William infamously describes as 'three feet long, and two feet wide') has led to local suspicion that this is the grave of her illegitimate child, whom she is believed to have murdered.

These two poems point us to another fascinating and familiar theme running through this poetry: abandoned women and children. *The Mad Mother*'s husband has deserted her and her child. The fiancé of the woman in *The Thorn* has jilted her on their wedding day, so that their baby is born out of wedlock. The wanderer in *The Female Vagrant* has lost her husband and children through poverty, disease and war. *The Complaint of a Forsaken Indian Woman*, though nominally about the Native American Indian practice of leaving behind the sick and dying, is actually about the woman's grief at having her child taken from her so that he can go on with the tribe. Illegitimacy, abandonment and mental instability were commonplace among the poor and therefore demanded a place in William's work. His recent reading in Erasmus Darwin's *Zoönomia* and William Godwin's life of his wife was demonstrably the impetus behind these themes, but it is difficult to avoid the impression that they were close to the poet's heart. How could William have written so extensively, and so often, on the subject without thinking of the woman and child he had, himself, left behind in France? Or without wondering what had been the effect of his action on them?

On an altogether lighter note, several of the new autobiographical poems sprang directly out of incidents at Alfoxton. Again, there is a discernible theme, the competing claims on the poet's time of the study of books and nature. It did not bode well for William's grand scheme of reading in preparation for *The Recluse* that nature won every time. Addressing Dorothy on 'the first mild day of March', he urges her to put away her books, put on her woodland dress and give herself up to 'the hour of feeling'.

> One moment now may give us more
> Than fifty years of reason;
> Our minds shall drink at every pore
> The spirit of the season.
> *Lines written at a small distance*
> *from my House, ll.1, 24–8*

In *Expostulation and Reply*, he answered the criticism that he had spent half the day dreaming, instead of drinking 'the spirit breath'd From dead men to their kind' in books, by declaring that the mind could also be fed by 'wise passiveness'. Or, as he put it in *The Tables Turned*,

> One impulse from a vernal wood
> May teach you more of man;
> Of moral evil and of good,
> Than all the sages can . . .
>
> Enough of science and of art;
> Close up these barren leaves;
> Come forth, and bring with you a heart
> That watches and receives.

William would always anxiously insist that he drew his inspiration from nature and personal observation, but books also made a vitally important contribution.

Even in this collection, as he acknowledged, they had directly provided him with the subject matter for at least two of his poems. The ballad of *Goody Blake and Harry Gill*, for instance, told the story of a farmer who can never again feel warm, after being cursed by an impoverished old woman he had captured stealing twigs from his hedge to feed her meagre fire in the depths of winter. William had read this tale in Erasmus Darwin's *Zoönomia*, where it had been cited as an example of 'Mutable Madness', or mistaking imaginations for realities. No doubt remembering those 'lying and picking and stealing' peasants of Racedown, William set the poem in Dorset and turned it into a warning against lack of charity.

Towards the middle of May, William took a short break from his studies. Together with Dorothy and Coleridge, he made an excursion to Cheddar Gorge, some twenty-five miles away. They broke their journey at Bridgwater and spent a second night at Cross, a village just outside Cheddar. William then went on to Bristol, while Coleridge escorted Dorothy back to Nether Stowey. One can only imagine the seething resentment that met them there, for poor Sarah Coleridge had, as usual, been left behind. In fact, her husband had actually set out on this jaunt only two days after Sarah had given birth to her second son. Like his elder brother, Hartley, the unfortunate baby was named after a philosopher, Berkeley.

When William returned from Bristol, he found that Coleridge had a visitor, a new disciple, picked up during his brief residence near Shrewsbury earlier in the year. This was the artist, essayist and critic William Hazlitt, then an impressionable young man of twenty. The son of a Unitarian minister, he had been swept off his feet by Coleridge's eloquence and jumped at his invitation to visit Nether Stowey. The very day he arrived, Coleridge carried him off to the more gracious surroundings of Alfoxton, where Dorothy gave them what Hazlitt later grudgingly remembered as a 'frugal' meal and invited them to stay the night. Hazlitt was given free access to William's manuscript poems and, to ensure that he learned his lesson properly, Coleridge accompanied him into the park after breakfast and, in the Alfoxton tradition, sitting under the trees, read him *The Idiot Boy*, *The Thorn*, *The Mad Mother* and *The Complaint of a Forsaken Indian Woman*. It was, as Coleridge intended, a revelatory experience for the young Hazlitt: 'the sense of a new style and a new spirit in poetry came over me'. As they walked back to Nether Stowey, Coleridge expounded at length on William's merits and demerits as a poet. He regretted particularly that William did not share his own belief in the traditional superstitions associated with places, claiming, in an apt image, that 'there was a something corporeal, a *matter-of-fact-ness*, a clinging to the palpable in his poetry, in consequence.' This criticism applied only to his descriptive poetry (as exemplified by the poems which would appear in *Lyrical Ballads*); his philosophic poetry, on the other hand, 'had a grand and comprehensive spirit in it, so that his soul seemed to inhabit the universe like a palace, and to discover truth by intuition, rather than by deduction'.

This was an analysis of immense significance, for it recognized and voiced William's rejection of Godwinian methodology in favour of the instinctive approach. The 'hour of feeling', the 'impulse from a vernal wood', were surer guides to moral truth than the chop-logic of the philosophers. This was the point at which Coleridge would always depart from William. Under the Wordsworths' influence, he had learned to 'love fields & woods & mounta[ins] with almost a visionary fondness'; like William, he had found 'benevolence & quietness growing within me as that fondness [has] increased'. But, unlike William, he was never content to rest at that point, because he was instinctively more of a philosopher than a poet, and here the youthful Hazlitt stood with Coleridge rather than William.

The following day, William arrived at Nether Stowey and there is a palpable air of disappointment in Hazlitt's description of the encounter. Unlike Coleridge, William did not have 'the poet's eye, in a fine frenzy rolling', which was the approved appearance for poets of the period. Instead, he was 'gaunt and Don Quixote-like', dressed 'quaintly' in a brown fustian jacket and striped pantaloons, which were probably his brother's cast-offs.

There was a severe, worn pressure of thought about his temples, a fire in his eye (as if he saw something in objects more than the outward appearance), an intense high narrow forehead, a Roman nose, cheeks furrowed by strong purpose and feeling, and a convulsive inclination to laughter about the mouth, a good deal at variance with the solemn, stately expression of the rest of his face.

The overriding impression was one of a 'drooping weight of thought and expression'.

Hazlitt's description is the first detailed word portrait of the poet. Coincidentally, however, not one but three portraits survive from this year. The other two, both pictures, were commissioned by Cottle, the only man of William's circle, other than Poole, sufficiently wealthy to afford such an extravagance. The first was an oil painting by a travelling artist, William Shuter. The second, a drawing in pencil and chalk, which was possibly intended as an illustration for *Lyrical Ballads*, was by Robert Hancock, a respected sixty-eight-year-old Bristol mezzotinter and engraver; it forms one of a set of four, Cottle also having commissioned Hancock to draw Lamb, Southey and Coleridge.

At first glance there is no obvious correlation between Hazlitt's description and Shuter's almost full-face portrait of a pleasant-looking, rather ordinary young man, with dark eyes and fine, dark hair worn loose at shoulder length. With the benefit of Hazlitt's analysis of his features, however, one perceives the distinctive vertical furrow in his right cheek, and a curiously coy half-smile, which was obviously meant to capture the 'convulsive inclination to laughter'. Hancock's altogether severer profile portrait gives a better idea of the Roman nose, and a receding hairline, which might indicate the 'worn pressure of thought about his temples'. Both portray William in what a later friend, Leigh Hunt, described as his 'habitual' pose, with one hand tucked beneath his jacket lapel. Neither portrait, however, supports Hazlitt's impression of either gauntness or 'a drooping weight of thought and expression', but one suspects that these, and indeed the other characteristics so graphically described, owe more to his later knowledge of the older William than to his first impressions in 1798. The attitude of pained thought, which is so typical of the later, better-known portraits, is entirely absent. This, as we shall see, was an innovation consequent upon William's public elevation to the role of philosopher-poet, after the publication of *The Excursion* in 1814. In 1798 the painters simply depicted what they saw before them: an unremarkable and, as yet, unknown young man of twenty-eight.

If William's appearance was not impressive, his manners were equally informal. He sat down and instantly began to 'make havoc' with a piece of Cheshire cheese on the table. Among other humorous asides, William remarked that Monk Lewis's dreadful play *Castle Spectre*, which he had been to see while in Bristol, 'fitted the taste of the audience like a glove'. The irony was not lost on Hazlitt, even though he did not know of the recent rejection of *The Borderers*.

The following day, Coleridge and Hazlitt came over to Alfoxton for an open-air reading of *Peter Bell*, William's latest long poem. Begun on 20 April, it was intended for inclusion in the forthcoming volume, but its rapid expansion and its controversial subject led to its being omitted. Written in ballad form, it told the story of Peter Bell, a drunken, dissolute, itinerant potter, who tries to steal an ass he finds standing by a river. The ass refuses to move until Peter recovers his master's body from the water, then voluntarily carries Peter back to the widow and fatherless children. For Peter, the journey becomes a spiritual one, effecting a complete character reformation. As far as William was concerned, it was his greatest experiment so far in pushing back the boundaries of poetic taste: both subject matter and language were aggressively lower class 'The *People* would love the Poem', he later wrote in its defence, 'but the *Public* (a very different Being) will never love it.' He was wrong on both counts; but though the poem has its admirers, for most readers it is an experiment too far. It teeters uneasily on the brink of doggerel, and occasionally slips over.

Hazlitt therefore found himself in the curious position of listening to William reading *Peter Bell* aloud 'in prophetic tones': 'and the comment made upon it by his face and voice was very different from that of some later critics!' he added unkindly. Whatever he thought of the poem, Hazlitt did have the perception to notice a key element in William's poetry. He attributed it to the hypnotic power of William's voice and intonation. 'There is a *chaunt* in the recitation both of Coleridge and Wordsworth, which acts as a spell upon the hearer, and disarms the judgment', he wrote. 'Coleridge's manner is more full, animated, and varied; Wordsworth's more equable, sustained, and internal. The one might be termed more *dramatic*, the other more *lyrical*.' Hazlitt could not resist an acerbic aside, 'Perhaps they have deceived themselves by making habitual use of this ambiguous accompaniment', but he had a point. Unwittingly, he had put his finger on one of the main reasons for the declining popularity of William's poetry in the twentieth century. It was meant to be read aloud to an audience, not, as it almost always is, silently in books.

Before the end of the month, Cottle came to stay at Alfoxton for a week. He may even have brought William back from Bristol in his gig, though if this were so, it is odd that neither he nor Hazlitt mentioned the other's presence. Perhaps

William walked over to Nether Stowey to meet him, for the gig played a vital role in Cottle's memories of this visit. Coleridge, Dorothy and the servant walked back to Alfoxton, while William accompanied Cottle in his gig. They carried with them a bottle of brandy, a loaf of bread and 'a stout piece of cheese' to enhance the table. When they drew up at Alfoxton, they discovered that the cheese had disappeared, presumably stolen by a beggar they had stopped to give alms to on the road. Coleridge released the horse from the gig, causing it to lurch forward, and the precious bottle of brandy fell out and smashed to pieces. Dinner therefore consisted of the loaf of bread and a plate full of cos lettuces, freshly culled from the vegetable garden, washed down with water from the Alfoxton spring. An empty plate at the bottom of the table bore witness to the cheese that should have been. To add insult to injury, when someone asked for salt, the servant admitted she had forgotten to buy any. The philosophers comforted themselves, as one does, with the thought of those less well off than themselves. Though Cottle's memoirs are notoriously inaccurate, one is irresistibly reminded of the frugal dinner offered to Hazlitt and, indeed, of little Basil and his complaints of being starved.

The main purpose of Cottle's visit was to determine the final form of the projected publication. Cottle wanted to include all William's unpublished poems in two volumes, a suggestion which to William was 'decisively repugnant & oppugnant'. Taken all together, he reasoned, they would lack variety, though he was prepared to consider publishing either *Peter Bell* or the Salisbury Plain poem separately. Coleridge was anxious to press ahead with publication of *The Rime of the Ancyent Marinere*, though Cottle does not seem to have been happy with its arch archaisms. Cottle was also opposed to the idea of a collaborative venture and, even more emphatically, to an anonymous one. Whatever the final configuration of the volume, or volumes, both poets were equally adamant that it, or they, should appear anonymously. Coleridge, still smarting from a personal attack in the *Anti-Jacobin*, explained why: 'Wordsworth's name is nothing – to a large number of persons mine *stinks*.'

By the time Cottle left Alfoxton, he had come to an agreement, in principle, that he would offer William the thirty guineas he had demanded as his price. He carried away with him Coleridge's manuscript of the *Ancyent Marinere*, which was to form the centrepiece of the publication. Apart from this, its contents were as yet undecided. When they finally settled on a single joint volume, twenty-two of the twenty-three poems it contained had already been written.

Cottle's accepted offer more than covered the cost of the journey to Hamburg, which, the Wordsworths calculated, would be between twenty and twenty-five guineas. William was expecting the final payment on Raisley Calvert's legacy soon. Additionally, he was due the tidy sum of £67 17s 3d, in the form of interest on the capital while it had remained in William Calvert's hands. In the event, it was 10 August before Calvert forwarded the full amount to Richard, including interest, and an extra half a crown 'to pay the postage of this letter'. And it was not until 4 December, by which time William had been out of the country for almost three months, that Richard finally invested the money in 3 per cent consols. Richard might have cavilled at his brother's casual manner of loaning money to his friends, but at least William obtained a far better rate of interest.

The plans for travelling to Germany were also taking shape. The original intention was to settle immediately in the neighbourhood of one of the German universities, so that they could take full advantage of the opportunities for studying while they learned the language. Their optimistic belief that they could live more cheaply in Germany than England soon proved misplaced. On inquiry, they discovered that lodgings were more expensive, and all the other costs of living far higher, in university towns. Of necessity, therefore, they would have to reside in 'some small town or village' till they had acquired sufficient German for William and Coleridge to take up places in a university. Saxony was recommended to them as being both extremely beautiful and very cheap. The Wordsworths intended to board with 'some respectable family' so that they would be obliged to talk German constantly; the Coleridges, because of their children and the need to have a servant, would have to take a ready-furnished house. They would be able to augment their finances by translating from the German, 'the most profitable species of literary labour'.

It all sounded wonderfully pragmatic and organized. Friends and relatives were naturally horrified, and their cluckings of disapproval reverberated the length and breadth of the kingdom. Southey was simply contemptuous: 'a wilder and more ridiculous scheme was never undertaken than this – to go with a wife and two infants merely to learn a language which may be learnt by his own fireside!' It was a fair criticism, particularly as the Wordsworths had reluctantly decided that they could not take five-year-old Basil Montagu with them 'as the experiment of taking a child of his age into a foreign country is at any rate hazardous'. He would now be passed on to the care of an aunt. But not until a month before their departure did Coleridge decide that it would be inappropriate for his wife and babes (Hartley almost two, Berkeley not yet six months old), to accompany him; even then, it was only on the grounds of expense. Not having consulted his wife, he could only guess that she would agree that this was the sensible thing to do. There was no question of his giving up the scheme: it was 'of high importance to my intellectual utility; and of course to my moral happiness'.

William went to Bristol to supervise the final selection and printing of his poems. He carried with him the two latest ones, *Expostulation and Reply* and *The Tables Turned*, which had been written in response to a conversation with Hazlitt, who was 'somewhat unreasonably attached to modern books of moral philosophy'. While in Bristol, he took the opportunity to pay several visits to James Losh and his wife. They had recently taken a small house on the Avon at Shirehampton, just north-west of the city, which had all the advantages of a pretty coastal village and yet was close to Bristol. As there would be a hiatus before departing for Germany and quitting Alfoxton, William engaged lodgings for himself and Dorothy with a view to spending two or three months in Shirehampton before their final departure.

On the morning of 25 June 1798, the day after their lease expired, the Wordsworths reluctantly left Alfoxton. It had proved a place of enchantment for them. The seeds of William's talent, which had sprouted at Racedown, had blossomed at Alfoxton and were about to bear fruit.

Had there ever been any chance of the Loshes accompanying them to Germany, it was now at an end. Shirehampton 'decidedly disagreed' with Losh, his nervous complaint had returned and he had been carried off to Bath. On 8 July the Wordsworths went over to visit him there, and had a chance meeting which would have important consequences. They dined twice in company with Losh's friend the Reverend Richard Warner, whose book, *A Walk through Wales in 1797*, was hot off the press. The Wordsworths had long planned to take a walking tour through Wales and their conversations with Warner prompted them to take the plunge. They caught the Severn ferry from Bristol to Chepstow and, retracing William's own route in the summer of 1793, walked the ten miles upstream to Tintern Abbey. The next morning, they followed the Wye up, through Monmouth, as far as Goodrich Castle, where they again halted for the night, before walking back to Chepstow. Instead of ending the tour there, however, they revisited Tintern Abbey, this time by boat. Braving the muddy, swirling tidal waters of the Wye in one of the little coracles which plied the route, they landed at Tintern, spent the night there and then returned to Bristol.

Sketching out this bare outline of their tour, the Wordsworths gave not the slightest hint that it was anything more than a simple tourist jaunt. Nothing could be further from the truth, for out of it would be born *Tintern Abbey*, the giant of *Lyrical Ballads*. As soon as William set foot on the banks of the Wye, it became an act of symbolic significance. He knew immediately that he was not just introducing his sister to a particularly lovely part of the country, but also revisiting his own past. He was aware that this was a time for personal reassessment, for taking stock. And he did so triumphantly. The last five years had wrought immense changes in William. Then he had been an ardent young revolutionary firing off salvoes at the British establishment; now, like Coleridge, he had become a man of no party, someone who could not, in conscience, vote for the removal of the present ministry, even though he thought them 'weak & perhaps unprincipled men', because he could see no one better to replace them. Then he had been a passionate lover of nature, constantly seeking the stimulus of new and different sights; now, 'with an eye made quiet by the power Of harmony, and the deep power of joy' he had learned to see 'into the life of things'. Then he had been in emotional turmoil, after leaving Annette and his unseen baby daughter behind in France; now, though still haunted by guilt, he had come to some sort of acceptance of the situation. Then he had been frustrated and purposeless: should he be a politician, a pamphleteer, a philosopher, a poet? How was he to earn a living? Now he had a vocation, which enabled him to combine all these things, but rendered him first and foremost a poet.

These reflections would probably have occurred to William had he returned to Tintern Abbey alone, but it was Dorothy's presence that brought them so forcibly home to him. For Dorothy, 'my dearest Friend . . . My dear, dear Sister!', who had loyally stood by him through thick and thin, was wild with delight and excitement. And she was the very image of his younger self.

>   in thy voice I catch
>   The language of my former heart, and read
>   My former pleasures in the shooting lights
>   Of thy wild eyes.
>
>   *Tintern Abbey, ll.116–20*

William was still a worshipper of nature, but his 'wild ecstasies' had been matured into 'a sober pleasure'. For him, that time, with all its 'aching joys' and 'dizzy raptures', was past, but other gifts had followed, which provided abundant recompense. He had learned to look on nature,

>   not as in the hour
>   Of thoughtless youth, but hearing oftentimes
>   The still, sad music of humanity,
>   Not harsh nor grating, though of ample power
>   To chasten and subdue. And I have felt
>   A presence that disturbs me with the joy
>   Of elevated thoughts; a sense sublime
>   Of something far more deeply interfused,
>   Whose dwelling is the light of setting suns,
>   And the round ocean, and the living air,
>   And the blue sky, and in the mind of man,
>   A motion and a spirit, that impels
>   All thinking things, all objects of all thought,
>   And rolls through all things. Therefore am I still
>   A lover of the meadows and the woods,
>   And mountains; and of all that we behold
>   From this green earth; of all the mighty world
>   Of eye and ear, both what they half-create,
>   And what perceive; well pleased to recognize
>   In nature and the language of the sense,
>   The anchor of my purest thoughts, the nurse,
>   The guide, the guardian of my heart, and soul
>   Of all my moral being.
>
>   *Tintern Abbey, ll.89–111*

Tintern Abbey was a mission statement by a mature and accomplished poet, confident in and at the height of his powers. It was William's equivalent of Martin Luther's 'Here I stand'. In the years to come, it was one of the very few poems he ever wrote to escape his revision almost untouched. 'No poem of mine was composed under circumstances more pleasant for me to remember than this:' he would later say. 'I began it upon leaving Tintern, after crossing the Wye, and concluded it just as I was entering Bristol in the evening, after a ramble of 4 or 5 days, with my sister. Not a line of it was altered, and not any part of it written down till I reached Bristol.' Once back in Bristol, William hastened to give the poem to Cottle. He knew instinctively that he had written something wonderful, but also that, being a summation of his own position, it was the perfect poem with which to conclude the volume.

Within five days of their return, *Lyrical Ballads* was in the press. Coleridge's *Rime of the Ancyent Marinere* was to take pride of place as the first poem in the book; at 658 lines, it was far and away the longest poem. Two extracts from his tragedy *Osorio* would appear in second and fourteenth place, as *The Foster-Mother's Tale* and *The Dungeon*. His fourth and last contribution, *The Nightingale*, was a last-minute substitution for *Lewti*, his reworking of William's juvenile poem *Beauty and Moonlight*. The replacement was probably dictated by the fact that *Lewti* had already appeared in the *Morning Post* on 13 April; it was one of six poems written by William but sent in by Coleridge in the first half of this year to fulfil his contract with Daniel Stuart. It may, however, have been prompted by Coleridge's sudden realization that, despite his *Ancyent Marinere*, he was being relegated to the role of minor contributor, for all the remaining nineteen poems in the volume were by William.

What is more, it was probably William who wrote the advertisement, which appeared as a preface to *Lyrical Ballads*. It was an oddly defensive, even pugnacious document, which appealed to the intelligent reader over the heads of the critics. 'It is the honourable characteristic of Poetry that its materials are to be found in every subject which can interest the human mind', it began, promisingly enough.

The evidence of this fact is to be sought, not in the writings of Critics, but in those of Poets themselves.

The majority of the following poems are to be considered as experiments. They were written chiefly with a view to ascertain how far the language of conversation in the middle and lower classes of society is adapted to the purposes of poetic pleasure. Readers accustomed to the gaudiness and inane phraseology of many modern writers, if they persist in reading this book to its conclusion, will perhaps frequently have to struggle with feelings of strangeness and aukwardness: they will look round for poetry, and will be induced to enquire by what species of courtesy these attempts can be permitted to assume that title. It is desirable that such readers, for their own sakes, should not suffer the solitary word Poetry, a word of very disputed meaning, to stand in the way of their gratification; but that, while they are perusing this book, they should ask themselves if it contains a natural delineation of human passions, human characters, and human incidents; and if the answer be favorable to the author's wishes, that they should consent to be pleased in spite of the most dreadful enemy to our pleasures, our own pre-established codes of decision.

In other words, put aside your prejudices, gentle reader, and enjoy. Well aware that most readers would find 'many lines and phrases will not exactly suit their taste', William attempted to forestall criticism by confessing that he might sometimes have gone too far; many of his expressions might appear 'too familiar, and not of sufficient dignity', but they were justified by the usage of centuries. 'An accurate taste in poetry ... is an acquired talent,' was William's lofty pronouncement, 'which can only be produced by severe thought, and a long continued intercourse with the best models of composition.' Though unintentional, the general implication of the advertisement was unfortunate: that the poet expected his offering to be disliked, and that the fault lay with the 'erroneous judgment' of the reader rather than the quality of the poetry itself. Like many deeply private people, William was acutely sensitive to both criticism and rejection. His way of forestalling or dealing with it was to go on the attack, even when this was not necessary. He did this particularly in conversation, where, as his friend Losh had discovered, he could be 'too earnest and *emphatic* in his manner of speaking'. It was an approach which antagonized and offended many of his contemporaries, who mistook his basic insecurity for mere egotism. And, of course, expressed in a preface to a book, it simply invited criticism. Reviewers might be able to ignore the poems, but they could not ignore the advertisement.

Even William's friends were uncomfortable with the inclusion of some poems. Cottle had succeeded in excluding *Peter Bell*, but James Tobin, who had seen some of the sheets as they were printing, earnestly entreated William to leave out *We are Seven*, 'for, if published, it will make you everlastingly ridiculous'. William refused and Tobin left 'in despair'. In this instance, William's instinct was right: it became one of his most enduringly popular poems.

At the beginning of August, while the poems were printing, Coleridge persuaded William and Dorothy to join him in a brief excursion into Wales to visit John Thelwall. A few days after their return, they set off again, this time on the first leg of their trip to Germany. Mrs Coleridge, Hartley and Berkeley remained at Nether Stowey, believing Coleridge would return in three or four months' time, either to take them back with him or to stay. Coleridge and the Wordsworths arrived in London on 27 August, but it did not augur well for the success of their emigration plans that, at the end of this short trip, their boxes had not arrived, a draft for £23 (possibly for the Alfoxton rent) had not been accepted and William had forgotten to bring a crucial letter from Cottle to Thomas Longman, asking him to undertake the London publication of *Lyrical Ballads*.

By 13 September the book had been printed, but it was still unpublished. Cottle could not afford to take the entire risk himself and needed a second, preferably London, publisher. There was a very real danger that the whole venture would founder, particularly as Cottle seemed to be in some financial difficulty. William had committed too much to *Lyrical Ballads* to allow this to happen. On the other hand, he was uncomfortably aware that his own insistence on receiving thirty guineas for his contribution had persuaded Cottle to be over-generous, and added considerably to his unavoidable costs in printing, distributing and advertising.

In an effort to sort the matter out to the benefit of all parties, William went to see Johnson, who had published *An Evening Walk* and *Descriptive Sketches* for him in 1793. He probably took Coleridge with him and introduced the two men. Coleridge, electric with charisma, immediately charmed the elderly publisher into undertaking a little collection of his own poems, *Fears in Solitude*, and giving him a credit note of £30 against the Hamburg bookseller, William Remnant. Johnson proved equally amenable to publishing *Lyrical Ballads* and was apparently willing to offer more than Cottle. It was the perfect solution. The day before he set sail, William wrote to Cottle pointing out all the advantages of this arrangement and requesting him to transfer his interest in *Lyrical Ballads* to Johnson. He also wrote to Johnson, asking him to deliver six copies of the book to Richard for distribution among his friends. Having done all he could, William sailed for Germany, leaving Cottle to finalize all the arrangements in his absence.

It was a big mistake. From the best of motives, Cottle had no intention of giving up his interest in *Lyrical Ballads*. Over the years, he gave several conflicting accounts of what happened, culminating in the obviously tall tale that the reviews had been so bad and he had sold so few copies that he had been forced to dispose of almost the entire print run to another London publisher, J. & A. Arch (the copies were actually with Arch before a single review appeared). From what one can glean from the muddle, it appears that Cottle took offence at William's assumption that he would not make a profit from the volume and at his making alternative arrangements with another publisher. He clearly believed that, without consulting him, William had entered into 'something like *an engagement*' with Johnson, whereas William thought he had left the decision in Cottle's hands. In any case, it appears that Cottle had already disposed of the copies (not the copyright) to Arch, so he was not in a position to sell to Johnson.

In William's absence, no one knew exactly what to do. There was a mildly acrimonious spat between Cottle and Johnson, but on 4 October 1798 *Lyrical Ballads* was finally published under the Arch imprint. A small, slim, insignificant-looking octavo volume, containing 210 pages of poetry and priced at 5s in boards, it bore neither Cottle's name nor those of William and Coleridge. It could hardly have been more anonymous. Its authors did not know of its publication and remained ignorant of its fate.

They had set off from London on 14 September, leaving Richard in charge of William's finances in his absence. The Wedgwoods, who had asked William to give them a copy of *The Borderers* before he left, were to be his bankers, since it was easy for them to transfer money abroad through their merchant contacts. The little party included not just the Wordsworths and Coleridge, but also John Chester, a young man from Nether Stowey. Hazlitt unkindly described him as low in stature, bow-legged and with a drag in his walk like a drover. He worshipped Coleridge, and scarcely ever spoke himself. This unlikely companion had the advantage of being wealthy enough to subsidize Coleridge's expenses, which is probably why he had been invited along.

They had what Coleridge sarcastically called 'an unusually fine passage of only 48 hours' to Cuxhaven at the mouth of the Elbe. To his evident glee, 'Chester was ill the Whole time – Wordsworth shockingly ill! – Miss Wordsworth worst of all – vomiting & groaning & crying the whole time!' Coleridge himself was 'gay as a lark'. Dorothy, emerging from her cabin for the first time in the still waters of the estuary, was surprised that she could not see the shores. Hamburg lay a further sixty-two miles further inland, and the captain agreed to take all the passengers there for half a guinea each.

Sailing up the winding and narrowing waters of the Elbe, the passengers were all sufficiently recovered from their seasickness to emerge from the cabin and get to know one another. Dorothy began a new journal, recording, with typical English intolerance of dirty foreign habits, a catalogue of foul smells, filthy hotels and cheating locals preying on innocent tourists. Coleridge had already attracted a motley party of rumbustious Scandinavians and Germans, with whom he had caroused his way across the Channel. William found a more congenial acquaintance in an amiable fifty-year-old French émigré, Monsieur de Leutre, who 'appeared [to be] a man of sense, & was in his manners a most complete gentleman'. They soon struck up what Coleridge called 'a kind of confidential acquaintance'. William discovered that de Leutre had managed to escape France with a large portion of his fortune intact and had settled happily in London. Like many émigrés, however, he had been the victim of intrigues among his fellow countrymen and was now being deported by the Home Office on suspicion of being an agent of the French government.

At Altona, the busy port of Hamburg, they disembarked into smaller boats and were rowed up to the steps of the Customs House. There, on 19 September, they set foot on German soil for the first time. Leaving Dorothy, Chester and de Leutre's French servant to guard the luggage from rapacious German porters, William and de Leutre set out to find accommodation, while Coleridge rushed into town to present his letters of introduction from the Wedgwoods. After scouring the city (all 'Huddle and Ugliness, Stink and Stagnation!', in Coleridge's memorable phrase), the only place they could find any rooms was Der Wilder Man, 'an hotel not of the genteelest Class'. The difficulty of travelling with an unmarried woman was immediately apparent: she had to have a room of her own. De Leutre shared with his servant, and Coleridge with Chester, but William was obliged to beg a bed off an old college friend, John Baldwin, who was in lodgings at the Duke of York's Hotel. Since de Leutre had the largest room, he agreed that they could all meet there for meals.

The next morning, while Dorothy, escorted by Chester, made a promenade of the town, William and Coleridge took advantage of Wedgwood's introduction to an English merchant, Mr Chatterley, to meet his German partner, Victor Klopstock. Klopstock was the proprietor of one of the Hamburg newspapers, but it was his older brother, the famous poet and dramatist Friedrich, who was the real object of their interest. Young Klopstock, as they jokingly referred to his younger, but elderly brother, proved kind and courteous. Speaking no English, he conversed with Coleridge in German and William in French, and took the two young men under his wing. He escorted them round the city in an effort to find them a carriage they could afford to buy so that they could travel more cheaply, and he introduced them to some of his own friends, including the deaf Professor Ebeling.

The next afternoon, after another fruitless search for a carriage, Victor Klopstock took William and Coleridge to meet his brother, who lived just outside the city. 'In chusing his residence', William remarked with all the disapproval of a man who chose his own carefully, 'the poet does not seem to have been influenced by poetic ideas.' Friedrich Klopstock lived in a row of similar houses at the intersection of several roads on dull, flat land. Now seventy-four, his personal appearance was equally disappointing, for this legendary figure of German poetry was virtually toothless, had monstrously swollen legs and wore a ridiculous powdered and frizzled periwig of enormous proportions. William was unable to discover marks of either sublimity or enthusiasm in his countenance, but was favourably impressed by Klopstock's manner of speaking 'with the liveliness of a girl of seventeen'.

Unusually, Coleridge seems to have taken a back seat, allowing William to do most of the talking; French had to be the medium of communication. They ranged over politics, including the recent French invasion of Ireland and rumours of Nelson's victory at the Nile. Klopstock had followed much the same path as our young poets. He had been a fervent Francophile, written odes in celebration of the French Revolution, and been sent gifts by the republicans; in the wake of French aggression against her neighbours, he had returned the presents with an ode of denunciation, and was now an equally fervent anti-Gallican. They also discussed the whole field of English and German literature. Unusually, again, Coleridge was severer in his judgement than William. 'He thought Glover's blank verse superior to Milton's – & knew nothing of the older German poets, & talked a great deal of nonsense about the superior power of concentering meaning in the German language.' William came to the more succinct conclusion that Klopstock's conversation was 'commonplace'.

William, however, was sufficiently interested to return again several days later, bringing with him a gift, a copy of the *Analytical Review*, which he had bought specially at Remnant's, the English bookseller in Hamburg. On this second occasion, without Coleridge's censorious presence, their conversation delved more deeply into the actual process of poetical composition and the role of the poet. Later that same day they met again, when they dined together at Victor Klopstock's house. This time, they were in a party of nine, which included Dorothy, but the two poets spent all afternoon in 'animated conversation'. They talked of Kant, whom Klopstock found unintelligible, French comedy and tragedy. 'He seemed to rate too highly the power of exciting tears', William recalled, adding his own acerbic response, 'I said that nothing was more easy than to deluge an audience. That it was done every day by the meanest writers.' Dorothy, finding the strain of trying to understand, and be understood, in a foreign language too great, retired to bed early with a bad headache.

Coleridge, meanwhile, was some thirty miles away in Ratzeburg, a pretty little red-brick town on an island in the middle of a lake, near Lübeck. He had gone there on the recommendation of Victor Klopstock, in the hope of finding cheap lodgings for them all. He was immediately undeceived, for Ratzeburg was a popular resort with the aristocracy and the cheapest to be had were twenty-one marks (£1 8s) a week, which was far more than the Wordsworths could afford. Seduced by the enchanting beauty of the place, however, Coleridge lingered on. The town was built on a hill, so there were lovely views over the lake on every side and delightful walks through groves on the shores. Almost equally attractive to Coleridge was the prospect of enjoying wealthy, and extremely Anglophile, German society, for there were concerts and balls every week. On the very day the Wordsworths were dining with the Klopstocks, Coleridge entered into an agreement with the local pastor for board and lodgings for himself and Chester at thirty-six marks (£2 8s) a week for both. There was no consultation with the Wordsworths, but Coleridge was obviously aware that they could not afford to join him in Ratzeburg, as he excluded them from his lodging arrangements. Quite what he expected them to do, knowing that they had followed him to Germany principally for the pleasure of his company, is not clear.

Staying in Hamburg was out of the question. Not only was it expensive, but they were cheated at every turn by the shopkeepers and innkeepers, who took advantage of their ignorance of the language and customs. There were also several incidents which left them feeling concerned and vulnerable. They saw a man beating a decently dressed woman on the breast with a stick but, despite the fact that the man was a stranger and this occurred in a public street, no one attempted to intervene. Another time, they saw a German swearing at and beating an unresisting Jew, again with a stick; a German bystander explained to them in broken English that this violence was quite legal, for 'the Jew had no right to *reign* in the city of Hamburg'. The Wordsworths were sickened, and Dorothy's headaches became semi-permanent.

They had three options. They could go with Coleridge and try to find cheaper lodgings, but he assured them it was impossible. They could cut short their residence in Germany and return to England, but, in that case, all the money they had already spent on travelling, and living in Hamburg, would have been for nothing. The only other option was to revert to their original plan, conceived at Alfoxton, and this is what they did. 'Wordsworth & Sister determined to go on, & seek, lower down, obscurer & cheaper Lodgings without boarding', Coleridge recorded in his notebook. Two days after his return to Hamburg, they booked their places in the coach to Brunswick at twelve marks (16s) a head for the following Wednesday, and William personally carried their two trunks to the departure point rather than pay the exorbitant price demanded by a German porter. The next day Coleridge and Chester took the coach to Ratzeburg, and, after barely twelve days together in Germany, that was the last the Wordsworths saw of them for several months.

The news of this unexpected separation was greeted with amusement and relief by their friends in England. 'I hear that the Two Noble Englishmen have parted no sooner than they set foot on german Earth,' Lamb wrote sardonically to Southey, 'but I have not heard the reason – Possibly to give Moralists an handle to exclaim "Ah! me! what things are perfect?"' Poole was, as usual, more down to earth. 'The Wordsworths have left you –', he wrote to Coleridge, 'so there is an end of our fear about amalgamation, etc.' This is often quoted as signalling Poole's disapproval of the relationship, but it is clear from what he goes on to say that this was not the case.

I think you both did perfectly right. It was right for them to find a cheaper situation; and it was right for you to avoid the expense of travelling, provided you are where *pure German* is spoken. You will, of course, frequently hear from Wordsworth. When you write remember me to him and to his sister, and thank him for his tragedy, which I am to receive from the Wedgwoods. Thank him in proportion as I value the present, which is indeed very highly . . .

Poole's great fear was that Coleridge would not make the best use of his time in Germany. 'Beware of being too much with Chester', he urged. 'Speak nothing but German. Live with Germans. Read in German. Think in German.' And, surprisingly, Coleridge did as he was told, making such rapid progress in his studies that within four months he was ready to put in place the second part of the original plan and enter a German university. The one he chose was Göttingen, some 140 miles due south of Hamburg, where the cost of living was less than half that of Ratzeburg.

On the evening of 3 October the Wordsworths set off from Hamburg in the diligence, a slow, heavy coach which, despite being half-lined with leather inside, was so full of cracks and crevices that Coleridge described it as 'a Temple of all the Winds of Heaven!!' They had a miserable journey. Only four miles outside Hamburg, Dorothy began to vomit at the shaking motion. Hour after hour, they jolted along on 'miserably bad roads', pausing occasionally at 'wretched' public houses which grew 'more strange and more miserable' as they entered Hanoverian territory, and passing through Lüneburg, 'a wretched miserable place . . . lifeless and dead'. After almost forty-eight hours of constant travel, they rolled into Brunswick and sank, with relief, into the unexpected comfort of the English Arms. With a schedule every bit as punishing as a modern coach tour, they were off again at eight o'clock the next morning, on the last twenty-five-mile leg of their journey. Between five and six in the evening on Saturday 6 October 1798 they finally reached Goslar.

Though the Wordsworths had always intended to go to Saxony, their ultimate destination had been vague. Goslar had been mentioned by Victor Klopstock as a possibility, but Dorothy's travel sickness was probably as compelling a reason as any to take at least temporary residence in the city. 'You can have no idea of the badness of the roads', she wrote feelingly to a friend soon after their arrival. Yet Goslar was by no means ideal. 'Goslar is a venerable, (venerable I mean as to its external appearance) decayed city', William informed Josiah Wedgwood after they had spent eighteen weeks there. 'It is situated at the foot of some small mountains, on the edge of the Harts forest. It was once the residence of Emperors, and it is now the residence of Grocers and Linen-drapers who are, I say it with a feeling of sorrow, a wretched race; the flesh, blood, and bone of their minds being nothing but knavery and low falsehood.'

It was impossible to find a family willing to take them in *en pension* as they had hoped. The Wordsworths innocently believed it was because the practice was rare and therefore very expensive in Germany; the more worldly-wise Coleridge realized it was actually because the Germans automatically assumed that 'sister' was a euphemism for 'mistress'. They found lodgings with Frau Depperman, widow

of one of the wretched race of linen-drapers, at 107 Breitstrasse, the main street in
the town. Despite being 'a civil and good kind of a respectable woman *in her way*',
even she indulged in the national pastime and initially cheated her new lodgers
out of petty amounts of cash. Neither she, nor her five children, spent much time
with the Wordsworths, but a young apprentice from her shop came up to sit with
them every evening. This was their only opportunity for daily conversation
in German; shared meals, which William knew from experience were the best
opportunity for learning the language, were 'utterly useless', as the Wordsworths
were obliged to dine together alone. There was no society of the sort Coleridge
was enjoying at Ratzeburg. The only congenial German they met, a 'dear and
kind creature . . . all kindness and benevolence', was unfortunately both deaf and
toothless; 'so that with bad German, bad English, bad French, bad hearing, and bad
utterance you will imagine we have had very pretty dialogues', William wrote
with grim humour, adding an unusually ardent, 'I shall never forget him'.

It was six weeks after taking up residence in Goslar before William wrote to
Coleridge. When he did, it was to say that though provisions and lodgings were
very cheap, there was no society, 'and therefore as he did not come into Germany
to learn the Language by a Dictionary, he must remove: which he means to do at
the end of the Month'. The end of November came and went, as did December,
January and most of February, but the Wordsworths were still in Goslar. What
they had not foreseen was the ferocity of a German winter. 'For more than two
months past we have intended quitting Goslar in the course of each week,' Dorothy
wrote to Christopher on 3 February 1799,

but we have been so frightened by the cold season, the dreadful roads, and the uncovered
carts; that we needed no other motives (adding these considerations to our natural aversion
to moving from a place where we live in comfort and quietness) to induce us to linger here.
We have had a succession of excessively severe weather, once or twice interrupted with a
cold thaw; and the cold of Christmas day has not been equalled even in this climate during
the last century. It was so excessive that when we left the room where we sit we were
obliged to wrap ourselves up in great coats &c in order not to suffer much pain from the
transition, though we only went into the next room or down stairs for a few minutes. No
wonder then that we were afraid of travelling all night in an open cart!

William's bedroom was particularly cold, because it lay over a passage that had
no ceiling. This was a source of grim amusement to Frau Depperman and her
family. 'The people of the house used to say, rather unfeelingly, that they expected
I should be frozen to death some night.' Dorothy could not bear to leave the house,
but William, wrapped up in fur gowns and caps, 'like any grand Signior', took his
daily walk alone on the old city ramparts, or in the public gardens, where a
kingfisher was his sole companion.

The Wordsworths made the best of their enforced isolation. They might not
get intellectual conversation in Goslar, but they corresponded regularly with
Coleridge, discussing his latest grand project, a life of the German dramatist and

critic Gotthold Lessing, to which he intended to add a survey of early German poetry. William could not share Coleridge's passion for Bürger, whose poems he had bought at Remnant's in Hamburg. Studying them now, he made perceptive criticisms which reflect his growing assurance in and understanding of his own role as a poet.

Bürger is one of those authors whose book I like to have in my hand, but when I have laid the book down I do not think about him. I remember a hurry of pleasure, but I have few distinct forms that people my mind, nor any recollection of delicate or minute feelings which he has either communicated to me, or taught me to recognise . . . It seems to me, that in poems descriptive of human nature, however short they may be, character is absolutely necessary, &c.: incidents are among the lowest allurements of poetry. Take from Bürger's poems the *incidents*, which are seldom or ever of his own invention, and still much will remain; there will remain a manner of relating which is almost always spirited and lively, and stamped and peculiarized with genius. Still I do not find those higher beauties which can entitle him to the name of a *great* poet.

William could afford to speak with such authority because he was practising exactly what he preached. The social and physical isolation of Goslar had forced him back on to his own resources: he was living on his thoughts, feelings and memories, and the poetry simply poured out of him. In just four months he wrote some twenty short poems, including the *Lucy* and *Matthew* poems, and over 400 lines of what would become the earliest version of *The Prelude*. There was no question that what William now produced was indeed 'stamped and peculiarized with genius', but undermining its value, at least in the poet's eye, was the fact that it was not *The Recluse*. The whole point of coming to Germany had been to equip himself for writing that poem. He was feeling his way towards it, but he had made no concrete advance. That was why he felt obliged to offer some sort of justification to Coleridge for his own failure to implement the necessary scheme of study. 'As I have had no books I have been obliged to write in self-defence', he told Coleridge apologetically. 'Reading is now become a kind of luxury to me.' In attempting to explain, he revealed just how absorbed in his poetry he had become. 'When I do not read I am absolutely consumed by thinking and feeling and bodily exertions of voice or of limbs, the consequence of those feelings.' Dorothy was more prosaic: 'William works hard, but not very much at the German.' Coleridge, far away in the social whirl of Ratzeburg, found this strange. 'I work at nothing else, from morning to night –', he boasted to Poole; 'my progress is more rapid than I could myself have believed.'

William's progress was of an altogether different kind. The poetry he was writing owed nothing to Germany, apart from the physical accident that Germany had separated him from Coleridge, books and social pleasure, and created the circumstances in which he was compelled to write. His fine ballad *Ruth*, for instance, could just as easily have been written at Alfoxton; indeed, it was actually suggested by the story of a Somersetshire vagrant, and told the now familiar tale of a woman, jilted by her lover and driven mad with grief. The exquisite *Lucy* poems were similarly sparked by an actual incident. Dorothy related the true story of a little girl from Halifax who was lost in a snow-storm; her frantic parents traced her footsteps to the edge of the canal, where her body was eventually recovered. Out of these bare facts, William conjured up a haunting evocation of an unspoilt child of nature:

> She lived among the untrodden ways
> Beside the springs of Dove,
> A maid whom there were none to praise,
> And very few to love;
>
> A violet by a mossy stone
> Half-hidden from the eye!
> Fair as a star when only one
> Is shining in the sky!
> *She dwelt among the untrodden ways (first draft)*

Playing around with this theme in what would become a whole group of poems, William mourned her early loss in spare, elegiac lines that are all the more powerful for being so restrained.

> A Slumber did my spirit seal,
> I had no human fears:
> She seem'd a Thing, that could not feel
> The touch of earthly years.
>
> No motion has she now, no force;
> She neither hears nor sees,
> Mov'd round in Earth's diurnal course
> With rocks, & stones, and trees!
> *A Slumber did my spirit seal (first draft)*

Coleridge, recalling this 'sublime Epitaph' when he belatedly learned of the death of his own infant son Berkeley, posed the question which has haunted biographers and critics ever since. Was there really a Lucy Gray in William's past? Or was she a figment of his imagination? Coleridge came up with the only solution he could think of: 'Most probably, in some gloomier moment he had fancied the moment in which his Sister might die.'

This reference, placed alongside Coleridge's comments about Dorothy being mistaken for William's mistress in Germany, has led to much prurient speculation about the relationship between brother and sister, particularly in the claustrophobic atmosphere of Goslar. Was it merely 'intense', or was it incest? Coleridge himself suggested the latter, but only many years later, when he was estranged from the Wordsworths and felt excluded by the closeness of their family circle. For all

Coleridge's undoubted genius, the one area of his life where he lacked any sort of perception was sexuality. When this was linked with his most emotional friendships, particularly those which included an element of jealousy, his judgement was completely unreliable. What one of his biographers has called his 'cuckoo in the nest mentality' would reassert itself every time: he would attach himself to the sister or sister-in-law of his friend, be it Southey, Morgan or, in this case, William, in an attempt to replicate the partnerships of his friends and their wives. When these attachments failed, or were rejected, he immediately perceived sexual relations between the relatives. He would do this twice with William, hinting at incest with Dorothy and, later, adultery with his sister-in-law Sara, which tells us rather more about Coleridge and his sexual hang-ups than about William and his relationships with the females in his family.

Coleridge's claims have been taken far more seriously than they deserve, not least because the post-Freudian world is incapable of believing that there could be anything innocent about intense sibling affection. The fact is that, before we were taught to see through Freud's distorting lens, such relationships were not only commonplace but also held up for admiration: Charles and Mary Lamb are typical examples, as are the Brontës. The latter, like the Wordsworths, have attracted this type of speculation because, unlike the Lambs, they did not live 'normal' lives, surrounded by London society, but alone in rural isolation. Inevitably that led to cosmopolitan suspicion about their motives for doing so. In William's case, it overlooks not only his compelling reasons for choosing to live in the country, but also the fact that he was already in love with Mary Hutchinson. Though it is indisputable that much, if not most, of William's poetry owed its vital spark to incidents drawn from real life, this does not mean that there had to be literal originals behind every one of his poetic creations. There is no reason to believe that Lucy, any more than Matthew, or the Pedlar, was anything other than an imaginary, composite figure.

In these winter months, frozen in at Goslar, William explored not only love and loss in his *Lucy* and *Matthew* poems, but also his own childhood in the Lakes. Each poem bore his distinctive hallmark: intense self-absorbed activity, followed by the shock of the intrusion of the outside world. Reading them for the first time, Coleridge could not suppress his excitement. 'I should have recognised [them] any where', he exclaimed, 'and had I met these lines running wild in the deserts of Arabia, I should have instantly screamed "Wordsworth!"' Though not originally intended as contributions to the same poem, they would eventually coalesce into the earliest version of *The Prelude*.

Dorothy copied out these scenes for Coleridge, deliberately choosing those which would have most appeal for him. He had described his own thrill at learning to skate at Ratzeburg, for instance, so she transcribed the lines on skating on Esthwaite and invited him to consider the greater pleasure of racing against William on his native Lakes. He had a beautiful German lake before him, so she offered him the description of Ullswater. William's recollections of his childhood had inspired both Wordsworths with a longing to return, they wanted Coleridge to go with them, and Dorothy was quite openly using these lines as lures to entice him up to the north of England. Wherever they finally settled, she told him, he must come with them at the end of the summer 'and we will explore together every nook of that romantic country'.

On 6 February Coleridge and Chester left Ratzeburg for Göttingen, an ancient town with a splendid university, founded in 1734 by George II, in his capacity as Elector of Hanover, and therefore much favoured by Englishmen. Coleridge had fulfilled his ambition of learning enough German to equip him for entering the university as a student; he was soon roistering in the company of his fellow countrymen. Living the high life in Ratzeburg had had its cost, at least £2 a week to be precise, and in reckoning over his expenditure at the beginning of January Coleridge realized he had already spent over £90 in just over three months. The Wordsworths' combined expenses had been less than half his alone.

Coleridge's progression to university simply reinforced William's own failure. He had not even learned sufficient German to earn money by translation. 'We must pursue a different plan', William informed Coleridge.

We are every hour more convinced that we are not rich enough to be introduced into high or even literary german society. We should be perfectly contented if we could find a house where there were several young people some of whom might perhaps be always at leisure to converse with us. We do not wish to read much but should both be highly delighted to be chattering and chatter'd to, through the whole day . . .

My progress in German considered with reference to literary emolument is not even as dust in the balance. If I had had opportunities of conversing I should not have cared much if I had not read a line. My hope was that I should be able to learn German as I learn'd French, in this I have been woefully deceived. I acquired more french in two months, than I should acquire German in five years living as we have lived. In short sorry am I to say it I do not consider myself as knowing *any* thing of the German language. Consider this not as spoken in modesty either false or true but in simple verity.

Determined to recoup something, William and Dorothy came up with a plan. They would walk the thirty or thirty-five miles over the Harz Mountains to Nordhausen, cutting twenty miles off the route taken by the public coach, which was an open cart. At Nordhausen, they had the option of taking covered diligences to any of the principal towns in Upper Saxony. As usual, they made no firm plans for a route, but intended to make a little circuit of towns, staying no more than a fortnight in each place. They had letters of introduction, presumably from the Klopstocks, to Weimar, the literary and intellectual centre of Germany, where the poet Goethe had lived since 1775. Even if they did not acquire greater familiarity with the language, at least they would have seen something more of the country.

On 23 February, they set off on foot from Goslar with a guide to lead them over the mountains. William carried with him the equivalent of £40 in cash, drawn on the Wedgwoods' account with a business associate in Brunswick. Together with the £32 he had already drawn in Hamburg, this was the entire sum he had allocated for their residence in Germany, but he had no contacts in Upper Saxony and was anxious that they should not have to curtail their trip for want of money. Instructing Richard to reimburse the Wedgwoods immediately, William was aware that his income would not be sufficient to cover this withdrawal, leaving him in debt to them for some £15 or £20, which he would not be able to repay till the end of the summer.

They made slow progress to Nordhausen. The first day they enjoyed a delightful walk through the pine forests of the Harz Mountains behind Goslar. Compared to the Lakes, or Wales, these mountains were merely high hills; even the waterfalls were 'kittenracts' rather than cataracts. They spent the night in the centre of the forest at Claustal, 'a large Hanoverian town cursed with the plague of a vicious population'; their inn, however, was excellent and cheap. Next morning, their eyes aching from the brilliance of the green moss beneath the trees after being so long accustomed to snow, they set off again. They had a glimpse of the Brocken, 'the Mont Blanc of the Hartz forest, and the glory of all this part of Germany', but 'it had nothing impressive in its appearance'. At four o'clock, they reached Osterode, another Hanoverian town, where they were stared out of countenance by the 'dirty, impudent, and vulgar' inhabitants and had a contretemps with some bloody-minded town officials who refused to allow them to proceed without a passport. This was not forthcoming till the following morning, when they were able to prove their identity by their letters of introduction, which were following behind in their trunk in the post waggon. Once off the hills, out of the forest and away from Osterode, the roads became increasingly impassable. Snow-melt had swept away the bridges and the ground, when it was not frozen, was waterlogged. They found themselves struggling up to their ankles in water and sometimes in clay. Nightfall caught them out before they reached their next destination and they might have been stranded had a waggon not stopped and given them a lift to Scharzfeld, the nearest town. The next day they made it as far as an inn ten miles from Nordhausen, where they spent the night, but as it was rainy the next morning, they gave up the unequal struggle and took places in the post waggon for the final leg of their journey. At the post house at Nordhausen, they found letters waiting for them from Coleridge. In her joy at seeing his handwriting again, Dorothy 'burst open the seals and could almost have kissed them in the presence of the post-master'. They responded immediately with a joint letter, Dorothy contributing an account of their journey, achieved, she noted, 'for a very trifling expense', and William a wide-ranging literary criticism, taking in the German poets, Bürger and his own favourite, Robert Burns. He had, he informed Coleridge, been hewing down *Peter Bell* for publication, as he was anxious not to be in debt on his return to England; he had also devoted two days ('O Wonder', he could not resist adding in self-deprecation) to the Salisbury Plain poem. It was their intention, he declared, to remain two or three days in Nordhausen and then, weather permitting, 'to saunter about' for a fortnight or three weeks before coming to pay a visit to Coleridge at Göttingen.

The projected two or three weeks eventually turned into seven and in the course of that time they managed to spend so much of their £40 that they were obliged to borrow three guineas from Coleridge to get to Hamburg, and draw a further £25 there for their passage home. This suggests that they had not found anywhere sufficiently attractive to take up lodgings again, and that they were travelling and staying in inns. The fact that no letters survive from this period also indicates that they were on the move, though Coleridge, their likeliest correspondent, preserved only a couple out of many from the Wordsworths during their entire seven months in Germany, so he may have lost or destroyed relevant material. The absence of a journal is more surprising, but Coleridge may again have been the culprit. The following year, when he was desperately trying to fulfil a contract with Longman for a publishable account of a German tour, William offered him 'the use of his Journal tho' not of his name'; Coleridge leapt at the chance to incorporate 'my friend's account of Germany farther south than I had been' but, in his usual dilatory way, failed to produce the promised publication.

Faced with an absence of record, one can only assume that the Wordsworths made their intended tour of towns in Upper Saxony. They are likely to have gone to Weimar, because they had letters of introduction there, but not to have met Goethe himself. William had a lifelong and violent antipathy to Goethe, whom he accused of 'wantonly outraging the sympathies of humanity' by an utter lack of moral sense; had he met him in person, this would surely have been reported. The only certainty is that on or around 20 April William and Dorothy arrived at Göttingen, 'burn[ing] with such impatience to return to their native Country'.

Their object, of course, was to visit Coleridge, who, despite the death of his son and the pleas of his anguished wife, was remarkably reluctant to return home. The question of where they would all eventually settle in England had been much discussed in their correspondence over the last few months, but a decision was now necessary. If nothing else the past few months had determined the Wordsworths that they wanted to go back to the north, and preferably to the Lakes. Coleridge wanted – and probably needed – to remain near Poole. William, he said, was affected to tears at the thought of a prolonged separation, 'but he deemed the vicinity of a Library absolutely *necessary* to his health, nay to his existence'.

William's sudden passion for a handy library was not just due to the book-deprivation of the last few months. In the white heat of poetic composition at Goslar he had discovered that only reading distracted him from thinking and feeling, the intensity of which had given him 'uneasiness at my stomach and side, with a dull pain about my heart'. Access to a library was also, of course, essential if William was ever to prepare himself properly for writing *The Recluse*. Nevertheless, for the rest of his life, including the immediate future, he would live miles from a major library. One cannot avoid the impression that Coleridge seized on this as an excuse to justify the separation to Poole. And he did not believe that the pull of the north would prove more powerful than that of his own society. 'I still think that Wordsworth will be disappointed in his expectations of relief from reading, without Society – & I think it highly probable, that where I live, there he will live, unless he should find in the North any person or persons, who can feel & understand him, can reciprocate & react on him.'

It is a measure of how far apart the two friends had grown that Coleridge simply did not know, or perhaps could not admit, that William was quite capable of living without him. The pleasure of his company could not even detain the Wordsworths now. A day was all they could spare him, then they were off again. Coleridge accompanied them five miles along the road, then they parted. They would not see each other again for six months.

The German adventure was over. The Wordsworths had gone there to be near Coleridge and to learn enough German to be able to earn money by translating. They failed on both counts. On one level, Coleridge was right in believing William 'might as well have been in England as at Goslar, in the situation which he chose, & with his *unseeking* manners'. On the other hand, William had made gigantic steps forward as a poet. For a year at Alfoxton he had been in almost daily contact with Coleridge, who had then been the assured and published poet, at the peak of his powers. In the year after parting at Hamburg, at the end of September 1798, they spent less than three days together. In that time, the whole balance of their relationship shifted. William had indeed assumed the mantle Coleridge had bestowed upon him, but in doing so he had also stepped into Coleridge's shoes. There could be little doubt in future who was the master poet.

9. The Concern

'I dare say you will be surprised when I tell you William and Dolly Wordsworth are arriv'd at Sockburne', Joanna, Mary Hutchinson's youngest sister, wrote to their cousin John Monkhouse on 12 May 1799. Mary was delighted to see them (they had been promising to return her visit to Racedown for two years) but her uncle and youngest brother, on a visit from Penrith, were not too sure, as Joanna described.

I cannot help telling you how genteely your <u>Pappa</u> and Poet George behaved – you must know your father got a fall from his horse, and got very much wet so much as to be fors'd to have his <u>Britches</u> change[d], as soon as he he[a]rd William and Dolly was comming he said he must be off – and that he would not have time to come back to Sockburne but upon examination his small close was so wet he could not possibly put them on therefore he was obliged to stay; However he and George sat all the afternoon in the Kitchen enjoying the company of the Blacksmith and Tailor, at last however they were prevail'd on to go into the Parlor and upon Mary's asking them where they had been Geo: reply'd why you would not have had us so unmannerly as to have left the Tailor and the Smith.

In the general laugh that followed, Mary's family discovered that the Words-worths might be intellectual giants with a reputation for doing the unconventional, but they were also pleasant and companionable people. William immediately acquired the family nickname 'the Great Poet', and he and Dorothy were welcomed into the extensive Hutchinson clan. They were made to feel so much at home, that it would be the end of the year before they left Sockburn.

The Wordsworths had arrived in England on or about 1 May and travelled straight from Yarmouth to County Durham, in fulfilment of their long-intended plans to visit Mary. It was an indication of how much she now meant to both of them that they chose to go to her rather than any of their relations, though they did pay a fleeting visit to Christopher, at Cambridge, where they caught the coach to Darlington. In their absence, Christopher had been awarded the fellowship at Trinity College for which he had worked so long and hard, and in January he had become engaged to Priscilla Lloyd, the sensitive and deeply unhappy seventeen-year-old sister of Coleridge's troublesome protégé Charles. The Lloyds were Quakers and therefore would not, indeed could not, give their consent to a marriage outside the faith, and particularly to a future Anglican clergyman, so Priscilla had been packed off to stay with the Clarksons, Quaker friends in the Lake District.

William's first priority was to sort out his financial affairs. He wrote immediately to Richard, asking for a statement of account, and to Josiah Wedgwood, informing him that he had had to draw the extra £25 in Hamburg but assuring him that he would reimburse this as soon as possible. Two days later, Richard dropped his bombshell. Instead of the £85 William had expected to come into his account during his absence, only £17 10s had been received. In the circumstances, Richard had not sent any money at all to the Wedgwoods. Heartily sick of dealing with William's affairs, he dumped them firmly back in his brother's hands. 'I expect to hear *from you* by the return of the Post', he ordered peremptorily, adding, 'I trust you will lose no time in endeavouring to effect a Compleat settlement.'

William now found himself owing the Wedgwoods over £120, with no prospect of repaying them unless his own debtors paid him. A flurry of correspondence chasing these and a mollifying letter to Richard were immediately dispatched, but all to little purpose. Only the good-hearted Cottle, about to quit the book-selling trade because of his own losses, came up trumps, sending William £5 in June and a draft for £15 at the end of July. He even offered William interest, which was indignantly refused. 'I am not poor enough yet to make me think it right that I should take interest for a debt from a friend, paid eleven months after it is due.'

He was poor enough, however, to have to think seriously about publishing more of his poetry. Repeated anxious queries to Cottle about the sale of *Lyrical Ballads* did not entirely reassure him, and Southey, calling in to Arch's bookshop early in May, was told by Arch himself that he expected to lose on the book 'as they sold very heavily'. A second edition was not a proposition but, in any case, William was not keen to commit himself to print again. His aversion to publication had been greatly increased by the reviews of *Lyrical Ballads*, which he now saw for the first time. The first had appeared in October 1798 in the *Critical Review* and it was by far the harshest. The *Ancyent Marinere* attracted particular contempt. 'We are tolerably conversant with the early English poets; and can discover no resemblance whatever, except in antiquated spelling and a few obsolete words.' It stood condemned as 'a Dutch attempt at German sublimity', *The Idiot Boy* as resembling 'a Flemish picture in the worthlessness of its design and the excellence of its execution'. There was high praise for *Tintern Abbey*: 'we scarcely recollect any thing superior . . .' to parts of it, 'in the whole range of English poetry', but even this compliment had a sting in its tail. 'On reading this production, it is impossible not to lament that he should ever have condescended to write such pieces as the Last of the Flock, the Convict, and most of the ballads.' The prefatory advertisement was skewered with clinical precision at the end. 'The "experiment," we think, has failed, not because the language of conversation is little adapted to "the purposes of poetic pleasure," but because it has been tried upon uninteresting subjects.' To add insult to injury, the author of this review was Robert Southey. Mortified, William could only affect an indifference he did not feel.

> He knew that I published those poems for money and money alone. He knew that money was of importance to me. If he could not conscientiously have spoken differently of the volume, he ought to have declined the task of reviewing it. The bulk of the poems he has described as destitute of merit. Am I recompensed for this by vague praises of my talents?

Later reviewers unfortunately took their cue from Southey. In December the *Analytical Review* praised the simplicity and tenderness of the poems, but dismissed the *Ancyent Marinere* as 'the extravagance of a mad German poet'. To the critic writing in the *Monthly Review* of June 1799, the *Ancyent Marinere* was 'the strangest story of a cock and a bull that we ever saw on paper'. Going through the poems, one by one, he disapprovingly exposed every trace of radical sentiment and attacked the presumption of the advertisement. 'The author shall style his rustic delineations of low-life, poetry if he pleases, on the same principle on which Butler is called a poet, and Teniers a painter: but are the doggerel verses of the one equal to the sublime numbers of a Milton, or are the Dutch boors of the other to be compared with the angels of Raphael or Guido?' Despite this, he confessed, the author 'has had the art of pleasing and interesting in no common way by his natural delineations of human passions, human characters, and human incidents'. It was just that it was not poetry. Nevertheless, he ended on an encouraging note. 'So much genius and originality are discovered in this publication, that we wish to see another from the same hand, written on more elevated subjects and in a more cheerful disposition.'

It was not surprising that William came to the view that the *Ancyent Marinere* had 'upon the whole' been an injury to the volume. 'I mean', he explained to Cottle, 'that the old words and the strangeness of it have deterred readers from going on. If the volume should come to a second Edition I would put in its place some little things which would be more likely to suit the common taste.' This was a far cry from his bold declaration to Klopstock that 'it was the province of a great poet to raise people up to his own level not to descend to theirs', but *Lyrical Ballads* was clearly not in the same category as *The Recluse*. William always claimed to regard the book solely as a money-spinner, though he never quite managed to remain emotionally disinterested about its reception. 'My aversion from publication increases every day,' he wrote Cottle, 'so much so, that no motives whatever, nothing but pecuniary necessity, will, I think, ever prevail upon me to commit myself to the press again'. Unfortunately for him, pecuniary necessity was to be the hallmark of most of his poetic career.

By August, he had succeeded in scraping together only £10 to set off against his

Wedgwood debt. Anxious and depressed, he tried to forget his problems in poetry, writing, not for sale, nor even for *The Recluse*, but for the poem on his own life which he had begun in Germany. In many ways, it was a self-indulgence, but it had him in its grip and he could not escape. Now he was welding into a continuous narrative all the fragments he had written earlier about his childhood, adding and expanding his descriptions of the 'spots of time', and trying to identify what had made him a poet. By the beginning of September, he was again troubled with a pain in his side, a sure sign that he had been working intensively. Dorothy and Mary were also hard at work, transcribing (no mean feat given William's execrable hand and disjointed composition) and making fair copies of the poem.

Coleridge, who had returned to Nether Stowey at the end of July, was concerned to learn that William was ill and apparently unhappy. He sought to rouse him in the only way he knew how. 'I am anxiously eager to have you steadily employed on "The Recluse"', he wrote.

My dear friend, I do entreat you go on with 'The Recluse;' and I wish you would write a poem, in blank verse, addressed to those, who, in consequence of the complete failure of the French Revolution, have thrown up all hopes of the amelioration of mankind, and are sinking into an almost epicurean selfishness, disguising the same under the soft titles of domestic attachment and contempt for visionary *philosophes*. It would do great good, and might form a part of 'The Recluse,' for in my present mood I am wholly against the publication of any small poems.

Instead of encouraging William, however, it reinforced his sense of inadequacy for the task. And, living with the Hutchinsons, with Mary daily before his eyes, who was he to condemn the soft title of domestic attachment? Nevertheless, in a fitting tribute to the man who had instigated the whole project, he decided that he would end his poem on his own life by dedicating it to Coleridge. Under the misapprehension that William had actually completed *The Recluse*, not just a prologue to it, Coleridge was in ecstasies. 'I long to see what you have been doing', he wrote impatiently on 12 October. 'O let it be the tail-piece of the "The Recluse!" for of nothing but "The Recluse" can I hear patiently ... To be addressed, as a beloved man, by a thinker, at the close of such a poem as "The Recluse," ... is the only event, I believe, capable of inciting in me an hour's vanity'.

A fortnight later, Coleridge arrived at Sockburn. The 'hovel' at Nether Stowey had flooded, Hartley had caught scabies so everything had to be fumigated and Sarah, obliged to part with her servant whom they could no longer afford, was tight-lipped and resentful. On the pretext of recovering his travel chests, he had abruptly left home and gone to Bristol; once there, he had discovered that Cottle was about to pay a visit to the Wordsworths and he immediately decided to accompany him, not bothering to inform his wife of his change of plans.

There was a joyful reunion at Sockburn, marred only by an insignificant incident which later festered in Coleridge's mind. Mary had never met Coleridge before and, immediately after tea on their arrival, Cottle asked her, 'Pray what do you

1. An early view of Cockermouth, painted from a point close to the Wordsworths' house, which stands just outside the picture on the right bank of the River Derwent. The smaller River Cocker flows into the Derwent from the right and the town is dominated, as it still is today, by its medieval castle.

2. An Edwardian photograph of the Market Place, Penrith. The Cooksons' drapery shop (with awning) stands at the top, facing into the square.

3. A photograph of Hawkshead Grammar School, taken by Herbert Bell of Ambleside before the 'restoration' of 1891 which completely altered its appearance. Note the typical Lake District round chimney pot and the plaque commemorating the school's foundation in 1585 by Archbishop Sandys of York.

4. *Belle Isle, Windermere, in a Calm*, painted in 1786 by Philip de Loutherbourg. The Windermere ferry, which provided the only lake crossing, ran just in front of the island and was often used by the boys from Hawkshead. In later life, the Wordsworths often visited Belle Isle as guests of their son John's wife's family, the Curwens, who owned the unusual round house, with its dome-shaped roof, built in 1774. This picture hung in the Curwens' main residence, Workington Hall.

5. William Wordsworth, aged twenty-eight, by William Shuter, 1798.

6. Dorothy Wordsworth, an anonymous and undated silhouette portrait.

7. *The High Sheriff of Lancashire Crossing Morecambe Sands*, undated watercolour by Thomas Sunderland (1744–1823). Travellers wishing to cross the treacherous sands of Morecambe bay were taken in convoy at low tide by experienced local guides. It was from just such a cavalcade as this that William learned the dramatic news of Robespierre's death in 1794.

8 and 9. John Harden of Brathay Hall, near Ambleside (1772–1847), was a talented amateur artist whose intimate portrayals of social life and the ordinary occupations of those around him form a unique record of the period. His pictures of the itinerants and poor of the Lakes complement those drawn by William in his poems. (*Above*) Beggar. (*Below*) Peasant women and children.

10. Mary Wordsworth, an anonymous and undated silhouette portrait.

11. Samuel Taylor Coleridge, aged twenty-four, by Robert Hancock, 1796.

12. The *Earl of Abergavenny* sank in only forty fathoms of water in Weymouth bay in February 1805. Ingenious attempts to salvage the treasure were made by divers wearing Mr Tonkin's patent diving machine (illustrated here), but the bulk of the cargo was recovered by the professional Braithwaites, who were employed by the East India Company. The three masts and their rigging were clearly visible from the shore, making the wreck a macabre but popular tourist attraction.

13. Sir George Beaumont, William's friend and patron, drawn by another of his protégés, the artist and architect George Dance (1741–1825), in October 1807.

14. Anonymous undated silhouette of Sara Hutchinson.

15. Grasmere, by Fennel Robson, 1830. The artist has omitted the island so that the village can be seen across the lake. Three Wordsworth homes are identifiable: Allan Bank, on the left-hand slope, the Vicarage to the left of the church, and Town End on the extreme right.

16. (*Opposite*) William's plan for the winter garden at Coleorton, Leicestershire, drawn upside-down in a letter from Dorothy to Lady Beaumont, 23 December 1806.

Coleridge & his Son Hartley arrived on Sunday afternoon My dear Lady Beaumont the pleasure of welcoming him to your house mingled with our joy, & I think I never was more happy in my life than when we had had him an hour by the fireside; for his looks were much more like his own old self & though we only talked of common things & of our Friends, we perceived that he was contented in his mind & had settled his affairs at home to his satisfaction. They had been tolerably well & cheerful ever since; & has brought his Books. Hartley poor Boy! is very happy & looks uncommonly well; but we are afraid of the hooping-cough; for there is now no doubt that the cough which our young ones have is the hooping cough. Thomas is better than when I wrote on Saturday. I long to know your opinion on & his George's of my Brother's plan of the winter garden. Coleridge (as our females are also) is much delighted with it, only he doubts about the fountain; & he thinks it is

Plan
of garden

possible that an intermingling of Birch trees somewhere on account of the richness of the colour of the naked twigs in winter might be very advantageous; & may add also, from myself, that we have often stood for half an hour together at Grasmere on a still morning to look at the raindrops glittering in sunshine upon the birch twigs — the purple colour & the sparkling drops produce a most enchanting effect. — All our family except the three children (for Dorothy is of this party) are gone to Grace dieu forth one ass to help — Miss & my sister over dirty places, the finess of the morning tempted them & I hope they will not be much fatigued as they will

17. No. 20, Great Russell Street, Covent Garden, by Herbert Railton. Charles and Mary Lamb lived in these rooms over an ironmonger's shop on the corner of Great Russell Street from 1817 to 1823. Looking down to Covent Garden theatre at the rear and Drury Lane at the front, Lamb told Dorothy, 'We are in the individual spot I like best in all this great city.'

18. Breakfast party at Samuel Rogers's, 1815, engraved by Charles Mottram. Portrait pictures of this type enjoyed great vogue in the nineteenth century and were compiled by the artist from extant images of famous men rather than from life. Rogers was unique in his ability to attract literary and artistic men to his breakfast parties, but this gathering is purely imaginary. (*Seated, l. to r.*) Sheridan, Moore, Wordsworth, Southey, Coleridge, Rogers, Byron, Kemble. (*Standing, l. to r.*) Flaxman, Walter Scott, Mackintosh, Lansdowne, Sydney Smith, Washington Irvine, Francis Jeffrey, Stothard, Lawrence, J. M. W. Turner, Tom Campbell.

think of Mr Coleridge's [first: deleted] appearance?' Coleridge was sensitive to his unprepossessing exterior, and four years afterwards would recall that this remark had first made him laugh, then melancholy. William had promised Cottle a tour into Cumberland and Westmorland, so, on the afternoon of 27 October, they set off on a leisurely amble, following the River Tees westwards. Cottle, who was lame from a childhood accident, rode a mare, while William and Coleridge walked by his side. The three young men made their way to Barnard Castle, taking in the churchyard at Gainford, where they lingered over the epitaphs, the grey ruins of Egglestone Abbey, and the battlemented bridge over the Tees at Barnard Castle. William and Coleridge were impervious to weather and distance, but Cottle soon found that the damp and riding brought on a convenient attack of rheumatism. Declining to accompany them into the Lakes, he parted from them at Greta Bridge, where he could catch the coach to London for a meeting with Thomas Longman, who was taking over his publishing business.

The mists and rain were too much even for William and Coleridge to contemplate walking over the bleak heights of Stainmore, which separated Yorkshire from Westmorland. They were obliged to seek refuge in the mail coach from Greta Bridge. Instead of travelling all the way to Penrith, however, they stopped seven miles short at Temple Sowerby, probably in the hope of meeting up with William's brother Christopher, who had been staying with their Cookson-Crackanthorpe relatives at Newbiggin Hall. Uncle Christopher had recently died; he had been buried in the pretty church adjoining the Hall on 17 October 1799. His brother, Uncle William Cookson, and his nephews attended the funeral. Either because they did not know or, more likely, because they chose not to go, only William and Dorothy were absent.

Arriving at Temple Sowerby, only two miles from Newbiggin Hall, William clearly hoped that Christopher would still be there. At the post office, however, he glimpsed a letter from his brother to their aunt, so he realized that Christopher had returned to Cambridge. Disappointment turned to unexpected joy, however, for in conversation with the woman there he discovered that John, whom he had not seen for more than four years, had returned to England in August. Being a dutiful nephew, he had hastened to Newbiggin on learning of Uncle Christopher's perilous state of health, and had remained there to comfort their aunt and her children. There was no way William could bring himself to pay a visit to the former Miss Cust, whom, if anything, he disliked more than his uncle, but he immediately dispatched a note to John at the Hall and shortly afterwards the two brothers were reunited. Frustratingly, William's account of this momentous meeting has been cut from the letter describing it: all that is left is the bald comment that John 'looks very well'. Fortunately, Coleridge was on hand and, after a few days spent in the company of this shy, sensitive, self-effacing man, he delivered his verdict in terms of awed reverence. 'Your Br. John is one of you;' he wrote to Dorothy, 'a man who hath solitary usings of his own Intellect, deep in feeling, with a subtle Tact, a swift instinct of Truth & Beauty. He interests me much.'

To the great delight of all concerned, John agreed to accompany William and

Coleridge for a few days on their walking tour to the Lakes. Next day, they set off together on an arduous route criss-crossing the fells that William had carefully and deliberately designed for maximum visual impact. Just as Dorothy had sought to woo Coleridge with William's descriptions from the poem of his own life, now William tried to convince him that he should settle there by introducing him to the reality.

Continually hampered by bad weather, the Wordsworths and Coleridge made their way up the western side of Windermere, where they roundly cursed the off-comers' new fashion for whitewashing their grand residences. Coleridge, William reported with obvious satisfaction to Dorothy, was 'enchanted' with the two vales of Rydal and Grasmere. For almost a week they made their headquarters at Grasmere, staying at Robert Newton's little inn, next to the church, and cradled on every side by soaring crags and sweeping fells. Bolstered by the approval of John and Coleridge, William began to think seriously about settling in Grasmere. 'You will think my plan a mad one,' he wrote to Dorothy, 'but I have thought of building a house there by the Lake side.' John, with typically selfless generosity, promptly offered to give his brother £40 to buy the land, but quite where William was to find the £250 he would need to build a house was anybody's guess. More practically, he had noticed a small, unfurnished house at Grasmere which was empty, 'which perhaps we may take'.

A week after joining William and Coleridge, John felt obliged to return to Newbiggin. 'We accompanied John over the fork of Helvellyn on a day when light & darkness coexisted in contiguous masses, & the earth & sky were but *one*!' Coleridge told Dorothy. 'Nature lived for us in all her grandest accidents'. It was the only fine day they had enjoyed so far and the three men seized the opportunity to head for the top of Helvellyn. Whichever route they took, it was literally a breathtaking climb, tearing at the calf muscles and bending the back double. They paused at the top, drinking in the glorious vista of a world in miniature below: ridges of rock clawed bare by the wind, encircling snow-capped mountains, the lead-grey flashings of half-glimpsed distant lakes and the expanse of sea beyond, before scrambling, half-sliding, down the dizzying slopes of Dollywaggon Pike to Grisedale Tarn. There, at the rock-strewn head of a deep cleft in the mountains, with the twin sentinel summits of Dollywaggon and Fairfield towering above them, they parted. William and Coleridge returned to Grasmere and John went forward alone to Patterdale and Penrith. It somehow seemed symbolic that, after he had gone, the clouds descended again.

Like every visitor to Lakeland in bad weather, William and Coleridge consoled themselves with the compensatory glory of the waterfalls. A trip to the spectacular Dungeon Ghyll over in Langdale had to be called off, but they visited the famous falls at Rydal in the gloom of an early November evening. From Grasmere, they went through the 'inverted arch' of Dunmail Raise to Keswick, from which centre they explored the northern lakes: Buttermere, where, at the humble cottage-inn, they were waited on by the soon-to-be-famous beauty, Mary, the Maid of Buttermere, and admired her grace and simplicity; Crummock Water; Ennerdale, where they learned the tragic story of James Bowman, who died after sleepwalking off a crag, leaving only his staff caught in a crevice on the cliff face; Wastwater, where the black screes plummet into the even blacker depths of the lake; Borrowdale, lake-less, but filled with angry brooks and waterfalls flashing through the mist; Derwentwater, where the Lodore falls thunder down a hidden, tree-lined crevasse; Aira Force, on Ullswater, where a permanent rainbow plays about the spray from the single cataract which plunges down a sheer rock face into the cupped hands it has itself worn out of the stone below. After more than a fortnight of such scenes, Coleridge's senses had taken such a battering that he was punch-drunk.

They ended their tour quietly, spending a peaceful day with the great anti-slavery campaigner Thomas Clarkson and his wife, Catherine, at Pooley Bridge. Neither William nor Coleridge knew the Clarksons personally, but they had mutual friends (of sorts) in Charles Lloyd and his sister, Priscilla, who had been dispatched to the Clarksons when her engagement to Christopher Wordsworth was announced. 'I must tell you that we [had] a Visit from Coleridge and W. Wordsworth who spent a whole day with us', the gossipy Catherine informed Priscilla.

C. was in high Spirits & talk'd a great deal. W. was more reserved but there was neither hauteur nor moroseness in his Reserve. He has a fine commanding figure is rather handsome & looks as if he was born to be a great Prince or a great General. He seems very fond of C. laughing at all his Jokes & taking all opportunities of showing him off & to crown all he has the manners of a Gentleman.

They might not have been so amused had they known that Coleridge, sitting in their garden overlooking the lake, was indulging himself by imagining that the combined effect of 'a round fat backside of a Hill' facing Eusemere, with a road running round its base, and its perfect reflection in the still waters of the lake, created an anatomically correct impression of the female pudenda. 'I never saw so sweet an Image!!' he wrote in his (secret) notebook.

It was, unfortunately, an indication of how his mind was working. He left Pooley Bridge on the coach to Scotch Corner, then he made his way back to Sockburn. With William out of the way and Tom Hutchinson busy on his farm, Coleridge had exactly what he wanted but so seldom enjoyed: the cuckoo in the nest had the undivided attentions of the females of the household. There were three of them. William's sister, Dorothy, his future bride, Mary, and, last but not least, Sara, Mary's twenty-four-year-old younger sister who had the misfortune to become the object of Coleridge's increasingly obsessive infatuation. Interestingly, she was physically more like Dorothy than Mary. In 1799, Sara was little more than five feet high, pert and attractive, though not pretty. She had boundless energy, good-humour and quick wits, and, like all the Hutchinsons, the twin gifts of tact and delicate sympathy, which would make her an indispensable member of more than one household. And what Sara lacked in looks Coleridge bestowed on her in his imagination. Increasingly frustrated and unhappy in his marriage with a real

Sarah, he turned an equally real Miss Hutchinson into his ideal Sara, 'Asra', who was all the more desirable for being unattainable.

In this visit of November 1799 there was only the tiniest hint of what was to come: an entry in Coleridge's notebook of the single enigmatic phrase 'The long Entrancement of a True-love's Kiss'. Four years later, reading this over in the depths of opium-addiction and depression, he would expand considerably on it. On the Sunday before he left, the oldest of the Hutchinson brothers, the jovial John, known as Jack, came over from Stockton. 'Conundrums & Puns & Stories & Laughter – with Jack Hutchinson – Stood up round the Fire', Coleridge now wrote in his notebook, adding guiltily in Latin 'and I held Sara's hand behind her back for a long time, and then, then for the first time, love pricked me with his arrow, poisoned, alas! & incurable'. Repeating his original phrase for the next day, Monday 25 November, he links it with taking leave of Sara and adds a cryptic, 'Ten Kisses short as one, one long as twenty'. Sara would always maintain a discreet silence on every aspect of Coleridge's infatuation, so we have only Coleridge's own, later, account of what happened (or what he hoped, or imagined, had happened). Was there a flirtation or did he simply read greater significance into entirely innocent gestures? Did he hold her hand behind her back as part of a parlour game? He could hardly do so in company without some such excuse. Did he extract a true-love's kiss from her on parting or was it wishful thinking? Whatever the truth of the matter, there can be no doubt that Coleridge looked back to this point as the moment he fell in love, and Sara would have to bear the consequences for years to come.

The day after Coleridge left, William arrived at Sockburn, where he found Mary alone and overjoyed to see him. He had important news. The walking tour of the Lakes had failed in its objective of persuading Coleridge to settle there, but it had determined William. He had taken the lease on the little house at Grasmere at a princely rent of £8 annually.

In the early hours of 17 December William and Dorothy left Sockburn on two horses borrowed from the Hutchinsons. They crossed the Tees at the Neasham ford by moonlight and rode eight miles beyond Richmond into Wensleydale. There they parted with Mary's youngest brother, George, who had accompanied them to take back the horses, and set off on foot to follow the stately Ure westwards towards Kendal. At six in the evening, having paused to view Aysgarth Falls and walked three of the last twelve miles in the dark, they reached Askrigg. Next morning, with a keen frost, showers of snow threatening and twenty-one miles to cover before nightfall, they still found time to turn aside to view two more waterfalls, including the spectacular Hardraw Force, a ninety-eight-foot-high sheet of water cascading in a single drop over a limestone crag. The spray from the force had frozen on the nearby rocks, encasing them in ice, so the Wordsworths made their way cautiously up the narrow cleft until they found themselves standing in a cave directly behind the fall, which shot out over their heads. The roof of the cave was swagged like a drawn-up curtain and festooned with icicles; mosses and water-plants lent it brilliant hues. 'What would I not give if I could convey to you the images and feelings that were then communicated to me,' asked William, before launching into an unusually long and lyrical description of the scene. They tore themselves away reluctantly and, with a following wind, travelled over the mountain road to Sedbergh. Next day, they walked the last eleven miles 'on a terrible up and down road' over the hills to Kendal. There, armed with £30 cashed for them by Jack Hutchinson, they bought and ordered the furniture they would need. On 20 December 1799 they hired a post chaise from Kendal and drove the final sixteen miles to Grasmere, drawing up, at half past four in the afternoon, at the door of the cottage which was to be their home for the next eight years.

The cottage stood on the roadside at Town End, a hamlet half a mile south of Grasmere village, on the main thoroughfare between Kendal and Keswick. Built in the early seventeenth century, it had, until very recently, been an inn, the Dove and Olive Branch; now it was simply a nameless cottage, at the foot of the steep and winding road over White Moss Common. Tucked into the mountainside, with the vast heights of Heron Pike towering above and behind, it looked straight out over open fields to Grasmere lake, with its tree-covered island, and the craggy eminences of Silver How and Loughrigg Terraces. Apart from a cluster of four or five cottages at Sykeside, just below the Wordsworths', and two others just above, their nearest neighbour was How Top, a small farm squatting in a hollow on the road up to White Moss Common.

The cottage itself was tiny and shambolic; originally two up and two down, an extension round the back and side had added a wash kitchen and two tiny unceiled rooms above. Because it was literally carved out of the fellside, the ground-floor rooms at the back lay below ground level. Behind the cottage, extending up a steep bank, was a 'little Nook of mountain-ground', which William would celebrate as his

> Sweet garden-orchard, eminently fair,
> The loveliest spot that man hath ever found
> *A Farewell, ll.5–6*

Long neglected, it was now completely overgrown with brambles, shrubs and moss. The Wordsworths, with their passion for gardening, were more interested in the potential for the surroundings than the cottage itself. 'D is much pleased with the house and *appurtenances*', William told Coleridge four days after they had moved in,

the orchard especially; in imagination she has already built a seat with a summer shed on the highest platform in this our little domestic slip of mountain. The spot commands a view over the roof of our house, of the lake, the church, helm cragg, and two thirds of the vale. We mean also to enclose the two or three yards of ground between us and the road, this for the sake of a few flowers, and because it will make it more our own.

The cottage itself was like a doll's-house, especially compared to the grandeur of Racedown and Alfoxton. Thomas de Quincey, who would later take over the

tenancy from the Wordsworths, described it on his first visit in 1807. Passing through
the garden gate, ten paces (but he was very short) brought him to the main door:

A little semi-vestibule between two doors prefaced the entrance into what might be
considered the principal room of the cottage. It was an oblong square, not above eight and
a half feet high, sixteen feet long, and twelve broad; very prettily wainscotted from the floor
to the ceiling with dark polished oak, slightly embellished with carving. One window there
was – a perfect and unpretending cottage window, with little diamond panes, embowered,
at almost every season of the year, with roses; and, in the summer and autumn, with a
profusion of jessamine and other fragrant shrubs.

The combined effect of the panelling and luxuriant vegetation (planted by the
Wordsworths) round the window was to make the room very dark. All the downstairs rooms had flagged floors, which contributed to the chill and damp which still
pervade the cottage. The main room, which had been the public room of the inn,
became the living room; the second room was turned into a lodging room, or
bedroom, with matting on the floor and a bed large enough to sleep two when
necessary. This was Dorothy's room. A little flight of fourteen stairs led up to the
main sitting room of the house, which William also used as his study or library. 'It
was not fully seven feet six inches high,' de Quincey reported,

and, in other respects, pretty nearly of the same dimensions as the rustic hall below. There
was, however, in a small recess, a library of perhaps 300 volumes, which seemed to consecrate
the room as the poet's study and composing room; and so occasionally it was. But far oftener
he both studied, as I found, and composed on the high road.

The second, smaller, room upstairs served as William's bedroom. Two single
beds were placed in here, so that William could accommodate a male guest when
necessary. The two remaining rooms were little more than walk-in cupboards.
Dorothy papered one with newspapers and put in a small uncurtained bed, so
that it could be used as an additional occasional bedroom; the other became a
lumber-room.

To complete the idyll, the manners of the neighbouring cottagers 'far exceeded'
the Wordsworths' expectations; the natives here were not like the 'lying and
picking and stealing' peasants of Racedown. 'The people we have uniformly found
kind-hearted frank and manly, prompt to serve without servility', William declared
with all the satisfaction of a man who has found his fellow northerners to be
infinitely superior to the rest of the human race. Sixty-year-old Molly Fisher, who
lived at Sykeside with her brother and sister-in-law, agreed to come in for three
hours daily to light the fires, wash the dishes and do the other hard work. On
Saturdays, when she was employed in scouring, or if required to do extra work
because of visitors, she was to receive her meals, in addition to her wage of 2s a
week. Dorothy soon discovered that Molly was not as useful as she might have
been. 'She was very ignorant, very foolish, and very difficult to teach so that I once

almost despaired of her,' she told Jane Marshall, 'but the goodness of her dispositions and the great convenience we knew we should find if my perseverance was at last sucessful induced me to go on.' Molly was eventually taught the basics of cookery and did all the washing for them and their guests, which was no small task. She also became a valued friend, who was 'much attached to us and honest and good as ever was a human being'.

The Wordsworths' arrival at Town End was not propitious. No preparation had been made for them 'except beds, without curtains, in the rooms upstairs, and a dying spark in the grate of the gloomy parlour'. Dorothy had raging toothache; they both developed colds. But they didn't care. 'We were young and healthy and had attained an object long desired, we had returned to our native mountains, there to live; so we cared not for any annoyances that a little exertion on our parts would speedily remove.' For once, their optimism was justified. Soon after their arrival, Molly Fisher popped round to see them. She would never forget Dorothy's first appearance: six years later, on the anniversary of that event, she would solemnly come up to Dorothy, who was standing by the parlour fire, shake her by the hand and say, 'I mun never forget t'laal striped gown and tlaal straw Bonnet, as ye stood here.' While Dorothy buried herself, her cold and her toothache under a mountain of needlework, making bedcurtains and the like, William established the pattern of his future life in Grasmere: he obtained a pair of skates, persuaded Dorothy to accompany him on a starlit walk up Easedale and he began to write *The Brothers*. The poem was a pastoral, based on the story he and Coleridge had been told of the Ennerdale shepherd who had fallen to his death while sleepwalking on the crags. It was a significant poem with which to begin his career as poet-in-residence of the Lakes.

Equally significant was the second poem begun at Town End and completed on 28 December 1799. It was the first of what would become the wonderful series associated with Grasmere, *Poems on the Naming of Places*. Coleridge had commented in his journal of the walking tour, 'In the North every Brook, every Crag, almost every Field has a name – a proof of greater Independence & a society more approaching in their Laws & Habits to Nature'. What William did was take this a step further, renaming features of the landscape after members of his circle who were particularly associated with that place or who shared its characteristics. This very first poem belonged to the latter category and it was dedicated to Mary Hutchinson. She may have been left behind at Sockburn, but she was pre-eminent in William's thoughts. The place was a hidden pool, 'a calm recess', in the woods at Rydal. The message was obvious.

> The spot was made by Nature for herself:
> The travellers know it not, and 'twill remain
> Unknown to them; but it is beautiful
> And if a man should plant his cottage near,
> Should sleep beneath the shelter of its trees,
> And blend its waters with his daily meal,

> He would so love it that in his death-hour
> Its image would survive among his thoughts,
> And therefore, my sweet Mary, this still nook
> With all its beeches we have named from You.
>
> *To M.H., ll.15–24*

The new century opened with what was to be an *annus mirabilis* for William. It began well enough, with the receipt on 1 January of an unlooked-for legacy of £100 to Dorothy from Uncle Christopher. She was the only one to benefit from his will, though John had received a loan of £100 for investment in his last voyage and Christopher had been generously supported through university by him. William, it was no surprise to learn, received nothing at all.

Towards the end of January, the first of the many visitors who would cram themselves into the cottage at Town End arrived. Overcome with habitual shyness, fear of intruding and emotion at the thought of meeting the sister he had not seen for so many years, John twice made his way to the cottage door, put his hand on the latch and then walked away. In the end, his courage failed him altogether, he retreated to Robert Newton's inn beside Grasmere church and sent a message up to say that he had arrived. 'This will give you a notion of the depth of his affections, and the delicacy of his feelings', Dorothy proudly reported to a friend.

John soon became an integral part of the little household at Town End. For eight 'blessed months' he lived with them, 'exulting within his noble heart that his Father's Children had once again a home together' and helping them turn the cottage into a home: 'he was so happy by the fire-side,' Dorothy remembered of this time, 'any little business of the house interested him, he loved our cottage, he helped us to furnish it, and to make the gardens – trees are growing now which he planted.' Every day, as they gradually came to know and love their reserved younger brother, they had abundant proof of Coleridge's judgement that he was, indeed, one of them. 'Of all human beings whom I ever knew, he was the man of the most rational desires, the most sedate habits, and the most perfect self-command', William would later say.

He was modest; and gentle: and shy, even to disease, but this was wearing off. In every thing his judgements were sound and original: his taste in all the arts, music and poetry in particular (for these he of course had had the best opportunities of being familiar with) was exquisite: And his eye for the beauties of Nature was as fine and delicate as ever Poet or Painter was gifted with; in some discriminations, owing to his education and way of life, far superior to any person's I ever knew.

Dorothy was equally captivated, reiterating that sensitivity to nature in her twenty-seven-year-old brother which had so impressed both William and Coleridge.

– he loved solitude and he rejoiced in society – he would wander alone among these hills with his fishing-rod, or led on merely by the pleasure of walking, for many hours – or he would walk with William or me, or both of us, and was continually pointing out with a gladness which is seldom seen but in very young people something which perhaps would have escaped our observation, for he had so fine an eye that no distinction was unnoticed by him, and so tender a feeling that he never noticed any thing in vain. Many a time has he called me out in an evening to look at the moon or stars, or a cloudy sky, or this vale in the quiet moonlight – but the stars and moon were his chief delight, – he made of them his companions when he was at Sea, and was never tired of those thoughts which the silence of the night fed in him –

Unwittingly, John provided William with just what he needed to turn his pastoral, *The Brothers*, into one of his most moving poems. Its evolution was a perfect example of the way William composed his poetry. At its heart lay the true story of the shepherd boy who had fallen asleep on the fells and sleepwalked to his death. The earliest drafts show that it was a simple retelling of the tale by the village priest. What turned it from a pathetic incident into a genuine tragedy was the introduction of another figure, the man to whom the priest tells the story, not knowing that he was actually the dead boy's brother. This man, Leonard, was based on John. At the age of twelve, Leonard had been taken from the country life he loved by 'an Uncle ... A thriving man [who] traffic'd on the sea', and sent to be a mariner, though 'his soul was knit to this his native soil'. Like John, who constantly reiterated his desire to work for William, Leonard had 'chiefly for his Brother's sake, Resolved to try his fortune on the seas'.

> but he had been rear'd
> Among the mountains, and he in his heart
> Was half a Shepherd on the stormy seas.
> Oft in the piping shrouds had Leonard heard
> The tones of waterfalls, and inland sounds
> Of caves and trees . . . .
>
> Below him, in the bosom of the deep,
> Saw mountains, saw the forms of sheep that graz'd
> On verdant hills, with dwellings among trees,
> And Shepherds clad in the same country grey
> Which he himself had worn.
>
> *The Brothers*, ll.41–6, 58–62

After an absence of many years, he returned to his native hills 'with some small wealth Acquir'd by traffic in the Indian Isles', determined to resume his former life with his brother. As he approached his paternal home, his heart failed him, just as John's had done, and, not daring to inquire tidings of one he so dearly loved, he had turned aside to the family plot in the churchyard. There he found a new, unmarked grave and discovered, through the priest, that it was indeed his brother who lay there. Not only that, but Leonard himself was indirectly responsible for his death: his brother had pined for him in his absence and, in dreaming that he was searching for him, had acquired the habit of sleepwalking. No longer able to bear the thought of living in the vale, Leonard returned to sea and became a grey-haired mariner. By this subtle change of emphasis and sympathy from one brother to the other, William transformed what might have been merely a voyeuristic account of an unusual accident into a deeply moving description of its effect on those left behind. It became the incarnation of one of William's most passionately held beliefs about his own poetry, which distinguished it from the popular poetry of the day: 'the feeling therein developed', William explained of his own poems, 'gives importance to the action and situation, and not the action and situation to the feeling'.

John, like Dorothy, believed passionately that William should not be distracted from his vocation by petty worldly concerns. 'He encouraged me to persist, and to keep my eye steady on its object', was William's grateful testimony. 'He would work for me, (that was his language), for me, and his Sister; and I was to endeavour to do something for the world.' Captain John Wordsworth had made his fortune and could afford to retire at the end of his current voyage in the *Earl of Abergavenny*. John had every hope that he would replicate his cousin's success and intended to apply for the vacant captaincy as soon as the *Abergavenny* returned to England. In the meantime he gave himself up to the simple pleasures of living at Grasmere and waited for his ship to come in.

Not long after his arrival, another welcome visitor came to stay at Town End: Mary Hutchinson. With John sleeping in the little unceiled room upstairs, there was nothing else for Mary to do but share Dorothy's bed.

Mary and John struck up an instant friendship. 'John used to walk with her every where, and they were exceedingly attached to each other', Dorothy would later write, adding that Mary had a 'tender love of John and an intimate knowledge of his virtues'. Mary herself had a slightly different slant on this. 'He loved every thing about this dear spot, and John was the first who led me to everything that I love in this neighbourhood.' This difference of emphasis is important, for there can be little doubt that John fell in love with Mary. There is no evidence to suggest that he ever declared himself. He may well have felt inhibited by the attachment between her and William, and he was not in a position to marry. He could offer neither a home nor a secure income, and he would be away at sea more often than not.

After they parted, however, they kept up a regular correspondence. Mary's letters are unfortunately lost. At least some of John's have been preserved. At first glance these may not seem like love letters: they are frequently taken up with everyday matters, or discussion of William's poetry, and there is not a single overt declaration of love. But John wrote to Mary with a tenderness that is unmistakable. He always addressed her, with old-fashioned intimacy, as 'thee' or 'thou', a term that never appears anywhere else in his letters, not even to his much-loved sister. He hated letter-writing, but always found time in the pressure of company business to scrawl a few lines to his 'dearest Mary'. 'As my time is precious I think I cannot

do better than by writing to *thee*', he wrote in February 1801, ending his letter by
begging her to write 'often and *long* letters': 'I make this request because my dear
Mary there is nothing that thou canst write but what will give me pleasure & to be
with *thee* I read thy letters over a *dozen* times in a day'. He worried endlessly about
Mary's lack of company, urging her to go visiting if only in order to make her
appreciate her own home and advantages; he sent her little presents and offered
his services in any way he could be useful; and he wrote often of his longing to be
with her and back at Grasmere. Most telling of all is the way their correspondence
ended. In September 1802, having just returned from his latest voyage, he met
William and Dorothy in London, and his sister handed him a letter from Mary. It
informed him of her forthcoming marriage to his brother. Dorothy had herself just
written to Mary and, unaware of the impact of this news on John, gaily left him
half a page to 'give you some account of his voyage'. John began his letter in
his accustomed way, 'My dearest Mary', then, realizing that this was now an
inappropriate form of address to another man's fiancée, he crossed it through. Even
when he began again, he immediately slipped into the same error, but he had not
the heart to erase it a second time. In a few brief lines, the most emotional he had
ever penned, marred by many errors indicating his inner turmoil, he wrote his last
letter to Mary.

> I have been reading your Letter over & over again My dearest Mary till tears have
> come into my eyes & I known [*sic*] not how to express my[s]elf   thou ar't [a] kind
> & dear creature But wh<t>at ever fate Befal me I shall love to the last and bear
> thy<y> memory with me to the grave
>   Thine affly
>   John Wordsworth

William called John a '*silent* Poet', an epithet nowhere more justified than in this
letter. Unable to find the words himself, John had been forced to borrow those of
his more eloquent brother. The last two lines were a quotation from William's
poem *Michael*. John never wrote directly to Mary again, though he would always
inquire tenderly after her in letters to Grasmere. Nor did he ever see her again.

All this was, of course, in the future. For the moment, in the early spring of 1800,
John and Mary simply enjoyed each other's company and the blissful sense of
being part of a closely knit group, bound together by deep affection and an identity
of tastes, sympathies and interests. One person was excluded, however, and he felt
his exclusion bitterly. Coleridge was accustomed to having a circle of his own
admirers; he was therefore baffled that William refused to fall prostrate at his feet.
What rankled particularly was that the one man whom he admired above all others
should prefer the company of his family and native mountains to that of Coleridge
himself.

'Coleridge has left us,' Charles Lamb informed a friend on 5 April, 'to go into the
North, on a visit to his God, Wordsworth.' If he could not persuade William to

come to him, he would have to go to William. He arrived in Grasmere the next day, probably just missing Mary, and stayed a month. It was symptomatic of the alteration in their respective creativity that Coleridge was currently working on a translation of Schiller's *Wallenstein*, 'a *Bore*' which 'wasted and depressed my spirits', while William was in the full flow of original composition. He was already planning to publish a second volume of *Lyrical Ballads*, together with a series of *Pastorals*, inspired by the Lakes, of which *The Brothers*, although first written, had now become the conclusion. Remarkably, too, he was also contemplating writing a novel.

Coleridge could not help but make comparisons. Perhaps a relocation to the Lakes might work wonders for him too? He sought shelter once more under Poole's wing at Nether Stowey. But he had come to a decision: if a suitable house could not be found there, then he would uproot himself, and his family, and settle at Keswick.

Within a few days of Coleridge's departure, William and John set off on a walking tour that would take them from one side of the country to the other. They had decided to visit Mary Hutchinson at Gallow Hill, a farm at Brompton-by-Sawdon, seven miles inland from Scarborough and the east coast of Yorkshire. Recent rent rises had made it impossible for her brother Tom to continue farming at Sockburn. At the beginning of the year he had sought, and found, the farm at Gallow Hill, where, for £120 a year he had more land (and better for growing corn) than the new tenant would have at Sockburn for an annual rent of £400.

What made it so different from Sockburn was the position: Gallow Hill stood on a gentle incline facing south over the flat, featureless Vale of Pickering, towards the distant low hills of the Wolds on the horizon. Next to the house was a curious and deceptively steep wooded knoll, like a barrow in its distinctive shape. A few hundred yards away lay the main Pickering to Scarborough road, which, then as now, was always busy with tourists: during the season the '*spaers*', as Sara called them, were 'thronging past daily ... we see Coaches *whirring* by for ever'.

William and John set off for Gallow Hill on 14 May in high spirits and with a pocket full of cold pork each to sustain them on their journey. Dorothy accompanied them as far as Lowwood Bay, just beyond Ambleside. 'My heart was so full that I could hardly speak to W when I gave him a farewell kiss –', she wrote in the journal she now commenced.

When William and John arrived at Gallow Hill, they found only three members of the Hutchinson family there: Mary, and her brothers Tom and George. Inspired by the Wordsworths' example at Town End, Mary was hard at work creating a garden, a corner of which she would name after John. Touched though he was by the sentiment behind this gesture, John was distinctly unimpressed by Gallow Hill. He bluntly called it 'a vile abominable place' and conceived an immediate dislike to the (as yet unseen) Hutchinson landlord, Mr Langley, and his wife, who, as daughter of Lord Middleton, gave herself airs and graces. 'How does her honour & its honour behave to you[?]', John inquired of Mary, 'are they like the lords and ladies I have seen very proud[?] pray have you got any body that you can *speak* to[?]' William too worried about Mary's lack of company, asking his old friend Francis Wrangham, who lived only twelve miles away at Hunmanby, to perform 'a great kindness . . . to me' and call on her. Despite their reservations about Gallow Hill itself, William and John found the company of the Hutchinsons so beguiling that they left Dorothy solitary for longer than they had intended, extending their visit to three weeks.

William returned to find good news awaiting him at Grasmere. Montagu's friend Charles Douglas had finally paid off his four-and-a-half-year-old debt; or rather, he had paid off £100 in capital, plus £4 17s in interest. The remaining £100 had been transferred to Montagu, from whom there was little or no chance of securing an early repayment. The repayment of Douglas's loan enabled William to pay back the money he himself owed for his advances from the Wedgwoods in Germany. This debt had weighed heavily on his conscience and his relief was palpable as he wrote to Josiah Wedgwood on 13 July, apologizing for the delay, explaining the circumstances and authorizing him to call on Richard for immediate payment of the £110 13s he was owed.

There was further good news from an unexpected quarter. Despite the reviews, the first edition of *Lyrical Ballads* had sold out and the booksellers were asking for a reprint. This was a far more valuable asset than it might have been, for Cottle had made William a gift of the copyright when he sold off his publishing business to Longman. Coleridge had approached Longman and negotiated an agreement which would give William £80 for two further editions of the original book, and two of the projected new volume. Writing to Richard, William said that he intended to accept this offer: 'if the books sell quickly I shall soon have the right of going to market with them again when their merit will be known, and if they do not sell tolerably, Longman will have given enough for them'. Anxious to avoid the confusion which had arisen over the publication of *Lyrical Ballads* on the eve of his departure for Germany, William spelled out his terms twice over in a letter to Longman.

On 29 June Coleridge arrived, this time to stay. As hostages to his decision, he brought with him his long-suffering wife, who was well advanced in pregnancy, and his child, Hartley, and all three squeezed themselves into the cottage at Town End. Whether it was the stress of committing himself to a life in the north, a retreat into the opium-taking which had now become a habit or simply, as he claimed, a cold which the damp climate exacerbated, Coleridge retired to bed at Town End, overcome with rheumatic pains, weakness, listlessness and, for good measure, swollen eyelids.

Despite Coleridge's illness, plans for the new edition of *Lyrical Ballads* proceeded apace. By the middle of July, Coleridge was writing to Cottle and his partner, Nathaniel Biggs, in Bristol, who were to print (but not publish) the poems, setting out the order for the edition. There were to be some significant changes. The Advertisement was to be dropped: in its place, at Coleridge's urgent request, William would prepare an expanded version of his poetic theory which would become the notorious preface. William would later claim that he 'never cared a straw about the theory' and that the preface was written 'out of sheer good nature'. 'I recollect the very spot, a deserted Quarry in the Vale of Grasmere where he pressed the thing upon me, & but for that it would never have been thought of.'

Like Topsy, however, once thought of, it just growed and growed. Almost as important as the introduction of a preface was the relegation of *The Rime of the Ancyent Marinere* from pride of place opening the volume, to second to last. What is more, Coleridge had agreed to amend its obscure, pseudo-medieval vocabulary. The poem would now appear as 'The Ancient Mariner, a Poet's Reverie'. Coleridge's *Foster-Mother's Tale* and *The Nightingale*, which had stood second and fourth, were pushed back to seventh and seventeenth respectively. In their place, as William had decided after reading the reviews, were six of his own shorter poems. William's poem *The Convict*, which had incurred critical wrath for its overtly political message, was to be omitted altogether and replaced by Coleridge's *Love*, the only new contribution to the volume. One other poem by Coleridge, *The Dungeon*, was allowed to remain at fourteenth position. The rest of the volume was entirely William's composition, and, as before, it would close triumphantly with *Tintern Abbey*. This time, however, the change in order of appearance placed the emphasis squarely on William.

In the flurry of activity caused by the Coleridges' arrival at Grasmere, nursing Coleridge himself and making preparations for the new edition of *Lyrical Ballads*, Dorothy was too busy to keep up her journal. William was unwell, suffering from the pain in the side which afflicted him when hard at work composing or revising his poems; Coleridge, unkindly but amusingly, diagnosed it as a pain 'in the right hypochondrium'. Nevertheless, it made a good excuse for turning down an offer from Daniel Stuart to write for the *Morning Post* on a regular basis. William was particularly anxious not to offend a man who had rendered him a considerable service by publishing seven poems from the original *Lyrical Ballads* between 2 April and 19 September. Their highly complimentary head-notes (which may have been written by Coleridge), as much as their republication to a wider readership, must have affected the level of sales and were probably responsible for it selling out. No doubt they also influenced Longman's decision to accept the new edition. William was the first to acknowledge his debt. 'Wordsworth requests me to be very express in the communication of his sincere thanks to you,' Coleridge wrote to Stuart, 'for the interest which you have been so kind as to take in his poems. We are convinced you have been of great service to the sale.'

On 23 July Coleridge left Town End for his new abode, Greta Hall, at Keswick; the next day he was followed by Sarah, Hartley, and the boxes containing their worldly goods. Coleridge was in hopeful mood. 'We drank tea the night before I left Grasmere on the Island in that lovely lake,' he wrote to Humphry Davy,

our kettle swung over the fire hanging from the branch of a Fir Tree, and I lay & saw the woods, & mountains, & lake all trembling, & as it were *idealized* thro' the subtle smoke which rose up from the clear red embers of the fir-apples which we had collected. Afterwards, we made a glorious Bonfire on the Margin, by some alder bushes, whose twigs heaved & sobbed in the uprushing column of smoke – & the Image of the Bonfire, & of us that danced round it – ruddy laughing faces in the twilight – the Image of this in a Lake smooth as that sea, to whose waves the Son of God had said, PEACE!

Leaving Grasmere, Coleridge consoled himself with the delusion that William would probably leave Town End the following summer and settle near him in Keswick. In his heart of hearts, he knew it would not happen. 'His cottage is indeed in every respect so delightful a residence, the walks so dry after the longest rains, the heath and a silky kind of fern so luxurious a bedding on every hilltop, and the whole vicinity so tossed about on those little hills at the feet of the majestic mountains, that he moves in an eddy; he cannot get out of it.'

Now that William, Dorothy and John had Town End to themselves again, work began in earnest on preparation for the second volume which was to be added to *Lyrical Ballads*. William revised, Dorothy transcribed and John kept the table going with a constant supply of fresh fish. By the end of July, Biggs and Cottle had printed the first volume and were ready for setting the proofs of the second. At Coleridge's suggestion, William decided to entrust the task of seeing the poems through the press to a man he had never met, Humphry Davy, Dr Beddoes's assistant at the Bristol Pneumatic Institution. This brilliant young chemist, who had discovered the laughter-inducing properties of inhaling nitrous oxide only the year before, was a Renaissance figure, equally at home with poetry as he was with chemistry; William even entrusted him with correcting his own punctuation, 'a business at which I am ashamed to say I am no adept'. Every three days, Davy received a set of sheets from Grasmere, checked them, then passed them on to the printer; as the proofs were printed they were returned to him for rechecking.

As all William's subsequent assistants were to discover, it was a thankless task. Delegation was absolutely necessary, but even when he had appointed a deputy, he undermined his position by writing directly to the publishers countermanding previous instructions.

Slowly, the second volume of *Lyrical Ballads* took shape. The Wordsworths walked almost daily, bathed, fished and sailed on the lake, tended their garden and rarely passed more than a few days without Coleridge. If he did not come to stay, then they went to Keswick. From the end of August, they had a constant stream of visitors: Anthony Harrison, a contemporary at Hawkshead Grammar School, now a Penrith solicitor; James Losh and his wife, who, in her brothers' absence, Dorothy proudly showed round the cottage, 'which is remarkably neat tho very plain, as far as I cou'd judge, it being dark'; Thomas and Catherine Clarkson of Eusemere, with whom William and Coleridge had stayed on their walking tour of the Lakes; John Marshall, husband of Dorothy's childhood friend Jane Pollard; perhaps most surprisingly of all, Robert Jones, William's college friend and companion of his walking tours in France and Wales, who stayed almost a week; the Wordsworths' uncle and cousin, Tom Myers, father and son; Christopher's future brother-in-law, Charles Lloyd and his wife, Sophia, who, much to the Wordsworths' dismay, had settled rather too close for comfort at Old Brathay, the other side of Ambleside. It was demonstrable proof that Town End, unlike Racedown or Alfoxton, was well and truly on the tourist circuit: love it or loathe it, the season would bring an annual tide of visitors to the Wordsworths' door for the next fifty years and more.

And there was also a parting of the ways. For more than a month, John had been in daily expectation of the return of the *Earl of Abergavenny* to English waters. On 28 September they learned that the ship had arrived. John had no option but to leave his Grasmere idyll and take himself off to London, there to begin the canvassing necessary to secure the captaincy of the ship for himself and, with it, the refoundation of the family fortunes. The following day was fine, but showery, with sunshine and clouds. William and Dorothy accompanied John up the stony beds of the precipitous becks leading up Fairfield and Seat Sandal to the eerie silence of Grisedale Tarn, clutched in the bony fingers of the unforgiving mountains. Loath to go their separate ways, they lingered by the still waters of the tarn, where the raucous cry of the raven and the plaintive bleating of a few scattered sheep echoed round the empty hills. Full of optimism, they talked over their plans for future happiness. John had even selected the field in which he intended to build his own house on the shores of Grasmere. As a pledge to the future, they agreed to lay the foundation stone of a little fishing hut by the side of Grisedale Tarn. Then they parted, John taking the plunging pathway down towards Patterdale, with Ullswater a dull gleam in the distance, and William and Dorothy retracing their route over the hills to Town End. 'Poor fellow my heart was right sad –', Dorothy recorded in her journal. 'I could not help thinking we should see him again because he was only going to Penrith.' In fact, though none of them knew it at the time, he would never return to Grasmere again.

10. *Home at Grasmere*

In the autumn of 1800 William struggled to put the final touches to his second volume. As the shape of the book emerged, it became obvious that it was something quite different from the first edition of *Lyrical Ballads*, and that the difference was the result of living at Grasmere. The poetic principle remained the same: simple tales about simple people, simply told. Instead of mad mothers, idiot boys and half-crazed peasants, the characters in these poems are the genuinely ordinary people who inhabited the Lake country, humble schoolmasters, shepherd boys and statesmen, living obscure lives, accepting and enduring their sufferings with quiet dignity. The result is both more lifelike and, consequently, more poignant. *The Childless Father*, for instance, depicts old Timothy, whose last child has died six months previously. Instead of giving himself up to extravagant grief, he keeps up the outward appearance of life. As he leaves his hut to join the rest of the villagers in coursing a hare and closes the door,

> Perhaps to himself at that moment he said,
> 'The key I must take, for my Ellen is dead,'
> But of this in my ears not a word did he speak,
> And he went to the chace with a tear on his cheek.

Though many of the poems are formal, or informal, epitaphs and inscriptions, emphasizing the elegiac quality of the verse, they are suffused with a new mood of serenity. There is a sense of completeness, an acquiescence in the natural cycle of life, which culminates in the inevitability of death.

And, more than ever before, the people are a part of the landscape – one which is defiantly Lakeland. The names of mountains are invoked like a roll-call of ancient deities, Loughrigg, Fairfield, Helvellyn, Skiddaw, Glaramara and Kirkstone, and poems such as *The Idle Shepherd Boys* and *Michael* are as much an evocation of their settings, at Dungeon-Ghyll Force and at the top of Greenhead Ghyll, as of the people that inhabit them. The Wordsworths themselves had staked their own claim to belong by the series of *Poems on the Naming of Places*. William had added several more since his first, written immediately after his arrival in Grasmere and addressed to Mary Hutchinson. Her sister, the flirtatious and merry Joanna, had one dedicated to her: curiously, despite its delightful and graphic description of her laughter echoing round the mountains, it was entirely a figment of William's imagination, for Joanna had not yet been to Grasmere. Dorothy, inevitably, had her place (if not her own name) in the poem describing Emma's dell, on the banks of the clear, pebbly brook running through Easedale. *Point Rash Judgement* commemorated a walk beside Grasmere Lake, taken by William and Dorothy with Coleridge, on his first visit to Town End. Seeing a man fishing in the lake, instead of joining his fellows in harvesting the fields, they leapt to the conclusion that he was an idle fellow. As they came closer, he turned and they realized he was mortally sick. Far from being idle, he was endeavouring to employ himself in the only useful activity he could, and his three observers were left to repent their hasty judgement.

Appropriately, the best of all the poems in this series is the one inspired by the poet himself. If one needs an excuse for quoting such a characteristic and exquisite poem in full, it is for what it reveals about William's (and Dorothy's) perception of his character and vocation.

> There is an Eminence, – of these our hills
> The last that parleys with the setting sun.
> We can behold it from our orchard-seat,
> And, when at evening we pursue our walk
> Along the public way, this Cliff, so high
> Above us, and so distant in its height,
> Is visible, and often seems to send
> Its own deep quiet to restore our hearts.
> The meteors make of it a favourite haunt:
> The star of Jove, so beautiful and large
> In the mid heavens, is never half so fair
> As when he shines above it. 'Tis in truth
> The loneliest place we have among the clouds.
> And She who dwells with me, whom I have lov'd
> With such communion, that no place on earth
> Can ever be a solitude to me,
> Hath said, this lonesome Peak shall bear my name.

It had always been William's intention to include some of Coleridge's work in this volume. Indeed, in the opening of his draft for the preface, he had actually declared that without *Christabel*, Coleridge's 'long and beautiful Poem', 'I should not yet have ventured to present a second volume to the public'. Unfortunately for both men, *Christabel* was incomplete and would never be finished. Coleridge had begun it in 1797 and, intending to include it in the new edition of *Lyrical Ballads*, had renewed his labours on it at Keswick. 'I tried to perform my promise', he told Josiah Wedgwood in November, 'but the deep unutterable Disgust, which I had suffered in the translation of that accursed Wallenstein, seemed to have stricken me with barrenness – for I tried & tried, & nothing would come of it.'

Though he claimed to have written up to 1,400 lines by early October, Coleridge lacked the will-power or interest to complete the poem. William even suspected that he did not know *how* to end it. More than a fortnight after they had expected *Lyrical Ballads* to be published, Coleridge had still not produced his poem. William tried to play for time by sending in more of his own poems to be inserted before *Christabel*, but this was only a short-term solution. A revised deadline of the end of September came and went. William had completed the notes and the lengthy preface, Dorothy had transcribed them and they had been sent off, together with a letter to the printers asking them to change the title of the book. A new volume of poetry, *Lyrical Tales*, by Mary Robinson, had just been published and William had an absolute horror of his poems being confused with the fashionable gushings of 'Perdita' Robinson, whose main claims to fame were that she had been both a successful actress and the Prince of Wales's mistress. He begged Biggs & Cottle to change his title-page to '*Poems in two Volumes* By W. Wordsworth'. Such a drastic change was not agreeable to Longman, and, in the end, they compromised. The title would now be '*Lyrical Ballads with other Poems in two volumes* By W. Wordsworth'.

For the first time, therefore, William's own name would appear on the title-page of *Lyrical Ballads*. It was a significant change, reflecting the fact that this was emphatically William's work, and that he was proud to claim it as such. But where did it leave Coleridge? Even if he had published a completed *Christabel* in the collection, he would still have contributed only six poems to William's fifty-nine. His contribution was also fully acknowledged and identified in the preface – which was more than Coleridge himself had done when publishing *The Fall of Robespierre* under his own name, despite the fact that Southey had written two-thirds of it. Both Coleridge's editions of his own *Poems* had included contributions from other poets whose names did not appear on the title-page; in 1796 Lamb had supplied four poems but, in 1797, he and Lloyd between them contributed almost 100 pages of poetry. At first Coleridge was unperturbed by the exclusion of his name. It was only later, when, frustrated by his own failures and increasingly jealous of William's sustained poetic power, he came to see this as a sinister denial of his abilities and of his own contribution to *Lyrical Ballads*.

At the time, Coleridge also accepted, with perfect equanimity, the decision to leave *Christabel* out of the second volume. For those who believe Coleridge's later view of this event, that William had rejected him as a man and a poet, this is proof of the Wordsworths' selfishness and ruthless determination to wrest *Lyrical Ballads* from the man who had given his all to promote William's poetry. In fact, as the contemporary evidence proves, it was nothing of the sort. On 4 October Coleridge walked into the cottage at Town End and read the Wordsworths the second part of *Christabel*, with which they were 'exceedingly delighted'. He read it again the following morning, to their 'increasing pleasure'. Next day, 6 October, Coleridge put off his intended departure, presumably because they were deep in discussion about *Christabel*. After tea, William read his latest contribution to *The Recluse*, which he called *The Pedlar*. Dorothy noted with characteristic baldness, 'Determined not to print Christabel with the LB'. This sequence of events is important, because, as Coleridge himself cheerfully reported three days later, 'We mean to publish the Christabel . . . with a long Blank Verse Poem of Wordsworth's entitled the Pedlar'. William had 'so much admired' Coleridge's '1300 lines', 'he thought it indelicate to print two Volumes with *his name* in which so much of another man's was included'. This was surely right, though one wonders if Coleridge himself would have been so scrupulous had their relative positions been reversed. Additionally, as Coleridge himself was the first to acknowledge, his Gothic tale of 'witchery by daylight' was totally out of step with the rest of the poems in the second volume and the poetic principles set out in the preface. Far from excluding Coleridge, William did his utmost to keep him involved.

A few days after he returned to Keswick, William and Dorothy took what they called a walk, but ordinary mortals would call a scramble, up Greenhead Ghyll, a precipitous path alongside a mountain stream which tumbled down a cleft between the swelling breasts of Stone Arthur and Heron Pike. Their object was to visit a ruined sheepfold which, they had learned from their neighbours the Fishers, had been built by a previous occupant of their own cottage. Whether it was the evocative shape of the sheepfold, 'in the form of a heart unequally divided', John Fisher's lamentations about the fate of the statesman (the local name for the Lakeland freeholder farmer), who was fast becoming an endangered species, or, more likely, a combination of both, William was instantly inspired. The next day he was out in the woods, walking and composing his sonorous and deeply moving pastoral poem *Michael*, which told the tale of an aged statesman forced to send his only son out into the world to earn a living. Before leaving for the city, Luke, a child of his parents' old age, went up Greenhead Ghyll with his father to perform the symbolic gesture of laying the cornerstone of a new sheepfold, as a covenant for the future and

> An emblem of the life thy Fathers liv'd,
> Who, being innocent, did for that cause
> Bestir them in good deeds.

After making a promising start, Luke was gradually seduced into profligate ways and had to flee overseas to escape his creditors. For seven long years, his father daily toiled up the mountainside to continue building the sheepfold, but it was unfinished when he died. When his wife died three years later, the little estate was sold and went into a stranger's hand.

> The Cottage which was nam'd The Evening Star
> Is gone, the ploughshare has been through the ground
> On which it stood; great changes have been wrought
> In all the neighbourhood, yet the Oak is left
> That grew beside their Door; and the remains
> Of the unfinished Sheep-fold may be seen
> Beside the boisterous brook of Green-head Gill.
>
> *Michael, ll.420–22, 485–91*

William really struggled composing this poem, spending day after day toiling away, often unsuccessfully, and making himself ill in the process. *Michael* was not finished until 9 December, but by then William knew he had succeeded triumphantly. In Michael he had created a man 'of strong mind and lively sensibility, agitated by two of the most powerful affections of the human heart; the parental affection, and the love of property, *landed* property, including the feelings of inheritance, home, and personal and family independence'. It was a summation of his own first year at Grasmere, and, like *Tintern Abbey*, it made the perfect ending to the volume.

Coleridge having failed to produce any *Poems on the Naming of Places*, despite the reprieve caused by William's lengthy struggle with *Michael*, the second volume, consisting of forty-one poems, would be entirely the work of William. As, also, was the preface, a lengthy disquisition on the purpose and nature of poetry in general. For such an important and influential document, it is extraordinarily dense and obscure in its language and argument. Time and again, struggling to understand some complex and grandiloquently expressed statement, one comes to the uncomfortable conclusion that it is either meaningless or blindingly obvious. The equally unpleasant alternative is that one is the only person in the world too stupid to understand its true meaning. It was this creation of an aura of élitism and exclusion that played an enormous role in spreading the popularity of William's poetry. The poems themselves are, for the most part, simple enough to understand. William's purpose in writing them is equally plain: his poems were intended to excite compassion and encourage benevolence. This is not a difficult concept to grasp, but it is nowhere stated in the preface.

Instead, we have an earnest and passionate defence of the style and subject matter of his poetry. Summarized, the arguments ran like this. William's poems needed some sort of introduction because they were 'materially different from those, upon which general approbation is at present bestowed'. The main 'mark of difference' was not, as one might expect, the lowly social class of most of the characters, but that each poem 'has a worthy *purpose*'. His object was to make 'the incidents of common life interesting by tracing in them . . . the primary laws of our nature'. 'Low and rustic life was generally chosen', he explained, '. . . because in that situation our elementary feelings exist in a state of greater simplicity and consequently may be more accurately contemplated and more forcibly communicated'. Simple countrymen spoke a 'more permanent and a far more philosophical language than that which is frequently substituted for it by Poets'; 'being less under the action of social vanity they convey their feelings and notions in simple and unelaborated expressions'.

In one of his least obscure (and therefore most often quoted) passages he blamed the current 'degrading thirst' for 'frantic novels, sickly and stupid German Tragedies, and deluges of idle and extravagant stories in verse' on 'the great national events which are daily taking place, and the encreasing accumulation of men in cities, where the uniformity of their occupations produces a craving for extraordinary incident which the rapid communication of intelligence hourly gratifies'. Hailed by modern academics as a radical new departure in poetical theory, this was in fact no more than an echo of those ancient Roman poets and historians whom William had loved since boyhood. Virtue was to be found in the simplicity of country life; unnatural vices, with fickle tastes and insatiable appetites, were the perversions caused by the unnatural way of life in cities. In 1800, when England was still a rural country, William's attack on city life must have seemed odd, exaggerated, even untrue, but as the Industrial Revolution gathered pace, it came to have a prophetic feel. It was no coincidence that the popularity of William's poetry increased in response to the swift progress of nineteenth-century urbanization and mechanization: his homely tales of rural virtue then seemed to hark back to a golden age and acquired the rosy blush of nostalgia.

More original was William's defence of his use of blank verse and everyday vocabulary. Rejecting the argument that poetry should have its own unique and elevated language, he argued convincingly, with an example quoted from Gray, that there 'neither is nor can be any essential difference' between the language of prose and poetry. He also remained impervious to the criticism that he had written on unworthy subjects in vulgar language which sometimes verged on the ludicrous. If he were convinced that he was mistaken, he would alter and correct.

But it is dangerous to make these alterations on the simple authority of a few individuals, or even of certain classes of men; for where the understanding of an Author is not convinced, or his feelings altered, this cannot be done without great injury to himself: for his own feelings are his stay and support, and if he sets them aside in one instance, he may be induced to repeat this act till his mind loses all confidence in itself and becomes utterly debilitated.

It was a fair point, but in stating it with typical bluntness, William laid himself open to the oft-repeated charge of arrogance. Similarly his claim that, if his poetic principles were followed, 'a species of poetry would be produced, which is genuine poetry; in its nature well adapted to interest mankind permanently, and likewise important in the multiplicity and quality of its moral relations'.

The preface built up a mystique around the poetry and endowed it with a didactic purpose that would speak only to a cultural élite capable of receiving and benefiting from his lofty message. Put simply, if you liked his poetry, you were members of an exclusive club; if you did not, you were unworthy of membership.

It is no coincidence that one of the two key phrases which appear repeatedly in the letters William received from his admirers in later years is gratitude for having their understanding enlightened, their taste exalted and their affections ameliorated by his poetry. What is significant about these phrases is that they are lifted directly from the preface; by quoting them, his admirers could congratulate themselves on being among the select and chosen few.

Coleridge had suggested that it might be useful to the sale of the book to send copies to 'different people of eminence'. His idea of eminence was eclectic, if not bizarre. The actress Dora Jordan, who had expressed an intention of singing stanzas from *The Mad Mother* if she acted Cora again in Sheridan's *Pizarro*; the popular poetess Mrs Barbauld; the society beauty and hostess Georgiana, Duchess of Devonshire; the politicians and men of letters Sir James Bland Burges and William Wilberforce. While the Wordsworths were with him, on a visit to Greta Hall, Coleridge dictated the accompanying letters in William's name to Dorothy.

Significantly, the only letter William composed and wrote himself was to Charles James Fox, the great Whig leader, who had been outspoken in his defence of the French Revolution and of civil and religious liberties in Britain, to the detriment of his own personal career. Despite being 'utterly unknown' to Fox, William explained at length why he had chosen him to be a recipient of his poems. Throughout his political career, Fox had consistently displayed a 'predominance of sensibility of heart', an ability to see and treat men as individuals rather than simply a body or class of people, and had fought to protect 'the most sacred of all property . . . the property of the Poor'. Such a man could not fail to be moved by the plight of the statesmen of the north of England, those 'men of respectable education who daily labour on their own little properties' whose 'little tract of land serves as a kind of permanent rallying point for their domestic feelings'. 'This class of men is rapidly disappearing', William bluntly told Fox. In words which recall the passion of his *Letter to the Bishop of L[l]andaff*, he argued that this was a national, and preventable, tragedy. Expanding on the hints he had given in the preface, he set out his political beliefs and purpose with a force and clarity totally lacking in that document.

It appears to me that the most calamitous effect, which has followed the measures which have lately been pursued in this country, is a rapid decay of the domestic affections among the lower orders of society. This effect the present Rulers of this country are not conscious of, or they disregard it. For many years past, the tendency of society amongst almost all the nations of Europe has been to produce it. But recently by the spreading of manufactures [factories] through every part of the country, by the heavy taxes upon postage, by work-houses, Houses of Industry, and the invention of Soup-shops &c. &c. superadded to the encreasing disproportion between the price of labour and that of the necessaries of life, the bonds of domestic feeling among the poor, as far as the influence of these things has extended, have been weakened, and in innumerable instances entirely destroyed. The evil would be the less to be regretted, if these institutions were regarded only as palliatives to a disease; but the vanity and pride of their promoters are so subtly interwoven with them, that they are deemed great discoveries and blessings to humanity. In the mean time parents are separated from their children, and children from their parents; the wife no longer prepares with her own hands a meal for her husband, the produce of his labour; there is little doing in his house in which his affections can be interested, and but little left in it which he can love. I have two neighbours, a man and his wife, both upwards of eighty years of age; they live alone; the husband has been confined to his bed many months and has never had, nor till within these few weeks has ever needed, any body to attend to him but his wife. She has recently been seized with a lameness which has often prevented her from being able to carry him his food to his bed; the neighbours fetch water for her from the well, and do other kind offices for them both, but her infirmities encrease. She told my Servant two days ago that she was afraid they must both be boarded out among some other Poor of the parish (they have long been supported by the parish) but she said, it was hard, having kept house together so long, to come to this, and she was sure that 'it would burst her heart.' I mention this fact to shew how deeply the spirit of independence is, even yet, rooted in some parts of the country. These people could not express themselves in this way without an almost sublime conviction of the blessings of independent domestic life. If it is true, as I believe, that this spirit is rapidly disappearing, no greater curse can befal[l] a land.

One can only lament that this powerful and moving plea was for Fox's eyes only; though overtly political, rather than poetical, it would have made a far more eloquent introduction to his poems than the verbose and otiose preface.

   Lyrical Ballads, with Other Poems. In Two Volumes by W. Wordsworth was finally published on or around 25 January 1801, though the title-page, due to all the delays, actually bore the date 1800. The first volume was effectively a reprint of the 1798 edition, with the addition of Coleridge's poem *Love* and the preface, which, after much indecision, appeared at the beginning. The second volume was entirely new. It was certainly an odd way to introduce a new collection of poetry to the world, though purchasers were able to buy the volumes separately for 5s each. Southey, for one, resented having to buy the first volume again: 'I am bitterly angry to see one new poem smuggled into the world in the *Lyrical Ballads,*' he complained to Coleridge, 'where the 750 purchasers of the first [edition] can never get at it.' John Wordsworth, visiting the London bookseller Arch, was told that, though the second volume sold well, the first did not, and customers complained of being 'cheated' out of the preface.

   In writing his preface, William had geared himself up for a reaction which he expected would be explosively hostile. In the end, it was a damp squib. There were only two reviews, one of them written by William and Coleridge's friend John Stoddart, who had visited the Wordsworths twice during their first year at Town End. Stoddart's review, in the February issue of the *British Critic*, was, as John declared, 'too flattering – I mean too much of a panegyric – they will see im[m]ediately that it has been written by a friend'. Stoddart had ploughed through the preface and accepted all its arguments at face value as proven by the poetry; the only hint of criticism was a rather weak and weary comment that it was written 'in some parts with a degree of metaphysical obscurity'. The poems themselves were treated favourably, but too briefly to give the readers any real idea of their merit or assist the sale. The *Monthly Review* gave the book only the shortest of mentions, declaring it unnecessary to enlarge on their review of the 1798 edition, except to say that 'the present publication [is] not inferior to its precursors [*sic*]'. This was, no doubt, the reason why there were so few reviews, though the tone of the preface may also have antagonized potential critics.

So it was left to William's friends to deliver their verdict. By far the most acute observations came from the '*silent* Poet'. 'Most of Wm's poetry improves upon 2d 3 or 4th reading', John pointed out, quite accurately, 'now people in general are not sufficiently interested with the first reading to induce them to try a 2d'. In time, he thought, they would become popular 'but it will be by degrees – the fact is there are not a great many that will be pleased with the poems but those that are pleased will be pleased in a high degree & they *will be people of sense* – this will have weight – & people who neither understand or wish to understand will buy & praise them'.

Charles Lamb, who could not wait for his complimentary copy to arrive, borrowed the second volume and read it with mixed feelings. Though he had measured praise for some of the poems, he reserved most of his energy for a spirited defence of the *Ancient Mariner* against William's criticisms of it in a published note to the poem. 'To sum up a general opinion of the second vol.', he wrote to William, 'I do not **feel** any one poem in it so forcibly as the Ancient Marinere, the Mad mother, and the Lines at Tintern Abbey in the **first**.' Much to Lamb's amusement, this letter provoked an immediate response. 'All the north of England are in a turmoil', he told a friend.

The Post did not sleep a moment. I received almost instantaneously a long letter of four sweating pages from my **reluctant Letterwriter**, the purport of which was, that he was sorry his 2d vol. had not given me more pleasure (Devil a hint did I give that it had *not pleased me*) and 'was compelled to wish that my range of **Sensibility** was more extended, being obliged to believe that I should receive large influxes of happiness & happy Thoughts' (I suppose from the L.B. –)

Coleridge was also galvanized into defensive action: 'four long pages, equally sweaty, and more tedious, came from him'. More seriously, Lamb privately expressed the opinion that the second volume 'too artfully aims at simplicity of expression. And you sometimes doubt if simplicity be not a cover for Poverty.'

Equally disappointing for William was the response of Charles James Fox. He told William that *Lyrical Ballads* had given him the greatest pleasure, but the ones he singled out for praise were *Goody Blake and Harry Gill*, *We are Seven*, *The Mad Mother* and *The Idiot Boy*. In other words, all poems from the first volume, and, apart from the first, none with a social message of the kind William had so anxiously drawn to Fox's attention. 'I read with particular attention the two you pointed out', Fox continued, 'but whether it be from early prepossessions, or whatever other cause, I am no great friend to blank verse for subjects which are to be treated of with simplicity.' And that was that. The social and moral dimensions of the poetry, which were what William really cared about, passed unnoticed.

The best answer to all the criticism, friendly or otherwise, was the level of sales. By June, only 130 copies remained in stock and Longman invited William to prepare a further edition. This should have been a simple enough exercise. A large number of printing errors had escaped Davy's less than vigilant eye. Some of them were horrendous: fifteen crucial lines describing Luke's childhood had been omitted from *Michael* and one ludicrous misprint made the sheep 'Panting beneath the burden of their wool' 'unborn' instead of 'unshorn'. No reissuing of his work was ever an easy task to William. He was constitutionally incapable of merely correcting errors; his perfectionism compelled him to re-examine every line of every poem, adding, deleting, relentlessly revising, until he made himself ill and drove his loved ones to distraction with what came to be known in the family as his 'tinkering'. It would be almost a year before he was well enough satisfied to submit his emended copy to the printers, but, for William, the process of revision would end only with life itself.

In the circumstances, it was not surprising that, after a period of such intense creativity, lasting throughout 1800, the following year was poetically unproductive. The presence of the Coleridges at Keswick and the Lloyds at Ambleside added considerably to the Wordsworths' social circle. Despite Dorothy's initial doubts about being so close to the unpredictable Charles Lloyd, they were soon on friendly visiting terms, calling on each other several times a week. Towards the end of October, they had a reason for increased intimacy. Charles's sister, Priscilla, came to stay with the newlyweds for the winter. This was the first time William and Dorothy had had the chance to meet and get to know their brother's fiancée. What they thought of her is not recorded, but John, who met her a few months later in London, had strong reservations. 'I think I am sorry for this connection [with] Miss L.', he told Dorothy privately. Though he thought Priscilla a 'fine looking woman ... upon the whole there was *that something* in her countenance that I could not bear to like'. Lloyd was equally unimpressed by a closer acquaintance with the Wordsworths: 'they are very unusual characters', he observed, 'indeed Miss Wordsworth I much like. but her Brother is not a man after my own heart. I always feel myself depressed in his society.'

On 14 November 1800 two letters arrived from Coleridge, informing them that he was very ill. William responded immediately to what was obviously a personal summons, setting off on foot for Keswick the next day, as soon as the driving rain had cleared. By the time Dorothy arrived two days later, Coleridge was better, but it was a sign of things to come. At the end of the month he came to Town End, retiring to bed early with a great crop of boils on his neck. In the early hours, he had a screaming, opium-induced nightmare in which a woman 'whose features were blended with darkness' tried to pull out his right eye and he caught hold of her arm; William called out three times to him before he woke – and then Coleridge thought it cruel that his friend had not come to his bedside. He returned at Christmas, preceded by his wife and children, and, having been soaked through during his walk, again took to his bed, this time with a rheumatic fever. He remained there until the New Year, waited on hand and foot by his friends, and forcing Dorothy to abandon her daily journal. When he was eventually carried home in a chaise, he retired once more to his bed, this time with a swollen testicle which, astonishingly, responded to the application of three leeches and a home-made poultice of grated bread mixed up with a strong solution of lead.

The nightmares and illnesses were symptoms of an acute underlying malaise. Coleridge was deeply unhappy. He owed money on all sides (including £20, soon to rise to £50, to William), he could not fulfil any of his literary engagements, even though he had received substantial advances for many of them and he was becoming increasingly disenchanted with his wife. When another bout of illness brought the Wordsworths scurrying over to Keswick again in April, Dorothy could no longer conceal her partisan dislike. Sarah Coleridge was entirely to blame: she was a bad nurse to her suffering husband and, worse still, enjoyed rude good health herself. She employed her time 'foolishly' with her children instead of tending Coleridge himself, and was such a 'sad fiddle faddler' that she spent three and a half hours on a Sunday morning just washing and dressing herself and her children. With spinsterish venom, Dorothy could not suppress the comment that, 'No doubt she suckled Derwent pretty often during that time.' Dorothy put on the black cap and piously pronounced her verdict: 'She would have made a very good wife to many another man, but for Coleridge!! Her radical fault is want of sensibility and what can such a woman be to Coleridge?' Dorothy, of course, was renowned for her sensibility.

But it was not Dorothy who was the object of Coleridge's increasing infatuation. It was Sara Hutchinson, who had begun her winter visit to the Wordsworths by spending the first week with them at Greta Hall. At this stage no one, possibly not even Coleridge himself, knew that she was about to become the object of his monomania. Her presence, however, exacerbated the situation. While Mrs Coleridge fretted and nagged her husband about money, work and his hugely expensive opium habit, and had the temerity to put her children's needs before those of her spouse, the Wordsworths and Sara took his side and encouraged, rather than condemned, him. Believing Coleridge's own story, that his inability to write and his addiction were merely the result of his unhappiness in his domestic situation and his financial difficulties, they thought that these problems could be overcome by effort of will. William lent Coleridge a further £30 he could ill afford, in the hope that this would ease his mind. More importantly, he fervently entreated Coleridge to abandon his distracting and futile studies of German metaphysics and urged him to apply himself to completing and publishing *Christabel*. Ominously, Coleridge was already beginning to associate his own writer's block with a sense of his inferiority to William. Inquiring whether Godwin had yet read *Lyrical Ballads* (and generous as ever in his praise of William's poems) led him to the bitter conclusion which would become his constant refrain. 'If I die, and the Booksellers will give you any thing for my Life,' he added, 'be sure to say – "Wordsworth descended on him, like the Γνῶθι σεαυτον [Know thyself] from Heaven; by shewing to him what true Poetry was, he made him know, that he himself was no Poet."'

From Keswick, the Wordsworths, accompanied probably by Sara Hutchinson, made their way over to Eusemere in January 1801, where they spent more than three weeks visiting the Clarksons. They made a very favourable impression on their kindly hosts, even though Catherine Clarkson stood somewhat in awe of William, who read her some of his *Lyrical Ballads* in manuscript and told her of his plans for *The Recluse*. 'I am fully convinced that Wordsworths Genius is equal to the Production of something very great, & I have no doubt but he will produce "*something that Posterity will not willingly let die*", if he lives ten or twenty years longer.' The Clarksons also introduced William to a fellow Quaker and campaigner against the slave trade, Thomas Wilkinson, who lived at Yanwath, a little village in a loop of the River Eamont just outside Penrith. The two men had much in common: they were both poets and shared an enthusiasm for landscape gardening. Wilkinson found William 'very sober and very amiable' and the two became fast friends. There were also meetings with Joseph Wordsworth, son of William's cousin Richard of Branthwaite, who came bearing a gift of bamboo fishing rods from John to his erstwhile angling companion, the Reverend Joseph Sympson; and with Joanna Hutchinson at Penrith, who was delighted to see the Wordsworths again. 'They are very nice folks – I love them dearly –', she enthused to her cousin. 'I don't admire Mr Coleridge half so much as William Wordsworth – Sara thought I would have liked him better he is not half so canny a man, Dorothy is a sweet woman – is not handsome but has a[n] uncom[mon] good countenance – and is very lively.'

Before they left the Clarksons, a letter arrived from their brother John, asking William to lend him the money he had invested in the funds. On 7 January 1801 he had been sworn as captain of the *Earl of Abergavenny*. 'the Ship is a very *noble ship* & I have every prospect of doing well & of being comfortable', he wrote proudly to Mary Hutchinson, 'indeed I do not know a man so lucky as myself'. It was more than just luck. The East India Company could not afford to risk its astronomic investments in one of its merchant ships by placing it in unsafe hands. For a young man who had only just had his twenty-eighth birthday, it was an awesome responsibility, though John took it in his stride. His brother Christopher was equally delighted. It was, he declared, 'a grand thing for him – effected without the expence of a farthing. If he is not unlucky, he may realize a handsome fortune out of the four voyages which the Ship has yet to run.' But that was the crux of the matter, for the fortune to be gained was not from earning a captain's salary, but from private investment in trade. Having next to nothing of his own, John was compelled to raise money by whatever means he could. Dorothy lent the £80 remaining from her Crackanthorpe legacy; William lent £277 10s of his meagre capital. In return, John arranged that Dorothy should be paid an annual allowance of £20 directly from his salary through East India House and gave William a legally executable bond and interest. By the time he sailed from Portsmouth, on 19 May, he had almost £10,000 personally invested in the voyage to China.

Towards the end of March, Christopher Wordsworth paid his first visit to his brother and sister at Grasmere. His motives were not entirely dictated by fraternal affection. As William drily observed to Calvert, 'he lodges at Ambleside being violently in love with Mr Lloyd's Sister, so of course we see so little of him, that it will not be worth your while to come over to Grasmere on his account'. His arrival coincided with the departure of Sara Hutchinson, who had been summoned to County Durham, where her youngest brother, George, at the age of twenty-three, had just taken his first farm and needed a housekeeper. He arrived at Town End at the end of March to escort Sara back to his vast but semi-ruined house, Middleham Hall, at Bishop Middleham. Within three months they would be joined by their sister Betsy, whose mental instability had apparently made her continued residence in Penrith impossible. Betsy could not go on her own, so Joanna was reluctantly and tearfully compelled to accompany her. It would not be long before Betsy would have to be consigned to the care of a nurse, but Joanna would never return to live in her beloved Penrith again.

Throughout the spring, William had been working hard on his revisions for *Lyrical Ballads* and slowly adding lines towards *The Recluse*. He wrote only one new poem, unexpectedly reverting to the *Lucy* series and producing the delightful 'I travell'd among unknown men', which William himself transcribed immediately for Mary Hutchinson. 'How we long to see you my dear Mary', he wrote. 'God for ever bless thee, my dear Mary – Adieu'. Dorothy was more wistful. 'I wish from my heart that William and I could be with you'. The new poem had done William good. His health had improved: 'he is always very ill when he tries to alter an old poem – but new composition does not hurt him so much. I hope he will soon be able to work without hurting himself.' If that was an implicit wish that William would resume *The Recluse*, Dorothy was to be disappointed. His 'tinkering' with old poems accelerated to such a pitch, with such dire consequences for his health, that Dorothy eventually persuaded him to put aside all his manuscript poems.

If William's health was a cause for concern this summer, Coleridge's was a cause for great alarm. He had spent nearly half the previous ten months confined to bed, unable to write and, consequently, unable to earn. The Wordsworths were deeply worried: even if the repeated bouts of illness did not kill Coleridge, as he feared, they must seriously undermine his constitution. There was nothing for it but to submit to his judgement that he needed to go abroad for at least six months to restore his health. William applied to John for information as to the best, most salubrious and cheapest places abroad. When John suggested San Miguel in the Azores, William took it upon himself to write to Poole, the only one of Coleridge's intimate circle who could afford, and might be prepared, to fund such an expensive trip.

Poor Poole had had his fingers burned once too often where Coleridge was concerned. He wrote to Coleridge, informing him that he had learned that Tom Wedgwood intended to spend the winter in Sicily for his health and had already suggested that Coleridge would be his ideal companion. If nothing came of this, he was prepared to lend £20, and he was sure other friends would do the same. And like Mrs Coleridge and the Wordsworths, he urged him to pull himself together. 'It seems to me impossible to imagine that you would not be well, if you could have a mind freely at ease', he wrote. 'Make yourself that mind. Take from it – its two weak parts – its tendency to restlessness and its tendency to torpor, and it would make you great and happy.' He was wasting his ink. Even as Poole wrote, Coleridge was snugly settled at Bishop Middleham with George Hutchinson, 'a young farmer . . . [who] . . . makes very droll verses in the northern dialect & in the metre of Burns, & is a great Humourist', and, of course, Sara, 'so very good a woman, that I have seldom indeed seen the like of her'. Joanna, who was also there, did not merit a mention. He managed to extend his stay for over a fortnight, then fortuitously acquired a swollen knee which required horse-exercise and sea-bathing. There was nothing for it but to pay a visit to Tom Hutchinson at Gallow Hill, where he could avail himself of the sea-bathing and 'frolick in the Billows' at Scarborough. Sara, naturally, accompanied him. It was 9 August before he tore himself away, and even then it was only to return to Bishop Middleham, where he lingered a few days longer. By the time he arrived in Keswick his interest in Sara had turned to obsession and the first of many fantasizings about her and cryptic groupings of the Wordsworth circle initials, all excluding his own, would appear in his private journal.

At the beginning of September, William set off on an expedition of his own. It was prompted by Basil Montagu, who had returned to the bar and had paid off some £50 of the debt he owed to William within the last year, and was now about to marry the eighteen-year-old daughter of a wealthy Suffolk landowner, Sir William Rush. The marriage was to take place in Glasgow on 6 September and the wedding party, which William was invited to join, passed through the Lakes on their way to Scotland.

It was not the sort of tour William liked to make, cooped up in carriages with Montagu, the Rushes and their six children, but it was an opportunity not to be missed. After the wedding ceremony, the whole party explored the area round Glasgow. They visited the Duke of Hamilton's picture gallery at Hamilton, just to the south of the city, and travelled north to Loch Lomond, whose spectacular setting, amidst wooded shores and craggy mountains, comes as such a shock when one suddenly emerges from the sprawling urban dereliction of Glasgow and Clydesbank. Thereafter, their route remains a mystery, but it is likely to have been eastward, through the Trossachs, to Edinburgh, for by the middle of September they were in Northumberland.

When William returned to Town End in the last week of September, the first person to arrive on his doorstep was Coleridge. He had already decided in his own mind that he had to separate from his wife: 'we are not suited to each other'. He would leave her and his children at Keswick, and take himself off to London or Somerset, once he had borrowed enough money from his long-suffering friends to finance his plan. In the circumstances, it was appropriate that, before he returned to Keswick, he helped the Wordsworths finish what they called Sara's seat on White Moss Common. Sara herself had chosen the site and laid the first stone on 26 March; now it was completed as a memorial to her.

On 16 October Sara's brother Tom Hutchinson arrived on a long-promised visit.

It was a much-needed distraction from Coleridge's woes, which had made Dorothy so sick and ill with worry that she too had resorted to laudanum. An enthusiastic admirer of William's poems, Tom did the now obligatory trip to the sheepfold up Greenhead Ghyll and even, one bright sunny day, climbed with the Wordsworths up Helvellyn. A week after his arrival, Mary Hutchinson came to Keswick and took up residence at Greta Hall. Quite what Mrs Coleridge thought about another of the Hutchinsons making free with her house we do not know. Mary was never an abrasive presence, but she was Sara's sister, and she did stay for more than two weeks, leaving only after Coleridge himself had departed.

Coleridge spent his last few days in the Lakes with the Wordsworths at Grasmere. Dorothy's journal is silent on what passed between them, but only because some officious censor has removed the relevant page, leaving just the words 'left us' still visible on the stub. One can only suspect the handiwork of Gordon Wordsworth, who, unlike his Uncle Christopher, destroyed primary evidence instead of merely editing it for publication. This in turn leads one to suspect that the reason why the page was torn out is that it contained information the Wordsworth family wished to suppress. In which case, one can only presume it included the revelation of Coleridge's love for Sara. Why else select this particular page for destruction? Dorothy's extravagant grief after Coleridge's departure also becomes more explicable if she had only just learned of his infatuation.

Life at Town End resumed its quiet outward tenor after Coleridge's departure, but significant developments were taking place. William had decided to ask Mary to marry him. There was no great fanfare or announcement; we do not even know when he proposed and was accepted. One can only pick up the nuances of Dorothy's journal which suggest that it happened on 12 November. On that Thursday, Dorothy lingered behind on their evening walk and returned to find William and Mary together at tea. The next day, they all three 'spent a happy evening' and went to bed late. Dorothy had a restless night and on Saturday 'lay in bed all the Day very unwell', which sounds like one of her typical nervous reactions. The following Monday, the servant, Molly Fisher, was 'very witty with Mary all day She says "Ye may say what ye will But there's no thing like a gay auld man for behaving weel to a young wife!"' William was, in fact, exactly the same age as Mary, though he looked older than his years. At thirty-one, neither of them needed to seek family approval or permission to marry. Nevertheless, a few days later Mary wrote to her aunt, which suggests some sort of announcement; more importantly, William wrote to Richard, asking him to draw up an account of all the money he and Dorothy had received through his hands for the past two years. And crucially, on 21 December, a letter arrived from France which can only have been from Annette. Viewed individually, these events seem insignificant, but as a body of evidence they point to the making of a formal engagement.

With marriage and future income in mind, William tried to kickstart himself back into a poetic routine. He had written nothing new for months other than a rather limp pastoral, *Repentance*, inspired by the complaints of their neighbour, Peggy Ashburner, whose statesman husband had sold their lands, leaving them with the unhappy thought, 'We've no land in the vale, Save six feet of earth where our forefathers lie!' For the moment, William occupied himself in translating Chaucer into modern verse. Towards the end of December, he returned to the poem on his own life, which he had now decided to expand to include his Cambridge education.

Heavy snow, followed by a rapid thaw, made the roads impassable, so an invitation to spend Christmas and the New Year with the Clarksons at Eusemere had to be deferred. They were also short of money, having lent Coleridge £10 which he had not repaid. In the end, they could not afford to pay for places in the coach and had to walk the long way round, over Dunmail Raise to Keswick, then along the River Greta to Pooley Bridge. At Keswick they had the good fortune to meet Joshua Wilkinson, the Cockermouth man who had shared Richard's chambers in London. He invited William to dine with him at the Royal Oak and they fell into conversation with a young man who was the heir to a marquisate. To the Wordsworths' evident pride, he not only knew all about *Lyrical Ballads*, but had even seen the Queen present a copy to Mrs Harcourt. The next day, cutting over the fells lining the northern shores of Ullswater, in driving wind and hail showers, Mary fell several times and Dorothy was sometimes forced to crawl, literally on hands and knees. With the help of a few kind souls who redirected their path, they eventually arrived safe and sound to a hearty welcome at Eusemere.

On New Year's Eve, Mary went to Penrith to stay with her aunt, returning to spend a few days at Eusemere before the Wordsworths left on 23 January, then departing for Bishop Middleham. William and Dorothy, with singular bravado, decided to risk going over the tops to Grasmere in conditions which would have appalled the Mountain Rescue Services. Grisedale Tarn was frozen solid, the ice cracked and split but waterless; they lost their way in the mists and snow and, by the time they reached Town End, it was dark. It was a foolhardy and unnecessary escapade, and all their neighbours rightly censured them for it, but it prompted two poems, *To a Young Lady Who Had Been Reproached for Taking Long Walks in the Country* and *Louisa After Accompanying Her on a Mountain Excursion*. Much ink has been wasted on trying to prove whether Dorothy, Mary or even Joanna was the subject of the poems. Both are very much in the *Lucy* genre and are probably composite portraits.

They were, in any case, unimportant poems as far as William was concerned, for, repeating a pattern of composition that had now become established, he had graduated from the poem on his own life to working on *The Recluse*. The section he was working on now, in the early months of 1802, was a development of the character of the Pedlar, the natural philosopher who would be the guide to the poem and link all the incidents and stories of rural life. In this he was considerably helped by a letter from Sara Hutchinson, containing her reminiscences of James Patrick, the husband of her mother's cousin Margaret Robison. Sara had been sent to live with this couple after her mother's death, when she was eight years old. Patrick, like his father-in-law, had begun life as a Scottish pedlar, before settling down in the hardware business at Kendal. 'My own imaginations I was happy to find clothed in reality & fresh ones suggested by what she reported of this man's tenderness of heart,' William wrote, 'his strong & pure imagination, & his solid attainments in literature chiefly religious whether in prose or verse.'

William's preoccupation with his poem had all the usual results. When he wanted to break off composing, he could not do so, and 'did himself harm', as Dorothy darkly described it. He was constantly tired and out of spirits. Like Dorothy, he suffered from bad headaches, minor bouts of illness and sleepless nights. These were not helped by 'heart-rending' letters from Coleridge, who, at the beginning of February, announced his decision to go abroad to the south of France for the sake of his health and, displaying an incredible lack of sensitivity, expected the Wordsworths (and Southeys) to accompany him. The news came as a considerable shock. 'I was stopped in my writing', Dorothy confided in her journal, '& made ill by the letters'. The very day Coleridge informed the Wordsworths of his plans, Southey repeated them to a friend as if everything had been settled and agreed between them. Always more robust in his opinions, Southey had no intention of going along with the scheme. 'I do not   wish that we should go abroad together. Our habits are not enough alike.'

Clearly the matter needed to be discussed with Mary: how would she feel about emigrating to the country where William's former mistress and child were living? On 14 February William walked over to Penrith to see her, dressing up like a proper suitor in his blue jacket and 'a pair of <u>new</u> pantaloons fresh from London'. What Mary's answer was we cannot guess, but Coleridge, writing to his wife on 24 February, blithely informed her that the marriage would take place in March and that, in July, all three Wordsworths would set sail with him, and his family, from Liverpool. They would go to Bordeaux and settle there, as 'companions, & neighbours', for a couple of years.

Sarah Coleridge would have no say in the matter, but would William really have repeated the mistake of uprooting himself and his family to live in a foreign land, simply so that he could be near Coleridge? The scheme put all his loyalties, to Coleridge, to Mary, even to Annette and Caroline, in conflict. It is tempting to dismiss the whole scheme as mere fantasy. On the other hand, Dorothy noted receiving a letter from 'the Frenchman in London' on 13 February and William writing to him on the 24th. Frustratingly, there is nothing to indicate who this Frenchman was, but, given the timing of the correspondence, it is likely that he was either connected with the emigration scheme or the bearer of letters from Annette.

Whatever the Frenchman's role, or non-role, something had gone seriously awry with William's marriage plans. He would always look back to this period as one of acute misery. He was haunted by his longing to see Mary, 'when I am away from you I seem to have heart for nothing and no body else', and tortured by sleepless nights of sexual frustration. The wedding did not happen until October. What went wrong? What little evidence there is suggests the possibility that Annette objected. It was only natural that she should do so. William's marriage to another woman ended any hope of his legitimizing her status, or that of their child. It also put her in a difficult position, since she had been passing herself off as William's wife and widow for almost ten years. If nothing else, Annette would have wanted some sort of security for Caroline. That William did not ignore her letters altogether, or go ahead with his wedding when he had intended, suggests that he acknowledged the justice of her claims. It may even raise the possibility that he wanted Annette's approval of, or, at least, her consent to his marriage.

The indications we have that negotiations were taking place are few but significant. What had been an intermittent correspondence suddenly leapt to life, and thirteen letters are recorded passing between the Wordsworths and Annette between 21 December 1801 and 5 July 1802. The first was actually from Annette, though this does not preclude the possibility that it was a reply to one from William. Dorothy thought it important enough to notice in her journal, as she did the following letters, so it may have come out of the blue; in which case, it must have been a rude shock to William, who had just proposed to Mary. Recalling how Annette had enlisted Dorothy's sympathy and support on her behalf once before, it is interesting to see that her third letter, written only a week after her second, was a joint one, from mother and child, and it was addressed, not to William, but to his sister. After the receipt of a fourth letter from 'poor Annette', on 22 March, William and Dorothy had a serious discussion: 'we resolved to see Annette, & that Wm should go to Mary'.

On 28 March they set off for Keswick to spend a few days at Greta Hall. Coleridge himself had returned to the Lakes only nine days before, shocking Dorothy by his 'half stupified' appearance. Though he had prepared for a reconciliation with his long-suffering wife, it did not augur well that, when he left London, he headed straight for Gallow Hill, where all his good intentions evaporated. This was not a happy visit. Coleridge's passion for Sara was self-evident and the atmosphere was tense. Sara herself seems to have tried to put a distance between them: 'Sara Hutcheson's new gospel – alias – Honesty–', he wrote witheringly in his private journal, accusing her of making him 'feel uncomfortable'. He left Gallow Hill on 13 March, without Sara, though he had been expecting to escort her to Town End, where he arrived on the 19th and stayed till the 21st.

At Keswick, the Wordsworths seem to have spent as much time with Calvert and his wife as with the Coleridges. Some sort of reconciliation had been patched up between husband and wife, for Sarah became pregnant about this time. It says little for Coleridge's loyalties that he was then employed in writing the first draft of his great poem *Dejection: An Ode*, which trumpeted his love for Sara Hutchinson, and his grief at having made her unwell and unhappy by his behaviour towards her. The poem was written in the form of a letter to Sara on 4 April, the day before William and Dorothy left Keswick.

That night, despite being ill in bed, Coleridge 'continued talking with Wordsworth the whole night till the Dawn of the Day, urging him to conclude on marrying Mary Hutchinson'. Coleridge, it would seem, had fewer scruples about abandoning Annette than William, but he was unable to convince his friend. The next day William set off for Eusemere, where he would leave Dorothy with the

Clarksons, while he went on alone to Bishop Middleham to tell Mary that, before he married her, he must have a personal meeting with Annette. Mary's reaction remains unknown, but one may guess it was not what the Wordsworths had hoped. William returned earlier than expected, on 13 April, retired early to bed and, when he finally rose at lunchtime the following day, his news made Dorothy 'ill – out of spirits – disheartened'. They returned to Town End, where it became Dorothy's first task to write a hearty admonition to Mary, who had, according to William, become very thin with anxiety.

Extraordinary as it may seem, throughout all the uncertainties of this period, William was deeply engaged in one of his most prolific outbursts of poetry. Between March and July, according to Coleridge's calculation, he wrote thirty-two poems, some of them of considerable length. Coleridge considered most of them were 'very excellent Compositions', but the first seeds of doubt were beginning to gnaw at his mind. William had taken yet another step in his radical revision of what poetry should be, and Coleridge genuinely, or perhaps motivated partly by jealousy, could not follow him. There was, he complained,

here & there a daring Humbleness of Language & Versification, and a strict adherence to matter of fact, even to prolixity, that startled me . . . and I have thought & thought again & have not had my doubts solved by Wordsworth . . . On the contrary, I rather suspect that some where or other there is a radical Difference in our theoretical opinions respecting Poetry –

Coleridge was uncomfortable with William's stubborn insistence on literalism of the kind displayed in one of his best poems written at this time, *Resolution and Independence*. The poet, meeting a leech-gatherer on a lonely moor, stops to inquire what he is doing and, while listening to the answer, drifts off into his own reveries and is obliged to ask the question and hear the answer again. Succinct and to the point the poem is not. But the repetition of question and answer reinforces the difference between the healthy young poet, preoccupied with imaginative fears for his own future, and the ancient, poverty-stricken leech-gatherer, 'carrying with him his own fortitude, and the necessities which an unjust state of society has entailed upon him'. Mary and Sara had the temerity to criticize the leech-gatherer's speech as 'tedious', earning themselves a sharp reprimand: 'everything is tedious when one does not read with the feelings of the Author . . . It is in the character of the old man to tell his story in a manner which an *impatient* reader must necessarily feel as tedious. But Good God! Such a figure, in such a place, a pious self-respecting, miserably infirm . . . Old Man telling such a tale!' Warming to his theme in defence of *Resolution and Independence*, William went to the heart of what his object was in writing poetry.

It is not a matter of indifference whether you are pleased with this figure and his employment; it may be comparatively so, whether you are pleased or not with *this Poem*; but it is of the utmost importance that you should have had pleasure from contemplating the fortitude, independence, persevering spirit, and the general moral dignity of this old man's character.

Like *Resolution and Independence*, many of the poems William wrote in the spring
and early summer of 1802 were about the beggars and itinerants who continually
passed through the Vale of Grasmere. He also embarked on a whole new range
of poetry, the short nature poems for which he is now best known. Instead of
celebrating the virtues of humble human life, he now chose to sing the praises of
the lesser members of the animal and plant kingdoms. The robin, skylark, green
linnet, cuckoo ('shall I call thee Bird, Or but a wandering voice?'), glowworm and
butterfly each earned their own dedicatory poems. Withering's *Botany* was pressed
into good service, with similar results for the daisy, barberry and, William's
favourite, the small celandine:

> Blithe of heart, from week to week
> Thou dost play at hide-and-seek;
> While the patient primrose sits
> Like a beggar in the cold . . .
>   *To the Same Flower*
>   *[The Small Celandine], ll.33–6*

What is self-evident in all these poems is the sheer delight which inspired them.
His beloved vale was now his established home: in his second year of residence,
the neat house and blooming garden could be enjoyed all the more since they were
the creation of the Wordsworths' own hands. William was not yet a statesman, but
he had made one corner of Grasmere his own.

On 25 May, William's cousin the retired Captain John Wordsworth, who was
now living at Brougham Hall, just outside Penrith, sent a cryptic note to Richard.
'Lord Lonsdale is no more . . . improve this Information if you can to your & your
Family's Advantage.' Living close to Lowther Park, he had been quick off the mark
with the news. 'Wicked Jimmy' had only died the day before, 'called to give an
Account where his Knavery & his money will nothing avail him', as Uncle William
put it. The Earl had no sons, so his earldom and viscountcy of Lonsdale died with
him. His heir was his forty-four-year-old cousin Sir William Lowther, whose
reputation as an 'exceedingly just and honourable' man preceded him. The Wordsworths swung into action. William suggested that they should draw up a memorial
stating their case and pointing out their sister's 'utter destitution' because of the
affair. They could get some of Uncle William's, or even brother Christopher's,
powerful friends to present it to Sir William. 'It can do no harm', he pointed out
to Richard, 'and may do good.'

On 18 June one of the Wordsworths' friends, Mr Luff, called in unexpectedly.
He had ridden over the fells in haste from Patterdale to tell them that Sir William
Lowther had placed advertisements in the local papers, stating his intention to pay
all the Earl's just debts. Mr Luff brought with him a memorandum from Thomas
Clarkson, drawn up in consultation with the Wordsworths' uncle, the Reverend
Thomas Myers, and Dr Lowther, the rector of Lowther church, who knew that the
debt was a just one and unpaid. It contained words of caution. 'It happens throughout

Life, that People often lose their Object, by asking too much, when, had they ask'd in Moderation they might have obtained it'. The considered opinion of all three men was that the Wordsworths' claim was no longer recoverable by law, so they should only ask for payment of the principal and forget any demand for interest. The new Lord Lowther would have so many debts to pay that he could not afford to set the precedent of paying interest; as an added inducement to accepting this lesser amount, they were assured that an application for the principal only would be dealt with, and paid out, in a matter of weeks.

With his marriage impending, William was more than prepared to settle for this, but Richard, whose whole life had been dedicated to recovering the debt, was determined to demand interest. Fearing that the whole would be lost when part might be gained, William wrote anxiously to him. Had Richard considered that Lord Lowther would not pay interest unless forced to do so by law? What hope would the Wordsworths have of pursuing their claim against the new Lord Lowther and his immense fortune? Lowther himself might be a fair man, but what about his attorneys and advisers? 'In whatever manner you proceed in the business, let me earnestly exhort you to avoid every thing which may appear like a manifestation of a disposition to challenge Lord Lowther to try the affair in a court of justice', William advised his lawyer brother. 'Shun this as you would do the pestilence.'

It was hardly surprising that Richard took offence. Nevertheless, he sent the requisite letter to Mr Richardson, Lowther's agent, pointing out that he had personally delivered an account of the debt, amounting to ₤4,660 4s 10¾d, on 30 August 1786, and that the amount still remained due to his father's estate, plus interest and costs. He also wrote a justifiably indignant letter to William.

It is proper that one Person should take ye lead in the affair. If you can find any Person better qualified than myself I beg you will let me know. We must not have a number of meddlesome Persons concerned in it. I think I have seen enough of the world to have reapeatedly [*sic*] observed meddlesome interfering Persons though meaning well have often done immense mischief to their Friends . . . If we remain united we shall do well . . . I have no desire to act in a Matter where my exertions are thought nothing of.

In the meantime, William had more immediate problems to overcome. On 9 July he and Dorothy left Town End for France and the prearranged meeting with Annette. Calais had been fixed as the rendezvous, and as a sort of reaffirmation of William's commitment to Mary, the Wordsworths travelled by Gallow Hill, even though it was an unnecessary detour which extended their journey by more than 100 miles. Coleridge was waiting for them at the Rock of Names, a wayside rock between Grasmere and Keswick on which Sara Hutchinson had carved her initials on her last visit. Since then Coleridge had returned several times to add further initials, which William had engraved more deeply. Now it bore those of not only Sara but William, Mary, John, Dorothy and Coleridge, a permanent reminder of the Grasmere power-house.

Coleridge escorted the Wordsworths to Keswick, but failed in his object of persuading them to give up Town End after William's marriage. He had hoped they might agree to settle in the other half of Greta Hall with him, but the Wordsworths were adamant, less from reasons of attachment to Grasmere, it has to be said, than from Dorothy's hostility to Mrs Coleridge. On 12 July, he accompanied them six or seven miles along their road, then, after sitting silently by the roadside together, they had a melancholy parting. It seems almost symbolic that Coleridge was left behind, alone and disconsolate, while William and Dorothy marched gaily and confidently forward towards Eusemere, Gallow Hill and, ultimately, a new life together with Mary.

At four o'clock in the morning on Sunday 1 August they arrived at Calais. They stayed on board the packet till half past seven, then William went ashore for the letters that would inform him where Annette and Caroline were staying. Dorothy's journal, which had been prolix to the point of tedium, falls silent just when we really want to know details. What did William and Annette make of each other after a separation of almost ten years? Had they changed beyond all recognition, or were they still recognizably the lovers of 1792? And Caroline, what was she like, this living, breathing progeny of that ill-fated union? How did she feel towards this stranger, the father who had abandoned her before she was born, and was only come to see her now because he was about to marry a woman other than her mother?

From Dorothy all we learn are the barest of bald facts, written in retrospect, after her return to England. The momentous meeting took place between eight-thirty and nine o'clock in the morning on 1 August at Annette and Caroline's lodgings in the Rue de la Tête d'Or. The two odd couples walked together 'almost every evening' and William bathed often. Caroline was 'delighted' watching the boats sail out at sunset. The Wordsworths left Calais on 29 August, landing at Dover the following day, and Dorothy was sick all the way. And that is that. Had it not been for William's lovely sonnet, composed on one of the evening walks with Annette and Caroline along Calais beach, we would know nothing at all about his feelings.

> It is a beautous evening, calm and free,
> The holy time is quiet as a Nun
> Breathless with adoration; the broad sun
> Is sinking down in its tranquillity;
> The gentleness of heaven broods o'er the Sea:
> Listen! the mighty Being is awake,
> And doth with his eternal motion make
> A sound like thunder – everlastingly.
> Dear Child! dear Girl! that walkest with me here,
> If thou appear untouched by solemn thought,
> Thy nature is not therefore less divine:
> Thou liest in Abraham's bosom all the year;
> And worshipp'st at the Temple's inner shrine,
> God being with thee when we know it not.

From this we can conclude that William's daughter was not the child of nature he had perhaps hoped to find. Affectionate though the tribute is, it does not thrill with the recognition of a kindred spirit. They had met as strangers and they parted a month later, apparently without any burning desire to meet again. There is less passion in this poem, addressed to his daughter, than in another William wrote at the same time to the Evening Star, visible across the Channel, shining on England.

> Blessing be on you both! one hope, one lot,
> One life, one glory! – I, with many a fear
> For my dear Country, many heartfelt sighs,
> Among men who do not love her, linger here.
> *Composed by the Sea-Side, near Calais,*
> *August 1802, ll.11–14*

Having done his duty, William returned to England with evident relief. Even Christopher, not noted for his sensibilities in such matters, noticed that his brother and sister 'seemed very glad to get home again' when he met them in London. Together, they paid a visit of a couple of days to Windsor, the first by William and Dorothy to the Cooksons for many a year. Uncle William was quite prepared to let bygones be bygones, so this meeting, too, was a reconciliation of sorts, though it is unlikely to have happened had news not greeted the Wordsworths, on reaching London, that John had also arrived back in England. The *Earl of Abergavenny* was off the South Downs and they could not leave without seeing him. So they waited for him, spending the interval in visiting the Cooksons in their canon's lodgings at Windsor and seeing the sights of London, including the hurly-burly of Bartholomew Fair, in the company of Charles Lamb.

On the evening of 11 September William and Dorothy returned to London and, as they crossed Temple Court, met Richard and John, pacing back and forth in the moonlight. They had much news to exchange, the good about the Lonsdale suit counterbalancing the bad about John's voyage, which had not been as successful as he had hoped. No doubt Richard had already informed John of their brother's forthcoming marriage, but when Dorothy put Mary's own letter into his hand the next day, John's usual self-control broke down. Overpowered by his emotions, he wrote her a brief but poignant farewell, to which he added the pragmatic gift of a new silk gown. It was the only wedding present the couple were to receive.

For eleven days, the Wordsworths lingered in London. But Mary had waited long enough. On 24 September William and Dorothy returned to Gallow Hill. 'Never shall I forget thy rich & flourishing and genial mien & appearance', William later wrote of the moment when Mary appeared at the end of the lane to welcome him. 'Nature had dressed thee out as if expressly that I might receive thee to my arms in the full blow of health and happiness.' The whole Hutchinson clan gathered in force. Sara, Joanna and Tom were already there; Jack and George arrived a few days later. Only Henry was absent, being now back at sea. Dorothy had to steel her nerves for the coming occasion. Ever since the engagement, she had been more than usually possessive about William, talking of him as if she, not Mary, were his lover. From plain 'William' or 'my dear Brother', he had been transformed into 'My Beloved'. When he was away for a couple of days at Keswick in March, she had confided in her journal, 'I *will* be busy. I *will* look well & be well when he comes back to me. O the Darling! here is one of his bitten apples –! I can hardly find in my heart to throw it into the fire.' 'I have long loved Mary Hutchinson as a Sister,' she now wrote to her erstwhile schoolfriend Jane, 'and she is equally attached to me this being so, you will guess that I look forward with perfect happiness to this Connection between us, but, happy as I am, I half dread that concentration of all tender feelings, past, present, and future which will come upon me on the wedding morning.'

She was probably not the only one dreading an outburst of emotion, though the preparations for the wedding went smoothly enough. Wisely, it was decided that Dorothy should not attend, on the pretext that she, and Sara, should be responsible for the wedding breakfast. The night before the wedding, William brought the ring to Dorothy for safekeeping, and she slept with it on her forefinger all night. Early next morning, he came upstairs to collect it and say goodbye. In an oddly repellent gesture, which was clearly meant to be an endorsement of his continuing love for his sister, William slipped the ring back on her finger and blessed her 'fervently'. Just after eight o'clock, the little wedding party set off on foot from Gallow Hill to walk the mile over the fields to Brompton-by-Sawdon. There, on 4 October 1802, in the pretty twelfth-century church of All Saints, William and Mary were married by the Reverend John Ellis; the only witnesses were Tom, Joanna and Jack Hutchinson. Back at Gallow Hill, Sara had been left to prepare the wedding breakfast alone. 'I kept myself as quiet as I could,' Dorothy confided in her journal,

but when I saw the two men running up the walk, coming to tell us it was over, I could stand it no longer & threw myself on the bed where I lay in stillness, neither hearing or seeing any thing, till Sara came upstairs to me & said 'they are coming.' This forced me from the bed where I lay & I moved I knew not how straight forward, faster than my strength could carry me till I met my beloved William & fell upon his bosom. He & John Hutchinson led me to the house & there I stayed to welcome my dear Mary.

It was characteristic of both women that Dorothy managed to upstage Mary on her wedding day and that Mary bore it with perfect equanimity.

II. *The Set is Broken*

There was no honeymoon. The newlyweds could not afford one. Instead, accompanied by Dorothy, they made a leisurely journey by post chaise to Grasmere, revisiting some of their favourite places, including the ruins of Helmsley Castle and Rievaulx Abbey, and the waterfalls in Wensleydale. They arrived at Town End at six o'clock in the evening on Wednesday 6 October.

It says much for Mary's tact and disposition that she was able to slip unobtrusively into the established pattern of the Wordsworths' lives. It could so easily have become an unbearably fraught situation, since Mary was effectively usurping Dorothy's place as mistress of the household and, more importantly, ending her exclusive relationship with her brother. Mary succeeded in making a place for herself and did not alienate or antagonize Dorothy in the process. One might almost argue the reverse, for Mary's quiet presence seems to have been a calming factor, and Dorothy actually benefited from the company of another woman. Apart from exchanging bedrooms, so that the married couple now had the double bed in the larger room downstairs, there was no visible alteration to the routine at Town End. Mary had inherited a small property from her father, but the income from the rents was only in the region of £30 a year, so there was no gain to the little household from a material point of view.

The only person who felt disadvantaged by the Wordsworths' marriage was Coleridge, for whom William's domestic happiness was increasingly a matter of envy. The night before the wedding, Coleridge had dreamt of William, Mary and a grotesquely transformed Dorothy in one of his nightmares about being pursued by a vengeful female. On the day itself, he published his poem to Sara as *Dejection: An Ode* in the *Morning Post*, addressing it deliberately to William as 'Edmund'. If this was not a sufficiently public hurling of a barbed spear, Coleridge also stooped to inflict a wound below the belt. The following week he published in the same paper a poisonous little satire, *Spots in the Sun*, which flaunted Annette's name and effectively accused William of being a hypocrite.

William nobly ignored the public manifestations of Coleridge's jealousy, but the contrast between their respective lives was growing ever deeper. Once more, Coleridge decided to flee, taking up Poole's suggestion (which he had earlier spurned in vituperative terms) of acting as companion to the chronically ill Tom Wedgwood. William seems to have tried to dissuade his friend from this second separation, not least because Coleridge's baby was due in December, but he failed. On 4 November Coleridge left Keswick again and spent the day with Sara Hutchinson at Penrith. By the middle of the month, he was jaunting round Wales with Wedgwood, loftily informing his wife that she was his inferior 'in sex, acquirements, and in the quantity and quality of natural endowments whether of Feeling, or of Intellect', and demanding, as of right, that she should 'love, & act kindly to, those whom I deem worthy of my Love'. With incomparable insensitivity to his wife's plight, he also told her to ask Sara over to nurse her when she gave birth: 'you will hardly have another opportunity of having her by yourself & to yourself, & of learning to know her, such as she really is'.

Sara had actually been on her way to Grasmere when Coleridge caught up with her at Penrith. She stayed at Town End for several weeks over the Christmas period, but apparently refrained from attempting to force her attentions on Mrs Coleridge, and left again soon after Coleridge's return. John saw Coleridge briefly when he passed through London, and thought that he looked poorly.

John also saw a good deal of Richard, and it was he who took the trouble to copy out Richard's letter to Sir William Lowther's solicitors, setting out the Wordsworth claim in full. The interest alone was now within £300 of the sum due for the original debt. In total, including legal costs, Richard was claiming £10,388 6s 8d. A vast amount in its own right, it paled into insignificance when compared to the full extent of the late Earl's debts, which now exceeded £200,000. John's forthcoming second voyage as captain of the *Earl of Abergavenny* provided the Wordsworths with the ammunition they needed to press home their claim to Lord Lowther. 'It is very desirable that he should be furnished with money for his Investment', Richard wrote. 'If Lord Lowther could let us have 3000 or £4000, it would be of most essential service to my brother before he sails.'

After much negotiation, Richard wrote privately to William, telling him that the most they could realistically expect to receive was between £8,000 and £8,500 and asking for his approval in accepting the offer. William had no hesitation in giving it and declared that he and Dorothy were 'so perfectly satisfied with your manner of conducting the business, that we leave the conclusion of it to your judgement entirely'. On 21 February Richard took out letters of administration enabling him to deal with his father's estate and, two days later, had the satisfaction of recording the receipt of £3,000 from Lord Lowther as the first instalment on the debt. A further £1,500 was handed over at the beginning of July, together with two promissory notes, worth £2,000 each, which were payable in twelve months' time, with interest. It had taken just six months short of twenty years for the Wordsworths to extract the money owed to their father by the Lowthers and, ironically, they owed their success not to persistence, or legal right, but to quixotic generosity.

For William and Dorothy, the payment of the debt meant the difference between a life of scraping together every penny and having sufficient capital to be comfortable, if not rich. Their joint share eventually amounted to £3,825, but, at John's request, Lord Lowther's first payment was entirely appropriated by him for investment in his voyage. Curiously, this rather than the Lowther debt brought the Wordsworths to the brink of a family quarrel. William and Dorothy wanted Richard to stand security for what, in effect, was a loan to John, but their other brothers saw no reason why Richard should always stand all the risk. Dorothy was incandescent with rage:

I am sure that William has never thought that it was fit you should *run all the risque*, only that it was *more* fit that John should call upon you to run a *further* risque rather than on him, for this plain reason that if you lost the whole of the money you would be, (taking in your profession) many, many degrees richer than he is, or has any grounds for hoping to be; and for me, I told you that I thought I ought not to be called upon to bear *any part* of the risque.

She explained to John that there were few sacrifices she was not prepared to make for him, but this was one of them. It was a matter of prudence. Old Molly Fisher was less cautious: 'if I could but see Maister John I would send all the money that ever I have for a venture with him!' she told Dorothy, who added wryly, 'you must know she has more than seven pounds'. William and Christopher gave their unconditional agreement to the loan, but Dorothy was moved to confront Richard again: 'as long as I am poor or in a state of dependence, I have claims upon you as your only Sister, and the only Daughter of my Father to which no other claims can be superior'.

Dorothy was right to be concerned, for John's voyage was troubled from the start. Even before he left English waters, in May, his crew, the ragtag and bobtail who had escaped impressment into the navy, were mutinous and had to be punished. More worryingly, the war against France had resumed. East Indiamen were a valuable prize for any marauding Frenchmen and, on his return voyage the following year, John was involved in an action against the French Admiral Linois, who was waiting to intercept the fleet before they entered the Straits of Malacca. What could have been a disaster was averted by the cool heads of the British commanders, who, despite being outgunned, managed to get the French in their cross-fire and drive them off. A suitably grateful Board of Directors rewarded captains and crews generously, and John personally received 500 guineas, a piece of commemorative silverware, worth fifty guineas, and a beautifully ornamented ceremonial sword.

All this was well into the future, however, and for the moment Dorothy had to be satisfied with her brothers' assurances that they would honour the informal promise they had made her when William announced his intention to marry: Richard, John and Christopher would each contribute £20 a year towards an allowance for their sister. It was just as well that they did, for she had gone on a spending spree in anticipation of her share of the Lowther claim and bought almost £20 worth of new clothes. Their new-found wealth also seems to have prompted the Wordsworths to consider moving from the tiny cottage at Town End. Mary was expecting a baby towards the end of July and it made sense for them to move into a larger house before the event. Quite where they intended to go is a mystery, but at the beginning of June, Dorothy told Catherine Clarkson that they hoped to get into their new house the following week, then have an enormous wash so that everything was ready before the baby arrived.

In the end, however, they were all taken by surprise, for just before six-thirty on the morning of 18 June 1803 Mary gave birth to 'a stout healthy Boy', whom they decided to call John. There was definitely something odd about the timing of his arrival. In theory, a full-term baby should not have been born until 16 July. Given that it was Mary's first child, a later date was likely, and despite arriving a full month before he was supposedly due, the baby was not undersized or weakly. The obvious inference is that he had been conceived before the marriage took place, which would not have been unusual at this period, when an engagement was commonly regarded as a licence for sexual relations to begin, but William was in Calais and London at the likeliest time of conception. He and Mary had parted on 26 July, which was too early for John to have been conceived, and William did not return to Gallow Hill until 24 September, a mere ten days before his wedding, which does not account for the disparity in dates. It is inconceivable (literally) that the child was not his, since there was never a breath of suspicion that Mary was anything other than totally loyal to William. She was also, it has to be pointed out, a month wrong in her dates for her second child, which was also born a month earlier than expected. Either Mary was careless in her computations, or she did not naturally carry babies full-term, in which case she was fortunate to have healthy children.

Dorothy was ecstatic. 'The Babe is a true Representative of the Wordsworths,' she told Richard, 'for he is very like his Father and our Family'. On 17 July a little party trooped into Grasmere church from Town End. Mary went through the old-fashioned ceremony of being 'churched', or purified after childbirth, and John was christened. Dorothy, of course, stood as godmother; the godfathers were Richard and Coleridge. As Richard could not be there in person, he was represented by one of the Wordsworths' earliest Grasmere friends, old Mr Sympson. A modest celebration was held afterwards at Town End, with tea, coffee and christening cake.

The baby's early arrival had effectively put an end to any immediate plans to move house. Instead, William, Dorothy and Coleridge began to contemplate the possibility of making a tour of Scotland. It says much for Dorothy's devotion to 'our own darling child' that she was now reluctant to go. The idea for the tour had been prompted by Coleridge's recent return to the Lakes. For most of the previous year he had been away, accompanying Tom Wedgwood in the hope of being taken abroad. On 24 December he had breezed unexpectedly into the cottage at Town End, with Tom Wedgwood 'worn to Skin and Bone' in tow, and it fell to the Wordsworths to inform Coleridge that he was now the father of a daughter, little Sara, born the previous morning. Before the end of January, he had gone again, and though he wrote confidently about taking up residence in Italy, Sicily, the Canaries, the South of France or even Madeira, nothing came of his plans. Wedgwood shook Coleridge off: he needed a companion who would look after him, not a liability for whom he did not wish to be responsible. He went abroad without Coleridge, who was forced to return to Keswick. A six-week tour of Scotland with William and Dorothy was not in the same category as a couple of years on the Continent with Wedgwood, but it was better than nothing.

William had more serious reasons for wishing to have a change of scene. For several months he had written nothing at all. The longer his fallow period dragged on, the more it became a matter for concern. His last great surge of creativity had been associated with his trip to France which inspired at least nine poems, beginning with his wonderful hymn to a still and silent London, viewed from the roof of the stage coach driving over Westminster Bridge in the early morning, on the way to France.

> Earth has not anything to show more fair:
> Dull would he be of soul who could pass by
> A sight so touching in its majesty:
> This City now doth, like a garment, wear
> The beauty of the morning; silent, bare,
> Ships, towers, domes, theatres, and temples lie
> Open unto the fields, and to the sky;
> All bright and glittering in the smokeless air.
> Never did sun more beautifully steep
> In his first splendour, valley, rock, or hill;
> Never saw I, never felt, a calm so deep!
> The river glideth at his own sweet will:
> Dear God! The very houses seem asleep;
> And all that mighty heart is lying still!

It was inevitable that William should contrast his first, hopeful visit to France at the dawn of the French Revolution with this, altogether sadder, occasion. The Peace of Amiens had been made possible by Napoleon Bonaparte's elevation to the office of consul for life; the great struggle for liberty had ended, as Burke had predicted it would, in substituting one tyranny for another. William was sickened at the sight of so many English tourists (who included Poole) pouring over the Channel to 'bend the knee . . . before the new-born Majesty' and scathing in his contempt for the 'men of prostrate mind . . . to slavery prone!' All his political instincts were also outraged by a different kind of slavery, that of the African negroes, whom the French republic refused to set free. He dedicated one great sonnet to Toussaint L'Ouverture, the former Haitian slave who had been an early supporter of the French Revolution, established free government on the island and, in resisting Napoleon's efforts to re-establish slavery there, had recently been captured and brought back to France as a prisoner. 'Thou hast left behind Powers that will work for thee . . .' William comforted him,

> There's not a breathing of the common wind
> That will forget thee; thou hast great allies;
> Thy friends are exultations, agonies,
> And love, and man's unconquerable mind.
>
> *To Toussaint L'Ouverture, ll.9–14*

On a more humble variant of this same theme, he wrote sympathetically of one of their fellow passengers from Calais, a negro woman expelled from France by decree of the government, contrasting her downcast, hopeless manner with her spotless white clothes and her eyes which still retained their 'tropic fire'. More than once he drew the obvious comparison between the spontaneous popular joy and 'faith ... pledged to new-born Liberty' which had greeted himself and Jones in 1791 with the servile pomp that was now displayed in Napoleon's honour. The contrast was all the more forcible on returning to England, 'Europe is yet in bonds ... Thou art free, My country!', but perhaps the finest of the series was written in London, after his return from France, and it invoked William's greatest hero, John Milton, the blind poet who had dedicated his life and work to the cause of liberty.

> Milton! thou shouldst be living at this hour:
> England hath need of thee: she is a fen
> Of stagnant waters: altar, sword, and pen,
> Fireside, the heroic wealth of hall and bower,
> Have forfeited their ancient English dower
> Of inward happiness. We are selfish men;
> Oh! raise us up, return to us again;
> And give us manners, virtue, freedom, power.
>
> *London, 1802, ll.1–8*

After this outpouring, occasioned by a deep sense of political grievance, William had fallen silent. He may not have been writing new poetry in 1803, but he was publishing extensively through the medium of Daniel Stuart's newspaper, the *Morning Post*. Over the course of that single year, at least fifteen of his poems appeared. More than half of them were published under an editorial banner which said that they were 'Sonnets of a Political nature, which are not only written by one of the first Poets of the age, but are among his best productions. Each forms a little Political Essay, on some recent proceeding.' In order to make them appear as a body, and in sequence, the *Morning Post* even went to the unusual lengths of reprinting on 29 January 1803 'I grieved for Buonaparté' and *Calais, August 1802*, which had already been published on 16 September 1802 and 13 January 1803. Although the editor had promised twelve of these poems, only seven eventually appeared, all of them under the initials WLD, which may have stood for something like 'Wordsworth libertatis defensor'. Apart from a single short epitaph and 'I find it written of Simonides', published on 14 January and 10 October respectively, the rest of the poems were translations from the Italian. All appeared without signature.

Other than the political sonnets, which had a serious purpose, William considered most of them ephemera and did not republish them in his lifetime. What he needed was something new to stimulate his interest and feeling, hence the Scottish tour.

The original plan was to walk, but Coleridge's uncertain state of health persuaded them to purchase what they called a jaunting car, but Samuel Rogers said 'looked very like a cart'. It was a low open vehicle, with a dicky box for the driver, hanging seats down each side capable of taking six people in all, and a space in the middle for luggage; to pull it, they purchased an 'aged but stout & spirited' horse. Sara could not come, as expected, to stay with Mary and little Johnny, but Joanna, 'a good hearted girl with a large share of the Hutchinson generosity and disinterestedness about her', stepped into the breach at the last minute. The evening before they were due to set off from Grasmere, Rogers and his sister, who were also on their way to Scotland on a tour, called for tea. The poet had met the Wordsworths before, in June 1801, when he and Richard 'Conversation' Sharp had called with a letter of introduction from Josiah Wedgwood. Though William greatly liked Rogers, Coleridge had thought him a 'drivelling Booby' then, and was now disposed to be outraged by the 'envy, the jealousy, & the other miserable Passions, that have made their Pandaemonium in the crazy Hovel of that poor Man's Heart'. William was simply amused by this display of pettiness, but Coleridge became 'melancholy', which was always a bad sign, indicating a resort to opium. Dorothy, nerves on edge, fell victim to one of her bilious attacks, delaying their departure from Grasmere. Not to be outdone, as soon as they reached Keswick, Coleridge diagnosed himself as suffering 'a compleat & almost heartless Case of Atonic Gout' and declared himself in imminent danger of a paralytic stroke.

At this point, most sane individuals would have abandoned the whole idea of going on a six-week tour of Scotland in such company, but William was not to be put off so lightly. When they eventually set off from Keswick, at twenty past eleven on the morning of 15 August, they must have made a hilarious sight: William up on the dicky box of the cumbersome cart, driving the ancient nag, like some nineteenth-century Don Quixote, and a miserable Dorothy and Coleridge hunched up in the rear, determinedly scribbling their notes for their journals of the tour. Less than four years later, Coleridge would complain that he could not recall a single image or conversation of the first week or more of the tour.

If true, this was extraordinary. Their route took them through Carlisle, where they arrived on 16 August, the very day on which the notorious bigamist and forger John Hatfield was sentenced to death. Coleridge had played a personal role in exposing Hatfield by writing a series of articles for the *Morning Post*, describing how he had passed himself off as Colonel Augustus Hope, MP, and bigamously married Mary Robinson, the beautiful Maid of Buttermere, in October 1802. The three travellers not only attended the assizes to see him condemned (Coleridge alarming the whole court by shouting 'Dinner!' to William who was on the other side of the hall), but also went to the gaol where he was being held. At Dorothy's ghoulish instigation, Coleridge obtained an interview with Hatfield, coming away with the impression that he was vain and a hypocrite. By a curious coincidence,

Dorothy, waiting outside, fell into conversation with a debtor at the prison, only to discover he had been a fellow sailor with John. William needed no persuasion to give him a shilling when they left.

At Dumfries, they unexpectedly found themselves staying in the same inn as Rogers and his sister; William and Dorothy called on them briefly but Coleridge remained aloof. 'Wordsworth and Coleridge were entirely occupied in talking about poetry', Rogers noted; 'and the whole care of looking out for cottages where they might get refreshment and pass the night, as well as of seeing their poor horse fed and littered, devolved upon Miss Wordsworth. She was a most delightful person, – so full of talent, so simple-minded, and so modest!'

Coleridge remained behind at the inn, presumably keeping out of the way of the Rogerses, while William and Dorothy went to pay homage to Robert Burns. With the help of a friendly bookseller they sought out his unmarked grave in a churchyard ironically full of expensive and fantastically wrought memorials. Afterwards, they called at Burns's house. Mrs Burns and her children were at the seaside, but the maid let them in and they viewed with approval its austere simplicity and cleanliness, which contrasted with the meanness of its external appearance.

The disparity in interest between Coleridge and the Wordsworths would only increase as the tour went on. By the evening of the fourth day, Coleridge declined to accompany them on their evening walks, claiming to be ill. When they were forced to dismount by the steepness of the rough road between Leadhills and Crawfordjohn, the three of them walked 'chearfully' along in the sunshine, but 'each of us alone'. As tension between them increased, so did the length of Dorothy's entries in her journal, as she chattered to herself rather than to her silent companions.

Hastening through a busy, noisy and dirty Glasgow, they made their way up the west bank of Loch Lomond (which continually reminded them of Ullswater), through Luss to Tarbet, at the northern extremity of the lake. As they set out to explore the Trossachs, the weather became increasingly cold and wet. The Wordsworths took every opportunity to travel by boat, but Coleridge preferred to walk on alone rather than face such exposure to the cold. There was clearly little point in going on together, so William suggested that perhaps they should part: the Wordsworths would continue with their tour and Coleridge could walk the twenty or so miles across the Trossachs to Stirling, where he could catch a coach to Edinburgh. The two poets and erstwhile friends both had an interesting gloss on their separation. 'Poor Coleridge was at that time in bad spirits, & somewhat too much in love with his own dejection', was William's analysis; Coleridge blamed William's 'Hypochondriachal Feelings' which 'keep him silent, & [self]-centered'. Dorothy pretended that nothing had happened. On 29 August they went their separate ways.

That it was only the company which had been ungenial became immediately transparent. Instead of heading straight for Edinburgh, 'poor Coleridge' decided to explore the Highlands, travelling 263 miles of mountainous terrain on foot in the space of a mere eight days. Much to their surprise, as they advanced deeper into the Highlands, the Wordsworths discovered that they had been anticipated by Coleridge; he had even stayed in some of the same inns and cottages. The

Wordsworths walked, rode and sailed along Lochs Awe, Etive, Linnhe, Tay and Tummel, travelling as far north as Fort William and as far east as Blair Atholl, before returning through the Trossachs to take the road they had themselves suggested to Coleridge, to Stirling and Edinburgh. Dorothy's response to the grandeur of the landscape was understandably rapturous: she saw everything with fresh eyes, and became neither jaded nor blasé. Again and again she declared she had never seen anything finer, more delicious or more delightful, reminding one of William's description in *Tintern Abbey* of 'the aching joys' and 'dizzy raptures' of his own youthful 'appetite' for nature, which

> ... had no need of a remoter charm,
> By thought supplied, nor any interest
> Unborrowed from the eye.
> *Tintern Abbey, ll.81–3*

At Edinburgh, the Wordsworths visited all the usual tourist sights, but apparently made no effort to be introduced to any of the literary society already flourishing there. On leaving, however, they made a detour eastwards to visit Walter Scott at his cottage in Lasswade.

William and Scott shared a mutual friend in John Stoddart, who supplied the introduction for this first meeting, but, more importantly, Scott, like William, was devoted to the land of his birth, knew all the local people, places and histories, and was the ideal guide to the borders. On 19 September, he conducted them round Melrose and the beautiful pale-red sandstone ruins of the Abbey, pointing out much that would otherwise have escaped them and regaling them with tales of its venerable history.

The Wordsworths were reluctant to part so soon from their new-found friend, who was on his way to the assizes at Jedburgh, so he agreed to meet them again, but begged that they would not enter the court, 'for I really would not like you to see the sort of figure I cut there'. Accidentally catching sight of him later, wearing a cocked hat and sword and marching in the judge's procession to the sound of a single cracked trumpet, they understood his embarrassment. After the business of the day was over, he joined them and greatly delighted them by partly reading and partly reciting, 'sometimes in an enthusiastic style of chant', the first four cantos of his as yet unpublished ballad the *Lay of the Last Minstrel*. But William found himself in a very awkward position indeed, for he immediately recognized that the poem was an imitation of Coleridge's *Christabel*, and included at least one phrase lifted straight from it. 'We were both equally convinced from the frankness of Walter Scott's manner that it was an unconscious imitation,' Dorothy wrote later. What is more, they understood how it happened. John Stoddart had 'a very wicked memory' and had repeated various passages from the then-unpublished *Christabel* to Scott. For years afterwards, William would reproach himself for not having said anything at the time, not least because the prior publication of the *Lay of the Last Minstrel* would pre-empt Coleridge's poem and steal its thunder. 'I did not expect that it [the *Lay*] would make much sensation', William admitted, 'but I was mistaken; for it went up like a balloon.'

On 23 September they were obliged to part from their genial friend and they turned their faces homeward. At Carlisle they paused to view the site of Hatfield's execution, and on 25 September, between eight and nine o'clock, they arrived at Town End, 'where we found Mary in perfect health, Joanna Hutchinson with her, and little John asleep in the clothes-basket by the fire'.

William and Dorothy had been away almost exactly six weeks. They returned in good health (though both whinged about minor ailments) and in high spirits, with a fund of material and memories from which they would both profit over the coming years. What William had not succeeded in doing was adding to his stock of poetry. He returned with only one completed sonnet, *Composed at [Neidpath] Castle*, attacking the Marquis of Queensbury for cutting down the ancient trees adorning the gorge of the Tweed below his castle, and three lines addressed to Kilchurn Castle.

Rumours of a French invasion of Britain had followed the Wordsworths even to the remoter regions of Scotland and returning to Grasmere, they found the whole vale literally up in arms. Lord Lowther had sent out a circular calling all loyal subjects to volunteer for the local militias in preparation for the defence of their country. On 3 October William 'with the greatest part of the Men of Grasmere' went to Ambleside to enlist. Ten years earlier he would have thought it impossible that he could ever contemplate fighting for England against the French, but France under Napoleon was not the same as France in the early days of the revolution.

The threat of invasion stirred William to poetry and he immediately dashed off a couple of sonnets, which did more credit to his patriotism than his talent. One he addressed to the 'Vanguard of Liberty, ye men of Kent', to assure them that

> We all are with you now from shore to shore:
> Ye Men of Kent, 'tis victory or death!
> *To the Men of Kent. October, 1803, ll.13–14*

The best one can say about both sonnets is that they suited the mood of the country, and quickly found a place in more than one publication.

One of the most urgent calls on William's duty was not connected with the war against France. Thank-you letters are never the easiest to write, but this one was particularly difficult. Just before he had set out from Keswick on the Scottish tour, Coleridge had presented him with an extraordinary gift. It was the title deeds to a little estate at Applethwaite, gloriously situated on the lower slopes of Skiddaw, just outside Keswick. The donor was Sir George Beaumont, a wealthy baronet, who was a talented amateur painter and a generous patron of artists and writers of every kind. With his wife, Lady Margaret, he had spent the summer lodging at Greta Hall with Mr Jackson, the owner and co-resident with the Coleridges. His object had been to sketch and paint in the Keswick area, but, like so many others, he had fallen under the spell of Coleridge's brilliant conversation. His wife was even more enthusiastic. Coleridge, as always, had been generous in his praise of

William's poetry and had lent the Beaumonts copies of the 1802 edition of *Lyrical Ballads*. By the end of July, they were 'half-mad' to meet William too. Even before the meeting came about, Beaumont decided that he had to make a practical gesture to show his appreciation of the two poets and encourage their respective careers. Discussion with Coleridge had led him to the conclusion that the best thing he could do was to bring the two men closer together: 'I thought with pleasure on the encrease of enjoyment you would receive from the beauties of nature', he told William, 'by being able to communicate more frequently your sensations to each other, & that this would be a means of contributing to the pleasure & improvement of the world by stimulating you both to poetical exertions'. Applethwaite was less than two miles from Greta Hall; it was worth £100 and consisted of a few old cottages and two small fields. An additional benefit was that ownership of a freehold estate in Cumberland also conferred the right to vote. Beaumont's intention was that William would 'patch up a house there if I liked to be near Mr Coleridge', as his recipient somewhat ungraciously phrased it.

It was an extraordinarily generous gesture, not least because the purchase was a *fait accompli*, made before Beaumont had even met William. Unfortunately, it was entirely misdirected. Had he consulted William, his family or even the unfortunate Mrs Coleridge, he would soon have discovered that living in closer quarters was not something anyone but Coleridge himself wanted. There was the added difficulty that William felt great reluctance to accept such a valuable present from someone he barely knew. What should he do? His indecision, combined with his incurable habit of putting off an unwelcome task, meant that it was 14 October, two months after he had received the deeds, before he wrote his acknowledgement. It was an awkward letter, struggling both to justify the delay by implausible accounts of ill-health, and to reject the proffered kindness without causing offence. 'It is a most delightful situation,' he told Beaumont,

and few things would give me greater pleasure than to realise the plan which you had in view for me of building a house there. But I am afraid, I am sorry to say, that the chances are very much against this, partly on account of the state of my own affairs, and still more from the improbability of Mr Coleridge's continuing in the Country ... what I sh[ould] wish is, that I might be considered at present as Steward of the land with liberty to lay out the rent in plant[ing] or any other improvement which might be thought [advi]sable with a view to building upon it. And if it should [be] out of my power to pitch my own tent there, I would then request that you would give me leave [to] restore the property to your own hands, in order tha[t] you might have the opportunity of again present[ing] it to some worthy person who might be so fortu[nate] as to be able to make that pleasant use of it which it was your wish that I should have done.

Beaumont was having none of it: 'talk no more of obligations', he roundly declared, 'plant it, delve it – & build upon it or not, as it suits your convenience, but let me live & die with the idea the sweet place, with its rocks, its banks, & mountain stream are in the possession of such a mind as yours'. He ordered William to keep the entire transaction a secret and forbade him to mention a word about it again. Applethwaite was his and so, in this most unexpected way, William had finally become a member of that class he so admired, a statesman of Cumberland.

Beaumont was not offended by William's refusal to build a house at Applethwaite, but Coleridge was, and his private comments about his old friend were becoming increasingly venomous. His relationship with the Wordsworths was not helped by the unexpected news that Sara Hutchinson was about to take up residence in the Lakes. Her brother had been given notice to quit Gallow Hill and, encouraged by the Wordsworths, as much as by his own links with Penrith, Tom came over to find a farm; by 22 October he had agreed to take Park House, on the Dalemain estate, overlooking Ullswater. Intimacy with the Wordsworths must have warped his judgement, for, though the house was gloriously situated, the farm itself would never be particularly successful.

As the late autumn slipped away there was much excitement at Keswick. William Hazlitt, Coleridge's former disciple, had come to the Lakes in July to paint portraits of William and Coleridge. At the end of October he returned to complete them. They were both dolorous and funereal efforts, which made the poets look twenty years too old. William's, as Southey humorously pointed out, looked like a man 'at the gallows – deeply affected by his deserved fate – yet determined to die like a man'. Coleridge had taken a dislike to the young Hazlitt: 'he is jealous, gloomy, & of an irritable Pride – & addicted to women, as objects of sexual Indulgence'. It was this last quality which got him into trouble. He made a number of 'gross attacks' on women at Keswick, even whipping one for not yielding to his advances, and brought the wrath of the town on him. He narrowly escaped being ducked, or even sent to prison, and only got away by slipping out under cover of darkness, arriving at midnight at Grasmere, where he threw himself on William's mercy. Hazlitt was lucky not only to find a refuge, but also to be given clothes and several pounds to make good his escape. No doubt he did not tell the full story, for, remembering William's reaction to the men who had publicly beaten women in the streets of Germany, it is difficult to imagine he would have assisted had he known.

Another visitor from the Alfoxton days also made a reappearance this winter. Towards the end of November, John Thelwall, the radical demagogue, whose arrival at Alfoxton had attracted the suspicions of the Home Office, paid a visit. He had embarked on a new lecturing career, this time avoiding politics and advocating an uncontentious system of elocution. He was in Kendal to give his public lectures, and drove out to see his old friends. He arrived at an inopportune moment. Mary, Dorothy and baby Johnny were alone at Town End. Alarming reports of Coleridge's health had compelled William to hurry over to Greta Hall. There he found his friend 'SO VERY VERY ill, with such a complication of bodily miseries', as Coleridge himself put it, that it was evident something would have to be done about him. Coleridge had no doubts about what he wanted to do. 'I have a Persuasion, strong as Fate, that from 12 to 18 months' Residence & perfect Tranquillity in a genial Climate would send me back to dear old England, a sample of the first Resurrection.' His drug-taking had reached such heights that he slept half the day, was awake half the night and suffered regular screaming nightmares. His brother-in-law, Southey, and his wife, who had lost their much beloved only child while the Wordsworths and Coleridge had been on their Scottish tour, now agreed to take up at least semi-permanent residence at Greta Hall. This meant that Coleridge could leave with a clear conscience, knowing that his family would have the Southeys' support in his absence. All that remained was to find the money. With a generosity he could ill afford (he had just received a demand for payment of college debts), William offered Coleridge a loan of £100.

On 20 December Coleridge and his younger son, three-year-old Derwent, arrived in a post chaise at Town End. It was supposed to be a farewell visit, for Coleridge had determined to go to Madeira. He intended to stay a single day, then walk on to Kendal for the coach to London. In the event, he stayed almost a month, reluctant to leave the genial atmosphere of the Wordsworths' home. Now that he was about to part from them for eighteen months or two years, he relearned to appreciate their virtues and temporarily forgot all his jealousies. For much of the time he was ill and, despite the inconvenience in the tiny household, made sure he was the centre of attention. His bed was moved into the sitting room and Mary and Dorothy nursed him 'with more than Mother's Love', sitting in turn by his bedside. With one of those flashes of endearing self-knowledge that were his saving grace, Coleridge admitted that the Wordsworths were 'in too great Sympathy with my Ill health' for his own good. On this occasion, however, he tried even Dorothy's patience; with unaccustomed asperity, she noted that Coleridge had been 'continually wanting coffee, broth or something or other'.

On 14 January 1804 Coleridge set off on foot for Kendal. William accompanied him the first six or seven miles, almost as far as Troutbeck, then the two friends parted. It would be more than two and a half years before they met again.

William now returned to the project of *The Recluse* with a vengeance. By 5 March he had written 1,200 lines, completing another book of the introductory autobiographical poem, and anticipated finishing the final one in two or three days' time. As the autobiographical poem neared its end, William became increasingly anxious to have Coleridge's long-promised notes containing his outline of how *The Recluse* itself was to take shape. 'I cannot say how much importance I attach to this,' he wrote to Coleridge, 'if it should please God that I survive you, I should reproach myself for ever in writing the work if I had neglected to procure this help.'

At Coleridge's request, Mary and Dorothy began to transcribe all William's manuscript poems, so that he could take a complete copy with him on his voyage. The manuscripts were in such wretched condition that William's almost constant superintendence was required, so Mary and Dorothy wisely took the precaution of making a second copy for themselves as they went along. It says much for the stamina and determination of the two women that they managed to transcribe about 8,000 lines in something under six weeks, and Coleridge had his own copy of William's entire unpublished opus before he set sail from Portsmouth on 9 April.

This spring, which saw one of William's most sustained efforts on *The Recluse* and what would become *The Prelude*, also witnessed the creation of about a dozen shorter poems which are among the most famous he ever wrote. Several of these were connected with the Scottish tour, such as *To a Highland Girl* and *Yarrow Unvisited*, but out of the former developed the lovely lines which became the poem addressed to Mary, 'She was a Phantom of delight':

> A perfect Woman, nobly planned,
> To warn, to comfort, and command,
> And yet a Spirit still, and bright
> With something of angelic light.

It comes as something of a surprise to learn that Mary, who is not usually credited with poetic insight, contributed what William considered the two best lines to perhaps his most famous poem. 'I wandered lonely as a cloud' was probably prompted by a visit he paid at the end of April to Gowbarrow Park, on Ullswater. His object was to see his friend Charles Luff, who was a captain in the Loyal Wedgwood Volunteers at Patterdale, exercising his militia in a 'Grand field day' at Gowbarrow. The site was renowned throughout the Lakes for its profusion of wild daffodils, which are much smaller, paler and more delicate than the cultivated varieties best known today. It was by no means the first time William had seen them, stretching in a golden band along the bay and fluttering and dancing in the breeze, and the poem celebrates not just the daffodils themselves, but also the power of memory:

> For oft, when on my couch I lie
> In vacant or in pensive mood,
> They flash upon that inward eye
> Which is the bliss of solitude;
> And then my heart with pleasure fills,
> And dances with the daffodils.
> *'I wandered lonely as a cloud', ll.19–24*

Two other important poems were written about this time. *Ode to Duty* was, as William admitted, modelled on Gray's *Ode to Adversity*, which was itself an imitation of the Roman poet Horace's *Ode to Fortune*, but it clearly arose from conversations with Coleridge on his last visit. Both men had reason to lament their lack of commitment to their work. Despite all his grandiose schemes and prospectuses, Coleridge had never yet written the great work which everyone expected of him; William, as friends and family continually reminded him, was supposedly dissipating his talents on small poems instead of dedicating his life to the completion of *The Recluse*. In his poem, which he addressed to Duty as the 'Stern Daughter of the Voice of God', William acknowledged his besetting sins of idleness and procrastination and effectively dedicated himself to *The Recluse*.

> ... oft, when in my heart was heard
> Thy timely mandate, I deferred

> The task, in smoother walks to stray;
> But thee I now would serve more strictly, if I may.
> *Ode to Duty, ll.29–32*

He was, of course, making himself a hostage to fortune; the *Ode to Duty* became a family joke and William was frequently teased by wife and sister for having forgotten this dedication of himself to the 'Stern Lawgiver!'

The second ode, *Intimations of Immortality*, was, quite simply, the greatest William ever wrote. So many of its lines and phrases have been used as titles for books and films, or become part of the common vocabulary, that it is difficult to come to it fresh. Reading it for the first time is like going through a dictionary of quotations. And yet it is impossible not to be impressed with its sheer grandeur and authority; it is emphatically the philosopher-poet speaking. The first four stanzas lamented the passing away of 'a glory from the earth' as we move from childhood to adulthood.

> Whither is fled the visionary gleam?
> Where is it now, the glory and the dream?

These lines had been written two years earlier, in March 1802, and then William had not known the answer. Coleridge, however, had characteristically reworked them and turned them into the self-explanatory *Dejection: An Ode*. Now William returned to his original lines and transformed the poem into a positive celebration of human nature. Taking his cue from Platonic philosophy, he argued for the pre-existence of the soul as the reason why childhood is 'apparelled in celestial light'.

> Our birth is but a sleep and a forgetting:
> The Soul that rises with us, our life's Star,
>   Hath had elsewhere its setting,
>   And cometh from afar:
>   Not in entire forgetfulness,
>   And not in utter nakedness,
> But trailing clouds of glory do we come
>   From God, who is our home:
> Heaven lies about us in our infancy!

This verse, in particular, would cause endless controversy because pre-existence is not a tenet of the Christian faith, but William flatly refused to withdraw or alter the lines. They were, indeed, central to the poem, for they conjured up the boy William, who could not believe in his own mortality, but expected, like Elijah, to be physically translated to heaven, and whose imagination was so strong that he could not conceive of external things having a separate existence from himself. Just as in *Tintern Abbey* the adult William had found compensation for the loss of childish glory.

> Though nothing can bring back the hour
> Of splendour in the grass, of glory in the flower;
> We will grieve not, rather find
> Strength in what remains behind;
> In the primal sympathy
> Which having been must ever be;
> In the soothing thoughts that spring
> Out of human suffering;
> In the faith that looks through death,
> In years that bring the philosophic mind.

He ended the poem with four deceptively simple lines which were the summation of his philosophy.

> Thanks to the human heart by which we live,
> Thanks to its tenderness, its joys, and fears,
> To me the meanest flower that blows can give
> Thoughts that do often lie too deep for tears.

It was no accident that William chose to end every future edition of his poems with these lines.

By the end of April 1804 William had added almost 3,000 lines to his poem on his own life, but the fit of creativity which had held him in its grasp since the beginning of the year gradually petered out. In Coleridge's absence, the Wordsworths felt an increased sense of responsibility towards his family, so there were regular visits to Greta Hall. An added bonus was the presence of Southey, to whom William, rather to his own surprise, took a liking. They had much in common: a shared republican past which had given way to a less radical stance in domestic politics, a commitment to their work as poets (and in Southey's case, as a historian and essayist as well) and a devotion to their families. That they had been wary of each other was principally due to Coleridge, whose bitter quarrels with his brother-in-law had drawn in their mutual friends. An uneasy truce now existed between the two men: 'my inclination to like him', Southey wrote of Coleridge, 'has always got the better of [my] judgement'. William discovered Southey was not only 'very pleasant in his manners' but also a man of 'great reading, in old books, poetry, Chronicles, memoirs, &c., particularly Spanish and Portuguese'.

Another shared bond, though not one that either man accepted, was that, with Coleridge and Lamb, they were now being classed as the 'modern school of poets', soon to be labelled, even more inaccurately, the 'Lake School of Poetry'. The man who coined these descriptions, and would be their scourge for years to come, was Francis Jeffrey, an Edinburgh lawyer, who had co-founded the *Edinburgh Review* in October 1802 and was its principal literary critic. Famed for his corruscating attacks on contemporary poets, his reviews made highly entertaining reading, unless you were the unfortunate author whose work was under scrutiny. In the very first volume of the new periodical, Jeffrey turned all the savagery of his undoubted wit on the '*sect* of poets, that has established itself in this country within these ten or twelve years'. The article purported to be a review of Southey's *Thalaba*, published the previous year, but almost half was dedicated to a scathing attack on the poetic principles of 'the modern school'. Almost as his starting point, Jeffrey took the much-enlarged preface to the 1802 edition of *Lyrical Ballads*, describing it as 'a kind of manifesto that preceded one of their most flagrant acts of hostility'. Without actually naming William anywhere, he tore him apart: 'It is absurd to suppose, that an author should make use of the language of the vulgar, to express the sentiments of the refined'. He attacked William's central thesis, that 'we have all of us one human heart'.

The love, or grief, or indignation of an enlightened and refined character, is not only expressed in a different language, but is in itself a different emotion from the love, or grief, or anger of a clown, a tradesman, or a market-wench. The things themselves are radically and obviously distinct . . . The poor and vulgar may interest us, in poetry, by their *situation:* but never, we apprehend, by any sentiments that are peculiar to their condition, and still less by any language that is characteristic of it . . . After all, it must be admitted, that there is a class of persons (we are afraid they cannot be called *readers*), to whom the representation of vulgar manners, in vulgar language, will afford much entertainment. We are afraid, however, that the ingenious writers who supply the hawkers and ballad-singers, have very nearly monopolized that department, and are probably better qualified to hit the taste of their customers, than Mr Southey, or any of his brethren, can yet pretend to be.

William dismissed the review with lofty disdain, 'the Fellow was a Blockhead and knew nothing about the Business'. He was wrong to be unconcerned. Jeffrey was being deliberately contentious and excessive, but his entertaining style quickly won him an enormous readership and a proportionately powerful influence on critical opinion.

Much of the summer of 1804 was taken up with visits to Greta Hall, and to Park House, where Tom, Sara and Joanna had been living since the beginning of April. A major disappointment for them was that the Clarksons were no longer their neighbours at Eusemere. Catherine had gone to Bristol the previous year to receive treatment from Dr Beddoes, leaving her husband at Eusemere to complete his book, *A Portraiture of Quakerism*, but when the anti-slavery movement demanded his presence in London Thomas, too, had left, and in July 1804 Eusemere was sold to Lord Lonsdale.

The Wordsworths spent three weeks at Park House. Dorothy, who remained at Grasmere, had dreaded the separation, but it was little Johnny, not her brother, for whom she pined: 'I shall be very lonely − at home without John − home without him will seem more lonely than it could possibly have been before his birth.' Dorothy's letters now were a continuous eulogy of this passionate child: even his fits of temper, when neither his mother nor his aunt could hold him, were recounted with admiration as proof of his remarkable strength.

The Wordsworths had not been home long when Mrs Coleridge and her three children descended on them for a visit. It must have been a trying time for Mary, who was heavily pregnant, though at least they now had more active assistance in the form of a fifteen-year-old servant girl who had come in May to take old Molly Fisher's place. Molly's sister-in-law had died suddenly, so she had been promoted to the 'high office of her Brother's Housekeeper and attendant upon his single Cow'. This enforced departure came as a great relief to the Wordsworths, for Molly, or 'the drollery belonging to the Cottage', as Coleridge called her, had been unfit for her duties for at least the previous six months. Entering on her third life, as Dorothy put it, Molly astonished them all by the transformation she wrought in the cleanliness of her brother's cottage; it was her great pride to be continually bearing little gifts from her garden and dairy to the Wordsworths. The new servant was active and strong (though nameless), and fortunately she loved children.

The Coleridges were still with them when Mary was delivered of her second child, a girl, whom they had already decided would be named Dorothy, on 16 August, her own birthday. Despite the fact that the baby was named after her, Dorothy could not conceal her preference for Johnny. 'She is a nice Baby, healthy enough – stout enough – pretty enough', she damned with faint praise, 'but in nothing *extraordinary*, as John certainly was . . .' Johnny, barely fourteen months old, was equally unimpressed, taking every opportunity to hit his new sister and make her cry, but William was besotted with his daughter: 'She is her Father's darling', Dorothy remarked, 'I think he is more tender over her than he ever was over her Brother.'

Sara came over the day after the birth and Mrs Coleridge and her children departed two days later. It was only a short breathing space, however, for less than a month later Mary's aunt and cousin, Elizabeth and Mary Monkhouse, arrived on a visit from Penrith and stayed a week. Little Dorothy, whom the family would later call Doro, or Dora, to distinguish her from her aunt, was christened on 16 September in Grasmere church, like her brother. Sara stood proxy for her godmother, Lady Beaumont, who, though a virtual stranger to the entire family, had been in regular correspondence with Dorothy since her husband had presented William with Applethwaite. As a christening gift, Lady Beaumont sent her goddaughter £10, which they decided to lay out in planting trees on a small plot of ground, to be called 'Dorothy's Grove': 'They will grow up *with her* at first, as brethren, with whom she may measure and compare herself from year to year, but if sun and wind prosper them they will be a shelter and a shade for her by the time she has lived twenty years, and who knows but they may be the nursery of her tenderest and best thoughts!'

Sara and the Monkhouses left Town End on 23 September, and on the first fine autumnal day that followed, William and Dorothy set off in the jaunting car for a short tour of Ennerdale and Wasdale.

They returned to find yet more visitors, but the one who would have been more than welcome at Grasmere but did not come, pleading pressure of business in

London, was John. He had returned from China at the beginning of August after an eventful voyage that had included the engagement with the French off Malaysia. He had not seen his brother and sister for two years and had never seen either of the children, but despite pressing invitations from both William and Dorothy, he did not come, and one is forced to the conclusion that he could not face the prospect of seeing Mary as his brother's wife.

Christmas passed quietly at Grasmere. Once the flood of visitors had slackened off, William returned to composition. Writing to Sir George Beaumont on Christmas Day, he could report that he had written 'upwards of 2000 verses during the last ten weeks', mainly for *The Prelude*. He now hoped to have completed it by May and then he intended to 'fall with all my might' on *The Recluse*, which he expected to be up to 12,000 lines in length. So far he had only some 2,000, most of them relating to the Pedlar, and composed long ago. He had also written 'a dwarf inscription' for a little circular summer-house which they had recently built at the top of the garden. The 'Moss Hut', as the family called it, commanded wonderful views over the lake and valley, marred only by the church, which had just been whitewashed and disturbed the proportions of the entire vale by standing out so incongruously. The moss hut was an ingenious solution to the lack of space in the cottage, serving as a refuge where William could retire for quiet, and a pleasure-house where the Wordsworths and their guests could take tea. They could get to it easily for, earlier in the year, at Catherine Clarkson's suggestion, they had replaced the window on the landing with a door, so that they could go straight out from the house into the back garden.

The New Year was ushered in by a series of sparkling days, brilliant sunshine, clear skies and keen frosts. Grasmere lake froze over and, with the help of Mary's energetic youngest brother, George, William took the entire family out on the ice, the two men on skates pushing chairs in which Mary and Dorothy sat, each holding a child in her arms. The next day, New Year's Day, they all packed into the jaunting car and, with George as their intrepid charioteer, drove over Kirkstone Pass to stay with the Hutchinsons at Park House. It proved to be a foolish escapade, for the severe cold and the strenuous exercise of having to walk up the hills carrying the children left Mary with toothache, Dorothy a bad cold and William an inflammation of the eyes. Almost the entire Hutchinson clan was waiting to greet them, only Jack, the oldest, being absent. Little Hartley Coleridge was there too, so the New Year began with a joyful family reunion.

John Wordsworth spent his thirty-second birthday and Christmas on board the *Earl of Abergavenny*. He had been assigned a new route to China which would take him to Bengal rather than Bombay and, so long as his was among the first ships to reach Canton, he stood to make immense profits in the way of trade. The cargo alone, which included £67,000 worth of dollars, packed in sixty-two chests, 200 tons each of copper, tin, lead and iron, and a vast quantity of cloth, haberdashery, millinery, glass, Wedgwood ware and military supplies, was valued at £200,000 (the equivalent of £7,046,000 today). John's personal investment amounted to some £20,000 in goods and money. He had thirty-five passengers dining at his table, nine of them civilians, the rest officers and cadets from the King's and the Company's own militia. As captain he was personally entitled to all the fees charged the passengers, including those for dining rights at his table.

John's crew numbered 164. His petty officers were all younger than himself, but were tried and trusted men with whom he had sailed before. They included, as third mate, his own twenty-three-year-old second cousin Joseph, the son of Richard of Branthwaite. The ordinary seamen were, in John's characteristically blunt words, 'only *trash*': slightly more than half were English, the rest, because of the shortage of experienced sailors caused by the war, a motley collection of Portuguese, Irish, Italians, Scandinavians and Germans. Thirty-two Chinese sailors, who were not allowed by Company law to crew an outward-bound ship, were returning as passengers, and there were approximately 156 soldiers, the majority of them little more than boys, cadets and recruits for the army and East India Company. Altogether, there were almost 400 people on board.

There was an unfortunate incident even before they set sail for China. During a gale off the Downs, another East Indiaman in the convoy, the *Warren Hastings*, drifted into the *Earl of Abergavenny*, damaging the starboard bow and carrying away the anchor fixings, necessitating minor repairs at Portsmouth. Contrary winds and heavy gales delayed their departure, but on 1 February the convoy finally put to sea, under the escort and overall command of HMS *Weymouth*. The orders were to sail through the Needles, 'a passage I do not like much but I hope will be attended with no accident'. In the hurry of departure, the first mate, Samuel Baggot, Joseph Wordsworth and two of the soldiers had to be left behind; so determined were they to reach their ship that they paid the master of an open boat forty guineas to follow and overtake the vessel, which, ironically, he succeeded in doing. Having safely navigated the Needles, the weather deteriorated fast and the slower merchant ships were in a quandary, for they lost sight of the *Weymouth*. The storms grew more violent and, at ten o'clock on the morning of 5 February, the signal was given to turn back and run for safety into Portland Roads, the natural harbour between Weymouth and the Isle of Portland. The *Earl of Abergavenny*, no doubt as a result of John's anxiety to be first out, was the furthest ship from shore. The three other East Indiamen managed to get the obligatory local pilot on board in order to negotiate the Shambles, a notorious shoal of shingles and rock to the south of the island, before the tides turned. John was not so lucky. It was three in the afternoon before his pilot came on board, and by then they had lost the benefit of a flood tide. To clear the Shambles the pilot should have taken a more southerly course than the one he chose, but he seems to have underestimated the clearance needed for the fully laden ship. John clearly distrusted the pilot, but having received an assurance in answer to his questioning, there was nothing he could do. They were in the pilot's hands.

At five o'clock disaster struck. The wind suddenly dropped and the strong ebb tide drove the ship straight on to the Shambles. For two and a half hours, they battled to get her off again, but when the wind veered round to the north-west, it was clear that she was doomed. The distress signal guns were fired to alert those

on shore and the rest of the convoy to their plight. Every time the wind drove them off
the rocks, the tide drew them on again. Under this battering, the hull was irreparably
damaged; even with all hands manning the pumps, the leaks continued to gain on
them. By seven o'clock, no assistance had arrived, so John gave the command for the
distress signal guns to be fired continuously. With great presence of mind, he also
sent off one of the ship's boats to fetch help. Aware this might be the only chance of
escape, he sent a crew of six and only two officers, the purser, Mr Stewart, who carried
the ship's log and all her documentation, and Joseph Wordsworth.

About seven-thirty in the evening the ship finally got clear of the Shambles, but
she was waterlogged. The best hope of saving all on board was to hoist all sails and
run for the nearest shore. There were several sloops in sight, but only one sent a small
skiff to assist. It was too small to make any effective rescue, so John ensured that the
few available places went to the civilian passengers, two Bengal merchants, John
Routledge and Thomas Evans, the latter's daughter and niece, and two of the military
officers. Mrs Blair, the only other woman on board, refused to go in the boat, too
afraid of the darkness and mountainous seas to leave the ship. Evans would later
recall how, as the little boat departed, John leaned over the ship's rails and said
'emphatically', 'God bless You!'

With the aid of his officers, John managed to maintain an air of calm and purpose
on the sinking vessel. The exhausted cadets who manned the pumps, many of them
only boys in their early teens, were encouraged by their superiors to keep up their
efforts and, when this failed, were issued with rations of grog. At around eleven
o'clock, the chief mate, Samuel Baggot, came to John, who had stayed on deck
throughout, and informed him, 'We have done all we can, Sir – she will sink in a
moment'. John replied, 'It cannot be helped – God's will be done'. They were his last
known words. The *Earl of Abergavenny* sank only a mile and a half from the safety of
Weymouth sands, in a mere sixty feet of water. The vast size of the ship meant that
between a third and a half of the upper rigging, top masts and yardarms were above
the level of the water. Some 180 survivors clung to them in the hope of rescue, but
though boats were heard paddling round in the darkness, it was between midnight
and two in the morning before any sort of attempt was made. Less than half of them
survived that freezing February night; benumbed by the bitter cold, many fell insensible from the rigging, or were swept away by the huge breakers of the winter storm.
As always in such desperate circumstances, there were individual acts of heroism.
Baggot died trying to save Mrs Blair, and the sixth mate, Herbert Mortimer, left the
safety of one of the boats to climb up the rigging and carry down, on his back, Sergeant
Heart of the King's Infantry. Thomas Gilpin, the twenty-four-year-old fourth mate,
made equally heroic efforts to save his captain, but they were in vain. John was last
seen clinging to the ropes of his lost ship, impervious to Gilpin's pleas that he would
save himself. No one would ever know whether he had been overcome by the cold
or had simply lost the will to live. Like the proverbial good captain, he went down
with his ship.

12. *Acquiring the Quiet Mind*

First reports of the disaster reached London on the morning of 7 February and it fell to Richard to inform the rest of the family. He wrote identical short notes immediately to both William and Christopher:

> My dear Brother,
> It is with the most painful concern that I inform you of the loss of the Ship Abergavenny off Weymouth last night.
> I am acquainted with but few of the particulars of this melancholy Event. I am told that a great number of Persons have perished and that our Brother John is amongst that number. Mr Joseph Wordsworth is amongst those who have been saved – The Ship struck against a Rock & went to the Bottom.

Knowing their sister's likely reaction, Richard added helplessly to William, 'You will impart this to Dorothy in the best manner you can'. The next day, *The Times* carried the first of many long, detailed accounts of the wreck which would appear in the press. And yet, unbelievably, the Wordsworths at Grasmere remained in ignorance of John's death until 11 February, six days after his ship went down.

It was Sara Hutchinson who brought the news. She was staying in Kendal with an old schoolfriend, saw the newspapers and came straight over to Grasmere to offer what comfort she could. Fortunately, she had the foresight to call at Rydal and intercept Richard's letter. When she arrived at Town End, William and Mary were out walking, and only Dorothy was at home. Realizing that they did not yet know, Sara had the unenviable task of breaking the news first to Dorothy alone, and then again to William and Mary. It requires little imagination to appreciate its devastating effect. Shocked and distraught, the Wordsworths could only weep together. 'I have done all in my power to alleviate the distress of poor Dorothy and my Wife', William wrote later that night, 'but heaven knows I want consolation myself.' Sara agreed to stay for as long as was necessary and, the next morning, a letter arrived from an unexpected quarter. Southey, belying his reputation for coldness, was swift to sympathize. 'I scarcely know what to say to you after the thunderstroke', he wrote,

– nor whether I ought to say anything. – Only – whenever you feel – or fancy yourself in a state to derive any advantage from company – I will come over to you, – or do you come here. It has been my custom when in affliction to force myself to mental exertion, a difficult thing – but possible. – but it made my sleep dreadful. – for grief – as far as it is a bodily feeling like disease will have its course . . . Come to me or send for me whenever you think society will not be impertinent.

'If you could bear to come to this house of mourning to-morrow,' William replied by return, 'I should be forever thankful.' Southey came, stayed two days, and left promising to return again before the week was out: 'he comforted us much, and we must for ever bear his goodness in memory'. Further comfort came from a host of unsolicited testimonials to John, all testifying to the love and respect he had inspired. Thomas Clarkson, who had been among the first to hear the news of the wreck, described how he had seen Wilberforce weep at the news and extol John's character at every opportunity. 'I mourn for my lost friend,' Clarkson wrote,

not only on account of his Loss to you, but of his Loss as a Man. I believe, that if he had returned, and settled in Life, he would have been useful in his Day, by the practical Duty of Benevolence, and by his Example to others. But it has so pleased Providence; and if we cannot call him back, we must reverence his Memory, by the Imitation of his Virtues.

'We loved and honoured your Brother', Lamb wrote, as his sister wept beside him, 'as long as we remember any thing, we shall remember your Brother's noble person, & his sensible manly modest voice'. Coleridge, far away in Malta, heard the news by chance in a social gathering in the drawing room of the governor, Sir Alexander Ball. He staggered to the door, almost fainting with shock, and gave way to his anguish in private.

O William, O Dorothy, Dorothy! – Mary – & you loved him so! . . . O dear John! and so ended thy dreams of Tairns & mountain Becks, & obscure vales in the breasts and necks of Mountains! So thy dream of living with or among thy Brother & *his* – O Heavens! Dying in all its Shapes; shrieks; and confusion; and mad Hope; and Drowning more deliberate than Suicide; – these, these were the Dorothy, the Mary, the Sara Hutchinson, to kiss the cold Drops from thy Brow, & to close thy Eyes! – Never yet has any Loss gone so far into the Life of Hope, with me. I now only fear.

Far more moving, in their simplicity and obvious sincerity, were the tributes paid by those who survived the wreck. From Thomas Evans, the wealthy Bengal merchant whose family owed their lives to John's ensuring that they had places in the rescue boat, down to the humblest, barely literate seaman, they one and all paid tribute to his kindness, cheerful disposition and calm authority in his final hours. His shipmates, the Wordsworths discovered, had called him 'the Philosopher'.

These were but small crumbs of comfort, however, in the face of the press reporting of the wreck. The scale of the disaster – one of the largest merchant ships in the country, laden with valuable cargo, not to mention the loss of some 300 lives – captured the public imagination. The wreck became a macabre tourist attraction: summer visitors to Weymouth (including the royal family) could see the masts of the sunken ship from the esplanade and were ferried out in small boats to view it at close quarters. Newspapers and a flurry of opportunistic pamphlets cashed in on the disaster, with increasingly lurid speculation about its cause. Nowhere was John's personal courage doubted, but questions were asked about his judgement. Why had he delayed firing the signal guns for an hour and a half after they first struck? Why had he not ordered the ship's boats to be cut free? Possibly even more distressing was the almost universal consensus that John had effectively committed suicide, rather than face the consequences of losing his ship and his fortune.

William was desperate for reassurance that his brother had died the hero, not just for his own satisfaction but because he could not bear the thought that the relatives of those lost would blame John. The *Earl of Abergavenny* was a Penrith ship and there was not a family in the town untouched by the tragedy. William knew he would never be able to look these people in the face again if he could not clear John's name. He turned to Charles Lamb, who was a clerk at East India House, and his own cousin Captain Wordsworth, who had been a major investor in the voyage. Both of them made enormous efforts to track down survivors and provide William with the answers he wanted. Unfortunately, this was not the same as the truth.

It proved impossible to scotch rumours that John had not wished to survive the wreck. But at least there was no question of misconduct. There was a logical, nautical, explanation for each of his decisions and an investigation by the Committee of Shipping reporting to the Court of Directors unanimously resolved 'that the Commander, Officers & Ship's company of the Earl of Abergavenny be fully acquitted of all Imputation of neglect or misconduct in respect to the Loss of that Ship'. The owners were also cleared of any neglect or misconduct in supplying and equipping the ship. All the evidence vindicated John and put the blame squarely on the pilot, who not only survived the wreck he had caused, but somehow managed to remain anonymous. The local community closed ranks. The suspicion must remain that the men of Portland and Weymouth also deliberately refrained from assisting the survivors. Indeed, they had an unenviable reputation for exactly that. Shipwrecks were commonplace on that notorious stretch of coastline but it was not often that the rich pickings of a fully laden East Indiaman were to be had. Many of the survivors reported hearing boats in the darkness after the ship went down, but their cries for help were ignored, because, it was later improbably claimed, of fears that they would be swamped in the rush for safety. Though there were important exceptions, boxes of personal belongings washed up on shore in the weeks that followed were plundered and left empty; no doubt valuables also went missing from the unidentifiable corpses.

For this reason, at Captain Wordsworth's instigation, a reward of £200 was offered for the recovery of John's body and, six weeks after the ship went down, it was found by dragging the wreck site. His sword, presented by the East India Company after the engagement with Admiral Linois the previous year, was missing; a reward was offered and, lo and behold, it too was recovered. On 21 March John was buried in the churchyard at All Saints' Church, Wyke Regis, overlooking the bay where he had lost his life. His funeral was attended by twelve mourners, including the mayor of Weymouth and representatives of the Company; 'by particular desire', presumably of the Wordsworth family, the burial arrangements were made by the widow of Thomas Fowell Buxton, whose country house, Bellfield, was just outside Weymouth in the parish of Wyke Regis. Mrs Anna Buxton, a Quaker, was a cousin of Christopher's wife, Priscilla, and her own son, Edward, was a midshipman in the service of the East India Company. John was interred next to the Buxton vault by the south door of the church; a large stone was laid on the grave, but was removed on the authority of a later bishop, who identified it as an altar table and removed it to the sanctuary. The daughter of John's cousin Robinson Wordsworth wrote to William in 1846 to point this out and suggest that it should be replaced. William thought a brass plaque within the church, recording the fate of the *Earl of Abergavenny* and pointing out the location of John's grave, might be more appropriate, but added, 'I should be somewhat more desirous of this being done if my own Poems had not widely spread the knowledge of my poor Brother's fate.' No plaque was put up so the silent poet, whose physical image was not preserved in either words or picture during his life, now sleeps anonymously in an unmarked grave. His lasting memorial was, as William rather egotistically claimed, the poetry his life and death inspired in his brother.

In the first shock of bereavement William could write no poetry at all but by 11 April he had begun work on a memorial poem. Inspiration was certainly not lacking, but it was too soon. Overpowered by his own feelings, he had to set the work aside until he was calmer, but, he knew, 'I shall . . . never be at peace till, as far as in me lies, I have done justice to my departed Brother's memory.'

Instead, he returned to *The Prelude*, adding a further 300 lines in the course of a week. The poem was now so long that William was rather embarrassed. 'It will not be much less than 9,000 lines, not hundred but thousand lines, long', he admitted to Beaumont; 'an alarming length! and a thing unprecedented in Literary history that a man should talk so much about himself.' It was not self-conceit that led him to this, however, but real humility. As he only had to describe his own feelings and thoughts, he was sure of success, unlike *The Recluse*, for which he still felt unprepared and diffident of his powers.

By the middle of May, William had put the finishing touches to *The Prelude*. It was a moment he had long anticipated as a joyous one, but it proved to be the inevitable anticlimax.

When I looked back upon the performance it seemed to have a dead weight about it, the reality so far short of the expectation; it was the first long labour that I had finished, and the doubt whether I should ever live to write the Recluse and the sense which I had of this Poem being so far below what I seem'd capable of executing, depressed me much: above all, many heavy thoughts of my poor departed Brother hung upon me; the joy which I should have had in shewing him the Manuscript and a thousand other vain fancies and dreams. I have spoken of this because it was a state of feeling new to me, the occasion being new.

John's unexpected death had forced William to re-evaluate his own life and define its purpose. Finishing the poem on his own life was merely the first stage of what had now become a three-part plan. 'This work may be considered as a sort of portico to the Recluse, part of the same building, which I hope to be able erelong to begin with, in earnest; and if I am permitted to bring it to a conclusion, and to write, further, a narrative Poem of the Epic kind, I shall consider the *task* of my life as over.'

To begin properly on *The Recluse*, however, he needed Coleridge's notes and detailed plan of the poem. These were still not forthcoming, despite all William's pleas, but, as William confidently assured Beaumont, 'I am sure he will return the first minute he can after hearing the news' of John's death. 'I am as sure of this as if I heard him say so.' It was not the first or the last time that such confidence would be misplaced. Coleridge had an almost pathological fear of facing up to the bereavements of those he loved: he had not returned home from Germany when his own son died and he did not come back now. He lingered at Malta until September, then set off for Italy, where he spent almost a year playing the gentleman of leisure in Rome and Naples. He did not set off for England until 23 June 1806.

At Grasmere the Wordsworths slowly picked up the shattered pieces of their lives. They had long neglected the garden, unable to bring themselves to work in it because it was so closely associated with John. It was three months after his death before they could summon up the courage to set it to rights. They also made some necessary improvements to the little cottage, easing the cramped conditions by raising the roof of the peat store, which created space for another bedroom, and by taking over another cottage at Townhead where they could do all their cooking and provide a bedroom for Sally Ashburner, who was now their servant.

On 8 June William and a neighbour went up to Grisedale Tarn to fish. It was the first time William had visited the place since John's death and he was so overcome he had to leave his companion in tears. Grisedale had been one of John's favourite haunts; significantly, it was also the scene of the brothers' last parting in the Lakes, and it was this that William memorialized in the *Elegiac Verses* he composed as he wept.

> – Brother and friend, if verse of mine
> Have power to make thy virtues known,
> Here let a monumental Stone
> Stand – sacred as a Shrine;

A couple of days later, with Mary and Dorothy to support him, William returned to the tarn and, taking leaving of them there, walked in his brother's footsteps to Patterdale, where he intended to spend a few days fishing and relaxing before he embarked on *The Recluse*. 'You will judge that a happy change has been wrought in his mind', Dorothy observed, 'when he chuses John's employments, and one of John's haunts (for he delighted in the neighbourhood of Patterdale) for such a purpose.' Before the end of the month, he had written two more memorial poems. One was the famous and beautiful poem inspired by, and echoing, a rare descriptive passage in one of John's letters. It was addressed to the daisy, John's favourite flower, and in appropriately simple and poignant lines it celebrated both John's life and death.

> Six weeks beneath the moving sea
> He lay in slumber quietly;
> Unforced by wind or wave
> To quit the Ship for which he died,
> (All claims of duty satisfied);
> And there they found him at her side;
> And bore him to the grave.
>
> Vain service! yet not vainly done
> For this, if other end were none,
> That He, who had been cast
> Upon a way of life unmeet
> For such a gentle Soul and sweet,
> Should find an undisturbed retreat
> Near what he loved, at last –
>
> That neighbourhood of grove and field
> To Him a resting-place should yield,
> A meek man and a brave!
> The birds shall sing and ocean make
> A mournful murmur for *his* sake;
> And Thou, sweet Flower, shalt sleep and wake
> Upon his senseless grave.
>
> *To the Daisy, ll.50–70*

The second poem, though inferior in every respect and never published by William in his lifetime, is important in a different way. It was prompted by the now redundant manuscript book of William's latest poems, which John had intended to carry with him on his voyage. Looking at it, with a heart oppressed by pain and grief, William was driven to cry,

> gracious God
> Oh grant that I may never find
> Worse matter or a heavier mind,
> Grant this, and let me be resigned
> Beneath thy chastening rod.
> *Distressful gift! this Book receives,*
> *ll.38–42*

It is hardly startling stuff, but it is the first explicit statement of belief in God in William's poetry. Coleridge, in the early days of their friendship, had suspected him of the atheism which usually went hand in hand with revolutionary politics; though this was not true, his poetry had veered between vague utterances on the eternal verities and outright pantheism (the worship of nature as the manifestation of God), and he was not yet a Christian. In the wake of John's death, he was forced to re-examine his spiritual beliefs in a way he had never done before. In an anguished letter to Beaumont he asked the questions most of us ask in the bitterness of bereavement.

Why have we a choice and a will, and a notion of justice and injustice, enabling us to be moral agents? Why have we sympathies that make the best of us so afraid of inflicting pain and sorrow, which yet we see dealt about so lavishly by the supreme governor? Why should our notions of right towards each other, and to all sentient beings within our influence differ so widely from what appears to be his notion and rule, if every thing were to end here? Would it be blasphemy to say that upon the supposition of the thinking principle being destroyed by death, however inferior we may be to the great Cause and ruler of things, we have *more of love* in our Nature than he has? The thought is monstrous; and yet how to get rid of it except upon the supposition of *another* and a *better world* I do not see.

William might have been arguing himself into an intellectual acceptance of faith, but in his wife, her family and Southey he had support from those with a more instinctive and emotional belief. By 16 April he could write to Richard to say how much comfort he derived from the idea that their brother had done his duty not only to his ship but also to himself: 'he went a brave and innocent Spirit to that God from whom I trust he will receive his reward'.

There was also comfort of a less elevated kind in learning that they were no worse off financially because of the shipwreck. With that delicate tact which marked all his dealings with the touchy members of the arts fraternity, Sir George Beaumont had conjured William 'by the obligation of our love, by the rights of our fellowship', to tell him if he had ventured his capital on the voyage. William was able to reassure him: John was well insured and Richard did not expect that any of the family would lose anything.

The summer brought the distraction of the usual flood of visitors. Mrs Coleridge and her daughter came on 18 June and stayed for between two and three weeks, enabling Dorothy to record with satisfaction that the two-and-a-half-year-old Sara was 'a Snarler – a little vixen'. They were followed immediately by two of the Halifax Threlkelds, the sister-in-law and niece of Mrs Rawson. Not having seen Dorothy for many years, they were shocked at her changed appearance: she was 'grown so thin and old that they shou'd not have known her, – lost many of her teeth and her cheeks quite sunk that it has entirely alter'd her profile, – yet she looks healthy'. They got over their revulsion pretty quickly, for a two-day visit turned into one of a fortnight.

Towards the end of July, the Clarksons came to Grasmere, taking up lodgings in a house belonging to Robert Newton close to the village inn. Catherine was now a confirmed invalid, but, having known John well, she insisted on coming to Grasmere to lend the Wordsworths her support. Despite her fragility, she was a cheerful and lively companion who brought some much needed merriment to the mourning household.

It cannot have been long after the Clarksons' arrival that a gruesome discovery was made by a shepherd on Helvellyn. Hearing barking, he went to investigate and found a small dog alone on the rocks at the head of Red Tarn. She led him to the headless corpse and bleached bones which were all that remained of her master. From a pocket book found in his clothes, Clarkson discovered that the unfortunate man was Charles Gough, a young artist from Manchester, who had fallen to his death from Helvellyn while on his way to fish in the tarn. As the dead man was a Quaker, it fell to Clarkson to arrange his interment in the Friends' burial ground at Tirril, and send news of his demise to his mother. The discovery caused a brief sensation, not least because of the loyalty of the dog in maintaining her lonely vigil beside the corpse for three long months. It was just the sort of pathetic incident to appeal to William, who set about commemorating it in verse. The resulting poem, *Fidelity*, is marred only by the rhetorical question at the end: how was the dog nourished 'through such long time'? – which invites the irreverent but obvious rejoinder, how was the corpse stripped of flesh in just three months? The more kindly disposed of the Lakers decided it ate grass.

Another visitor, in August, was Walter Scott. William went to Keswick to meet him and repay his courtesy two years previously by giving him a guided tour. It turned into quite a party, for they were joined by Southey and his brother Harry, Humphry Davy, who had seen *Lyrical Ballads* through the press, and Southey's friend Charles Danvers. From Greta Hall they had an expedition to the Lodore Falls, Watendlath and the Bowder Stone, the vast boulder resting in splendid isolation on the lower slopes of Borrowdale, returning to Keswick over Castle Crag. The following day, William, Scott and Davy went to Patterdale, spent the night at the inn there, then, bright and early, climbed Helvellyn together. It was a day they would always remember. Their progress was slow, for Scott was lame from birth, but this did not deter him, and he beguiled the time by telling stories and amusing anecdotes. Over thirty years later, William remembered with admiration the vigour with which Scott had then scrambled along the treacherous horn of Striding Edge:

> Where once together, in his day of strength
> We stood rejoicing, as if earth were free
> From sorrow, like the sky above our heads.
>   *Musings near Aquapendente, ll.63–5*

No doubt William pointed out the place where Gough's body had been found, for Scott too, quite independently, wrote his own poem on the subject of the devoted dog. Davy grew impatient with the two dawdlers, and, having reached the summit, set off on his own to the rendezvous at Town End. The little party were then joined by Mrs Scott, dined together and, next day, sailed on Windermere, before going their separate ways. Scott left the Lakes with a profound admiration for both Southey and William.

They are certainly men of very extraordinary powers, Wordsworth in particular is such a character as only exists in romance virtuous, simple, and unaffectedly restricting every want & wish to the bounds of a very narrow income in order to enjoy the literary and poetical leisure which his happiness consists in.

Richard paid a fleeting visit to Grasmere this summer too. He had decided to purchase some tenanted land on Ullswater to add to his Sockbridge estate. Dorothy's appearance shocked him as much as it had her Halifax cousins. He was convinced she was doing too much walking for her own good, so, before he left, he made arrangements for the purchase of a pony for her. It proved an invaluable gift and the pony was pressed immediately into service by all the family.

Even after the last visitors departed, William still could not settle to any serious employment. On 9 October *Lyrical Ballads*, a reissue of the 1802 edition, was published by Longman. Even for what should have been a reprint, William could not resist tinkering with both poems and preface, though his changes this time were restricted to punctuation and odd words. The reprint of his most successful publication to date set William thinking. Perhaps he should publish another volume of small poems? He had enough in hand to do so, and throughout the late autumn and winter continued adding to his stock. *Fidelity* prompted two more poems on canine devotion, and the Scottish tour of 1803 was still proving fertile ground for poetry, not least because William was continually reminded of its salient images by Dorothy's recent completion, and multiple copying, of her journal. *Rob Roy's Grave* and *To the Sons of Burns, after Visiting the Grave of their Father* were both rather dull meditations arising out of visits to the graves of two famous Scotsmen during the tour. A third, lovely poem, *The Solitary Reaper*, which bears all the hallmarks of William's art of recalling and investing an image with later meaning, was deceptive. Though the Wordsworths had seen, and commented on, many striking instances of solitary figures in otherwise empty landscapes, they had not seen this Highland lass, whose sweet and plaintive song filled the vale and was borne away in the poet's heart long after he had last heard it. She had actually been seen and described by Thomas Wilkinson, the Quaker poet of Yanwath, in his manuscript journal of his own tour of Scotland in 1787, which William had just read.

By the beginning of November, William had 'entirely given up the idea' of publishing some of his smaller poems. It was not just that he had a great dislike to the whole business of publishing: 'that is not his reason –' Dorothy informed Lady Beaumont, 'he thinks that having been so long silent to the world he ought to come forward again with a work of greater labour'. In other words, the elusive *Recluse*. Instead he went on a three-day exploration of the tributary vales of Ullswater, which he had never visited before. He set off on 7 November, walking beside Dorothy, who rode her new pony. They were dogged from the first moment by bad weather, and, though they had assured accommodation with their friends, the Luffs, at Patterdale, their wanderings were curtailed to the lake shores. Dorothy minutely recorded descriptions of everything they saw in a journal dedicated to the 'tour', probably written for Lady Beaumont. It was while staying with the Luffs at what is now Side Farm that William found what he considered the perfect spot for building a cottage. It lay quarter of a mile from the village of Patterdale, across the deep, wide, clear, slow running waters of Goldrill Beck, which bisects the broad vale, and it is surrounded by the fells, which rise sheer and bare and crested with rock. With views up the valley to Kirkstone Pass, across to the heights of Helvellyn and down to the waters of Ullswater, with the shadowy fells looming beyond the lake, it was indeed a perfect setting. What distinguished this particular spot, Broad How, from those around it, was the large wooded and rocky knoll, dominated by a great yew tree, which was a vantage point for the whole vale.

On the last morning of their visit, as they sat at breakfast, the maid-servant 'with an uncouth stare and grin of pleasure' announced that there had been a great British victory at Trafalgar and that Lord Nelson was dead. Rushing over to the village inn, they learned that it was indeed true and were shocked to hear that there had been great rejoicings at Penrith; for Dorothy at least, the loss of Nelson outweighed the joy of victory. Returning to the Luffs' house, they made a detour to walk by 'William's rock & grove', and William came to an uncharacteristically swift decision. Perhaps the shock of the news of Nelson's death at sea brought back thoughts of that similar, yet so much more personal, 'thunderstroke' earlier in the year, reinforcing the knowledge that John had particularly loved Patterdale, but William decided to buy Broad How. The Wordsworths set off immediately to see Thomas Wilkinson, hoping that he might know the owner and negotiate a deal on William's behalf. Having begged beds for the night from the Hutchinsons at Park House, William called on Wilkinson that very evening and authorized him to offer up to £800 for the site.

Next morning was fine, so they decided to go to Lowther. The bad earl had left both house and grounds to fend for themselves, but Sir William had appointed his neighbour, Wilkinson, as his 'Arbiter Elegantiarum, or Master of the grounds at Lowther'. Wilkinson was an 'amiable inoffensive man, and a little of a Poet too', as William rather patronizingly, if aptly, described him. He had earned something of a reputation for the way he had laid out his own little estate at Yanwath; now he was busily at work, transforming the grounds at Lowther, for which he received a half-hearted endorsement from William: 'what he has done hitherto is very well', he told Beaumont, 'as it is little more than making accessible what could not before be got at'. Where the two men parted company was Wilkinson's manufactured riverside walk. William admitted it was 'absolutely necessary in many places' but lamented that it would efface a natural forest pathway which he had loved since childhood. Dorothy, oblivious to the devastation Wilkinson had wreaked on the ancient woodland, recorded 'three delightful hours [spent] by the River-side' in her journal, and later described it as 'a marvellously beautiful walk'. The next day, she and William retraced their steps through Patterdale and over a starlit Kirkstone to Grasmere, where they found Mary and the children all retired to bed.

The exposure to the rain and cold brought on one of Dorothy's chest infections, 'a slight attack of *Peripneumony*', but she was sufficiently recovered by 25 November for Mary to leave her in charge of the children while she went on a fortnight's visit to Park House. William joined his wife a few days later, and Dorothy was left alone with the children and her own thoughts. William had deliberately left her with an important task to complete: the transcription of the entire *Prelude*, but it failed to keep her thoughts from John. 'The Children are now in bed', she wrote to Lady Beaumont on 29 November.

The evening is very still, and there are no indoor sounds but the ticking of our Family watch which hangs over the chimney-piece under the drawing of the Applethwaite Cottage, and a breathing or a beating of one single irregular Flame in my fire. No one who has not been an Inmate with Children in a *Cottage* can have a notion of the quietness that takes possession of it when they are gone to sleep. The hour before is generally a noisy one, often given up to boisterous efforts to amuse them, and the noise is heard in every corner of the house – then comes the washing and undressing, a work of misery, and in ten minutes after, all is stillness and perfect rest. It is at all times a sweet hour to us; but I can fancy that I have never enjoyed it so much as now that I am quite alone – yet it is a strange kind of pleasure for the Image of our departed Brother haunts me with many a pang in the midst of happy recollections of him . . .

As the winter progressed, William became increasingly anxious to get on with *The Recluse*, but he was at a loss how to proceed. The non-appearance of Coleridge had left them all in limbo. As the vale was battered by one winter storm after another, and the anniversary of John's death came and went, Dorothy spent sleepless nights conjuring up images of shipwrecks and imagining that Coleridge too had drowned at sea. Even if he escaped such a fate by travelling overland, there was every possibility that he might be captured by the French. The news from the Continent was so depressing that she dreaded the arrival of the newspapers. Napoleon's armies were sweeping across Europe and in March his brother Joseph Bonaparte was crowned King of Naples and Sicily. In the midst of this crisis, William Pitt, the Prime Minister, died. As the nation mourned the loss of the man who had kept Britain at the forefront of opposition to French aggrandizement, William, his radical sympathies rising to the fore, offered only muted praise.

I have never been able to regard his political life with complacency: I believe him, however, to have been as disinterested a Man, and as true a lover of his Country as it was possible for so ambitious a man to be. His first wish (though probably unknown to himself) was that his Country should prosper under his administration; his next, that it should prosper: could the order of these wishes have been reversed, Mr Pitt would have avoided many of the grievous mistakes into which, I think, he fell.

'We are crammed into our little nest edge-full', Dorothy told Catherine Clarkson at the beginning of March. They had taken on an additional temporary nursemaid while Mary visited Park House, but she had been so useful that they had kept her on. Mary had brought Sara back with her and she too was still with them. All three women were hard at work, transcribing copies of William's poem on his own life. Every bed in the house was shared by two people, and Mary was pregnant again, though, as usual, casually unaware whether the baby was due in May or June.

William decided to get out from under everyone's feet. The Beaumonts had repeatedly offered him the use of their house in Grosvenor Square and, on 29 March, William set out on his first trip to London in two and a half years. He arrived in town at the beginning of April and went immediately to Lambeth, to stay with his brother Christopher, who was now chaplain to the Archbishop of Canterbury. This was William's first visit to his brother's home since Christopher's marriage; he already had one son, like William's named John, after their lost brother, and Priscilla was expecting a second child in August.

As William informed Mrs Clarkson soon after his arrival, 'I am here to see everything and every Body good bad great little &c &c that I can.' Old friends and new were on his agenda. Having stayed with Christopher, he paid visits to both the Montagus and the Lambs, probably saw his brother Richard, and the Clarksons, and paid a three-day duty visit to the Cooksons at Binfield, where his uncle now had a rich living in addition to his canonry at Windsor. William Godwin, another figure from his past, soon found him out, and there were regular calls on, and from, him. Through Godwin and Sir George Beaumont, William met once again the radical lawyer Horne Tooke, and a host of up-and-coming artists: James Northcote, the historical and portrait painter, who had been an assistant to Sir Joshua Reynolds; Henry Edridge, the brilliant society miniaturist, who had called at Town End in the late summer of 1804; Richard Duppa, Southey's friend; David Wilkie, the young Scottish artist and portrait painter; Joseph Farington, an artist-friend of Uncle William Cookson, now probably better known for his voluminous and splenetic diaries than his landscapes. Southey too brought his friend John Rickman, the statistician and founder of the decennial census, and Lamb his friend Thomas Manning, the mathematician and linguist, who was on the point of departure for Canton, where he would practise as a doctor.

It was a glittering array of the brightest and best London had to offer. And what did they make of William? The general opinion (as reported by the arch-gossip Farington) was that he was considered a better poet than conversationalist. Northcote whispered that Godwin, considering the relative merits of William and

Coleridge, preferred the poetry of the former and the conversation of the latter. John Taylor, who had just started his own publishing business, invited William to dine and was startled to find him 'strongly disposed towards Republicanism.'

At the beginning of May, Beaumont acquired tickets for the Royal Academy exhibition, where three of his own paintings were on show. Showing yet again that delicacy of feeling which made him such a genuinely good man, Beaumont showed William the one inspired by his own poem from *Lyrical Ballads*, *The Thorn*, but did not draw his attention to one of Piel Castle, near Rampside. The reason was that the painting depicted a storm and a ship about to be wrecked beneath the castle, which Beaumont feared 'might raise painful sensations in your mind'. This was exactly what did happen, but it proved to be an unexpectedly positive experience, for out of it came *Elegiac Stanzas suggested by a Picture of Peele Castle*. A measured, multi-layered poem, it contrasted William's memories of the calm, glassy sea he had witnessed daily while staying near Piel Castle in 1794 with the storm painted by Beaumont. At its core lay William's abiding grief for John, and the fact that it had permanently altered his outlook on life. It was a moment of self-recognition comparable to that in *Tintern Abbey* and the *Ode: Intimations of Immortality*.

> A power is gone, which nothing can restore;
> A deep distress hath humanized my Soul.
>
> Not for a moment could I now behold
> A smiling sea, and be what I have been:
> The feeling of my loss will ne'er be old;
> This, which I know, I speak with mind serene.

While he was in London, William sat for his portrait to Henry Edridge. The delightful little pencil drawing represents the thirty-six-year-old William in solemn pose, the half-turned face giving peculiar prominence to the heavy-lidded eyes and thoughtful expression. His hair is still worn democratically short and unpowdered.

The highlight of William's visit was his attendance at a ball given by Mrs Charles James Fox. He was taken there by his friend Rogers, whose wealth, as much as his literary reputation, opened every door in London. It was the first and last time William would ever meet Fox, the man to whom he had so hopefully sent *Lyrical Ballads* with such disappointing results. When Rogers introduced William to him, Fox said '"I am very glad to see you, Mr Wordsworth, though I am not of your faction," ... meaning', as Rogers explained, 'that he admired a school of poetry different from that to which Wordsworth belonged.' Southey, who had not been invited to Mrs Fox's ball, remarked sourly, 'Wordsworth flourishes in London, he powders and goes to all the great routs. No man is more flattered by the attentions of the great, and no man would be more offended to be told so.' Allowing for exaggeration (William is unlikely to have powdered his hair), there is more than a grain of truth in this. William had always been sociable and, for someone who lived and wrote in the comparative solitude of the Lakes, it was thrilling to come to the centre of literary life and find everyone knew his name and his work. He would have been less than human had he not been flattered.

William returned to Grasmere on 25 May, much improved in health. The cottage at Town End was in chaos. They were without a servant, both Johnny and Sara Hutchinson, who had come to assist her sister at the birth, were ill, and Mary showed no signs of going into labour. The one bright spot was little Dora, now twenty-one months old, who had grown into 'the most delightful Chatterer ever seen', as her proud father noted, 'all acquired in two months; nor is it the least of her recommendations that she is more delighted with me than with a new Toy; and is never easy, if in my sight, when out of my arms'. Even Dorothy was won over: 'she is so full of life and sensibility and has so many pretty tricks'. She called William 'Dear 'Ather', and he could refuse her nothing. All the neighbours were equally enchanted with the little girl, though they, and Dorothy, muttered darkly about her being 'too wise for this world'. Even at this age, it was obvious that she was much cleverer than Johnny, but she did not enjoy his robust constitution, having been subject to croup since birth.

Four days after William's return, Johnny was sent over to Park House for two months, to be out of the way when his mother was confined. That childless household had become something of a convenient nursery, for both Hartley and Derwent Coleridge had separately enjoyed lengthy visits there during their father's absence. Unfortunately, Park House had little else to recommend it and Tom was already looking for a new farm. It was Tom who arranged the sale of Dorothy's pony, which was now badly lame, and the purchase in its place of a cow, to supply the growing family with milk and butter.

Thomas Wordsworth made his belated appearance on 15 June, just three days short of three years since Johnny's birth. It was a coincidence they all found peculiarly affecting, and Dorothy immediately felt 'a double rushing-in of love' for the new baby, 'as if I had both what had been the first-born infant John's share of love to give it, and its own'. At first they decided to call him William, but Southey, who called two days later, was decidedly against it: there should not be two *William Wordsworths*. As Tom was to be his godfather, they therefore settled on Thomas, by which name he was christened at Grasmere church on 13 July.

At the beginning of August, William was startled to get a letter from Wilkinson informing him that he had come to an agreement with the vendors of Broad How and, on William's behalf, had agreed to purchase the nineteen-acre estate for £1,000. William had given the idea up completely before he went to London, knowing that £800 was the most the estate was worth and having failed to persuade the wealthy rector of Patterdale, who owned the adjoining land, to give up his interest in it. He had thought no more about it, but Wilkinson had been so grieved at his failure that he poured out the whole story to Lord Lowther, who immediately offered to make up the difference, with or without William's knowledge. Wilkinson had insisted that William had to know, but had gone ahead and signed the agreement, at the asking price. William was thus in a quandary. He could not undo the agreement, which was legally binding; he did not wish to pay more than he could afford out of his own pocket, which would, in any case, appear to be an ungracious rejection of Lord Lowther's generosity; yet he did not wish to be under obligation to Lowther. 'Strange it is that W[ilkinson] could not perceive, that if I was unwilling to pay an exorbitant price out of my own money, I should be still more unwilling to pay it out of another's', William fretted to Beaumont, who hastened to reassure him. 'I know no man to whom I would sooner be under obligations than Lord Lowther – he is candid, he is sincere, & generous – he esteems worth, & he admires genius'. If William could not bear the thought of accepting the money as Lowther's gift, Beaumont suggested he might consider it as a loan or even sell the Applethwaite property he had himself presented to William to make up the shortfall.

William swallowed his pride. In offering the money, Lowther had expressed a wish to meet him, so William called on Wilkinson, and together they went to Lowther. Sir William was not at home. They had to make do with escorting the Lowther daughters as far as Yanwath, where William showed his appreciation of his friend's efforts by assisting him in building one of his beloved riverside paths. He also seized the opportunity to tell Wilkinson, frankly but gently, that he would not have accepted Lord Lowther's offer had he been consulted. Wilkinson not only accepted the implied rebuke 'very well', but also seemed quite happy that he had *not* consulted William. When William returned home, he wrote a surprisingly gracious letter of grateful acceptance and thanks to his new benefactor.

It had been an unusually quiet summer at Grasmere. There were fewer tourists than usual, though annual visitors, like Sharp, called in as they always did. With the two older children away at Park House, the cottage was also 'strangely dull' and quiet. For once, therefore, William was able to work, and this time he turned to *The Recluse*. By 1 August, he had written 700 additional lines. 'Should Coleridge return, so that I might have some conversation with him upon the subject,' he informed Beaumont, 'I should go on swimmingly.'

Exactly a fortnight later, 'the blessed news' arrived: Coleridge was in English waters, confined to his ship by quarantine restrictions, but within sight of Portsmouth. Ominously, the tidings came not from Coleridge himself, but from one of his fellow passengers. Once the quarantine was over, he went straight to London, took up residence with the Lambs and began working for Stuart again. He was, he said, 'shirtless, & almost penniless'. He had nothing to show for his two years abroad. The Wordsworths had had only a single letter from him since John's death, and his wife not many more, but they all excused him. 'I have no doubt (as Mrs Coleridge thinks also) that he is afraid to inquire after us lest he should hear of some new Sorrow.' They were wrong. Coleridge had decided to separate permanently from his wife but lacked the courage to tell her in person or by letter. It was Mary Lamb who eventually persuaded Coleridge to write his first letter to his wife, a month after his arrival. Even then, he wrote as if nothing had changed between them. He did not mention separation and talked of her joining him in London.

The Wordsworths had seen much of Sarah Coleridge and her children during their friend's long absence and had come to appreciate her worth. Even Dorothy realized that if Coleridge would just accept his wife for what she was, instead of what he wanted her to be, they ought to be able to live together in peace and quiet. But on such things many a marriage founders and, in the meantime, William lost patience. He wrote a brief note expressing his disappointment at not hearing from, or seeing, Coleridge, offered to go to London 'if a meeting there would be more acceptable to you' and championed the abandoned wife. 'This is absolutely necessary either that you should decide upon something immediately to be done; or that Mrs Coleridge should be furnished with some reason for your not coming down as her present uncertainty and suspense is intolerable.' William's letter probably crossed in the post with the one Mary Lamb had compelled their friend to write, but it did no good. Coleridge remained paralysed in London, refusing to write or answer letters, to the great distress of many old friends.

All this could not have come at a worse time for William. The children had succumbed to whooping cough, and the family were preparing to leave the cottage at Town End. In the summer months they could manage by using the moss hut at the top of the garden as a sanctuary and additional room for visitors, but it was not practical to do so in winter. The three permanent adult members of the household could not face the prospect of being cooped up in the confined quarters of the cottage throughout the long dark days which lay ahead, especially with three children. No other house in the area being available, William had gratefully accepted the Beaumonts' offer of the use of the Hall farmhouse on their Coleorton estate in Leicestershire.

In the midst of all this domestic upheaval, William had serenely continued to add to *The Recluse* and, having read in the papers that Charles James Fox was dying, had composed his wonderful poem while walking that evening at Grasmere.

> A Power is passing from the earth
> To breathless Nature's dark abyss;
> But when the great and good depart
> What is it more than this –
>
> That Man, who is from God sent forth,
> Doth yet again to God return? –
> Such ebb and flow must ever be,
> Then wherefore should we mourn?
> *['Loud is the Vale! the Voice is up'], ll.17–24*

Such lines could not have been written before John's death.

At the end of October, the Wordsworths set out for Coleorton. Sara, who was to accompany them, met them at Kendal with the news that they had only just missed Coleridge: he had arrived at Penrith half an hour after she left it but would not come to meet them at Kendal if it was only to part again immediately. Nevertheless, the Wordsworths sent a special messenger over to Keswick, begging him to come and telling him they would delay their departure for another day. At seven o'clock in the evening he arrived at the inn and summoned William to him. Dorothy, Mary and Sara had no intention of being left behind, so it was a joyful party that descended on Coleridge. 'Never, never did I feel such a shock as at first sight of him', Dorothy later confided to Catherine Clarkson. Lack of exercise and an increased dependency on opium had made him so grossly fat that his eyes were lost in flesh. Worse still was his mental state.

We all felt exactly in the same way – as if he were different from what we have expected to see; almost as much as a person of whom we have thought much, and of whom we had formed an image in our own minds, without having any personal knowledge of him . . . He is utterly changed; and yet sometimes, when he was animated in conversation concerning things removed from him, I saw something of his former self. But never when we were alone with him. He then scarcely ever spoke of anything that concerned him, or us, or our common friends nearly, except we forced him to it; and immediately he changed the conversation to Malta, Sir Alexander Ball, the corruptions of government, anything but what we were yearning after. All we could gather from him was that he must part from her or die and leave his children destitute, and that to part he was resolved.

The Wordsworths were bewildered and distraught. All they could extract from him was a promise that he would join them as soon as he had come to an arrangement with his wife.

The Beaumonts, though they had met only William before, gave all his family a kind and affectionate welcome at Coleorton. 'They are the best of people,' William told Coleridge, 'and their kindness to us most delicate and unbounded'. To Beaumont himself, William was quite candid: 'I esteem your friendship one of the best gifts of my life . . . I speak of soul indebted to soul.' The feeling was genuine and mutual. 'Were I to express to you how much our interest & if possible our regard is encreased by a personal knowledge of your family of love, it might appear like affection,' Beaumont wrote shortly after he and his wife departed for London. 'I never see you, or read you but I am the better for it – & at least make resolutions which I hope in time I shall perform.'

The farmhouse at Coleorton was to be the Wordsworths' home for more than seven months. It lay two miles east of Ashby de la Zouche, in the midst of what would have been pleasant, rolling Leicestershire countryside, had it not been for the open-cast coal-mining surrounding it. The coal pits were the main source of Beaumont's wealth and, in 1804, he had begun to build a vast mock-baronial castle on his estate, just a mile outside the village of Coleorton; he had also decided to redevelop all his grounds to make an apt setting for his grand new house. William had strong views on landscape gardening and he did not fail to make them known to his patron. He believed passionately, with Coleridge, that a house should belong to the country and that the country should not be an appendage to the house. He deplored the recent fashion for formal gardens, with their topiary, exotic trees and plants, and pristine pathways: 'Let nature be all in all,' he urged Beaumont. He was glad to learn that Beaumont did not intend moving the village: 'for my part strip my Neighbourhood of human beings and I should think it one of the greatest privations I could undergo. You have all the poverty of solitude, nothing of its elevation.' Having set out his views so forcefully, and at such length, William ruefully concluded his letter was 'something like [a sermon], upon the subject of natural beauty'.

When Lady Beaumont asked William to plan and supervise the planting of her latest scheme, a winter garden, he was in his element. It was a practical opportunity to put into practice his belief that laying out gardens was a liberal art and to prove that a poet was the best person 'to assist Nature in moving the affections'.

From the extant letters of this period, one might be forgiven for thinking that William had abandoned poetry in favour of gardening, but this was not the case. In June he had told Walter Scott that he had 'some thoughts of publishing a little Volume of miscellaneous Poems, to be out next Spring'. Immediately after his arrival at Coleorton, he began to put the collection together, assisted by Sara, who did all his transcribing for him. 'I publish with great reluctance,' he told Scott on 10 November,

but the day when my long work will be finished seems farther and farther off, and therefore I have resolved to send this Vol: into the world. It would look like affectation if I were to say how indifferent I am to its present reception; but I have a true pleasure in saying to you that I put some value upon it; and hope that it will one day or other be thought well of by the Public.

Just as had happened in 1800, the process of selecting poems for publication seems to have ignited a spark. New composition flowed from revising the old, and a dozen or more short poems were written, all but two of which found their way into the new book. Among them were two short ballads, *The Horn of Egremont Castle* and *Song at the Feast of Brougham Castle*, both tales of medieval chivalry, based on local Cumberland tradition.

More characteristically Wordsworthian were two wonderful sonnets he wrote in reaction to the desperate state of affairs on the Continent, where, in October, Napoleon's armies had crushed the Prussians at the battles of Jena and Auerstadt, and added Prussia and its dependencies to an increasingly long list of annexed territories.

> Another year! – another deadly blow!
> Another mighty Empire overthrown!
> And We are left, or shall be left, alone;
> The last that dare to struggle with the Foe.
> 'Tis well! from this day forward we shall know
> That in ourselves our safety must be sought;
> That by our own right hands it must be wrought;
> That we must stand unpropped, or be laid low.

Having taken up this determinedly patriotic stance, William ended the sonnet in distinctly downbeat fashion. Victory would be won only if Britain's leaders were

> Wise, upright, valiant; not a servile band,
> Who are to judge of danger which they fear,
> And honour which they do not understand.
>
> *November, 1806, ll.1–8, 12–14*

The second sonnet was a more oblique reflection on the same subject.

> Two Voices are there; one is of the sea,
> One of the mountains; each a mighty Voice:
> In both from age to age thou didst rejoice,
> They were thy chosen music, Liberty!
>
> *Thought of a Briton on*
> *the Subjugation of Switzerland, ll.1–4*

The voice of the mountains, Switzerland, had been silenced by the French, so William appealed to Liberty to 'cleave, O cleave to that which still is left' – that is, to Britain, the voice of the sea.

On 21 December Coleridge arrived at Coleorton to 'an uproar of sincere Joy'. He brought with him his eldest son, Hartley, now aged ten, and the news that he had persuaded his wife to accept that their marriage was over. They had agreed to separate permanently: for the moment, Coleridge and Hartley would live with the Words-worths, while his wife would remain at Greta Hall, under Southey's protection, with Derwent and little Sara. The Wordsworths were naïvely convinced that Coleridge would be transformed back into the creative, charismatic figure of the Alfoxton days. With the confidence born of ignorance, Dorothy gaily declared to Lady Beaumont that Coleridge would be 'tolerably safe' with them: 'I think, if he is not inclined to manage himself, *we* can manage him'. She could not have been more wrong.

Unable to drink brandy, because there was none in the house, he drank strong beer at night, mid-morning and dinner-time. The Wordsworths were apparently unaware that he had a supply of opium and they did not know, because they did not have access to his private thoughts recorded in his journal, the perverted turn his drug-induced fantasies had taken. His obsession with Sara had grown stronger and he could not face the reality that she did not return his feelings. 'I know, you love me! – My reason knows it, my heart feels it', he confided in his journal. 'Do you command me to abide Asra's neglect?' he wrote in an accusing poem, written in Latin, and addressed to William as 'Vilmum Axiologum',

and submit to the sight of Asra's estranged eyes? and know for certain that she who was – and always will be – dear to me is false and cruel? And you bid me endure the daylight when I am crazily in love with an empty woman and my whole wide world quivers and totters? Why not, William, order me – with mock grief – to let my guts be pierced with a knife? Why not tear out my heart, or my eyes, or whatever – if possible – is more precious! I shall command my failing spirit to observe your wish – though I am dying – as long as faith in Asra lingers ... My life is finished; yet Asra lives on, heedless of me.

William's kindly meant warnings served only to divert Coleridge's warped imagin-
ings into new channels. On 27 December Coleridge wrote in his journal 'The
Epoch.' in large, bold lettering centred on the page, adding beneath it the cryptic
comment, 'Saturday, 27th December, 1806 – Queen's Head, Stringston, 1½ a mile
from Coleorton Church, 50 minutes after 10'. Three subsequent pages recording
what had happened (or, rather, what he imagined had happened) have been torn
from the journal, but later entries make it all too clear what this was. 'But a minute
and a half with ME – and all that time evidently *restless & going* – An hour and
more with [Wordsworth] *in bed* – O agony!' For years afterwards he was haunted
by the image of Sara, her breasts exposed, in bed with William. Some biographers
have chosen to regard this as proof that William had an adulterous relationship
with his sister-in-law, but this is simply not credible. If William had wanted a
secret tryst with Sara, the local inn was hardly the place to do it. In any case,
Coleridge later admitted that the whole scenario was simply a lurid product of his
own imagination. 'Yes! Yes! I *knew* the horrid phantasm to be a mere phantasm: and
yet what anguish, what gnawings of despair, what throbbings and lancinations of
positive Jealousy!'

Instead of confronting his friend, as honesty demanded if what he had seen was
real, Coleridge kept his gnawings, throbbings and lancinations (shooting pains) to
himself. What is even more peculiar is that he was able to maintain such a
convincing façade of ordinary life that no one had the slightest inkling of the
suspicions and jealousies festering in his heart. And, ironically, when the family
gathered round for a ceremonial reading by William of *The Prelude*, which was
dedicated to Coleridge himself, he was moved to write a generous tribute in some
of the finest lines he had ever composed.

> And when – O Friend! my comforter and guide!
> Strong in thyself, and powerful to give strength! –
> Thy long sustainèd Song finally closed,
> And thy deep voice had ceased – yet thou thyself
> Wert still before my eyes, and round us both
> That happy vision of beloved faces –
> Scarce conscious, and yet conscious of its close
> I sate, my being blended in one thought
> (Thought was it? or aspiration? or resolve?)
> Absorbed, yet hanging still upon the sound –
> And when I rose, I found myself in prayer.
>   *To William Wordsworth, ll.102–12*

It should have been one of the happiest evenings of their lives, a joyful celebration
of mutual achievement. Instead it was symbolic of all that had gone wrong in their
relationship.

13. The Convention of Cintra

William's new book progressed slowly, not least because he insisted on correcting the proofs himself this time. The projected single volume had become two smaller ones, each containing miscellaneous poems and sonnets. A thousand copies were to be printed by Longman, the publisher of *Lyrical Ballads*, for which William was to receive 100 guineas. It was hardly a princely sum for the product of more than six years' labour.

Of greater concern to them all was the problem of where they should live. Coleridge had decided to make his home permanently with the Wordsworths, a decision which gave his brother-in-law a certain grim satisfaction: 'It is from his idolatry of that family that this has begun –', Southey told Rickman, 'they have always humoured him in all his follies, listened to his complaints of his wife, and when he has complained of his itch, helped him to scratch, instead of covering him with brimstone ointment, and shutting him up by himself.' With rather less justice, he accused William and Dorothy of being the 'most intensely selfish' people he had ever known. They had only offered Coleridge a home because it suited William.

The one thing to which W would sacrifice all others is his own reputation, concerning which his anxiety is perfectly childish ... and so he can get Coleridge to talk his own writings over with him, and criti[ci]se them, and (without amending them) teach him how to do it – to be in fact the very rain and air and sunshine of his intellect, he thinks C is very well employed and this arrangement a very good one.

It was hardly fair comment, but then Southey had every right to feel bitter, having had Coleridge's wife and children dumped on him.

Providing Coleridge with a home also meant providing one for his sons, and the

Wordsworths were in despair. Where could they find a house sufficiently large to take them all? The Beaumonts were happy for them to remain at the Hall farm but William was unwilling to trespass further on their kindness. On 25 March William completed the purchase of his little estate at Patterdale. It might have been possible to build there, but he had neither the money nor the time to do so.

Such was his determination to offer accommodation to all his entourage and to return to the north that William submitted to the mortification of taking a lease of Allan Bank at Grasmere. Standing on 'that beautiful ridge that elbows out into the vale (behind the church and towering far above its steeple)', Allan Bank was, in William's own phrase, 'a temple of abomination'. It had been built by a Liverpool attorney who had bought the site early in 1805. A year later, to Dorothy's undisguised glee, it had become a 'ruinous mansion' when a third of it collapsed while being built. A year further down the line, it was still not ready for habitation, but the plasterers and painters were putting the finishing touches.

In April William, Mary and Sara accompanied Coleridge and Hartley to London, leaving Dorothy in charge of the children at Coleorton. The Wordsworth contingent took up residence in Thornhaugh Street, with the recently widowed Basil Montagu, moving, at the beginning of May, to stay with Christopher and Priscilla at Lambeth. From a social point of view, it was a relatively quiet trip. Mary and Sara were eager to play the tourist and declined to join the dinner party circuit, but they breakfasted twice with Walter Scott, who was also in town, and persuaded him to return to Coleorton with them on his way home. They were also, of course, regular visitors to the Beaumonts in Grosvenor Square.

The main purpose of the visit, however, was business. On 28 April 1807 Longman published William's new book, succinctly titled *Poems, in Two Volumes*. The title-page bore his name as 'William Wordsworth, Author of *The Lyrical Ballads*', a significant association, since it reminded purchasers of the success of the earlier work, which was now in its fourth edition, and of the pioneering nature of that publication. This latter was particularly important, because *Poems, in Two Volumes* had nothing to prepare the reader for its contents: there was no advertisement, no preface, no attempt to explain or justify William's poetic theory or method, just the poems themselves. *Lyrical Ballads*, *The Recluse*, even the poem on his own life, all owed their inception to Coleridge. *Poems, in Two Volumes* did not. The very fact that William chose to publish it at all was a repudiation of Coleridge's insistence that writing so many small poems was 'hurtful' to his poetic genius. It was a sign of his confidence in his own powers. As one modern critic has put it, '*Poems, in Two Volumes* presented [William's] claim to be the most original, copious, and various lyric poet since the seventeenth century.'

William had chosen the poems, and their order of appearance, with his usual care. The first volume contained sixty-nine poems, beginning with *To the Daisy* and ending with the sonnet *November, 1806*; the second, forty-six, opening with *Rob Roy's Grave* and closing with *Ode: Intimations of Immortality*. The publication therefore began and ended with lines celebrating the humblest of flowers.

Almost before they left London, the adverse criticism of *Poems, in Two Volumes* began. Even William's friends showed no mercy. Rogers declared it a pity that so many 'trifling things' should be allowed to obscure the poems that had real merit. Sharp was scathing, saying, 'He had carried His system of simplicity too far, and had proceeded to puerility.' Lady Beaumont was so upset on his behalf by the virulence of the mounting tide of criticism that William had to reassure her. 'It is impossible that any expectations can be lower than mine concerning the immediate effect of this little work upon what is called the Public.' He looked to future reputation, not current reception, trusting that the destiny of his poems would be 'to console the afflicted, to add sunshine to daylight by making the happy happier, to teach the young and the gracious of every age, to see, to think and feel, and therefore to become more actively and securely virtuous; this is their office, which I trust they will faithfully perform long after we (that is, all that is mortal of us) are mouldered in our graves'. How could fashionable society possibly understand his poems: 'the thoughts, feelings, and images, on which the life of my Poems depends ... what have they to do with routs, dinners, morning calls, hurry from door to door, from street to street, on foot or in Carriage[?]'

These people in the senseless hurry of their idle lives do not *read* books, they merely snatch a glance at them that they may talk about them. And even if this were not so, never forget what I believe was observed to you by Coleridge, that every great and original writer, in proportion as he is great or original, must himself create the taste by which he is to be relished; he must teach the art by which he is to be seen;

In the short term, William failed to create the taste or teach the art. The reviews were venomous. Francis Jeffrey summed up the reaction in the *Edinburgh Review*. 'If the printing of such trash as this be not felt as an insult on the public taste, we are afraid it cannot be insulted.' Had the reviews been unmitigated spite, it might have been easier to dismiss them. What complicated the picture was the constant refrain that *Poems, in Two Volumes* did not live up to the expectations created by *Lyrical Ballads*. William had promised to be 'the poet of the heart', and instead had become 'the capricious minion of a debasing affectation'. To a certain extent, William was shielded from the full force of the critical onslaught by the very isolation which the critics so despised: most of the periodicals simply did not make their way to Grasmere unless specifically requested. And the Wordsworths were, at last, on their way back home.

On 10 July they returned together to Grasmere. Allan Bank was not yet ready for them and they would have to manage in the cottage at Town End a little longer. All they could do was hope for fine weather. Fortunately, it was an un-usually quiet summer. The Beaumonts arrived at Keswick a few days after the Wordsworths at Grasmere, and much of the time was spent in their company. The wretched Mr Crump, who owned Allan Bank, arrived, and turned out to be a most kind-hearted and good-natured man who was quite prepared to leave all the planting of trees and laying out of grounds at Allan Bank entirely in William's hands.

It was an indication of how firmly William was already identified with the Lakes that he had become something of a tourist attraction himself. On 26 August he was summoned as 'one of the Lake poets' to dine at the Lowwood Inn with an aristocratic party led by Lord Holland, the nephew of Charles James Fox, and his wife, Elizabeth, the beautiful society hostess. It was a perfect example of the gulf that William had recognized as existing between his own life, sympathies and tastes, and that of fashionable London society. Lady Holland was suitably condescending. 'He is much superior to his writings,' she wrote in her journal,

and his conversation is even beyond his abilities . . . He holds some opinions on picturesque subjects with which I completely differ, especially as to the effects produced by *white* houses on the sides of the hills; to my taste they produce a cheerful effect. He, on the contrary, would brown, or even black-work them . . . His objection was chiefly grounded upon the distances being confounded by the glare of white . . .

William refused to be intimidated, maintaining his opinion 'with a considerable degree of ingenuity'.

William was received with rather less condescension and amusement by his benefactor Sir William Lowther, newly created Earl of Lonsdale. The new Earl had great plans for the family estate. Not only had he employed Wilkinson to lay out the grounds, but he had begun to rebuild the dilapidated house. The new Lowther Castle would be a fantastic fairy-tale creation, with soaring turrets and battlements, and the Earl was anxious that it should have an appropriate setting. William's new-found status as landscape gardener made his advice indispensable.

Once their last visitors, the Beaumonts, had gone, towards the end of the second week in September, William and Mary seized the chance to make a three-day tour of the north-western corner of the lakes, visiting Wasdale, Ennerdale, Whitehaven and Cockermouth.

Returning to the cottage at Town End, William threw himself into composition. He had an entirely new subject, inspired by visiting Bolton Abbey that summer, and, for him, an equally new way of handling it. The project was *The White Doe of Rylstone*, a narrative poem in cantering octosyllabics, almost 2,000 lines in length. It neatly interwove what William took to be historical fact, the tragic story of Emily Norton's father and nine brothers, who were all killed in the futile northern uprising of 1569, with the legend of a white doe which, after the rebellion, frequented the churchyard of Bolton Abbey. William would always indignantly deny that it was an attempt to cash in on the lucrative seam of medieval romance opened up by Scott's *Lay of the Last Minstrel*. He pointed out, with some justification, that Scott's poems were purely concerned with action, whereas *The White Doe* began and ended with the spiritual. The stirring events of the uprising are not an end in themselves, but merely a backdrop to the state of mind of the heroine of the tragedy, who is entirely passive in the midst of action. She knows

Her duty is to stand and wait,
In resignation to abide
The shock, and finally secure
O'er pain & grief a triumph pure.
The White Doe of Rylstone, ll.1069–72

The white doe, which becomes the companion of her solitude in bereavement, has 'a tender & humanizing influence' upon her. The twin points at which the poem aimed were the 'anticipated beatification . . . of her mind' and the 'apotheosis' of the doe. The comparison with Scott was 'inconsiderate': the true subject of William's poem was not the fate of the Nortons, but Emily's struggle over and conquest of her own sorrows. 'How insignificant a thing, for example, does personal prowess appear compared with the fortitude of patience & heroic martyrdom, in other words with struggles for the sake of principle, in preference to victory gloried in for its own sake.' It is unfortunate, therefore, that *The White Doe* invites, and suffers from, comparison with Scott's *Lay of the Last Minstrel,* and his *Marmion,* which would appear in 1808. Even the secondary title, *The Fate of the Nortons,* appears calculated to mislead the reader into thinking that this is a tale of chivalric derring-do.

The poem was finished by 16 January 1808, despite a number of distractions, the most important of which was the much anticipated meeting with Thomas de Quincey on 4 November. Four and a half years earlier, in May 1803, de Quincey, then a troubled young man about to go up to Oxford, had written an extraordinary fan letter to William in which he expressed his fervent admiration, literally on bended knee, for *Lyrical Ballads* and 'earnestly and humbly sue[d]' for William's 'friendship'. William was touched; he replied tactfully and with just the right amount of encouragement and reserve. He pointed out that de Quincey had already achieved his main aim: how could William feel anything but kindly feelings towards one who had written so enthusiastically about his work? 'My friendship', he added more sternly, 'it is not in my power to give: this is a gift which no man can make, it is not in our power: a sound and healthy friendship is the growth of time and circumstance, it will spring up and thrive like a wildflower when these favour, and when they do not, it is in vain to look for it.' He ended the letter with a casual, if sincere, invitation: 'I shall indeed be very happy to see you at Grasmere; if you ever find it convenient to visit this delightful country.'

Ironically, William thought he had recognized in de Quincey a version of his youthful self, a comparison that was inevitably strengthened when the latter's beloved younger brother was apparently lost at sea. In fact, de Quincey might more aptly be likened to Coleridge: he was also an opium addict, with all the delusions and paranoia which that induced, he had the same desperate need to be loved by those whom he admired and he was promiscuous as Coleridge had been in his youth. Like Coleridge, too, he was acutely aware of his lack of physical attractiveness (de Quincey was small to the point of dwarfism), but he lacked the compensatory charisma, personality and verbal fireworks of Coleridge on a good day. Quiet, observant, shrewd and well read, he was willing to please and desperate for admission to what Coleridge called the Concern, the magic circle of William's devoted family and friends. Several times over the intervening years he had made arrangements to meet William, but his courage had always failed him at the last moment. Now he had a legitimate reason to do so, having offered to escort Mrs Coleridge and her children from Bristol back to Keswick, enabling Coleridge to go to London alone as he wished and relieving him of an uncomfortable duty.

On 4 November a trembling de Quincey finally found himself face to face with William, 'a tallish man, who held out his hand, and saluted me, with the most cordial manner, and the warmest expression of friendly welcome that it is possible to imagine'. Entering the cottage, he encountered Mary, 'a tall young woman, with the most winning expression of benignity upon her features that I had ever beheld', and Dorothy, shorter and slighter, whose unladylike 'determinate gypsy tan', glancing quickness of motion and ungraceful 'even unsexual' deportment, startled him. De Quincey was one of the few people who knew the Wordsworths well in this early period to attempt to describe them fully, though his account has to be treated with some caution. It was written as a piece of journalism, long after he had become disenchanted with the whole Wordsworth circle, and most of all with William. Nevertheless, despite its jaundiced colouring, it is a fascinating insight by an intelligent and perspicacious observer.

De Quincey described William as being 'upon the whole, not a well-made man', five feet ten inches tall, thick-limbed, with legs that were 'serviceable beyond the average standard of human requisition ... [but] certainly not ornamental'. A narrowness of chest and a droop about the shoulders added to what de Quincey called the 'absolute meanness' of his figure, especially when viewed from the back and not counteracted by his countenance, which 'was one which would have made amends for greater defects of figure; it was certainly the noblest for intellectual effects that, in actual life, I have seen ...' It was a variety of the indigenous face of the Lake District, like that of a courtier in a painting by Titian or Van Dyck, not oval, but long, with a broad and expansive forehead, large, rather arched nose, eyes which, after a long walk, assumed the most solemn and spiritual expression possible, and a prominent mouth. Both he and Dorothy always looked fifteen or twenty years older than they were, because they shared 'the secret fire of a temperament too fervid; the self-consuming energies of the brain, that gnaw at the heart and life-strings for ever'.

For Mary, so often overlooked or ignored by observers, de Quincey immediately conceived, and (unusually) preserved, profound respect and admiration. Physically, she was tall, with a good figure, though too slender for de Quincey's taste, and possessed of natural dignity: 'she furnished a remarkable proof how possible it is for a woman, neither handsome nor even comely, according to the rigour of criticism – nay, generally pronounced very plain – to exercise all the practical power and fascination of beauty'. Her 'sunny benignity – a radiant gracefulness – such as in this world I never saw equalled or approached' transformed her. (Sir George Beaumont had been equally struck by this, telling William that no one could be more sensible of Mary's 'angelic kindness & goodness of heart ... indeed it is not possible to be two minutes in her company without perceiving it, it beams from her countenance & shines out in all her actions & expressions'. If all men and women were like her, there would be something approaching perfect happiness in this world. 'This is not a compliment –', Beaumont assured William, 'I seriously declare it to be the conviction of my heart & I have repeatedly said the same thing to Lady Beaumont who feels exactly as I do upon the subject'.) Intellectually, de Quincey described her as 'inactive'; blue-stocking loquacity, discussion and analysis were not her natural *forte*. Indeed, she talked so little that Clarkson used to say of her that she could only say '*God bless you!*' What she did have was 'a luxurious repose of mind', 'a quiescent, reposing, meditative way' which was perfectly suited to the needs and tastes of her husband.

Having described Mary as a paragon of femininity, de Quincey rounded on Dorothy with a brutality which is all the more shocking for the contrast. It was a deliberate juxtaposition, for the whole thrust of his portrayal was that Dorothy was 'unfeminine'. The italics in the following descriptions are mine.

Her manner was warm and even ardent; her sensibility seemed constitutionally deep; and some subtle fire of impassioned intellect apparently burned within her, which, being alternately pushed forward into a conspicuous expression by *the irrepressible instincts of her temperament, and then immediately checked, in obedience to the decorum of her sex and age*, and her maidenly condition, (for she had rejected all offers of marriage, out of purely sisterly regard to her brother and his children,) gave to her whole demeanour and to her conversation, an air of embarrassment and even of *self-conflict*, that was sometimes distressing to witness ... At times, the *self-counteraction* and *self-baffling* of her feelings, caused her even to stammer, ... The greatest deductions from Miss Wordsworth's attractions ... was the glancing quickness of her motions, and other circumstances in her deportment, (such as her stooping attitude when walking,) which gave an *ungraceful*, and even an *unsexual* character to her appearance when out of doors. She did not cultivate the graces which preside over the person and its carriage ... she ought to have been the more polished of the two; and yet, from greater natural aptitudes for refinement of manner ... Mrs Wordsworth would have been pronounced the more *lady-like* person.

Writing in 1839, in *Tait's Edinburgh Magazine*, de Quincey could do no more than hint that Dorothy was a lesbian, by suggesting that she had a masculine mind and spirit trapped in a female body. It was almost as an afterthought that he paid tribute to her 'very remarkable' intellectual endowments, and her 'sympathizing attention', 'by which she made all that one could tell her, all that one could describe, all that one could quote from a foreign author, reverberate as it were, *à plusieurs reprises*, to one's own feelings, by the manifest impression it made upon her'. Dorothy's sexuality would always intrigue her male friends, just as it does modern commentators, but de Quincey was the only one to postulate the possibility of lesbianism. At the time, however, it did not lessen her personal interest in de Quincey's eyes, for it seems that he was one of those rejected suitors for her hand in marriage.

Welcoming de Quincey to their cottage, the Wordsworths had no idea that he would one day expose them to the prurient gaze of magazine readers. For the moment, they were completely taken up with the Coleridges. Sarah brought news that nothing had changed: her husband had parted from her, just as he had done before, assuring her that he would never live with her again, but he did not have the courage to make the separation public knowledge. This suited Sarah, who was afraid that a formal separation would bring disgrace on herself and the children, but, as the Wordsworths feared, the uncertainty was not in Coleridge's interest. Accusations that he had forsaken his family would be made and, while his marital affairs remained unsettled, he would be unhappy, and therefore unable to fulfil the promise of his great genius. In the meantime, he had gone to London, to undertake a series of twenty lectures on poetry for the Royal Institution. 'I will not say, how dearly I love you all;' he now wrote to Dorothy, 'as perhaps it is a misfortune, that so enormous is the difference between my Love of you & of others, that it seems as if I loved nothing & nobody else. O God! has there been a single hour of my Life, even in sleep, in which I have not been blending with you in my Thoughts!' To his private journal, he was confessing something quite different: 'It is not the W's knowlege of my frailties that prevents my *entire* Love of them No! it is their Ignorance of the Deep place of my Being – and o! the cruel cruel misconception of that which is purest in me', which was, of course, his love of Sara. Even now he was still haunted by jealousy of William, whom he held responsible for teaching Sara 'to pity & withdraw herself from my affections – Whither? – O agony! O the vision of that Saturday morning – of the Bed – O cruel! is he not beloved, adored by two   & two such Beings – and must I not be beloved *near* him except as a Satellite?'

De Quincey stayed with the Wordsworths for five days; they showed him the sights, walked him up Easedale and round the lakes of Grasmere and Rydal, and took him to Keswick by the picturesque route over Kirkstone Pass and round Ullswater. De Quincey had already been unnerved by the Wordsworths' 'modest hospitality': he woke to find he was sharing a room with Johnny and, at breakfast, Dorothy herself boiled the kettle on the fire in the little sitting room. 'I had never seen so humble a *ménage*', he admitted. He was in for another shock when they went to Eusemere, for they travelled in 'the common farmers' cart of the country'. A further one was in store at Greta Hall, where he listened with horror as William and Southey casually revealed their republican sympathies by suggesting that Britain would never come to any good till the royal family should be 'expatriated'. De Quincey returned to Oxford with his ideas in turmoil and his admiration for 'the Lake Poets' greatly increased. He left a good impression at Grasmere, as 'a remarkable and very interesting young man; very diminutive in person, which, to strangers, makes him appear insignificant; and so modest, and so very shy that even now I wonder how he ever had the courage to address himself to my Brother by letter'. Dorothy thought of him with particular pleasure, proudly believing de Quincey to be 'a remarkable instance of the power of my Brother's poems, over a lonely and contemplative mind, unwarped by any established laws of taste'.

Soon after de Quincey left, there was one of the greatest falls of snow in living memory. The mountains were impassable and all the roads were blocked for weeks on end. Mary, whom Joanna had persuaded to accompany her to Stockton, to visit their brother Jack, was stranded there. It was 1 December before the roads were clear enough for William to join her and 23 December before they returned home. At Penrith, they chanced upon a copy of the *Edinburgh Review* and there read Jeffrey's scathing criticisms of *Poems, in Two Volumes*. The Wordsworths maintained an air of calm indifference. Their only fear, a justifiable one, was that it would affect the sale of the book.

This mattered more than ever, for William was putting the finishing touches to his new poem, *The White Doe of Rylstone*, and he was determined that it should be a financial success. He had made up his mind that his poem was to be published in quarto (unlike his previous two publications, but, significantly, like Scott's *Lay of the Last Minstrel*) and that he would accept nothing less than 100 guineas for an edition of 1,000 copies. Southey, to whom William read the completed poem, was all encouragement. 'The story affected me more deeply than I wish to be affected ... nothing was ever more ably treated', he reported to Scott. William had already decided that he would go in person to London to sell his book for the best possible price when news came that Coleridge was so seriously ill that he had had to give up his lectures at the Royal Institution after delivering only two. William decided to go to London immediately. Coleridge was lodging in a pair of rooms above the *Courier* office; the state of his bowels was such that, as Lamb put it, he 'receives visitors on his close-stool'.

By the time William arrived in town, on 27 February, Coleridge had rallied a little, having been drawn out of the contemplation of his own miseries by those of Henry Hutchinson. The Hutchinson name 'would be a Spell to recall me for the time even from the verge of death ... he is the Brother of the two Beings, whom of all on Earth I most highly honor, most fervently love'. Henry had had a disastrous seafaring career. He had been captured at sea, held prisoner in Guadeloupe, released, become a successful privateer, been impressed (and relieved of his winnings) by HMS *Fortunee*, recaptured and held prisoner for twenty-two months in Mexico, released again in a second exchange of prisoners and sent back to Plymouth, where, as his impressment was still in force, he was expected to rejoin the *Fortunee*. 'He has done enough – he has suffered enough', Coleridge pleaded, as he enlisted Beaumont and Clarkson to lobby all their Admiralty contacts on Henry's behalf. By 3 March he was able to announce triumphantly that he had secured Henry's immediate discharge and earned the undying gratitude of all the Hutchinsons for his prompt and energetic intervention. The effort of this campaign probably did as much to revive Coleridge's flagging spirits as William's presence. By 30 March, Coleridge had recovered sufficiently to resume his lectures, after a break of two months, and William was able to attend two of them before returning to Grasmere.

As usual, William packed as much into his visit as he possibly could. There was the usual round of breakfast, dinner and tea parties, including a dull evening dining with William's publisher, Longman, and his partner, Rees, in a company which included an antiquarian friend of Scott's, Richard Heber, and the historian Sharon Turner; Coleridge was in belligerent mood and gave them all 'some good haranguing, talk I cannot call it' in denunciation of the clergy, for which he later had to apologize.

The Lambs played host to several gatherings. On the evening William finally yielded to their entreaties and brought *The White Doe* to read, he was disconcerted to find that Hazlitt and his fiancée, Sarah Stoddart, were fellow guests. William's personal dislike of Hazlitt had intensified since they last met; the latter had published a political pamphlet in 1806 denouncing as 'apostates' those who, like William, Southey and Coleridge, had changed their attitude towards France as Bonaparte rose to power. In the circumstances, William at first refused to read his poem, but then grudgingly relented and read a single canto. He had not expected a rapturous reception, and he did not get one. Lamb complained that the principal characters 'did nothing'. It was an understandable complaint, given the expectations roused by the form and title of the poem, but if friends like Lamb so completely missed the point, then how would the public react? William's frustration boiled over: in another of those long, sweating letters he poured out his defence of the spiritual object at the heart of the poem, and urged that Lamb should 'learn to be ashamed of himself in not taking some pleasure in the contemplation of this picture'. Poor Lamb was roundly condemned for having the temerity to dislike the poem (or rather, as William would have said, to misunderstand it): 'of one thing be assured,' William wrote to Coleridge, 'that Lamb has not a reasoning mind, therefore cannot have a comprehensive mind, and, least of all, has he an imaginative one'.

It was comments like these – sadly all too frequent when William felt driven to justify his poetry in both his conversation and his correspondence – which so often provoked charges of arrogance and egotism against him. Southey regarded this unlikeable trait with amused contempt. 'It would amuse you to hear how he talks of his own productions, – his entire & intense selfishness exceeds anything you could have conceived.' Hazlitt suggested that William's temper had been soured by a 'sense of injustice and of undeserved ridicule'. The most perceptive response, however, came from Henry Crabb Robinson, to whom William was introduced by the Lambs during this visit to London. Robinson was a barrister, five years younger than William, and an intimate friend of the Clarksons. He had long been an admirer of William's poems and would become a lifelong friend. 'Wordsworth quotes his own Verses with pleasure', he told his brother after he had enjoyed two têtes-à-têtes with the poet, but he had an unfortunate habit of judging the moral worth of his audience by their reaction to his poems. As Robinson observed, there were many who could fully appreciate the moral truths and sentiments of the poetry, but could not overcome their dislike of his style; William did not make any allowance for the influence of 'conventional & habitual taste'.

That there was this confusion in William's mind is evident from his barely suppressed anger at Lamb's reaction to *The White Doe*. Anyone who appreciated the moral truths at the heart of the poem *must* like the poem itself was his argument;

it therefore followed that disliking the poem could result only from moral ignorance or turpitude in the reader. It was a logical extension of his belief that 'Every Great Poet is a Teacher: I wish either to be considered as a Teacher, or as nothing', and also that his works would never be appreciated until the depraved tastes of his generation had been reformed.

Lamb was not alone in being critical of *The White Doe*. Lady Beaumont and her sister, Frances Fermor, 'liked' it (not a good sign, as they were both noted enthusiasts), but 'it did not much interest Sir George'. Coleridge also had considerable doubts; he found the battle scenes and Francis's delivering up of the family '*comparatively* very heavy' going, and, in terms of Francis's motivation, 'quite obscure'. These were significant censures, particularly coming from a critic as astute as Coleridge. William's confidence faltered. He had carried out his intention to offer Longman the right to publish a first edition of 1,000 copies of *The White Doe* in return for 100 guineas, but when Longman insisted on having the manuscript referred to an independent editor for approval before he agreed to accept it, William seized on this as an excuse to back out and refused. 'I do not chuse to send it to be thumbed by his criticasters', he informed the family at Grasmere. 'I do not think it likely I shall publish it at all – indeed I am so thoroughly disgusted with the wretched and stupid Public, that though my wish to *write* for the sake of the People is not abated yet my loathing at the thought of publication is almost insupportable. – Therefore trouble yourselves no more about it.' William might have been prepared to abandon the project out of principle, but his wife and sister had more pragmatic concerns at heart, as Dorothy did not hesitate to remind him.

We are exceedingly concerned, to hear that you, William! have given up all thoughts of publishing your Poem . . . without money what *can* we do? New House! new furniture! such a large family! two servants and little Sally! we *cannot* go on so another half-year; and as Sally will not be fit for another place, we must take her back again into the old one, and dismiss one of the Servants, and work the flesh *off our poor bones*. Do, dearest William! do pluck up your Courage – overcome your disgust to publishing – It is but a *little trouble*, and all will be over, and we shall be wealthy, and at our ease for one year, at least.

Coleridge came to the rescue. He suggested that William leave the manuscript with him and authorize him to make what arrangements he could for its publication. On 3 April William left London, ironically recalled home early by news that Sara was seriously ill. He parted from Coleridge at seven o'clock in the morning and walked towards the City

in a very thoughtful and melancholy state of mind; I had passed through Temple Bar and by St Dunstan's, noticing nothing, and entirely occupied with my own thoughts, when looking up, I saw before me the avenue of Fleet street, silent, empty, and pure white, with a sprinkling of new-fallen snow, not a cart or Carriage to obstruct the view, no noise, only a few soundless and dusky foot-passengers, here and there; you remember the elegant curve of Ludgate Hill in which this avenue would terminate, and beyond and towering above it was the huge and majestic form of St Pauls, solemnised by a thin veil of falling snow. I cannot say how much I was affected at this unthought-of sight, in such a place and what a blessing I felt there is in habits of exalted Imagination. My sorrow was controlled, and my uneasiness of mind not quieted and relieved altogether, seemed at once to receive the gift of an anchor of security.

It was the perfect subject for a poem, yet another of those 'moments of time' when the outside world suddenly and unexpectedly impressed its presence on a preoccupied mind. The resulting blank verse lines, 'Pressed with conflicting thoughts of love and fear', drew heavily on the imagery and vocabulary of this prose description to create a wonderful meditative poem. Despite its obvious quality, William deliberately suppressed it during his lifetime, for reasons which remain obscure.

He returned home to scenes of more than usual chaos. Sara was in a very delicate state, though no longer in danger, but Johnny, who had been ill with influenza, suddenly developed alarming symptoms of meningitis on the very day of William's return. For more than a week his parents and aunts were frantic with worry; doctors were brought in from Ambleside and Keswick and, despite their best efforts (purgatives, bleeding and blistering) Johnny recovered. The burden of the nursing fell on Mary, who was herself unwell, being in the fourth month of pregnancy; their servant had left to get married and she had only two young girls to help her, one of whom, Sally Green, had just suffered a terrible bereavement. On the night of 19 March her parents had been caught in a snowstorm returning over the tops from Langdale to their isolated cottage in Easedale, where they had left their six youngest children in the care of the oldest, a girl of eleven. For two days the children waited for their parents to return, thinking that they had stayed in Langdale, so the alarm was not raised till the oldest went to borrow a cloak so that she could go out to look for them. Realizing what must have been their fate, between fifty and sixty men turned out and the bodies were found, forty-eight hours later, lying at the foot of the precipice from which they must have fallen. They were buried in a single grave in Grasmere churchyard on 25 March. The Greens had been typical Lakeland statesmen, fiercely independent, struggling to provide for themselves and their family on a small, heavily mortgaged farm and refusing to go to the parish for assistance. 'See them when you would,' Dorothy remarked, 'they were always chearful, and when they went from home they were decently dressed. The children, too, though very ragged, were clean; and are as pure and innocent, and in every respect as promising children as I ever saw.'

It was not until after their deaths that the full extent of their poverty became known. Mary and Dorothy, who visited the orphans almost immediately, were shocked and distressed to find that there was virtually no food in the house. They determined that something would have to be done. There were twelve orphans: the five oldest were already in employment and one of them could take a younger brother into his house and business. The Wordsworths offered a home to Sally. She had been with them as a nursemaid to the children since their return from

Coleorton, but, before the tragedy, they had decided that she would have to be replaced by someone older and more authoritative. Now they volunteered to keep her as a member of their household, sending her to Grasmere school and teaching her sewing to enable her to go out and earn her own living in due course. Only the five youngest children were left without any means of support. It was decided to raise a public subscription to enable the Greens to be boarded with families in the vale, sent to school and trained as servants and apprentices. Mary joined a committee of local ladies at Ambleside to supervise the care of the orphans and personally took charge of keeping the accounts. William, immediately on his return from London, drafted a short account of the fate of the Greens and circulated it among his rich and powerful friends, appealing to them to assist this 'cluster of little orphans, who have been left such in a most afflicting manner'. He was phenomenally successful. As the result of his efforts, over a third of the total sum of £500 was raised. After visiting the new grave, William composed a poem which he dismissed as 'a mere pouring out of my own feeling', but nevertheless asked Coleridge to utilize for 'any profit for the poor Orphans' by reciting, circulating or publishing it. William was justifiably proud of the way the whole vale had united to help the orphans, suggesting to Dorothy that she should make 'a minute narrative' of all the circumstances. It would, he said, 'throw much light upon the state of the moral feelings of the inhabitants of these Vales'. To those who complained that his own poetry celebrated a way of life and a spirit of benevolence long since passed away from the Lakes, Dorothy's *A Narrative Concerning George and Sarah Green* furnished a practical example that they had not.

At the beginning of May, Henry Hutchinson paid his first visit to Grasmere. His discharge from the navy had come through at last and he was a free, if impecunious, man. Henry proved to be not only a raconteur who had them all hanging on his every word, but also 'the handiest creature in the world – can sew, cook, wash dishes – put up beds – any thing that you can name'. He stayed only for a few days, but long enough to make himself so indispensable that they all begged him to return to help them make the long-awaited move to Allan Bank.

It was fortunate that he did, for Sara was too ill to do anything other than a little light sewing, Mary had sprained her wrist in a fall just before the move and William was generally regarded as useless in such situations. The whole burden of packing and unpacking papers, linen, books and all the paraphernalia of daily life fell on Dorothy. She and Henry worked body and soul, determined to save as much money as possible by making their own carpets and curtains. Reluctant as Dorothy had been to move from the cottage, she, and indeed all the family, felt the advantages of Allan Bank immediately. The children thought they were in Paradise: they were free to play all over the surrounding fields without fear of being run over by the horses, waggons and carriages which daily passed the old cottage door.

Allan Bank was unquestionably a gentleman's house. Externally it was imposing, if brutally symmetrical, with large sash windows and semicircular bays to take full advantage of the views offered by its elevated situation. Internally, a surprisingly modest entrance porch gave way to a vast, square hall, with a highly impractical glass roof. From this central hallway opened out a series of huge, ornately plastered reception rooms, each one large enough to swallow the cottage at Town End whole. Up a sweeping staircase, a rabbit warren of bedrooms led off the galleried landing which ran right round the upper floor. For the first time in years the Wordsworths had space and privacy. They each had a room of their own and the views from every window were spectacular.

Now that the Wordsworths had room to accommodate any number of guests, they were inundated. Mary's family descended *en masse* from Penrith, and an invitation was offered to de Quincey. There were visits to the Lloyds at Old Brathay, a disastrous picnic party to the island on Grasmere lake as guests of Crump, which was rained off, and a renewal of an acquaintance struck up the previous year with John Wilson, a wealthy young Scotsman who was building a new house, Elleray, on Orrest Head, overlooking Windermere. Wilson, like de Quincey, had been drawn to the Lakes by his personal admiration for William. Still only twenty-three, this 'very amiable young man' had become a friend, as well as an '*adorer* of William and his verses'; the friendship was to prove enduring, though it was not without its difficulties once Wilson was drawn into the ambit of *Blackwood's Magazine*.

The one visitor who was most anxiously expected did not make his appearance at Allan Bank till 1 September. Coleridge had gone with Stuart to Margate, then to stay with the Clarksons at Bury St Edmunds. Both Coleridge and the Wordsworths looked forward to their reunion with mixed feelings. The previous December, Dorothy had confided her fears to Catherine Clarkson:

we had long experience at Coleorton that it was not in our power to make him happy; and his irresolute conduct since, has almost confirmed our fears that it will never be otherwise; therefore we should be more disposed to hesitation; and fear, of having our domestic quiet disturbed if he should now wish to come to us with the Children. I do not say that we *should not consent*; but it would be with little hope; and we shall never *advise* the measure.

Since then, relations between Coleridge and William had hit a new low. The ostensible cause was William's sudden decision in May to cancel publication of *The White Doe*. Coleridge had fought long and hard on his friend's behalf to secure the terms he wanted from Longman and had succeeded where William himself had failed. On 1 May Dorothy had written to Coleridge, saying,

We are very anxious that 'the White Doe' should be published *as soon as possible* ... Our main reason (I speak in the name of the Females) for wishing that the Poem may be *speedily* published, is that William may get it out of his head; but further we think that it is of the *utmost importance*, that it should come out before the Buz of your Lectures is settled [Coleridge's emphases].

Coleridge naturally took this to be an authorization to send the manuscript immediately to the publisher, not realizing that when Dorothy said she spoke for the 'Females', she spoke for them alone. They were certainly pushing William to go ahead, but he proved obdurate, being increasingly convinced by the reaction of those permitted to read the poem that it would neither sell nor add to his reputation. When he learned that Coleridge had given the go-ahead to Longman's, he wrote at once to countermand the order, suggesting that Coleridge had exceeded his authority.

There had been a perfectly genuine misunderstanding, but the stress of delivering weekly lectures, a run-in with the *Edinburgh Review* and being 'on show' in London society had driven Coleridge to drinking and opium-taking of heroic proportions. As a result, he was both paranoid and psychotic, believing that he had been 'Cruelly' treated by 'almost every one'. The suggestion that he might have exceeded his authority was the catalyst to ignite all his festering grievances, both real and imagined. He wrote William a long and bitter letter, articulating for the first time all the complaints which he had previously confided only to his private notebooks. Worse still, he charged the Wordsworths with turning Sara against him. Her letters to him had been written under their censoring eye, but 'the keystone' of their 'offences' was their 'cruelty' in instilling into Sara's mind the notion that his attachment to her had been 'the curse' of all his happiness.

William refused to take offence: he understood that it was not the true Coleridge speaking, merely 'a man in a lamentably insane state of mind'. Though he considered all the accusations 'utterly unworthy of notice', he would not have been human had he not wished to refute them. He tried hard to remain both calm and reasonable, drafting the letter twice, but it was an effort that could not be sustained, particularly when it came to Coleridge's 'unmanly and ungentlemanly' accusation that he censored Sara's correspondence. 'She is 34 years of age and what have I to do with overlooking her letters!' As for trying to make her believe she was the curse of Coleridge's happiness, 'the very reverse is the truth'. Mary and Dorothy had told Sara that it was in Coleridge's nature to conceive such an infatuation; she was therefore not the cause of his unhappiness, but the innocent occasion of it. What is more, she could congratulate herself, for *his* sake, that she was the object of his passion. Had he fixed on a less virtuous woman, what might his sufferings then have been?

What the Wordsworths believed was true, but then Truth is not always comfortable or acceptable, especially when preached to the suffering. Having given vent to his own feelings, William did what Coleridge should have done and did not send his letter. Coleridge also seems to have realized that he had gone too far. When he went to stay with the Clarksons, they found him a Quaker doctor and he made a serious attempt to overcome his addiction. By the time he arrived at Grasmere, he had reduced his opium intake to a sixth of his former consumption and, as a result, was in better health and spirits than he had been for years. He arrived on 1 September, making a spectacular entrance at half past eleven at night, which roused the whole household from their beds.

Coleridge would share the Wordsworths' home at Allan Bank for the next two years. A few days after his arrival, William accompanied him to Keswick, where there was an amicable meeting with his wife. She not only agreed that her two sons should live with their father at Allan Bank during school terms and with her during the holidays, but also that little Sara should pay him an extended visit. Sara was now almost six and barely knew her father. She returned with him to Allan Bank, where her delicate beauty and quiet manners won all hearts – and provided a striking contrast to naughty Dora, with her long blonde ringlets, wild eyes and even wilder motions. Johnny was instantly smitten and, to the amusement of all the adults, the pair decided that he would be her future husband. The relationship with her father proved less successful. When her mother arrived to carry her back home, Sara flew to her and 'wished not to be separated from her any more'. Her father could not hide his annoyance at this understandable preference and, more than forty years later, Sara could still recall vividly both her distress at his accusing her of 'want of affection' and her jealousy when he contrasted her coldness towards him with the childish caresses which the young Wordsworths lavished on him.

On 6 September, while William was at Keswick with Coleridge, Mary gave birth to her fourth child and second daughter, Catherine, who was named after her godmother, Catherine Clarkson. At the end of the month, Hartley and Derwent Coleridge, aged twelve and eight, arrived. They were to go to Mr Dawes's school at Ambleside as weekly boarders, but would spend every weekend at Allan Bank. At the beginning of November, they were joined by another permanent guest, de Quincey, who had thrown up his studies at Oxford. As Dorothy wearily pointed out to Catherine Clarkson, they regularly had thirteen people in the household, rising to fifteen at weekends.

Given the size of Allan Bank, this should not have been a problem. Unfortunately, the autumn closed in cold, wet and windy. Not only were they all confined to the house, but they now discovered the fatal flaw in its design: the chimneys did not work. 'You can have no conception of the uncomfortableness, not to say *misery*, of this House in these storms –', Sara complained to her cousin; 'not a chimney will draw the smoke! and one day we could not have a fire except in the Study; & then you could not *see* each other. In the rest of the rooms the fire was actually blown out of the Grates'. The combination of cold and smoke was so great that they were forced to go to bed in the middle of the day with the baby, just to keep her warm. A chimney doctor was summoned, worked for a month and did no good. 'We females wish to quit the Premises immediately but the Men will not hear of it', Sara sighed. The Men were hard at work and happy. The grounds were taking shape rapidly under William's eye; more importantly, he had become caught up in the latest political controversy. British troops, under the command of Sir Arthur Wellesley (the future Duke of Wellington) had landed in Portugal at the beginning of August and inflicted a crushing defeat on the French army of occupation. Instead of insisting on an unconditional surrender, his superiors agreed that the French could retreat, with their arms, honour and plunder from Portuguese palaces, museums and churches completely intact, and French collaborators in Portugal were guaranteed immunity from prosecution and persecution. The blindingly obvious outcome was that the retreating French army was free to reinforce

Napoleon's armies in Spain and assist in crushing the native Spanish revolt against the imposition of Joseph Bonaparte as their king. The terms were set out in the notorious Convention of Cintra on 30 August 1808, which was widely regarded as a betrayal of Britain's Portuguese allies and the Spanish resistance.

William was mortified. Coleridge, Southey and de Quincey were equally incensed: little Sara Coleridge would never forget how the four men 'gravely and earnestly' paced the room, discussing the affairs of the nation 'as if it were their private concern'. Reverting to the idealism of his radical youth, William decided to turn political pamphleteer. By the beginning of December, he was 'very deep in this subject' and believed he would soon be ready to publish, 'first, I believe in a newspaper for the sake of immediate and wide circulation; and next, the same matter in a separate pamphlet'. Coleridge wrote to Stuart, offering him William's 'series of most masterly Essays on the affairs of Portugal & Spain' for the *Courier*. Stuart was delighted. 'The subject is extremely important; the present situation of Spain abounds with new & important subjects for reflexion ... Never did I hear any Measure so universally execrated as the Cintra Convention.'

Fired with enthusiasm for his project, William would frequently stay up into the early hours, writing or talking with Coleridge, with shy little de Quincey a rapt and silent auditor. Anxious for the latest news from the Peninsula, he would leave the house at midnight and walk up the Keswick road to meet the carrier bringing the *Courier* from London. Despite the acrid smell of smoke pervading the house, and the fact that the study fire had frequently to be used for cooking and heating water, William composed rapidly. With Coleridge's assistance and Mary as his amanuensis, five instalments were sent off to London before Christmas, and the first, some 2,500 words long, appeared in the *Courier* on 27 December. There was a short delay, caused when the manuscript of the next essay was lost in London and had to be completely rewritten, then it was followed, on 13 January 1809, by a further 4,250 words.

At this point it must have been obvious to Stuart that he was not getting what he had anticipated. Instead of a hard-hitting *exposé* of the military and administrative failings which had led to such a shameful episode, he had received two essays which, despite their length, were merely introductory and mentioned the Convention only four times in passing. Had there been no other news, Stuart would have continued the series, but a sensational investigation by a House of Commons Committee was about to begin. Mrs Clarke, the mistress of the Duke of York, was accused of accepting bribes to influence military appointments by the Duke, who was Commander-in-Chief of the army. It was not merely hot news, but it went to the heart of what was wrong with the British administration and its handling of the war. Reports of the committee proceedings filled the *Courier* throughout February and the newspaper serialization of William's pamphlet ended before it had properly begun.

William was rather relieved, as his style and method of writing were not adapted to the pressures of meeting newspaper deadlines; now he could afford to take a more leisurely approach. He decided to widen his reading and eagerly accepted

Stuart's offer to find him both relevant reports and pamphlets and a publisher for his own work. Nevertheless, he was still acutely aware that the pamphlet had to be published as soon as possible if it was to be pertinent and effective. Sheets of copy were duly dispatched in batches to the printers as soon as they were written, but the post was so dilatory and haphazard that direct supervision of the proofs from Grasmere proved impractical. De Quincey, delighted to have an opportunity to render practical service to his hero, volunteered to go to London to see the pamphlet through the press. William accepted gratefully: it would save him time and expense, and Stuart the trouble which had, by default, fallen to him.

De Quincey arrived on 25 February to find London agog with the news that Sheridan's splendid new Drury Lane theatre had burnt down in the night. In his anxiety to please, he sent long chatty letters, full of all the latest gossip, every few days to Allan Bank. They were clearly designed to entertain the Grasmerians, but ultimately led to (unfounded) suspicions that he had not dedicated himself to the task in hand. The printers had already received between a half and two-thirds of William's text. The tasks of punctuating the rest of William's manuscripts, as they arrived, passing them on to the printer and correcting the proofs would fall to de Quincey. It was a grave mistake. He had no practical experience of proofreading or editing, and would often fail to pick up misprints until printing was far advanced. He was too young, stood too much in awe of William and lacked the self-confidence to take decisions without referring to Grasmere, which rather undermined the whole purpose of his being there. Like everyone who had ever undertaken the thankless task of seeing William's work through the press, he was also deluged with last minute emendations, cancellations and second thoughts, all of which caused delay and confusion.

His problems were aggravated by the fact that this was not a volume of poetry, but a commentary on contemporary politics, which was inherently liable to be wrong-footed by the pace of events. The appearance in March of the official Report of the Board of Inquiry on the Convention of Cintra meant that the Appendix, which had been compiled from newspaper reports, had to be completely remodelled. The fall of Saragossa under a second siege, after a successful resistance to a first, necessitated comment or changes. De Quincey provided a lengthy and painstakingly compiled footnote, which, to his mortification, William cancelled as unnecessary. The death of the British commander Sir John Moore at Corunna on 16 January and his widely publicized aspersions on the Spanish also had to be taken into account. Nevertheless, by the end of March de Quincey had received all the copy, and corrections, and William confidently expected the pamphlet to be published within the next fortnight. In the event, it was not published until eight weeks later, by which time the French, under Marshal Soult, had reinvaded Portugal, a revolution in Sweden had led to the abdication of the monarch, France and Austria were at war and Napoleon had annexed the Papal States. The Convention of Cintra was no longer a topical subject.

What caused the delay? De Quincey laid the blame squarely on the printers and a drunken compositor. Stuart blamed de Quincey, saying that the printers had never known 'so much chopping & changing, so much cancelling & correction'. Coleridge, who seems to have taken a certain malicious and jealous delight in fomenting trouble for de Quincey, encouraged both the Wordsworths and Stuart to believe that it was entirely de Quincey's fault.

William himself was unconcerned, and, indeed, contributed to the delay by a last-minute panic of his own. He suddenly realized that he might be fined or imprisoned for remarks which might be construed as libellous, particularly against Arthur Wellesley, who had just been sent back to Portugal as Commander-in-Chief of the British forces there. Stuart and de Quincey were urgently requested to read the pamphlet through before publication and cancel any defamatory passages. 'We Females', as Dorothy, Mary and Sara had taken to calling themselves, thought the whole notion extremely funny. 'We Females . . . have not the least fear of Newgate', Sara informed de Quincey; '– if there was but a Garden to walk in we think we should do very nicely – and a Gaol in the Country would be quite pleasant'. Taking his tone from her letter, de Quincey replied that there was 'no hope of Newgate', but rather spoilt the joke by admitting that he and Stuart could not agree which passages might be libellous.

William tried hard to keep his nerve, but admitted to being 'ruffled . . . not a little' when he learned that all 500 copies of the pamphlet had been run off before Stuart had completed his read-through for libel; worse still, after all the delays, the completed pamphlet then lay for ten days at the printers instead of being forwarded to Longman's for publication. Belatedly, William realized that de Quincey was temperamentally unsuited to the task he had been given. William could not bring himself to give the heartfelt thanks and unqualified approval which the young man believed he had earned and deserved for his selfless labours. His praises were at best half-hearted – 'I am surprized how you have been able to get it done so correctly'; his most fulsome compliment was a congratulation 'on your escape from so irksome an employment and . . . my sincere thanks for all the trouble you have undergone'. When Mary chivvied him into expressing 'stronger language of approbation', he had the grace to repeat her rebuke to de Quincey, but followed it with a string of regrets about misprints which negated its value. It was hardly surprising that de Quincey would later publicly complain that William had never made 'those returns of friendship and kindness [to] which most firmly I maintain [I was] entitled'.

And what of the pamphlet itself? It was finally published on 24 May 1809 by Longman, who set the price at 5s. William personally bore the entire cost of printing and publishing, a sure indication of how much the pamphlet meant to him. He had not been sanguine about its prospects, even before publication. 'What I have written has been done according to the best light of my Conscience;' he told his old friend Wrangham; 'it is indeed very imperfect, and will I fear be little read, but, if it is read, it cannot I hope fail of doing some good – though I am aware it will create me a world of enemies, and call forth the old yell of Jacobinism.'

He had every reason to be wary. He had accused the government of preparing to lay further restraints upon freedom of speech and of the press 'in contempt of the rights of the nation'. He declared that the purpose of his pamphlet was to instruct men in authority, who, 'if they possess not talents and acquirements, have not title to the high stations which they hold', and 'to assert the sanctity and to display the efficacy of principles and passions which are the natural birth-right of man'. He attacked the self-serving, place-seeking spirit of those in Parliament, who had refused to bow to popular demand and censure or condemn the Convention of Cintra. 'If the People would constitutionally and resolutely assert their rights, their Representatives would be taught another lesson; and for their own profit', he thundered. And, though speaking of Spain, the lesson for British politics was implicit when he asserted that a nation 'determined to be free' could overcome the mightiest power which a foreign invader might bring against it: 'the cause of the People ... is safe while it remains not only in the bosom but in the hands of the People; or (what amounts to the same thing) in those of a government which, being truly *from* the People, is faithfully *for* them'.

No one could doubt what he held dear and precious on reading his pamphlet, or, to give it its proper title, which was an essay in itself: *Concerning the Relations of Great Britain, Spain, and Portugal, to each other, and to the Common Enemy, at this Crisis; and Specifically as Affected by the Convention of Cintra: The whole brought to the test of those Principles, by which alone the Independence and Freedom of Nations can be Preserved or Recovered.* (William remarked, with typically wry humour, 'This is less a Title than a Table of Contents'.) In just over 200 pages of sizzling prose, he lambasted the British generals for exceeding and perverting their powers by pretending to be diplomats, and the injustice and consequent evil of the Convention itself. 'The evil is incalculable, and the stain will cleave to the British name as long as the story of this island shall endure.'

They were fine words, and the reviewers responded with surprising sympathy. The *Eclectic Review* could not resist a snide comment on the style, which, it said, 'resembled nothing so nearly as the blank verse of the Westmoreland triumvirate of Bards', but went on to praise the pamphlet.

In these Sibylline leaves, (full of portentous and awful denunciations,) snatched from the winds, and stitched loosely together to make a pamphlet of only one day's longer life than a newspaper, there is more of the spirit and fire of genuine poetry, than we have found in many a cream coloured volume of verse ... there is a pulse of philanthropy, that beats through every page (though not through every line), and a soul of patriotism that breathes through the whole body of this work, which raises it, as an off-spring of intellect, far above the political ephemera, quickened from the carcasses of transient events which Time leaves behind him in his devastating march to Eternity.

Stuart, an experienced journalist and political commentator, had every confidence that the pamphlet would be a success 'in all ways, – in political influence – in popularity & in money'. He was wrong on every count. It sank, virtually without trace. William needed to sell all 500 copies to recoup his costs. By 7 July, 170 copies had been purchased. Two years after publication, the remaining 178 copies were sold as waste paper.

14. *The Blessedest of Men!*

Throughout the winter and spring of 1808–9, William had been engaged 'head, heart, soul, and fingers in the Spanish Business'. Not only had he composed his *Convention of Cintra* pamphlet, but also some ten sonnets celebrating the struggle of the Spanish patriots against the French, which would later be published among his 'Poems Dedicated to National Independence and Liberty'. Since then, he had done some desultory tinkering with *The White Doe*, but his heart was not in it, and he did not allow it to go to press.

In February, there were three departures from the household at Allan Bank. De Quincey went off to London to deal with William's proofs, Coleridge set out on what was supposed to be a short visit to the Lloyds which turned into an absence of four months, and little Dora, just four and a half years old and the apple of her father's eye, was carried off to Penrith by her Aunt Sara and John Monkhouse to stay with her great-aunt, Elizabeth Monkhouse, who had brought up all her own orphaned nephews and nieces and was about to be left bereft by the departure of her two youngest charges, Joanna Hutchinson and Mary Monkhouse: 'if she is any comfort & gratification to my Aunt we shall think ourselves well repaid for the want of [Dora]', her mother wrote. When Aunt Monkhouse was ready to part with her, Dora was to go to Appleby to visit her cousins from Stockton, Bessy and Jane Hutchinson, who were at Miss Weir's school there, and bring them back to Grasmere for the summer holidays. 'She ... is the sweetest little creature in the world', her besotted Aunt Joanna declared, 'is so tractable, & behaves to admiration.' William, however, missed his daughter so much that he suffered severe headaches after her departure and seized any opportunity to visit her.

Joanna and Mary's departure from Penrith was part of a major change of circumstances which would permanently break up the extended Hutchinson clan. They were going to join their respective brothers Tom and John in the Welsh borders. Since giving up Park House, Tom had acted as a carrier between Penrith and Stockton, then taken a situation as steward to Sir Francis Blake, which he left after only a few months. John had been depressed and ill since the death of his wife soon after their marriage and had sold his father's wine business, intending to go to Portugal; prevented by the Peninsular War, he agreed to throw in his lot with Tom. Efforts to find a farm near the Clarksons, in Suffolk, proved futile, but a trip down 'the *Sylvan Wye*', as John pointedly called it (quoting *Tintern Abbey*), was more successful. John found a farm belonging to the MP, Sir Frankland Lewis, at Hindwell in Radnorshire (now Powys), and was immediately offered a sixteen-year lease at a reasonable rate. By the middle of April 1809 the four cousins were settled in their new home, or, as Mary and Sara complained, were '*buried* in Wales'.

Amidst all these comings and goings, William was also heavily caught up in Coleridge's plans for a revival of his youthful scheme to write and publish his own weekly newspaper. This was aimed only at those 'who either by Rank, or Fortune, or Official situation, or by Talents & Habits of Reflection, are to influence the multitude'. Its object was philosophical rather than rabble rousing. 'I write to found True PRINCIPLES,' Coleridge declaimed. 'To oppose false PRINCIPLES in Legislation, Philosophy, Morals, International Law.' His record was not such as to inspire anyone with confidence that he would be able to carry out his scheme, but, as Dorothy pointed out, he would never embark upon it unless and until he committed himself. The Wordsworths therefore set to and circulated his prospectus to all their friends and acquaintances, as did Southey and Coleridge himself, building up a list of 500 subscribers so that the venture could be launched. Inevitably, the fact that this was done under the auspices of the Wordsworths raised the expectation that William would also be a contributor, which had never been his intention.

The prospectus promised the opening issue of the *Friend* for the first Saturday in January. It finally appeared on 1 June 1809. Coleridge had written it at Yanwath, where Wilkinson had taken him in, deprived him of spirits and opium, and urged him to work. It was ironic that a Quaker thus became 'the Father of *The Friend*'. Having published his first two editions, and left the third with the printer at Penrith, Coleridge returned to Allan Bank, not only sober and on restricted use of opium, but resolved to remain so. Reading the first issues, the Wordsworths were distressed to discover that he had referred to William as 'the *one* poet of his own time', which they knew would hurt Southey's feelings, and that he had stooped to deny ten-year-old accusations about his Jacobinical past again; they also thought the first number 'very obscure' and lacking *joie de vivre*. On the other hand, they had to admit that 'everywhere the power of thought and the originality of a great mind are visible'; almost more important, from a purely personal point of view, was their delight in his achievement. 'I cannot enough admire his resolution in having written at all', was Dorothy's heartfelt comment.

The *Friend* turned out to be Coleridge's most sustained literary achievement. It ran for twenty-eight weekly issues, contained over 140,000 words of his own composing and gave voice to some of his most brilliant insights. It was, as he declared towards the end, 'the History of my own mind'. And therein lay the problem, for it was also chaotically organized (some issues ending mid-paragraph, mid-argument and even, on occasion, mid-sentence!), full of disproportionate digressions and convoluted footnotes and, finally, so densely and obscurely written that most readers were simply left bewildered.

The women had rather hoped that William would return to his poetry once he had exhausted his enthusiasm for the *Convention of Cintra*. Instead, he had redis-covered his raw passion for politics. Even before his pamphlet was published, he had startled them all by announcing that he had decided to write upon 'publick affairs' in the *Courier*, or some other newspaper. 'Two things are absolutely wanted in this Country;' William announced to Stuart at the end of March; 'a thorough reform in Parliament and a new course of education.' Reform, he thought, would never be effected unless the people took up the cause in public meetings. It was natural at such gatherings that the most violent men should be the most applauded, but it did not necessarily follow that their words would be realized in action.

The misfortune of this question of reform is, that the one party sees nothing in it but dangers, the other nothing but hopes and promises. For my part I think the dangers and difficulties great but not insurmountable, whereas, if there be not a reform the destruction of the liberties of the Country is inevitable.

Such views seem moderate enough now, but they were radical by the standards of the day. So much so, indeed, that Sir George Beaumont felt obliged to caution his visitors against William's 'terrific democratic notions'.

William was equally passionate on the subject of educational reform, believing that it should be preceded 'by some genuine philosophical writings from some quarter or other, to teach the principles upon which that education should be grounded'. There is no indication that he saw himself as being the quarter in question, but it was about this time that, through Coleridge, he became a disciple of Dr Andrew Bell. While Coleridge had been lecturing in London in the spring of 1808, he had been drawn into the debate then raging between two new rival systems of education. Both relied on the use of 'monitors', older pupils who supervised the efforts of younger ones, to maximize the effectiveness of the teacher, and there was some controversy as to who had first invented the idea. Bell, a Scottish clergyman, had successfully pioneered his scheme in an Indian orphanage (hence its name, the Madras System), and saw its potential for making a national system of education available even in the poorest districts of Britain. Joseph Lancaster, a Quaker, had also introduced similar ideas (the Lancasterian System), but, being a dissenter, wished the schools to remain independent of any establish-ment control. Coleridge and William both believed that education should be the responsibility of the state and should be conducted under the banner of the Anglican Church. For this reason, they supported the Madras System. Where he and Coleridge also parted company with Lancaster was over the Quaker's enforcement of learning and discipline by punishments of extraordinary ferocity and humiliation.

William had philosophical and personal reasons for supporting Bell. He had long believed that education was the vital means by which the moral state of society could be transformed, and in his own way, in his poems, he had sought to assist the process. 'I am a teacher or I am nothing', he had insisted. Since the cataclysm of his brother John's death, he had been forced to re-examine his religious beliefs and had become a committed deist and practising Anglican, though the emphasis was definitely on practice rather than commitment.

There had been little incentive to attend the Anglican church at Grasmere. The rector, John Craik, had been insane for sixty-three years until his death in 1806. His curate, Edward Rowlandson, who officiated in his stead for forty years, was if anything even more infamous. William was unusually caustic in his judgement. 'Two vices used to struggle in him for mastery, avarice & the love of strong drink: but avarice as is common in like cases always got the better of its opponent, for though he was often intoxicated it was never I believe at his own expence. As has been said of one in a more exalted station he could take any *given* quantity.' Craik's successor, Thomas Jackson, was inevitably an improvement, but it was at Coleorton that the Wordsworths began to attend church regularly, more from a desire to set a good example to the children than from personal preference.

Even in old age, despite a revolution in the quality of Anglican clergymen, thanks to the Evangelical and Puseyite movements, William remained unimpressed by most village sermons, confiding to an amused Moravian minister, 'with a peculiar expression of countenance & intimation, "Ah, well! I go to church for the sake of the Prayers – the Sermon you know is an Accident." ' He supported the Anglican Church because, unlike its sectarian opponents, it was comprehensive, inclusive and tolerant. It was therefore a unifying force for moral good nationally and, in its parish system, a focal point and exemplar for benevolence, even in the remotest regions.

But William had more personal reasons also for supporting the Madras System. Despite his insistence that young Basil Montagu should not begin formal learning too early, all his own children began school at the age of three – indeed, little Thomas was a couple of months short of his third birthday when he went for the first time after Easter this year. They all attended the village school in Grasmere, at the gate of the churchyard. Clever, wilful Dora was a great favourite with the schoolmaster, but poor Johnny, who struggled with his alphabet and was slow to learn to read, was beaten regularly. (The family did not discover this punishment until a new master came and Johnny revealed that, since then, he had only been beaten once.) His Aunt Sara was indignant: 'He is not to be dealt with by severity – it would make him quite obstinate and stupid.' In sharp contrast, he made great progress over the summer, motivated solely by the desire to be an assistant to de Quincey, who was thinking of setting up a private press at Grasmere. De Quincey had tactfully encouraged and enthused him by pointing out that, if he wanted to be a printer, he would first have to be a good scholar. As Sara observed, 'the hope of being with Mr de Q. would stimulate him to any thing – for he loves him better than anything in the world!' In the circumstances, it was not surprising that William favoured the Madras above the Lancasterian System.

After his labours on William's behalf in London, de Quincey did not return to Grasmere until the autumn. In his absence, there was a host of visitors. In addition to the family visitors, who each spent more than a month at Allan Bank, Southey came with a party of his friends and Clarkson arrived with his son Tom and his friend Samuel Tillbrooke, who would later become a friend and neighbour of the Wordsworths at Rydal. They stayed only a few days, but were followed by Catherine Clarkson's aunt, uncle and cousin, the Hardcastles, who arrived at the worst possible time. An army of workmen had descended on the house, determined to eradicate the problem of the smoking chimneys before the onset of winter. They were assisted by the gift of a 'patent *Smoke-Dispenser*', purchased in London by de Quincey as 'my offering to Allan Bank'. Under Crump's instructions, they were also adding a bow window to William's study. In the circumstances, the Wordsworths seized every opportunity to get away.

Towards the end of October, to the great delight of the Wordsworth children, de Quincey returned to Grasmere. It had been agreed that he should become the new tenant of the cottage at Town End. Dorothy, Mary and Sara had jointly taken on the task of redecorating and refurnishing it to his requirements. With new wallpapers, a ceiling in the kitchen and mahogany furniture (mainly bookshelves to contain de Quincey's vast library), it was unrecognizable as the Wordsworths' former home.

As the frosts and snows returned to the vale with the approach of winter, a financial crisis threatened the Wordsworths. William had lost money on his *Convention of Cintra* pamphlet and Coleridge could contribute nothing to the household as he was heavily in debt: until the twentieth issue of the *Friend* had been published, he could not call in the subscriptions and was having to fund the production costs personally. William was therefore having to subsidize not only Coleridge's living expenses but also those of his children, as well as to support his own extended family. To add to their problems, Mary was pregnant with her fifth child, due in May, and living at Allan Bank was once again intolerable as the workmen had failed to cure the smoking chimneys.

The need to earn money had become pressing and William embarked on a prose work, which was commissioned from him by the Reverend Joseph Wilkinson, former rector of Ormathwaite, near Keswick. Now resident in Norfolk, Wilkinson was an amateur artist much admired by his friends Coleridge and Southey for his fidelity in depicting landscapes. In the summer, he had asked Coleridge to write a text to accompany the publication of forty-eight engravings of his drawings of the Lakes. Fully occupied with the *Friend*, Coleridge had declined, but suggested William in his stead.

It is an indication of how desperate the Wordsworths were for money that William, for the first and last time in his life, hired out his pen and submitted to the drudgery of writing on commission. What Wilkinson expected from William is not clear, but it was probably an appreciation of the scenery and instructions to the traveller on how to find the best vantage points from which to see the sublime and beautiful vistas depicted in his prints. What he cannot have expected was the idiosyncratic document he eventually received as the introductory essay to open the series.

It began, uncontentiously enough, with a general topographical and historical description of the Lake country, which Dorothy proudly declared to be 'the only regular and I may say *scientific* account of the present and past state and appearance of the country that has yet appeared'. As it progressed, however, it turned into a lengthy lamentation for the passing of a 'perfect Republic of Shepherds and Agriculturists' and a diatribe against inappropriate development by wealthy incomers. William pinpointed the date when the old ways ended – small, self-sufficient estates, 'perfect equality' among the inhabitants, even transportation by packhorse instead of on carriage roads – very precisely, though the significance of this is not immediately apparent until one sees that in subsequent editions of the work the date was altered. In 1810, for example, when it was first published, it was 'within the last forty years'; in 1820 it became 'within the last fifty years' and, subsequently, 'within the last sixty years'. In other words, William felt that the golden age had ended with his own birth in 1770. This was clearly poignant symbolism rather than historical fact, for some of William's strictures on the changes which had taken place, such as denuding the lake shores of their mature native trees, which read as though he had personally seen them take place, actually occurred when he was too young to observe them or even long before he was born.

It would be wrong, however, to dismiss this introduction as just a misty-eyed exercise in nostalgia, for what William was attempting to do was as revolutionary as anything he had ever done in his poetry. Once again his aim was to change and educate prevailing tastes. In doing so, he rejected the perceived wisdom of a generation of topographical writers who judged landscapes solely in accordance with their own preconceived images of what constituted perfection. 'What I wished to accomplish was to give a model of the manner in which topographical descriptions ought to be executed', he told Lady Beaumont privately, expressing quiet satisfaction with his own wonderfully apt, yet totally original, simile, comparing the eight main valleys stretching out from a central point between Great Gable and Scafell as 'like spokes from the nave of a wheel'. William described this comparison as being both 'useful' and 'intelligible'. Just as he had done in his poetry, he was applying the simple language and homely imagery of everyday life to a literature which had developed its own highly specialized and esoteric vocabulary.

In the late eighteenth and early nineteenth centuries, the fashion was for the 'picturesque', a word which then meant, quite literally, 'like a picture', and specifically the idealized landscape paintings of the schools of Claude Lorrain, Gaspard Poussin and Salvator Rosa. No self-respecting tourist in search of the picturesque travelled without his Claude-glass, a plano-convex mirror of convenient pocket-book size through which he would view the scenes and objects to be admired. It seems wholly appropriate that to do so he had to turn his back on the real living landscape in order to see its image reflected in miniaturized form and neatly contained within the mirror's frame. In other words, reduced to a picture. Not surprisingly, the devotees of the picturesque rarely saw '*real views* from Nature in this country . . . equal to the poorest imitations of Gaspar or Claude'. (A statement, astonishingly, made by Thomas Gainsborough, one of the most evocative of English landscape painters.) Gilpin, whose works William had admired as a young man, suggested that the 'practised eye would usually wish to correct' the 'deformities' of nature; he even recommended judicious use of a mallet to 'improve' the ruins of Tintern Abbey.

The tourists who flocked to the Lakes came clutching their guidebooks, Claude-glasses and preconceived ideas. If they used their own eyes at all, it was only to make the obligatory (and usually denigratory) comparison with the Alps. It was against this fashion that William took up cudgels. 'My object is to reconcile a Briton to the scenery of his own country', he proclaimed, 'Nothing is more injurious to genuine feeling than the practice of hastily and ungraciously depreciating the face of one country by comparing it with that of another'. To do so inevitably led to disappointed expectations: '. . . the best guide to which, in matters of taste we can entrust ourselves, is a disposition to be pleased'. He illustrated this with an example that will strike a chord with the modern visitor to the Lakes. The perceived wisdom was, and is, that water-falls are scarcely worth seeing except after much rain, and that the more swollen the stream, the more fortunate the spectator. This is a fallacy, as William argued:

what becomes, at such a time, of that sense of refreshing coolness which can only be felt in dry and sunny weather, when the rocks, herbs, and flowers glisten with moisture diffused by the breath of the precipitous water? But, considering these things as objects of sight only, it may be observed that the principal charm of the smaller waterfalls or cascades consists in certain proportions of form and affinities of colour, among the component parts of the scene; and in the contrast maintained between the falling water and that which is apparently at rest, or rather settling gradually into quiet in the pool below. The beauty of such a scene, where there is naturally so much agitation, is also heightened, in a peculiar manner, by the *glimmering*, and, towards the verge of the pool, by the *steady*, reflection of the surrounding images. Now, all these delicate distinctions are destroyed by heavy floods, and the whole stream rushes along in foam and tumultuous confusion.

What this perceptive comment (one of many) illustrates so beautifully is William's instinctive belief that nature cannot be improved: beauty is there to be seen by the discerning eye and feeling heart. The fashionable habit of comparison and demand for spectacle and sensation, fed by more conventional guides, served only to obscure the genuine 'spirit of the place'.

This blindness among tourists was bad enough, but among the new inhabitants of the Lakes it was unforgivable. In the longest and most important section of his introduction, 'Changes, and Rules of Taste for Preventing their Bad Effects', William launched a blistering attack on unsympathetic development in the Lakes. He did not mince his words: '. . . in truth, no one can now travel through the more frequented tracts, without being offended, at almost every turn, by an introduction of discordant objects, disturbing that peaceful harmony of form and colour, which had been through a long lapse of ages most happily preserved'. He attacked the 'gross transgressions' and the 'disfigurement' which incomers had inflicted on this 'country so lavishly gifted by nature': their 'immoderate' 'craving for prospect' which led them to build on 'the summits of naked hills in staring contrast to the snugness and privacy of the ancient houses'; their affectation and pretension which dictated that every new house should be a mansion sufficiently grandiose to attract comment; their anxiety to sweep away ancient woodlands and introduce 'the whole contents of the nursery-man's catalogue', foreign plants and exotic trees all 'jumbled together – colour at war with colour, and form with form ... everywhere discord, distraction, and bewilderment!' These people were, as William pointedly reminded them, 'liable to a charge of inconsistency, when they are so eager to change the face of that country, whose native attractions, by the act of erecting their habitations in it, they have so emphatically acknowledged'. Worst of all, because their impact was so visually intrusive, were the plantations now springing up over the Lakeland hills: serried ranks of larches and firs marching inexorably and indiscriminately over all terrain, lacking variety of shape, colour, size or movement.

This was not just a negative and reactionary piece of what might now be called 'Nimbyism', for what William sought to do was to re-educate the perpetrators. Mansions are inappropriate in mountain regions, he reasoned, because they can never have sufficient dignity or interest to become the focal point of the landscape and must always be subordinate to the view. In building houses, one should consult antiquity, 'the co-partner and sister of Nature'. In laying out grounds, 'The rule is simple ... work, where you can, in the spirit of nature, with an invisible hand of art.' Houses, grounds and, most of all, plantations should be so constructed as 'to admit of [their] being gently incorporated into the scenery of nature'.

By 18 November William had completed the introduction and Sara transcribed a fair copy to send to Wilkinson. Dorothy, ever mindful of the Wordsworths' precarious financial position, was convinced that William should now apply himself to writing a proper guide of his own. William demurred. Wilkinson's publication ought to have its fair run before he attempted anything independently.

While he waited for the arrival of the first batch of Wilkinson's plates, so that he could embark on the accompanying text, William found himself temporarily at leisure. He occupied himself by translating eleven epitaphs from the Italian of the poet Gabriello Chiabrera. Six of these he allowed Coleridge to print in the *Friend*, even though, in doing so, he lost the opportunity of earning any money for them. Coleridge's enthusiasm and energies were beginning to flag and he had begun to solicit contributions from some of his friends. William supplied not only the epitaphs but also hitherto unpublished extracts from *The Prelude* and *The Recluse*, as well as seven of his latest sonnets written in the autumn of 1809. These were inspired by the heroic resistance of the shepherd patriots of the tiny Tyrol, who, led by a charismatic innkeeper, Andreas Hofer, repeatedly defied the might of Bavarian and French armies in a doomed struggle to retain their liberty. For William, this unlikely hero was a 'godlike Warrior' who embodied the spirit of William Tell and had fought, with his humble compatriots, for 'a *moral* end' which had not been vainly sought.

At Christmas the whole household decamped to Elleray to join the Kendal Cooksons for two days of 'merriment and thoughtful discourse'. From Elleray they all proceeded to Brathay to dine with the Lloyds, then on to Town End, where de Quincey entertained them to a New Year dinner and the entire village to a firework display.

It was a short respite, because it was increasingly clear that Coleridge could no longer sustain the *Friend*. Sara, who had worked tirelessly as his amanuensis and exerted all her influence over him to the full, bullying and harrying him to keep to his deadlines, was exhausted and ill. They were all well aware that if the journal folded, Coleridge would once again face total mental and physical collapse, so they rallied round to support him. William contributed an essay on 22 February, but the last issue of the *Friend* appeared on 15 March. This would become apparent only in retrospect, for Coleridge blithely continued to speak of it 'as if it were going on, and would go on'. The Wordsworths had no such delusions. 'The fact is that he either does a great deal or nothing at all' was Dorothy's tart but accurate assessment. The sheer volume of material he had produced for the *Friend* belied the fact that there had been weeks on end when he had not written a line, for he would suddenly compose a whole issue in two days, drawing on his prodigious stores of knowledge and relying on his facility in conversation to dictate verbatim to Sara.

The pressure had told, however, particularly on Sara. Her situation was bizarre. Not only was she living in the same house as the married man who loved her, but for hours on end she was cooped up with him, acting as his secretary, and effectively at his beck and call. He was still haunted by his fantasy that he had seen William and Sara in bed together three years previously at Coleorton, racked by sexual torment, forced to acknowledge that Sara was strictly off-limits: '*a mother of my children*', he wrote in cipher, '*how utterly improbable* – how utterly improbable dared I hope it!'

It was an impossible situation and when, in the new year, Coleridge became tired of his work, depressed by his loss of subscribers and reverted to his usual comforter, opium, it became intolerable. Sara took the first opportunity to flee. She had a standing invitation to visit her brother and cousins at Hindwell, their new farm in Radnorshire, and this she now accepted. In the middle of February, her cousin John Monkhouse came to collect her.

Sara had been a vital part of the Wordsworth household for more than four years and she would be sadly missed. That she chose to leave so soon before her sister was due to give birth is an indication of how desperate she was to get away from Coleridge; that the family were relieved by her decision also speaks volumes. 'I need not tell you how sadly we miss Sara', Dorothy confided in their mutual friend, Catherine Clarkson, on 12 April,

– but I must add the truth that we are all glad she is gone. True it is she was the cause of the continuance of The Friend so long; but I am far from believing that it would have gone on if she had stayed. He was tired, and she had at last no power to drive him on; and now I really believe that *he* also is glad that she is not here, because he has nobody to teize him.

His spirits have certainly been more equable, and much better. *Our* gladness proceeds from a different cause. He harassed and agitated her mind continually, and we saw that he was doing her health perpetual injury. I tell you this, that you may no longer lament her departure.

Having unburdened her heart thus far, Dorothy could no longer hold back the pent-up frustration, bewilderment and despair, which had clearly been building for months.

As to Coleridge, if I thought I should distress you, I would say nothing about him; but I hope that you are sufficiently prepared for the worst. We have no hope of him – none that he will ever do anything more than he has already done. If he were not under our Roof, he would be just as much the slave of stimulants as ever; and his whole time and thoughts, (except when he is reading and he reads a great deal), are employed in deceiving himself, and seeking to deceive others. He will tell me that he has been writing, that he *has* written half a Friend; when I *know* that he has not written a single line. This Habit pervades all his words and actions, and you feel perpetually new hollowness and emptiness. I am loth to say this, and burn this letter, I entreat you. I am loth to say it, but it is the truth. He lies in bed, always till after 12 o'clock, sometimes much later; and never walks out – Even the finest spring day does not tempt him to seek the fresh air; and this beautiful valley seems a blank to him. He never leaves his own parlour except at dinner and tea, and sometimes supper, and then he always seems impatient to get back to his solitude – he goes the moment his food is swallowed. Sometimes he does not speak a word, and when he does talk it is always very much and upon subjects as far aloof from himself or his friends as possible.

In a final, bitter coda, she entirely (and surely unfairly) rejected the idea that Sara's departure had in any way contributed to the demise of the *Friend*.

With respect to Coleridge, do not think that it is his love for Sara which has stopped him in his work – do not believe it: his love for her is no more than a fanciful dream – otherwise he would prove it by a desire to make her happy. No! He likes to have her about him as his own, as one devoted to him, but when she stood in the way of other gratifications it was all over. I speak this very unwillingly, and again I beg, *burn* this letter. I need not add, keep its contents to yourself alone.

What lies unspoken at the heart of this indictment, and explains its bitterness, is that the Wordsworths had always believed that, once Coleridge had separated from his wife and come to live with them, they would be able to restore him to his former glory. That they had failed to do this must have seemed like a rejection of them personally – particularly as Coleridge seemed to wish to avoid their company and conversation, even while living in their midst. All the habits which Dorothy complained of had been known to them of old, but it was a different matter having to deal with their consequences on a daily basis, particularly in such a large household, full of children, where every penny counted. Economies had been implemented, and it must have been yet another source of aggravation that Coleridge did not play his part. 'We drink (*none of us*) any thing but water', he feelingly informed Poole, admitting, however, that he could not give up tea at breakfast: 'it is, for *me*, an absolute necessary, if not of Life, yet of literary exertion'. And he still had a daily fire in his study.

Coleridge's self-centredness must have grated particularly in the crisis which occurred a few days before Dorothy let slip her criticisms. On 7 April little Catherine, who was eighteen months old, was suddenly taken seriously ill with a brain seizure. Richard Scambler, the apothecary from Ambleside, was called, and the poor infant was subjected to warm baths, blistering, lancing of her gums and half-hourly doses of purgatives. Seven hours later, the convulsions ceased, and she fell into a deep and continual sleep. When she eventually woke, she was paralysed down the right side of her body. In the days and weeks that followed, she gradually recovered movement in her arm and leg, but her right hand remained useless and she was unable to walk without limping. Afraid Mary would go into premature labour with the shock and distress, Scambler assured the Wordsworths that Catherine's prognosis was bright; what he did not tell them was that another similar seizure would probably kill her.

The imminent arrival of the new baby finally persuaded Coleridge to do what Catherine's illness did not. At the beginning of May he left Allan Bank to pay a ten-day visit to his wife and daughter at Greta Hall. Not even Dorothy suspected that he had left for good. It is not even clear whether Coleridge himself knew it, but the longer he stayed at Keswick, the more difficult it became to return to Grasmere, for then he would have to face the Wordsworths in the full knowledge that he had abandoned the *Friend* and, once more, become a slave to opium. He shut himself up in his study at Greta Hall and nurtured a growing sense of grievance against the Wordsworths. Opium-induced dreams and reality once again began to fuse: Sara, he dreamt, was about to marry John Monkhouse, and William and Dorothy had left for Wales to give her away.

On Saturday 12 May, at quarter past two in the morning, Mary gave birth to her fifth child, 'a fine Boy', who looked just like Johnny and was 'stout and healthy with the Wordsworth nose'. The Wordsworths were determined to call this son William and on 24 June a second William Wordsworth was christened at Grasmere church. His godparents were Joanna and two of his father's young admirers, Wilson and de Quincey.

A few days after the christening, William and Dorothy left for Coleorton. They were both reluctant to leave Mary, especially with five children to look after, the oldest of whom was only just seven, and the hay harvest to supervise. But she had the assistance of three servants and she was insistent that they should go. William needed a holiday after his labours over the winter and spring. In addition to his contributions for the *Friend*, he had been producing copy for Wilkinson's prints and managed to complete three books of *The Recluse*. More importantly, the Beaumonts had asked them, and the Wordsworths were duty-bound to oblige the friends who had been so kind to them.

At Coleorton, their days passed in leisurely fashion: they breakfasted between eight-thirty and nine, William rode out with Beaumont from eleven till two-thirty, they dined at three, had tea between six and seven and then walked till nine. A couple of times, they had a little reading in the afternoon. It was an undemanding routine which suited Dorothy, whose health and appearance improved dramatically. William, however, pined for home. A series of seven letters passed between husband and wife this summer. Unlike all previous extant letters, which were usually joint efforts with Dorothy, they were entirely private and written for each other's eyes only. And they are revelatory. For, aged forty, and after eight years of marriage and five children, their passion for each other shines out with all the ardour of a pair of teenage lovers. What is more, this rare expression of their love is convincing proof that, however deeply William cared for his sister, his love for her was altogether of a different kind. Had these letters been available to earlier biographers, it would have been difficult for them even to have posited the case for an incestuous relationship between brother and sister.

William wrote the first letter on 22 July, seizing the opportunity while Dorothy was at church to address Mary, 'my dearest Love', 'sweet love', 'my joy, my repose, my hope, and my support in every good thought or profitable feeling that enters my spirit'.

We have now been here a fortnight and every thing has been done which kindness could do to make us happy ... For my own part though I should feel it a disgrace to be discont[ent]ed to any oppressive degree, with so much affectionateness, & tranquil and innocent pleasure about me, yet I do feel, that to no place where I am stationary some time can I ever be perfectly reconciled, even for a short time. When I am moving about I am not so strongly reminded of my home, and you and our little ones and the places which I love. Therefore I must say[,] though not without regret do I say it, that I cannot help being anxious that I were gone, as when I move I shall feel myself moving towards you; though by a long circuit. O my beloved how my heart swells at the thought; and how dearly should I have enjoyed being alone with you so long! ... How do I long to tread for the first time the road that will bring me in sight of Grasmere, to pant up the hill of Allan bank to cross the threshold to see to touc[h] you to speak to you & hear you spea[k] ...

Alluding delicately to his overwhelming physical desire for her, he compared his sufferings during this separation to those he had endured while she was at Middleham and Gallow Hill before they married, made heavier and more uneasy by 'a thousand tender thoughts intermingled, and consciousnesses of realized bliss and happiness'. The Beaumonts were already talking about a repetition of the visit next year, but William would not even consider it. 'I cannot think of any thing of the kind; nor will I ever, except from a principle of duty, part from you again, to stay any where more than one week. I cannot bear it.' He ended the letter with a passionate appeal. 'Fail not to write to me with out reserve', he begged her; 'never have I been able to receive such a Letter from you, let me not then be disappointed, but give me your heart that I may kiss the words a thousand times!'

Receiving this letter at Allan Bank, Mary was overwhelmed. She literally shed tears of happiness, much to the puzzlement of little Dora. 'O My William!' she replied,

it is not in my power to tell thee how I have been affected by this dearest of all letters – it was so unexpected – so new a thing to see the breathing of thy inmost heart upon paper that I was quite overpowered, & now that I sit down to answer thee in the loneliness & depth of that love which unites us & which cannot be felt but by ourselves, I am so agitated & my eyes are so bedimmed that I scarcely know how to proceed ... Indeed my love it has made me supremely blessed – it has given me a new feeling, for it is the first letter of love that has been exclusively my own – Wonder not then that I have been so affected by it.

Despite constant interruptions from the children, she managed to pour out her heart to her husband. 'I am SORRY for what causes in me such pious and exulting gladness –', she told him, 'that you cannot fully enjoy your absence from me – indeed William I feel, I *have felt* that you cannot, but it overpowers me to be told it by your own pen'. She responded with equal ardour and modesty to his expressions of sexual longing. 'I did not *want thee* so much *then*,' she wrote, referring to an earlier letter where he had spoken of coming home, 'as I do now that our uncomfortableness is passed away – if you had been here, no *doubt* there would have existed in me that underconsciousness that I had my *all in all* about me – *that* feeling which I have never wanted since [I slept with: deleted] the solitary night did not separate us, except in absence.'

Mary made a telling reference to Dorothy, to whom she had written only a short letter: 'do not give her to understand that you have recd. a longer one – this would make her uneasy – and I have not had it in my power to do any better'. Allusive though the remark is, it is an indication of some of the difficulties inherent in the Wordsworth relationships. It is a tribute to Mary's remarkable generosity of spirit that she not only understood her sister-in-law, but was constitutionally incapable of feeling jealousy or resentment towards her.

William and Dorothy spent just over a month at Coleorton before going their separate ways. William and Beaumont travelled together to Birmingham, where they visited the Leasowes, former home of the poet William Shenstone, and attended a performance of Thomas Otway's tragedy, *Venice Preserv'd*. Beaumont would look back on the three days he spent in William's company as 'amongst the whitest of my life'. Having parted from his generous host, William joined his brother Christopher and his family for dinner at the Lloyds', before setting off on the final leg of his journey to visit Sara at Hindwell. He went with the utmost reluctance, since it delayed his return home, but it was a sacrifice he felt he had to make for both Sara and Mary. 'You often laugh at me about Duty,' he told Mary, 'but this [is] a pure march of duty, at vast expence of inclination if ever one was made by man.'

William arrived at Hindwell on 11 August and, having quickly ascertained that all were well, wrote immediately to his wife. 'We have been parted my sweet Mary too long, but we have not been parted in vain, for wherever I go I am admonished how blessed, and almost peculiar a lot mine is. – ... O Mary I love you with a passion of love which grows till I tremble to think of its strength'. Having only just arrived at Hindwell, he was already making plans to depart. 'I shall move heaven and earth to be with you by this day three weeks', he reassured Mary.

Dorothy, by contrast, had prolonged her absence from home. She left Coleorton a few days after William and travelled alone to Cambridge, where she packed in a crammed sightseeing schedule before Thomas Clarkson carried her off to Bury St Edmunds. There she was welcomed with open arms by his wife, Catherine, and the friends spent the ensuing two months quietly and happily enjoying each other's company. When she finally left Bury, it was for London, where the Lambs had offered her accommodation (unwittingly sparking off another of poor Mary's mental breakdowns). There was also a joyous reunion at Binfield. The Cookson children had all come home from university and school to see her, Uncle William was all affection and his wife still the same admirable, cheerful woman who had been so kind to Dorothy in her youth, though, as the latter could not forbear remarking, 'she would look as if she were dead if her eyes were shut'. Christopher and his family were all there too, but Dorothy's plans to return with them to her brother's new country parish of Bocking were pre-empted when a letter arrived from William, informing her that the children had all taken the whooping cough and little Catherine was dangerously ill. She arrived in style, by gig, at Grasmere on Thursday 25 October.

Johnny came bounding down the field to greet her, followed by the two Williams and then Mary, bearing Catherine in her arms. The child was worn to a skeleton: constant coughing and vomiting had reduced her to a sickly pale, hollow-cheeked shadow of her former self. In Dorothy's shocking phrase, 'She looked to me – when I could *think* at all – like a child bred and born in a Gin-Alley.' The next morning, the entire family packed their bags and decamped to stay with the parents of one of their servants, Sally Yewdale, who lived at High Hacket, an ancient, rambling, cottage-style farmhouse clinging precariously to the rocky ridges high on the fells above Little Langdale. Dora and Thomas had been sent to recuperate there a fortnight earlier, and the sunny, sheltered location, fresh air and kindly attentions of their hosts had gone some way to restore them.

They had not been back home for long when a deadlier disease struck the vale. Scarlet fever made its way insidiously towards Allan Bank. When it reached the two houses next to them and a previously fit and healthy man died of it, they knew that they would have to leave immediately. In their weakened state, the children were desperately vulnerable. But where to go? William set off at once to see Wilson and, less than a fortnight after their return from High Hacket, the Wordsworths were established at Elleray. Wilson proved to be a genial host who took evident pleasure in the Wordsworths' company. His servants were kind, good-natured and fond of the children, the situation of the house, on the shores of Windermere, was 'enchanting' and, as Dorothy noted with satisfaction, 'we could not have been so well off anywhere.'

The children escaped the scarlet fever, but they could not shake off the whooping cough, which still had them in its thrall six months after its first appearance. As soon as one child seemed to improve, another took a turn for the worse. Tom became so ill that Mary took him, and the baby, who was still at the breast, into lodgings at Ambleside, simply so that they could be near Scambler. Thomas and Catherine were the worst sufferers, coughing and vomiting day and night until they were both weak and undernourished. Catherine, in particular, gave cause for concern. A semi-permanent invalid, she had become so dependent on her mother that she refused to allow anyone else to nurse her and would not let Mary out of her sight. Fortunately, the baby, though suffering from whooping cough himself, was not so 'very troublesome' and, apart from feeding him, Dorothy was able to assume all responsibility for his care.

In the circumstances, it was not surprising that the Wordsworths had little thought for anyone or anything outside the family. It explains, at least in part, why they remained oblivious for so long to a second catastrophe that struck them in the autumn of 1810.

At the time, there was nothing to alert them to anything unusual. William and Mary had been alone together for a mere three weeks after his return from Hindwell when Montagu and his third wife, the former Anne Skepper, arrived at Allan Bank. The ostensible reason was to visit Algernon, Montagu's oldest son by his second wife, Laura Rush, who had been sent to join Hartley and Derwent Coleridge at Mr Dawes's school in Ambleside. It had been left to the Wordsworths to find him lodgings with Mrs Ross at Ambleside and to manage the boy's finances. Like the Coleridge boys, he would also become a regular weekend visitor at Allan Bank.

The new Mrs Montagu was as much an admirer of William as her husband, but for different reasons. A self-important woman, she was something of a trophy hunter and liked to be seen to be on intimate terms with the poets. 'Our Children are brought up with the highest reverence for Mr Wordsworth,' she wrote soon after her marriage in 1808, 'and I hope that one day they will be nearer to him.' Having achieved this aim, she was now seeking to accomplish her second, which was to lure Coleridge within her ambit, by offering him 'a quiet Bed room whenever you choose to occupy it' at their house in Frith Street, London, and suggesting that he submit himself to the latest fashionable doctor, Sir Anthony Carlisle. William positively loathed the new Mrs Montagu: 'the Creature is utterly odious to me', he confessed to Mary.

Despite the children's illness, the Montagus stayed almost a month at Allan Bank. It was not until 18 October that they finally took their leave, and when they did so they took Coleridge with them.

Coleridge's decision to go to London placed his friends in a dilemma. It was patently obvious that the Montagus had no idea what they were letting themselves in for; like the Wordsworths before Coleridge moved in with them, they thought that Montagu's own industrious habits and spartan regime (he rose early and worked late, drank no alcohol and had an almost vegetarian diet) would inspire a reformation in Coleridge himself. Well aware that any disruption of his orderly existence would cause Montagu severe problems, and that the two men would inevitably quarrel, since Montagu was the last person to tolerate habits so discordant to his own, especially in an inmate of his house, William took Montagu on one side and suggested that it would be better for them both if Coleridge did not take up residence at Frith Street. His arguments were in vain. Montagu 'was resolved. "He would do all that could be done for him and would have him at his house."' In the circumstances, William felt that he had no other option but to speak the plain truth.

Quite what that truth was remains a matter of dispute to this day, dividing Wordsworthian and Coleridgean sympathizers as effectively as it divided the two men themselves. Given the tenor of William's recent letters to Poole, and Dorothy's to Catherine Clarkson, it is likely that William said that the Wordsworths no longer had any hope of Coleridge either reforming his habits or producing anything more, or better, than he had already done. He undoubtedly described Coleridge's antisocial and disruptive habits: the gruel, toast and water, and eggs at unreasonable hours of the day and night; his long fits of depression and silence and his screaming nightmares. Coleridge's opium addiction was an open secret, but William pointed out that, in his current state, he would not be able to sustain the sort of severe regimen which Carlisle proposed to put him on immediately, and that he would therefore be driven to deception. As Dorothy indignantly complained to Catherine, this was a private conversation between mutual friends who were both anxious to do their best for Coleridge. What William had confided was nothing more than common local knowledge. Nevertheless, a monstrous spectre had unwittingly been conjured up which would tear open a breach in the friendship between Coleridge and the Wordsworths, and destroy their intimacy for ever.

Montagu gratefully accepted William's warning and his advice that, rather than actually live with them, Coleridge should be found lodgings nearby. William had intended to speak privately to Coleridge and make the same suggestion, but in the bustle between his arrival and departure there was no opportunity to do so. Coleridge therefore left Grasmere under the impression that he was going to stay with the Montagus. If Montagu had suspected William had exaggerated Coleridge's faults, only a few days on the road served to convince him as he saw, with his own eyes, 'confirmation of all that W. had said'. Instead of seeking a diplomatic way of informing Coleridge that he no longer wished to offer him a home, or taking responsibility for that decision on his own shoulders, Montagu took the easy option, used William's warning as his excuse and repeated his comments verbatim to Coleridge. What poisoned an already unpalatable draught was that Montagu told Coleridge (or Coleridge believed Montagu had told him, which distressed him no less) that William had 'commissioned' or 'authorized' him to repeat these comments to Coleridge himself.

Coleridge was understandably devastated. 'W. authorized M. to tell me, he had no Hope of me!' he wept into his notebooks. 'No Hope of me! absol. Nuisance! God's mercy is it a Dream!' Instead of confronting William, Coleridge did what he always did. He pretended that nothing had happened. Only in his notebooks did he admit his distress, and, repeating a now familiar pattern, lapsed into accusation and self-pity.

To the Wordsworths, he maintained a pained and prolonged silence for eighteen months. Soon after his arrival in London, Montagu wrote to confess what he had done and revealed that Coleridge had been 'very angry', but Mrs Montagu assured them that he was well, powdering his hair (a sign that he was enjoying an active social life) and 'talked of being busy'. Confirmation of this came from the Lambs: 'if I had not known how ill he is I should have had no idea of it,' Mary wrote on 13 November, 'for he has been very chearful'. He had not yet begun Carlisle's regimen, as Lamb mischievously informed them.

Oblivious of the storm brewing, the Wordsworths returned to Allan Bank from their self-imposed exile at Elleray on 18 December preoccupied with their own problems, but the new year brought no relief from sickness. William suffered a recurrence of the trachoma – a disease of the eyelids causing painful swelling and affecting his vision – which had afflicted him the previous summer on his way to Coleorton, and the children could not rid themselves of whooping cough. By the middle of February, Catherine was so reduced and feeble that change of air again became imperative. At this crisis, one of their friends, Miss Knott, came to the rescue, sending her carriage round to fetch the little girl and her aunt to stay at her house in Ambleside. Against the odds, Catherine rallied once more.

William's literary activities were understandably at a standstill. Since going to Coleorton, he had produced almost nothing. Writing the text for Wilkinson's prints had theoretically been a continuing project throughout 1810, but William had composed the bulk of it before leaving for Coleorton, including a detailed itinerary and advice to tourists on the best approaches to and viewing points for the Lakes. Again, however, his approach to the work did not suit Wilkinson, who seems to have thought the text too long. As a result of this disagreement, William refused to waste any more time or energy on work. By November, when the final sheets were being prepared for publication, he had farmed out the composition of some of the descriptions to Dorothy.

Probably as a result of having to live so many months with the daily prospect that one or more of his children would die from the whooping cough, William was suffering from a new malaise in the spring of 1811. 'I am shocked to find how indifferent I am becoming concerning things upon which so much of my life has been employed', he wrote in March. 'I am not quite 41 years of age, yet I seem to have lost all personal interest in everything which I have composed.' When he read his own poems, he explained,

I often think that they are such as I should have admired and been delighted with if they had been produced by another, yet, as I cannot ascertain how much of this approbation is owing to self-love, and how much to what my own powers and knowledge supply to complete what is imperfect in the poems themselves, upon the whole my own works at present interest me little, far too little . . .

He would not write another poem for many months to come.

15. *Suffer the Little Children*

At the beginning of April 1811, the Hutchinsons descended on Allan Bank for a family reunion and conference. Jack came from Stockton, Tom and Joanna from Radnorshire and Aunt Elizabeth Monkhouse from Penrith. Henry Hutchinson, their wealthy bachelor uncle, had died on 78 January, leaving his vast estates to be divided among his nephews and nieces. Jack, Tom and their three male cousins were each to receive between £8,000 and £10,000; Mary and Joanna were to share the income of an estate near Stockton let at £100 a year; and a similar arrangement was put in place for Sara and Betsy. Their other brothers, Henry and George, were comparatively hard done by, being left only the interest on £500 each. For the Wordsworths, an additional £50 a year was more than welcome.

Joanna's presence and nursing skills freed Mary and Dorothy to do some urgently needed sewing, for on 25 May they were due to move house. The lease of Allan Bank had come to an end and they were to move into smaller, cheaper quarters at the Parsonage in Grasmere. The incumbent, Thomas Jackson, lived at Langdale and had agreed to create a library out of the adjacent barn and build a back kitchen before the Wordsworths entered the house. Despite Mary and Dorothy's determination not to move in until all the work had been completed, the workmen were dilatory and much remained to be done.

The Parsonage could not have been more different from Allan Bank. Built in 1687, it lacked all pretension and was nothing more than a traditional Lakeland farmhouse. Long and low, with thick walls and cottage windows, it stood in the bottom of Grasmere Vale, only yards from the church, and close to Robert Newton's lodgings, where so many of their family and friends had stayed. Downstairs there were two parlours (the smaller one, assigned to William as a study, was a mere 'cabin', but the larger one was bigger than that at Town End), two good kitchens with a back porch, a dairy and large storeroom, a small cellar and a good pantry;

upstairs there were four bedrooms, including one assigned to Sara, a maids' room and a lumber room. The barn was at least as large again, attached to the southern end of the house, but set back from it. Though partially filled with the parson's tithe hay, there were stalls for the Wordsworths' two cows. To the front of the house lay a small rectangular courtyard, enclosed within ugly white walls, but otherwise the property was unfenced. The Wordsworths soon discovered that the location of the Parsonage left much to be desired. It lacked privacy, because it stood in the fork of the roads into Grasmere village and over Red Bank into Langdale, but this they planned to remedy by planting shrubs and trees. Irremediable, however, was the fact that one end of the property was bounded by the River Rothay, running crystalline clear over its stony bed in good weather, but apt to rise and flood its banks after heavy rains or snow-melt. The field in which the Parsonage stood was therefore a permanent bog, delightful for the children, but not conducive to health or cleanliness.

By early June the Wordsworths were firmly established in their new home. The children were all better, even the three youngest, who had been most ill. Five-year-old Thomas was well enough to go off to Keswick to stay for a month on his own at Greta Hall, where little Herbert Southey was a playmate of the same age. The Coleridge boys and Algernon Montagu were still regular weekend visitors, even though the comparatively cramped accommodation of the Parsonage meant that they could no longer stay overnight.

There was now only one cloud on the horizon and that was Coleridge. The Wordsworths had heard nothing from him since his departure for London, but, as they knew he had not written to Southey or his own children, they had not been worried by his silence. The first intimation that something was wrong came from Mary Lamb, who wrote to say that she knew that 'a coolness' existed between the two men, and urged William to come to town immediately, as Coleridge's mind was seriously unhinged. (Coleridge had visited her that day, burst into tears and declared, between sobs, 'Wordsworth – Wordsworth has given me up. *He* has no hope of me – I have been an absolute Nuisance in his family'.) Dorothy had replied, denying any coolness on William's part and telling her what had passed between her brother and Montagu. She, or perhaps her brother himself, also reported William's remark which, according to Coleridge, who learned it only from an indiscreet third party, 'amounted in substance to a Sneer on my reported high Spirits & my wearing Powder'. (Coleridge's hilarious excuse for adopting powder was to prevent his catching cold because his hair was thinning.) The fact that a third person saw the letter to the Lambs, and reported its contents to Coleridge, is symptomatic of the whole affair. It is ironic that the indiscreet repetition of comments made in a private conversation should have caused the quarrel, for it was envenomed and prolonged by similar revelations from both William's and Coleridge's private correspondence to third parties.

Believing that Coleridge would eventually come to his senses, the Wordsworths dismissed him from their thoughts. Dora, who was a month short of her seventh birthday, was about to go away to school. With her brothers, she had been attending the village school at Grasmere, but while Johnny and Thomas plodded through their lessons, she was quick, clever and easily bored. Neither Mary nor Dorothy had sufficient time to keep her 'regularly and steadily to work, which is absolutely necessary for a learner of her airy dispositions'. Reluctantly, therefore, they had decided that she should join her cousins at Miss Weir's school in Appleby, at least until September, when her Aunt Sara would return and more time and attention could be devoted to her. The school was small, only nine boarding pupils, so it was more like a large family than an institution, and they were all young girls about Dora's own age. Dora had no qualms. She left Ambleside in great glee, perched on top of the coach with Miss Jameson, one of the Wordsworths' friends, who taught at Miss Weir's school. She was followed by a box containing spice cake, tea, sugar and a letter from Johnny, the first he had ever written.

Shortly after Dora's departure, William, Mary, Thomas and Catherine, accompanied by one of their servants, Fanny Turner, set off to spend six weeks by the sea, leaving the oldest and youngest children at Grasmere in Dorothy's care. Thomas and Catherine were still delicate after their whooping cough, and it was hoped that sea-bathing would restore their health and even relieve the little girl's lameness. This was a significant step. William had deliberately avoided the sea ever since his brother's death and only his concern for his children could persuade him to go there now. At Bootle, on the Cumberland coast, they took up residence in a cottage seven minutes' walk from the seaside. It was a 'dreary' place, bleak and treeless, but abounding in cornfields, miles of empty beach and ravishing views of the Isle of Man, whenever it fleetingly emerged from its bed of clouds. They had typically English weather, but this did not prevent them walking as far as Muncaster Castle, where William was distinctly unimpressed to find every estate entrance locked up and the castle itself invisible behind impenetrable plantations.

From Bootle, William wrote his first letter to Sir George Beaumont in almost a year, enclosing a transcript of his latest poem as a peace-offering for his silence. It was a sonnet, inspired by one of Beaumont's own pictures, which now occupied pride of place over the mantelpiece of the parlour in their new home at Grasmere. In a graceful and subtle tribute to his friend and patron, William praised the power of the art which could capture 'one brief moment caught from fleeting time' and cast over it 'The appropriate calm of blest eternity'. Apart from a short burst of enthusiasm for *The Recluse*, which had ended almost as soon as it had begun, this was all he had written since the spring of 1810. The holiday proved to be just the incentive William needed to return to composition – though boredom seems to have been the catalyst rather than inspirational sights and experiences. The prose letter to Beaumont prompted a verse *Epistle* describing their journey, and the vicinity of Black Combe, the lofty mountain whose brooding heights dominate the upper Furness peninsula, inspired two shorter poems.

At the beginning of September, they returned to Grasmere, and at the end of the month, William rode over to Warrington to meet Sara and escort her back to Grasmere. It was now eighteen months since she had parted with the Wordsworths and her delight in her return was palpable. She plunged into a whirl of social activity: walks, rides, excursions and parties with de Quincey's mother and sisters, who were on a visit to Grasmere; exchanging visits with the Luffs at Patterdale and the Southeys at Keswick. Casting an acerbic eye over the scarlet cloaks and silk pelisses of the grand summer visitors arriving at Grasmere church in their landaus and carriages, she could not resist reporting Peggy Ashburner's comment that, surely, 'Miss Joanna' would like Grasmere now that there was so much visiting; 'I never expected to see Grasmere come to sic a pass.' William, Sara noted, 'is always the soul of the Parties – the Ladies say they are nothing without him'.

Rather more surprising was the fact that William was now involved in the village school on a daily basis. A new curate, William Johnson, had arrived the previous summer and made an immediate impression with his 'jingling' sermons, good plain discourses of the kind William advocated for country churches. He had also endeared himself to Mary by the eagerness with which he accepted a proffered volume of William's poems, 'went smiling off like a shot with the book open, & ere he crossed the threshold to which I followed him he had begun to read'. Young and ambitious, he was determined to transform the school and was in the process of introducing the Madras System. Not content with being merely a theorist, William spent two or three hours in the school every morning and evening, teaching and helping to set up the system. He was justifiably proud of this achievement and when, in the middle of October, Southey brought Dr Bell himself to call, William instantly rushed him off to the school to hear the children at their lessons and give Johnson and himself the benefit of his advice. Bell was sufficiently impressed to declare that he would like to steal Johnson from them. The following spring, he was as good as his word, offering Johnson the post of headmaster of his newly established Central School in London. This was done not only through William but with his active support. It was, he admitted, one of the most disinterested acts of his life. 'For besides his general usefulness to the parish, I feel how much my own children will lose in him.'

In addition to his voluntary labours in the school, which would soon involve all the female members of the family, William was hard at work on his poetry. This, however, was a chore, for he was belatedly responding to a request from Sir George Beaumont that he would write some inscriptions for decorative features in the gardens at Coleorton. William could hardly refuse his friend and patron, but his distaste for the task was self-evident. Not only was he having to write to order again, but the Beaumonts were politely insistent on certain changes. The reference to 'Female and Male' in one poem, for instance, 'some would find ludicrous'. A rewrite was also sought for the final lines of the inscription for an urn dedicated to Beaumont's old friend Sir Joshua Reynolds. To Beaumont it appeared a relatively simple matter to transpose these lines from the first person to the third, but to the author it was almost impossible. William then had the frustration of finding that Lady Beaumont had lost the first versions of his poems, so he could not compare them with the alterations he had laboured so long and hard, and against his better judgement, to produce. Worse was to come, for by the end of November the Beaumonts had changed their minds once more and decided that, on the whole, they preferred the first versions after all. In the circumstances, it was remarkable that the finished inscriptions were so good.

Beaumont was too generous-spirited not to feel at least a twinge of guilt about his imposition on William's time. At the end of one of his letters containing emendations, William casually mentioned that he was about to go to Lowther to seek a personal interview with Beaumont's friend, Lord Lonsdale. The purpose of his journey was an embarrassing one: he would go as a suppliant in the hope that Lonsdale might be able to offer him one of the thousands of posts, many of them sinecures, within his extensive patronage. 'In fact, whatever sacrifice it cost me,' a chagrined William wrote to Beaumont, 'a considerable portion of my time *must* in some way or other be devoted to money-making. The expences of living encrease so fast, and my family necessarily as the Children grow up requires more to support it.' Beaumont immediately dispatched a letter wishing William success in his application and enclosing a banknote from himself. William was mortified that his words should be so misinterpreted. He refused the money immediately, and, anxious not to appear ungrateful, assured Beaumont that if he ever found himself in real financial difficulties, he would not hesitate to inform him. The tact which both men displayed in handling such a delicate matter was a tribute to the genuine friendship between them.

Towards the end of November Sara and her sailor brother, Henry, went to visit Miss Weir and their three nieces at Appleby. They found all three girls well, happy and delighted to see them, but it was Dora who entranced Sara. 'I thought her the most beautiful Creature I ever saw in my life ... *bewitchingly* so – for your life it seemed impossible not to admire her – there is such a life and variety in her countenance as I never saw – then she was so modest & pretty-behaved that it gave her face a milder & sweeter expression than I thought it capable of'. When Dora herself returned to Grasmere for the Christmas holidays, the general opinion of her progress was favourable. According to her Aunt Dorothy – her severest critic – Dora 'reads very tolerably – spells well – writes decently and sews as well as one could expect'. Another half-year at school, it was decided, would set her well and truly on the path of regular advancement in learning.

Writing her usual end of the year summary for Catherine Clarkson, Dorothy reported that Johnny had made some progress with his books in recent weeks, but his 'duncery' was unconquerable; Thomas was also slow, but lack of inclination rather than intellect was his problem; Catherine, 'almost as broad as she is long', was 'uncommonly good-tempered', but at three years old was hardly more articulate than her eighteen-month-old youngest brother. Dorothy herself was in fine fettle, walking between ten and twenty miles daily without the least fatigue, and William had at last resumed work on his 'great poem'. After the trials and tribulations of the last eighteen months, the outlook now seemed bright. 'We had the finest Christmas day ever remembered, a cloudless sky and glittering Lake; the tops of the higher mountains covered with snow.' The Wordsworths celebrated, as usual, with roast beef and plum cake; William walked with his sister in the morning, while the rest of the family were at church, then by moonlight with his wife.

Dorothy played cards with the children, a treat she promised to repeat on New Year's Day, and there was dancing in the kitchen when the Grasmere fiddlers arrived on their annual round.

At Keswick the new year was greeted with alarms and fears of an uprising among the manufacturing population. 'Half the people in Keswick sat up on Thursday night last', Southey reported, 'because two "ugly fellows" had been seen in the town. I have been obliged to load an old Spanish fowling piece to keep up the courage of the family, and to write to London for a brace of pistols and a Watchmans rattle.' Grasmere remained tranquil, but courage of a different kind was required, for William addressed himself to Lord Lonsdale. His own instinct had been to make the first approach informally in person, but he had been thwarted by Lonsdale's absence from Lowther for the winter. The letter he now wrote, though seasoned with a little judicious flattery of His Lordship's 'gracious manners' and 'attachment to Literature', was remarkably frank and to the point. 'Literature has been the pursuit of my Life', he wrote,

... I long hoped, depending upon my moderate desires, that the profits of my literary labours added to the little which I possessed would have answered to the rational wants of myself and my family. But in this I have been disappointed; and for these causes; 1st the unexpected pressure of the times falling most heavily upon men who have no regular means of increasing their income in proportion; and 2ndly I had erroneously calculated upon the degree in which my writings were likely to suit the taste of the times; and, lastly, much the most important part of my efforts cannot meet the public eye for many years through the comprehensiveness of the subject. I may also add (but it is scarce worth while) a fourth reason, viz. an utter inability on my part to associate with any class or body of literary men, and thus subject myself to the necessity of sacrificing my own judgement, and of lending even indirectly countenance or support to principles either of taste, politics, morals, or religion, which I disapproved; and your Lordship is not ignorant that except writers engaged in mere drudgery, there are scarcely any authors but those associated in this manner, who find literature, at this day, an employment attended with pecuniary gain.

Having established himself firmly on the moral high ground, William then proceeded to the main thrust of what was, after all, a begging letter. He had just learned of the death of John Richardson, Lonsdale's principal agent, and the opportunities thus created for new appointments:

if any Office should be at your Lordship's disposal (the duties of which would not call so largely upon my exertions as to prevent me from giving a considerable portion of time to study) it might be in your Lordship's power to place me in a situation where with better hope of success I might advance towards the main object of my life; I mean the completion of my literary undertakings; and thereby contribute to the innocent gratification, and perhaps (as the Subjects I am treating are important) to the solid benefit of many of my Countrymen.

Lonsdale replied that he had no suitable vacancies available on this occasion, but assured William of his respect for his talents and character, and urged him to get in touch again 'whenever you think I can be of use to you'.

There was nothing William could do but return to his poetic labours. He took the time to revise *Peter Bell*. That he did so now, and that Sara made fair copies of it, and of *Benjamin the Waggoner*, suggests that he was considering the possibility of raising some money by their publication. However, his reluctance to publish soon overwhelmed him, the manuscripts were again returned to the drawer and neither poem saw the light of day for another seven years.

William was restless and uncharacteristically edgy in these early months of 1812. There were a number of factors, but dwarfing everything was the quarrel with Coleridge. On 19 February Coleridge called at Ambleside to collect Hartley and Derwent from school and carry them home to Greta Hall. 'I passed thro' Grasmere; but did not call on Wordsworth', he airily informed his friend Morgan. What he did not say was the effect that this omission had on his children, who, though still in the habit of paying weekly visits to the Wordsworths, had no idea that anything was amiss. 'Poor Hartley sat in speechless astonishment as the Chaise passed the turning to the Vicarage where W. lives,' his mother told Poole afterwards, 'but he dared not hazard one remark and Derwent fixed his eyes full of tears upon his father, who turned his head away to conceal his own emotions.' It was left to Mrs Coleridge to explain their father's conduct, and the reason for it, to her sons.

When the Wordsworths learned what had happened, they were deeply hurt, particularly on Dorothy's behalf. Whatever Coleridge's quarrel with William, she had played no part in it. 'Numerous were the letters and messages I received from Miss W. to urge C. to write to her and not to leave the country without seeing them,' Mrs Coleridge told Poole, 'but he would not go to *them* and *they* did not come to him'. This was something of a simplification, for, as Coleridge himself declared at the time, what he wanted from William was not just a visit but an apology for his remarks to Montagu. 'I have refused to go over,' Coleridge wrote on 24 March, '& Wordsworth has refused to apologize and has thus made his choice between me and Basil Montagu, Esqre'. The affair, he prophesied, 'will end in complete alienation'.

For six weeks, there was an *impasse*. Then, as suddenly as he had arrived, Coleridge left, not having seen any of the Wordsworths, nor, indeed, Sara. What none of them knew was that he would never return to his home or the Lakes again. From Penrith, on the eve of his departure, he wrote bitterly to Morgan, complaining that he had received four letters in the last three days

about my not having called on Wordsworth as I passed thro' Grasmere – & this morning a most impassioned one from Mrs Clarkson – Good God! how could I? how can I? – I have no resentment – and unless Grief & Anguish be resentment, I never had – but unless I meet him as of yore, what use is there in it? What but mere pain? I am not about to be his Enemy – I want no stimulus to serve him to the utmost whenever it should be in my power. – And can any friend of mine wish me to go without apology received, and as to a man the best-beloved & honored, who had declared me a nuisance, an absolute nuisance – & this to such a Creature as Montagu?

A well-meant intervention by Southey only added to Coleridge's misery. Relying on William's own word, as well as 'on the common sense of the thing', Southey had 'denied most peremptorily' that William had ever commissioned Montagu to tell Coleridge that he had no hopes of him. This meant only one thing to Coleridge: William believed Montagu in preference to him and was therefore accusing him of being a deliberate liar as well as an absolute nuisance. On 27 March the Wordsworths learned from Mrs Coleridge that her husband had gone. It clearly came as an unwelcome surprise.

A fortnight later, William also left for London. The visit had been planned since the beginning of the year and was originally a purely social one, but it had now assumed a more immediate importance. He was determined to 'confront' both Coleridge and Montagu 'upon this vile business'. His first duty was to escort Mary and five-year-old Thomas to Chester to meet Tom Hutchinson. Mary and Thomas would then go on to Hindwell, where they would stay for the next two or three months, while William made his way to London. He travelled via Birmingham, staying overnight there with the Lloyds, to Oxford, 'an enchanting place', where he spent thirty-six hours exploring everything but the museum. He called on his cousin William Cookson, a student at Brasenose, and on William Jackson, son of the rector of Grasmere, who was an undergraduate of Queen's College; with Jackson, he attended the examination schools and, by chance, heard Coleridge's nephew, John, give an impressive performance. He reluctantly left for Binfield, to spend a few days with the Cooksons, before travelling up to London, where, on 27 April, he took up residence with the Beaumonts in Grosvenor Square.

William's first priority on arriving in town was to get to the bottom of the whole affair with Coleridge. This had now become urgent, for reports had already begun to reach him that the quarrel was the subject of dinner and tea-table gossip. The Beaumonts had received letters and a visit from Coleridge himself in which he had tried to enlist their sympathy by telling his side of the story, with 'plentiful abuse' of William, to which they refused to listen. As William had carefully refrained from confiding in Sir George, because he was a mutual friend and he had not wanted to cause him pain, this was particularly hard to bear. 'This conduct is insufferable', William complained to Mary, 'and I am determined to put an end to it.'

The indiscreet revelations by Coleridge and the Montagus had been improved upon by scandalmongers in London society. Catherine Clarkson, a friend of Robinson, Coleridge and, of course, William himself, was horrified that matters had come to such a pass. 'I hope you will either see [Coleridge] or at least take some measures to put a stop to the reports which are in circulation respecting your conduct towards him', she urged William. 'My dear friend! There has been downright <u>lying</u> somewhere not mere misrepresentations & dressing up of facts but inventing against you – and if I were in your place I would take Mr Montagu & C Lamb with me & force an interview with C.' This was precisely what William decided to do. It was hardly subtle, but at least it was honest. His first call was on Montagu, but no opportunity presented itself for raising the matter. He therefore wrote instead to Coleridge's oldest friend, Lamb, asking to see him alone at home: 'as I wish to have the business sifted to the bottom, and will take his opinion how it may be done in the most unexceptionable manner'. Lamb thus became the unofficial go-between.

Coleridge's reaction to William's suggestion of a meeting was to point out, quite rightly, that it would turn into a confrontation. Only one version of events could be true: either William had indeed said what Montagu had told Coleridge he had said, or Montagu, or Coleridge, was lying. Faced with one man's word against the other, what could be achieved? William suggested that the two men should prepare a written statement of what they each believed had been said. The two could then be compared and William would write his own, adding 'under what circumstances I spoke, with what motive, and in what spirit. And there, I believe, the matter must end'.

At this crucial point, a cool head was desperately needed, and fortunately for everyone concerned one was found. Henry Crabb Robinson was the epitome of discretion, and motivated by liking both parties. He had a genuine desire to bring the quarrel to an end, but he needed all his considerable diplomatic skills, as well as his legal training, to do so. Robinson's diary is frustratingly discreet. Many of the entries are in code and a number of the conversations with William are simply noted as being 'confidential', 'of a kind not to be repeated' or 'I ought not to put in writing what he said'. As an insight into the quarrel, however, it is unique, for the admirable Robinson managed not only to remain impartial, and to perform his task as intermediary punctiliously, but also to ensure that anything inflammatory was quietly suppressed.

It was Coleridge who first involved Robinson by relating his grievances and giving him permission to repeat them to William, probably because William had refused to open letters from him on the subject. Robinson duly conveyed the message, and in return was asked to give William's verbal answers to Coleridge's charges. There were three absolute denials: he had never 'commissioned' Montagu to say anything, used the expression '*rotten drunkard*' or said Coleridge himself was a 'nuisance', only that some of his habits were. He admitted that he had expressed no hopes of Coleridge, but indignantly repudiated the suggestion that he would ever have said so, directly or indirectly, to Coleridge himself. He did, however, blame himself for forgetting that Montagu 'was not a man whose discretion could be safely trusted with even so much as he did say'. He no longer wished to confront Coleridge and Montagu and was content to leave undetermined who was at fault, but he expected Coleridge to give him credit for the truth of this declaration, 'And not continue to use that langu[age] abo[u]t him which he had done'. These points Robinson duly repeated to Coleridge, 'Except perhaps the conclusion of the last which I might not distinctly state to C— W added other remarks which I was careful not to repeat as they co[ul]d not tend to the reconciliation so desireable, [*sic*] And perhaps so important to the future happiness of C.'

Coleridge's immediate reaction was simply to reiterate all his complaints, but

Robinson, though 'apprehensive of saying too much', would not allow him to dwell on them.

I endeavoured to draw C's attention *from* words w[hi]ch are so liable to misrepresentation – And w[hi]ch in repetition so entirely change their character, to the fact so positively denied by W that he ever intended (least of all commissioned) M to repeat what W stated to him – This in my mind is the only material fact. Every thing else admits of explanation. This does not.

And so a compromise was finally beaten out. Coleridge wrote out his statement which, 'tho' not elaborately drawn up, or artfully written' contained 'the most indubitable internal evidence of truth'. As such, it had its due effect on William. Convinced now that Coleridge had genuinely believed William's reported comments to be true, and of the sincerity of his unhappiness, William drew up his own statement. It proved a difficult task, 'because he had to reconcile things very difficult to unite – The most exact truth & sincerity with the giving his friend the least possible pain'. What facilitated the writing of a conciliatory letter was William's bad opinion of Montagu and his wife. Robinson seems to have asked the obvious question. Why was William so reluctant to put an end to his friendship with Montagu, if he believed Montagu was responsible for causing the quarrel between himself and Coleridge? William's answer impressed him: he 'spoke eloquently of the difficulty of breaking off an intimacy early formed, more especially where a benefit is conferred by that intimacy And where by the influence of friendship characters are preserved from lapses that might otherwise prove their shipwreck'.

In the end, 'the great part' of William's statement was actually written by Robinson, who found him 'willing to say anything he could truly, to give Coleridge satisfaction'. No doubt this explains why it bears more resemblance to a legal document than a letter to a friend. 'The conversation that accompanied the writing it was highly interesting & exhibited W in a most honourable light', Robinson noted in his diary on 11 May. 'His integrity his purity, his delicacy alike are eminent'. Having carefully preserved his impartiality throughout the affair, Robinson now let slip that, as far as conduct went, he had learned to admire William more than Coleridge: 'How preferable is the *coolness* of such a man to the heat of C.'

Having drawn up at least two drafts of his statement, a shorter final form was agreed with Robinson, written out by William and delivered to Coleridge the same day. That evening, when Robinson called on Coleridge, he had the immense satisfaction of learning that it was considered 'perfectly satisfactory'. Reporting the glad news to Greta Hall, a jubilant Coleridge announced that William had given him an 'unequivocal denial of the Whole *in spirit* & of the most offensive passages in letter as well as Spirit', and that, in response, he had 'instantly informed [Wordsworth] that were ten thousand Montagues to swear against it, I should take his word not ostensibly only but with inward Faith!' The level-headed Robinson was rightly more sceptical: 'the Wound is healed,' he wrote in his diary, 'but . . . probably the Scar remains in Coleridge's bosom'.

When the two men finally met, face to face, it was something of an anticlimax. William called on Coleridge. 'I felt no awkwardness at the meeting,' William told Dorothy, 'nor was he much agitated.' Both behaved as if nothing had happened. At neither this meeting nor the ones that followed did either of them touch upon the subject of the quarrel which had consumed so much of their time and energy and caused them both so much pain. They met frequently on social occasions, even at each other's residences, and William attended Coleridge's lectures, but the old intimacy had gone for ever.

The very day of the reconciliation, 11 May, a shocking event took place which threw the whole country into a state of panic. The Prime Minister, Spencer Perceval, was shot dead in the lobby of the House of Commons by John Bellingham, a Liverpool merchant. William was at a dinner party at Rogers's house when the dramatic news was announced by no less a person than Lord Byron. William's first thoughts were for his family, for the murder had been greeted with joy by the lower orders; in the streets and in the pot-houses they were toasting the radical Francis Burdett as 'the People's Champion', who would rid them of all sufferings, real and imaginary. It was revolutionary France all over again and William's blood now ran cold at the thought. 'Oh my Joy & my comfort, my hope & my repose,' he wrote to Mary, 'what awful thoughts passed through my mind of thee & Dorothy and home'. Only ten days earlier, he had seen Perceval in the House of Commons 'and admired the spirit and animation with which he suppressed & chastized that most dangerous & foolish Demagogue Sir Francis Burdett ... The country is no doubt in a most alarming situation; and if much firmness be not displayed by the government confusion & havoc & murder will break out & spread terribly.'

Having 'settled the business with Coleridge', as he always referred to the reconciliation, William now found himself more at liberty to enjoy all London had to offer. The rest of his visit passed in a hectic round of social engagements. He breakfasted, dined, went to the theatre and partied with many old friends, including the Lambs, Rogers, Sharp, Stoddart, Davy and Stuart, but his circle of acquaintance was expanding rapidly. He met Lord Byron, whose recent publication of *Childe Harold* had made him all the rage. William admitted the power of his writing, but dismissed his style as un-English and the man himself as 'somewhat cracked'. Robinson took him to meet the Aitkin family, editors of and contributors to the *Annual Review*, which had so viciously reviewed *Poems, in Two Volumes*. There he met the 'old snake' Mrs Barbauld, whose poetry he despised almost as much as her political opinions, and the poet James Montgomery, who appeared feeble but amiable. At Beaumont's many grand dinners he met a wide range of people, from artists such as the American, Washington Allston, to the highest in the land. On one occasion he was even introduced to the Princess Regent, the notorious Caroline of Brunswick. It was, as William cheerfully admitted, 'an empty honour, for her RH– was at some distance from me, and I had no conversation with her. She is a fat unwieldy Woman, but has rather a handsome & pleasing Countenance, with an expression of hilarity that is not however free from Coarseness.' (At this particular party, William was obviously fascinated by a woman with a 'huge & tremendous' bosom: 'Her Breasts were like two great hay-cocks or rather hay-stacks, protruding themselves upon the Spectator,' he told Mary, 'and yet no body seemed to notice them'.)

With such a busy social calendar, it was not surprising that William occasionally found himself double-booked, but after a while it began to pall. He had to spend £8 12s on a new suit, hat and silk stockings, an enormous sum to lay out for a man who was usually to be found wearing the cast-off clothing of his brothers and brothers-in-law. He was also increasingly frustrated and bored by the constant round of engagements.

Despite all the claims on him, William found time to perform a number of quiet kindnesses. He went several times to visit the former Grasmere curate William Johnson and was somewhat dismayed to find him 'in a nasty Dirty place' which was the temporary school. 'Johnsy' was also having difficulties with Dr Bell, who, though an 'excellent Creature', had frequent changes of mind and 'something of a plaguy manner'. In an effort to ease tensions, William agreed to undertake a most disagreeable chore: 'viz to select and compose with Mr Johnson's assistance 20 pages of monosyllabic lessons for Children.'

William also spent considerable time and effort in trying to secure the release of a French prisoner-of-war. It is a very odd story, made all the more strange by the fact that it can only be pieced together from scattered and allusive references which raise more questions than they solve. The Frenchman was Eustace Baudouin, whose elder brother, Jean Baptiste, married William's daughter Caroline in 1816. It has been assumed that the Baudouins and Vallons became acquainted because, after his release, Eustace carried messages from the Wordsworths to the Vallons. In fact, this is an inversion of the true order of events, for it is clear that the Baudouins were already friends of the Vallons, and Eustace's plight was brought to William's attention by a letter from Annette in the spring of 1812. (This is also the first indication we have that there was still a correspondence with Annette; whether this letter broke a ten-year silence or was simply the first to register in the wider correspondence remains a mystery.)

The first reference to Eustace Baudouin appears in Mary's letter to William, written from Hindwell on 23 April. Describing her journey after she and Thomas had parted from William, she says they dined at Oswestry in Shropshire. 'Oh with what a fervent heart did I greet the river Wye for thy sake & for its own loveliness!' she wrote. 'I looked for our friend in the face of every Frenchman we met, & never before was sorry that I could not speak their language I was sorry for his sake that you had not come so far with us – for I dare say he has never recd. his father's . . . letters.'

By 29 April William had received a letter 'from the French Prisoner at Oswestry', forwarded from Grasmere, 'telling you that he has no present want of money having received a supply – that he wished much that by applying to the Transport office you could assist him in obtaining his release but seemed to have little hope; and requested to hear again, telling him your address – where he might *always* find you, and saying you might write in English'.

'I wish you may be able to serve Annette's friend', Mary responded, and William did attempt to do so, seeking the advice of Daniel Stuart, 'a most able man' whose 'good sense & knowledge of things are consummate', and whose contacts, through his editorship of the *Courier*, were second to none. Having made his inquiries, Stuart informed William that nothing could be done. Unable to secure Baudouin's release, William sent him £20, half of it borrowed from Mary's cousin Tom Monkhouse.

The correspondence with Annette continued, however, for in bringing Baudouin to their attention she had also referred to her own straitened circumstances. The Wordsworths were determined to assist her and wrote to ask her for a detailed account of her situation. Throughout most of May, they waited anxiously for her response. The letter they eventually received was written jointly by Annette and Caroline, who was now almost twenty years old. It described how their days were confined to an office, where Annette had managed to secure some sort of official post which required their constant attention. They could not take holidays and had no time for exercise or recreation; all their pleasure in life they found in each other. They had supported themselves, however, had no present need of money, and Caroline's devotion to her mother was a credit to the way she had been brought up. It was, the Wordsworths agreed, a deeply affecting letter. 'Does not Annette appear to have behaved well (& even in a dignified manner[)?];' William asked his wife. Mary responded with her usual generosity. 'I do indeed think Annette's conduct very dignified & most heartily wish we were rich enough for you to settle something handsome upon dear Caroline.'

Throughout the eight weeks of their separation, William had belied his reputation as a poor correspondent by writing almost daily to his wife. Twenty-four letters passed between them, every bit as ardent as the ones of the previous year. 'My sweet Love how I long to see thee;' he wrote on 13 May; 'think of me, wish for me, pray for me, pronounce my name when thou art alone, and upon thy pillow; and dream of me happily & sweetly. – I am the blessedest of Men, the happiest of husbands'.

On 4 June he wrote to tell Mary that his visit to London was at last drawing to a close. In a month's time he would meet her at Hindwell and, together with Thomas, they would return home for a grand family reunion. It was not to be. The very day he wrote, tragedy struck at Grasmere. Little Catherine died. It was as much a shock to her aunts Dorothy and Sara, who had been looking after her in her parents' absence, as it was to William and Mary. 'For several days the Child had been in the most joyous spirits', wrote Dorothy.

On the Sunday afternoon and the Monday I had been for several hours with Willy and her in the Churchyard and they had run races and played on the very ground where now she lies. I then particularly noticed how little was to be seen of her lameness, and several persons who came up to speak to us while we were there observed how trifling the lameness was, and how thriving and healthy she looked.

Sara had noticed a corresponding improvement in her paralysed hand. The afternoon before she died, Catherine had surprised Sara by turning over a playing card with it and had eaten her dinner with a fork 'as steadily as any Child'. After a supper of porridge, she had run up to bed, 'in such glee striving to get before William, and proud that she was going to sleep in her *Mother's* bed, an unusual treat'. It was not until Johnny went up to join her later that anyone realized anything was wrong. He found that she had been sick and was lying with her eyes fixed. Dorothy, who had been present when Catherine had her last seizure, instantly knew what was to come. Fanny, the servant, galloped off immediately on Sara's pony to fetch Scambler, and while they waited his arrival, they tried all the remedies they had applied before. Scambler arrived an hour later, by which time Catherine was completely convulsed down her right side. He examined her and announced that the brain was 'very much affected'. When Dorothy asked him if it was more dangerous than the previous attack, he simply replied 'undoubtedly', '& by his manner we saw that he had no hope'.

For hour after hour through that terrible night, Sara, Dorothy and the two servants took turns to nurse the dying child on their knees. As death approached, Sara could bear it no longer and had to leave the room.

I went down stairs & could hear her moaning & could even fancy she spake – once after she begun she said Aunt Ant or something like it but it was mechanical for she had no sense. I stayed down stairs & walked in the court knowing I could do nothing & fearing to witness the change but at last my anxiety got the better of my fear & I went up & looked at her & saw the film was spread over her eyes D felt that her feet were growing cold & I bade the old woman raise her head a little higher & soon after the noise of phlegm in her chest & her moaning ceased D got up & gave her place to Fanny & the Angel breathed about 20 times after this every breath lower till it died away & seemed to have no struggle at the last her face did not the old woman said move. I have not seen her since but she is beautiful they say as an angel her own sweet countenance with something more heavenly ... D has had much comfort in looking at her in her present peaceful state. I cannot bear to see her for I hope to forget all but her own dear sweet living face but the countenance of death would I know be never forgotten.

Catherine died at quarter past five on the morning of 4 June 1812. She was three months short of her fourth birthday. Four days later, she was buried in the quiet north-east corner of Grasmere churchyard, beside the river, and under the hawthorn tree where she had played so happily such a short time before. The little coffin was carried by the mothers of four of the Wordsworths' past and present servants, and followed by Dorothy, Sara and Johnny, the two servants, Fanny and Sarah, and Hartley and Derwent Coleridge. In Dorothy's opinion, 'All who attended her Remains ... were sincere mourners.'

Somehow the news had to be broken to the bereaved parents. Dorothy and Sara decided that Mary would be better able to stand the shock if the news was broken to her by her husband. Dorothy wrote immediately to William. Forced to keep her own emotions on a tight rein, her letter was brutal in its baldness. 'My dearest Brother,' she began, 'Sara and John and William and I are all in perfect health, but poor Catherine died this morning . . .' Scambler fulfilled his promise and wrote by the same post, briefly describing Catherine's symptoms and the treatment he had applied. 'I hope it will be some consolation to you to know,' he ended his letter, 'that from the first she appe[ared] quite insensible to her sufferings; & that every attention was paid to her that possibly could be'. Sara did her part, writing a long and detailed description of Catherine's last hours. Nominally, it was addressed to Tom Hutchinson, but it was meant for Mary, once she had recovered from the shock of hearing the news.

Unfortunately, Dorothy's letter reached the Beaumonts' an hour after William had left and had to be forwarded to Bocking, so it was not until 11 June, a week after Catherine's death and three days after her funeral, that he finally learned the dreadful news. His first impulse was to rush straight to Hindwell, but on his return to London the next day, he realized that it was probably too late. He was right. Sara's letter had already arrived at Hindwell and Mary had been in the room when it was handed to Tom. There was, of course, no way that the news could be kept from her and her reaction was everything they had most feared. Racked with guilt that she had not been there when she was most needed and tortured by the belief that, had she been there, a mother's instinct might have enabled her to save her child, Mary's grief was unassuageable.

In London, William had consoled himself with the thought that having his arrival to look forward to would be of far more use to Mary than his actual presence, at least in the first instance. Several days after his arrival, he had to admit that she was

yet little recovered from the deploreable dejection in which I found her. Her health has suffered: but I clearly see that neither thought nor religion nor the endeavours of friends, can at once quiet a heart that has been disturbed by such an affliction. We must wait patiently and do what we can ... She suffers more than in the ordinary course of nature from the tender connection and dependence in which this child has long existed with her, or hung upon her maternal care; and I feel that the privation will be a sorrow for life; though I hope at some future period she will be able to draw consolation from her very source of encreased suffering.

It was the beginning of July before Mary was well enough to make the journey home. It could not, of course, be a happy homecoming, but it was some comfort to be reunited with her remaining children. Six-year-old Thomas returned with his parents. Living on the farm at Hindwell had suited him down to the ground; but though the suggestion had been made that he should stay on after his parents left, his sister's death made this unthinkable. Dora had returned from Appleby a couple of weeks earlier, and both aunts expressed themselves indebted to Miss Weir for her care. Dora, now almost eight, had become an inseparable companion to her brothers, looking after Willy and encouraging Johnny in his lessons. Johnny himself had left Grasmere school and on 9 June, just before his ninth birthday, had joined Hartley and Derwent Coleridge and Algernon Montagu at Mr Dawes's school at Ambleside. Instead of being a weekly boarder, however, he walked happily to and from school each day. Though deeply distressed by Catherine's death, his sensitivity and good sense in his affliction were a great comfort to his aunts. Two-year-old Willy, whose most recent illness had been kept from his mother (though it had been sufficiently alarming to send Dorothy scurrying off to Ambleside to see Scambler), was fully recovered and as lively as ever.

The Wordsworths tried hard to pick up the threads of their life. A couple of days after William and Mary's return, Dorothy went off to Eusemere to spend four days with her cousin Captain John Wordsworth and almost a fortnight with her 'aunt', Elizabeth Rawson. Only a couple of days after Dorothy's return to Grasmere, Mary Monkhouse arrived from Hindwell on a visit that would last three months. Her presence was a comfort to them all. She was 'a *perfect Woman*', Dorothy said admiringly, 'the only one I ever knew – except Mrs Rawson. I *know* not one fault she has'. Mary brought good news to cheer the mourning family. She was engaged to be married to her cousin, Mary's brother Tom, and the wedding would take place at Grasmere in October.

There was the usual influx of annual summer visitors: Samuel Tillbrooke and his friend Charles Blomfield, from Cambridge, stayed at Robert Newton's lodging house next to the Parsonage. Blomfield, a future bishop of London, provided them with a rare treat by taking duty at Grasmere church in place of the incumbent, Thomas Jackson, who, in Dorothy's acerbic phrase, 'is a worthy man – very good as a Steward or a Farmer; but totally unfit to preach or read prayers'. When they left, Dr Bell took over their lodgings and soon had Dorothy constantly employed in helping him to arrange and correct his various publications for reissue as a single work. On 8 August Bell carried William, Mary, Dorothy, Dora and Johnny off to Keswick to pay a visit to Greta Hall. They left Dora there, wild with joy at the prospect of staying with her friends Sara Coleridge and Edith Southey, and brought Herbert Southey back to stay with Thomas, who was his great friend. Despite all these distractions, William and Dorothy were deeply concerned that Mary's usually sunny nature failed to reassert itself.

At the end of October, the Monkhouses and Hutchinsons gathered at Grasmere for what was truly a family wedding. At the last minute, there was a crisis. The bride's brother Tom, who was to give her away, was recalled to London by his partner because of a threatened bankruptcy. It proved to be a false alarm, but the bride was naturally disappointed. 'I was grieved on your account, as well as mine,' she told him,

because if you had staid you would have seen so much of William's goodness, and how nice and entertaining he can be some times, and I fear from what you saw of him you will have rather an unfavourable impression upon your mind – he apologized to me for his strange behaviour on the day of your first arrival at Grasmere, and said he had been very uncomfortable about it ever since –

By way of compensation, on the eve of the wedding William presented Mary with 'too valuable a present for any body to share in', a sonnet he had written specially for the occasion, praising the quiet simplicity of the wedding and the bride herself. William's unexplained 'strange behaviour' might have been the result of his struggle to compose the poem, but it is more probably attributable to his preoccupation with his financial affairs. At the beginning of September he had received an unexpected letter from Sir George Beaumont. Lord Lonsdale was anxious to assist William in securing a suitable post, but was concerned that the opportunity of doing so might be very distant. Until that moment arrived, it was his wish to offer William an annuity of £100. Knowing how proud William was about accepting anything that smacked of charity, he had made his proposal through their mutual friend, who proffered his 'sincere opinion that you may accept it without degradation, circumstanced as you are'. To sugar the pill, Beaumont also suggested that a refusal would give Lonsdale 'more pain than you would be willing to inflict'.

It was a subtle argument, not to mention a tempting offer, but Beaumont was wasting his time. William would not even consider it, though he was grateful for this evidence of Lonsdale's willingness to help him. He now wrote to Stuart, asking to be informed of any likely vacancies and assuring him that, if the salary were adequate and the duties 'what I am equal to, without being under the necessity of withdrawing myself wholly from Literature', he had no objection to leaving the Lakes. 'Of course', he added, 'all this is *between ourselves.*'

Stuart identified several possibilities, so, early in November, William decided to go over to Lowther to seek Lord Lonsdale's assistance in applying for them. Hoping that a short excursion might benefit Mary, he took her, and Dora, with him as far as Keswick, where they all stayed together for a few days. It proved to be a pleasant visit, but it failed to raise Mary's spirits. As soon as she returned to Grasmere, she went straight to the churchyard 'to throw herself upon the poor Child's grave –', Sara sadly noted.

Worse was to come. The Wordsworths' third child, Thomas, had always been delicate and whooping cough had left him with a permanent weakness in the chest. Nine days after his parents' return, Thomas developed a cough and showed all the symptoms of measles. For several days he ran a high fever, but on the morning of 1 December, when Richard Scambler called, his temperature had returned to normal and he was thought to be going on as well as possible. An hour after the apothecary left, Thomas was seized with a violent coughing fit and sickness. Shaking with fear and panic, he cried out to his mother, 'I shall die, I shall die'. William rushed off to fetch Scambler back; in his absence, his son grew calmer and declared that he was getting better, but it was obvious he was failing fast. When William returned from Ambleside, Sara told him that there was no hope. The little boy died just before six in the evening.

After a sleepless night, William rose early next morning and set off to intercept Dorothy, who was on her way to Keswick from Watermillock, where she had spent the previous fortnight with the Marshalls. He met the coach at Threlkeld, broke the news to her and brought her straight home in a state of collapse. This time it was Mary who displayed what her husband admiringly called 'striking fortitude'. 'She received me with the calmness of an Angel –', Dorothy wrote; 'she comforted me, – and in truth I was ashamed of my own weakness; and bitterly reproached myself that I could not bear the sorrow as she did.' That evening, William somehow found the strength to write brief businesslike notes to their closest friends informing them of this second tragic loss. Only to Southey, who had been such a comforter in the dark days after John's death and was himself the father of Thomas's best friend, could William betray a glimpse of the emotion he was struggling to keep at bay.

For myself dear Southey I dare not say in what state of mind I am; I loved the Boy with the utmost love of which my soul is capable, and he is taken from me – yet in the agony of my spirit in surrendering such a treasure I feel a thousand times richer than if I had never possessed it. God comfort and save you and all our friends and us all from a repetition of such trials – O Southey feel for me! If you are not afraid of the complaint, I ought to have said if you have had it come over to us!

On 5 December Thomas Wordsworth was buried beside his sister. All the family attended the coffin to the grave, except his Aunt Sara, who was literally ill with grief. 'Nothing . . . can sustain us under our affliction but reliance in God's Goodness,' William wrote the next day,

and a firm belief that it is for *our* Good, as we cannot doubt it was for his, that he should be removed from this sinful and troublesome world. He was too good for us; we did not deserve such a blessing – and we must endeavour to correct and amend every thing that is wrong in us and our bitter sorrow will in time become sweet and kindly, and never such, at no moment such, as we should wish to part with –

William's hard-won resignation to the will of God was about to be tested to the full. No sooner had he penned this statement of faith than all three of his remaining children were struck down with measles. The entire family packed their bags and left immediately for Ambleside, so that they could be near Scambler. For the rest of the month, they lived in an agony of hope and fear, as they had to contemplate losing first one child, then another. Just when it seemed that they had weathered the storm, and were about to return to Grasmere for Christmas, Willy had a relapse. As Johnny and Dora were both recuperating, Sara and Dorothy took them home. William and Mary were therefore left to spend an anxious and exhausting week in lodgings, nursing a desperately ill toddler.

While they were at Ambleside and Willy was at the height of the measles, William received a letter from Lord Lonsdale informing him that there was no prospect, within any foreseeable period, of obtaining any of the offices suggested by Stuart. The new Tory Prime Minister, Lord Liverpool, had expressed 'the strongest inclination' to assist William, but candidly said he saw no means of doing so, except by presenting him with a pension. Lonsdale's own offer still remained open 'which you can revert to whenever you think proper, or find occasion'. William was too distraught even to consider the matter. Once Johnny and Dora were on the mend, however, he turned again to Lonsdale's letter. Though he nominally canvassed the opinions of his friends, his own preference was obvious, for as early as June he had identified what seemed to him to be the ideal government office. The post of Distributor of Stamps for Westmorland, based at Appleby, was held by one of his own distant relatives, who had recently suffered a paralytic stroke. Death, or incapacity, was certain to ensure a vacancy sooner or later. '400£ per ann. in Westmorland would be to me more desirable than 800 in London, and I must rest content with that expectation; for as to the pension, I do not see how I can accept it'. His friends were less scrupulous. Stuart sent a robust response.

You hesitate more at taking a Pension, I think, than is reasonable. What is the difference between a Pension & such a Place as you describe? The one would lay you as much under an obligation to the Government or the Ministry as the other but the pension would be more honourable to a literary man, I think, & more consistent with his character & pursuits. Surely, surely a Literary Man might most honorably deserve a Pension for his writings? . . . If you dread the reproach of a certain class of scandalous writers and politicians, that would meet you on the ground of Place quite as much as Pension. If a man does nothing dishonorable to obtain a Pension I have no objection to his taking it . . .

Beaumont had a less forceful argument, but one that spoke to the heart. Were he in William's position, he would accept Lonsdale's offer without hesitation: 'I had far rather receive it from him than from government'.

Cowed by the threat to what remained of his family, William gave up the fight. On 27 December he wrote to Lord Lonsdale and accepted the proposed annuity. He would, he declared, 'rather . . . owe any addition to my income, required by my present occasions, to your Lordship's friendship than to the Government, or to any other quarter where it was not in my power to return what in the common sentiments of men would be deemed an equivalent'.

For the second time in six months, William and Mary had to face a dismal homecoming to Grasmere. Mary's courage and strength, which had borne up under her son's death and throughout her children's illnesses, now deserted her completely. 'She is as thin as it is possible to be except when the body is worn out by slow disease, and the dejection of her countenance is afflicting', Dorothy wrote miserably; 'wherever we look we are reminded of some pretty action of those innocent Children.' The unaccustomed stillness of home and the unavoidable view of the churchyard oppressed all their spirits. William grew 'very thin, and at times I think he looks ten years older since the death of Thomas', but Mary seemed to have given herself up to her grief. 'I feel that it knits about the heart strings and will wear her away if there is not a turn in her feelings.' It was obvious to them all that they would have to leave Grasmere.

16. The Excursion

On 8 January 1813 William received a letter from Lord Lonsdale, enclosing a draft for £100. It could not have come at a more opportune moment, and it was to transform the Wordsworths' lives in ways far beyond its material value. The money would enable them to move 'to a most desirable Residence soon to be vacant at Rydale' in the certain knowledge that they could now afford the higher rent. The residence was Rydal Mount, 'a place that ten years ago I should have almost danced with Joy if I could have dreamed it would ever be ours', according to Dorothy. The current owners, the Norths, had sold it to their wealthy aristocratic neighbours, the Le Fleming family of Rydal Hall, and would leave in February. As it would then stand empty until May Day, the Wordsworths hoped to be allowed to move in immediately.

Lonsdale's money would also allow William to return to his poetry. Until his son's death, William had been working rather half-heartedly on what he called 'a task undertaken for profit', which was probably his expanded guide to the Lakes. He had even sought the assistance of his friend, Rogers, in finding an appropriate publisher. Now he could set aside that work and return, with a clear conscience and palpable relief, to his unprofitable poetry.

It is significant that, at this juncture, he went back to *The Recluse*. While Mary wept inconsolably from morning to night and Dorothy poured out her grief uncontrollably in page after page to her friends, William retreated into himself, adding a large section to the autobiography of the Solitary, describing the deaths of his son, daughter and wife, and his subsequent retreat into the mountains to live a hermit-like existence, which excluded not only all human contact but also all human emotion. Much of this section was eventually omitted from publication within the long poem, but it was reshaped into, and inspired other, shorter poems, which were to form a lasting memorial to his lost children. Included for the first

time were the lovely lines he had written about Catherine, after her return from
the seaside holiday, *Characteristics of a Child Three Years Old.*

> Loving she is, and tractable, though wild;
> And Innocence hath privilege in her
> To dignify arch looks and laughing eyes;
> And feats of cunning; and the pretty round
> Of trespasses, affected to provoke
> Mock-chastisement and partnership in play.
> ... this happy Creature of herself
> Is all-sufficient; solitude to her
> Is blithe society, who fills the air
> With gladness and involuntary songs.

In describing the response of the Solitary's wife to the loss of her children,
William drew a touching portrayal of Mary's initial 'striking fortitude', followed
by her collapse.

> The eminence whereon her spirit stood,
> Mine was unable to attain. Immense
> The space that severed us!
> ... overcome with speechless gratitude,
> And, with a holier love inspired, I looked
> On her – at once superior to my woes
> And partner of my loss. – O heavy change!
> Dimness o'er this clear luminary crept
> Insensibly; – the immortal and divine
> Yielded to mortal reflux; her pure glory,
> As from the pinnacle of worldly state
> Wretched ambition drops astounded, fell
> Into a gulf obscure of silent grief,
> And keen heart-anguish – of itself ashamed,
> Yet obstinately cherishing itself.
>
> *The Excursion, iii, 659–61, 666–77*

William's own fears for Mary were reflected in the fate he assigned the Solitary's
wife, who, consumed by her sorrow, 'melted from my arms; And left me, on this
earth, disconsolate!'

The greatest of all the poems William wrote as a result of his children's deaths
– in fact, one of his finest by any standards – was the exquisite sonnet he wrote
about Catherine 'long after her death'. In this sonnet, more perhaps than any other,
he gives us a poignant glimpse of a heart that was no less feeling for not being worn
on his sleeve.

> Surprised by joy – impatient as the Wind
> I turned to share the transport – Oh! with whom
> But Thee, deep buried in the silent tomb,
> That spot which no vicissitude can find?
> Love, faithful love, recalled thee to my mind –
> But how could I forget thee? Through what power,
> Even for the least division of an hour,
> Have I been so beguiled as to be blind
> To my most grievous loss! – that thought's return
> Was the worst pang that sorrow ever bore,
> Save one, one only, when I stood forlorn,
> Knowing my heart's best treasure was no more;
> That neither present time, nor years unborn
> Could to my sight that heavenly face restore.

The loss of two of his beloved children in such a short space of time, and so unexpectedly, affected William profoundly at the time, but it was to be an abiding and ineradicable sorrow. Forty years later, he would describe to Aubrey de Vere 'the details of their illnesses with an exactness and impetuosity of troubled excitement, such as might have been expected if the bereavement had taken place but a few weeks before'.

One of the immediate consequences of the bereavement was that they all became understandably over-anxious and over-protective of the remaining children. Johnny was removed from Mr Dawes's school at Ambleside and sent back to the greatly inferior village school. Dora too became a pupil there. Every ailment, however minor, became a cause for panic, and Willy, being the youngest, was particularly mollycoddled.

A more insidious trait, of which they were completely unaware, was that the adults, particularly Dorothy, could not forbear making comparisons between the living and the dead. Catherine and Thomas became apotheosized into perfect children, their faults (of which she had complained frequently when they were alive) forgotten, their undoubted virtues magnified into saintliness. Dora's thoughtless, wilful ways would be contrasted with Catherine's affectionate, sunny nature and poor Johnny's duncery with Thomas's belatedly discovered book-learning and quickness of intellect, which had manifested itself only in the last six months of his life. Both children grew up to feel instinctively that they had somehow let the family down by living when their 'better' siblings had died. This was by no means intentional. It was not even completely true, for they were both deeply loved for themselves. Nevertheless, the feeling was there and the Wordsworths were at fault in failing to eradicate it. Johnny would never completely rid himself of the belief that his failure to shine intellectually was a disappointment to his father, and would become a sullen, jealous and dissatisfied man. Dora reacted by trying to become the perfect dutiful daughter, even to the point of sacrificing her own happiness by refusing to marry the man she loved, so that she could stay at home with her parents.

A further, indirect, consequence of the bereavement was that it became clear that the previous year's reconciliation with Coleridge had merely papered over irreparable cracks in their friendship. William had written to him immediately after Thomas's death and had received a confused and self-involuted, but well-meant, reply, the gist of which appeared to be that he would come to them as soon as possible. But the weeks stretched into months and he did not come. When they finally learned that he had left town and gone to the seaside, they knew he never would.

The move from the Parsonage at Grasmere to Rydal Mount was both literally and metaphorically one from darkness into light. 'I was the last person who left the [Parsonage] yesterday evening', Dorothy wrote. 'It seemed as quiet as the grave ... the house only reminded me of desolation, gloom, emptiness, and chearless silence.' Next morning at Rydal Mount, however, the weather was 'delightful, and the place a paradise'. As Sara smugly commented a few weeks later, 'It is the admiration of every body – the *crack* spot, and the envy, of the whole neighbourhood.'

Rydal Mount was, and is, a lovely house, with a delightful split personality. The oldest part is a simple sixteenth-century farm cottage, little more than one-up, one-down, with three-foot-thick stone walls and what might politely be called random mullioned windows. In the mid-eighteenth century it was transformed into a gentleman's house by its owners, the Knotts, who added a west wing twice as large as the original building. This wing, facing due south, was typically Georgian: neat and symmetrical, with two large sash windows either side of the central glazed folding doors, which opened out on to a terrace, and five identical ones above. By thus reorienting the house, the Knotts took full advantage of the incomparable view. The house stands on the lower slopes of Rydal Fell, a few hundred yards from the road from Ambleside to Grasmere, which snakes along the valley bottom. All the main windows therefore look out over the beautiful little Vale of Rydal, towards Ambleside, which is hidden behind the fold in the hills, where the craggy peaks of Wansfell Pike and Loughrigg Fell fall away to reveal the distant grey glimmer of Lake Windermere. Immediately in front of the house, across the terrace, is an ancient mound of indeterminate age and origin, which was traditionally believed to be a ninth-century Northumbrian observation post. From this spot, which was William's pride and joy, there is a panoramic view over the ancient woodlands of Rydal Hall to the east, the parkland and lush pasture running down to the sparkling waters of the River Rothay and, to the west, one of the most beautiful of all the lakes, Rydal Water, a limpid pool reflecting in mirror image the precipitous slopes of the fells which cradle it and scattered with tiny rocky islands. (Grasmere lake, which lies just beyond Rydal Water, is clearly visible only from the westernmost end of the garden.) Looming above and around on every side are the fells, dwarfing the scenes below. If one imagines them as a giant clawed hand poised above Patterdale, then Fairfield, rising to 2,864 feet high, would be the back of the hand, from which extend the crooked thumb, Wansfell Pike, and the four fingers of Red Screes, High Pike, Heron Pike and Stone Arthur. Kirkstone Pass, the main route to Ullswater, lay between thumb and first finger, Rydal Mount between second and third, and the cottage at Town End between third and fourth. Facing Rydal Mount was Loughrigg Fell, standing in moated isolation, with its distinctive grey rocky outcrops, almost 2,000 feet high; walking out on to the terrace after tea to watch the sun set and the evening star rise behind its parapets would become a daily ritual for William which never lost its potency to move him.

Eager for an outlet for their pent-up energies and a distraction from their personal sorrows, they flung themselves into home-making. William wisely decided that it was time for a little extravagance. 'We are going to have a *Turkey*!!!! carpet – in the dining-room, and a Brussels in William's study', Dorothy reported in high glee to Catherine Clarkson. 'You stare, and the simplicity of the dear Town End Cottage comes before your eyes, and you are tempted to say, "are they changed, are they setting up for fine Folks?"' Even Mary and Dorothy balked at the idea of buying a Brussels carpet as well, but William had a fancy to make his study smart. With a bookcase, some chairs from Allan Bank, newly painted black, a writing table, new curtains and Sir George Beaumont's pictures on the walls, it looked 'very neat'. Economy was satisfied by purchasing the carpets cheaply in London, through Tom Monkhouse, and the furniture at local sales. The excitement of attending the auctions and bidding for bargains was in itself a tonic to them all. They stayed till the bitter end, walking home by moonlight from Dove Nest proudly carrying their breakable purchases, a decanter and glass and a gilt-framed mirror, while Fanny, their servant, drove a full cart-load home. Though they tried not to get carried away, like most bidders they ended up with far more chairs than they knew what to do with. Dorothy's pleasure in these activities is evident in her racy accounts, very differently written from the tearful outpourings of earlier in the year. Mary benefited too. Dorothy observed that she was looking better and in good spirits, 'the sales were the very thing for her'.

The Wordsworths were able to justify their unusual profligacy by the fact that William had, at last, secured the post he had earmarked as the most suitable for his purposes. Wilkin, the current Distributor of Stamps, had been unable to resume his duties after his stroke and agreed to retire, on the customary understanding that he would receive, as a pension, an annuity for life of £100 from his successor. There was no official salary, but William had been led to believe the annual profits would be between £400 and £500, so he accepted Wilkin's terms. On 27 March the Treasury approved William's appointment, on Lord Lonsdale's nomination, as Distributor of Stamps for Westmorland, Whitehaven and the Penrith area of Cumberland. William signed a personal bond on 26 April for £15,000, forfeitable for malpractice or maladministration, and, with Lord Lonsdale and Sir George Beaumont as his sureties for a further £8,000, he officially assumed his duties. These were not particularly onerous, for the stamps were not postage stamps but sheets of stamped paper, issued by the Treasury, upon which legal documents were written and newspapers printed. The day-to-day business of issuing them and receiving payment was handled by sub-distributors throughout the area.

William was required to act as an intermediary between them and the Treasury, overseeing his subordinates, ensuring that they had an adequate supply of stamped papers and accounting for the money raised to the Board of Stamps. He had to make a quarterly return, which entailed visiting each of his sub-distributors, auditing their accounts and forwarding the receipts to London. Legacy receipts, which often involved large sums of money, had to be made up monthly. The accountancy side of the business could all be safely delegated to a clerk and William was extraordinarily fortunate, right at the outset, in finding John Carter. Competent and entirely trustworthy, he remained in the Wordsworths' employment for forty-three years, becoming such a trusted friend and intimate of the family that he was even appointed executor of their wills. Bizarrely, he combined his Stamp duties with the role of gardener and general handyman at Rydal Mount, as well as acting as an amanuensis for William's poetic output.

William took both his duties and his responsibilities very seriously. Obliged to keep a supply of stamped paper and money at Rydal Mount, he ensured that it was kept locked in a designated chest and that it was never left unattended. If he had to be absent, he made sure that a member of the family was in his place, refusing even to leave Carter in sole charge without prior authority from the Stamp Office. He was equally scrupulous in ensuring that his sub-distributors were as conscientious as himself, taking particular care over their appointment.

The erstwhile poet thus became a government tax collector. While he was able to see the humour in the situation, many of his idealistic young admirers could not. Keats, Byron, Shelley, the rising generation of poets, accused him of being a political turncoat, abandoning his youthful radicalism and becoming a Tory hireling. As Stuart had prophesied, few could see the difference between accepting a government place and a government pension. Even today it is still used as a stick with which to beat his reputation. But what else could he have done? He had a wife and dependent children to support and, however high his poetic calling, he believed it was 'his duty to turn to some meaner employment' to provide for them. That he chose to earn money rather than live on the bounty of politicians or private patrons ought to be a matter for congratulation, not reproach.

Throughout the spring and summer, William was constantly occupied in 'dancing about the Country' in the performance of his new duties. By the middle of September, Dorothy was complaining that he had done nothing else for weeks and had been away from home two-thirds of the time. Fortunately, both she and Mary were too busy to repine, for they were inundated with visitors. In addition to all the Ambleside gentry coming to pay their house-warming visits, there was the usual flood of summer visitors. Among them were many old friends, including Stoddart and his wife, Sharp and Stuart and his eighteen-year-old bride ('more like Father & Daughter than Husband & Wife' was Sara's acerbic comment). Dr Henry Parry, the Inspector of the Stamp Office, stayed several days and turned out to be a perfectly pleasant man, though he confirmed the Wordsworths' worst suspicions, that Wilkin had inflated the value of the Distributorship. Already it looked as though William would clear only £100 a year, after paying

Wilkin's pension and Carter's salary, instead of the £200 or £300 he had expected.

Family visitors were also very much in evidence. Twenty-three-year-old William Crackanthorpe, son of the hated Uncle Christopher, came to stay in July with his sisters. Much to everyone's surprise, the younger generation of 'Cousin Cracken crokes', as Willy called them, proved very likeable. The purpose of the visit was not entirely social, though it did coincide with the Regatta. Crackanthorpe was about to go abroad and was anxious to settle his late father's debts to the Wordsworths, incurred during the years he had acted as their guardian and administrator of their father's estate. As a result of this visit, both Dorothy and William wrote to Richard, urging him to send a statement of the account. For once they got a swift reply, possibly because the debt now amounted to almost £1,000 and most of it was due to Richard personally. A final settlement was reached by the end of the year.

Early in September Elizabeth, the wife of William's cousin Richard Wordsworth of Branthwaite, her son, John, and three daughters came to stay. The Wordsworths had a particular liking and empathy for one of the latter, Mary Peake. She had visited them earlier in the year, when they were still at Grasmere, and had been full of hope and joy because her husband, captain of the Royal Navy frigate *Peacock*, had just received a posting which would enable him to spend several years on shore. Before he could get home, his ship was destroyed in enemy action, and the same cannonball which killed him wounded Mary's fifteen-year-old brother, the same John Wordsworth who now visited Rydal Mount. It could not be anything but a painful visit for all concerned, reviving memories of the death at sea of their own John, but it was a salutary reminder that others had suffered as much, if not more, than themselves. Mary and her siblings stayed a fortnight, but Dorothy, the youngest sister, became a member of the Rydal Mount household till the following summer. Though very backward in her books, she proved to be a steadying influence on Dora, and Dorothy found the two girls far easier to teach than she had ever found her restless niece alone.

The frenetic activity of this first summer at Rydal Mount proved beneficial to them all, but by the beginning of October they were looking forward to 'long evenings and winter's quiet'. The women had comparatively few domestic chores. The house was fully fitted out and, as they were now so much closer to Ambleside, Johnny had returned to Mr Dawes's school. Willy, now three years old, had also begun to attend school; like his sister, he proved to be quick and clever, but not fond of his books. Only Dora and Dorothy were still being taught at home, spending four hours a day in lessons with Sara and the elder Dorothy. The Coleridge boys were regular weekend visitors, but Algernon Montagu's elder brother, Basil, was 'a constant dish with us every evening'. Basil was now almost twenty-one. After leaving school, he had become a midshipman in the navy, but hated every minute of the two years he served at sea. In May, after months of importuning his father, he had obtained his discharge on the grounds of ill-health, leaving 'with an excellent character from his officers, but with scarcely any hope of life'. Having exhausted the goodwill of all the friends and relatives to whose care he had since been dispatched, Basil was sent back to his old lodgings at Ambleside, intending to renew his classical studies under the watchful eye of the Wordsworths. Basil gave his father the impression that he would 'atone' to William for the malicious stories he had spread about the way he had been treated by the poet and his sister as a boy, which may account for his daily visits. If so, either he must have been a consummate actor or he failed, for his letters home reveal that he had nothing but contempt for the Wordsworths and their friends, and preferred the company of the Lloyds.

At the end of November Sara returned to Rydal Mount, after an absence of three months at Stockton. Only a sense of duty to her brother Henry had dragged her away, but her absence made them all realize how much she had become part of the family. Their sufferings had brought them together in a way nothing else could. The two aunts had become fast friends. Sara had been an 'inexpressible comfort . . . to all of us, but to me especially', Dorothy wrote. On their wedding anniversary, William and Mary both wrote to her: 'every year whether fraught with joy or sorrow has brought with it additional cause why I should thank God for my connection with your family', William wrote, ending his letter, 'wishing ardently to have you here again'. Sara herself was miserable at Stockton, declaring that she had caught the '*indifferentism*' which affected everyone in that corner of the world.

Christmas seems to have been an understandably subdued affair. Dorothy took the children to Ambleside, to see Mr Polito's wild beasts and a Punch and Judy show. As it rained, they were obliged to spend the night at Basil's lodgings, an experience he did not relish: 'I contrived to be gracious all the time', he told his stepmother, 'tho' Miss Wordsworth (that is old Dorothy) contrived to fidget most amazingly'.

A few weeks later he had cause to be deeply grateful to Dorothy. Mary Barker, who lived in the half of Greta Hall not occupied by the Southeys and Coleridges, had invited him to stay. He disliked the woman, but he was tired of his lodgings and wanted a change. While there, he suffered a serious relapse, vomiting so much blood that he was not expected to live. Dorothy went immediately to his assistance and, as he was too weak to be moved from his bed, she agreed to stay and help nurse him. Three months later, to her great frustration, she was still there. Basil had recovered. He rode out daily on horseback, but he was, she remarked with pardonable asperity, 'loth to remove from good quarters where he lives *Scot Free*'. The reason Dorothy herself had not gone home was that she had become indispensable to Mary Barker, who was desperately lonely after a quarrel with Southey's womenfolk had left her cut off from their company. Wisely refusing to be drawn into openly taking sides, Dorothy nevertheless felt she could not leave her friend alone. So she stayed on at Keswick, homesick and heart-sore in the knowledge that, by this self-exile, she was denying herself a part in William's most important publishing project to date.

'*Now* above all other time I should have wished to be at home,' she confessed miserably to Catherine Clarkson, 'for William is actually printing 9 books of his long poem.' That William should have decided to publish part of *The Recluse* at this point in his life is astonishing. Everything militated against it. He had been working on it for sixteen years and it was meant to be the goal and summation of his poetic career, yet it was unfinished. He had convinced himself that it would be badly received, because the world was not yet ready for his work. So why did he decide to lay part of it before the public now?

Two possibilities present themselves. First that William felt it necessary to respond to the derogatory comments of the literary critics. Despite the fact that he had not published any poetry for the last six years, they still continued to ridicule the childishness, vulgarity and affectation of his verse. That this was done simply by coupling any passing mention of his name with a contemptuous reference was probably more damaging than a full-frontal assault, because it implied a consensus of critical opinion. The main offender was Francis Jeffrey, who had been nipping at the heels of the 'Lake Poets', as he called them, for the last ten years in the *Edinburgh Review*, but he was not alone. Publishing part of *The Recluse* would prove that William was capable of writing a grand philosophical poem.

There is, however, a key phrase in Dorothy's letter which suggests a more powerful motive than simply a desire to confound the critics. 'We are all most thankful that William has brought his mind to consent to printing so much of this work;' she wrote, 'for the MSS. were in such a state that, if it had pleased Heaven to take him from this world, they would have been almost useless.' The uncertainty of life, the suddenness with which it can be cut off, *is* a new and constantly reiterated theme in the Wordsworth correspondence. It had arisen as a natural consequence of the deaths of Catherine and Thomas, and all the Wordsworths dwelt on it. The fact that both children had appeared well and happy only a few hours before they had been so unexpectedly snatched from life forcibly impressed on the survivors the insecurity of their own existence. There had been no time to prepare for death. William's decision to publish part of *The Recluse* at this point bears all the hallmarks of having been forced upon him by the fear that he might die with the greatest part, in every sense, of his work unpublished.

The surprisingly ambitious nature of William's publication scheme did not stop at *The Recluse*, but embraced a new, two-volume, edition of his shorter poems, and also the hitherto unseen *Peter Bell*, *Benjamin the Waggoner* and *The White Doe*. In other words, before the end of the year William expected to see his complete works in print, leaving only his autobiographical poem (*The Prelude*) to languish in his desk until he had completed *The Recluse*. *The Excursion*, as he now grandly named the nine books of *The Recluse*, was to be published in an edition of 500 copies by Longman in two magnificent quarto volumes, costing the princely sum of two guineas. Appropriately, it was dedicated to the man to whom he owed so much, William, Earl of Lonsdale. Having benefited so much from Lonsdale's goodwill, he was able to acknowledge publicly his own 'high respect and gratitude sincere' in a dedicatory sonnet. Surprisingly, it was here that William came closest to admitting why he now published only part of *The Recluse*.

Gladly would I have waited till my task
Had reached its close; but Life is insecure,
And Hope full oft fallacious as a dream:

After this dedicatory sonnet there followed another of William's combative prefaces. As he himself admitted there, *The Excursion* was a self-contained unit which was perfectly capable of standing alone. Nevertheless, in both the title (*The Excursion, Being a Portion of The Recluse, A Poem*) and at length in the preface William unnecessarily advertised to the world that it was just 'a portion of a poem'. As this 'portion' was just short of 9,000 lines long, his admission was a gift to hostile critics. Conversely, it raised expectations among his well-wishers that the remainder of the poem would follow, putting him under intolerable pressure to do the impossible. Why did he do it? Partly honesty, but partly from a desire to prove that he was a poet of far greater vision, depth and power than his published works had so far indicated. Just as he had done in the preface to *Lyrical Ballads*, he set out a chronology of his composition which was not strictly accurate, but suggested that his whole life and all his poetic labours had been dedicated to the fruition of a single grand plan. He claimed that when he retired to his native mountains, 'with the hope of being enabled to construct a literary Work that might live', he had undertaken a review of his own mind to see how far Nature and Education had qualified him for this purpose. The result of this review was a determination to write *The Recluse*, which he described once again, repeating the usual mantra, as 'a philosophical poem, containing views of Man, Nature, and Society', with a significant addition, '. . . having for its principal subject the sensations and opinions of a poet living in retirement'. *The Prelude*, he now claimed, was a subsidiary outcome of the review, but it was inextricably linked with *The Recluse*, as he explained in a magnificent analogy:

the two Works have the same kind of relation to each other . . . as the ante-chapel has to the body of a gothic church. Continuing this allusion, . . . [the] minor Pieces, which have been long before the Public, when they shall be properly arranged, will be found by the attentive Reader to have such connection with the main Work as may give them claim to be likened to the little cells, oratories, and sepulchral recesses, ordinarily included in those edifices.

Without stooping to debate with his critics, William thus dismissed their accusations that his published poems were trite, silly and puerile. He ended his preface with an earnest for the future, offering an extract 'from the conclusion of the first book of The Recluse . . . as a kind of *Prospectus* of the design and scope of the whole Poem'. Speaking in his own voice as the poet, he invoked the Muse, Urania:

. . . upon me bestow
A gift of genuine insight; that my Song
With star-like virtue in its place may shine,
Shedding benignant influence . . .

Deliberately echoing Milton, he claimed that Paradise was not lost, but could be regained if the 'discerning intellect of Man' were 'wedded to this goodly universe In love and holy passion'. In describing the subjects he would cover in *The Recluse*, William again reverted to Milton, this time actually quoting *Paradise Lost*:

> Of Truth, of Grandeur, Beauty, Love, and Hope,
> And melancholy Fear subdued by Faith;
> Of blessed consolations in distress;
> Of moral strength, and intellectual Power;
> Of joy in widest commonalty spread;
> Of the individual Mind that keeps her own
> Inviolate retirement, subject there
> To Conscience only, and the law supreme
> Of that Intelligence which governs all –
> I sing: – 'fit audience let me find though few!'

Though this '*Prospectus*' applies to the whole of *The Recluse*, it is equally applicable to *The Excursion* alone. Indeed, it is perhaps the best summary of a poem which is impossible to summarize, for *The Excursion* is very much more than the sum of its parts. The plot is easily sketched. The poet accompanies the Wanderer, the 'intellectual Pedlar', on a pedestrian tour of the Lakes. Together they visit the Wanderer's friend, the Solitary, a pessimistic misanthrope living in self-imposed isolation by Blea Tarn, and endeavour to persuade him that his unhappiness is caused by want of faith in religion and in the virtue of humanity. The three men then visit another friend of the Wanderer, the Pastor, who, in a series of oral epitaphs of the dalesmen buried in his village churchyard, gives practical examples of the importance of religion and virtue in daily life. The poem ends with a visit to the Pastor's house, and a sail on the lake, while the Wanderer draws together the threads of their discussions, lamenting the ignorance and degradation brought about by excessive industrialization, advocating a system of national education as the solution and ending with a joyful prayer of thanksgiving to the Almighty.

Such a summary can be nothing more than the sloughed skin of a snake: the bare dry outline which retains the shape, but gives no idea of the colour, vitality and movement of the living creature which has emerged. *The Excursion* is formidably long, often obscure in meaning, and has many a dull moment, but it is one of those rare books which rewards persistence. It improves out of all proportion to the initial struggle and yields new treasures on every reading. The language is sonorous, majestic and hypnotic, carrying the reader irresistibly forward; there are touching stories of human suffering told so tenderly that they cannot fail to move; and above all broods what can only be called the gigantic spirit of Wordsworth, patient, wise, empathic, sympathetic, suffering, yet sustained by faith. This is not the appropriate place for extensive quotation, but two passages, both from the fourth book, *Despondency Corrected*, are fundamental. Not only do they go to the didactic heart of the poem, but also to the core of William's own philosophy, for they are the hard-won result of his personal experience in trying to come to terms with the trials of his own life. Having heard the Solitary's tale of bitter disillusionment and personal loss (not unlike William's own), the Wanderer says:

> One adequate support
> For the calamities of mortal life
> Exists – one only; an assured belief
> That the procession of our fate, howe'er
> Sad or disturbed, is ordered by a Being
> Of infinite benevolence and power;
> Whose everlasting purposes embrace
> All accidents, converting them to good.
> – The darts of anguish *fix* not where the seat
> Of suffering hath been thoroughly fortified
> By acquiescence in the Will supreme
> For time and for eternity.

The second extract is the famous analogy of the child, who puts a shell to his ear and hears the sea from which it came.

> Even such a shell the universe itself
> Is to the ear of Faith; and there are times,
> I doubt not, when to you it doth impart
> Authentic tidings of invisible things;
> Of ebb and flow, and ever-during power;
> And central peace, subsisting at the heart
> Of endless agitation. Here you stand,
> Adore, and worship, when you know it not;
> Pious beyond the intention of your thought;
> Devout above the meaning of your will.
>   ... the Man –
> Who, in this spirit, communes with the Forms
> Of nature, who with understanding heart
> Both knows and loves such objects as excite
> No morbid passions, no disquietude,
> No vengeance, and no hatred – needs must feel
> The joy of that pure principle of love
> So deeply, that, unsatisfied with aught
> Less pure and exquisite, he cannot choose
> But seek for objects of a kindred love
> In fellow-natures and a kindred joy.
>   ... he looks round
> And seeks for good; and finds the good he seeks:

The Excursion was published in August 1814, while the poet was taking his own excursion in Scotland with his wife and sister-in-law. As a gesture of lofty indifference to the fate of his poem, this was somewhat spoilt by the way he rushed straight to a bookshop the moment they reached civilization 'with a sneaking hope that I might hear something about the Excursion'. Not only was there 'not a word' about his own poem, but he had the additional mortification of hearing the bookseller in rhapsodies over a joint publication of Byron's *Lara* and Rogers's *Jacqueline*, which sold faster than copies could be obtained. 'Now dont you think I am quite a hero not to be envious[?]' he inquired, pointing out what a blow this would have been to 'poor me if I had been of the commonly supposed poetic constitution'.

The trip to Scotland had been planned for many months. Mary had long dreamt of making such a tour with her husband, but had always been prevented, first by child-bearing and rearing, then by fear of what might happen if she left her children again. William was determined that she should go this summer, in an effort to restore her health and spirits. His own inclination was to go to London, not just because his book was printing there, but mainly because he longed to see all the festivities in the wake of the Armistice with France. After his disastrous march on Moscow in 1812 and consequent retreat, with enormous losses, from Russia, Bonaparte had suffered a further humiliating defeat at the hands of the Allies at the battle of Leipzig in October 1813. Wellington had then crossed the Pyrenees into France and the Prussians and Russians, advancing from the east, had entered Paris in March 1814. They established a provisional government and, much to the disgust of the Wordsworths, allowed Bonaparte to abdicate on a fat pension and go into exile on Elba. Following the First Peace of Paris, signed on 30 May, Field Marshal Blücher, the Prussian King and his two sons were among the Allies to come to London, where they were showered with honours. As an active member of the war faction, as he called himself, William would have loved to see Bonaparte's conquerors, but he could afford neither the money nor the time to go to London and Scotland, and therefore sacrificed the former for the sake of his wife.

'It is like a dream', Dorothy wrote of this sudden ending to a war which had lasted most of her adult life; ' – peace peace – all in a moment!' One of the immediate personal consequences to the Wordsworths was the arrival at Rydal Mount in June of Eustace Baudouin, newly released from prison and come to pay his respects before returning home to France. It is inconceivable that the Wordsworths made no comment on his visit, so it must have been a significant one, prompting the later destruction of the evidence. Were it not for the fact that Baudouin accompanied Sara on a visit to Southey at Keswick, we would not know that it had taken place. Southey found the young man 'apparently one of the best of these Frenchmen' who had the grace to admit that the war in Spain had been an unjust one, despite his complaint, which greatly amused Southey, that the Spaniards were 'very hard-hearted' towards their conquerors.

The Wordsworths set out on 18 July, armed with a copy of *The Traveller's Guide through Scotland*, presented the day before by John Marshall. They travelled in the old jaunting car which had served William, Dorothy and Coleridge so well on the

Scottish tour of 1803. To begin with, they were quite a large party, for in addition to William, Mary and Sara they had Johnny, who was now a sturdy eleven-year-old, and a friend of the Lloyds, Miss Alms, who had begged a lift home to Carlisle. For William, this third tour of Scotland was a reprise of his earlier ones, with a northern detour after Longtown to Burnfoot, where they were to leave Johnny with the Misses Malcolm until their return to England.

Throughout the seven and a half weeks of the tour, Sara jotted down notes which were intended to form the basis of a journal similar to Dorothy's *Recollections*. Though it was a self-conscious exercise, the notes she made were little more than an *aide-mémoire* and were never worked up into the finished article. Even in this form, Sara's pungent sense of humour and sharply observant eye produced some characteristic vignettes of Scottish life: the 'screaming minister' of the Established Kirk at Lanark, for instance, who screamed 'with his whole might ... & seemed not the least fatigued by it', the mother of seventeen children living at the toll-bar house at Garelochhead 'in the midst of dirt & wretchedness scarcely to be met with in an English cottage', yet wearing 'silver rimmed spectacles', possessing ladylike manners and conversation, and paying £30 a year to educate each of her sons; the disagreeable inn at Luss, where the waiters ran around as if they were cracked in the head, the baker called once every ten days '& the possibility of making bread at home never entered their heads'.

Sara was struck by the contrast between the poverty of the Scots and their innate intelligence and good breeding. 'Men living in such hovels as you would not think good enough for Cattle you will find far more intelligent & expressing themselves much better than any person you can meet with in England who has not had, as I may say, an *university* Education or one as liberal.'

Having completed their tour of the Highlands, the party arrived on 25 August at Edinburgh, where they were immediately drawn into literary circles. They dined out every evening, twice with their friend Mrs Wilson, mother of John, of Elleray, once with Mrs Taylor and, on their final evening, with a new acquaintance, Robert Pearce Gillies. William was particularly drawn to this young man, who was twenty-six years old and seemed to be a version of his younger self. He was a struggling poet who believed that originality was all-important and, failing to achieve this, was subject to overpowering fits of dejection. William befriended Gillies and took him under his wing. He attempted to persuade him that morbidity and peculiarity should never be the chosen material of poetic composition, and urged him to imitate Cowper, who was constitutionally morbid but 'wisely *tried* to help it by looking abroad on nature and society, by endeavouring to do good, and in that pursuit to lose himself'. Before he left Edinburgh, William composed a sonnet to Gillies, assuring him there was 'immortal seed' in his mind, and exhorting him to free himself from the chambers of dejection and trust to his youth, genius and ambition:

> A cheerful life is what the Muses love,
> A soaring spirit is their prime delight.
> *From the dark chambers*
> *of dejection freed, ll.13–14*

The kindly interest William had shown and Gillies's gratitude for his concern would ripen into a friendship that would last many years.

Another poet who was introduced to William at Mrs Wilson's was the remarkable James Hogg, whose life was a romance in itself. 'The Ettrick Shepherd', as he was commonly known, had been snatched from obscurity as a shepherd in his native Ettrick Forest by Walter Scott, who had recognized his poetic gift and published his ballads. He now lived in Edinburgh, where he had found fame as a poet and contributor to the *Edinburgh Review*. William would remain ambivalent about both the man and his work. Soon after meeting Hogg and, as a result, reading his poems for the first time, he described him as 'too illiterate to write in any measure or style that does not savour of balladism', sugaring the pill by adding 'this is much to be regretted; for he is possessed of no ordinary power'. Many years later, he reaffirmed that Hogg 'was undoubtedly a man of original genius, but of coarse manners & low & offensive opinions'. (William was offended by Hogg's 'self-conceit' in pronouncing judgements on classical literature about which he knew nothing, but was also not best pleased to see himself parodied by Hogg in the *Poetic Mirror*.) Hogg himself was overjoyed to meet William. He escorted him on his first emotional visit to the River Yarrow and listened to his conversation 'as to a superior being, far exalted above the common walks of life. His sentiments seemed just, and his language, though perhaps a little pompous, was pure, sentient, and expressive.'

The tour had been a great success. It had provided material for new poetry, but this was almost incidental: 'dearest Mary is much improved by her journey', Sara wrote a fortnight after they set out; 'she truly enjoys herself; & William is happy that the journey has accomplished this his chief aim'. They returned to Rydal Mount on 9 September to find that Dorothy and the children were well and nothing of note had occurred in their absence. There was, however, a curious coda to the Scottish tour. James Hogg had anticipated them by a couple of days and, while he awaited their arrival, Dorothy had made an immediate conquest of him by her kindness and conversation, 'a true mental treat'. Hogg became a regular visitor during his stay in the Lakes. One evening a comet blazed across the sky, creating a lingering trail of light that arched from horizon to horizon. According to Hogg, there was a large party of literary gentlemen at Rydal Mount that night, including de Quincey, and the poets, Wilson, Lloyd and himself. On being told of the phenomenon, they all went out on to the terrace in front of the house to observe it, and Dorothy, who was walking arm in arm with Hogg, expressed the fear that it might prove an ominous portent. Hogg gallantly declared that it was nothing more nor less than a triumphal arch, raised in honour of the meeting of the poets. Wilson was gratified and laughed, but William, who had overheard the remark, apparently turned on his heel and disdainfully asked de Quincey, 'Poets? Poets? – What does the fellow mean? – where are they?' 'Who could forgive this?' Hogg asked, when he published the story in 1832; 'for my part, I never can, and never will!' Apocryphal as William's words probably are – even Hogg admitted he did not hear them personally – it is indicative of William's reputation for egotism that they were, and are, widely believed to be true.

When he left Rydal, Hogg took with him a copy of William's latest verses, *Yarrow Visited*, which William had agreed he could publish in an anthology intended to include a poem from every living author in Britain. 'Nothing but a wish to show to Mr Hogg that my inclination towards him, and his proposed work were favourable, could have induced me to part with it in that state', he wrote to Gillies in November, as he substituted a virtual rewrite for the original poem. Even then, he was still unhappy with it.

The first copies of *The Excursion* had been released during the second week in August. Robinson actually stole out of the theatre to see an early copy and, after hastily scanning the preface and a few extracts, proffered a hesitant, but all too accurate, verdict.

It is a poem of formidable size, and I fear too mystical to be popular. But it will, however, put an end to the sneers of those who consider him or affect to consider him as a puerile writer [who] attempts only little things. But it will draw on him the imputation of dullness possibly. Still it will, I trust, strengthen the zeal of his few friends.

The first review was by Hazlitt, who carried off Lamb's complimentary copy and rushed into print on 21 August. It was a beautifully written, clever and discerning critique, which both eulogized and as heartily damned. 'In power of intellect, in lofty conception, in the depth of feeling, at once simple, and sublime, which pervades every part of it, and which gives to every object an almost preternatural and preterhuman interest, this work has seldom been surpassed', it began. Having defined *The Excursion* (inadequately) as 'a philosophical pastoral poem ... a scholastic romance', Hazlitt launched a thinly veiled attack on the egotism of its poet, who could not paint a scene, delineate a character or tell a story, either ordinary or remarkable, without clothing it in his own thoughts, recollections or imagination.

It is less a poem on the country than on the love of the country. It is not so much a description of natural objects as of the feelings associated with them; not an account of the manners of rural life, but the result of the poet's reflections on it. He does not present the reader with a lively succession of images or incidents, but paints the outgoings of his own heart, the shapings of his own fancy. He may be said to create his own materials; his thoughts are his real subjects.

Though some would feel that this is William's greatest attribute, for Hazlitt it was detrimental to the poetic process: 'The image is lost in the sentiment, as sound in the multiplication of echoes.' 'An intense intellectual egotism swallows up everything', he complained. Seizing upon the preface, Hazlitt cleverly turned the argument against William in a way that would be repeated by future reviewers. The 'poet living in retirement', far from being a seer who could view the world dispassionately, was his own worst enemy. 'The power of his mind preys upon itself. It is as if there were nothing but himself and the universe. He lives in the busy solitude of his own heart; in the deep silence of thought. His imagination lends life and feeling only to the "bare trees and mountain bare," peoples the viewless tracts of air, and converses with the silent clouds.'

Hazlitt's review was bad enough, but Jeffrey's in the *Edinburgh Review* would have destroyed a lesser man than William. Jeffrey adopted an air of amused contempt, as if he were a rather superior and sardonic teacher reproving a foolish child. The infamous opening sentence, 'This will never do.', launched thirty pages of criticism of the poet, his 'system' and his poem, which is all the more devastating for making the reader smile guiltily in recognizing the undoubted truths behind the malice. William's 'imprudent candour' about *The Recluse* in the preface was a gift to Jeffrey. 'What Mr Wordsworth's ideas of length are, we have no means of accurately judging; but we cannot help suspecting that they are liberal, to a degree that will alarm the weakness of most modern readers.' If the 9,000 lines of *The Excursion* covered a period of precisely three days, Jeffrey argued, tongue-in-cheek, 'by the use of a very powerful *calculus*, some estimate may be formed of the probable extent of the entire biography'. More seriously, he too attacked 'the poet in retirement' as being, not above society, but out of touch with it.

The Excursion, Jeffrey declared, was 'a tissue of moral and devotional ravings' which displayed the author's talent for 'enveloping a plain and trite observation in all the mock majesty of solemn verbosity'; it might contain 'salutary truths' but these were inculcated 'at far greater length, and with more repetitions, than in any ten volumes of sermons that we ever perused'. Where the moral was not trite, it was so obscurely phrased that 'if our readers can form the slightest guess at its meaning, we must give them credit for a sagacity to which we have no pretension'.

The odd thing about this review is that, despite the relentlessly hostile tone, it is clear to the dispassionate reader that Jeffrey was not entirely convinced by his own arguments. By his extensive quotation from *The Excursion*, Jeffrey inadvertently undermined his own stance. The influential blue stocking and evangelical Hannah More cannot have been alone in deciding that she would purchase the book even though she had never seen the poem or any other review except Jeffrey's.

Most of the later reviews were paler versions of the two first trend-setters. Both the reviewer in the *British Critic* and James Montgomery, who wrote an otherwise enthusiastic piece in the *Eclectic Review*, raised the question of the religious ortho-doxy of the poem. Depending on one's viewpoint, this is either the greatest strength or the greatest weakness of *The Excursion*. The poem is saturated with the spirit of religion – but quite which religion is never made explicit. It is therefore either ecumenical, embracing all Christian sects (and some paganism and pantheism besides), or doctrinally unsound. Robinson's perceptive comment about William himself, that his religion 'would not satisfy either a religionist or a sceptic', was equally applicable to his great poem.

William was bitterly disappointed by the critical reception of his great poem, but, once again, he tried to hide the hurt behind a cloak of dignified indifference. Fortunately, he had the unwavering support not only of 'the Concern', his family circle, but also a much wider group of devotees, who were growing in number and importance. All these converts were themselves keen proselytizers, spreading the word among their friends and publicly reading William's poetry aloud at every opportunity, so, like the ripples from a stone flung in a pool, his work was gradually reaching a wider audience. Neither Lamb nor Southey had been uncritical in the past, but both were now ardent in his defence. Lamb thought *The Excursion* 'the best of Books'. Southey openly declared his 'full conviction that posterity will rank [Wordsworth] with Milton', and ridiculed Jeffrey's claim to have written a '*crushing review*'. Though he had just published his own *Roderick* and had every reason to fear the same treatment, Southey wrote to Hogg, '*He* crush the *Excursion*!!! Tell him that he might as easily crush Skiddaw.' Robinson and the Beaumonts were particularly active. Through them, and others like them, the Wordsworths were informed of favourable opinions: the Bishop of London was 'in raptures', Sergeant Rough thought there had been nothing to equal it since Milton and young Tom Clarkson had stayed up all night to read it. Particularly gratifying were the unsolicited letters which now began to arrive from 'ordinary' people who had no contact with the Wordsworth circle. Even Uncle William Cookson was moved to write a sincere appreciation.

There was one opinion, however, which mattered more than any other to William, and from that quarter there was a deafening silence. It was not until some eight months after the publication of *The Excursion* that Coleridge broke his silence. Even then, it was only to make a passing remark in a letter to Lady Beaumont that he did not think *The Excursion* equal to *The Prelude*, followed by perhaps the most cutting criticism he could make of what was, after all, the second book of William's great philosophical poem.

I have sometimes fancied, that having by the conjoint operation of his own experiences, feelings, and reason *himself* convinced *himself* of Truths, which the generality of persons have either taken for granted from their Infancy, or at least adopted in early life, he has attached all their own depth and weight to doctrines and words, which come almost as Truisms or Common-place to others.

However hurtful this disclosure must have been, William managed to keep his feelings in check, writing a pleasant if somewhat formal letter directly to his old friend, admitting perplexity at Coleridge's '*comparative* censure'. 'One of my principal aims in the Exn: has been to put the commonplace truths, of the human affections especially, in an interesting point of view; and rather to remind men of their knowledge, as it lurks inoperative and unvalued in their own minds, than to attempt to convey recondite or refined truths.'

Whatever the original schematic for *The Recluse* had been, it was certainly not this, as Coleridge rightly reminded him. Putting commonplace truths in an interesting point of view was all very well for the *Poems, in Two Volumes*, but *The Recluse* was to have been 'the *first* and *only* true Phil[osophical] Poem in existence'. It should have been a profound insight into the whole truth, bottomed in human nature, not an assertion of mere commonplace truths. The greatest irony of the entire history of *The Recluse* is that it was only now, when William had spent sixteen years of his life working on the poem, and a portion of it was irrevocably in the public demesne, that Coleridge at last produced the coherent, cogent and detailed plan for which William had so long and so fruitlessly begged him. As a description of the poem that never was (or could have been), it is fascinating. As an indication of how far apart the minds, as well as the hearts, of the two men now were, it is heartbreaking.

I supposed you first to have meditated the faculties of Man in the abstract, in their correspondence with his Sphere of action, and first, in the Feeling, Touch, and Taste, then in the Eye, & last in the Ear, to have laid a solid and immoveable foundation for the Edifice by removing the sandy Sophisms of Locke, and the Mechanic Dogmatists, and demonstrating that the Senses were living growths and developements [*sic*] of the Mind & Spirit in a much juster as well as higher sense, than the mind can be said to be formed by the Senses –. Next, I understood that you would take the Human Race in the concrete, have exploded the absurd notion of Pope's Essay on Man, Darwin, and all the countless Believers – even (strange to say) among Xtians of Man's having progressed from an Ouran Outang state – so contrary to all History, to all Religion, nay, to all Possibility – to have affirmed a Fall in some sense, as a fact, the possibility of which cannot be understood from the nature of the Will, but the reality of which is attested by Experience & Conscience – Fallen men contemplated in the different ages of the World, and in the different states – Savage – Barbarous – Civilized – the lonely Cot, or Borderer's Wigwam – the Village – the Manufacturing Town – Sea-port – City – Universities – and not disguising the sore evils, under which the whole Creation groans, to point out however a manifest Scheme of Redemption from this Slavery, of Reconciliation from this Enmity with Nature – what are the Obstacles, the *Antichrist* that must be & already is – and to conclude by a grand didactic swell on the necessary identity of a true Philosophy with true Religion, agreeing in the results and differing only as the analytic and synthetic process, as discursive from intuitive, the former chiefly useful as perfecting the latter – in short, the necessity of a general revolution in the modes of developing & disciplining the human mind by the substitution of Life, and Intelligence (considered in it's [*sic*] different powers from the Plant up to that state in which the difference of Degree becomes a new kind (man, self-consciousness) but yet not by essential opposition) for the philosophy of mechanism which in every thing that is most worthy of the human Intellect strikes *Death*, and cheats itself by mistaking clear Images for distinct conceptions, and which idly demands Conceptions where Intuitions alone are possible or adequate to the majesty of Truth. – In short, Facts elevated into Theory – Theory into Laws – & Laws into living & intelligent Powers – true Idealism necessarily perfecting itself in Realism, & Realism refining itself into Idealism. – Such or something like this was the Plan, I had supposed that you were engaged on –.

Though Coleridge said nothing about *The Excursion* itself, only attacking what it was not, his criticism was absolutely devastating. It cut the ground from under William's feet as a man, as a philosopher and as a poet. Quite simply, it told him that he had failed in the most important work of his life. And reading this critique, this prospectus for a poem of which a third was already written, William must have been forced to accept his failure. If he responded, or made any sort of protest, the letter has been lost. But it was the end of the dream which had motivated almost the whole of his literary life. *The Recluse*, whose future completion he had so confidently announced a few months earlier in his preface to *The Excursion*, was quietly abandoned.

17. *Increasing Influence*

Throughout the autumn and winter of 1814 William was hard at work preparing a new edition of his shorter poems for the press. As so often happened when revising his work, he was inspired to compose at least one wholly new poem. Unusually for him, its origins were purely literary, for it was a reworking of the classical legend of Laodamia, cribbed from Virgil's *Aeneid*. It was in some ways an unfortunate departure, because it encouraged William to go reading and hunting through his old books in the hope of further inspiration, 'for no *good purpose*', as his wife noted. As usual, also, he made himself ill with the stress, suffering night sweats and a painful boil between his thumb and forefinger, which infected his arm to his armpit and crippled his right hand.

The burden of preparing the text for the printers now fell entirely on Mary. Dorothy and Sara had gone on a long visit to Hindwell in the middle of September, expecting to be back around Christmas. Much to Mary's distress, Tom had bought an estate in Wales, so it was obvious he did not contemplate a return to the Lakes; his brother-in-law John Monkhouse, with whom he was in partnership, had also established himself on a farm of his own, the Stow, twelve miles south of Hindwell, looking over the flat Wye valley to the Black Mountains beyond. Dorothy was delighted with her first visit to Hindwell; 'it is a thousand times more beautiful than she expected & as she has become a <u>compleat</u> horsewoman since she came', Mary Hutchinson wrote. 'I hope she will see every thing that is worth seeing before she leaves us.'

It was not to be. At the beginning of December Dorothy received a carefully written note from William which opened with the words, 'At the sight of this short Letter do not be alarmed'. Little Willy had been seriously ill with what Scambler diagnosed as inflammatory croup and her presence was needed urgently at home.

Dorothy was back at Rydal Mount by 15 December, and was thrown straight into nursing duties, for Dora too was ill, and neither child recovered as quickly as they had hoped. 'Our own anxieties have been dreadful,' William wrote to Catherine Clarkson on New Year's Eve,

and I seem to possess all my children in trembling, the youngest in particular after so narrow an escape. The ordinary health of them all is excellent, but they are all subject occasionally as all my Father's family were to bad Catarrhs. Wm is a charming Boy; beautiful and animated; I wish you could see him, he is the delight of my eyes; pray heaven that I may not have to say with Ben Jonson, 'My sin was too much hope of thee loved Boy.'

The same could not be said of Johnny, who was still at Mr Dawes's school and 'for book-attainments the slowest Child almost I ever knew', according to his father. Dora was quick and clever, but as careless and inattentive as ever, despite the fact that she had been attending a school at Ambleside since April. William said she knew no French and only half the Latin she had learned the previous winter. 'I have not the least hope that any regular progress, (let what pains there may be taken with D.) will be made', her mother wrote despairingly, 'until her own sense and pride bring her to it – her temper is so much against her improvement.'

William had hoped that the new edition of *Poems* would be ready for publication by the beginning of January, but he was to be disappointed. The printing proved slower than expected, but the main cause of delay was his decision to include an engraving as the frontispiece to each volume. The other cause was that William belatedly decided he would have to include a preface to the *Poems*. For once, a preface was essential to explain the innovatory system under which William classified his poems. He had introduced a rudimentary categorization in 1807, dependent on subject matter, but now he implemented a far more complex system. What he wanted to do was to break away from the idea of chronological progression. He would blend together all his poems, irrespective of their dates of composition or publication, and then redivide the whole body into groupings dictated principally by their subject matter. The basic scheme had been outlined to Coleridge in 1809 and consisted of allocating the poems into categories roughly equating to the periods of human life. By 1812, when William expounded his theory to Robinson, it had become more complicated and involved a psychological approach: the poems would also be arranged 'with some reference either to the fancy, imagination, reflection or mere feeling contained in them'. That the two methods of classification were incompatible did not matter to William, but, as Robinson admitted to his diary, it made explanation and justification difficult.

Nevertheless, in his preface, William tried to explain as logically as he could. Six powers were requisite for writing poetry: observation and description, sensibility, reflection, imagination and fancy, invention and, finally, judgement. There were also six types of poetry: narrative, dramatic, lyrical, 'the Idyllium', didactic and philosophical satire. It therefore followed that 'poems, apparently miscellaneous, may with propriety be arranged either with reference to the powers of mind *predominant* in the production of them; or to the mould in which they are cast; or, lastly, to the subjects to which they relate'. As far as possible, he also tried to place the poems in order of time, beginning with Childhood, and ending with Old Age, Death and Immortality. The result was a grouping of poems under such headings as 'Poems referring to the Period of Childhood', 'Poems Founded on the Affections', 'Poems of the Fancy', 'Poems of the Imagination' and 'Poems proceeding from Sentiment and Reflection'. 'My guiding wish', William declared in the preface, 'was, that the small pieces of which these volumes consist, thus discriminated, might be regarded under a two-fold view; as composing an entire work within themselves, and as adjuncts to the philosophical Poem, "The Recluse."'

The problem with the new arrangement was that it was almost entirely subjective. And as William not infrequently moved poems from one category to another in future editions, it would appear that it was neither obvious nor definitive, even to the author himself. Though one might not wish to go as far as the critic in the *Monthly Review*, who declared the system 'a pompous classification of trifles', it is impossible not to feel some sympathy with his bewilderment: 'in the present volumes we have a poem belonging to the class of "Fancy", with no possible distinguishing characteristic from another in the class of "Imagination"; the "Affections" lay claim to a third, which might as well have been ranked under the head of "Sentiment and Reflection"'.

William's classification of his poems might have exposed him to ridicule, but it was hardly contentious. Unfortunately, once again he could not leave it at that, but felt obliged to hit back at his critics, and more specifically at one critic in particular. Francis Jeffrey's review of *The Excursion* had been the final straw. Not only was it likely to damage the sales of the book, but also it threatened to undermine William's poetic reputation permanently. William had written to Stuart, asking him to print in the *Courier* a series of letters from de Quincey 'upon the subject of the stupidities, the ignorance, and the dishonesties of the Edinburgh Review; and principally as relates to myself, whom, perhaps you know, the Editor has long honored with his abuse'.

Perhaps because Stuart declined, William decided to retaliate himself, in an 'Essay, Supplementary to the Preface'. Written in magisterial prose, it was a covert attack on all his critics. The Unitarians, though not named, were implicitly taken to task as being 'men who read from religious or moral inclinations'. They were therefore 'prone to over-rate the Authors by whom those truths are expressed and enforced' and could not enjoy poetry which seemed to them to endorse doctrinal errors; 'at all seasons, they are under temptation to supply by the heat with which they defend their tenets, the animation which is wanting to the constitution of the religion itself'. The real enemies of poets of original imagination, however, were 'critics too petulant to be passive to a genuine poet, and too feeble to grapple with him . . . men of palsied imaginations and indurated hearts . . . judges, whose censure is auspicious, and whose praise ominous!' Citing a long list of major poets whose works had not achieved immediate popularity, such as Spenser, Shakespeare and Milton, he compared them with their ephemeral contemporaries, who had blazed into fame but then left scarcely a trace behind them. Naturally, William placed himself in the former category. 'Grand thoughts', he wrote, '. . . as they are most naturally and most fitly conceived in solitude, so can they not be brought forth in the midst of plaudits, without some violation of their sanctity.' He ended by assuring his readers that he would immediately destroy 'the contents of these Volumes, and the Work to which they are subsidiary', were he not convinced that they revealed something of the 'Vision and the Faculty divine'.

The preface and the essay were remarkably free from bitterness, but as a defence of William's poetry they were a pointless exercise. His enthusiasts did not need one and his critics could not be converted by one. Indeed, it played into the latter's hands by inviting a response to it, instead of to the poetry. The *Quarterly Review* was comparatively polite.

For a writer to protest that he *prides* himself upon the disapprobation of his contemporaries, and considers it as an evidence of the originality of his genius, and an earnest of the esteem in which he will be held by succeeding generations, is whimsical enough, to say the least of it   He should remember, moreover, that the public, and those who profess to be the organs of the public voice in these matters, have at least as much right to dislike *his* poetical taste, as he has to dislike *theirs*.

The *Monthly Review* was less restrained, adopting a note of facetious contempt worthy of Jeffrey himself.

We are so thoroughly overwhelmed by the high and mighty tone of this author's prose, that we really must have immediate recourse to his verse, in order to get rid of the painful humiliation and sense of inferiority which he inflicts on his readers. There, (Dieu merci;) we are comforted by silliness instead of system; by want of harmony instead of abundance of pride; by downright vacancy instead of grandeur and presumption.

By the end of February the two volumes were nearly through the press and the Wordsworths believed it would be possible to publish by the second week in March. At the same time, however, the first proof sheets were beginning to arrive for *The White Doe of Rylstone*. It had originally been William's intention to go to London in April to bargain with his publisher about this book in person and then see it through the press. When or how he changed his mind is not clear, but it was a deeply significant decision. Longman would, as usual, be the publisher of the poem, but, for the first time, it would be printed by James Ballantyne of Edinburgh, who was first and foremost the printer of Walter Scott's immensely popular ballads. To have Ballantyne's name on the title-page of *The White Doe* was therefore to identify with a distinctive and highly successful genre of book-production. It was William's one act of cynical and naked literary ambition: perhaps the Ballantyne name might do for *The White Doe* what his own could not and make his poem sell like Scott's. 'Never more would I have a Book printed in London –', Dorothy declared. 'Ballantyne goes on like Buonaparte in his march to Paris, and the White Doe will, if they do not make haste in London, beat the Poems.'

The reference to Bonaparte was portentous. On 25 February he had escaped from Elba and the spectre of war loomed large over Europe once more. The Wordsworths had more reason than most to be deeply concerned at this unexpected turn of events. The previous autumn, the Vallons had announced that a marriage treaty was under discussion between Caroline, then twenty-one, and Eustace Baudouin's brother, Jean Baptiste, a thirty-three-year-old government officer. Caroline needed her father's permission to marry and the settlement of an annuity upon her in order to do so. William willingly consented, but only on the understanding that the marriage would bring an increase of income to the Vallons. Annette and Caroline were anxious that there should be a representative of the Wordsworth family at the wedding and Dorothy was the obvious candidate. Dorothy herself was equally keen to go.

As she clearly could not travel so far unaccompanied, it was arranged that either Joanna or Sara Hutchinson would go with her, and the wedding was tentatively fixed for April 1815. They could not have chosen a worse time. Bonaparte's resurrection put an end to all their plans. 'For the sake of our Friends I am truly distressed', Dorothy wrote as the news filtered slowly through to Rydal.

The Wordsworths were in a fever of anxiety. The next letters from Annette and Caroline contained high drama. They were written on the eve of Bonaparte's entry into Paris. Eustace Baudouin had set off to join the royalist forces, but his old loyalty to the emperor had overcome his new to the king and he returned without striking a blow. As Annette finished her letter at midnight, she heard troops advancing which she guessed were the vanguard of Bonaparte's army. The last words of her letter were, 'Good God what is to become of us?'

At the beginning of May William and Mary set off on the long-projected visit to London, leaving Dorothy in charge of the children and the Stamp office. They were accompanied by Hartley Coleridge, who was now eighteen and about to take up a place at Merton College, Oxford. This was something of a personal triumph for William and Southey, because it was almost entirely due to their efforts that Hartley had secured a place at university. One by one they had approached Coleridge's relations and old friends for funds. Hartley's Coleridge uncles offered £40 a year, Lady Beaumont £30, Poole £10 and Cottle £5. With the assistance of a college office, worth £50 annually, it was hoped that Hartley would do well, but William was not confident: 'he is too much inclined to the eccentric'. Was William aware of the irony, bearing in mind his own youthful rebellion, as he now lectured his friend's son just as his own uncles had once lectured him? 'I have done all in my power to impress upon H.'s mind the necessity of not trusting vaguely to his talents, and to an irregular sort of knowledge, however considerable it may be, in some particulars; and of applying himself zealously and perseveringly to those studies which the University points out to him', he told Poole. 'His prime object ought to be to gain an independence.'

The Wordsworths left Hartley at Oxford in the care of his cousin, William Hart Coleridge, on 6 May, then travelled on to London, where they were to rendezvous with Sara. William usually stayed with the Beaumonts or Montagus, but Mary could not face all the hectic socializing which this inevitably involved, so they went into private lodgings at 24 Edward Street, Cavendish Square. This was fortunate, because the guards on the coach lost most of their luggage and they were stranded in town at a weekend without any appropriate clothes.

Lady Beaumont had expressed the hope that they would meet 'in a quiet way', knowing large parties did not suit Mary, but for William this London visit was as busy as ever. There were several dinners at the Beaumonts' and it was through them that William had his first introduction to William Wilberforce, the anti-slavery campaigner and friend of his Uncle William Cookson. The two men were in instant sympathy on at least one issue which dominated home politics. They were both in favour of the Corn Laws, which protected the market of English farmers by prohibiting the importation of foreign corn, if the price at home was less than 80s a quarter. With hindsight, it seems obvious that such a measure would cause immense hardship among the poor by keeping the price of bread artificially high at a time of falling wages and rising unemployment. At this time, however, when the new laws were being introduced, the issue was by no means clear-cut. Having witnessed bread riots in revolutionary France, William was all too well aware of the dangers of an inadequate supply. He was therefore convinced that, without some form of protectionism, no native corn would be grown: unless farmers were assured of a decent return on their crops they could not afford to pay their rents, which had risen 'unnaturally' in recent years. If Britain became reliant on foreign imports, then corn would become insupportably dear and perhaps could not be got at all. Conversely, with protection in place, once the price had reached the ceiling where foreign imports would be allowed, the resulting influx would immediately and inevitably drive down the cost of corn and bread. 'The advocates for the Corn Laws are in fact the friends of the poor', he declared, and, having read one of Wilberforce's speeches in favour of the Bill, it was 'almost word for word what I had said by our fireside before'. Like Wilberforce, William had one serious reservation: that the ceiling price had been fixed too high. So they had much to talk about on their first meeting, which turned out to be a long one, and Wilberforce was 'much pleased' with his new acquaintance.

At both the Lambs' and Robinson's, the Wordsworths attended many small, informal gatherings and were introduced to a number of young men who counted themselves among William's small but growing band of devotees. These young men were the seed-corn of William's future reputation, for they would all achieve eminence in their chosen fields, and possess power and influence which they would exert on his behalf. They included Thomas Alsager, a musician and scholar who wrote for *The Times*, Thomas Noon Talfourd, a fledgling writer and barrister, and the unfortunately named Barron Field, also a barrister, who, rather touchingly, showed the Wordsworths his copy of the *Poems*, which he had interleaved with his own handwritten transcripts of William's unpublished poems, copied from Lamb's manuscripts.

One person who was deliberately excluded from these gatherings was Hazlitt. William had not been in his company voluntarily since Hazlitt's escapade in the

Lakes in 1803, but the key factor was his review of *The Excursion*. Hazlitt himself expected gratitude for what he considered a laudatory piece; when William did not visit him to proffer thanks, he was deeply offended. For William, Hazlitt's sneering remarks about, and abuse of, the natives of the Lakes in his review had been a forcible reminder of the whole degrading episode, which had caused him so much embarrassment. Unfortunately, Hazlitt's 'acid feelings' were roused by what he regarded as this public and deliberate snub, and William would bear the consequences for years to come. Hazlitt had never missed an opportunity to snipe at William's politics. Now he would turn a stream of vitriolic and belittling comment on his poetry as well, and it would have a corrosive effect on public opinion. Even while William was in London, he launched the attack by publishing an article in the *Examiner* on 11 June which honoured Milton as a consistent patriot and disparaged William as the author of 'paltry sonnets upon the royal fortitude'.

Leigh Hunt, the editor of the *Examiner*, disclaimed the article when William called on him the day it was published, but his attitude towards the poet was always what one mutual friend aptly described as 'weathercock'. The two men had never met before but in 1811 Hunt had satirized William in his *Feast of Poets*, having him driven from the feast for 'gath'ring the refuse that others reject'. After the publication of *The Excursion*, Hunt privately retracted his opinion, and when William learned from Henry Brougham that Hunt admitted 'valuing' his poetry, he sent him a complimentary copy of *Poems*. Thanking him for it in a letter written on 28 May, Hunt declared himself 'one of the most ardent of your general admirers'. When they met again on 13 June, he paid William 'the highest compliments' and told him that 'as he grew wiser & got older he found his respect for his powers & enthusiasm for his genius encrease'. In a facetious account of his distinguished visitor, written many years later, Hunt described the poet as having a dignified manner, 'a deep and roughish but not unpleasing voice, and an exalted mode of speaking'. He noted William's habit of keeping his left hand tucked into the bosom of his waistcoat while he sat, 'dealing forth his eloquent but hardly catholic judgments'. Though Hunt gently mocked William's manners and opinions, he was mesmerized by his eyes: 'certainly I never beheld eyes that looked so inspired or supernatural', he wrote. 'They were like fires half burning, half smouldering, with a sort of acrid fixture of regard, and seated at the further end of two caverns. One might imagine Ezekial or Isaiah to have had such eyes.'

Another new acquaintance of this London visit who was also impressed by William's physical appearance was Benjamin Robert Haydon. A twenty-nine-year-old artist who famously quarrelled with almost everyone he met, he shared with William an exalted sense of his vocation. Unfashionably, and much to the detriment of his purse as well as his career, Haydon painted huge historical canvases in which he struggled for anatomical accuracy. He had been an admirer of William's poetry for many years and had written to him as an eighteen-year-old student to praise his 'sublime, enthusiastic hymn' and assure him 'if you never write again, this will immortalize you'. The two men met, possibly not for the first time, at one of William's literary breakfasts, where Haydon spent a 'delightful two hours'.

Three weeks later William returned to Haydon's studio to sit for the artist. Haydon did not paint a picture, however, but took a 'life mask', a plaster cast of William's face. It was an uncomfortable, lengthy and undignified process, but as Haydon wrote in his diary, 'He bore it like a philosopher.' John Scott, who was to meet William at breakfast, arrived while the plaster was still in place, so his head was wrapped in cloth and straws were sticking out of his nostrils to enable him to breathe. Haydon invited Scott 'as a curiosity to take a peep, that he might say the first sight he ever had of so great a poet was such a singular one as this'. William was sitting, in Haydon's dressing gown, 'with his hands folded, sedate, steady, & solemn ... there he sat innocent & unconscious of our plot against his dignity, unable to see or to speak, with all the mysterious silence of a spirit'. When it was all over, he came into breakfast 'with his usual cheerfulness, and delighted & awed us by his illustrations & bursts of inspiration'.

John Scott's enthusiasm for William's poetry was new and important. He too was young and influential, for, at the age of thirty-two, he was already editor of the *Champion*. He had been what William called 'a desperate Enemy of mine', but after reading *The Excursion* he had undergone a Damascene conversion. Only a fortnight after his first meeting with William, he published a review of the new edition of *Poems* and *The White Doe* which he had personally written for the *Champion*. It was a significant moment, for Scott was a poacher turned gamekeeper and was determined to recruit an audience for William's poetry.

When William left London, on or about 19 June, he could do so secure in the conviction that he had indeed found 'fit audience ... though few' for his poetry. He had been introduced to a whole new range of people, principally young men, who were fervent in their admiration. (Two of them, Talfourd and Haydon, would even name their sons after him.) He had won over two more editors of influential journals, Hunt and, more particularly, Scott, to add to the faithful Stuart. The reviewers might, and would, continue to pour scorn on him, but now William had conclusive evidence to prove that his poems were valued outside the tight-knit loyal band of relatives and friends.

Before the Wordsworths left London, William's latest book, *The White Doe of Ryl-stone, or The Fate of the Nortons*, was published by Longman. This time there was no preface to aggravate the critics, only an uncontentious introductory sonnet on the sacred power of imagination. There were, however, a large number of notes to the text, rooting it in its historic, geographic and balladic setting. The reviews trickled out over the next six months and were a mixed bag. Hot on the heels of Scott's praise in the *Champion* came a similar review in the *New British Lady's Magazine*, which began by pointing out that it seemed 'strange that the works of the author now before us should have met with such unmerited obloquy'. Declaring *The White Doe* 'almost entirely free' from all William's 'peculiarities', the critic opined, 'we think [it] will be perused by all classes, by all poetical sects, with a pleasure that experiences no drawback by the insertion of passages for which the reader's mind is not prepared'. The review ended on a curiously humble note entirely alien to all William's previous critics. Only an imperfect sketch of the poem had been given, partly from want of room, and partly (with unfeigned diffidence we say it) from incapacity to estimate worthily a man of Mr Wordsworth's mind. This feeling is, we are happy to say, becoming more general; and although perhaps the poem now before us will not contribute to raise him in the admiration of his friends, we doubt whether it will not render him more popular.

Instead of returning home after their six weeks' residence in London, William, Mary and Sara travelled by coach to Bury, to pay a visit to their friends the Clarksons. While they were there, the stunning news of Bonaparte's defeat at Waterloo on 18 June was announced, followed shortly afterwards by that of his abdication and recapture. A placard on the Ambleside coach bearing the slogan 'Great News. *Abdication of Buonaparte*' brought the first tidings of this event to Rydal. It revived all Dorothy's hopes of going to France for Caroline's wedding, and Annette, writing in great joy after the return of Louis XVIII, urged her to come immediately, saying all was safe and quiet. Nevertheless, Dorothy demurred, preferring to wait until she could be certain that peace and stability had been re-established. A proposal that Caroline should come over also foundered, as they could find no one to escort her to England or to whom they could 'with propriety' entrust her once she arrived in London.

On 21 August there was a huge bonfire on the top of Skiddaw to celebrate the victory at Waterloo. William, Mary, Dorothy and Johnny went over to Keswick to join Southey, his wife and children, and Miss Barker, who were the instigators of the event. Together with a huge party of neighbours, they made their way up the mountain. They roasted beef and boiled plum puddings on the bonfire and drank hot rum punch – until William, who was notoriously clumsy, tripped over the kettle and spilt all the boiling water. The irrepressible Southey immediately set about exposing the culprit and punished him by singing a parody, which all the party joined in, "Twas *you* that kicked the kettle down! 'Twas you, Sir, you!' They sang 'God save the King' round the bonfire, fired cannons at every toast and rolled blazing balls of tow and turpentine down the steep side of the mountain. 'The effect was grand beyond imagination', Southey enthused. 'We formed a huge circle round the most intense light, and behind us was an immeasurable arch of the most intense darkness, for our bonfire fairly put out the moon.' It was an event which, not surprisingly, entered the folklore of the Lakes.

Less memorable, but equally special in its own way, was a personal memento of Bonaparte which found its way to the Wordsworths. Henry Parry, the Inspector of Stamps who had stayed at Rydal Mount two years earlier, had found himself on board a ship moored alongside that in which Bonaparte was imprisoned, before his exile to St Helena. The former emperor's chamberlain cut a profile portrait of the prisoner. Parry obtained permission to trace it, and sent it to William, 'thinking it might be acceptable'. As William had been disgusted by the crowds flocking to see David's portrait of Bonaparte in London, this was debatable, but he nevertheless preserved the profile among his letters.

As the summer drew to a close, the Wordsworth circle was hit by a series of tragedies. Charles Lloyd, who was subject to occasional bouts of insanity, had become significantly worse. For three months he had been confined to his room and would allow no one except his wife near him; it was only at the end of September that he allowed her to have some relief from her constant attendance, but even then he could not bear to have anyone near him, except Mary or Dorothy. The two women therefore took it in turns to go to Brathay on a daily basis, taking over Sophia Lloyd's nursing duties, or looking after her eight children for her. It was clear that things could not continue in this way, so Sophia decided that she would take her husband to his native Birmingham, where there were medical men devoted to the management of insanity in whose care he could be placed. On 12 October William escorted the afflicted husband and his wife as far as Manchester, leaving Dorothy in charge of their children at Brathay. The night before they set off, the shocking news arrived that Priscilla Wordsworth had died on 7 October, probably from septicaemia. Lloyd was in no fit state to learn of his sister's death, so his wife and William had to keep the news to themselves.

As Priscilla had no unmarried sisters, Dorothy was the obvious choice to look after her widowed brother and three nephews, the oldest of whom was not yet eight. Though she was prepared to do this on a temporary basis, she had no intention of doing so permanently. 'I have no thoughts of residing with him', she wrote to Jane Marshall, eight days after her sister-in-law's death. 'I could not give up my present home for any other.' She was equally dismissive about the unfortunate Priscilla. With terrible irony, bearing in mind what she herself would one day become, she described Priscilla's tendency 'if not to insanity, to that excess of nervous irritability which puts our feelings and actions almost as much out of our own power as if we were actually what is called insane' and Christopher's tenderness and patience in looking after her as 'almost beyond belief'. Her conclusion? A crisp 'Priscilla might have suffered less if she had had a less indulgent Husband.' It was perhaps fortunate that Christopher decided he did not wish to bring Dorothy from home 'unless absolutely necessary'; his father-in-law had come to him immediately, and Sophia offered to visit when the doctors decided it would be expedient for her to be separated from Charles for a while. Thereafter, he would manage on his own. He never married again, devoting himself instead to his three young sons and his career.

Hard on the heels of these calamities came news that Mary Lamb had suffered another mental breakdown and again been confined. And then, from Catherine Clarkson, they learned that William's old and dear friend from Patterdale, Captain Luff, had died in Mauritius. 'We are truely afflicted by the event;' William told Catherine, 'as he was much valued by us all; and we looked forward to their resettling themselves in our neighbourhood as one of the pleasantest hopes that this Family entertained.' William felt strongly that there should be a memorial of some kind: 'Luff was a genuine lover of his Country, and a true and enlightened Friend of Mankind.'

In the midst of all these sorrows, William had little time or inclination for poetry. The sales of *The Excursion*, *Poems* and *The White Doe* had all been very poor and

Dorothy now resigned herself to the idea that her brother's poetry would never sell. There was clearly no point in proceeding with the plan to publish *Peter Bell* and *Benjamin the Waggoner*, so this part of William's grand scheme for laying his works before the public was shelved once more.

There were crumbs of comfort, not the least being a small but steady stream of poems dedicated to William himself, suggesting that he was beginning to win approval among his peers. His Edinburgh protégé Robert Pearce Gillies, Keats's and Haydon's friend John Hamilton Reynolds and the Quaker poet Bernard Barton all sent him poems and letters detailing their indebtedness and it was just such a letter from Haydon which sparked William's first creative effort of the winter. Writing to thank William for the gift of a pencil case, Haydon had been embarrassingly grateful: 'I have the highest enthusiasm for your genius & purity of mind –', he wrote. 'I have benefitted & have been supported in the trouble of life by your Poetry.' William was equally convinced of Haydon's genius and in a moment of artistic solidarity, composed a sonnet addressed to him, 'High is our calling, Friend!', which urged faith 'in the whispers of the lonely Muse, While the whole world seems adverse to desert' and ended with the triumphant rallying cry, 'Great is the glory, for the strife is hard!' It was not a poem of which William was particularly fond or proud, but to Haydon it became a talisman: it was 'the highest honor that ever was paid or ever can be paid to me'. His first instinct was to ask if he could give it to John Scott to publish in the *Champion* '& might he say it was written by you to me [?]', but over the coming years, as his own fortunes declined, he would quote it with monotonous regularity, until William must have been heartily sick of hearing it. William reluctantly gave his permission to publish on condition it was made clear that this was a private tribute and had not been written for the papers. 'I naturally shrink from solicitation of public notice', he told Haydon. 'I never publish any thing without great violence to my own disposition which is to shun, rather than court, regard.' The sonnet, with two others enclosed in the same letter, was duly published in both Scott's *Champion* and Hunt's *Examiner* the following spring. The three sonnets had been written on three consecutive days, but the last proved to be more prophetic than the first, for it welcomed the first blasts of winter air which

> Announce a season potent to renew,
> 'Mid frost and snow, the instinctive joys of song,
> And nobler cares than listless summer knew.
> *September, 1815, ll.12–14*

Sending these off to Haydon on 21 December, William confessed, 'I am grieved to think what a time has elapsed since I last paid my devoirs to the Muses, and not less so to know that now in the depth of Winter when I hoped to resume my Labours, I continue to be called from them by unavoidable engagements.'

The most urgent of these engagements was a final settling of the accounts between himself, Dorothy and their brother Richard. It had become imperative for two reasons. While in London, William had obtained confirmation from Richard's partner, Richard Addison, that his brother had invested all his and Dorothy's money in purchasing land. Rents were low, and neither he nor Dorothy had any legal security for their money. This was a particular worry for Dorothy, who had no capital or income other than that in Richard's hands.

To add to their problems, Richard was now the father of a son, John, born in January 1815, to whom his estate would pass on his death. After years of leading an entirely dutiful and respectable life, Richard had scandalized all his acquaintance by suddenly marrying, at the age of forty-five, his twenty-two-year-old servant at Sockbridge, Jane Westmorland. The Wordsworths could not help but disapprove of him marrying one so young, and one of his own servants to boot, but when they actually met her they were won over. Their little boy, who would be known as 'Keswick' John, to distinguish him from his cousin at Rydal Mount, was 'a sweet creature,' his aunt enthused, 'very pretty, and most intelligent and engaging. This in an extraordinary degree, for he forces every one to admire him.'

In January, William obtained a bond for £3,000 as security for his and Dorothy's money invested in Richard's land. What he still needed was Christopher's approval for their decision to set off the debt paid by William Crackanthorpe to the estate against that due to Uncle Richard. The latter debt had almost wholly been incurred by William's own education, but, as he pointed out, it was hardly fair that he should have to repay it personally, as Christopher's had been entirely paid for by the Crackanthorpes.

Despite all these harassments, William found that the winter had indeed been a 'season potent to renew . . . the instinctive joys of song'. On 29 January he wrote to John Scott, offering him three new sonnets, belatedly inspired by the Allied victory at Waterloo. The last six lines of the third poem were intended to stand alone, if required, as an inscription for a memorial to the English who had fought there.

> Heroes! – for instant sacrifice prepared;
> Yet filled with ardour and on triumph bent
> 'Mid direst shocks of mortal accident –
> To you who fell, and you whom slaughter spared
> To guard the fallen, and consummate the event,
> Your Country rears this sacred Monument!
> *Occasioned by the Battle of Waterloo, ll.9–14*

England did not take the hint, but Scott was thrilled to be offered the first chance to publish the lines.

It was no accident that William's poetic response to Waterloo was so tardy, for the sonnets marked the beginning of a whole series of poems, mostly odes, written in the spring of 1816, which would reflect on the victory. They were by no means jingoistic or triumphalist. In fact, they were rather subdued. The problem, as William tacitly admitted in the prefatory advertisement, was that it was hard to see any superior moral virtue in a post-war Britain, where much of the populace was starving, the mills were idle, Luddites were smashing machines and even the countryside was subject to riots. Everywhere one looked there was poverty, distress and discontent.

William completed the odes by 11 March, admitting privately that he feared he had laboured too long and hard on the style, at the expense of the spirit. Taken together with the handful of sonnets which also belonged to the collection, he had written just over 700 lines of poetry, his most sustained effort for several years. The manuscript was parcelled up and posted off to Longman, with instructions that it should be printed in the same size and style as the 1815 edition of *Poems*, so that the two could be bound up together by collectors.

The slim volume appeared in May, with a price tag of 4s on its sixty-one pages, and a title out of all proportion to its size: *Thanksgiving Ode, January 18, 1816: With Other Short Pieces, Chiefly Referring to Recent Public Events.* The reaction was predictable. A few weary reviews, and a sale so poor that he was driven to declare 'as to Publishing I shall give it up, as no-body will buy what I send forth: nor can I expect it seeing what stuff the public appetite is set upon'.

Life at Rydal Mount continued on an even tenor throughout the spring of 1816. The education of the children was still a priority. Dora was introduced to music, a subject in which she would excel, during a two-month visit to Keswick with her Aunt Sara. No one else in the family had musical skills, so it was Miss Barker who began to teach Dora to play the harpsichord. Johnny was boarding at Mr Dawes's and improving steadily. Willy, who had proved as inattentive and easily bored as Dora when taught by the Wordsworth women, began to take lessons from John Carter and, to everyone's delight and astonishment, made rapid progress.

Dorothy was still hoping rather forlornly that she might get to Paris to see Caroline, but William and Mary were unwilling to let her go until France was more settled. The main reason for the trip had been removed, for in February Caroline had married Jean Baptiste Baudouin. Despite the family's straitened circumstances, the wedding was a glittering occasion at which Annette's royalist friends turned out in force. They witnessed the civil marriage contract, which was signed by the groom, his bride as 'A. C. Wordsworth' and her mother as 'M. A. Vallon *dite* William', and specifically stated that the marriage had the consent of 'M[onsieur] W. Wortsworth'. Annette was determined to see her daughter married in style, providing a dinner, ball and supper for thirty people, even though, as Dorothy remarked, she would feel the financial penalty for months to come. Thanks to the efforts of a number of the guests, Annette herself had secured the promise of a royal pension or place, as soon as one became available. The financial future of the newlyweds did not look as promising. William's annuity of £30, rising to £35 the following year, would be an important part of his daughter's future income, and a millstone round his neck.

William's own financial situation was still far from secure. In February Richard and his wife went to London, partly on business but partly to consult doctors about his continuing bilious attacks. They proved to be the symptoms of fatal liver disease. In the confined quarters of their lodgings, he became so seriously ill that

Montagu, redeeming himself for his former mischief-making, took pity on him and carried the couple off to his own house. When he discovered that Richard had not made a will, or appointed guardians for his child, he made haste to report this to William. At first William was concerned only about his infant nephew, but, consulting an attorney in Kendal a couple of days later, he discovered that, if Richard died intestate, his bond would be unenforceable during the twenty-year minority of his son. It was therefore imperative that Richard should be persuaded to make a will. William wrote immediately to Montagu, begging him, 'as a friend and a man of business acting as my *representative*', to put the matter to Richard. 'Do think of my poor sister's situation at present,' he pleaded, 'forty-four years of age, and without the command of either principal or interest of her little property'.

A similar letter went to Christopher, who, having taken possession of his new rectory at Lambeth a fortnight earlier, was now in a position to offer his brother and sister-in-law a home. They arrived on 1 May and it was obvious that Richard's case was hopeless. On 6 May he formally executed his will, appointing his widow, his brothers and Thomas Hutton, his Penrith lawyer, as his executors. His widow and brothers were also to be guardians of his one-year-old son. The end came fairly quickly. Christopher sent daily bulletins to Rydal Mount, in answer to anxious queries and expressions of love to Richard and his wife. Like the Rydalians, Christopher was impressed with his sister-in-law. 'His Wife watches and nurses him most attentively – and shews him all possible tenderness', he wrote, adding that he feared her own health would be undermined by her devotion. Richard died at five in the morning on 19 May; he was forty-seven years old. As he had never expressed any opinion about where he wished to be interred, he was buried in the chancel of Christopher's new church at Lambeth. Though 'the contemplation of the death of a *Brother* was solemn and distressing', Richard's passing was not the devastating blow to his surviving siblings that John's had been. The consequences of his death, however, were to reverberate for years to come.

Both William and Christopher feared that Richard's affairs would turn out to be in a worse state than he himself had believed, but even they were not prepared for what they found. Their first intimation came when Hutton refused to act as a trustee of the will. On 31 May William went over to Sockbridge to see him and to meet the widow, who had returned that day from London. The inability to find a third trustee would delay the administration of the will for months, causing great frustration to Richard's many long-standing creditors, who included not only his business partner, Addison, but also Lord Abergavenny. It was not until the autumn that steps could finally be taken to put Richard's lands on the market, and the following spring before they could rent out the Sockbridge estate and hold a sale of his effects.

By this stage, Lord Abergavenny, who was owed over £4,500, lost patience and threatened the estate with a suit in chancery. The direct personal intervention of Christopher prevented the suit going ahead, but the threat was only suspended, since his sole bargaining counter was that they would pay as soon as possible. Probate was finally granted on 24 April 1817, but it was the end of the year before the trustees were in a position to offer any payment to creditors. Richard's simple contract debts then amounted to almost £12,500, but the sale of his effects had grossed less than £10,000. The immediate objective of paying off the creditors 'of any material importance' could therefore be achieved, but Christopher balked at William's suggestion that they should contribute to the shortfall, because he was himself in debt to the tune of £500. In the end, all that was left to Richard's son and heir was a very uncertain £300 a year in rents, half of which would pay the widow's annuity, the rest the interest on William and Dorothy's bond. Their capital, to all intents and purposes, was irrecoverable.

Richard's death was followed by that of two local grandees. The Bishop of Llandaff, whose lamentations on the execution of Louis XVI had inspired William's first political pamphlet, died at his estate on Windermere and was buried at Bowness. The second death was more regretted: Lady Diana Le Fleming of Rydal Hall died in London, but her remains were brought back to be buried next to those of her husband. 'Poor Lady F[leming; the daughter] has lost her *only* Friend –', Sara wrote, 'the Poor a most benevolent one – and we, and the country round, an excellent neighbour.' The cortège was a fortnight on the road and the funeral was conducted with great pomp. Much to the Wordsworths' amusement, the master-undertaker in charge of the proceedings brought his wife with him, all the way from London, not as an indispensable part of the ceremony, but simply to show her the Lakes.

No fewer than fourteen 'Cantabs', as the Wordsworths called the members of the University of Cambridge, took up residence in Ambleside and Bowness for three months during the summer. 'Some have been introduced,' Sara noted in July, '& I suppose most of them will find means to get a sight of the Poet before the summer is past.' The Wordsworths were in no doubt that, though William's poems did not sell, his reputation was growing.

Among the visitors who came to stay at Rydal Mount was Southey. He brought with him his friend the artist and miniaturist Edward Nash, who produced such delightful portraits of the Southey children, and also a telling pencil sketch of William. Southey himself looked like a ghost. His beloved nine-year-old son Herbert, 'the very heart and life of my happiness and my hopes', had died on 17 April. With his usual self-command, Southey had buried himself in his work, but it was clear to him, and to all who knew him, that he was no longer his old cheerful self. The Wordsworths, whose own dead son had been Herbert's best friend, knew better than most what he was suffering and were quietly, but steadily, supportive.

One of the most welcome visitors of the late summer was Robinson, whom William took on a personal guided tour of the Lakes. It was, as Robinson gloomily noted, 'uninterruptedly rainy', but when he finally parted from William, on 24 September, he did so 'under the impression of thankfulness for personal attentions in addition to the high reverence I felt for his character before'. Mary Lamb reported in November that Robinson still spoke 'in raptures' of the days he had spent with the Wordsworths, adding, 'He says he never saw a man so happy in *three wives* as Mr Wordsworth is.'

Less happy had been Robinson's meeting with de Quincey, whom he found 'very dirty and even squalid' in appearance, and bitter against the Wordsworths, from whom he was estranged. The Wordsworths had known that de Quincey was an opium addict for at least two years. His health had suffered in consequence, but he was still capable of rabble-rousing with the best of them. 'He doses himself with Opium & drinks like a f[ish]', Sara had commented the previous autumn, observing his painful determination to match Wilson in his debaucheries. Worse still, he had notoriously acquired a mistress in Margaret Simpson, who was only just seventeen when she caught his attention. The daughter of a local statesman, who lived at Nab Cottage on Rydal Water, she was barely out of childhood. Rumours that they were to marry had reached the Wordsworths as early as November 1815, but a year later, when Margaret produced their first son, the parents had still not made it to the altar. The Wordsworths did not approve of this conduct, and had left de Quincey in no doubt of their opinion, so he had broken off all contact with them.

William greeted the birth of William de Quincey on 15 November with heavy irony which, as the father of an illegitimate child himself, was inexcusable. 'Such, in these later times, are the fruits of philosophy ripening under the shelter of our Arcadian mountains', he informed Lamb. 'A marriage is expected by some; but, from the known procrastination of one of the parties, it is not looked for by others till the commencement of the millenium.' Confounding these expectations, the marriage did take place, ten weeks later, on 15 February 1817, in Grasmere church. Dorothy was so vitriolic that one is inclined to suspect some jealousy of the woman who had won de Quincey's affections. 'Mr de Quincey is married; and I fear I may add he is ruined', she wrote. 'He utter'd in raptures of the beauty, the good sense, the simplicity, the "angelic sweetness" of Miss Sympson, who to all other judgments appeared to be a stupid, heavy girl, and was reckoned a Dunce at Grasmere School; and I predict that all these witcheries are ere this removed, and the fireside already dull.'

She was quite wrong. Margaret was to prove a devoted wife and mother, enduring much unhappiness and abject poverty in her marriage, as well as regular abandonment by her erring husband. It was not long before the Wordsworths realized her value, and, having done so, they did everything in their power to assist her and her children.

The year ended with two unsolicited, and very different, tributes to William's growing reputation as a poet. The first was the anonymous publication of Hogg's *Poetic Mirror*, which contained parodies of the poetry of Byron, Scott, Southey, Coleridge, Wilson and William himself, as well as a self-parody. William's three 'contributions', the *Stranger*, the *Flying Taylor* and *James Rigg*, each mischievously purporting to be 'a further portion of *The Recluse*,' were all in blank verse. William at first suspected Lamb might have had a hand in this, but then, realizing that Scottish poets were disproportionately represented, he guessed that it probably originated over the border. For all that it mocked his style, the fact that it was so instantly recognizable to the reading public as to be an appropriate subject for parody was in itself a compliment, of sorts.

The second tribute came from the pen of a new disciple, a man who, at twenty-one, was younger than William's eldest daughter, had published his first poem in the *Examiner* only in May and, before his death less than five years later, would leave behind a body of poetry which would establish his reputation as one of the greatest of all lyric poets. The man was John Keats and the tribute was a sonnet, written on 21 November and forwarded to William by their mutual friend the artist Haydon, on 31 December. 'The Idea of your sending it to Wordsworth put me out of breath', Keats wrote to Haydon; ' – you know with what Reverence – I would send my Wellwishes to him'.

The sonnet itself is an exquisite work of art in its own right but it is also important because, at every level, it reveals Keats's debt to William. Not only is he obviously familiar with all William's poetry, but he has adopted his mentor's style and language, and, most important of all, his philosophy.

> Great Spirits now on earth are sojourning
>   He of the Cloud, the Cataract, the Lake
>   Who on Helvellyn's summit wide awake
> Catches his freshness from Archangel's wing
> He of the Rose, the Violet, the Spring
>   The social smile, the Chain for Freedom's sake;
>   And lo! – whose stedfastness would never take
> A meaner sound than Raphael's Whispering.
> And other Spirits are there standing apart
>   Upon the Forehead of the age to come;
> These, these will give the World another Heart
>   And other Pulses – hear ye not the hum
> Of mighty workings? –
>   Listen awhile ye Nations and be dumb!

18. Bombastes Furioso

William, Mary and the children spent Christmas alone at Rydal Mount. Dorothy was on a visit to her 'aunt', Elizabeth Rawson, at Halifax. By the time she returned home, on 15 February 1817, she had been away for five months. The days had been spent very pleasantly in a quiet routine of social visiting, walking and reading. With only two elderly people in the house, servants to perform the work 'as if by magic' and no children's voices disturbing the perfect stillness, it was a complete and, for a time at least, not unwelcome contrast to Rydal Mount. 'I was very happy there', she wrote, 'yet now that I am placed again in the perfect freedom of home, I rejoice many times in every day that I am here saying, "how glad I am that I am among you once again"!'

Sara had also been away since the middle of December, staying with Mary Barker at Greta Hall, but spending most of her time with the Southeys. She was devoted to Southey's five little daughters, who ranged in age from eleven to four, loving them almost as much as the Wordsworth children. Southey was preparing to write a history of the Peninsular War and Wellington had lent him all his personal papers, including officers' letters, secretarial journals and memoranda. He asked Sara to transcribe them and she was in her element: 'We have had the secret history of all these affairs', she confided with glee.

The bustle of literary activity round Southey was in stark contrast to the atmosphere at Rydal Mount, where, in Sara's typically pithy phrase, William was 'doing nothing'. This was undoubtedly true in the sense she meant it, for William had not touched poetry in a long time, but his time was fully occupied. One of William's sub-distributors, John Hall at Kirkby Stephen, had stolen almost £300 from legacy receipts, which he had not recorded in his returns. The money was legally due to the government, but as William had no sureties from him William himself was personally liable for the whole sum. He therefore had the distasteful duty of going over to Kirkby Stephen, seizing all his sub-collector's movable goods and selling them to raise the amount due. Just to complicate matters, Hall was then arrested for other debts and all William's prompt and diligent efforts to procure the money were threatened by the demands of other creditors. It would be more than three weeks before he knew for certain that the government's money had been secured and he would not have to reimburse the sum from his own pocket.

Southey, in flight from his inextinguishable grief for the loss of his only son, had decided to take a trip to the Continent. William wanted to go with him, but could not afford to do so. Instead he charged Southey with a commission to do what none of the Wordsworths had been able to do, visit his daughter in Paris. On 16 May Southey called at 47 Rue Charlot, 'small lodgings, pleasantly situated', only to find Caroline alone with her daughter. She spoke no English, his French was halting, but as soon as he mentioned that he had met Baudouin in William's company Caroline said that William was her father 'and we had a tete-a-tete of about an hour long, much like a scene in sentimental comedy', during which Caroline wept copiously and appeared 'much affected'. Southey's eagerly awaited impression of Caroline was that she was 'a very interesting young woman, with much more of natural feeling than of French manners, and surprizingly like John Wordsworth, much more so than his own sister. The little French Dorothy [Caroline's daughter] is very like her mother, a sweet infant, in perfect health and good humour.'

Southey arranged to call back the next morning to meet Annette and Baudouin. Baudouin was like his brother, but taller, and 'very fond of his child, a fair presumption that he is not less fond of his wife'. Both Caroline and Annette spoke of him as the best of husbands. 'We parted sworn friends,' Southey told his own wife.

One longs to know how William reacted to this account. He was, after all, a grandfather of a child he had never seen, as well as father of a girl he had known only for less than a month when she was eleven years old. His passionate love for his other children is well documented. Even now, in the fifth year after the loss of Catherine and Thomas, he could not bear to look at John Scott's newly published poem about the death of his own son, *The House of Mourning*, because the subject was too painful to contemplate. Catherine and Thomas 'are perpetually present to my eyes –', he admitted to Haydon. 'I do not mourn for them; yet I am sometimes weak enough to wish that I had them again.'

A similarly poignant, reflective mood pervades the poetry that William wrote this spring and summer. It was in many ways an unexpected return to verse, which Dorothy hailed with heartfelt relief and delight. 'To-day he has composed a Sonnet,' she observed on 13 April, 'and in our inner minds we sing "Oh! be joyful!" It has indeed been most melancholy to see him bowed down by oppressive cares, which have fallen upon him through mismanagement, dilatoriness, or negligence.' The poems he wrote, however, were anything but joyful. Like those he had written the previous spring, they were principally odes, but the new ones were less strictly constrained by classical models. Instead, they referred back, quite consciously and deliberately, to the great ode, *Intimations of Immortality*, he had written in 1804.

While echoing both its sentiments and its language, the new mood was altogether less optimistic. *Vernal Ode*, for instance, has a lovingly and wonderingly observed description of a bee, but ends by looking back sadly to the golden age, when all creatures met in peace and the bee itself did not need its sting.

Composed upon an Evening of Extraordinary Splendour and Beauty is more explicit in its borrowings from *Intimations*. The poem is a wonderful evocation of a sunset, observed from the mount in front of the house. These are the closing lines.

> Such hues from their celestial Urn
> Were wont to stream before mine eye,
> Wher'er it wandered in the morn
> Of blissful infancy.
> This glimpse of glory, why renewed?
> Nay, rather speak with gratitude;
> For, if a vestige of those gleams
> Survived, 'twas only in my dreams.
> Dread Power! whom peace and calmness serve
> No less than Nature's threatening voice,
> If aught unworthy be my choice,
> From THEE if I would swerve;
> Oh, let Thy grace remind me of the light
> Full early lost, and fruitlessly deplored;
> Which, at this moment, on my waking sight
> Appears to shine, by miracle restored;
> My soul, though yet confined to earth,
> Rejoices in a second birth!

Had the poem ended there, it would have struck the same note of renewed optimism as *Intimations of Immortality*, but it does not. The final two lines are a claustrophobic return to the 'prison-house' of mortal flesh.

> – 'Tis past, the visionary splendour fades;
> And night approaches with her shades.

The same sense of time running out for the poet haunts the first *Ode to Lycoris*, which draws on William's own youthful preference for twilight rather than dawn, and autumn rather than spring. The second *Ode to Lycoris*, celebrating an ascent of Helvellyn with Dorothy in June, ends with a version of lines he had written as long ago as 1798 and last revised in 1802.

Should we look at the poems of 1817 and see them as a poet coming to terms with the idea that his best work is behind him? With the benefit of hindsight, we know that this was true, on the whole. William would never recapture the vitality, originality or prolific output of his earlier years. We know that he would never write the rest of *The Recluse*. On the other hand, William could not know this, and did not. He had always found revision of his work a fruitful source of inspiration for new poetry and, as late as October, he was planning 'to work hard at the Recluse in Winter'.

The most important visitor to Rydal Mount this summer was a completely unknown northern artist, just twenty-five years old, called Richard Carruthers, whom Tom Monkhouse had commissioned to paint a portrait of William. It was the first of all William's portraits to be engraved, and every picture of the poet published in the next fourteen years would be based on it. As much as the likeness, it was the pose which made this portrait famous. Carruthers was determined to capture not just the man but also the poet. He painted him sitting under a tree and leaning on a boulder, against a backdrop of mountains and cloud on one side and a river, with tumbling cataracts, on the other. While his left hand is tucked into his waistcoat, his right props up his head, the hand being carefully placed so that the fingers rested on the part of the forehead which, according to the popular pseudo-science of phrenology, was the seat of poetry.

The importance of this pose was recognized by both the Wordsworths and the artist himself. Carruthers's first attempt was almost completed when it was abandoned by mutual agreement. 'He erred in chusing the attitude – one in which William is never seen – and the face is too fat & the expression unnatural – but this was not the artist's fault for Wm himself sate, as Joanna told him, in "*a perpetual smirk*" – and would not put on one Schedoni glance'. The 'Schedoni glance' was all-important, for this was the impressively blood-chilling look cast by the monk in Ann Radcliffe's romance *The Italian*, improbably set during the Inquisition. The second portrait, with its look of pained world-weariness and heavy-lidded eyes, was judged a great success.

The Wordsworths had looked forward to a quiet winter in the Lakes once all their visitors had gone, but towards the end of November William, Mary and Sara suddenly packed up and rushed off to London. Christopher had been pressing William to come for some time as he was reluctant to take the decision about settling Richard's debt to Lord Abergavenny alone. William had some business affairs of his own to sort out, and Sara had promised to spend the winter with Catherine Clarkson at her new house, Playford Hall, near Ipswich. They arrived in London around 26 November and divided their time between Christopher's house in Lambeth, his 'nice old-fashioned crincum-crankum' country parsonage twenty-two miles away at Sundridge, near Sevenoaks, Tom Monkhouse's lodgings in Mortimer Street and his house at Hampstead.

William had brought with him the poems he had written earlier in the year, planning to publish them. The idea was abandoned, probably because of William's reluctance to go into print and the exorbitant cost of publishing such a small collection. There was little hope of even recovering his expenses: his income from Longman the previous year had amounted to the princely sum of £17.

While in London, William met Coleridge several times at the Lambs' and at Tom Monkhouse's. They had not seen each other since they had patched up their quarrel in the summer of 1812. The meetings witnessed by Robinson were not entirely comfortable. In the summer Coleridge had published his *Biographia Litera-ria*, which purported to be his autobiography, but was actually his most important work of literary criticism to date. The book had not pleased William: 'he finds just fault with Coleridge for professing to write about himself and writing merely about Southey and Wordsworth', Robinson observed. 'With the criticism on the poetry too he is not satisfied. The praise is extravagant and the censure inconsiderate. I recollected Hazlitt say that Wordsworth would not forgive a single censure mingled with however great a mass of eulogy.' Conversely, Coleridge was piqued that William, in his 'Essay, Supplemental to the Preface' of 1815, had credited the Germans, instead of himself, with introducing a correct appreciation of Shake-speare. He resented this particularly because he blamed William indirectly for the reviewers' hostility towards himself. He had, he said, fought for William's poetic fame 'with an ardour that amounted to absolute Self-oblivion'. This was entirely true, but it did not follow, as Coleridge claimed, that this had caused the 'ranco[u]r of the Edinburgh clan and . . . the coldness, neglect, and equivocal compliments of the Quarterly Review' towards himself.

With both men harbouring these resentments, and on opposite sides on the burning political issue of the day, the prosecution of William Hone for blasphemy, it was not surprising that the conversation was 'not altogether as it ought to have been'. On 27 December Robinson dined at Tom Monkhouse's with William, Mary, Sara, Cole-ridge and his son Hartley and Samuel Tillbrooke. Charles and Mary Lamb joined them after dinner. 'I was for the first time in my life not pleased with Wordsworth, and Coleridge appeared to advantage in his presence', Robinson wrote.

Coleridge spoke of painting in that style of mysticism which is now his habit of feeling. Wordsworth met this by dry, unfeeling contradiction. The manner of Coleridge towards Wordsworth was most respectful; but Wordsworth towards Coleridge was cold and scornful. Coleridge maintained that painting was not an art which could operate on the vulgar, and Wordsworth declared this opinion to be degrading to the art. Coleridge illustrated his assertions by reference to Raphael's Madonnas. Wordsworth could not think that a field for high intellect lay within such a subject as a mother and child, and when Coleridge talked of the divinity of those works, Wordsworth asked whether he thought he should have discerned those beauties if he had [not] known that Raphael was the artist; and when Coleridge said that was an unkind question, Wordsworth made no apology.

While one might not agree with Robinson that William was 'substantially wrong' in his opinion on art, one cannot quarrel with his verdict that William's conduct had been at fault. Perhaps he felt this himself, for when they met again three days later at the Lambs', he was content to remain tête-à-tête with Talfourd for the evening, leaving Coleridge to hold the floor to an admiring crowd. Catherine Clarkson thought it a pity that the two friends had met in company. 'Men of the world have a certain tact by which they regulate their conduct in society & which seems to have been wanted upon the occasion to which you allude', she wrote to Robinson. 'A man of the world in W's place would have been kind before strangers cold in private. W's better nature I have no doubt would make him affectionate in private & only cold before strangers because his whole mind could not be expressed before them.' The justice of this remark soon became apparent. Before he left London, William wrote privately to a mutual friend, John Payne Collier, asking him to attend Coleridge's new series of lectures and help make them a success. His sympathy for Coleridge was explicit, generous and warm.

He talks as a bird sings, as if he could not help it: it is his nature. He is now far from well in body or spirits. The former is suffering from various causes, and the latter from depression. No man ever deserved to have fewer enemies, yet, as he thinks and says, no man has more, or more virulent. You have long been among his friends; and as far as you can go, you will no doubt prove it on this as on other occasions.

The Wordsworths' visit passed swiftly in a round of entertainments, parties, plays, operas, dinners and breakfasts. Tom Monkhouse held open house for artists and writers, and Carruthers's portrait was on constant display. The likeness did not impress as much in London as it had done in the Lakes. Robinson thought it 'strong', but complained that there was 'a languor approaching to disease in the countenance'. Carruthers tried his hand at a pencil portrait of Mary on 3 January, but this was even less successful and the attempt was abandoned.

The argument surrounding his portrait of William prompted two other artist friends to see what they could do. Edward Nash's miniature pencil sketch was simply a sleepier, hairier version of Carruthers's painting, but Haydon produced something strikingly different. A pencil and chalk study of William's head, it needs only a bolt through its neck to complete a more than passing resemblance to Frankenstein's monster. Dorothy was dismayed by this portrait: 'all that there is of likeness makes it to me the more disagreeable'; William himself preferred the Carruthers, prompting a characteristic sarcasm from Sara: 'The Painters who flatter are quite in the right – Truth gives no satisfaction.' Within the family, it was aptly known as 'the Brigand'.

Haydon was also responsible for the highlight of this winter visit to London. On 28 December he held his 'Immortal Dinner' in his studio, with his vast painting of *Christ's Entry into Jerusalem* towering behind as a backdrop. It was a small and select party, all friends and all at ease with each other: William, Monkhouse, Lamb, Haydon himself and Keats, for whom Haydon had organized the event, so that he could meet his fellow poet. 'Wordsworth was a fine cue, and we had a glorious set-to, – on Homer, Shakespeare, Milton and Virgil', Haydon wrote in his *Autobiography*. 'Lamb got exceedingly merry and exquisitely witty; and his fun in the midst of Wordsworth's solemn intonations of oratory was like the sarcasm and wit of the fool in the intervals of Lear's passion.' Lamb was the life and soul of the party, teasing everyone mercilessly and contributing to the general tipsiness by offering toast after toast. 'Now, you old lake poet, you rascally poet, why do you call Voltaire dull?' he demanded of William. He then attacked Haydon for including Newton in his picture, agreeing with Keats that Newton had destroyed all the poetry of the rainbow by reducing it to the prismatic colours, and proposing that they drank a health to Newton 'and confusion to mathematics'. Lamb was irresistible and William laughed as heartily as the rest. When they retired to tea, however, they found an intruder, a self-confessed enthusiast for William's poetry, who had begged Haydon for an introduction on the basis that he had corresponded with the poet. What Haydon 'forgot' to tell William was that this admirer was John Kingston, Deputy Comptroller and Accomptant General of the Stamp Office in London.

Kingston was stone-cold sober, prosaic, self-important and completely out of his depth, but he tried to make appropriate conversation. 'Don't you think, sir, Milton was a great genius?' he asked William. Keats looked at Haydon, William looked at the comptroller. Lamb, who was dozing by the fire, turned round and said, 'Pray, sir, did you say Milton was a great genius?' 'No, sir; I asked Mr Wordsworth if he were not.' 'Oh,' said Lamb, 'then you are a silly fellow.' William remonstrated in vain, 'Charles! my dear Charles!' After an awful pause, the comptroller broke out again. 'Don't you think Newton a great genius?' While Keats and Haydon struggled to keep their countenances, William stared at Kingston as if asking himself, 'who is this?' The irrepressible Lamb, however, got up, seized a candle and advanced on the poor man, saying, 'Sir, will you allow me to look at your phrenological development?' All further attempts at serious conversation were interrupted by Lamb singing nursery-rhyme ditties and begging, 'Do let me have another look at that gentleman's organs'. Keats and Haydon hurried Lamb out into the painting room, shut the door and collapsed with laughter. While William, who had just made the alarming discovery that Kingston was his superior, tried to smooth the ruffled man down, Monkhouse managed to spirit Lamb away, though his struggles and cries of 'Who is that fellow? Allow me to see his organs once more' were all too embarrassingly audible. 'It was indeed an immortal evening', Haydon reminisced many years later. 'Wordsworth's fine intonation as he quoted Milton and Virgil, Keats' eager inspired look, Lamb's quaint sparkle of lambent humour, so speeded the stream of conversation, that in my life I never passed a more delightful time.'

Kingston's discomfort was amusing, but it was also highly embarrassing, not only to him, but also to William. In front of a crowd of literary people, including some of his young admirers, he had been unexpectedly confronted with a man who clearly expected the deference due from a government official to his superior. The dead silence with which he greeted Kingston's complacent announcement that he was a comptroller of Stamps was surely an indication of his embarrassment. Haydon did not realize this, but the more sensitive Keats did. It was anathema to Keats to see the 'great spirit' whose poetry he worshipped in worldly bondage to a humble tax collector. The two men dined together at Monkhouse's two days later, on 5 January, in company with Mary and Sara, whom Keats described as William's 'beautiful Wife and his enchanting Sister'. Again there was a small incident which irritated Keats. When he tried to intervene in one of William's lengthy disquisitions on poetry, Mary laid a restraining hand on his arm and murmured, 'Mr Wordsworth is never interrupted.'

The two men met again several times, but Keats could never quite forgive or forget his idol's feet of clay, which made him all the more susceptible to Hazlitt's jaundiced views of William's politics and character. So much so that, after attending Hazlitt's lectures, he remarked to his brothers, 'I am sorry that Wordsworth has left a bad impression wherever he visited in Town – by his egotism, Vanity and bigotry'. In justice, he could not refrain from adding, '– yet he is a great Poet if not a Philosopher'.

Keats's image of William would have been dented even further had he known of the correspondence then under way between the poet and the Lowthers. Astonishingly, despite this encounter and his unpleasant experience with the sub-distributor at Kirkby Lonsdale earlier in the year, William was anxious to expand his income by acquiring more Stamp distributorships. Just as he had done with the office he now held, he had earmarked the one he thought most suitable. It was that of Carlisle, which was said to be worth £600 a year to the current distributor, Mr Ramshay, who was seventy-one years old. With the backing of the Lowthers and Parry of the Stamp Office, William had entered into negotiations with Ramshay, but before these could be brought to a conclusion they were overtaken by events.

In 1818 there was to be a general election and, for the first time in many years, there was to be a contest in Westmorland, where both seats were held by the sons of Lord Lonsdale. The elder, thirty-year-old William, Viscount Lowther, was a career politician who had entered Parliament in 1808. The younger, twenty-seven-year-old Henry Cecil Lowther, had performed distinguished service in the army, fighting under both Sir John Moore and the Duke of Wellington in the Peninsula, and had risen to the rank of Lieutenant Colonel in the 12th Foot; he had joined his brother in the House of Commons in 1812.

Rumours that a contest was likely began to circulate in December 1817. Tom Monkhouse learned that there had been a meeting in the name of Westmorland Freeholders on 10 December at the City of London tavern; £3,000 had been subscribed to support a candidate against the Lowthers and no lesser person than William Crackanthorpe had agreed to stand. A few days later, William offered his services to the Lowther cause. 'I need not say how happy I should be if I could be of any use', he informed the Earl; '. . . your Lordship has only to point out the way in which you wish me to exert myself.' His ink was hardly dry before his offer was accepted and he was swept up into the maelstrom of an election campaign which, even in those days of entrenched interests and minority representation, was distinguished for its bitterness and violence.

The enthusiasm with which William flung himself into the Lowther cause was, and remains, a matter of acute embarrassment to his apologists. Quite apart from the fact that he had once been an ardent republican, here he was actively supporting hereditary wealth and power in the face of popular demand. The poet who had championed the common man, the pedlar, tinker, shepherd and beggar, was now on the side of aristocratic reaction and conservatism. He was a hypocrite and a turncoat, a government hireling and an aristocratic toady. Or, at least, so said the likes of Hazlitt; and, as we are all democrats now, we are inclined to agree.

Yet we should not judge the past by the standards of today. There are two keys to understanding William's stance in 1818 and beyond. The first is his belief that, though his opinions had changed, his *principles* remained the same. The second is his personal experience of the French Revolution, which led him to fear the mob (as opposed to the people) above all else. 'A representative legislation is still in my opinion the best of political blessings when a Country has materials fit to compose it', he wrote in 1816. Though most people would put the emphasis on the first half of this sentence, the second half was just as important, if not more so, to William. That was why he had always been a fervent advocate of national education, believing that it was the means by which the 'fit materials' could be created for greater representation. As a young man, he had believed it 'derogatory to human nature to set up Property in preference to Person, as a title for legislative power'. He still believed it would be better to widen the franchise, but only so long as it remained in the hands of those with property. 'I should think that I had lived to little purpose if my notions on the subject of Government had undergone no modification –', he wrote to Losh in 1821.

My youth must, in that case, have been without enthusiasm, and my manhood endued with small capability of profiting by reflexion. If I were addressing those who have dealt so liberally with the words Renegado, Apostate etc, I should retort the charge upon them, and say, *you* have been deluded by Places and Persons, while I have stuck to Principles – I abandoned France, and her Rulers, when they abandoned the struggle for Liberty, gave themselves up to Tyranny, and endeavoured to enslave the world.

Ever since the end of the war with France, poverty among the rural and urban poor had escalated, bringing with it the threat of disaffection and even riot. Though the Wordsworths read about such things in the papers, the Lakes seemed impervious to such problems. It was only when Dorothy went to stay with the Rawsons at Halifax that she began to appreciate the enormity of the problem among the manufacturing population. 'The wealthy keep their mills going, chiefly for the value of employing workmen', she observed,

– and few get more than *half* work – great numbers none at all, so that really a great part of the population is reduced to pauperism – a dreadful evil. Things cannot go on in this way. For a time whole streets – men, women and children may be kept alive by public charity; but the consequence will be awful, if nothing can be manufactured in these places where such numbers of people have been gathered together.

William, like most of his friends of his own age and class, was full of fears. 'A Revolution will, I think, be staved off for the present,' he wrote to Stuart.

Nevertheless I am like you, an alarmist, and for this reason, I see clearly that the principal ties which kept the different classes of society in a vital and harmonious dependence upon each other have, within these 30 years either been greatly impaired or wholly dissolved.

Everything has been put up to market and sold for the highest price it would bring. Farmers used formerly to be attached to their Landlords, and labourers to their Farmers who employed them. All that kind of feeling has vanished – in like manner, the connexion between the trading and landed interests of country towns undergoes no modification whatsoever from personal feeling, whereas within my memory it was almost wholly governed by it. A country squire, or substantial yeoman, used formerly to resort to the same shops which his father had frequented before him, and nothing but a serious injury real or supposed would have appeared to him a justification for breaking up a connexion which was attended with substantial amity and interchanges of hospitality from generation to generation. All this moral cement is dissolved, habits and prejudices are broken and rooted up; nothing being substituted in their place but a quickened selfinterest, with more extensive views, – and wider dependencies, – but more lax in proportion as they are wider. The ministry will do well if they keep things quiet for the present, but if our present constitution in church and state is to last, it must rest as heretofore upon a moral basis; and they who govern the country must be something superior to mere financiers and political economists.

In this penetrating and perceptive analysis of the problems facing post-war Britain, William obliquely explains his own fervent attachment to the Lowther cause. If there was anywhere in the country where the 'moral cement' was still effective in binding society together, it was the Lakes, and it could only be attributed to the pervasive influence of the Lowthers, and, more particularly, of the 'Good Earl' himself, Lord Lonsdale.

The news that Henry Brougham, owner of Brougham Castle, near Penrith, and a leading Whig, had accepted the invitation to stand against the Lowther brothers sent the Wordsworths racing back home. This was an altogether more serious challenge than that posed by young Crackanthorpe. By 29 January they were in Kendal, and William immediately set about investigating the loyalties of the freeholders and compiling lists of lawyers whose assistance would be essential in deciding who was eligible to vote. 'I do not like the appearance of things in this Town', he wrote the day he arrived. 'If your Lordship fails, it will be owing to the hostility of little people; blind in their prejudices and strong in their passions.'

Kendal was to prove a thorn in the flesh of the Lowthers throughout the campaign, not least because it was a manufacturing town (its main industries were the production of snuff and 'Kendal Green' cloth) with a high proportion of dissenters among its population. William was on good personal terms with many of these men, but it was difficult for him to intervene too openly because, as the holder of a government office, he was officially disbarred from canvassing. '*We* do nothing, you know', Mary wrote, warning Tom Monkhouse not to say a word about William's activities behind the scenes. Yet these were substantial and influential. William was, in effect, acting as the Lowthers' political agent, albeit unpaid. It was William, for instance, who urged them to change the second part of the 'Lowther and Loyalty' slogan from 'Church and King' to 'King and Constitution', so as not to exclude or offend dissenting voters.

Again and again, throughout the election campaign, William drew parallels with his own experience of revolutionary France. Brougham, for instance, immediately assumed a Robespierre role. 'Mr B. may at this moment be regarded as the most prominent Demagogue in the Kingdom', William wrote in March.

I am convinced, at this moment there is such a hostility among the lower Ranks, including servants, day-labourers, handicraftsmen, small shopkeepers, to whom must be added many who from education and situation in life ought to know better, that if it went by counting heads Mr B. would sweep all before him, and be triumphant to a degree which I fear to contemplate.

These fears seemed to be justified by the reaction of what William significantly referred to as 'the Mob', who rioted violently in Kendal when Viscount Lowther made his first attempt to canvass the town. When 'the great Demagogue', Brougham himself, appeared in Westmorland, he reinforced these fears by refusing to address the freeholders, who were the only men entitled to vote. Instead, he always made a play for the sympathies of the wider, unenfranchised, audience. Dorothy's account of his first speech at Kendal is significant in its terminology. 'I could have fancied him one of the French Demagogues of the Tribunal of Terror at certain times, when he gathered a particular fierceness into his face. He is very like a Frenchman', she wrote. 'Oh! he looked ready to lead a gang of Robespierrists set to pull down Lowther Castle and tear up the very trees that adorn it.'

William was less hysterical, but he was deeply concerned at Brougham's attempts to pressurize the electorate by means of the unenfranchised crowds who followed him from hustings to hustings. Well aware of the role journalists and pamphleteers had also played in inciting violence in France, William had quickly identified the Kendal newspaper, the *Westmorland Advertiser and Kendal Chronicle*, as a source of much anxiety. Even before the campaign began, he thought it propagated 'Jacobinical principles', and it became increasingly and more openly anti-Lowther.

To counteract its inflammatory rhetoric, William first of all attempted to persuade the editor, his friend the Unitarian minister John Harrison, at least to be even-handed; when that failed he urged the Earl to buy it, and when that proved impossible, he recommended, and assisted in, setting up a rival newspaper, the *Westmorland Gazette*. Stuart advised him to secure a writer as editor, preferably a man of 'good sense, steadiness & integrity, he having been bred a Printer & having a common Education'. Unfortunately, William ignored this voice of experience. When de Quincey wrote asking for the post, promising that he was now a reformed character as far as 'punctuality . . . and power of steady perseverance' went, William backed his appointment, admitting reservations only on the score of his punctuality.

William was also actively involved in writing, printing and circulating pro-Lowther literature. Unable to write under his own name, he chose a variety of pseudonyms. As 'A Friend to Consistency' he appealed to voters not to split their votes by choosing between one of the Lowthers and Brougham; as 'A Friend to Truth' he defended Viscount Lowther against accusations that he lived off government sinecures and Colonel Lowther against insinuations that he had not earned his military rank. These letters were published in the *Kendal Chronicle*, but were also circulated in their thousands by the Lowther committee as handbills. (Ironically, they achieved a far higher print run than any of William's poetry.) As 'A Freeholder', he also wrote two lengthy *Addresses to the Freeholders of Westmorland*, extolling the virtues of the Lowthers and the Tory government and lambasting the Whig record in opposition.

Despite his strenuous efforts for the Lowther cause, William was not blind to its failings. 'The more I see of this Contest the more I regret that circumstances should have thrown the representation upon both your Sons', he wrote to the Earl. 'This is unpalatable to many respectable people wellwishers to your Lordship's family … "Two Brothers, and these Sons of a Peer, for one County!" is a frequent exclamation from quarters entitling it to regard.' He was similarly outspoken in his relief when the Earl refused to support the government's proposal to pay a huge annuity to the German princeling who was the widower of the late Princess Charlotte. 'There is scarcely any part of the conduct of Government which I have found so difficult to defend (or indeed which I have been so little inclined to defend) as the grant to Prince Leopold.'

By the third week in February, William's role in the campaign was already an open secret. His authorship of the *Two Addresses* was also swiftly detected, earning him the soubriquet 'Bombastes Furioso' in the *Kendal Chronicle*. Worse still, it was also known in London, where Clarkson heard it, and wrote post-haste to warn William, in case he was unaware that he should remain neutral as a government official. Clarkson found himself in a very difficult position. He admired the Earl personally, but Brougham had been such an active opponent of the slave trade, even to the point of introducing one of the anti-slavery bills, that he could not, in conscience, vote against him. More importantly, Clarkson carried with him the votes of the large Quaker community in Kendal, so his intervention could have been a decisive factor. Ultimately, he decided to play a low-key role, writing a couple of letters in support of Brougham, but refusing to campaign more actively or in person. This was fortunate for Sara Hutchinson, who was in the even more embarrassing position of being a guest in the Clarkson household throughout the election campaign.

All the family, except Dora, were in Appleby, the county town, for the closing of the polls on 4 July, when both Lowthers were returned to Parliament by a substantial majority, but the after-effects of Brougham's campaign continued to reverberate. The next day there were riots in Kendal and troops had to be called out to restore order. It was essential, as William advised the newly returned MPs, that they should do everything in their power to conciliate the disaffected and make themselves personally known to their electorate. At the Appleby poll, Brougham had threatened that, to strengthen his hand for a future election, the Whigs would make a concerted effort to purchase and create freeholds in the county. There could be only one response to this, and once again William led the van in identifying potential freeholds and persuading friends to buy them. Within a month of the closing of the polls, he was in negotiation for an estate which could be divided into twelve freeholds. This sale seems to have fallen through, but on 15 November he agreed the purchase of Ivy How farm, 'a sweet sunny place with beautiful rocks. Yew trees and hollies around two comfortable dwellings', just below High Hacket, in Little Langdale. 'Already we see in imagination Betty [Yewdale] an inhabitant of one of these Cottages', Mary wrote, as William tried to set up a syndicate of Lowther supporters to put up the money. Southey could not afford to join them, but Christopher Wordsworth, Jack, Tom and Henry Hutchinson, Tom and John Monkhouse, Eldred Addison (son of Richard's business partner) and George Gee, the Wordsworths' neighbour at Rydal Mount, all contributed to the 700 guineas, and eight freeholds were squeezed out of the little property.

Despite the disruption caused by the election, the summer saw an endless stream of visitors to Rydal Mount. On 25 August the Wilberforce family arrived in style for a visit that would last two months; as there were nineteen in their party, planning for their accommodation proved a major headache for Dorothy. On 28 August Thomas Arnold, the future headmaster of Rugby school, but then a twenty-three-year-old graduate of Oxford, called at Rydal Mount. Arnold immediately fell in love with the house and the vale, 'one of the most beautiful Situations I ever saw'.

As the winter closed in, comparative peace and quiet returned to the Wordsworth household, and William was suddenly seized with the desire to write. 'W is at this moment sitting, as he has been all the morning, except while he dashed off a letter to Till[brooke] with his feet on the Fender, and his verses in his hand –', Mary wrote with pride and delight on 1 December; 'nay now they have dropped upon his knee and he is asleep from sheer exhaustion – he has worked so long. He has written 21 Sonnets (including 2 [o]ld ones) on the river Duddon – they all [to]gether comprise one Poem'. Over the years William had written a number of sonnets inspired by the River Duddon, which had been a favourite haunt since childhood. Now he had had the idea of drawing these together, adding more and creating a single body of work.

Strictly speaking, as William was uncomfortably aware, it was not his idea at all. Coleridge had first suggested writing a poem about a river twenty years ago at Alfoxton. More importantly, only eighteen months previously he had referred to it in his *Biographia Literaria*. There he explained that he had intended to call his poem 'the Brook', and trace its route from its source among the lonely hills, through farms, villages, market towns and manufactories, to a great seaport. The river image was the perfect vehicle for a poet, Coleridge added, offering a unifying theme with 'freedom for description, incident, and impassioned reflections on men, nature, and society'. This familiar phrase was, as we know, shorthand for *The Recluse*. Anticipating both the obvious inference that he was also indebted to Coleridge for the concept of this new work, and Coleridge's inevitable criticism that, like *The Recluse*, it did not live up to the grandiose philosophical ideas proposed for 'the Brook', William wrote a characteristically aggressive postscript to accompany the final published text. The sonnets were 'the growth of many years', he stated; as he had added to them, he had 'proceeded insensibly, without perceiving that I was trespassing upon ground pre-occupied, at least as far as intention went, by Mr Coleridge'. Acknowledging that Coleridge had described his scheme in 'a recent publication', William went on the offensive.

a particular subject cannot, I think, much interfere with a general one; and I have been further kept from encroaching upon any right Mr C. may still wish to exercise, by the restriction which the frame of the Sonnet imposed upon me, narrowing unavoidably the range of thought, and precluding, though not without its advantages, many graces to which a freer movement of verse would naturally have led.

He concluded by expressing the hope that his own publication would spur Coleridge to fulfil his 'own more comprehensive design'.

Despite these protestations, it is impossible to avoid the suspicion that reading about 'the Brook' in the *Biographia Literaria* planted the seed in William's mind for *The River Duddon*. Only a handful of the thirty-three sonnets were old ones, and at least nineteen were demonstrably written this winter. What is more, linking them together created a poem that was much more than the sum of its parts. This was very important to William, for he was sensitive to the criticism that he had done nothing towards *The Recluse* since publishing *The Excursion*.

A sustained return to poetry was under threat from a new quarter in the winter of 1818–19. The problem was Johnny. He was now fifteen and, if he was to go to university, as the family hoped and planned, he needed to have a better education than that afforded by Mr Dawes. The brilliant Hartley Coleridge had just taken his degree at Oxford, but had only been placed in the second class, a failure which was generally attributed to the defects in his early education. The Wordsworths were anxious to avoid the same mistake with their son and the only option open was for William himself to teach Johnny. 'It is very unfit that his Father's time should be consumed in a task that an inferior Person could perform much better', Sara complained. Even Christopher added his voice: 'I hope you will not think of preparing him for College yourself. You have be[en] already too much and too long separated from the Recluse, by executorship & election matters.' Determined to do the best for his son, William ignored this advice, preferring instead to consult the founder of the Madras System, Dr Bell, and Johnson, both of whom visited Rydal Mount in the new year.

Bell arrived just as the Wordsworths were decorating Rydal Mount with evergreens as they prepared to host a grand ball on 7 January 1819 for Dora and her friends. Mrs Coleridge had brought her daughter, Sara, and niece, Edith Southey, to stay on New Year's Eve and, on the day of the ball, they were joined by Dora's fellow pupils from Ambleside. Miss Fletcher's little boarding school had been taken over by Miss Dowling, a former governess, who ran it on the Madras System and had rapidly achieved excellent results. Dora had recently been joined there by Mary Calvert, the daughter of William's old friend from Keswick, and Sophia

Crump, from Allan Bank, both of whom were to be among her closest confidantes for the rest of her life.

Against the odds, literary matters did take precedence throughout the spring of 1819. Much to William's impotent fury, three sonnets he had written in the winter appeared without his prior knowledge or permission in the January edition of *Blackwood's Magazine*. The poems had been inspired by William Westall's recently published *Views of the Caves near Ingleton, Gordale Scar, and Malham Cove in Yorkshire*. William had presented Westall with copies of the sonnets when he stayed at Rydal Mount the previous November and Westall had passed them on to Wilson, the editor of *Blackwood's*. This was a significant coup for Westall and, more especially, the magazine, for William loathed *Blackwood's* heartily. To vent his indignation a little, William sent newly revised and updated versions of the poems to de Quincey, suggesting he might like to include them in the *Westmorland Gazette*, where they duly appeared, with his letter, on 6 February.

The same month, an engraving of William's portrait by Carruthers appeared in the *New Monthly Magazine* as part of a series of literary profiles. Southey remarked that William had got off lightly, for it was 'a respectable likeness', but the accompanying brief memoir was so extravagantly laudatory as to be embarrassing (and unrecognizable). It read more like Squire Wordsworth than Wordsworth the revolutionary poet, describing him as 'a good husband, father and friend, esteemed in his neighbourhood ... a loyal subject of the King, and a sincere member of the Church of England'. The mystery becomes a little clearer when we discover that the information had been supplied by Scambler, the well-meaning Ambleside physician, who shared William's enthusiasm for the Lowther cause.

Oddly, Scambler's opinion was borne out by a distinguished visitor to the Lakes in March, the American George Ticknor, who had just been appointed Professor of Belles Lettres at Harvard University. 'He is about fifty-three or four,' Ticknor noted in his journal (William was actually forty-eight), 'with a tall, ample, well-proportioned frame, a grave and tranquil manner, a Roman cast of appearance, and Roman dignity and simplicity ... His conversation surprised me by being so different from all I had anticipated. It was exceedingly simple, strictly confined to subjects he understood familiarly, and more marked by plain good-sense than by anything else.' It was, Ticknor added, with evident feeling, only when he talked poetry that he became metaphysical and extravagant. 'It was best of all, though, to see how he is loved and respected in his family and neighbourhood ... The peasantry treated him with marked respect, the children took off their hats to him, and a poor widow in the neighbourhood sent to him to come and talk to her son, who had been behaving ill'. In the evening, William showed Ticknor the manuscript of *The Prelude* and read to him *Peter Bell* and *Benjamin the Waggoner*. The choice of these two poems, rather than any of the Duddon sonnets he was then writing, was significant, because William was, at long last, about to publish them.

Peter Bell had, quite literally, come of age; it was now twenty-one years old. Why William decided to publish it at this point is unclear, for its reception was entirely predictable. The poem was duly advertised to be published early in April, but before it reached the shops an extraordinary thing happened. Keats's friend Reynolds, who had once addressed an admiring sonnet to William, hastily composed a parody of the as yet unseen poem and got it into print a week before the genuine article. *Peter Bell, A Lyrical Ballad* is a very funny romp through a graveyard where all the characters of the *Lyrical Ballads* lie buried. Even funnier is the accompanying prose, for Reynolds decked the poem out complete with Wordsworthian Preface, Supplementary Essay and Notes, which are wickedly accurate in lampooning William's style.

Reynolds's witty parody enjoyed great success: it was reviewed in at least thirteen journals and went into three editions. Against the odds, William also benefited. The first edition of *Peter Bell* sold out within a fortnight and a second one had to be printed to meet the demand. It was a popular success of a kind William had never before experienced. What is even more striking about the reviews which followed is that, although they were almost universally condemnatory, the tone changed from bitter invective to what one can only describe as good-humoured indulgence of the poet's foibles.

This is all the more extraordinary because *Peter Bell* is one of the most defiantly mould-breaking of all William's poems, with an ass and a womanizing, heavy-drinking, thieving potter as its subjects, and a belligerently 'unpoetic' vocabulary. William was equally confrontational in his dedication of the poem. *Peter Bell* was dedicated to the beleaguered Poet Laureate, Robert Southey. This was undoubtedly a public gesture of political solidarity, for Southey had been under sustained and bitter attack in the press since the publication (without his consent or knowledge) of his radical drama *Wat Tyler* in 1817. Written in 1794, the poem was used as a stick to beat all those who, like Southey, Coleridge and William himself, had turned from youthful republicanism to middle-aged Toryism. Coleridge had reacted by blustering denials of his past, but both Southey and William candidly acknowledged it. *Peter Bell*, as William unnecessarily pointed out in his introductory remarks, had been written in 1798. By dedicating it to Southey, he effectively stood up to be counted alongside his friend.

There had been a sea-change in opinion. The *Eclectic Review*, for instance, mocked the name and subject of the poem, but closed with the telling comment, 'he is a poet that, after all, cannot be laughed down'. Reviewing the poem in greater depth a couple of months later, the critic explained, 'In spite of the imbecilities of style which run through the narrative, and in spite of our determination not to allow *Peter Bell*, the potter, to gain upon our feelings, the Poet got the better of us, and we closed the Tale resolved, even at the imminent risk of being set down for *Lakers* ourselves, to do its Author justice.'

William naturally felt the criticisms more than the appreciation, but the females of his household could see that the reviews indirectly admitted the importance and pervasiveness of William's influence on contemporary poetry, and therefore urged him to publish *Benjamin the Waggoner* with the second edition of *Peter Bell*, 'just to give them another bone to pick'. These reviews were a mixed bag. Some liked its light, playful mood and simple, unaffected lyrics; others could not resist the opportunity to mock. Benjamin's waggon was said to carry heavy loads from the Lakes to London, 'Mr W's own works included', and the accuracy of William's description of the drinking scene in the inn prompted tongue-in-cheek insinuations that he was drawing on personal experience.

Letters arriving at Rydal Mount suggested a happier reception among the reading public. De Quincey wrote a graceful tribute: 'In common with all Englishmen who know anything on the subject of Poetry, – I feel more and more how great a debt of gratitude is owing to you for the vast services which you have rendered to the literature of the country and eventually to the interests of Human Nature.' William Pearson, a friend from Kendal, was more forthright. 'You may not dislike to hear the <u>real</u> opinions of some of your less learned admirers', he wrote. The Waggoner, he declared, was the most lively and humorous of all William's poems, and therefore more accessible: 'it comes more home to the business and bosoms of <u>every-day</u> Man'.

The summer of 1819 was unusually quiet. Many of the former Lakers were now abroad, enjoying the first opportunity to travel in comparative peace and security in Europe for many a long year. William had been sorely tempted by the idea of a trip to the Continent, or even to Norway, but he was obliged to conceal his disappointment as best he could. His self-imposed task of teaching Johnny effectively tied him to home. The difficulty of fulfilling this commitment was now forcibly brought home to him when he suffered another severe bout of trachoma. He could neither read nor write, let alone supervise his son's studies; any sort of strain on his eyes aggravated the condition. His eyelids were so painful and swollen that he could not appear in public and he was even obliged to give up an invitation to meet Prince Leopold at Lowther on 23 September.

Reluctantly, William allowed himself to be persuaded that Johnny should go away to school, to Sedbergh, a grammar school of sixteenth-century foundation which, like Hawkshead, had strong links with Cambridge University. The appointment of the master and the control of the school's income were all in the hands of William's own *alma mater*, St John's College. Just ten miles east of Kendal, the school was gloriously situated in the pretty market town of Sedbergh, at the confluence of the lush pastoral dales which lie in the shadow of the tumescent Howgill Fells. The problem was that the school was in sharp decline. There were no longer any boarders, only eight day pupils, and William Stephens, the headmaster, whose wife had died giving birth to her twelfth living child in August, was obviously at death's door himself when the Wordsworths visited in October.

As soon as they left the school, William immediately sent the Kendal doctor over to see Stephens and, when he died a week later, the whole family were active in seeking donations towards a private subscription to support his destitute orphaned children. William also enlisted Lord Lonsdale's support in pressurizing St John's into appointing a more able successor. When the twenty-seven-year-old Henry Wilkinson, a Second Wrangler and fellow of St John's, took up the post, Johnny entered the school in April 1820. This time he went fearlessly, secure in the knowledge that his academic studies had blossomed under his father's tuition.

Six months earlier the decision to part with Willy, who was almost nine and a half, was less easily taken, but acted upon with less difficulty. His aunts were anxious to prise him away from his father, who, they were convinced, was spoiling the boy, and to get him into Charterhouse before it was too late. Johnson, the former curate of Grasmere church who was now the headmaster of the Central School in London, willingly agreed to admit Willy immediately and prepare him for entrance to Charterhouse in six months' time. Despite his youth, Willy was far more able and sociable than his elder brother. He settled quickly into his new school, piously informing his sister by letter that, 'for my own credit and your satisfaction, I mean to do my utmost that not one defect may be left and that I may get to the top of the Tree'.

Any hopes that he would be less indulged at boarding school proved ephemeral. His father's friends and relations fell over themselves in the mad scramble to entertain him. Nevertheless, despite his junketings and his fondness for over-eating and visiting the zoo, Willy did well enough at the Central School to secure a place at Charterhouse, to which he transferred at the beginning of April 1820.

For the first time, the Wordsworths could congratulate themselves on the fact that all three children were placed in good schools, doing well and promising better. The drawback was the financial cost. Unable to risk losing any of his small capital, but anxious to secure the best return for it, William sold off one of his small estates for £2,000, sought Lord Lowther's advice and invested the money for his children's education in the French Funds.

Having done his duty by his children, it was now high time that William should return to his own poetic labours and do his duty by himself. 'William has done nothing lately except a few Sonnets,' Dorothy apologized to Catherine Clarkson on 1 August, adding defensively, 'but these are exquisitely beautiful.' The sonnets were the final contributions to the River Duddon series, which William intended to publish the following spring. 'Then, *he says*', Sara wrote with an emphasis which all too clearly indicated her disbelief, 'he will never trouble himself with anything more but the *Recluse*'.

19. Rydal Water, a pencil and wash drawing by Thomas Chubbard, 1796. Rydal Mount lies just out of sight at the far end of the lake, on the lower slopes of Rydal Fell, which is the mountain on the left.

20. George Webster's architect's drawings for the north elevation of the Wordsworths' new house, which was to be built in the field in front of Rydal Mount if Lady le Fleming ended their tenancy, as she threatened to do in 1826. Note the vernacular round chimney stacks, pillared frontage, symbolic poet's lyre carved into the end gable and grand stone-built terrace.

North Elevation of a Residence.
designed for William Wordsworth Esq.
at Rydal.

Kendal
Abril 1826

ROOM AT RYDAL MOUNT.

21. The drawing room at Rydal Mount, drawn by William Westall and published by Edward Moxon in 1840. A crucially important picture in the iconography of the poet, this widely circulated engraving depicts William, aged seventy, standing before his fireside in his favourite pose (his hand tucked into his waistcoat), dictating to his wife. The image is deliberately domestic, but the portraits, busts and, above all, the book-lined shelves testify to the poet's calling. Westall's meretricious use of perspective makes the room appear far larger than it was in reality.

22. William Westall's delightful watercolour of Rydal Mount, painted in 1831 in Dora's sketchbook. Dora herself is in the garden.

23. The garden entrance to Rydal Mount, drawn by K. J. Bennett, one of a family of Quakers who visited the Wordsworths in 1846. The picture was drawn to sell at the Belfast Ladies' Bazaar for the Relief of Irish Destitution and was authenticated by William as 'A most correct Drawing of Rydal Mount'.

24. A highly dramatized painting of the Lower Falls at Rydal, to which all visitors to Rydal Mount, including the dowager Queen Adelaide, were escorted by the Wordsworths. Watercolour of 1780 by C. W. Bampflyde.

25. An early photograph of Rydal Mount, with the terrace steps leading to the overgrown mound, which gave the house its name, on the right.

26. William Wordsworth, aged seventy-two, painted by Benjamin Robert Haydon in 1842 as if the poet were standing on Helvellyn.

27. Mary Wordsworth, aged sixty-nine, miniature painted in oil on ivory by Margaret Gillies in November 1839.

28. Christopher Wordsworth, William's brother, painted as Master of Trinity College in 1824 by George Robson.

29. Henry Crabb Robinson, an undated portrait by J. J. Masquerier.

30. A slightly bizarre image of the tall William Wordsworth walking with short Hartley Coleridge, sketched from life in 1844 by John Peter Mulcaster. This is a watercolour copy by Tom Monkhouse's daughter, Mary Elizabeth; the original is lost.

31. Mary Elizabeth Monkhouse, daughter of Mary Wordsworth's cousin Tom Monkhouse, whose childish beauty and happy disposition inspired William's poem *The Infant M– M–*.

32. The Reverend Owen Lloyd, hard at work on a sermon, observed by Jessy Harden and H. Almack at Brathay Hall, *c.* 1827; an ink and wash drawing by John Harden, whose daughter, Jane, Owen hoped, but failed, to marry.

33. Dorothy Wordsworth, aged
sixty-one, painted by Samuel
Crosthwaite in 1833, during a
period of remission before her
final mental and physical collapse.
The dog, Miss Belle, was a stray
which the family did not have the
heart to turn away after it
followed William and his
son home.

34. Isabella Fenwick, aged
fifty-six, painted in 1839 by
Margaret Gillies. Miss Fenwick
was described by William as 'The
star which comes at close of day
to shine' and by Dora as her 'good
angel'; this picture inspired
William's poem *Upon a Portrait*.

35. John Wordsworth's
Vicarage at Whitwick,
Leicestershire, drawn by
his sister, Dora, in August
1828. It was here that
Dorothy, living out her
dream of keeping house in
a country parsonage,
caught the illness which
eventually led to
permanent mental and
physical impairment.

36. Samuel Taylor Coleridge, aged about fifty-two, drawn by Charles Robert Leslie, *c.* 1824.

37. Sir Francis Legatt Chantrey's bust of the Poet Laureate, Robert Southey, aged fifty-eight, taken in 1832.

38. A re-creation of the famous visit by William Wordsworth (*standing*) and Sir Walter Scott to the Yarrow in 1831, which inspired William's *Yarrow Revisited*. After a painting by George Cattermole (1800–1868), illustrator of Scott's *Waverley Novels*.

39. Dora Wordsworth, painted by Margaret Gillies in November 1839. Dora later visited Miss Gillies's studio in London 'to have my nose reduced a little'. After Dora's death, at Quillinan's request, Miss Gillies retouched the portrait again to make her appear more 'spiritualized'.

40. (*Below left*) John Wordsworth, the only known portrait of Dora's brother as a young man.

41. (*Below right*) Willy Wordsworth, with his daughter, Mary Louisa, who was born in 1849. Willy's strong resemblance to his father is a family characteristic still in evidence among Wordsworth descendants to this day.

19. A Tour of the Continent

On 29 January 1820 King George III died. His reign had been distinguished by its length, the loss of the American colonies and the struggle against, and final defeat of, Bonaparte. For the last nine years, he had been a pitiable figure, blind and insane, a 'dread Shadow of a King! Whose realm had dwindled to one stately room'. According to the Constitution, the death of the reigning monarch demanded an immediate dissolution of Parliament and the calling of a general election. After a lull of only eighteen months, William would again be dragged from Parnassus into the muddy waters of politics. Once again he found himself in almost daily correspondence with one or other of the Lowthers, reporting local sentiments, drawing attention to dissatisfaction among the voters and identifying attempts by Brougham's supporters to create more freeholds.

Fortunately, there was not the same need to become a propagandist in this election. De Quincey's dilatory habits had forced his resignation from the editorship of the *Westmorland Gazette* on 5 November 1819, so the paper had become less controversial, and William's intervention was no longer required. Nevertheless, much of his time was taken up with visits to the hustings throughout the county, leading Sara to complain in April, 'This work will never have an end – Poetry & all good & great things will be lost in Electioneering.' When the poll finally did close, the Lowther brothers retained their seats and Brougham was discomforted once more.

Throughout this winter and spring, William was putting the finishing touches to the River Duddon volume. There were now thirty-three sonnets. As a note to that on Seathwaite Chapel, William added a twenty-page memoir of 'Wonderful Walker', the humble pastor who had faithfully served his flock there for sixty-six years and whose memory was still revered in the Duddon valley. The book closed with a revised version of William's *Guide to the District of the Lakes*, now published independently of Wilkinson's plates for the first time. The inclusion of these two long prose digressions from the poetry was important, for together they proved a potent combination. They not only staked William's claim to be the Poet of the Lakes (rather than just one of the Lake School, as Jeffrey had so often taunted him), but each piece underpinned and reaffirmed his profound belief in the unique moral character of his corner of England. Like *The Excursion*, which he reissued at the same time, in a second, smaller-format edition, the *River Duddon* was imbued with William's politics. The memoir of Walker was simply a historic example of the independent rural virtues of the Lakeland statesmen. The dedicatory poem to Christopher Wordsworth emphasized this point.

> Hail, ancient Manners! sure defence,
> Where they survive, of wholesome laws . . .
> Hail, Usages of pristine mould,
> And ye that guard them, Mountains old!

In *After-Thought*, the final sonnet of the series, which is incomparably the best, William assumed an elegiac note in bidding farewell to the Duddon as it reached the sea.

> I thought of Thee, my partner and my guide,
> As being past away. – Vain sympathies!
> For, backward, Duddon! as I cast my eyes,
> I see what was, and is, and will abide;
> Still glides the Stream, and shall for ever glide;
> The Form remains, the Function never dies;
> While we, the brave, the mighty, and the wise,
> We Men, who in our morn of youth defied
> The elements, must vanish; – be it so!
> Enough, if something from our hands have power
> To live, and act, and serve the future hour;
> And if, as toward the silent tomb we go,
> Through love, through hope, and faith's transcendent dower,
> We feel that we are greater than we know.

The air of finality which pervades this poem was indicative of William's own mood. *The River Duddon, A Series of Sonnets: Vaudracour and Julia: and Other Poems. To Which Is Annexed, a Topographical Description of the Country of the Lakes, in the North of England* was printed and published by Longman in April 1820. Purchasers were informed that it completed 'the third and last volume of the Author's Miscellaneous Poems'. The implication, as the *Eclectic Review* was quick to point out, was that the poet would write no more. What William actually meant was that there would be no more miscellaneous poems because from now on he intended to work solely on

The Recluse. However, he did not intend to advertise the fact to the world again. It would be time enough to talk of *The Recluse* when – if – it was completed.

In what was probably intended as a final clearing of the decks in preparation for embarkation on *The Recluse*, William also performed a complete overhaul of all his published work, reissuing it in July in what Sara described as '4 nice pocket volumes – far more agreeable to my mind than the last ones'. This was not simply a cynical exercise in commercialism, but a comprehensive revision, re-editing and, in some cases, rewriting of all his poems which had ever appeared in print. What is more, many of the changes were a response to criticism, particularly by Coleridge, whose judgement in such matters was incomparable.

All this was achieved despite continuing trouble with his eyes which prevented him reading or writing by candlelight. The recurrence of the trachoma had raised a very real fear in William's mind that, like his hero, Milton, he might be going blind. This was an added incentive to get his poems republished in what might be regarded as the definitive version, though labouring over the proofs aggravated the condition. In January he had decided that he would go to London in May and, if possible, spend the summer in Switzerland. Sara had nobly volunteered to stay behind in charge of the Stamp Office, since Dorothy was determined to accompany her brother and Mary too had a rare opportunity to go, with all three children away at school.

Dorothy had gone to London at the beginning of April, partly to take personal charge of the printing at Longman's, but mainly to see a London dentist. She was now forty-nine years old and, though remarkably fit for her age, she had 'a true old woman's mouth and chin' because she had just six teeth left. She had long contemplated acquiring false ones but had balked at the hazards of provincial dentistry and the cost of a London orthodontist. Emboldened by the imminent departure for the Continent, she took the plunge. She paid fifty guineas to a Mr Dumergue, had her remaining teeth pulled and, while she waited for her gums to heal and the new set to be made, took refuge with Christopher at Lambeth.

When the Wordsworths arrived in London, their plans for going abroad had to be put on hold. Christopher was dangerously ill and it was impossible for Dorothy to leave him. Overworked and disinclined to pamper his own ailments, his recovery was slow, but towards the end of June he went to Hampstead to stay with the Hoares, and Dorothy, sporting her new set of false teeth, was free to join the touring party. This had now grown considerably in size. Tom Monkhouse had long been included in their plans, but at the beginning of June he announced his engagement to Jane Horrocks, sister of the MP for Preston, and, according to Robinson, 'a young and very beautiful woman'. The bride and one of her sisters would accompany them, and the Wordsworths' Continental tour was thus transformed into the Monkhouses' wedding tour.

After a final consultation with a London oculist, to ensure that William's eyes would be up to the journey, the Wordsworths finally left Lambeth for Dover on 10 July. There they were joined by the newlyweds, who had married on 8 July, and Miss Horrocks. Next day, after a swift passage of less than four hours, they landed at Calais on the first stage of a tour that was to last four months and take them through France, the Low Countries, Germany, northern Italy and Switzerland. As they soon discovered, the Wordsworths and the Horrockses were chalk and cheese. The Wordsworths, and Dorothy in particular, were on a pilgrimage to re-create William's tour of 1790; they wanted to see all he had seen, stay where he had stayed and literally walk in his footsteps. Jane Monkhouse and her sister (plus maid) were on a fashionable Continental tour. They wanted to visit all the usual places frequented by English society travellers, do it as easily as possible and mix only with their fellow countrymen. Poor Tom was torn between the two, with unfortunate consequences for his marriage and his future happiness.

Everyone in the party kept a travel diary, apart from William. Three survive, Dorothy's, Mary's and Robinson's, and of the three only Mary's has not been published. This is unfortunate. It is every bit as observant and perceptive as her sister-in-law's, but spiced with her own brand of mordant humour.

At Calais, they bought two second-hand travelling carriages and set off at a cracking pace through what is now Flanders and Belgium as far as Cologne, where they turned southwards and followed the Rhine for almost 280 miles before entering Switzerland. On the field of Waterloo they were fortunate to encounter a man who had been compelled to act as Bonaparte's guide on the battlefield and had been at his side until he fled in defeat. He escorted them round, as he had Southey some time before, pointing out to them all the memorable places where the action had taken place. For the Wordsworths it was the equivalent of a trip today to the killing-fields of the Somme. 'We stood upon grass, and corn fields where *heaps* of our countrymen lay buried beneath our feet', Dorothy wrote in her journal. 'There was little to be seen; but much to be felt; – sorrow and sadness, and even something like horror breathed out of the ground as we stood upon it!' William worked this moment up into one of the best of his sonnets memorializing this tour. It opens with an image of the goddess of victory hovering above the 'far-famed Spot' and bestowing her crowns and garlands, but ends on an altogether more sombre note.

> She vanished; leaving prospect blank and cold
> Of wind-swept corn that wide around us rolled
> In dreary billows, wood, and meagre cot,
> And monuments that soon must disappear;
> Yet a dread local recompense we found;
> While glory seemed betrayed, while patriot-zeal
> Sank in our hearts, we felt as men *should* feel
> With such vast hoards of hidden carnage near,
> And horror breathing from the silent ground!
> *After Visiting the Field of Waterloo, ll.6–14*

William's occasional fits of poetic inspiration on the tour were not always welcome, for he became morose and introverted until he had finished to his own satisfaction.

After only eighteen days of this hectic pace, the cracks began to show. Mrs Monkhouse had been constantly 'unwell' with headaches and sickness, retreating early to her bed and opting out of the daily pedestrian exploration of the towns in which they stayed. As they made their way to the borders of Switzerland, she decided she wanted to go to Baden-Baden, the fashionable spa in the foothills of the Black Forest. Tom was determined to humour her, so the party temporarily went their separate ways: the Monkhouses, Miss Horrocks, the maid and Dorothy making a three-day detour to Baden-Baden, and William and Mary travelling on to Schaffhausen alone. This was a considerable sacrifice on Dorothy's part, for she was longing to get to Switzerland, but none of the Monkhouse party could speak sufficient German, so her services were required as interpreter. As they finally crossed over from Germany into Switzerland, Dorothy abandoned the carriage and walked. It was a symbolic gesture, a conscious re-enactment of her brother's pedestrian tour of 1790.

The Wordsworths took on a new lease of life in Switzerland. The carriages were abandoned and they took to their feet, determined to cross and recross the Alps with all the vigour of people half their age. The problem, once again, was the Monkhouse party. It was not to be expected that the ladies would be capable of such exertion and another parting of the ways was inevitable. What was unexpected, and deeply shocked everyone who found out, was Tom's decision to go with the Wordsworths. For all her selfish and self-pitying behaviour, it is impossible not to feel sorry for Jane Monkhouse, married for only a month and then abandoned by her husband in a foreign country while on her bridal tour. With her sister and maid she would take up residence in Geneva and await the return of her husband and the rest of the party.

The carriages were disposed of at Berne and a large portion of their luggage was forwarded to Geneva, in the care of John Wedgwood, whom William had not seen for twenty one years and unexpectedly bumped into at the Staub-back falls. At Lucerne they were joined by Robinson, and the Wordsworth party took to the hills. They climbed every mountain, forded every stream, visited the waterfalls, traversed the glaciers and sailed on the lakes. Everywhere they went, they constantly compared all the sights to those of their own lakes and mountains – despite William's strictures against tourists doing the reverse in his *Guide to the Lakes*. Most of all, they saw everything through the filter of William's earlier experience, as portrayed in *Descriptive Sketches* and *The Prelude*. 'I find that my remembrance for thirty years has been scarcely less vivid than the reality now before my eyes!' William declared. Significantly, though all their minds were constantly recurring to that earlier, profoundly important tour, not a single poem in *Memorials of a Tour on the Continent, 1820* would look back or refer to it. For a poet whose work was built upon the subtle fusion of past and present experience and remembered emotions, this was extraordinary.

They were reunited with Mrs Monkhouse, her sister and maid at Geneva, and from there the entire party made a swift dash through Dijon and Sens to Paris, where it was now possible for them all to go their separate ways without inviting comment. The Monkhouses and Robinson found accommodation in hotels, while the Wordsworths stayed in Rue Charlot, taking lodgings next door to Annette and Caroline. 'Mr Eustace Baudouin met us at the door of our lodgings; –', Dorothy wrote for her entry on 1 October, 'and here ends my Journal.'

Her discretion is infuriating, for one longs to know how they all reacted to this long-anticipated meeting between William's two families. There are hints in Dorothy's sketchy notes and from Robinson's diary that it was not without its emotional cost. Nor is it surprising that the person who suffered most was Mary, who found it hard to come to terms with meeting William's first family face to face. Indeed, Robinson consistently showed a delicate sympathy for Mary's plight, visiting her and chaperoning her round Paris while her husband and sister-in-law were with the Baudouins. Meeting them himself, he found Caroline 'a mild amiable little woman in appearance' and liked everything about her, 'except that she called Wordsworth "father" which I thought indelicate'. What Robinson found 'indelicate' must have been painful to Mary, and perhaps explains why, for the first time in four months, she became 'poorly'.

Both Eustace Baudouin and his brother, the Colonel, escorted the Wordsworths round the sights of Paris: they went to Fontainebleau, Versailles, the Palais Royale, the Père Lachaise cemetery, Notre-Dame, the Louvre and the Jardin des Plantes. Helen Maria Williams was still a resident of Paris and Robinson, who was involved in her latest publication, effected the introduction which had eluded William in 1791–2. Then it had been the young unknown poet, whose sole publication had been his sonnet to Miss Williams, who sought the introduction; now it was she who anxiously and rather touchingly assured him 'how deeply she has felt the power of his compositions' and 'how much she would regret losing an opportunity of being introduced to him'.

The Wordsworths left Paris at the end of October and made their way to Boulogne. They were eager to be back in England, and when the packet boat could not sail on the day appointed for their departure, they foolishly took passage on a smaller boat which, alone of all the ships in harbour, was willing to defy the contrary winds and huge breakers. Ten minutes after leaving harbour, their boat struck the rocks, water began to pour in and it looked as if they would all be lost. Fortunately, the tide was running in their favour, the boat was soon left stranded high and dry, and the Wordsworths had an undignified return to Boulogne in the carts sent across the bay to rescue them. It was 7 November before they finally set foot on English soil again, prompting not one but two heartfelt sonnets from William addressed to Dover.

It is possible, but unlikely, that they arrived in London in time for William to attend the final day of Queen Caroline's trial for adultery, as his portrait was included in a curious picture depicting this scene in the House of Lords. At Lugano they had actually stayed in the same rooms occupied by Caroline and her alleged paramour, Count Bergami, but as the painter, James Stephanoff, also included a number of other celebrities, including Byron and Moore, who were demonstrably unable to attend, William's inclusion was not so much a record of fact, or even a statement of sympathy, as simply a recognition of his growing public reputation.

This was immediately apparent during this visit to London, for the reviews of the *River Duddon* had been uniformly the best William had ever received. Though Mary was 'painfully anxious to be at home' and Sara, who had been left holding the fort at Rydal Mount, was now 'quite *angry*' with them for prolonging their absence, the Wordsworths lingered almost a month in London, spending most of their time in social parties and attending exhibitions.

At the end of November, the Wordsworths left London for Cambridge, where they were to spend a fortnight with Christopher, who had just taken up residence in the magnificent Master's Lodgings of Trinity College. With his usual talent for finding work, Christopher had not only taken on the mastership but also the vice-chancellorship of the university, and he was determined to reform and liberalize the Cambridge syllabus. William was impressed with what he now saw of a Cambridge which was very different from that of his youth. Observing the 'great ardour of Study among the young Men', their more temperate habits, and the zeal with which their masters, tutors and lecturers discharged their duties, he could not but augur well for the rising generation.

Dorothy would remain in the south until the end of January, dividing her time between her brother and his three sons at Cambridge and the Clarksons at Playford Hall. William and Mary left Cambridge for the north on 6 December, breaking their journey at Coleorton, where Lady Beaumont wanted William's advice on replanting some of the winter garden. The Beaumonts were always congenial hosts and the intended week-long visit turned into a fortnight, so it was 20 December before the Wordsworths finally turned their faces towards home.

William and Mary had been away for six long months and much had happened in their absence. Their old friend and trusted physician in so many times of need, Richard Scambler, had died, leaving a widow and nine children in straitened circumstances. John Wordsworth, the younger brother of Mary Peake, had fallen victim to the sailor's scourge, yellow fever, and died on board ship. The districts of Maryport, Cockermouth and Workington had all been added to William's Stamp Distributorship in his absence, and Carter had assimilated them smoothly and without difficulty.

There were some things Carter could not do, however, and within days of his return William had to go off to Appleby to dismiss the sub-distributor and inform the Stamp Office of his new appointments to this office and the three new districts. He had barely returned home again when he had to go chasing off to Millom, on the Duddon estuary, on distressingly personal business. John Myers, his cousin and inseparable friend at university, had been found dead on the floor of his bedroom. The news was not unexpected to the Wordsworths, who were all too aware of his intemperate habits since the death of his wife, but it was a profound shock to his father, the eighty-five-year-old Reverend Thomas Myers. It fell to William to break the news to John's only child, nine-year-old Julia, who was Dora's fellow pupil at Miss Dowling's school at Ambleside. He also had to organize the funeral at Millom and, in March, a sale of his cousin's household effects and livestock. Myers's death was the fourth in the Wordsworth family in just over twelve months. Another cousin to whom they had been very close, Captain John Wordsworth, had died in December 1819, and on 23 February 1820 Uncle William Cookson had died after a lingering illness. William was rapidly acquiring the unwanted position of head of the family.

Two more deaths in February 1821 affected William deeply, but in a profoundly different way. On the 23rd, twenty-five-year-old John Keats coughed his last in Rome, his early demise attributed by common report to his sensitivity to the hostile reviews. Four days later, John Scott, the youthful editor of the *Champion*, died of wounds received in a duel over a literary squabble with Lockhart. William had liked Keats and admired his talent, believing him to be 'a youth of promise too great for the sorry company he keeps', but Scott's unnecessary and futile death was more distressing. And, as always, he was among the first to make discreet inquiries about the financial circumstances of Scott's bereaved family.

William's own work progressed swiftly this spring, despite recurrent problems with his eyes. His first priority was not poetry, however, but a new edition of his *Guide to the Lakes*. The decision to expand and publish it separately was prompted by the commendation of this section in at least four important reviews of the *River Duddon*. And every visitor to Rydal Mount, friend or stranger, wanted the benefit of William's advice on how to make the best of their tour of the Lakes. There was clearly a demand for such a publication, and in fulfilling it there was a chance of recovering some of the cost of the Continental tour.

The direction of his poetic endeavours surprised even his sister. 'William is quite well, and very busy,' she informed Catherine in March, 'though he has not looked at the Recluse or the poem on his own life; and this disturbs us.' With an unintentional pun, she announced, almost apologetically, to her Quaker friend that William was now composing a series of sonnets on a subject 'which I am sure you would never divine, – the Church of England, – but you will perceive that in the hands of a poet it is one that will furnish ample store of poetic materials'. Southey was also struck by William's choice of subject. 'Wordsworth was with me last week', he wrote on 15 April.

Oddly enough, while I have been employed on my Book of the Church, he has been writing a series of historical sonnets upon the same subject, of the very highest species of excellence. My book will serve as a running commentary to his series, and the one will materially help the other; and thus, without any concerted purpose, we shall go down to posterity in company . . .

The coincidence was not as remarkable as either man supposed, for they were both reacting to one of the burning political issues of the day, the perceived threat to the Established Church from the relaxation of constitutional rules excluding Roman Catholics from positions of secular authority and power. 'I cannot but tremble at the prospect of introducing men who *may* turn, and (if they act consistently with the spirit of their Religion and even with its open profession) *must* turn their mutual fidelity against our Protestant Establishment', he wrote to Viscount Lowther; 'till in co-operation with other Dissenters and Infidels, they have accomplished its overthrow'.

As long ago as 1812, William had declared that he would shed his blood in defence of the Church of England. (He rather spoilt the effect by confessing 'he knew not when he had been in a church at home "All our ministers are such vile creatures" '.) Ink was a more appropriate commodity for a poet than blood, and William shed a great deal of it, writing 102 sonnets descriptive of the history of the Church in England. The subtext was a celebration of the Church of England as a unifying force for moral good and its clergymen as a civilizing and elevating influence, particularly in rural communities. Its doctrines were, in some senses, irrelevant. It was still literally a broad church, encompassing many shades of opinion. As an institution, it remained a bulwark against sectarianism and factionalism, a final defence against anarchy. The poems were much admired in their day, but even then it was their pious sentiment, rather than their poetical quality, which drew approval. They are not the sort of work which a modern reader, however religiously inclined, would choose to read voluntarily.

It was not just the Church of England that was under threat in the spring of 1821. On 22 March Joseph Hume, a radical MP, made a speech in the House of Commons proposing the abolition of the posts of Receiver-General and Distributors of Stamps, on the grounds of economy and a reduction of the influence of patronage. Distributors, he argued, were sinecurists who received too high a percentage of the public money passing through their hands and earned interest on it too. Viscount Lowther leapt to William's defence, armed with a list of his duties and responsibilities and a candid account of his profits. Recently, he had been collecting £18,000 a year, of which more than half was always forwarded direct to the Stamp Office; the remainder was sometimes banked, but rarely earned interest because it was mostly paid in provincial and Scottish notes, on which the banks refused to pay interest until they had been in their hands for six weeks. From interest he therefore received next to nothing; from the 4 per cent he was allowed to deduct for his own profit (£720 in total out of the £18,000), he had to pay a pro rata percentage to each of his sub-distributors. Despite the Solicitor-General being favourably impressed with William's submission, Hume succeeded in getting his motion referred to an investigative Commons committee, changes would become inevitable and William would never again be able to view his government office as a certain source of income.

The summer proved to be one of the busiest in many years and there was not a spare bed in the house for months on end. Sara, who had left for Stockton as soon as William and Mary returned from the Continent, came back in May, bringing her oldest niece, Bessy, with her for the grand Ambleside ball, though bad weather frustrated the usual picnics and excursions. To the initial joy of the entire family, Joe Monkhouse suddenly announced his intention to pay them a visit. Joe, the youngest of the three brothers, had lived for many years in the West Indies, where he was the manager of sugar plantations on Jamaica. He had made money not only by slave labour on the plantations, but also by speculating in selling them. As his shocked family were about to discover, he had also used them in other ways, having fathered several children, all by different slave women. One of these, his three-year-old son George, he now brought with him to England, with the obvious intention of leaving him in the care of his relations. 'I am not partial to such like progeny', his sister wrote coldly, 'and shall feel great reluctance to have it introduced amongst mine which I suppose he will expect.'

Whether it was the thought of little George's illegitimacy, his slave descent or his negroid blood which had so alienated his English relations, when Joe died, on 2 September 1822, leaving him penniless, they all rallied round. His Uncle John offered him a home at the Stow, Tom undertook to pay for his clothing and education and Mary, in a sudden sympathetic return of maternal feeling, welcomed him into the bosom of the family. 'He is a sweet little fellow as can be –,' Tom wrote with surprise and delight, 'of a mild disposition & very interesting & pensive Countenance'.

Rydal Mount was, as usual, a refuge for waifs and strays this summer. Richard's widow and her six-year-old son came to stay for five weeks. 'Keswick' John was 'a pretty genteel looking child – but when he speaks the revolution is astonishing! he has the very worst and most barbarous of all the dialects of Cumberland'. It was hoped that sending him to Sedbergh the following year would prove an effective cure. The orphaned Julia Myers also spent her summer holidays with the Wordsworths, before returning to Miss Dowling's with Dora, who was entering upon her last term at the school.

The most significant newcomer, however, was a half-pay Irish dragoon who had retired from the army and taken up residence in the Lakes. Edward Quillinan was thirty-one years old, a veteran of the Peninsular War, a minor poet and a fervent admirer of William's work. He was, quite literally, to become one of the Wordsworth family. Within a matter of weeks of his first meeting with William, Quillinan had left the army for good and taken up residence with his wife, Jemima, and their eighteen-month-old daughter, Mima, at Spring Cottage, under Loughrigg Fell in the Vale of Rydal. The two families were instantly on intimate terms. Quillinan almost succeeded in persuading William to accompany him on a five-week tour of his native Ireland that summer and, though this project fell through, he did join him on a short excursion into the Yorkshire Dales at the beginning of November.

Quillinan was an intelligent and agreeable companion for William, but he secured a lasting hold on the entire family's sympathies and affections by the sufferings which the autumn and following spring would inflict. In September, his wife gave birth to a second daughter, whom, at William's suggestion, they named Rotha, after the river flowing through the Vale of Rydal. A proud and delighted Dora was invited to join her father in standing as the baby's godparents, but they had to enter on their duties sooner than expected when Jemima failed to recover from the birth. Suffering from what would now be diagnosed as postnatal depression, she became so ill that Mary, her constant nurse, could do nothing for her, and she had to be removed to Lancaster for mental treatment. When Mary took her babes over to see her in the new year, she seemed to be making an excellent recovery, and the Wordsworths all looked forward to their return in April.

Throughout the year, Mary and Dorothy had been employed in writing up their journals of the previous summer's Continental tour. Mary dismissed hers as 'a mere transcript' of her notes, copied at her daughter's 'earnest request', because Dora could not read the hastily scribbled originals. Her transcript was ready by May, but she was 'so very shy of exposing it' that Sara made a fair copy of her own, 'that I might lend to whom I liked'. Their fellow traveller, Robinson, read the journal during his brief stay at Rydal Mount in August, and was 'greatly delighted with its minuteness and faithfullness; and liveliness of observation.' He was also permitted to read Dorothy's journal, as far as it went. It was a chastening experience for the habitual diarist. 'They filled me with shame at the comparison with my own … [they] drew my attention to a great and unobserved distinction. The ladies' journals abound in observations, and contain no reflexions.'

Anxious not to be influenced by Mary's work, Dorothy refused to read Mary's journal until she had completed a first draft of her own. This proved to be a far more laborious task. 'Had not my Brother so very much wished me to do my best,' she explained to Catherine Clarkson, 'I am sure I should never have had the resolution to go further than just re-copy what I did by snatches, and very irregularly, at the time; but to please him I have amplified and arranged; and a long affair will come out of it, which I cannot think any person can possibly have the patience to read through'.

The most effective way William found of motivating his sister was to offer to write poems for her to intersperse with her text, just as he had done with her *Recollections of a Tour in Scotland*. However, as with *Ecclesiastical Sketches*, it is as if his head, rather than his heart, was engaged in the work. Dorothy's comment on her own journal, 'you will be frightened when you see so many pages – all written about the outside of things hastily viewed!', is also a peculiarly apt description of the poems. The few poems intended for the journal soon swelled into thirty-eight, to which would be added a dedicatory poem to the fellow travellers, and a concluding poem, written when William received the proof sheets. As late as the end of November, when William was still trying to complete his sonnets for *Ecclesiastical Sketches*, which he intended to publish in the spring, there were no plans to publish the tour poems. Sara then made a fair copy of them for Tom Monkhouse, but he was strictly prohibited from recopying them for anyone else, even Robinson, though he was to be allowed to read them, if he wished. By the middle of January, Dorothy for one was convinced that they should be published: 'his work has grown to such importance (and has continued growing) that I have long ceased to consider it in connection with my own narrative of events unimportant, and lengthy descriptions'.

The conviction of all those of his fellow travellers who read the poems was that they ought to be published. Robinson advocated the idea of printing one of the journals with the poems intermixed, believing this would be more popular. It was a suggestion which had been mooted at Rydal Mount, as Mary admitted: 'we sometimes jestingly talk of raising a fund by such means for a second and a further trip into Italy!' Once William had decided to publish his poems as an independent collection, such a joint venture could not go ahead. Nevertheless, Dorothy could not quite let go of the idea. The thought that publishing her journal might raise enough money for her to afford a second tour was too alluring. In September William, who was even more anxious to see the journal in print than his sister, wrote to Rogers on her behalf, taking him up on his offer to assist in securing her a London publisher. Dorothy would not sacrifice her privacy by becoming a published author, she told Rogers, for less than £200. Whether he was unable to secure such a sum or her doubts finally got the better of her, the journal did not appear in print until long after the reluctant authoress was dead and buried.

Throughout January William revised his poems and added new ones. By the beginning of February *Memorials of a Tour on the Continent, 1820* was in the press and *Ecclesiastical Sketches* about to join it. The two little books were published by Longman in March to reviews which generally acknowledged William's staying power as a poet. Only two reviews struck a discordant note. The *Literary Gazette*, which paradoxically was part-owned by Longman, dismissed the *Memorials* with the pungent phrase 'there is hardly one . . . worth reading at all' and took William severely to task over *Ecclesiastical Sketches*. 'It is astonishing to see a man of genius so far delude himself as to fancy he can render any thing popular, no matter how untractable the subject, how prosaic the verse, and how absurd the plan.' And in November the acrid giant of the *Edinburgh Review* waded in with his customary arresting opening sentence: 'The Lake School of Poetry, we think, is now pretty nearly extinct.' William, Jeffrey went on, had 'exchanged the company of leech-gatherers for that of tax-gatherers' and had fallen into a distasteful way of writing, which was 'a sort of prosy, solemn, obscure, feeble kind of mouthing'. As both reviews were so obviously dictated by political enmity rather than literary judgement, they could be dismissed out of hand, more particularly as they were so out of tune with the general reception accorded the poems.

A third volume completed the trilogy of William's publications in 1822. This was his *Guide to the Lakes*, which he now republished as a separate volume for the first time. Substantial revision had taken place. Newly retitled with one of those comprehensive titles so beloved by the youthful William, *A Description of the Scenery of the Lakes in the North of England. Third Edition, (Now First Published Separately) with Additions, and Illustrative Remarks upon the Scenery of the Alps*, it too was published by Longman. Unlike William's poetry, it was to prove a great success, the 500 copies of the first edition selling out within the year, and double that number being printed for the next edition of 1823.

The publication of the three volumes of 1822 was to become a milestone in William's literary career. Everything he had ever written and wished to preserve for posterity was now in print, except for *The Prelude* and *The Recluse*. Once again, he was ready for a fresh start on his life's work. '*The Recluse* has had a long sleep, save in my thoughts,' he confessed to Walter Savage Landor in April; 'my MSS.

are so ill-penned and blurred that they are useless to all but myself; and at present I cannot face them.' He never would. And as far as the public were concerned, he now ceased to be a writing poet. It would be thirteen years before his name again appeared on the title-page of a new work.

This withdrawal into a silence of such duration was neither premeditated nor intentional. It simply arose from circumstances. Domestic concerns were at the forefront of William's mind throughout most of 1822. Dora had left Miss Dowling's school at Christmas, having regularly carried off prizes for her application and attainments. She was now almost eighteen: her education was complete, a career was out of the question and, like most girls of her age and class, she would remain at home until she married. In the summer she was joined by Willy, whose career at the Charterhouse was ignominiously cut short by the discovery that despite the 'enormous expense' lavished on his education, he had made very little progress. 'It does not appear to me –', wrote his Uncle Christopher, after examining him during the Christmas holidays, 'that his being at the Charter house hitherto has been very profitable: and yet I am far from seeing any natural deficiency about him.' It was clearly folly to keep him at the school: 'if he will be idle he must be idle at less cost!' Sara declared, feeling sorry for his elder brother. 'What would [Johnny] not give now for the advantages that this little *Monkey* has thrown away!'

At the beginning of May Willy was dispatched to join his brother at Sedbergh, but within weeks of his arrival he had to be sent home again. He was clearly very ill, dropsical as his anguished father described it, and for three weeks his family despaired of his life. Scambler's replacement, Thomas Carr, and a physician from Kendal were both brought over to treat him, and gradually he recovered his health and spirits, though he remained so delicate that he would not be sent away to school again. For the rest of his life William would be tortured with guilt, blaming himself for destroying Willy's health and education by sending him to the Charterhouse so young, and doing his best to compensate for what he considered the irreparable wrong he had done his son.

For the Wordsworths, Willy's brush with death was just the latest in a series of calamities. The Quillinans had returned to Rydal from Lancaster in March, taking up residence at Tillbrooke's Ivy Cottage, at the foot of the hill to the Mount. Jemima was apparently quite recovered but, a few weeks later, she accidentally set her clothes on fire and was horribly burnt. The Wordsworth women nursed her devotedly, day and night for a fortnight, but other than change her dressings there was little they could do to ease her suffering. Then Mary and Dora were suddenly called away to Lowther by the news that William had had an accident. Riding near Lowther with Tom Monkhouse and George Gee, his horse had taken fright and thrown him against a stone wall, gashing the back of his head. In this crisis, Dorothy was worse than useless: she simply took to her bed until reassurance arrived from Mary and Dora that her brother was on the mend. William's accident detained the family several days at Lowther rectory, where James Satterthwaite had kindly offered them all accommodation until the invalid was fit to travel home. As Sara was away sampling the waters at Harrogate, Dorothy was thus alone with Jemima

when she died, and it fell to her and Gee to arrange the funeral on behalf of
Quillinan. With strange prescience, Dorothy chose a site adjoining the graves of
the Wordsworth children as the place where Jemima would lie in Grasmere
churchyard. On 12 June Quillinan left Ivy Cottage, his dreams of settling permanently in the Lakes shattered by this unforeseen tragedy. Leaving his children with
his wife's family at Lee Priory, in Kent, he embarked on a series of lengthy
Continental tours in a fruitless flight from guilt and grief.

The summer saw an unusually large gathering at Rydal Mount. This was
occasioned, in part, by the christening of Tom Monkhouse's baby daughter, Mary
Elizabeth, who had been born the previous December. Jane had been slow to
recover from the birth and it was thought she might benefit from a change of air;
they were also about to move house and would have to go into temporary lodgings
until the new one was ready. It therefore made sense to do as Sara suggested and
take a cottage at Rydal from April till October. The christening was to be held on
9 August and the family gathered in force. Mary Hutchinson, who was to be
godmother, and her aunt, Elizabeth Monkhouse, who would remain at Rydal for
the winter, came up from Hindwell, Joanna, with Mrs Ellwood, from Penrith.

Coincidentally, too, Christopher Wordsworth and his three boys, aged seventeen, sixteen and fourteen, were taking their first ever holiday in the Lakes. Despite
seven weeks of incessant rain, both families took great delight in each other's
company. Christopher's boys were immediately enslaved by their lively, affectionate cousin Dora, and when they parted in September it was with genuine regret.
Charles was even prompted to verse.

> Fare thee well! Dear couzin Dora
> And believe me when I tell
> That my heart was never sorer
> Than at bidding thee Farewell –

Their father was equally smitten, this being the first chance he had ever had to get
to know his goddaughter.

As the Wordsworths left, Jack Hutchinson came, escorting two of his sons to
Sedbergh, where they were Johnny's fellow pupils, and taking Dora and her Aunt
Sara back with him to Stockton on a visit that would last till Christmas. They were
accompanied over Kirkstone Pass by William, who was on his way to Lowther,
and Dora's aunts Dorothy and Joanna. These two middle-aged ladies, in an unlikely
pairing and even more unlikely mood of adventure, were embarking on a tour of
Scotland together, without the benefit of masculine company or escort. Travelling
mostly by coach and steamboat, they made their way to Edinburgh, Stirling,
Glasgow, Inverary, as far north as Skye, then back down the western coast by
steamboat to Glasgow and home by the Lanark road. Dorothy was, once again,
assiduous in writing notes for her journal but without William to draw attention
to striking images, particularly in scenery, her own description was less vivid and
less original. As both Coleridge and de Quincey had recognized, her greatest gift

was to empathize and respond. It was essentially reactive. And without William to evoke a response, her journal lacks its usual sparkle.

Dorothy's return coincided with an unexpected and severe recurrence of Willy's summer illness. For ten days he stared death in the face, but once more he recovered. The doctor ordered a complete rest from all application to books and said that, for the next few months, he was to be watched over and treated like an invalid.

In the circumstances, it was not surprising that William found it hard to settle to poetry, though Quillinan's request that he would write an epitaph for his wife weighed heavily on his conscience. Mary tactfully suggested to Quillinan that, 'judging from many of your own elegant verses', the best and speediest solution would be if he wrote a draft himself, which would either give William something to work on or prompt him to write new verses of his own. She was right, as usual. William gratefully seized on Quillinan's thirteen lines, reduced them to ten, added an introductory six lines of his own and made several emendations. His comments on why he made these changes are more interesting than the finished lines. He thought that the cause of Jemima's death should be specified, and he substituted 'patient' for 'lovely' in the description of her virtues, because he did not think personal beauty should be dwelt on in an epitaph. It was a measure of how seriously he had taken his task that, when Quillinan responded with a letter of fervent thanks, expressing his sense of obligation, William was affected 'to tears'. The lines would be engraved in marble by Chantrey for a memorial in Grasmere church.

Apart from these lines, and a couple of other short poems, written in December, William's poetry was at a standstill. As Christmas approached and the family gathered together at Rydal Mount, he and Dorothy embarked on a revision of the *Guide to the Lakes* in preparation for a second edition. 'He is now giving his mind to Poetry again,' Dorothy wrote on 21 December, 'but I do not think he will ever, in his life-time – *publish* any more poems – for they hang on hand – never selling'.

20. *Idle Mount*

On 18 February 1823, William and Mary left Rydal Mount to pay a three-week visit to the Beaumonts at Coleorton. Sara accompanied them as far as Derby, then went on to London, to stay with Tom Monkhouse, whose wife was confined to the couch by that affliction beloved of Victorian ladies, 'spinal weakness'. The Wordsworths' visit to Coleorton was 'of *infinite service*' to William: the stimulus of the Beaumonts' society was even more valuable to him now, when his eyes were so weak and easily irritated by light and heat that he was unable to read for himself. As usual, the three weeks turned into four, and on 19 March they left Coleorton to meet their son John at Birmingham.

After all his years of schooling at Sedbergh, John was now, aged almost twenty, at last about to achieve his own, and his parents', dream of going to university. Cambridge had been the natural choice, but the great stumbling block was the mathematics, which still formed the core of the curriculum. He applied instead to Oxford where his father's contacts did much to smooth the way. John Keble, soon to be famous as a founder of the Oxford Movement, had long been a devotee of William's poetry and, having been introduced to him by Coleridge's nephews in 1815, admired the man as much as the poet. Now a fellow and tutor of Oriel, he willingly gave his advice on where and how to apply. Augustus Hare, a fellow and tutor of New College, who had been a regular summer visitor at Rydal Mount since 1819, lent his support and was a decisive influence in the ultimate choice of New College for John. Unlike his father, John would enter university with every possible advantage. Not for him the lowly status and despised gown of a sizar; this Mr Wordsworth would be a true gentleman of the university, a gentleman commoner, wearing a silk gown, and costing his father more than half his annual income to support.

Having seen John safely matriculated at Oxford, the Wordsworths travelled on to London to join Sara at the Monkhouses' new home in Gloucester Place. The highlight of their stay was a dinner, on 4 April, hosted by a proud Tom Monkhouse, who could scarcely contain his glee when Rogers described it as 'the *most brilliant Thing* this Season'. The Beaumonts and Lord Lowther were unable to come, but '*five of the most distinguished Poets of the Age*' were present: William, Coleridge, Lamb, Tom Moore and Rogers. Coleridge, who was in fine health and spirits, dominated the conversation, talking mainly metaphysical criticism to William. Lamb was on his best behaviour, did not get drunk and 'was only cheerful at last'. How Sara must have laughed inwardly when all five poets concurred in Robinson's gallant, but all too true, diagnosis that Jane Monkhouse was 'an Imposter . . . she looks so well it is impossible that she can ail anything'.

From London, William and Mary travelled to Lee Priory, in Kent, to stay briefly with Quillinan and his family, before embarking on a short tour of the Low Countries. From the outset, the journey was dogged by ill-luck. Bad weather and a virulent attack of William's trachoma delayed their departure for five long weeks. When they did set off, on 16 May, the sea was so rough that they both began vomiting before they even got on board the steam packet, then lay in their bunks, rigid with fear and sickness, throughout the crossing. Travelling mainly by barge, but also by road, the Wordsworths made a circular tour through Bruges, Ghent, Antwerp, Dort, Rotterdam, Delft, The Hague, Leiden, Haarlem, Amsterdam, Utrecht and Brussels. They visited churches, looked at paintings and walked quietly round the streets of the towns, but their activities were curtailed by the state of William's eyes. It proved a gratifyingly 'cheap excursion!', but, as Robinson observed when the travellers returned to London on 17 June, William had not 'laid in many poetical stores'. After a leisurely journey northwards, they arrived home in the early hours of 15 July to find Dorothy and Willy well, and John returned from Oxford for the vacation. Hartley Coleridge, who had been staying at Rydal Mount with his mother and sister, was unimpressed by the Wordsworth children. 'John is laborious as an Ass', he told his brother. 'Dora is a sweet, good humour'd girl. Little Will is a bore.' His venom was understandable, given that laborious John was likely to make a success of his Oxford career, whereas brilliant, eccentric Hartley had been expelled from his fellowship at Oriel, for allegedly heavy drinking and bringing the college into disrepute by his erratic behaviour. Now, aged twenty-seven, he was reduced to the position of master in the school at Ambleside where he had once been taught himself, tutoring young Willy Wordsworth, and being lectured like an errant child by Dorothy for his sudden and unexplained absences from Rydal Mount.

There was only one memorable visitor this summer, the actor William Charles Macready, who had made his name playing Shakespearian characters on the London stage. William received him cordially, if gloomily, in the dining room, where the blinds were pulled down to exclude the painful daylight from his sensitive eyes. Finding an avid listener in Macready, William soon perked up, reciting his poetry sonorously and impressively. He and John accompanied the actor back to his lodgings in Ambleside that evening, took him on an evening excursion on Lake Windermere and sat with him while he ate his dinner. Like the pastor in his *Excursion*, Macready commented, William held their attention with his comments on the beauty of the evening and the scenery.

Throughout the winter William worked 'very hard' at his latest project, a translation of Virgil's *Aeneid*. Two books were complete by 23 January 1824, and these he forwarded to Lord Lonsdale, with an apologetic note, stressing the 'good deal of pains' he had taken over the work. The versification also called for an apology, or at least an explanation. William found 'long narratives in couplets ... very wearisome', so he had run them together freely, in an effort to recapture the movement of the Virgilian original. It was not, as William came to realize, a happy experiment and he suppressed the translation during his lifetime.

In the middle of February William and Dorothy left Rydal Mount for Coleorton, where they were to spend a month, before calling in at Oxford on a 'very very industrious' John for a couple of days and then travelling on to London. There they were to meet Dora, who, in a first attempt at independence, had gone in December to stay with her friends the Gees at Hendon.

As usual, the Wordsworths stayed at Gloucester Place with the Monkhouses. Every night they dined with innumerable old friends: Coleridge, Rogers, the Lambs, the Beaumonts, Quillinan, Robinson, Christopher's sons. Every day they were out seeing the sights, from exhibitions of old masters and modern painters to panoramas and dioramas of Switzerland, Mexico (ancient and modern) and Pompeii, and even the Swiss Giantess, 'a strapping wench of six feet two inches ... But she was not worth paying money to look at'.

Despite all the gaiety, the Wordsworths were deeply concerned about their genial host. Even Dora had swiftly realized that all was not as it should be in Gloucester Place. 'Mrs M is on the Sofa –', she wrote to Quillinan the day she returned there from Hendon, 'she looks very well & is in excellent spirits. Mr M looks miserably ill but says he is better.' While he (and everyone else, including the susceptible Robinson) danced attendance on the beautiful pseudo-invalid, the Wordsworths could not fail to see that Tom was genuinely ill.

On 23 April William, Dorothy and Dora set off for Lee Priory to see Mima and Rotha Quillinan for the first time in almost two years. They could stay only a week, for Dorothy had promised to return home before the end of June so that Mary could visit her brother and cousins in Wales. A tearful Dora had then to be parted from her goddaughter so that the Wordsworths could visit Christopher and his sons at Cambridge before setting off homeward. It was at this point that Dora staged a quiet rebellion. Her father and aunt had intended that she should return to London and accompany the Monkhouses to Ramsgate. 'It will be a most uncomfortable disagreeable visit as I plainly saw that neither Mrs M. nor Miss H[orrocks] wished me to go –', Dora confessed miserably to Quillinan; '– I know nothing more disagreeable than to feel yourself where you know you are not wanted – indeed where you are I may say a complete Nuisance'. Dorothy was adamant that she should go and was thoroughly exasperated to find that William was entirely on his daughter's side. The combined forces of father and daughter were enough to carry the day and they 'absolutely made an elopement', riding off in triumph and leaving a disgruntled Dorothy to write Dora's apologies. Her own arrangements could not be so easily abandoned: she had to go to Playford Hall to meet her friend Mrs Luff, who was returning to live in the Lakes, bringing with her two cart-loads of goods and her African menagerie.

Mary's visit to Wales was now deferred till the autumn, and it was agreed that both William and Dora would accompany her. The Wordsworths spent the interval pleasantly enough, surrounded by family and friends. All the Robinsons came over from York and there were regular musical parties at the Mount. They were often joined by the summer tenants of Spring Cottage, a likeable pair of sisters from Sussex, Frances and Emma Ayling, with their clergyman brother and Frances's intended, 'an antiquated Baronet', Sir William Ashburnham. The two Miss Aylings charmed everyone and were soon on intimate terms with the Wordsworths: 'they play and sing beautifully –', Mary enthused, 'come here every morning to practice, and poor Willy is half in love – cannot sleep for making rhymes about his own happiness, ventures to rally the Ladies on the old Gentleman, all which is taken in good part – and they never tire of his company'. On 3 August one of Dora's closest friends, Mary Calvert, married her neighbour Joshua Stanger at Keswick. Dora, Sara Coleridge, Mary's cousin and Isabella Curwen, a young woman who was to play an important future role in the Wordsworth family, were her bridesmaids. As Sara commented, somewhat bitterly, few of her circle would be so fortunate in their love affairs as Mary.

On 24 August William, Mary and Dora set off from Rydal Mount for Liverpool, where they stayed with the Crumps, the owners of Allan Bank. The Crumps and William Jackson, the former curate of Grasmere, accompanied them on the first stage of their journey, by steamboat under Penmaenmawr and by Puffin Island to Bangor, where they admired the 'stupendous preparations' for Thomas Telford's great suspension bridge linking Anglesey to the mainland across the Menai Straits. The next day they spent three hours exploring Conwy Castle, 'which I think the King of castles', Dora wrote. 'All that I have heard of it, all that I have seen – even Sir George's picture – nothing gives one a sufficient idea of its grandeur ... The longer I stayed the longer I wished to stay.' Her father was equally entranced by the journey from Conwy to Llanberis.

There was no carriage road from Llanberis, so the Wordsworths walked the eight miles to Capel-Curig, along the Pass of Llanberis, with the Snowdonian range of mountains towering above them. They had arranged to meet William's old friend Robert Jones at Llanrwst, in the Vale of Conwy, but it was symptomatic of William's growing reputation that, before they did so, they had a prearranged meeting with John Hobart, Bishop of New York. A leading reformer in the Protestant Episcopalian Church in America, he had visited Rydal Mount just before the Wordsworths' departure, and had been invited to join them at Llanrwst. 'The day when you honored me with your attentions at the Lakes and that which I subsequently passed with you in Wales, I shall always look back to with pride &

with the highest pleasure', he wrote afterwards, with all the enthusiasm of one of William's young university disciples.

It was a great pleasure to see Jones again, particularly in his native element, for once again, just as he had done on the Continental tour of 1820, William was consciously retreading old ground. Jones brought his carriage and a servant, which made travelling more comfortable, and he was quite happy to set a leisurely pace far different from the frenetic sightseeing of 1820. 'Jones was the best of companions,' William told Christopher, 'being master of the language, very extensively known in the Country, a most affectionate Man, and, I verily believe, the best-tempered Creature imaginable; to me, who am apt to be irritable in travelling, an inestimable qualification.' Jones introduced them to his friends in the Vale of Clwyd and to the famous 'Ladies of Llangollen', Lady Eleanor Butler and the Hon. Sarah Ponsonby, the aristocratic eccentrics whose dedication to reclusiveness, celibacy and Rousseau (not necessarily in that order) had ironically made them a tourist attraction.

Mary could scarcely contain her joy at the success of this tour – so different from their most recent jaunts on the Continent. William had been well and in excellent spirits for the three weeks they had been away, Dora had been 'enchanted' with everything they had seen, '*I* could not therefore but be happy'. To crown her pleasure, this tour had at last awakened the poet: her husband had been 'murmuring verses' throughout their wanderings. From Ruthin he addressed a sonnet to the Ladies of Llangollen, christening their Dee-side home 'the Vale of Friendship'. Exploring the ruined castles of North Wales, with their 'shattered galleries, 'mid roofless halls', inspired a characteristic meditation on the changes wrought by passing years:

> Relic of Kings! Wreck of forgotten wars,
> To winds abandoned and the prying stars,
> Time *loves* thee! at his call the Seasons twine
> Luxuriant wreaths around thy forehead hoar;
> And, though past pomp no changes can restore,
> A soothing recompense, his gift, is thine!
>
> *Composed among the Ruins of a Castle*
> *in North Wales, ll.9–14*

At the Devil's Bridge, where they parted from Jones, the waterfalls were 'in perfection', after heavy overnight rains. William 'poured out' a sonnet 'in the chasm there, during a heavy storm, while Dora was at my side endeavouring to sketch the body of the place, leaving, poor Girl! the soul of it to her Father'. As in most of William's better poems, it was a coming together of past and present, interfused with his own personal memories. The rocky chasm with its raging torrent reminded him of the infant Rhine he had seen in the ravines of Viamala in 1790. It was, as Mary said, 'a sublime finale' to the tour.

Except that it was not the end, only the beginning, for the main object of this absence from home was to visit Mary's brother and cousins in Radnorshire. It was a last chance to do so, for Tom had lost hope of ever making a success of the farm at Hindwell, given notice on his lease and engaged to take a new one just outside Hereford. Looking at the magnificent Brinsop Court today, with its fourteenth-century great hall, mellow golden stone, half-timbering and encircling moat, it is difficult to imagine it being the residence of a penurious farmer obliged to give up his former property because he could not afford the rent. It is emphatically a gentleman's residence, an ancient manor house set in a natural bowl amidst gently rolling hills which are crowned with woodland. Secluded but not isolated, it is surrounded by cereal fields so rich and productive that the gorged pheasants stagger drunkenly under their own weight, barely able to strut, let alone fly. In 1824, however, the estate had recently been purchased by David Ricardo of Gatcombe Park, its manorial rights granted to Sir Uvedale Price, and the house and farm were suffering from years of neglect. It was, as they say, a place with potential.

One of its advantages was that it was still less than ten miles from the Stow, where John Monkhouse was at last beginning to see an improvement in his farming concerns. Unfortunately, this was counterbalanced by his failing eyesight: aged forty-two, he was gradually going blind, a particular problem for him, since he lived alone and his greatest pleasure in life was reading. Sara, always desirous to make herself 'useful as well as ornamental', had been his guest since the spring, helping to train his servants for him and acting as his amanuensis and reader.

When the Wordsworths arrived at Hindwell for a grand family reunion, however, it was not John but his brother Tom whose appearance shocked them. His foray to Ramsgate had done nothing for him, and he had prevailed on his wife to try a visit to his family in Wales. It was obvious to the Wordsworths that he was suffering from pulmonary tuberculosis and 'travelling slowly, but I fear surely, to the grave'. The Wordsworths extended their stay as long as they could, leaving only when Jane Monkhouse finally succeeded in carrying her husband off to Torquay for the winter, even though she knew he was happier with his brother and sister in Wales than anywhere else. Sara, determined to prevent her beloved cousin being left to the not-so-tender mercies of his wife, went with them, devoting herself for four long and miserable months to the dying man.

The Wordsworths left Hindwell on the same day. Instead of going straight home, however, they went to Coleorton, 'to secure to ourselves a long sojourn when we do arrive [at Rydal Mount] – thinking it better to lengthen our long absence, than be called upon in the early spring by our Friends here to perform Wm's *half* promise of making our annual visit to them'. Mary's contrivance to obtain a long period at home was a little wifely plot, inspired by William's recent return to verse. 'I trust after we feel ourselves settled at Rydal, he will be able seriously to address himself to the Recluse –', she confided to Quillinan. It was a fallacious hope. Though Dorothy colluded, even she had to admit on 13 December that her brother had not yet looked at *The Recluse*: 'he seems to feel the task so weighty that he shrinks from beginning with it –'.

What William had written was a number of small poems, for the poetic mood which had overtaken him in North Wales had never left him. Most of them were associated with Tom's approaching death, one in praise of his little daughter, Mary Elizabeth, who was now three years old and the light of her father's life. Dorothy, who had met 'Good-good', as the family called her, in London in the spring, simply marvelled. 'She is a child by herself – Such an one as was never born before and never will be again. There seems to be no seed of evil in her ... She is constantly happy – and everything that is new and everything that is old affords her amusement.' William's tribute was a lovely sonnet, beginning with the memorable lines, 'Unquiet Childhood here by special grace Forgets her nature, opening like a flower', and ending by comparing Mary Elizabeth's placid innocence to that of the infant Virgin.

Less elevated in sentiment, but no less sincere, were two poems William addressed to his own Mary, which reveal that twenty-two years of marriage had done nothing to diminish his love for her. Even after all these years – perhaps, indeed, because of them – Mary still needed reassurance about her lack of conventional beauty. 'Let other bards of angels sing, Bright suns without a spot;' William wrote, adding honestly, if ungallantly,

> But thou art no such perfect thing:
>   Rejoice that thou art not!
>
> Heed not though none should call thee fair;
>   So, Mary, let it be
> If naught in loveliness compare
>   With what thou art to me.
>
> True beauty dwells in deep retreats,
>   Whose veil is unremoved
> Till heart with heart in concord beats,
>   And the lover is beloved.

The second poem is the other side of the coin, for it reveals William's emotional dependence on his wife. Though not well known, it is fascinating on many counts, not least because it is a rare and uncharacteristic admission in verse of religious doubt. As Tom began to spit blood, and was reduced to speaking in a whisper, 'dying very, very slowly', William found himself

> Trembling, through my unworthiness, with fear
> That friends, by death disjoined, may meet no more!
> Misgivings, hard to vanquish or control,
> Mix with the day, and cross the hour of rest;

For Mary, secure in her faith, there was no such uncertainty, and William, in his anguish, appealed to her for reassurance, and through her for unquestioning belief for himself. 'Yet bear me up', he begged,

– else faltering in the rear
Of a steep march: support me to the end.

Peace settles where the intellect is meek,
And Love is dutiful in thought and deed;
Through *Thee* communion with that Love I seek:
The faith Heaven strengthens where *he* moulds the Creed.

       ['O dearer far than light and life are dear'], ll.3–6, 11–16

That the author of *The Excursion,* one of the greatest affirmations of faith, could be so stricken with personal doubt is ironic and instructive.

The uncertainties of human life were reinforced by changes in the vale. In the Wordsworths' absence, there was a freak storm which wreaked havoc on the ancient woodlands of Rydal, though, miraculously, Rydal Mount had escaped untouched. What threatened to change totally and permanently the whole character of the vale was enclosure. The scheme had been initiated by Lady le Fleming, or rather her agents, in response to what William admitted were encroachments and abuses committed by many who had an interest in these commons. William leapt into action in defence of his beloved mountains and the dwindling band of small statesmen whose livelihoods would most be threatened by enclosure. The threat was beaten off for the time being, but it was not the last time William would have to be an active and vocal champion of the silent fells.

A second violent storm, the worst William ever remembered, struck on Christmas Day. In some ways this was unfortunate, for it was the day Lady le Fleming's Rydal Chapel opened its doors for the first time. 'I never was out in such a storm', Dora declared, but, with some sixty or seventy other worshippers, she and her family struggled through the wind and rain to attend the service. 'The sight must have been highly gratifying to the munificent Foundress', William remarked, adding somewhat crisply that the cost of building the church had 'much exceeded what was needful'. Nevertheless, the Wordsworths were almost entirely reconciled to the new chapel built in front of their house. William was still somewhat grudging, 'when time has softened down the exterior a little it will prove a great ornament to the Village', but both Mary and Dorothy were enthusiastic. 'Nothing can be more lovely than the prospect from the "red room window" at which I write', Mary told Quillinan; '... the frosty mist glistening and curling over the rich tawny hillsides and the *steeple tower* gleaming between the branches of the laurel upon the Mount'. Dorothy thought the outside of the church 'very pretty' in itself, but 'you can have no idea how beautiful in connexion with the village, especially seen from the other side of the lake'. Even the clergyman was more than satisfactory. Fletcher Fleming, distantly related to Lady le Fleming, was the son of William's old school and college friend John Fleming of Rayrigg. The Wordsworths were unanimous in declaring the young man 'a Treasure in these parts where, as my Father says, we are so ill parson'd'; he was 'very earnest', gave 'beautiful' sermons and his only fault was that he read too slowly.

The opening weeks of the new year were marred by news of Tom's worsening health. He loathed Torquay and daily regretted having left the Stow. Sara's reports were so heart-rending that John, despite his blindness, went in person to Torquay and organized Tom's immediate removal. The journey had to be taken in easy stages, but by 9 February they had reached Clifton, on the outskirts of Bristol. Another fashionable society resort, Clifton suited Mrs Monkhouse very well, and it was agreed that they should spend a month there, before moving on to the Stow. In the end death cheated them all. Tom died suddenly, but peacefully, at Clifton on 26 February.

Writing to Rogers, William added a personal note which went beyond the usual platitudes of obituary: 'he was not bright or entertaining, but so gentle and gracious, and so much interested in most of what ought to interest a pure mind, that his company was highly prized by all who knew him intimately'. His death removed not only 'one of my most valued friends' but 'one of the strongest of my inducements, and the most important of my facilities for visiting London, and prolonging my stay there'. It was some small comfort that he had left his widow and daughter well provided for. Technical problems with the will deprived John of the family estate at Sebergham which Tom had left him, but he, his sister and even little George Monkhouse, the half-caste son of their late brother Joe, each benefited by legacies of several thousand pounds. As Tom's executor and guardian of little Mary Elizabeth, John was also presented with the *de facto* and unwelcome legacy of the merry widow. Mrs Monkhouse had, in Sara's sarcastic phrase, borne her loss 'with wonderful fortitude', and scampered off to the delights of Clifton as soon as she was able to escape the mourning household at the Stow. Within two years she had married again, to the bizarrely named Dr Paris Dick, but her unconscionable demands for money and, worse still, her refusal to allow Tom's family to see his daughter were a constant source of aggravation and worry for years to come.

Tom's death, at the age of only forty-two, affected the poet profoundly. It effectively put an end to the stream of poetry which had flowed slowly, but steadily, since the tour of North Wales. William now had some 500 or 600 lines of verse in hand and once again he began to consider publishing a new edition of his poems. Since 1798 his poetry had been published exclusively by Longman, but, comparing his reputation to the profits from his sales, William could not help but feel that he might do better elsewhere. William wrote to his old (and highly successful) friend Rogers to ask for his advice. Was there any publisher 'more liberal, more adventurous, or more skilful in pushing off unfashionable books than Messrs Longman'? The new poems could not make a volume of themselves, but they could be incorporated into a new edition of his *Miscellaneous Poems*. And, he suggested, it might be possible to rearrange these in a new way which would be more attractive to purchasers: a volume of local poetry, for instance, and a volume of sonnets.

Now you may think that I ought to undertake this disagreeable business myself, and so I should think, if I had not so kind a Friend who has 50 times the talent for this sort of work which I possess, and who besides could say 100 handsome things, which, egotist as I am described to be, and as *in verse* I am *willing* to be thought – I could not say of myself.

Rogers could not refuse, but he did dare to suggest that perhaps the best way to achieve a profit was to publish a selection 'of the most admired, or the most popular' of his poems. This seems such an obvious solution that William's rejection of it out of hand appears incredible. Yet reject it he did, because he was, quite genuinely, 'utterly at a loss how to proceed in that selection'. The negotiations for a new publisher would drag on tediously, and ultimately unsuccessfully, for almost two years, but William spent the spring 'tinkering' with his poems in preparation for the new edition, which had already swollen to six volumes by April.

As always, the desire to earn a just financial reward for his poetical labours conflicted with William's high-minded notions of the integrity of his work. He did not scruple to reject the increasing number of requests which were now being made for him to contribute poems to the new monthly magazines and annuals, simply because these were ephemeral publications deliberately aimed at the popular market and he did not approve of their partisan attitudes. The very fact that his contributions were being sought at all was an indication that astute editors and publishers recognized his importance as a poet, and thought his name would sell their titles, but this in itself was objectionable to William. He wanted his work to sell on its own merit, not because it was being puffed in fashionable magazines.

Mary might not have succeeded in encouraging William to return to *The Recluse*, but she did achieve her objective of obtaining a more settled period at home. There were great temptations to go off on another tour. Beaumont's sister-in-law, Frances Fermor, had died the previous December and, though the Wordsworths barely knew her, she had read *The Excursion*, derived great pleasure from it and unexpectedly left William a legacy of £100 'as a small mark of her esteem and regard'. Informing him of this, Beaumont had dropped a hefty hint, 'O for a Muse to consecrate her Memory', to which William had dutifully responded by writing not one but two poetic tributes. Beaumont was delighted and promptly offered William £100 of his own, in the hope that the two sums would enable William, Mary and Dorothy to finance a tour of Italy. It was an offer that William could not, and did not refuse, but simply put on hold. He could not think of going to Italy until John was nearer the end of his university career.

Instead of travelling to foreign parts, the Wordsworths had to make do with a trip to Kents Bank, on the northern coast of Morecambe Bay, where they rented lodgings for six weeks. As is the way with such things, it turned into one of their happiest ever holidays. This was in no small part due to a young lady who, until May, had been a complete stranger to them all. Maria Jane Jewsbury was twenty-five years old and a budding authoress. The previous year she had published her first work, *Phantasmagoria, or Sketches of Life and Literature*, which she had dedicated 'to him whose works occasioned whatever merit this possesses'. William had been deeply touched: 'I am not altogether free from reflections natural to my time of life,' he replied, 'such as, that I have lived and laboured to little purpose, – assurances like yours are correctives of this mistake, for how can it be other than one, when I receive blossoms of such promise with declarations so fervent, yet evidently sincere!'

William left the happy party at Kents Bank on 7 August, to pay his annual visit to Lord Lonsdale at Lowther Castle and to attend some splendid festivities at Storrs, the grand house on Windermere belonging to John Bolton, a Liverpool merchant and prominent Lowther supporter. The celebrations were in honour of the Foreign Secretary, George Canning, and a great assembly turned out to fete him. William and John Wilson, now the Professor of Moral Philosophy at Edinburgh University, heading the local intelligentsia, were unexpectedly joined by Sir Walter Scott and his son-in-law, J.G. Lockhart. Lockhart, who seems to have been under the impression that the annual Windermere regatta had been laid on especially for his father-in-law and Canning, was impressed.

The weather was as Elysian as the scenery. There were brilliant cavalcades through the woods in the mornings, and delicious boatings on the lake by moonlight; and the last day, 'the Admiral of the Lake' [Wilson] presided over one of the most splendid regattas that ever enlivened Windermere. Perhaps there were not fewer than fifty barges following in the Professor's radiant procession, when it paused at the point of Storrs to admit into the place of honour the vessel that carried kind and happy Mr Bolton and his guests. The Bards of the Lakes led the cheers that hailed Scott and Canning; and music and sunshine, flags, streamers, and gay dresses, the merry hum of voices, and the rapid splashing of innumerable oars, made up a dazzling mixture of sensations as the flotilla wound its way among the richly-foliaged islands, and along bays and promontories peopled with enthusiastic spectators.

On 23 August, Scott, Lockhart and Wilson accompanied William home to breakfast at Rydal Mount, then Dora and her father 'spouting his own verses very grandly all the way', escorted Scott and Lockhart to Keswick.

'We have had the finest weather, and the most bustling summer ever remembered', Dorothy wrote breathlessly. 'We never in our lives had so many visitors.' On 21 October Bertha and Kate Southey came to stay. All the young people at Greta Bank had been struck down with whooping cough, Sara Coleridge particularly badly, and it was thought wise to send her two cousins out of the way for a time. It is only thanks to this coincidence that a momentous event in the Wordsworth household was preserved from oblivion. One of the most assiduous visitors to Rydal Mount at this time was a thirty-one-year-old Royal Navy Lieutenant, Tom Robinson, Dora's second cousin. He arrived at Rydal on 8 October and left on 23 November, staying with his widowed mother and his many siblings in Ambleside – when he was not having breakfast, dinner or tea at Rydal Mount, accompanying Dora to visit 'Cousin Dorothy' at Coniston, walking with her to the waterfalls or to pay local visits, or playing cards with the young ladies in the evenings.

Tom was quite the dashing naval lieutenant. Bertha Southey, who was only sixteen at the time, remembered him almost half a century later as 'a very handsome & delightful man'. Dora, at twenty-one, was far more innocent than young Bertha. She treated Tom just as she treated every other member of the family, admitting him to a degree of intimacy which was both flattering and misleading. No one, except Dora, could have failed to see what Tom's intentions were, Bertha remarked indulgently. Fail she did, however, and after her parents' return, the smitten young man made a formal application to William for his daughter's hand in marriage. William replied instantly, and in a kindly manner, but with a decided negative. In a rather clumsy attempt to lighten the mood, he added this advice.

If you have thoughts of marrying, do look out for some lady with a sufficient fortune for both of you. What I say to you now I would recommend to every naval officer and clergyman, who is without prospect of professional advancement. Ladies of some fortune are as easily won as those without, and for the most part as deserving. Check the first liking to those who have nothing.

Tom behaved impeccably. He neither made a parade of his feelings nor tried to wound Dora in any way. As Bertha put it, he behaved under his trial like a gentleman ought. What did Dora think about her first romantic encounter? As she had never considered the possibility that Tom could be interested in her, she emerged heart-whole, though deeply grieved at unintentionally causing her would-be lover pain.

It was not Dora, but John, whose future was uppermost in William's mind at the end of 1825. In twelve months' time he would be a graduate, and he would have to decide what career he wished to pursue. John had a romantic hankering to be a soldier, but he was left in no doubt that the army was 'out of the question'. His father could not afford to purchase a commission for him and no one, least of all John himself, wished him to enter the army without one. When John decided he would like to become a fellow at Merton, William pulled every string he could, but it was to no avail: as a resident of the diocese of Chester, John was debarred from holding a fellowship.

The bitter disappointment the Wordsworths felt at this blow to John's career prospects was rendered insignificant in the scale of the disasters which overtook them this autumn. The lease of Rydal Mount was fast running out. Earlier in the year, Lady le Fleming had granted an extension until May 1827, but rumours began to circulate that she intended to install her widowed aunt in the house. William reacted with remarkable speed and decisiveness. He went straight to James Backhouse, owner of the Rash, a field which lay in front of Rydal Mount, between the house and the church, and agreed to buy it for £300. Next morning, he wrote to Lady le Fleming, asking to know if the rumours were true, and informing her of his purchase and his intention to build a house upon it, if he were forced to vacate Rydal Mount. Lady Fleming's answer was a verbal one, that Mrs Huddleston was coming in 1827.

As if it was not bad enough to lose their beloved home, the Wordsworths also faced the prospect of losing everything else they had. At Christmas there was a national financial crisis which caused a run on the banks. This was the period before the Bank of England: all the banks were privately owned, most of them an extension of a business or manufactory, and many were simply overwhelmed. Among them was Jack Hutchinson's Tees Bank, in which every member of the extended family was involved to a greater or lesser degree. All of them would suffer losses, but Jack, as one of the partners, was ruined. Lands which had been in the family since the time of Henry VIII would have to be sold, but the haunting fear was that they might not be able to raise the £100,000 necessary to cover their losses. And then what would happen to them all? It was hardly surprising that Sara literally became ill with worry.

At precisely the same time, and for much the same reasons, William's new-found publisher, Hurst & Robinson, also collapsed. Only a few days earlier, on 30 December, Wordsworthian enthusiast Alaric Watts, whose annual, the *Literary Souvenir*, was published by Hurst & Robinson, had finalized a deal with them, contracting for an edition of 1,000 copies of William's complete poems, to be published entirely at Hurst & Robinson's risk and expense, allowing William twenty-five copies for personal distribution, and paying him £300. John had carried the first volume ready for the press to Manchester on 18 January and on the very next day William read in *The Times* that Hurst & Robinson were stopping payments. He wrote a letter of controlled desperation to Watts, seeking to prevent the manuscript being handed over, and waited in an agony of suspense to learn his fate. Watts had not forwarded the manuscript and, by the grace of God, William escaped unscathed. His old friend Scott was not so fortunate. The collapse of Constable's publishing house in Edinburgh left him personally bankrupt, and, in his determination to pay back his creditors, he worked so hard that he ruined his health and shortened his life.

William, however, had already spent the £300 he was to receive from Hurst & Robinson in buying the Rash. Somehow or other, he would have to raise the money from an alternative source if Lady le Fleming's plans were to be thwarted. Though the Wordsworths hoped against hope that it would not be necessary for them to build, William summoned George Webster, the architect who had designed Rydal Chapel, from Kendal in February to draw up the plans. Remembering William's scathing comments and earnest advice about new building in his *Guide to the Lakes*, it is not surprising to find that the new house, which now took shape on the drawing board, was very much in the vernacular, though grandiose, style. The Wordsworths would not be bullied into leaving Rydal.

Though forewarned and forearmed, it was still a profound shock when, in May, Lady le Fleming served them with a legal notice to quit Rydal Mount. William mourned in verse.

> The doubt to which a wavering hope had clung
> Is fled; we must depart, willing or not,

Sky-piercing Hills! must bid farewell to you
And all that ye look down upon with pride,
With tenderness imbosom; to your paths,
And pleasant Dwellings, to familiar trees
And wild-flowers known as well as if our hands
Had tended them:
  Composed When a Probability Existed of Our Being
  Obliged to Quit Rydal Mount as a Residence, ll.1–8

Rydal Mount had been a refuge in the days of their greatest suffering, had exerted its healing power and, together, they had made it into a family home. In the thirteen years they had lived there, they had shaped the house and, more particularly, the garden. The lower terrace, which William had carved out of the mountainside, was inextricably associated with everything that mattered most to him.

A Poet's hand first shaped it; and the steps
Of that same Bard – repeated to and fro
At morn, at noon, and under moonlight skies
Through the vicissitudes of many a year –
Forbade the weeds to creep o'er its grey line.
No longer, scattering to the heedless winds
The vocal raptures of fresh poesy,
Shall he frequent these precincts; locked no more
In earnest converse with belovèd Friends,
Here will he gather stores of ready bliss,
As from the beds and borders of a garden
Choice flowers are gathered! But, if Power may spring
Out of a farewell yearning – favoured more
Than kindred wishes mated suitably
With vain regrets – the Exile would consign
This Walk, his loved possession, to the care
Of those pure Minds that reverence the Muse.
  ['The massy Ways, carried across these heights'], ll.6–22

21. *Shades of the Prison-house*

At the beginning of 1826 Robinson wrote a mock obituary for William, anticipating the comments of future generations of literary critics with uncanny accuracy.

This great poet survived to the fifth decennary of the nineteenth Century, but he appears to have dyed [*sic*] in the year 1814 as far as life consisted in an active sympathy with the temporary welfare of his fellow creatures – He had written heroically & divinely against the tyranny of Napoleon, but was quite indifferent to all the successive tyrannies which disgraced the succeeding times – The Spaniards the moment they were under the yoke of the most odious & contemptible tyrant that ever breathed – ceased to be objects of interest – The Germans who emancipated themselves were most ungratefully neglected by their sovereigns & the poet – The Greeks began a War as holy as that of the Spaniards He was silent – He had early manifested a feeling for the negroes & the poet did honour to his friend Clarkson – That source of sympathetic tears was dried up – A new field of enterprise was opened in America – The poets eye was not a prophetic one – There is proof that he was alive abo[u]t 1823–4 when new churches were built in London but otherwise he took no care about any of the events of the day –

It was not meant to be entirely serious, and Robinson had not intended that William himself should read it. Nevertheless, he did so, and it touched a nerve. 'Your supposed Biography entertained me much', he informed Robinson, adding drily, 'I could give you the other side.' His poems were all out of print, no publisher seemed eager to take them on and now he was about to lose his much-loved home. It was hardly surprising that William felt his whole life was crumbling to the touch. And, as he had confessed to Maria Jewsbury the previous year, he had reached the age when he had begun to think 'I have lived and laboured to little purpose'.

There was little to cheer him at home. Dorothy had left for Brinsop and the Stow on 8 February, and William was supposed to join her in May, to fulfil his dream of making another tour of North Wales, culminating in an ascent of Snowdon. The notice to quit put paid to these plans, as William sorrowfully informed Jones. 'Do come and see *us*,' he begged, 'we are growing old and ought to make the best of our time to keep up long tried affections.' As if to underline the uncertainties of life, news arrived that his brother Christopher was seriously ill. A brief note, tacked on to one from his son John, asked William to take care of his boys if he should not recover.

The election of June 1826 provided a welcome relief from personal troubles and passed off relatively peacefully. William performed his by now customary role of sending daily reports to Lord Lonsdale from the hustings, but his heart was not in it. It somehow seemed a fitting close to the campaign that, when Lord Lowther called to see Lady le Fleming, to plead on William's behalf that he might be allowed to remain at Rydal Mount, her Ladyship claimed to be indisposed and refused to see him. There were still some things even the mighty Lowthers could not have their own way.

There were only a couple of bright spots during the election. Tom Hutchinson and John Monkhouse were obliged to make a welcome visit to the Lakes, in order to place their votes, and Southey returned from a Continental tour to find that, in his absence and without his knowledge, he had been returned as a Member of Parliament for Downton. Lord Radnor, who 'owned' the rotten borough, had conferred this honour on him because he approved of Southey's *Book of the Church*. 'Keswick was in an uproar when I arrived', Southey told his brother. 'The Band had assembled to salute the Member for Downton, the people here having agreed that my election is greatly to the credit of the place; and a crowd of men women and children among whom I have lived three and twenty years were collected to see me in my new character! There was music on the lake in the evening!' At any other time, Southey would have been hugely amused, but he had returned to find his youngest daughter, Isabel, who was not yet fourteen, seriously ill. A week later, she was dead. Her suffering parents were outwardly the 'pattern of resignation and patience', but Kate, her sister and inseparable companion, was desolate. The Wordsworths could not fail to be moved by their friends' affliction, knowing from bitter experience how much it cost to maintain a façade of composure.

In the summer, Joanna and Henry Hutchinson spent six weeks at Rydal Mount, by way of saying farewell. The collapse of the Tees Bank had reduced their tiny income even further and they had decided to move to the Isle of Man, where they could live respectably, but cheaply, on their combined income. Poor Jack, meanwhile, had literally fled the country. Sara and Mary had both escaped without loss, as had Tom Monkhouse's estate – though, in the last case, only through the 'over liberality of his high-minded Brother, who means to bear the loss himself'. As William remarked, this was all the more admirable in view of the fact that John Monkhouse had been deprived of his own legacy through a technical fault in the will.

Another visitor who stole all hearts was Miss Emma Ayling. She and her brother came to Spring Cottage in the autumn, bringing with them a young friend, Lionel

Fraser, who was a grandnephew of William's acquaintance the poetess Charlotte Smith. The rapport the Aylings had enjoyed with the Wordsworths on a previous visit was instantly re-established. 'She is certainly a charming person ... such delightful spirits I never before saw – nor any one who was so *instantaneously* attractive', Sara mused. Beautiful, accomplished and yet also 'a truly useful female of the old-fashioned kind', Dora's '*Syren* friend' had at least two old bachelors, Tillbrooke and Rogers, eating out of her hand.

The fascinating Emma succeeded in catching one of her matrimonial prizes, Samuel Tillbrooke, but her brother, the Reverend William Ayling, did not. A thirty-three-year-old clergyman, without a benefice but with an independent income, Sara thought him 'a very agreeable Person – of mild manners with a spice of humour'. Dora thought differently, merely tolerating his presence for the sake of his sister, an interpretation of appearances which never crossed the unfortunate clergyman's mind. At what point William Ayling proposed to Dora is not clear. On 1 October she was taken 'very ill' with an attack of biliousness and nerves, which lasted several weeks. This might pinpoint the date, for Ayling unfortunately chose not to accept Dora's word for it that she could not return his affection. On the other hand, Dorothy's journal records him coming to tea on 26 November, supper two days later (when Dora was 'very nervy'), walking with William, Dorothy and Dora to Grasmere on 30 November and 2 December, and dining with the Wordsworths at Ivy Cottage on 3 December. The following day, he abruptly left Rydal for good, despite his stated intention of remaining there for the winter.

What made this affair so unpleasant was Ayling's response to his rejection. He simply refused to believe that Dora was not interested in him. Almost fifty years later, Bertha Southey's blood still boiled whenever she thought of what happened next. Ayling 'went about & told every one that Mr W would not let his daughter marry him & that she was breaking her heart in consequence'. His sisters sided with him and, according to Bertha, 'turned against her also and behaved shamefully – no wonder poor Dora was made really ill by such base conduct on the part of friends'. Letters were exchanged between Dora and Emma for 'a little while' after the refusal, until it became clear to the Wordsworths that the Aylings were spreading malicious gossip about them. The most regrettable casualty of the whole sorry business was the Wordsworths' long-standing friendship with Tillbrooke.

Dora's health continued to give cause for concern throughout the winter. She began a regular regime of warm bathing and, when she was well enough to do so, took daily exercise riding on her pony. There were no consumptive symptoms, her aunt explained defensively, she was just 'debilitated'. Dora's brother John was also 'debilitated'. As his university examinations loomed ever nearer, he suffered 'a rush of blood to the head', which a doctor conveniently diagnosed as the result of too much study. The remedy was even more convenient: he was to lay aside his books for a month and then read only in moderation. For a young man who did not stand a chance of winning the honours his family hoped for, it was a timely rescue from disappointment and shame. John's health was far more important to them than academic glory. He went into the examinations secure in the knowledge that his father would be satisfied with a common degree and dutifully returned to Oxford in January to read divinity and prepare himself for ordination.

Dorothy was in better health than any of her nephews and nieces. She had arrived home on 4 November, having spent seven months at Brinsop and the Stow, and two more on the road to the Lakes. She had visited, and exhausted, Maria Jewsbury, who took to her couch while the indefatigable Dorothy played the tourist and got to know Kenilworth 'by heart', 'absolutely digested' Warwick, and 'swallowed whole' Stratford and Charlecote. She had also paid a quiet visit to Coleorton, spending her time reading and walking, when she was not lecturing Lady Beaumont over the changes she planned to make to the winter garden.

William, too, was enjoying a sudden resurgence of health and purpose after a year of somewhat aimless drifting. One of his summer visitors, the editor of the *Keepsake*, Frederic Reynolds, had suggested that he should rub his eyes with the blue stone (copper sulphate) to cure the trachoma. Miraculously, it worked. Within weeks they were as good as any eyes in the house. This remarkable recovery just happened to coincide with the joyful news that Lady le Fleming had abandoned her determination to force the Wordsworths out of, and her aunt into, Rydal Mount.

Relieved of two of his long-standing problems, William now turned his attention to his third. His poems had been out of print too long and none of his negotiators had succeeded in finding him a publisher. It was time to take matters into his own hands, and he did so decisively. He offered John Murray first refusal of the complete poems, with the proviso that, if Murray did not reply '*immediately*', his silence would be interpreted as a rejection. Murray did not respond, so William offered the same terms to his old publisher, Longman, who promptly accepted. His perseverance had paid off: from now on, he would meet two-thirds of the expense and risk of publishing (which, as William had learned from his dealings with other publishers over the past year, was no risk at all), and would receive two-thirds of the profit. By 2 January 1827 the first volume was winging its way to London on the Manchester Mail, and the first proof sheet arrived ten days later.

On 10 May William received a parcel from Longman containing six copies of the new edition, in five volumes, grandly titled *The Poetical Works of William Wordsworth*. 'I am pleased with the appearance of the books', he informed Longman, 'except an error in apportioning the matter in the third vol. which is too large, the miscalculation was my own fault.' Complimentary copies were scattered with his usual prodigality, though one of William's closest friends, his earliest patron, Sir George Beaumont, had not lived to see the publication of the new edition. He had suffered a seizure while standing at his easel and died eight days later, on 7 February, aged seventy-three.

Beaumont's death struck William hard. It was not just his friend's unstinting support and many tactful kindnesses over the long period of their intimacy, but the intensity of the artistic sympathy between the two men. A perfect example of this occurs in an anecdote William himself told Scott to illustrate the poet George Crabbe's lack of imagination. The three men had been sitting together when Beaumont blew out a candle, 'and exchanging a look with Wordsworth began to admire in silence the undulating thread of smoke which slowly arose from the expiring wick'. Crabbe, however, put on the extinguisher. 'In two other men I should have said "this is affectations," with Sir Hugh Evans', Scott remarked, quoting from *The Merry Wives of Windsor*, but in this case he knew it was sincere. It was typical of Beaumont's modesty that, despite decades of patronage of the arts, he declined any personal ostentation in death, requesting only a simple marble tablet with nothing but his name, dates and the legend 'Enter not into judgement with thy servant, O Lord!' engraved upon it, to commemorate his long and useful life. In a final act of generosity, he left William a legacy of £100 outright, together with a life annuity of £100.

The Wordsworths' columns of births, marriages and deaths filled up rapidly. A third daughter, Sarah, was born at Brinsop Court in January, bringing the number of little Hutchinsons to five, while poor Jack lost not one but two daughters within a month to consumption. Bessy and Jane, the only children of his first marriage, were buried together in the little churchyard at Sockburn-on-Tees, close to their mother and aunt. Not one of them had reached her thirtieth year. It was rumoured that Owen Lloyd, Christopher's nephew, who had just been ordained curate to Mr Dawes at Ambleside, was on the brink of marriage with Jane Harden, of Brathay Hall, much to Dora's delight; 'they are as nice a pair as I could wish to see'. Owen, bright, cheerful, affectionate, and a regular visitor at Rydal Mount since childhood, was the 'delight of all this household'.

'Sickness is an humbling thing', Dora wrote to her old schoolfriend Mary Stanger; '– it shows one what poor weak mortals we are'. She had never recovered from the Ayling débâcle and, throughout the winter and spring, had been confined to the house, even, at times, to her room. Reluctantly, the Wordsworths came to the conclusion that she should not spend another winter at Rydal. The Southeys hatched a plot to carry Dora and her Aunt Sara off with them to Harrogate in May. It was not entirely successful – the Southeys had to content themselves with Sara – but on 2 June Dora joined them, her father having driven her over by slow stages in the pony chaise. She returned 'a new creature!', ready to enjoy the social delights of a Lake summer. Her cousin Richard's son, now twelve years old, was to spend his holidays at Rydal Mount, and all three of Christopher's sons were expected as part of a Cambridge reading party, based in Ambleside.

On 15 August they were joined by Edward Quillinan, returning to Spring Cottage for the first time since the death of his wife five years earlier. Joined by his Portuguese half-brother, he flung himself wholeheartedly into all the gaieties, including a grand picnic under Raven Crag, near Wythburn, where the families of Greta Hall and Rydal Mount, with assorted hangers-on and 'vagrants', made a merry party of thirty as they sat round a gypsy fire on the rocky shore of the lake. Dora was in her element, 'is become as strong as I ever remember her to have been', her mother noted, but she was a complete barometer, her state of health depending on the weather. Before the next rainy season began, she would have to be out of the weeping climate of the Lakes.

On 4 September Dora and Mary left for Brinsop, their journey brought forward by the news that Mary's aunt, Elizabeth Monkhouse, was 'diseasedly anxious lest she should die before their arrival'. They had barely time to say hello and goodbye to Dorothy, who had returned the day before after a ten-week visit to the Rawsons in Halifax, and they missed John Monkhouse altogether. He arrived the day after their departure, just in time to join the Southey and Wordsworth households in an assault on Blencathra, in which they were accompanied by their old friend Blomfield, the Bishop of Chester, and three not-so-young American visitors.

'The dissipation of our family since the departure of Mary & her Daughter has exceeded all former dissipations of the kind', Sara proudly reported, as the whole household, young and old, trooped gaily from one ball to another and attended races not only at Penrith but even as far away as Doncaster. Idle Mount well and truly lived up to its reputation. This was all very well for Christopher's sons, who were enjoying a well-earned vacation, and even for young Owen Lloyd, who was already on the ladder of ecclesiastical preferment. It was not so healthy for John and Willy, neither of whom revealed any real sense of purpose. John seemed quite happy to sit back and let his father do everything for him. He could not be ordained until he found a curacy and such was William's anxiety on behalf of his son that, when his old friend Satterthwaite, rector of Lowther, died, he wrote with unseemly haste to Lord Lonsdale to ask if there was an opening for John.

In the end, John had to accept the only curacy which had been offered to him, that of Whitwick, in Leicestershire. The greatest objections to the place were the fact that John would have to furnish part of the rectory there and keep house for himself, but Whitwick itself was not attractive, especially to a young clergyman in his first post. A grim village in the industrial desolation of the coalfields on the edge of Charnwood Forest, his parishioners would be miners and stocking weavers, impoverished, illiterate and stridently Nonconformist. John's rector would be the Wordsworths' old friend Merewether of Coleorton, and the hospitality of his house, and Lady Beaumont's, both less than three miles away, would constantly be open to him. As none of William's friends could come up with anything better, Whitwick it had to be. John was packed off to his uncle for last-minute cramming for his examination before the bishop and, on 2 March 1828, he was ordained deacon. A few weeks later, his father accompanied him to Whitwick, leaving him in his new home with Mary, one of the Wordsworths' own Rydal Mount housemaids, now elevated to the rank of housekeeper. Short of performing John's duty for him, there was little more William could do for his son.

Willy was, if anything, more of a problem than his elder brother. He was now seventeen, but he had little inclination for university, and even less for study. 'His thoughts turn (I fear constantly) on the Army', Dorothy wrote to Quillinan in November, but he was forced to accept that a military career was out of the question. For the time being, until something could be found for him, he would have to continue his studies at home.

On 13 November William left Rydal Mount to join Mary at Coleorton, where they were to spend three weeks with Lady Beaumont, before going on together to Brinsop Court. Their route took them through Birmingham, where, as usual, they stayed with the Lloyds. Christopher, just disappointed of his ambition to become Regius Professor of Divinity at Cambridge, joined them for Christmas at Brinsop Court. The Christmas party included not just the seven resident Hutchinsons and two Monkhouses, but William, Mary and Dora, Christopher and Edith Southey. Even the fact that Mary's seventy-seven-year-old aunt, Elizabeth Monkhouse, was now genuinely dying did not put a damper on the party: she herself was always cheerful and sometimes 'as merry as her *great-nieces*'. Dora, too, was fully restored to health and happiness, writing cheekily of her father's saying 'in his pompous way' that he did not like the weather because it had 'none of the <u>dignity</u> of rain or the <u>beauty</u> of sunshine'.

Satisfied that it was in his daughter's best interests to see out the winter at Brinsop, William returned alone to Rydal Mount on 29 January. 'You, I hope, are now seriously set down to the Recluse', Christopher wrote sternly a few days later, but, of course, he was not. Instead, after years of implacable resistance to the idea of writing for periodicals, he had finally succumbed to the siren call. He had, quite simply, been made an offer he could not refuse. Reynolds (he of the blue stone cure for trachoma) had called on him in early February and offered him the princely sum of 100 guineas for just twelve pages of verse to be published in the *Keepsake*. The offer was very timely, since William was now faced with 'formidable' bills for John. In addition to more than £60 owed to his college, excluding tailor's bills, there was money to find for his new furniture at Whitwick, his journey there and his other incidental expenses on taking up his living.

Within days of agreeing to contribute William was hard at work, and by the end of the month had produced three of the five poems which would appear in the *Keepsake*. The best of them, *A Tradition of Oker Hill, in Darley Dale, Derbyshire*, was a sonnet as good as any he had written. It was based on a story told him by the coachdriver as they were passing through Derbyshire, but what makes it so successful is that it was informed by William's own feeling for the brother he had lost so long ago. Even now, John's death had power to move him.

> 'Tis said that to the brow of yon fair hill
> Two Brothers clomb, and, turning face from face,
> Nor one look more exchanging, grief to still
> Or feed, each planted on that lofty place
> A chosen Tree; then, eager to fulfil
> Their courses, like two new-born rivers, they
> In opposite directions urged their way
> Down from the far-seen mount. No blast might kill
> Or blight that fond memorial; – the trees grew,
> And now entwine their arms; but ne'er again
> Embraced those Brothers upon earth's wide plain;
> Nor aught of mutual joy or sorrow knew
> Until their spirits mingled in the sea
> That to itself takes all, Eternity.

Dorothy, it would seem, did not approve of the *Keepsake* contribution. 'My Brother is writing verses – but has not yet turned to the Recluse – and we shall lose him again so soon that I fear this winter will produce nothing – and how years roll away!' It is significant that William deliberately did not show his sister the alterations he had made to a fourth poem, *The Triad*, which he had promised Dora and Edith he would write several years previously. As in all such requested poems, he had difficulty engaging with the subject, a celebration of the close friendship and differing characters of the three poets' daughters, Dora Wordsworth, Edith Southey and Sara Coleridge, but the fancy now seized him and the poem was 'thrown off rapidly – and afterwards revised with care'. Of all the poems he contributed to the *Keepsake*, this was William's particular favourite: 'I think [a] great part of it is as elegant and spirited as any thing I have written – but I was afraid to trust my judgement – as the aery Figures are all sketched from living originals that are dear to me.'

On 17 April, having completed something above 300 lines of verse for the *Keepsake*, William left Rydal Mount for Cambridge, where he was to meet Mary and Dora. John went with him as far as Whitwick, having practised for his new role by reading prayers at Grasmere and Rydal, to his father's satisfaction and even greater pride. After a series of grand dinners in the lodge at Trinity College (meals being the only time they saw Christopher, who was always fully occupied), the Wordsworths went up to London for what William had said would be 'a short, very short, visit'. As usual, it turned out to be nothing of the kind. The object of the visit was supposed to be to find a situation for Willy who was now eighteen and had agreed to be a merchant – but on condition that he could do so abroad. Once they had reached London, however, where they stayed with the hospitable Quillinan in Bryanston Street, their good intentions soon went by the board.

By the beginning of June, Mary had had enough. She was also anxious to fulfil her promise to visit John at Whitwick. William saw her on to the stagecoach on 3 June and she drove off, expecting that her husband and daughter would join her before the end of the month. They, however, had other ideas. 'You will be not a little astonished at our plans –', Dora wrote to Mrs Hoare on 16 June. 'We are going up the Rhine the *We*, Mr Coleridge my Father & myself – going to visit a Lady who lives in the most interesting part of that interesting country.' It was an improbable scheme and the choice of companion even more so. The intimacy of the old friendship between the two poets had never been restored: they were not even on letter-writing terms. What is more, apart from an annual trip to the seaside at Ramsgate, Coleridge had not left London since taking up residence in Highgate. And he had never gone anywhere without his minders, the Gillmans, who controlled his opium habit, as far as anyone could do so.

The unlikely trio set off on 21 June for Margate, where they were to take the steam packet to Ostend. Dora was beside herself with joy at the thought of her first Continental tour, and determined to maintain the female family tradition by keeping a journal. Her father, without his 'three wives' to run round after him, was in an almighty panic, firing off a last-minute letter to Reynolds telling him not to

publish his poems in the *Keepsake* until his return, and trying desperately to
borrow a carpetbag from Robinson for his luggage. Coleridge floated along in a
drug-induced haze, the personification of benevolence. Poor Mary, stranded for
she knew not how long at Whitwick, was reduced to writing exasperated letters to
Quillinan, asking to be enlightened as to how, when, where and with whom her
'Vagabonds' were travelling.

During the seven weeks they were away, Dora faithfully kept her journal and
her ready wit, sense of fun and sheer enjoyment shine through on every page. The
poets were her 'tutors', pointing out the best pictures in the Dutch galleries and
churches, but her own views were pungently matter-of-fact. Viewing a celebrated
statue of the Virgin and Child in the Church of St Salvador in Bruges, she was
unimpressed, noting indignantly, 'they have given the Virgin a double chin'! No
man is a hero to his daughter, even if he is a romantic poet. Driving to Waterloo
on the coach, she observed that William and Coleridge were 'perched on the roof
exactly like a pair of monkies', and she recorded without scruple how they had all
laughed when, William having offered one of the men selling souvenirs on the
battlefield two sous, instead of the two francs he was asking, the man had turned
to her and said, 'Ah Mademoiselle you have a very miserly father'. As Dora
mischievously noted, having two elderly poets as guardians gave her plenty of
opportunity for flirtation with fellow travellers.

'The two Poets and their amiable Daughter', as Dora put it, arrived on Quillinan's
accommodating doorstep in London on 6 August. After a fortnight spent at Whitwick, where they were reunited with Mary, and found John happy in the discharge
of his duties, the travellers returned to Rydal Mount on 27 August. It was almost
exactly a year since Mary and Dora had left home. They arrived just in time for
the annual Keswick and Windermere regattas, with all the balls and fêtes attendant
on them. Nor were they too late for the summer visitors who flocked to Rydal, the
most eminent of whom was Andrews Norton, Professor of Sacred Theology at
Harvard.

All his father's attempts to find Willy a situation had been fruitless; there were no
opportunities in business, though William tried as far afield as America, and even the
mighty Lowthers could not identify a suitable opening in a government office. There
was nothing for it but to fall back on the idea of sending him to university. Before he
could go there, however, he required a more intensive course of study than his father,
brother or Carter could offer him. To Willy's delight, a foreign education proved
more easy to find than an opening in foreign commerce. Just before Christmas, the
Wordsworth network managed to locate a Mr Papendick, the British vice-consul in
Bremen, a town in the north-west corner of Germany. Not only was he the English
master in a school, but he took a few boarding pupils himself; Willy would have
the opportunity to learn both the classics and modern languages. The Wordsworths
jumped at the opportunity, and it was agreed that when Papendick came over to
England in April, Willy would return with him for two years. In the meantime,
like Mr Micawber, they hoped something would turn up.

Something had turned up for John. At the beginning of December, Lord Lonsdale offered him the living of Moresby, a small village on the coast between Whitehaven and Workington. It was an infinitely preferable posting to Whitwick, and John had no hesitation in accepting. His rector, Merewether, graciously agreed to allow him to give up his curacy on condition that he remain at Whitwick for a further six months, until a replacement could be found. His Aunt Dorothy, who had been with him since the middle of November, was happy to stay. 'In fact, if he had continued here another winter, I should have done so also; as, in the first place, I am more useful than I could be anywhere else, and, in the second, am very comfortable.' It was a long time since Dorothy had been in sole charge of a household, and she clearly relished this Whitwick reincarnation of keeping house for her brother at Town End. One wonders if it ever occurred to her that she was now, at the age of fifty-seven, finally realizing her youthful dream of living in a country parsonage, albeit with her nephew, rather than her brother.

Sara, too, had left Rydal Mount for the winter. After recurrent attacks of spitting blood, it was thought wise that she should take advantage of the milder climate of Herefordshire. As one invalid left, her place was taken by another, her sister Joanna, who was still very lame two years after an accident, and had great hopes that Carr, the Ambleside physician, might be able to cure her. Amidst all these comings and goings, and the uncertainties over his sons' futures, William's poetic confidence also deserted him. 'I have not written a verse these 9 months past –', he wrote miserably on 11 November, 'my vein I fear is run out.' What was almost worse was that the sale of his new edition of *Poetical Works* was now threatened from an unexpected source. A Parisian publisher, Galignani, had taken advantage of the absence of international copyright law to print a pirated edition of William's own five volumes, reduced to a single volume, for which the author received nothing. Selling at only twenty francs, it was a mere third or quarter of the price of Longman's edition. As the disconsolate poet gloomily remarked, 'Everybody goes to Paris nowadays' and not everybody was as high-minded as Robinson, who declined to purchase a copy on principle. Galignani did send a beautifully got-up presentation copy, which William was forced to admit had been printed with admirable accuracy, but it was 'a poor Compensation for his Piracy'. Urging Robinson, as a lawyer and a man of letters, to reflect and write in the periodicals on the subject of copyright, William sounded the first clarion-call in a campaign to rectify the injustice to authors. He could not have foreseen that it would take fourteen years of intensive lobbying to achieve any satisfaction.

After a long fallow period – and indeed within weeks, if not days, of bemoaning the fact that his 'vein had run dry' – William suddenly embarked on a new poem. It was new in every sense, for it was his first (and thankfully his last) excursion into Arthurian romance. *The Egyptian Maid; or, The Romance of the Water Lily*, described how a fair Egyptian princess, shipwrecked through the malevolence of Merlin, is brought back to life by the touch of Sir Galahad. 'It rose from my brain, without let or hindrance, like a vapour', William wrote happily on 25 November, when he had completed all 360 lines, though he would later admit that its halting metre was not well suited to narrative poetry. *The Egyptian Maid* is not one of William's most memorable poems, but it broke through his writer's block and prepared the way for what he considered one of his most important. This was his ode *On the Power of Sound*, which he began to compose in December, though it was not completed until some nine or ten months later.

This sudden outpouring of poetry was brought to an abrupt end by a nasty accident. Running down from the mount, where he had been entertaining a small party of visitors, William caught his toe in the turf and was thrown head-first down to the bottom of the hill. 'He fell like a log of wood', his daughter observed; 'having one hand in his breast & the other in his Trowser's pocket he had no power of balancing or saving himself'. He landed on his head, gashing the bridge of his nose, giving himself a black eye and straining the muscles in his neck, which altered his voice, so that he sounded as if he had a cold. The leather front of his cap was broken in two by the force of the fall, but fortunately William himself was made of hardier stuff.

Throughout the spring of 1829 William watched, with increasing dismay, as a Tory government, led by the Duke of Wellington and Sir Robert Peel, pushed the Roman Catholic Emancipation Act through stormy sessions in both Houses of Parliament. The act, which secured its final passage in June, allowed Catholics to vote, sit in Parliament and hold civil office, provided that they met the necessary property qualifications and took an oath of loyalty to the Constitution. It was undoubtedly an act of expediency, designed to alleviate the rising demands for Catholic equality, behind which loomed the spectre of rebellion in Ireland. This made it seem even more of a betrayal to those, like William, who opposed it root and branch, on moral, as well as practical, grounds. At the heart of his argument was his fear that the act would lead to the disestablishment of the Church of England. Rather touchingly, William naïvely believed that, because a Catholic's first duty was to obey the Pope, every Catholic was therefore absolutely committed to the restoration of papal supremacy in Britain. To ask a Catholic to take an oath to protect the Church of England was therefore '*monstrous*' and immoral, because it forced him to prefer a civil duty above a religious one. The proposal that the government would pay the salaries of Irish Catholic priests was similarly immoral, because it was a disingenuous attempt to bribe men of sacred calling to act contrary to their sense of duty. Sincere priests would find it impossible to accept such a salary, knowing it was granted with that expectation; the more worldly minded would simply take it, and continue to undermine the government, while pretending to support it. Once Catholics were admitted to civil office themselves, they would be morally obligated to disestablish the Church of England. All William's experience of travelling on the Continent, he declaimed, had taught him that it was impossible for the Catholic and Protestant Churches to share power in a free country and preserve Christian belief as a vital principle of action.

As for the very real threat of civil war in Ireland (a country he had never visited), William argued that making concessions to the Catholics would not solve the problems there. 'The chief proximate causes of Irish misery and ignorance are twofold – Papacy and the tenure and management of landed Property'. His answer was simple, as those of theorists usually are. The Catholic clergy should be prevented from punishing any of their flock found in possession of the Bible or attending Protestant churches, and the consolidation of Protestant parishes should be reversed, so that Protestant clergymen were more in evidence throughout the country. First and foremost, however, the security of person and property should be re-established, if necessary by military force, so that absentee landlords would return, rents would be kept within the country and a flow of 'English Arts, Manners, refinements and aspirations' into Ireland would be encouraged. In time, William believed, 'the grovelling Peasantry' of Ireland would realize the 'Social blessings which Protestants have acquired by being delivered from Spiritual thraldom', be encouraged to accumulate property and therefore be less liable to become the tools of political and religious agitators.

There was little William could do to oppose the Catholic Emancipation Act, but that little he did, to his utmost. He wrote to his old friend Blomfield, Bishop of London, for instance, putting his case as strongly as he dared, and entreating the bishops to stand firm in the House of Lords. And, in common with Anglican clergymen and laymen throughout the country, he was personally responsible for organizing a local petition against the passing of the act. Quillinan, a Catholic, could not resist teasing his gloomy friends.

I am sorry you are such an intolerant set . . . but you will learn charity from the papists in time; especially after we have had a few holy bonfires on Penenden Heath near Maidstone, & Martyr's Field near Canterbury, where the chiefs of the Brunswick Heresy [i.e. Protestants] are to be boiled, broiled, grilled, roasted, or stewed, according to the pleasure of His Holiness the Sovereign Pontiff.

It was not a happy spring in other respects. William was very anxious about Dora, who, having spent the winter at Rydal Mount, had been afflicted with persistent colds. As Sara Coleridge observed, she had also an 'unpleasant, obstinate cough' which 'often drives him out upon the terrace when he would otherwise make one of the social circle: I suppose this cough has an ominous sound to him but I trust his apprehensions will prove ground less'. After a trouble-free two years, and more, William also suffered three consecutive attacks of trachoma, of increasing severity, culminating in a large abscess on his eyelid. Unable to read or write, and forced to leave off composition, he tried to bear his privations patiently, but the same east wind which he believed had caused the initial inflammation claimed another victim.

On 3 April Dorothy was suddenly struck down with one of those irritatingly vague nineteenth-century illnesses which William described as an 'internal inflammation' and Dorothy, probably more accurately, as 'Cholera morbus'. She and John had both had influenza, but a week before her attack Dorothy had paid a round of visits to the parish sick of Whitwick, including a poor woman and a child, both of whom she described as 'very ill'. Whether she caught something from them or had some chronic illness of her own, for forty-eight hours she suffered agonies of griping pain in her bowels, sickness and violent perspirations, both hot and cold. Fortunately, Willy had been at Whitwick since 6 March and, according to his grateful aunt, he proved 'the tenderest nurse possible'. By the time Mary arrived, on the first available coach, the crisis had passed, but Dorothy was left so weak she could scarcely speak, let alone stand, and it was a full month before she was able to do anything more than potter round the house and garden.

By the second week in May, Dorothy was well enough for Mary to feel able to return home. Willy had departed the day before, and on 22 June John and Dorothy said their farewells to their kind friends the Merewethers and Lady Beaumont and set out for Halifax, where Dorothy had reluctantly agreed to pay a visit to her 'aunt', Elizabeth Rawson. Only the knowledge that her 'aunt' was so old, and had been newly widowed, persuaded Dorothy to relinquish her intention of going straight to Rydal, for she was longing to be home after such a long absence. She was also in a very delicate state of health. Lady Beaumont was so concerned that she wrote to warn William that he would have to watch his sister carefully, as she could not bear any excitement or fatigue. Earlier in the month (despite the doctors' assurances), she had suffered a severe relapse.

It was not Dorothy, however, but Lady Beaumont herself who died, suddenly, a mere three weeks after they had parted at Coleorton. It was a painful shock to the Wordsworths, as William wrote in his letter of condolence to her husband's cousin and heir, the new Sir George. It went without saying that everyone expected a suitable poetic tribute from William: 'I have only to say that to make any promise of the kind would be the surest way of defeating the object altogether –', William responded. 'You may be assured however generally that if I live and have health and spirits to write verses, a tribute will not be wanting, some where or other, among my works to the Memory of so dear a friend and so excellent a person'.

Dorothy returned to Rydal Mount on 8 September, just in time to welcome Sara Coleridge's bridal party from Keswick. The 'Celestial Blue' was now 'quietly *happy* and chearful – and not abstracted as she often used to be'. Five days earlier, she had at last become Mrs Henry Coleridge, marrying her cousin after a lengthy engagement. Dora, and Sara's three Southey cousins, Edith, Bertha and Kate, were among the eight bridesmaids, and John Wordsworth officiated at the ceremony. The newlyweds, accompanied by an uncomfortable Dora, who did not appreciate playing gooseberry, honeymooned in the Lakes and stayed twice at Rydal Mount. The second visit was a momentous one, for it closed another chapter in the Coleridge family's life in the Lakes. With both Sara and Derwent married, there was no longer any reason why their mother should remain at Greta Hall. She had come to Keswick most reluctantly, and would leave it with even deeper regret, but her home in the future would lie with her son, in Cornwall, and, ultimately, her daughter in London. Only one Coleridge would remain in the Lakes, 'li'l Hartley', gifted but flawed, son of a gifted but flawed father. And like his father, he could not face an emotional parting from his mother, disappearing before she arrived at

Rydal Mount and not reappearing till she had gone. Deeply sensitive to his own failings and peculiarities, he concluded, 'I remain alone, bare and barren and blasted, ill omen'd and unsightly as Wordsworth's melancholy thorn on the bleak hill-top. So hath it been ordain'd, and it is well.' It was not well, for he would never see her again, and the knowledge that he had avoided this chance to say goodbye would haunt him for the rest of his life.

Within a month of returning to Rydal, Dorothy had again to take to her bed with a recurrence of all the symptoms which had first attacked her at Whitwick. As she approached her fifty-eighth birthday, it was apparent to them all, Dorothy herself included, that her constitution was shattered. There would be no more foreign tours, no more excursions and no more walking fifteen miles a day. William's 'exquisite sister' had become a permanent invalid.

22. *Furiously Alarmist*

Dorothy's illness prevented William fulfilling a promise, made more than thirty years earlier, that he would take her on a tour of North Wales. Even when she recovered, she was obviously not physically capable of the exertion of a Wordsworthian tour. He toyed with the idea of accompanying Joanna and Henry Hutchinson to Norway, but with the passage of the Roman Catholic Emancipation Act, there was only one place he felt he should go, and that was Ireland.

Two years earlier he had met a young Irishman, William Rowan Hamilton, a brilliant mathematician, polyglot and poet who, at twenty-two, was already Professor of Astronomy at Trinity College, Dublin. With two friends, Alexander Nimmo, a civil engineer, and Caesar Otway, a Church of Ireland clergyman, Hamilton had visited Rydal Mount in September 1827 and struck up an instant rapport with William. Despite the disparity in their ages, each man was dazzled by the talents of the other. They had spent all evening together conversing, then, reluctant to part, took a midnight walk together, 'for a long, long time, *without any companion* except the stars and our own burning thoughts and words', as Hamilton put it. William afterwards wrote, 'Seldom have I parted – never I was going to say with one whom after so short an acquaintance, I lost sight of with more regret. I trust we shall meet again'. On his return to Dublin, Hamilton sent William a poem he had written at Ambleside, prompting an intelligent and sympathetic critique from the poet which ensured that the correspondence would continue.

When William decided to go to Ireland, he immediately turned to Hamilton for advice: 'I am ignorant of so many points, as where to begin, whether it be safe at this *rioting* period, what is best worth seeing, what mode of travelling will furnish the greatest advantages at the least expence.' A prompt and helpful reply encouraged him and he laid tentative plans to go with Dora in August, but, at the last minute, he got cold feet. 'I dread the risks as to health, the fatigue, and the expenses of taking Dora and the long sea sickness.' Luckily, his old friend John Marshall had planned a visit to Ireland himself, with his son, James, and offered William a place in his carriage. The little party set off from Kendal on 25 August. For several days before they sailed, there had been terrific storms and at least two ships were wrecked at Whitehaven, but William was blessed with a calm voyage, arriving in Dublin on 30 August. While the Marshalls spent a leisurely three days exploring the city, William took up residence with Hamilton at the Observatory, just outside Dublin, and embarked on a whirlwind series of social engagements and tourist visiting.

It was a visit that was even more exhausting mentally than physically. 'Mr Hamilton is a most interesting person quite a man of Genius and always very lively – but I was over stimulated; and could not have stood it long.' The over-stimulation did not make itself apparent to his host's family, who were charmed with the poet's 'slight touch of rusticity and constraint about his perfect gentlemanliness of manner ... everything he said and did had an unaffected simplicity and dignity, and peacefulness of thought that were very striking'. Once again, by reading his poems aloud, in his sonorous voice and dignified manner, he succeeded in winning over an audience which, if not actually hostile, had not been predisposed in his favour.

On the third day William rejoined the Marshalls and they set off, in their private carriage, on a five-week clockwise tour of Ireland, which would take them through 'all the crack places of the Wicklow Mountains and Country – the Devils glen excepted', Wexford, Waterford, Cork, Limerick, Sligo, Londonderry, the Giant's Causeway, Antrim and Belfast. 'You cannot guess how hard I work to see and hear all I can', William wrote from Enniskillen. 'I am never in bed later than half after five, and often rise at five.' On one occasion, he and James Marshall

breakfasted at 5, set off from Kenmare at half past, rode 10 Irish miles, took to our feet, ascended nearly 15,00 feet, descended as much, ascended another ridge as high, descended as much, and then went to the top of Carrantuohill, 3000 feet, the mountain being the highest in Ireland, 3410 feet above the level of the sea. We then descended, walked nearly two hours, and rode on bad horses an hour and a half or more, and reached Killarney at ten at night, having eaten nothing but a poor breakfast of spongy bread without eggs and one crust of the same quality, and drank milk during the whole day. I reached Killarney neither tired nor exhausted after all this. We were richly recompensed by a fine day, and most sublime views.

This was by no means an untypical day, as William's purpose in rising early was to explore the country on foot before the Marshalls set off on the next stage of the journey in their carriage. Not only was this a preferable way of seeing the scenery, but it gave him a much-needed opportunity to meet and converse with the Irish people, for, despite his prejudice against Catholicism, he was anxious to see and learn for himself. And he was pleasantly surprised. At St Kevin's Pool, in County Wicklow, he was deeply moved by the sight of a peasant woman bearing her sickly child in order to dip him nine times in the holy waters in the hope of a cure. 'It would have affected you very much to see this poor confiding creature – and to hear the manner in which she expressed her faith in the goodness of God and St Kevin', William told his brother. 'What would one not give to see among protestants such devout reliance on the mercy of their Creator, so much resignation, so much piety – so much simplicity and singleness of mind, purged of the accompanying Superstitions[?]' Talking to the ordinary people, he discovered that the Catholics among them believed that Protestants were attached to their religion by personal interest, not genuine conviction. Much to his surprise, he also discovered that they spoke well of their priests; 'this was not so in Italy where the commonalty treated them with derision'. When he asked them what they hoped to gain from Catholics being eligible to sit in Parliament, the universal response was to be relieved of Church rates and for tithes to be apportioned between the two churches. After mixing with many Catholics among the wealthy, educated classes, he was also forced to the conclusion that he had overestimated their desire to exalt their Church at the expense of the Protestant establishment. When he reported home comments by Lord Lorton's brother, that 'the country [was] more unquiet than ever, and [that he] forbode the very worst from Catholic bigotry and intolerance in alliance with political Demagogues', William added an important caveat: 'But remember Lord Lorton and his family are Brunswickers [Protestant hard-liners] of the first water.'

William returned to Rydal Mount on 11 October with much matter for thought, but none for poetry. Out of all the sights he had seen, only one, admittedly magnificent, image, that of a pair of eagles off Fairhead Promontory, in County Antrim, found its way into a poem (on Scotland!) two years later.

> The last I saw
> Was on the wing; stooping, he struck with awe
> Man, bird, and beast; then, with a consort paired,
> From a bold headland, their loved aery's guard,
> Flew high above Atlantic waves, to draw
> Light from the fountain of the setting sun.
> *Eagles, ll.4–9*

William was later ashamed of 'this want of notices, in my verse, of a country so interesting', ascribing it to lack of time, due to the shortness of the autumnal days and speed at which he had travelled. This was not true, as is clear from his enthusiastic and detailed observations of both people and scenery in his letters home. What is undoubtedly true is that politics, rather than poetry, had always been uppermost in his mind, and above all else the apparently insoluble problem of Irish poverty. 'The subject of the Poor Laws was never out of my sight whilst I was in Ireland', he admitted on his return. Though it was a system he favoured in principle, he now realized that it simply would not work in Ireland: there were too many poor with equal claims for relief, and not enough people of sufficient income to support or administer it.

As Quillinan, the last of the summer visitors, took his leave, the annual cry went up from Rydal Mount. 'He does intend to fall to the "Recluse" being seriously impressed with the faith that very soon it must be too late (His next Birth day will be his 60th)', Dorothy wrote hopefully to her Cambridge nephews,

– but, in the mean time he has been busy with less important matters, polishing the small poems he wrote last year, and actually he has written another *Sonnet.* This we were not glad of, fearing it might be but the beginning as heretofore, of a *Batch.* he has, however, promised that he will write no more. Now I should have little faith in this promise, if it were not plain that his mind is set upon doing its best at the great Work.

William began by altering and, ominously, completing *On the Power of Sound.* 'We all think there is a grandeur in this Poem', Dora wrote, 'but it ought to have been in the "Recluse" & Mother on that account but half enjoys it'. The frustration of all the Wordsworth females would only increase. Even Dorothy – especially Dorothy – was perplexed by William's failure to engage with *The Recluse.* 'He is still the crack skater on Rydal Lake,' she boasted on 9 January 1830,

and, as to climbing of mountains, the hardiest and the youngest are yet hardly a match for him. In composition I can see no failure, and his imagination seems as vigorous as in youth; yet he shrinks from his great work, and both during the last and present winter has been employed in writing small poems . . . in the course of man's life, but a few years of vigorous health and strength can be allotted to him. For this reason, my sister and I take every opportunity of pressing upon him the necessity of applying to his great work, and this he feels, resolves to do it, and again resolution fails. And now I almost fear habitually, that it will be ever so.

It was the first time any of the Wordsworths had voiced the fear that *The Recluse* might never be written. Even William had not yet admitted this to himself, though in his heart of hearts he must have known that he no longer had the necessary energy, or, indeed, poetic powers.

Christmas at Rydal Mount was a relatively quiet affair this year. Sara and Joanna, who were expected on Christmas Eve, did not arrive until New Year's Eve. John could not be spared from his duties at Moresby and Willy was still in Germany, where he had abandoned the classics, and, at his father's suggestion, was now studying mathematics, drawing and architecture, in addition to modern languages, in preparation for a career as a landscape gardener. Willy had been honest enough to admit he did not particularly like the proposal, as there was not much prospect of making money, and he felt it was 'somewhat beneath' him, but Papendick agreed with William that it was the only respectable profession where Willy could enjoy the outdoor life he craved.

Unfortunately, it was a profession better suited to his father, who, as soon as the winter snows had cleared, threw aside his poetical labours with obvious relief and began 'draining a bit of spungy ground' to build a new terrace at Rydal Mount.

Supervising the workmen, and sometimes wielding a spade himself, were thera-
peutic employments for William as, on 7 April, he reached the milestone of his
sixtieth birthday. 'I have given over writing verses till my head becomes stronger
or my fancy livelier', he informed his daughter a few weeks later. A new edition of
his poems would soon be needed and William could not decide what to do. Dorothy
had no doubts. 'We females wish him to publish the numerous poems now in store
immediately, in one small volume, that they may have a Boom, and the Edition
get sold off before the 5 vols. are again printed'. The new volume could then be
incorporated with the complete poems. William was not convinced. His reluctance
to publish was not just for the usual reasons, dislike of the trouble and fear of
critical reaction. Since publishing his last edition, he had come to realize that public
taste was changing. The runaway success of the cheap pirated copies of his works
in France and America, combined with that of the annuals, which Southey wittily
called 'picture-books for grown children', had shown that there was a voracious
market for poetry. When yet another reader, a complete stranger, John Gardner,
wrote to inform him that the pirated Galignani edition was being widely sold in
England, and urged him to publish a cheap edition of his own, he merely confirmed
what had already become a growing conviction. 'I am inclined to think with my
Friend Mr Southey that shortly few books will be published except low-priced
ones, or those that are highly ornamented, for persons who delight in such luxuries.'

Inquiries at Longman's revealed that they had little enthusiasm for the idea of a
cheap edition, maintaining the traditional line that purchasers of poetry were 'of
that class who do not regard prices'. William's experience had taught him otherwise
– and he had been listening to what his readers told him. With or without his
publisher's support, William had already decided that his next edition would have
to be compressed into four volumes, simply to make the price more affordable.
And when the young and enterprising Edward Moxon wrote, at the beginning of
June, to inform him that he had left Longman's to set up on his own, William not
only offered his active support for the venture but immediately inquired about the
potential for a cheap edition of his poems.

Early in June John sprang a surprise on his unsuspecting family by announcing
that he was engaged to be married. It was, as his father commented laconically, a bold
step, for John's income as rector of Moresby was a mere £100 a year. (What he did not
say was that John was already living beyond it, having just purchased a horse, which
he considered a necessary luxury 'for various reasons'. He had also cost his father
more than £255 in the past two years, despite being employed for most of that period
at Whitwick.) Fortunately, John's intended bride was Isabella Curwen, oldest daughter of Henry Curwen, of Workington Hall and Belle Isle, on Windermere. 'The
Father's allowance to his Daughter is so liberal as to remove every objection upon
prudential grounds', William assured his brother. 'The young Lady is in her 23d
year, bears the highest character for feminine virtues, and in her demeanour and
appearance is truly engaging, but her health is, I grieve to say, delicate.'

Given that Isabella's grandfather, John Curwen, had been an outspoken political
opponent of the Lowthers for many years, it was something of a relief to find that

her father had no taste for active politics. After only a couple of meetings, William's verdict on his new relation was positive: 'he is a man of extensive reading, accurate memory, and very intelligent: His habits are those of a retired Man, and I like him the better on that account.' The two men exchanged cordial letters agreeing the match, met again on Belle Isle, and the wedding was arranged for October.

Isabella herself came to stay at Rydal Mount in July, giving the Wordsworths their first opportunity to get to know their future daughter-in-law. Predisposed in her favour as they all were, she did not disappoint them. 'She gains daily and hourly on our affections', Dorothy reported, '... in every thing she does or says, you can trace the best of dispositions.' The engagement naturally led to intimacy with all the Curwen family, who were frequent visitors over the summer months. They were not alone. 'The house has been more like an Inn, for the last six weeks, than a private one', Sara pretended to complain to Quillinan. She was not exaggerating, for thanks to the Rydal Mount Visitors' Book, which was started in May of this year, we know that more than 166 people crossed the Wordsworths' threshold before the end of the year. Among them was Mrs Felicia Dorothea Hemans, popular authoress of such gems as 'The boy stood on the burning deck', who owed her introduction to her friend Maria Jewsbury, but behaved as though she were bestowing the favour. 'For one *long* fortnight we had Mrs Hemans & one of her boys –', Sara wrote feelingly to Quillinan. When she left Rydal Mount on 2 July it was only to go as far as Dove Nest, on Windermere, where she took up residence for the summer, happy in her conviction that she had conquered the poet with her charms and taking a malicious glee in his foibles. 'Imagine my dear – a Bridal present made by Mr Wordsworth to a young lady in whom he is much interested – a poet's daughter too!' she confided in a letter, later published in the *Athenaeum*, which reveals as much about her as it does about William.

You will be thinking of a brooch in the form of a lyre or a butterfly shaped [aigette?] or a forgetmenot ring, or some such 'small gear'. Nothing of the sort – but a good, handsome, substantial, useful-looking – pair of scales to hang up in her storeroom! 'For you must be aware, my dear Mrs Hemans' added he gravely 'how necessary it is for every lady to see things weighed herself!' <u>Poveretta me</u>! I looked <u>as good as I could</u>, & happily for me the poetic eyes are not very clear sighted, so that I believe no suspicion derogatory to my notability of character has yet flashed upon the mighty master's mind; indeed I told him that I looked upon scales as particularly graceful things & had great thoughts of having my picture taken with a pair in my hand.

It does not seem to have occurred to Mrs Hemans that the 'poetic eyes' were indeed clear-sighted, and that the poet himself was having a little private joke at the expense of a 'literary lady'.

The wedding was celebrated with great panache on 11 October. Dora, the eternal bridesmaid, did her duty once more, accompanying the bride and her father in the first of five carriages which carried the wedding party from Workington Hall to the church. The whole of Workington turned out to cheer the bride to and from church, and when the newlyweds emerged, they scattered silver among the crowds, guns were fired and all the ships in the harbour hoisted their flags. Fifty guests sat down to the wedding breakfast, after which the married couple set off for a honeymoon in Scotland. It was a far cry from the walk across the fields and quiet village church ceremony which had marked the start of William and Mary's married life together, twenty-eight years earlier.

The bridegroom's parents and sister returned briefly to Rydal Mount, where Dorothy and Sara had remained in companionable seclusion during the wedding festivities, before setting out again, on 1 November, to spend the winter in Cambridge. Throughout the year, Dora's health, or lack of it, had been a cause of deep concern. Afraid that she would not be able to withstand the usual winter coughs and colds in her weakened state, her parents were determined that she should stay in the south, at least until the spring. As they thought it would be useful if Dora could ride her pony regularly, they decided to take it with them, her sixty-year-old father undertaking 'very valiantly and economically' to ride it all the way to Cambridge himself, while Mary and Dora travelled by more conventional means.

It was just the sort of eccentric gesture William loved. Ambling along, with only the silent pony for companionship, he made his way through Lancashire and the Peak District, revelling in this rare chance for unhurried observation. By the time he reached Chatsworth, he was beginning to murmur verses for the first time in twelve months.

The poetic spirit fled as soon as William reached Cambridge, for the whole university was abuzz with the news that Wellington had resigned as Prime Minister and that Lord Grey had formed a ministry committed to parliamentary reform, with Brougham as his Lord Chancellor. From the sanctuary of Trinity Lodge, William watched in dismay as the fires of reform, both metaphorical and literal, began to blaze in the surrounding countryside. Everywhere he looked, it seemed as if the old order was being destroyed. In the space of just a few months, there had been popular revolutions in France, Belgium and Poland, which were now spreading to Germany and central Italy. The king of France had been deposed and the king of Holland ousted from a Belgium which now claimed its independence. The new king of England, William IV, had refused to go to Guildhall for fear of riots on the streets of London, and Ireland, tinder-dry, was awaiting the explosion.

At such a crisis, William could not return to the Lakes for Christmas, as he had intended to do. Instead, when the university broke up for the vacation, he allowed Christopher to persuade him to go to his country parsonage at Buxted, a village just outside Uckfield, in Sussex. This was a convenient place to leave Mary and Dora, while he took advantage of an open invitation from Quillinan to make frequent excursions into London. In London he now had a voice in the highest and most influential circles in the land. He dined several times with the Bishop of London and the Archbishops of Canterbury and York. He was continuously in the company of the new Lord Liverpool, half-brother of the former Prime Minister, who was also opposed to reform. The very fact that he was so often in such company reflected the respect in which his opinions were held.

What comes as more of a surprise is to find that he was also mixing regularly with radicals and reformers. Henry Taylor, a poet and playwright, who worked in the Colonial Office and had met William on earlier visits to London, hosted at least four breakfasts to which William was a welcome guest. 'Though he was old, and the rest so young, and he was opposed to them in politics, yet the force and brightness of his conversation, his social geniality, and the philosophic, as well as imaginative largeness of his intellect, delighted them all', Taylor wrote afterwards. Both Taylor and a young John Stuart Mill were flattered to receive an invitation to call at Rydal Mount, and another radical, Charles Greville, was won over by William's 'chearful', 'courteous' behaviour and his generous tributes to Brougham's talents and moral virtues, particularly his devotion to his family. That William was capable of distinguishing between Brougham's personal attributes and his politics, at a time when the latter seemed about to triumph over everything he believed in, is a remarkable instance of his generosity of spirit.

Through thick and thin, William clung to the belief that the Reform Bill was morally and politically wrong. Morally, because it was unjust, allowing the bare 5,000 inhabitants of Cockermouth to retain a Member of Parliament, but granting Manchester, with all its hundreds of thousands, a mere two. Politically, because it was the first step on a road which would lead inevitably to universal suffrage and annual elections. 'In the present stage of our affairs,' he wrote in December, 'the class that does the most harm consists of well-intentioned men, who, being ignorant of human nature, think that they may help the thorough-paced reformers and revolutionists to a *certain* point, then stop, and that the machine will stop with them.' William's own experience of the French Revolution had taught him otherwise. 'You mistake in supposing me an Anti Reformer –', he corrected Robinson, '*that* I never was – but an Anti-Bill man; heart and soul. – It is a fixed judgement of my mind, that an unbridled Democracy is the worst of all Tyrannies.' It was obvious to him, as to many of his contemporaries, that the equally inevitable result of universal suffrage and annual elections would be a government dependent on the whim of the mob and at the mercy of the popular press. 'I have witnessed one revolution in a foreign Country,' he wrote with sad dignity, 'and I have not courage to think of facing another in my own.'

Christopher, Lord Liverpool, and indeed many others, urged him to write publicly against the Reform Bill, but he could not be persuaded to do so. 'Your exhortations troubled me in a way you cannot be in the least aware of; for I have been repeatedly urged by some of my most valued friends, and at times by my own conscience, to undertake the task you have set before me', he answered one Cambridge friend.

But I will deal frankly with you. A conviction of my incompetence to do justice to the momentous subject has kept me, and I fear will keep me, silent. My sixty-second year will soon be completed, and though I have been favoured thus far in health and strength beyond most men of my age, yet I feel its effects upon my spirits; they sink under a pressure of apprehension to which, at an earlier period of my life, they would probably have been superior.

It was ironic that William's sense of impotence was increasing at a time when his influence was gaining ground every day. During his visit to London this spring, he had accepted not one but four separate requests to take his portrait. Perhaps more flattering than any of these attempts at portraiture was an extraordinary visit William paid, by invitation, to a Brixton school on 1 March. 'On Tuesday Captain Todd and I accompanied him to Brixton, not to the tread-mill, but to see a mad Schoolmaster named Hine or Hind', Quillinan informed Dora.

Now listen. This broad shouldered muscular Theban had one advantage over us besides his learning. His eyes are so arranged that you never know when he is looking at you; so that he may be staring hard at you all the time that he seems to look quite the other way. I shouldn't like to have such a cunning-eyed Schoolmaster . . . There were 54 boys at desks in rows of 8; as in the pit of a theatre. We were on the stage . . . pencils and slates were brought out at word of command; pedagogue gave out, line by line, the Sonnet supposed to be written on Westminster Bridge. All the Boys wrote it, one echoing the Master, as the clerk in certain cases, does the clergyman. When finished, several boys in turn, read it aloud: very well too. They were then called upon to explain the meaning of 'the river glideth at its own sweet will.' One boy . . . made a dissertation on the influence of the moon on the tides &c &c, and seemed rather inclined to be critical; another said there was no wind; another that there were no water breaks in the Thames to prevent its gliding as it pleased; another that the arches of the bridges had no locks to shut the water in or out: & so forth. One Boy said there were no boats – that was the nearest – Poet explained: was then called on by Pedagogue to read his sonnet himself: declined. Ped. entreated: Poet remonstrated: Ped. inexorable: Poet submitted. I never heard him read better. The Boys evidently felt it; a thunder of applause; Poet asked for a Half Holiday for them – granted – thunders on thunders Seriously speaking, the whole scene was indescribably animated and interesting.

To a man who loved children, was passionately interested in education and yet was riven with doubt about his own poetic powers, there can have been no more powerful, or touching, affirmation of his own achievement.

Joesph Hine was a teacher committed to the idea of reading poetry aloud to his pupils 'as a mode of culture profitable to health, to manners, to the understanding, and the social affections'. Having given William such a practical example of the effectiveness of this method, he succeeded where everyone else had failed. He persuaded the poet to sanction the publication of a not-so-slim volume, *Selections from the Poems of William Wordsworth, Esq. Chiefly for the Use of Schools and Young Persons*. Equally important, he also persuaded another Wordsworthian disciple, Edward Moxon, to print and publish it. The selection William left entirely to Hine. For a poet who had been painstaking, to the point of obsession, in the arrangement of his editions of his poetry, this was a rare tribute. The proof sheets, though, would be sent to him, scrutinized with his usual meticulous eye for detail and returned to Moxon suitably corrected. The pocket-sized volume, just over 380 pages long, contained 'I should suppose, at least 1100 verses', cost just 5s 6d, fully bound, and, as William remarked, 'would be found a good travelling companion for those who like my poetry'. Within days of publication, in June, Rogers wrote to tell William that the little book was selling fast '& giving an animation to Moxon which he has not known for some time'. And, within months, its success would encourage Southey to embark on a similar experiment with his own poetry.

The Wordsworths left London on 21 April, taking William and Dora's goddaughter, Rotha Quillinan, with them, but they were forced to halt at Nottingham, when Mary was struck down by so severe an attack of lumbago that she could not get up from bed. Fortunately, William remembered that William and Mary Howitt, Quaker poets who had presented him with a copy of their first publication, lived in the town. Though he had never met them personally, he sought them out and asked them to recommend a doctor. Not only was their brother a physician, but they gladly offered Mary, and Dora, who stayed behind with her mother, accommodation in their own house. The awkwardness of the situation was increased by the discovery that their kind hosts were radicals and actively involved in the election which was about to take place. They had landed, Dora said, 'in a hot bed of Reformists – in a wasps nest positively, & it drives me mad to hear of the "enlightened mob" – "the poor neglected" "their rights trampled upon" – "laws made for the rich & not for the poor" . . .' Mrs Howitt was 'a red hot Reformist', but she was also 'a charming Creature much the most fascinating of the Authoresses I have seen', and when they parted, twelve days after the Wordsworths' arrival in Nottingham, it was with genuine regret on both sides. William invited them to Rydal Mount in the autumn; Howitt 'consoled himself' with writing a sonnet to Dora. Another unlikely friendship across the political divide had been established.

William had been forced to abandon his wife and daughter, as it was imperative that he return to Westmorland immediately. Not only was he anxious to be there for the general election, but he had to attend to urgent Stamp Office business. The districts of Cumberland and Westmorland were to be amalgamated, under William's sole distributorship, and his sub-distributors were to have their salaries doubled, though their responsibilities remained unchanged. In other words, Dora complained on her father's behalf, 'my Lord Althorp has been most liberal, just given him double risk, double duty, & no more pay'.

The Stamp Office reforms provided William with the opportunity he had been looking for to place his second son in employment. Willy had returned to England in March, his sojourn on the Continent cut short by the revolutions sweeping Europe. William's first idea was to dismiss his clerk, Carter, and employ Willy in his place, 'which I believe the youth does not consider a very dignified employment'. But he simply could not bring himself to dismiss someone who had served him so long and so well, just to find a job for his own son. Besides, Carter was indispensable. Not only did he single-handedly run the office, but he was always willing and able to lend a hand around the house, even though he had officially given up his gardening duties in 1824. His services would be vital in amalgamating the administration of the huge new district with that of the old, and, as William and Carter did their annual round together, William realized that there was a better opening for his son as a sub-distributor in Carlisle. His duties would be less complicated than Carter's, he would earn in the region of £180 a year, and enjoy all the benefits of city life without being banished from the bosom of his family.

William had been depressed by his tour of his new district. He was even more depressed by the result of the general election a few days later. Another Lowther, Sir John, who had sat for Cumberland for thirty-five years, had declined to stand again. At the last minute, his place had been taken by Lord Lowther and, in a shock result, the Cumberland electors rejected him and returned two radical Members of Parliament. Even in Westmorland, the Lowthers avoided outright defeat only by coming to an arrangement with their opponents, whereby a single candidate from each party was put forward for unopposed election. Embarrassingly, John's father-in-law, Henry Curwen, had contributed to the Lowther defeat by putting up £500 to support the radical candidates. 'Poor Father is quite overpowered by the horrors & sorrows which seem to him hanging over this hitherto favo[u]red spot of earth', Dora wrote. With the return of a Parliament committed to reform, there was nothing more William could do, except resign himself to the inevitable passage of the bill. Though he complained that his Muse had forsaken him, 'being scared away by the villainous aspect of the Times', he made a great effort on behalf of his old friend Haydon, who had requested a sonnet to his picture of 'Napoleon on the Island of St Helena'. Knowing that Haydon was in dire financial straits, William sent him the sonnet 'not "warm" but piping hot from the brain, whence it came in the wood adjoining my garden not ten minutes ago, and was scarcely more than twice as long in coming', and gave him permission to publish it wherever he wished. This was generous, for Haydon immediately offered it to Samuel Carter Hall for his annual, the *New Monthly Magazine*, where it appeared in the July issue as a splendid piece of publicity for the picture. A few days later, William composed a second short poem, which he intended as an inscription for a stone in 'a hazel nook' in the garden, but was more like an epitaph for himself.

> In these fair Vales, hath many a tree
> At Wordsworth's suit been spared,
> And from the builder's hand this Stone,
> For some rude beauty of its own,
> Was rescued by the Bard;
> Long may it rest in peace! and here
> Perchance the tender-hearted
> Will heave a gentle sigh for him
> As One of the Departed.

In stark contrast to the doom and gloom pervading spirits at Rydal Mount, the summer proved a brilliant one for weather and 'unexampled gaiety in Regattas, Balls, Dejeuners, Picnics by the Lake side, on the Islands, and on the Mountain tops – Fireworks by night – Dancing on the green sward by day'. Even the Wordsworths were not immune, holding a dance for 'forty beaus and belles, besides

Matrons, ancient Spinsters, and Greybeards' and a 'Venison feast' at the beginning of September.

On 13 September William, Dora and Sara went over Kirkstone Pass in a little four-wheeled open carriage, pulled by a horse purchased by William and Willy. Sara was bound for Patterdale, to stay with the Marshalls, but father and daughter were setting out on a tour of Scotland together. To their frustration, they were delayed for several days, both at Rydal Mount and at Patterdale, by a severe recurrence of William's trachoma, but they could wait no longer, for it was imperative that they should reach Abbotsford before the end of the month. William had been summoned by Scott, who had sent 'an affectionate message' saying that 'if I did not come soon to see him it might be too late'. For months they had heard reports of his declining health; now he was so ill that he was about to leave for Italy, in the fragile hope of prolonging his life beyond the winter.

The Wordsworths found all Scott's family gathered at Abbotsford, together with Sir William Allan, the Scottish historical painter, William Laidlaw, Scott's steward and secretary, and the eldest son of Lord Ravensworth, Henry Liddell, his wife and brother-in-law. They were also joined, at William's invitation, by his own nephew, Charles Wordsworth, who was on a walking tour of Scotland. The highlight of the visit was an emotional trip to the Yarrow, so that the two poets could retrace their footsteps one last time in one of their favourite haunts. As they crossed the Tweed in their carriages on the way back to Abbotsford, a setting sun bruised the clouds above the Eildon Hills with a purple light. It was a moment when the elegiac moods of poet and nature synthesized, prompting William to begin his sonnet *On the departure of Sir Walter Scott from Abbotsford, for Naples*, which mourned the departure of a 'kindred Power' and assured him that 'the might Of the whole world's good wishes with him goes'. He was also, of course, duty bound to produce the inevitable *Yarrow Revisited*, which became a tribute to his old friend, the 'last Minstrel'.

> For Thou, upon a hundred streams,
>   By tales of love and sorrow,
> Of faithful love, undaunted truth,
>   Hast shed the power of Yarrow;
> And streams unknown, hills yet unseen,
>   Wherever they invite Thee,
> At parent Nature's grateful call,
>   With gladness must requite Thee.

The evening before the Wordsworths' departure, the two poets, one dying, the other half-blind, sat quietly together in the library. In the course of their conversation, Scott dwelt at length on the singular fact that both Fielding and Smollett had been driven abroad by declining health and had never returned. William was equally struck that neither of these authors had inspired due marks of respect at the close of their lives. It was, undoubtedly, these remarks which lent a sense of urgency to the composition of the tributes to Scott; both poems were sent to him personally, as he was *en route* to Italy, and William had the satisfaction of learning that he had been 'delighted' with them.

On the final morning before their departure William and Scott said their farewells in private, and Scott wrote a faltering few lines of verse in Dora's album. Handing the album back to Dora, in William's presence, he told her, 'I should not have done any thing of this kind but for your Father's sake; they are probably the last verses I shall ever write.'

While Scott and his family made their way slowly southwards to embark for Italy, William and Dora parted from Charles and took the road to the Highlands. 'From Abbotsford we went to Roslin, Edinburgh, Sterling, Loch Kettering, Killin, Dalmally, Oban, the Isle of Mull – too late in the season for Staffa – and returned by Inverary, Loch Lomond, Glasgow, and the falls of the Clyde', William reminisced to another poet, Rogers, after their return.

For William it was that most potent of mixtures, past and present, combined with a state of heightened feeling, brought on by the emotional parting from Scott. He forgot, or laid aside, all his troubles and gave himself up to sheer enjoyment.

On 7 October Dora was able to send her mother six new poems her father had composed in the eight days since they had parted from Charles at Callander, adding that he was, even as she wrote, 'hammering at a horrid sonnet & he cannot give me his ear at the moment'. The momentum did not leave him once they returned home and before the end of the month he had added several more, including *Yarrow Revisited* and the wonderful sonnet *Eagles*, contrasting an imprisoned eagle seen at a castle near Oban with the freewheeling birds he had watched off Fairhead in Ireland.

Reinvigorated by his Scottish tour, William promised his daughter that *The Recluse* would be this winter's employment, but 'entre nous', Dora whispered to Maria Jewsbury, 'I think his courage will fail him when winter really arrives.' The females were taking no chances. They had invited William's oldest nephew, John Wordsworth, twenty-six years old, a fellow of Trinity and a brilliant scholar, yet also a shy, eminently likeable young man in delicate health, to spend the winter at Rydal Mount. The unspoken hope was that his companionship would provide William with the intellectual stimulus he needed to go on with *The Recluse*. It was too much to ask of anyone, but the four months John spent at Rydal Mount were both productive and important: 'having John to talk to in his walks', Christopher proudly reported, William 'was very industrious through the whole winter at all other times of the day – and worked very hard, specially in the revising and finishing of his long autobiographic poem'. 'Cambridge John' won all hearts at Rydal Mount. Even Quillinan, who came to collect his daughter Rotha in the spring, was deeply impressed. 'I like him much', he confided to his diary. 'What a contrast are his modesty & courtesy to the manners of that little queer will o the wisp of conceit Hartley Coleridge. Yet John W has more learning than HC & perhaps as much natural aptitude if not more.'

For five weeks over Christmas, the Wordsworths also enjoyed the daily society of the Arnold family, who were staying in the cottages at the foot of the hill. Thomas Arnold, who had first paid homage to William at Rydal Mount in 1818, was now headmaster of Rugby school, married, with seven children of his own and another due in May. The little Arnolds were as taken with their neighbours as their parents: the Wordsworths were themselves so fond of children, and knew so well how to amuse them, their mother affirmed, that she had never seen the four eldest in such high spirits. There were tea-drinkings and parties, presided over by Dora and her great Newfoundland dog, Neptune, and the little Arnolds made lively companions for the Wordsworths' own winter house-guests, their niece Mary Hutchinson and Rotha Quillinan. More importantly, Thomas Arnold and William delighted in each other's company, despite being diametrically opposed in politics. 'My almost daily walks with him were things not to be forgotten', Arnold recalled months later.

The year 1832 was not to be a happy one for any of the Wordsworths. For William, it was dominated by the passage, in June, of the Reform Bill. All his worst fears for the preservation of the Constitution were realized, in that it required the threat of a mass creation of peers to force the House of Lords to allow the bill through. Advising Lord Lonsdale to trust to his principles rather than expediency in determining how to vote, William asserted that, in the Earl's position, he would vote against the bill, 'tho' with my eyes open to the great hazard of doing so'.

Once the bill was passed, William's anxiety was succeeded by 'dejection to despondency'. Parliament, he declared, had given birth to a monster. Accurately predicting that out of nine members to be returned by Cumberland under the new arrangement, only two would be Tory, the rest 'down right Jacobin Republicans' or, more dangerous still, 'rash or complying Whig Innovators', he waited impotently for the coming revolution.

Had all been well at home, his spirits might have rallied; but Dorothy, confined to her room after her last attack, before Christmas, had another relapse at the end of April. What frightened William most was that there was no apparent cause – and if a cause could not be identified, then future relapses could not be prevented. The only consolation was that Dorothy herself remained cheerful, even when unable to leave her room. When Dora carried up the first spring flowers, it prompted her aunt to compose what Dora rightly called an 'affecting poem', despite its 'limping measures'.

> I felt a power unfelt before
> Controlling weakness, languor, pain,
> It bore me to the terrace walk,
> I trod the hills again.
>
> No prisoner in this lonely room
> I <u>saw</u> the greens [*sic*] banks of the Wye
> Recalling thy prophetic words
> Bard! Brother! Friend from infancy!

No need of motion or of strength
Or even the breathing air
I thought of Nature's loveliest scenes
And with Memory I was there.

While Dorothy was in her most precarious state, news came from Stockton that Mary's younger sister, Betsy, had died. 'She has always been of weak faculties; and latterly her mind was disordered; so that it is a happy deliverance', William commented. Nevertheless, it was a breaking of the Hutchinson circle; the first death among Mary's siblings since that of Margaret, thirty-six years earlier.

In June 1832 a new edition of William's *Poetical Works* was published by Longman. This was the long-heralded, cheaper edition of his poems, which, by dint of printing the lines closer together and two sonnets a page, instead of one, had been compressed from five volumes into four. Despite these economies, the price could not be reduced below the magic figure of £1 without incurring a loss to both publisher and author. It would therefore sell for £1 4s, which was almost half the price of the last edition. Prudence dictated that the new edition should not appear until the last copies of the old had been sold, and that no new, unpublished, poems would be included, these being reserved either for separate or posthumous publication. It was characteristic of William's thoughtfulness in these matters, that he did not forget to send a complimentary copy to John Gardner, the London surgeon who had written to him two years earlier, suggesting he should publish a cheap edition.

Gardner had proved himself useful in other ways. William had written to him earlier in the year, asking his advice on how to place his nephew, 'Keswick' John, on a medical apprenticeship. John was now seventeen, so shy that he was still called 'Dora's child' because she was the only one who could get him to speak, and eager to do something for himself. Though he had spent two years at Hawkshead Grammar School, the quality of the teaching was not what it had been, and even his uncle had to admit that he was not a good scholar. Gardner, who was already training his own nephew, offered to take John himself and allow him to live with the family, so that he would not be alone in London. As his father's estate could not stand the costs, his guardian uncles had to find the money for John's maintenance, and the £200 indenture fee. Both William and Christopher were generous, ensuring that the indenture was paid for out of their own pockets as a gift to the young man. Fortunately, the amenable John was happy in his new-found profession, liked all the Gardners, and, as Quillinan observed, with a new London haircut, he already looked 'sharper'.

William's own son John also had a stroke of luck. In May Lord Lonsdale and Lord Lowther offered to present him to the living of Brigham, two miles from Cockermouth, on the River Derwent. It was a huge parish, including part of the town of Cockermouth itself, as well as several chapelries, worth £190 a year to its vicar, who would be able to hold it jointly with Moresby. It was a considerable advance for John, but there was no doubt at all on whom the Lowthers were conferring their favour: the letter offering the presentation was addressed to William.

In normal circumstances, William would have been happy in the knowledge that his sons and nephews were all provided for, but he could not rid himself of a depression he had not felt so strongly since his late twenties at Racedown. Then he had sought to come to terms with political disillusionment in the wake of the French Revolution, his guilt about Annette and Caroline, and his growing love for Mary. Now he had to face his fears about the consequences of the Reform Bill and the realization that Dorothy, if not actually dying, would never be restored to health and strength.

The summer saw literally hundreds of visitors (more than 267, according to the Rydal Mount Visitors' Book). There was the usual crop of Americans, 'Cantabs' and relations, but also a first-time visitor who came with an important mission, which proved indisputably that William's poetic reputation had risen to hitherto unimagined heights. Henry Pickersgill was an artist and Royal Academician who had been commissioned to paint William's portrait for St John's College, Cambridge. It was a signal honour. William's undistinguished university career, his youthful republicanism, his years as the butt of literary critics' contempt were all forgotten. William insisted that Pickersgill was to be his guest at Rydal Mount. At first the Wordsworths found him 'so odd & pompous', but they soon warmed to him, to the point where Dora jokingly threatened to reveal the 'flirtation' between him and Sara to Mrs Pickersgill. 'The 10 days Mr Pickersgill was with us were the happiest and most memorable I had well nigh said, of my life', Dora enthused.

There were the usual battles – to wrinkle or not to wrinkle – which Pickersgill clearly won, as neither the preliminary chalk drawing nor the finished portrait bear the tell-tale furrow down his cheek. Looking at the latter, which still hangs in St John's College, it is hard to see why the Wordsworths were all so pleased with it. William sits, in the half-reclining pose only poets in portraits adopt, on the green terrace with Rydal lake beyond. He is swathed in what Quillinan describes as a 'dandy military sort of cloak', clutches a cap in his right hand and, improbably, a pencil and paper in his left. Given the unnaturalness of the pose and background, the head looks as though it has been grafted on to a mannequin, and, unlike the chalk drawing, which is both dignified and powerful, the face is that of a weak and senile old man. Nevertheless, in the first flush of enthusiasm, they all felt 'deeply grateful to Pickersgill for giving us such a likeness of such a Father! We all agree that Rotha's . . . picture & this are the only <u>perfect</u> likenesses that is <u>living</u> likenesses, we ever saw.' Dora declared she could not look at it for five minutes without tears welling up, a reaction with which one cannot fail to agree, though for entirely different reasons.

Dora's tearful enthusiasm, combined with a feeling that this first public honouring of William's poetic career ought to be recognized by the poet himself, led to the obligatory sonnet: 'Go, faithful Portrait! and where long has knelt Margaret, the saintly foundress, take thy Place'. A workmanlike effort rather than an inspired piece, it centred around the appropriate image of the poet, immutably fixed on the canvas by his hills and streams, 'tho' Kingdoms melt Before the breath of Change', and referred to Dora's tears. Quillinan, in particular, had strong reservations about William publishing a sonnet to his own portrait: 'they seem to be lines purely domestic, and not proper, as yet at least, for the eye of the public: it would be impossible to explain to Strangers their full meaning, and many are the ungenerous who would pretend to find in them matter for sarcasm.' The sonnet was not intended for publication Dora replied, 'but more copies have been given than my Mother & I like – my Father as you know in such matters – is all dove no serpent. We are truly obliged by your hint for he will not always give ear to our notions but you have put him on his guard as to whom & where it is repeated.'

As one of the most momentous years in parliamentary history drew to a close, William was more than ever convinced that the country was on the brink of disaster. 'A spirit of rash innovation is every where at war with our old institutions', he wrote in October. Two months later, he wrote to urge all those members of his family with votes to come to Westmorland to support the Lowther cause: 'having spent nearly 160,000 pounds in resisting the enemy in this County they deserve the generous support and the personal exertions of all friends to good order and the British Constitution'. This personal plea and a signature on a petition requesting Lord Lowther to stand again for Westmorland, rather than Cumberland, was the extent of William's involvement in this election. The Lowther brothers were duly returned, but this was no cause for rejoicing, for all the towns in both counties returned reformers to a man, and the tidal wave of reform would continue. As the old year passed away and a new one dawned, William felt tired, defeated and depressed.

23. Falling Leaves

'You will grieve to hear that our dear Sister is very poorly and seems to grow weaker every day', William informed Christopher on 29 January 1833. Dorothy had suffered another relapse, this time accompanied by alarming new symptoms, swelling in her legs, blackness about her ankles and distressing spasms. 'Alas! my dear Friend, I fear she will not be long with us', Sara wrote to Mrs Coleridge; '. . . her weakness & languor are truly deplorable – indeed without the help of stimulants you could scarcely believe her alive – but with these she is kept at times tolerably easy – & even comfortable & *cheer*ful – which is always the case when free from pain & languor'. Entirely confined to her bed, Dorothy amazed them all with her patience and gaiety, greeting everyone who entered her sick chamber with her usual 'bright smile so full of love & tenderness'. The Ambleside surgeon, Carr, warned them there was no hope, so it came as no surprise when, at the beginning of February, she suffered another attack. Everyone thought her last hour had come, but still she clung to life. 'I wash her face as she used to do mine some thirty years ago', Dora wrote, 'she dear creature not having the power to do so much for herself without great exhaustion – but she is happy & contented & only has one regret – that she cannot read or even bear to be read to & as she cannot gain new ideas she knows she must lose some old ones – so she tells us'.

It seemed that everyone was ill. Dora had had another of her severe winter colds and ate so little that her parents could not help being anxious about her. 'Keswick' John was reported to have suddenly grown extremely thin and was suffering from a return of his cough, symptoms which did not bode well to a concerned guardian uncle's ear. Most dramatically of all, however, a series of shocking revelations about Tom Monkhouse's widow, Mrs Paris Dick, reached the Wordsworths from unimpeachable quarters. First of all, she wrote to inform Richard Addison, the London solicitor who had been Richard's business partner, that due to a 'long continued series of Injuries & provocations', she had separated from her husband. Towards the end of November Addison discovered that she was 'a confirmed Drunkard'. Her daughter, who was not quite eleven years old, was said to appear 'low-spirited'; she was living in lodgings in Blackpool with her mother and a governess who was nearly as bad as her mistress. It was an intolerable situation and, as the Horrockses refused to intervene, it was left to Tom's family to act to save his child. At the suggestion of Mrs Dick's own solicitor, they therefore kidnapped her. Mary was invited to Brinsop Court for the Christmas vacation and simply not returned, a place being found for her at boarding school, a solution which the Wordsworths welcomed with relief.

Happier news came from Moresby, where on 7 March the first Wordsworth grandchild, Jane Stanley, made her appearance. 'Her father thinks it the prettiest little thing that ever was', Dora reported, 'but if the truth were known I dare say it is a perfect little fright.' The proud grandfather was persuaded to pay her a brief visit, and ended up staying three weeks, executing family shopping commissions and paying visits to the Curwens at Workington Hall, Lord Lowther at Whitehaven and the theological training college at St Bees. He threw himself into his son's plans to build a rectory at Brigham, accompanying John and the architect to the chosen site on the banks of the Derwent. He walked twelve miles a day, and discovered, for the first time, that the sea, which he had shunned since his brother's death, could be a delightful companion. 'Nothing can be more charming, especially for a sequestered Mountaineer, than to cast eyes over its boundless surface, and hear as I have done almost from the brow of the steep in the Church field at Moresby, the waves chafing and murmuring in a variety of tones below, as a kind of base of harmony to the shrill yet liquid music of the larks above.'

Before he left, he composed several poems, including one, as he had promised Dora, on the new baby. He also wrote a sequel, 'which I fear none of you will like', lamenting the state of the nation. 'Who shall preserve or prop the tottering Realm?' he cried. 'What hand suffice to govern the state-helm?' It was a poem written for the best of reasons, 'viz. that the author could not help writing it', but he refused to publish it, also for the best of reasons. As he explained to a lady member of the Sheffield Female Anti-Slavery Society, who wrote to solicit a contribution from him for an anthology of anti-slavery poetry and prose, this was not the time to be publishing inflammatory, politically motivated, material. However good the cause – and he thought slavery abhorrent – he was not prepared 'to add to the excitement already existing in the public mind upon these, and so many other points of legislation and government. Poetry if good for any thing, must appeal forcibly to the Imagination and the feelings; but what at this period we want above every thing, is patient examination and sober judgement.'

Dorothy continued to improve very slowly throughout the spring and early summer. Twice a day William would come up to her bedroom and massage her swollen feet and ankles, to keep the circulation going; he read to her and, when the weather was fine, even took his turn in pulling her out on the terraces in her invalid carriage. By the beginning of May she was well enough to walk a little, with the aid of two sticks. By 16 July she had recovered sufficiently, mentally and physically, to resume her journal.

Sara had reluctantly left on 2 July to pay her triennial visit to Brinsop Court. 'I have almost a dread not to say horror of the thought of leaving Rydal Mount even to go into Herefordshire lest I should not return & end my Days here', she confessed in a moment of uncharacteristic weakness. It was a fear Dora shared: 'years rob one of ones joyous spirits – & now gloomy forebodings of what may happen before we meet again press upon me sadly & unwisely nay well nigh wickedly'.

Even William was persuaded to take a tour, his companion being Robinson, who took up residence in the Salutation Inn at Ambleside on 14 June, was summoned to Rydal Mount on the 18th, when a bed came free, and then had to kick his heels for a month while William dithered over the weather, his engagements and whether or not he could leave Dorothy. Robinson was an equable soul, content to 'lounge agreeably' round Rydal Mount, occupying himself with reading, chat and, when it was fine, walking with William. Their talk, naturally, was almost entirely on politics. The great difference between them, according to Robinson, was that he was a *hoping* alarmist and William a *despairing* one. Dorothy thoroughly enjoyed the company of Robinson, who, in the Hutchinson family terminology, was known as her 'lover', because of his kind attentions to her: he would sit by her bed trying to entertain her, help her on her short rambles into the garden and escort her back to bed when she was tired.

When Robinson had almost given up hope that they would ever get away, William suddenly announced it was time to go. They set off on 13 July, sailing from Whitehaven, where they were joined by John, who left his own wife and child at Rydal Mount. William had also invited Dora, but she declined, thinking she ought to stay behind to look after her aunt and her cousins Tom and George Hutchinson, who spent their Sedbergh school holidays with the Wordsworths. 'I think too I must have died from <u>talk</u> before we had reached the Island –', she added.

William's principal object was to visit the islands of Staffa and Iona, but they began their travels by taking a circuit of the Isle of Man, prompted by Dorothy's journal of her own visit in 1828. In a rare instance of William himself writing a descriptive letter during a tour, we get a tantalizing glimpse of the entertaining and perceptive journal writer he could have been, and the immediate impressions, captured in prose, which would later lead to a whole series of poems celebrating the island. They called on Mr and Mrs Cookson, their friends from Kendal, who had settled in Ballasalla, after the failure of their business in 1830. 'Bala Sala is a little wood-embosomed Village by the side of a stream upon which stands the ruined walls of an old Abbey, a pretty sequestered place – thronged with Blackbirds and thrushes of extraordinary size and power of song –', William enthused; 'the upper part of the old Tower is overgrown with a yellow Lychen which has the appearance of a gleam of perpetual evening sunshine'. From Ballasalla, they followed Dorothy's pedestrian route around the island. At Castletown they admired King William's College, against the backdrop of the 'grand slopes' of South Barule; on the road to St John's they halted under some sycamores by a waterfall and the two elderly travellers took a nap 'to the great delight of the neighbouring cottagers'. At St John's itself they stopped to view Tynwald Hill, and, surrounded by eleven cottage children, were amused by the sight of 'an old Gullion', sitting almost at the top of this 1,000-year-old seat of government, 'with a telescope in his hand through which he peeped occasionally having the advantage of seeing things double, for as he frankly owned he had got a drop too much'. At Peel they took an evening trip round the castle by boat, 'to the great dismay of my Companion though the sea was calm as glass, but it broke unintelligibly with noise and foam over the sharp black rocks on which the Castle stands'. After spending some time with Joanna at Ramsay, the travellers sailed from there to Greenock, ready to begin their tour of the Scottish islands.

'Upon the whole, Dearest D., I liked your Isle of Man better than I expected', William observed, but its subtle delights were lost on the urbane Robinson. Like the good lawyer he was, he had found his greatest amusement in looking over the Manx laws, 'which contain some amusing illustrations of Etymology'. Robinson was equally unimpressed by William's beloved Scotland. 'The greater part of our journey was a threading of the Scotch isles of which I have now had more than enough –', he informed his brother. 'Rocks are pretty in pictures, will do very well in poems, but one does not want them for daily companions.' From Greenock, they travelled by steamboat down the Firth of Clyde (during an eclipse, which their fellow travellers ignored) to Oban, and then through the Inner Hebrides, calling at Mull, Coll, Staffa and Iona. Only the two last were distinguished in Robinson's mind. Staffa he forbore to describe – 'You may consult any book you like' – though it drew from him unexampled praise – 'truly a marvellous sight and well worth a voyage to be seen'.

William's impressions are not recorded in prose, but this short tour, only a fortnight from start to finish, provided a wealth of material for poems. From them, it is clear that William's own reactions were out of step with his friend's. His first visit to Staffa was a major disappointment. He arrived expecting to enjoy silent communion with its isolation and the awesome wonder of Fingal's Cave. Instead, he arrived on a steamboat with the nineteenth-century equivalent of a coach party.

> We saw, but surely, in the motley crowd,
> Not One of us has felt the far-famed sight;
> How *could* we feel it? each the other's blight,
> Hurried and hurrying, volatile and loud.
> *Cave of Staffa, ll.1–4*

Unwilling to quit the place with only this memory of it, he became that traditional scourge of the coach party, the One Who is Always Late. 'At the risk of incurring the reasonable displeasure of the master of the steamboat, I returned to the cave,' he explained, 'and explored it under circumstances more favourable to those imaginative impressions which it is so wonderfully fitted to make upon the mind.' Not one, but three more sonnets were the result, which was probably little consolation to those left on board ship, waiting for him to make his reappearance.

The ravaged abbey ruins and lonely Celtic crosses on Iona, sixth-century home of St Columba, and birthplace of Christianity in the north of Britain, could not fail to move William. In one of four sonnets inspired by the place, he checked a lament for the contrast time had wrought between its glorious past and forlorn present: though ruined now, the abbey had fulfilled its purpose in spreading the Word to the heathen.

> And when, subjected to a common doom
> Of mutability, those far-famed Piles
> Shall disappear from both the sister Isles,
> Iona's Saints, forgetting not past days,
> Garlands shall wear of amaranthine bloom,
> While heaven's vast sea of voices chants their praise.
>
> *Iona, ll.9–14*

Even the beggar children, who irritated Robinson by offering their pathetic array of shells and stones for sale to wealthy tourists, provoked a kindlier response in William. 'How sad a welcome!' he mused, contrasting it with the glory days of Iona's Celtic past.

When they reached Inverary, 'this pleasing little place', Robinson decided that the weather was so gloomy, he could not face travelling on to Loch Lomond and Glasgow with William and John. Instead, he remained there, waiting for better weather, then set off alone to explore eastern Scotland, not forgetting, because of William's poems, to visit the Yarrow, before rejoining them at Rydal Mount. The Wordsworths, meanwhile, returned home, arriving, unexpectedly, on 25 July, to find Dorothy improved beyond their wildest dreams.

William had been at home for less than a fortnight when, in his official capacity as Distributor of Stamps, he was summoned to Carlisle to attend a suit for libel brought by the Earl of Lonsdale against several local newspapers. It was an opportunity to pay Willy a visit, so Mary went with him, and, instead of returning by the direct route through Penrith, they made a slight detour to the east, down the lovely Eden valley. Still vibrant with poetry after his Scottish tour, this little excursion was to furnish William with material for seven more sonnets, including one of his most moving, inspired by Nollekens's sculpted monument in the chapel at Wetheral, just outside Carlisle. It portrayed Maria Howard, whose sole claim to immortality was that of domestic tragedy. She had died giving birth to a still-born son when she was twenty-three.

> Stretched on the dying Mother's lap, lies dead
> Her new-born Babe; dire ending of bright hope!
> But Sculpture here, with the divinest scope
> Of luminous faith, heavenward hath raised that head
> So patiently; and through one hand has spread

> A touch so tender for the insensate Child –
> (Earth's lingering love to parting reconciled,
> Brief parting, for the spirit is all but fled) –
> That we, who contemplate the turns of life
> Through this still medium, are consoled and cheered;
> Feel with the Mother, think the severed Wife
> Is less to be lamented than revered;
> And own that Art, triumphant over strife
> And pain, hath powers to Eternity endeared.

The wide, rust-coloured waters of the Eden itself, flowing slow and deep through woods and blushing rocks, earned its own tribute: its name was 'rightfully borne', since its beauties were indeed those of Paradise. Nunnery Walks, near Penrith, which William had loved since childhood, prompted a sonnet. So did Long Meg and her Daughters, seventy-three standing stones in a circle eighty yards in diameter, with a single larger stone apart from the rest. More surprisingly, the railway viaducts spanning the Eden and a neighbouring ravine at Corby also won praise; though trains and steamboats were at war with 'old poetic feeling', and marred the loveliness of nature,

> Time,
> Pleased with your triumphs o'er his brother Space,
> Accepts from your bold hands the proffered crown
> Of hope, and smiles on you with cheer sublime.
> *Steamboats, Viaducts and Railways, ll.11–14*

The Wordsworths ended their little excursion by spending a couple of nights at Lowther Castle (a rare visit by Mary) and three with the Marshalls at Hallsteads, on Ullswater.

They returned to find Rydal Mount in the full throes of the Lakers' season. More than 268 visitors called or stayed this year, among them a young clergyman, Robert Perceval Graves, who was tutor to Mrs Hemans's son, Charles. Graves received the usual kind reception, and returned to Dublin determined to exchange the Church of Ireland for the Church of England and secure a curacy in the Lakes. Afraid of appearing to presume on so brief an acquaintance, he persuaded Mrs Hemans to enlist William's assistance in procuring him one. 'I should much rather owe my settlement as a Pastor to your interposition & recommendation than to any other channel of interest which I possess', Graves wrote gratefully, adding that both he and his brother would treasure their memories of their meeting with the poet as 'setting the seal to our knowledge of your Poetry, [which] has become an efficacious influence upon our lives'.

On 28 August, William was visited by a thirty-year-old Bostonian who had just resigned his Unitarian ministry and would later become internationally famous as one of America's most eminent essayists, poets and preachers. When he met

William, however, Ralph Waldo Emerson was virtually unknown outside the confines of Boston society. Nevertheless, he brought with him a highly unusual degree of New World and youthful arrogance, which stood in the way of his appreciation of both the man and the poet. William was dismissed (in print, not just a private journal) as 'a plain, elderly, white-haired man, not prepossessing, and disfigured by green goggles', who talked with 'great simplicity'. William spoke at length on his favourite themes, politics and education, assuring Emerson that he did so to impress upon him '& all good Americans, to cultivate the moral, the conservative, &c. &c. & never to call into action the physical strength of the people; as lately had been done in the Reform Bill, &c. in England'. 'He was so benevolently anxious to impress upon me my social duties as an American citizen', Emerson added in a private letter, 'that he accompanied me near a mile from his house talking vehemently & ever & anon stopping short to imprint his words.'

As they walked in the garden along the terraces, William offered to recite the three sonnets on Fingal's Cave he had composed within three days of leaving Staffa, and proceeded to do so with such gravity and power that Emerson was convinced they were more beautiful than anything which had appeared in print. Nevertheless, he found the spectacle amusing.

This reciting was so unexpected & extraordinary, – he, the old Wordsworth, standing forth & reciting to me in a garden walk, like a schoolboy 'speaking his piece,' – that I at first had nearly laughed; but, recollecting myself, that I had come thus far to see a poet, & he was chaunting poems to me, I saw, that he was right, & I was wrong, & gladly gave myself up to hear.

Emerson went away impressed by William's kindness but 'surprised by the hard limits of his thought. To judge from a single conversation, he made the impression of a narrow and very English mind; of one who paid for his rare elevation by general tameness and conformity. Off his own beat, his opinions were of no value.' This was the opinion he published, together with an account of his visit, the following year, in the book of his tour, *English Traits*. It was hardly a generous return for the time and kindness William had devoted to him, but it was neither the first nor the last time that the privilege of meeting with, and talking to, the poet in the privacy of his own home would be abused.

By the beginning of October William had composed more than forty sonnets arising from his forays to the Isle of Man and Scotland and down the Eden. It was a level of sustained creativity unparalleled in recent years, and he paid the price with a bout of trachoma so severe that he was temporarily blinded and had to be confined to a darkened room for ten days. Even this could not stem the flow, for as he had told Emerson, he was quite capable of composing several hundred lines of poetry and holding them in his head without writing them down. 'I cannot muster courage to publish them, or any thing else', William told Kenyon. 'I seem to want a definite motive – money would be one, if I could get it, but I cannot.' The print run of the cheap four-volume edition was 2,000, but a year later only 400 had been sold, leaving both author and publisher considerably out of pocket. William circulated copies of the new sonnets privately among his friends and even, with a lack of caution he later regretted, in response to a heartfelt request from a stranger.

Though Dora and Mary reported that William was 'very, very patient' under his blindness, his progress was so slow that he began to get 'very nervous & <u>very</u> anxious'. For the first time, the seat of the infection was in his eye, rather than the eyelid. Reports of his blindness began to appear in the newspapers, and though he hastened to contradict them, in his heart of hearts, he feared they might prove true.

The arrival of William's nephew, Chris, on 29 December was greeted with relief and joy by the beleaguered household. 'My Uncle's eyes are ... much better,' he told his father, 'indeed they would be quite well, if he did not write verses: but this he *will* do; and therefore it is extremely difficult to prevent him from ruining his eyesight.' Convinced that blindness would be his fate, sooner or later, William consoled himself with the idea of going to Italy, 'to lay in a store of images, poetical and others', to feed his imagination in the darkness to come.

He stood in need of consolation, for he had not just his blindness to contend with but also, in his mid-sixties, he had reached the age when death was reaping a plentiful crop among his friends. He had lost no fewer than fourteen relatives, friends or 'valued acquaintance' within the previous three or four months. The most important of these was Jack Hutchinson, Mary's oldest brother, and Thomas Cookson, one of their oldest friends, died of cholera only a very short time after William had composed the sonnet celebrating his pretty cottage refuge at Ballasalla in the Isle of Man. Two of William's young Cambridge admirers and friends had also died suddenly, Arthur Hallam (the subject of Tennyson's *In Memoriam*), at the age of twenty-three, and Lionel Fraser at the age of twenty-six.

It was a trend that was set to continue throughout the spring and summer. Sara Coleridge gave birth to twins seven weeks prematurely on 14 January; born on the Tuesday, they were baptized on Wednesday, died on Thursday and buried on Saturday. The poor mother herself was in an apparently hopeless state, suffering in mind and body, and ironically, like her father, dependent on opiates. The list seemed endless. William Sotheby, a London friend of more than thirty years' standing; Mary, widow of William Calvert; Barratt Brydges, Quillinan's kindly brother-in-law; Maria Jane Jewsbury, of cholera, in India; Mrs Paris Dick of typhus, at Clifton, leaving her orphan daughter to the happier fate of informal adoption by the Hutchinson and Monkhouse clan in Herefordshire.

And then there was Coleridge. The Wordsworths had seen so little of him over the previous twenty years, he had survived so many crises, and declined so steadily and slowly, that his death came as a tremendous shock to them all. More than any other, it was a severing of William's poetic ties with the past. By great good luck, both Poole and Sara Hutchinson, who rarely went to London, had visited him several times in the weeks before he died. Though he had then been unwell, no one, except the woman who had carried the oppressive weight of his love so long, guessed dissolution was so close. 'Yesterday I was at Highgate & greatly was I shocked with the changed appearance of my dear old Friend', she confided in

Quillinan. '. . . He will never rise from his bed more I fear tho' this does not seem to be the opinion of his relatives'.

When death came, it came suddenly. He was seized with acute pains in his bowels and difficulty in breathing and speaking. Opium, which had so long been his enemy, proved his friend at last, easing him to a painless death five days later, on 25 July 1834, aged sixty-one. As he had requested, his body was opened after his death, to identify the cause of the internal pains from which he had suffered all his life and for which he blamed his dependency on opium. Nothing was found. His will left what little money he had to his widow, for life, and then to his children; a gold mourning ring, enclosing a lock of his hair, was bequeathed to each of his oldest friends, Lamb, Montagu, Poole, Josiah and Lancelot Wade, and Sara Hutchinson. To William and Southey, who, more than anyone else, had done so much to support him and his family over the years, Coleridge left the 'Gratitude and Reverential Affection' of his children, 'and the sentiments I have left on record in my Literary life and in my Poems, . . . which . . . supersede the necessity of any other Memorial of my Regard and respect'.

If this was an intentional slight, William refused to take it as such. 'I cannot give way to the expression of my feelings upon this mournful occasion; I have not strength of mind to do so –', he confessed to Sara's husband, Henry Nelson Coleridge. In private conversation with Robert Graves, Mrs Hemans's protégé, who arrived at Rydal just as the news of Coleridge's death was announced, William was generous about his old friend, calling him

the most <u>wonderful</u> man that he had ever known, wonderful for the originality of his mind & the power he possessed of throwing out in profusion grand central truths from which might be evolved the most comprehensive systems. Wordsworth, as a Poet, regretted that German metaphysics had so much captivated the taste of Coleridge – for he was frequently not intelligible on this subject – whereas if his energy & his originality had been more exerted in the channel of poetry, an instrument of which he had so perfect a mastery, Wordsworth thought he might have done more, permanently, to enrich the literature & to influence the thought of the nation than any man of the age. As it was, however, he said he believed Coleridge's mind to have been a widely fertilizing one, & that the seed he had so lavishly sown in his conversational discourses & the Sibylline leaves (not the poem so called by him) which he had scattered abroad so extensively covered with his annotations, had done much to form the opinions of the highest-educated men of the day; although this might be an influence not likely to meet with adequate recognition.

William read Henry Nelson Coleridge's moving account of his father-in-law's death to Graves, his voice faltering, and then breaking down completely when he reached the part where Coleridge had expressed the hope, in his final moments, that his end would manifest the depth of his trust in his Saviour, Jesus Christ.

As soon as they learned of Coleridge's death, the Wordsworths immediately sought out Hartley. 'Poor fellow! in such distress –', Dorothy noted in her journal; '[he] bitterly regrets he has seen so little of his Father except in early childhood.'

Only Sara, pardonably, gave way to any bitterness, accusing Coleridge's relations of having more pride in him than love for him. She had returned to Rydal Mount on 21 June, after an absence of almost a year, escorted by her nephew, 'Keswick' John.

Sara now lent her voice to the females' campaign to persuade William to publish another volume of poetry. 'Reluctant as I am, I have at last given way', William wearily informed Moxon, to whom he wished to offer the book, though he felt honour-bound to continue with Longman. He toyed with the idea of including illustrations, as Rogers had done in his latest edition, but, unlike Rogers, he did not have a private fortune and the extra expense was prohibitive. Instead, he settled for a single volume, of the same size and format as the last, 1832, edition, so that former purchasers could buy it to complete their set. The decision was not entirely altruistic: Longman assured him that this edition had sold better than any former one. The choice of title, too, was deliberately popularist. It was to be called *Yarrow Revisited, and Other Poems*, invoking memories of the two earlier Yarrow poems, which had been widely praised.

As Dora, with characteristic lack of deference, put it, 'a little *stuffing*' would be required to make the volume up to size. Henry Hutchinson's delightful little autobiographical poem, with its refrain 'poor to Sea I went, and poor I still remain', would thus be set among the poems relating to the Isle of Man, duly attributed to 'a Retired Mariner (a Friend of the Author)'. Another 'friend of the author', his sister, was less easily persuaded to contribute. Curiously, it was Rogers, to whom *Yarrow Revisited* would be dedicated, who succeeded where everyone else had failed. Visiting Rydal in August, 'He sate a while with me', Dorothy wrote in her current journal, '& determined me not to withhold my consent'. What arguments he used to convince her remain a mystery.

Rogers's visit and the birth of a first grandson, Henry Curwen Wordsworth, were the only bright spots in the autumn of a year which ended as miserably as it had begun. In September *Tait's Magazine* published the first in what became a series of four 'kiss and tell' articles about Coleridge by de Quincey. Like modern tabloid journalism, they were vastly entertaining to the casual reader, but to Coleridge's family and friends they were utterly abhorrent, especially because one and all regarded them as a breach of trust and friendship. William was so incensed that he wrote to Green, Coleridge's literary executor, suggesting that he should attempt to stop, or at least contradict, the articles.

At the end of September, Sara Hutchinson received a note from Southey, begging her to go to Keswick immediately. His wife had been increasingly depressed since Edith had married and left home in January; the imminent departure of Cuthbert, her only son, who was going to live with Edith, and be tutored by her husband in preparation for university entrance, triggered a mental crisis. She became so wild and unmanageable that she had to be removed to the Retreat at York. 'I have been parted from my wife by something worse than death', Southey wrote on 2 October. 'Forty years has she been the life of my life; and I have left her this day in a lunatic asylum.' 'Miss Hutton', as the young Southeys had called Sara from childhood, went at an hour's notice to care for the afflicted family, and remained with them, not having the heart to leave and they being unwilling to part with her.

At the beginning of November, Dora became very unwell. Carr diagnosed an inflammation of the spine and put her on a drastic course of treatment. She was consigned to the sofa, where she was to lie all day and be bled and blistered. Remarkably, she survived, but unremarkably, she grew steadily weaker. Aunt Joanna had to be summoned to assist poor Mary, who had far too much to do. As Dora miserably admitted to her cousin, she was worse than useless; Dorothy could not do much and her father required constant attention. 'We are a bright trio are we not [?]'. The basic problem, as everyone knew, was Dora herself. She had long ago convinced herself that a spare diet was good for her: perhaps she feared that she was too fat (she was certainly tall in an age when this was not fashionable for women), but publicly she would say only that it was necessary for her health. As she now appeared to accept the doctor's diagnosis, her family hoped that she would start to eat properly again, but this she refused to do. She lay on the sofa, read novels and was, to all appearances, perfectly cheerful, complaining only of 'not wellness', rather than illness. 'She persists in living upon *prison fare* – bread & water – ie Tea as weak as water –', Sara told Quillinan two months later, 'though the medical men are of opinion that this spare diet is the cause, in her case, of the complaint – & cannot therefore be the remedy also!' Her family begged and pleaded, to no avail, and it was only a forthright letter of rebuke from an unexpected source which had any effect at all. Quillinan, who was temporarily living in Portugal on business, responded to Sara's letter by writing directly to Dora herself. It was an important letter, and it was a significant intervention.

I long, long ago, perceived that you were destroying your health by that pernicious system of starvation; but you were always so wilful on the subject that I could not presume to venture on anything like repeated remonstrance, which indeed could have produced no effect but irritation, when none better was produced by the interference of those who had a right to remonstrate. But, at this distance, when I learn that you are reduced to serious illness, and that you still persist in your <u>determination to be unable to eat</u> (for that is <u>my</u> construction of the fact) I do take upon myself to implore you to be persuaded into the <u>duty</u> of habituating yourself to a more generous diet. If you continue obstinate, I shall still think of you fifty times a day, but it will always be as <u>Dora Wordsworth the Wilful</u>. – I did hope that your good sense would rid you of your infatuation on this subject. I will say no more; I fear what I have already said may sound harsh if not impertinent; and God knows I am far from intending harshness to <u>a poor sick Girl confined to her sofa</u> ... God bless you, Dora: make haste and repent of your sin of self-condemnation to 'Prison Fare,' and turn <u>Gourmande</u>.

'I confess I was hurt that <u>you</u> should think so ill of me –', Dora replied; 'if ever we meet again you will have no cause to complain on this head <u>I guess</u>.'

At the beginning of December, it was Dorothy's turn. A severe bilious attack kept her confined to her bed for three long weeks and to cap a bleak year, Lamb, whom William lovingly described as 'a good man if a good man ever was', died on 27 December, aged fifty-nine. The Wordsworths' first thought was for his poor sister, who was suffering one of her periodic fits of insanity. It was imperative that she should be well cared for, and, though they rightly suspected that Lamb would have made that provision, William immediately offered to contribute whatever she might need.

This was particularly generous, for William's finances were more than usually under strain. Due to the Stamp Office reforms, his post was now worth only £400 a year, but William decided that it was his duty to hand over the Distributorship to his son. It was the only way he could advance Willy's career and secure him enough income to enable him to marry. It was, of course, impossible for William simply to step down in favour of his son; the resignation and appointment would have to be made formally, through official channels. There was also the risk that William might resign and his post be given to someone else. When William IV suddenly dismissed Melbourne's Whig administration, on 15 November, and invited Sir Robert Peel to form a government, it was an opportunity which his friends urged William not to miss. He hoped to have the support of Peel himself, knowing him to be an admirer of his poetry and that Peel's nephew was serving a farming apprenticeship with the Hutchinsons at Brinsop Court.

What he had reckoned without was the Duke of Wellington's opposition to the appointment of sons as successors to their fathers – because it reduced the range of government patronage. In arguing his case, William revealed just how out of step he was with the times. Now, as in 1813, he sought the post not on the grounds of his own or his son's fitness, but as a reward for his poetical labours:

I have myself some claim upon my country as a man who in the most disinterested way has devoted his life to the service of sound literature; and now, when the success with which this has been done, is generally acknowledged, and a pecuniary return might be expected to be made to my family, the Law respecting copyright steps in, and declares that the greatest part of my productions, shall be public property the moment I cease to breathe; it would be surely therefore hard, if under these circumstances, my wish to resign in favor of my son were not complied with.

Peel was sincerely committed to the idea of supporting the arts. He had just offered Southey a baronetcy, which was declined, and an additional pension of £300 from the Civil List, which was gratefully accepted. Peel hoped to do the same for William, but William was implacably opposed to the idea of either himself or his wife becoming a government pensioner. Besides, a pension for either of them would not help Willy. Nevertheless, Peel's gracious letter, acknowledging the justice of William's claims on men in power and begging him to communicate 'without reserve' if there was any other way he could help, was a consolation and it was encouraging. Lord Lowther, in office as Treasurer of the Navy and Vice-President of the Board of Trade, was equally positive. 'I think you had better get into the mail coach and come to London when we with other of your friends might decide the specific mode of serving yourself and family, that would be most agreeable to you.' This was advice that could not be ignored. Less than a week after receiving it, William and Mary were in London.

The Wordsworths spent five weeks in town, lobbying everyone they knew but the Tory administration fell before any decisions had been taken and they were left exactly where they had been. For the time being, all they could do was urge Willy to economize, improve his presentational skills and be happy and hopeful.

William was also anxious to settle another financial matter which had assumed a greater importance since he contemplated giving up the Distributorship. This was the annual payment of £30 to the husband of his French daughter, Caroline, to which he was bound by the terms of her marriage contract. Finding the sum, and the complications arising out of remitting it, had become an increasing problem. What William now wished to do instead was to settle a lump sum of £400 on his daughter, investing it in the French Funds, so that the interest could pay the annuity. It was a perfectly reasonable plan, to which Baudouin at first assented. When he discovered that the capital sum was not large enough to produce the equivalent of £30, however, he demanded more. Annette was dragged in, to apply moral pressure on the father of her daughter. Robinson, who acted as an intermediary in the affair, took a dim view of these proceedings. 'It is quite clear to me that the Baudouins are trying to extort money without any good feeling or excuse whatever'. As a compromise, William offered the £400 outright, in lieu of the annuity, for the Baudouins to do with as they pleased. To Robinson's great relief and pleasure, this was accepted, and, as far as William was concerned, he had fulfilled his duty.

A fortnight of the Wordsworths' visit to London was spent staying with Henry Taylor and his step-aunt, Isabella Fenwick, a woman who was to play an increasingly important role in their lives. Taylor was naturally anxious to show off his celebrated guest and at one of his gatherings William had his first encounter with Thomas Carlyle, the great essayist and historian. 'I did not expect much; but got mostly what I expected', Carlyle told his brother. Echoing his American friend Emerson, Carlyle declared William to be, 'A genuine man (which is much) but also essentially a *small* genuine man'. He criticized the poet's handshake, 'feckless, egotistical', his conversation, 'for prolixity, thinness, endless dilution it excels all the other speech I had heard', and his wife, 'the oldest looking woman I ever saw; winking, withered, sleepy-fidgetting, as if she were all dried to a *Kipper* without and within. A silly woman (probably) from the first.' Given the shallowness of his observations, founded upon a single meeting at a party where William was expected 'to perform' by his host, one can only comment that Carlyle got not only what he expected, but also what he deserved.

While the Wordsworths were in London William's new volume of poetry was published. As it was his first collection of new work to appear in thirteen years, it should have been a major event, announced with public and private fanfares. Instead, it crept out almost unnoticed, even by its author. It was to have been published the previous autumn, but there had been delays in printing, which

William considered fortunate, as it would have appeared during the political crisis caused by the dismissal of the Melbourne ministry. As he remarked, 'neither Othello, Mackbeth [*sic*] nor the Paradise Lost, if now first produced, would be attended to'. For the same reason, it was withheld from circulation throughout the early part of the year. This unexpected postponement affected the final shape of the volume, for it allowed William to add to it, in response to the pace of political events. Though he had earlier refused to publish the poem, for fear it was too inflammatory, he now decided to include *The Warning*, with its bleak prophecy that the labouring multitudes, deceived by the flattering hopes held out by reformers, would rise 'in marshalled thousands, darkening street and moor' to exact violent revenge for imagined wrongs. 'I felt it due to myself to give this warning to my Countrymen, at this awful Crisis – utterly useless it may prove, but I should have suspected myself of cowardice or selfish caution, if I had suppressed what I had thought and felt'.

Even more important was a lengthy prose postscript on the subject of the Poor Laws which William added in London. Robinson was troubled by it – 'Wordsworth will aggravate antipathies by his polemical notes' – but politics had always been more important than poetry to William, and what he now wrote was as radical as anything he had written in his youth. Returning to a theme he had first publicly espoused in 1798, in *The Old Cumberland Beggar*, he extolled the moral benefits to both recipient and donor of charitable giving to the needy, but now he argued that the poor had a *right* to public support. The principal object of his attack was the Poor Law Amendment Act, passed in August 1834, which had put an end to the old system of 'outdoor relief'. Within two years, no able-bodied persons would be able to claim poor relief, for themselves or their families, except in 'well-regulated' workhouses – 'well-regulated' meaning that husbands, wives and children were separated according to gender, labour on the treadmill was enforced, and food and drink were doled out, not according to need but in predetermined and miserly quantities set out in the act. As William pointed out, the whole basis of the act was punitive. In the interests of humanity at large, William declared, it was better that ten undeserving poor should have relief than that one worthy man should suffer. In a subsidiary section, he also made an enlightened call for the repeal of the laws governing joint-stock companies, arguing that if workmen were allowed to invest their savings in manufacturing, they would then have a stake in its success.

His sympathy for the plight of the modern labouring poor was articulated most strongly in a poem, *Humanity*, in which he lambasted his countrymen for priding themselves on the abolition of slavery.

> . . . that boast
> Is but a mockery! when from coast to coast,
> Though *fettered* slave be none, her floors and soil
> Groan underneath a weight of slavish toil,
> For the poor Many, measured out by rules
> Fetched with cupidity from heartless schools,

That to an Idol, falsely called 'the Wealth
Of Nations', sacrifice a People's health,
Body and mind and soul; a thirst so keen
Is ever urging on the vast machine
Of sleepless Labour, 'mid whose dizzy wheels
The Power least prized is that which thinks and feels.

Southey, for one, wrote to congratulate him for touching upon 'our white slavery' and annexing 'such a postscript'.

Most purchasers of *Yarrow Revisited, and Other Poems*, however, bought it for the quality of the verse, the tour poems in particular appealing to the age of steamboats and trains, and to a growing number of people able to travel faster and more easily to the very places William celebrated in his poetry. And buy it they did, in their hundreds. To William's bemusement and delight, within two months of going on sale *Yarrow Revisited* had sold 900 copies. It was a palpable hit, by anyone's standards. Even the reviews were laudatory John's wife, Isabella, however, noted, 'it is extraordinary how he is puffed in all the Whig and Radical publications; and scarcely noticed in the Tory and Conservative Papers'. Was it discreditable to admit, William asked Robinson, that the reviews interested him only so far as they were likely to affect the sale?

The private testimonies which I receive very frequently of the effect of my writings upon the hearts and minds of men, are indeed very gratifying – because I am sure *they* must be written under *pure* influences – but it is not necessarily or even probably so with strictures intended for the public. The one are *effusions*, the other *compositions*, and liable in various degrees to inter-mixtures that take from their value –

Though he highly valued the private testimonies, William was no more inclined to accept their judgement than that of the professional critics. 'Take care', he wrote to one enthusiastic admirer who had just addressed a letter and a sonnet to him, bewailing the harm the critics had wrought on his works over the years, '. . . that the sense of injustice both to yourself and me, in having neglected, or rather disregarded them so long, does not by a natural reaction of the mind impel you now to overrate them'. For himself, William remained convinced that, irrespective of what any critics thought, his writings would endure only if they truly illustrated the principle he had so long espoused, 'That we have all of us one human heart!' That he should quote now from *The Old Cumberland Beggar* was significant evidence that, as he always claimed, his politics remained fundamentally unaltered, even if he had changed his mind on how they should be implemented.

Not long after their return to Rydal Mount, Sara was seized with lumbago, all three invalids then caught influenza and, as Anne, the cook who had been with them for twelve years, was also confined to bed with a rheumatic fever, Mary and her niece, fifteen-year-old Ebba, were run off their feet trying to nurse them all. Ebba's mother, Mary Hutchinson, came from Brinsop in answer to their plea for help, and proved invaluable. It was obvious to them all that Dorothy was dying, as she grew daily weaker and weaker. Sara, though frequently delirious with fever and pain, even in her wanderings could not forget the miseries of the Southey household and begged Mary to explain why she seemed to neglect them. Sara grew better, Dorothy worse.

And then, as they waited in daily and hourly expectation of Dorothy's demise, Sara slipped quietly away. 'One of our anxieties is over and not that which we thought would first cease', William wrote to Robinson on 24 June; 'on Monday she sunk alarmingly, yesterday at noon a change took place that left no hope of saving her life, and before seven all was over'. Shortly before the end, Dora had asked Carr if anything could be done to ease her, at which Sara had opened her eyes and said 'in a strong and sweet voice ... "I am quite, I am perfectly comfortable"'. 'O, my dear Southey, we have lost a precious friend', William mourned; 'of the strength of her attachment to you and yours, you can but imperfectly judge. It was deep in her heart.' Informing Christopher of Sara's death, he paid her a tribute that was all the more touching for its simplicity. 'She was to this House an inestimable Friend, disinterested, generous, noble-minded, a sincere and pious Christian, and we trust her Spirit will receive its reward.' To everyone, he described how he had seen her, within an hour after her decease, 'in the silence and peace of death, with as heavenly an expression on her countenance as ever human creature had'. This 'Vision sanctified' would both haunt and comfort William, resulting eventually in a moving poetic tribute to Sara. All traces of pain had been removed, he declared, age smoothed from her brow, and her face revealed 'A loveliness to living youth denied'.

> Oh! if within me hope should e'er decline,
> The lamp of faith, lost Friend! too faintly burn;
> Then may that heaven-revealing smile of thine,
> The bright assurance, visibly return:
> And let my spirit in that power divine
> Rejoice, as, through that power, it ceased to mourn.
> *November, 1836, ll.9–14*

Tributes flowed in from all over the country. The most significant, given the difficulties of Sara's relationship with Coleridge, was that from his wife and daughter. It is so oddly worded that it can be understood only as making deliberate, if elliptical, reference to the past. 'It is impossible not to regret dear Miss Hutchinson,' Sara wrote,

who never was anybody's hindrance, and who occupied no place which any other person would be glad to fill ... She was an excellent kind hearted creature, and possessed a fine clear understanding, which was never put to any but good purposes and was always ready when wanted ... Her kindness to me I shall ever remember with gratitude. Mama is greatly distressed at this event and keeps saying that she has lost a good friend in Miss Hutchinson and one who has been long tried.

Dorothy, who was particularly close to Sara, suffered a shock from which she would never recover. She clung to life with remarkable tenacity, but now began to lose her mind. Her short-term memory disappeared and she craved food incessantly. As she stridently maintained that 'She knows best what is good for her', her sickroom became a battleground. Convinced at first that this weakening of the mind was a result of the opiates her physical condition required, the Wordsworths gradually weaned her off them, to no avail. A slight improvement in her short-term memory was more than counterbalanced by 'increasing irritability, which when her wishes are necessarily opposed amounts to rage and fury'. She was never happy except when she was eating, she told her brother, a claim that was pitifully substantiated when her old schoolfriend Jane Marshall sent a turkey and two chickens as joint Christmas and birthday presents. Though she had been 'in her disturbed way' when they arrived, the sight of them transformed her. 'she stroked & hugged the Turkey upon her knee like an overjoyed & happy child – exulting in, & blessing over & over again her dear, dearest friend'. When Dora happened to say it was a pity that such beautiful white chickens should have been killed, Dorothy scorned the regret, saying 'what would they do for <u>her</u> alive, her friend knew best what she wanted – & she should eat them every bit herself'. Nothing more clearly illustrates the loss of the sensibility which had been the most striking feature of her character.

Dorothy was to continue in this state for the rest of her life. Unable to walk or retain what she read, though still capable of surprising her nearest and dearest with an occasional brief letter, she alternated between '<u>mental feebleness</u>', in which she was 'as happy & as amiable as possible', and 'impatient discomfort', when she behaved 'exactly like a very <u>clever, tyrannical spoilt</u> Child'. The Wordsworths tried always to remember the better days and lavished love and attention on her. She had constant attendance and companionship from servants and members of the family; she was taken out in her bath-chair whenever the weather permitted and one of the bedrooms was given up to her as an upstairs sitting-room. (When the summer visitors started to arrive, this had to be exchanged for one at the back of the house, as Dorothy had discovered a new amusement in drawing attention to herself by shrieking, and startling the tourists in the house or grounds.)

'Books are to me as a dead Letter, and so must they be for some time', William had written in the summer of 1835, but as the autumn closed in he turned again to poetry. This was partly through necessity. *Yarrow Revisited* had been so successful that a second edition was called for, which he could not allow to go to press without revision. Walking from Lyulph's Tower to Hallsteads, on his way to Lowther Castle in September, he was still capable of finding comfort in the landscape, and throwing off some lovely descriptive lines.

> Not a breath of air
> Ruffles the bosom of this leafy glen,
> From the brook's margin wide around, the trees
> Are stedfast as the rocks; the brook itself
> Following, in patient solitude a course
> Old as the hills that feed it from afar,
> Doth rather deepen than disturb the calm
> Where all things else are still and motionless.
>
> *Airey-Force Valley, ll.1–7*

His main preoccupation, however, was to write an epitaph for Lamb, a task which was the sort of request piece he hated, and a troublesome responsibility, because it was Lamb's sister who asked for it. He laboured long and fruitlessly until, at Mary and Dora's suggestion, he took Chiabrera as his model and, on 19 November, composed the entire poem at one sitting. 'By sending it immediately, I have prepared the way, I believe for a speedy repentance – as I dont know that I ever wrote so many lines without some retouching being afterwards necessary.' As Moxon learned to his cost, it was a true prophecy: six months later, William was still sending revisions, and the epitaph, at thirty-eight lines already too long for engraving on the memorial, had swollen to more than 130. The first version was infinitely the best, a tender and truthful evocation of a man, full of 'Humour, and wild instinctive wit', but also troubled by depression; who had 'humbly earned his bread', but whose genius had triumphed over adversity. The new lines were added because William felt it imperative to write 'a few lines' celebrating the love between Lamb and his sister. Though they certainly do this, at length the suspicion is inescapable that William would not have felt so compelled to dwell on this aspect of Lamb's life if his own sister had been in health. Death had broken 'the sacred tie' between the Lambs, but Dorothy's descent into senile dementia had effectively done the same for his own relationship with her. It was a lament for the Wordsworths, as much as for the Lambs.

Eleven days after composing the first version of the epitaph William read in the *Newcastle Journal* that Hogg, the Ettrick Shepherd, had died on 21 November. It was just the latest in a growing list of friends he had lost over the year: Sharp, whose financial advice and touring journals had been invaluable, Tillbrooke of Ivy Cottage, the literary lady Mrs Hemans and the companion of his walking tour of France and Switzerland in 1790, Robert Jones. Hogg had guided William on his first visit to Yarrow, just as Scott had been William's companion on his second visit. They, together with Coleridge and Lamb, had all been younger than William, yet he had outlived them all. Within half an hour of reading the notice of Hogg's death, William had composed his great tribute to these friends and fellow poets.

> The mighty Minstrel breathes no longer,
> 'Mid mouldering ruins low he lies;
> And death upon the braes of Yarrow,
> Has closed the Shepherd-poet's eyes:

Nor has the rolling year twice measured,
From sign to sign, its stedfast course,
Since every mortal power of Coleridge
Was frozen at its marvellous source;

The rapt One, of the godlike forehead,
The heaven-eyed creature sleeps in earth:
And Lamb, the frolic and the gentle,
Has vanished from his lonely hearth.

Like clouds that rake the mountain-summits,
Or waves that own no curbing hand,
How fast has brother followed brother,
From sunshine to the sunless land!

Yet I, whose lids from infant slumber
Were earlier raised, remain to hear
A timid voice, that asks in whispers,
'Who next will drop and disappear?'

*Extempore Effusion upon the Death
of James Hogg, ll.9–28*

Observing her husband's depression of spirits, Mary wrote to Robinson, begging him to come to them for Christmas. 'It must be purely a work of charity – Your presence to W. would be inestimable – he wants such a friend to take him out of himself and to divert his thoughts from the melancholy state in which our poor Sister is *struggling* (to use her own word).' Robinson could not refuse. He arrived at Rydal Mount on Christmas Day and remained until 1 February 1836, spending the greater part of the day either at Rydal Mount or walking with William, but lodging at the foot of the hill, an arrangement which suited them all. Robinson saw Dorothy only a couple of times, when she was 'in her better way', but even then, she had 'offensive practices' (Mary told Catherine Clarkson that these were the cause of Dorothy's greatest discomforts, but she could not describe them, as it would be too distressing for them both), had a habit of shouting and screaming, without obvious cause, and demanded constant and unbearable heat. The most painful aspect of Dorothy's imbecility was its effect on Dora, who was distressed beyond measure, aggravating her own deplorably weak state of health.

There was little anyone could do to alleviate these problems, but the Wordsworths consulted Robinson on others, where his legal training and discretion were invaluable. When he left, on 1 February, he carried with him the oft-reiterated gratitude of the entire family, though the moment he cherished most was an unsolicited compliment, heard by accident and proudly enshrined in his journal. 'I overheard Wordsworth say last night to the Doctor [Arnold] that I had helped him through the winter and that he should gratefully recollect my kindness as long as he had any memory!'

24. *Coming Home*

In looking over William's finances, Robinson made a significant discovery. For the last few years (and for the first time in his life), William had been making in the region of £200 a year from his writings. This was due to the increasing popularity of his poetry, his renegotiated terms with his publishers and his recent policy of making his poems available as cheaply as possible. The second edition of *Yarrow Revisited, and Other Poems*, which was published early in the spring of 1836, was a case in point. On Longman's advice, it was printed in stereotype, a cheap system, used mainly by newspapers, because large quantities could be printed from a single stereotype. The quality of print was not as good as traditional printing methods: as the bibliophile Robinson sourly commented, *Yarrow Revisited* was 'the worst-printed book that ever came from the press'. More importantly, especially for an author like William who persisted in making changes until the book was irrevocably bound and could not be 'tinkered' any more, once the plate had been produced, it could not be altered. Any changes necessitated the making of replacement plates, the most expensive part of the process.

William realized the full implication of this only when Longman announced that the last edition of *The Excursion* had sold out, and that just 180 copies of the four-volume *Poetical Works* remained on hand. Longman was anxious to go ahead with a reprint, but William demurred. As always, he was concerned that his purchasers should be able to buy the books individually, but end up with a matching set of volumes; this was now impossible, unless the next edition was also stereotyped. To do so would mean not only that it would be prohibitively expensive to 'tinker' future editions, but also that he was effectively tied permanently to Longman as his publisher. He sought advice from his nephews Chris and John, both of whom were experienced authors, and, as he had increasingly done, from Edward Moxon. Rather than enter into complicated negotiations by letter,

William decided that he would have to go to London and sort the matter out in person.

His departure was delayed on several counts, most notably by the baptism of his third grandchild, a third William Wordsworth, who made his appearance on 27 December 1835. William was allowed to choose the godparents for his namesake, 'from among *my particular friends*', and the honours fell to Isabella Fenwick, William Rowan Hamilton and Robert Southey. William attended the christening at Workington, where John was acting as locum for his brother-in-law, and returned as delighted with his three grandchildren 'as any fond grandfather ever was since the world begun'.

William's presence was also required in Bowness on 13 April, at a ceremony to mark the foundation of a new free school. The project had been entirely funded by his old friend, 'the Liverpool Croesus', John Bolton of Storrs, who had requested William to stand in for him, as he was too old and ill to attend. Astonishingly, this was the first time William had ever made a speech in public, and he was consumed with nerves. His sister, in one of her rare moments of complete sanity, wrote immediately to her nephew Chris, who had just been appointed Public Orator of Cambridge University, and laid this 'case of distress' before him: 'alas! the poet is no Orator and he knows not what to say on this important occasion. I therefore request *you* the first Orator of the Nation to make a speech for him which I will answer for it he will pronounce verbatim, his diffidence of his own powers being so overwhelming.'

Preceded by a band and the schoolchildren of the neighbourhood, and to the sound of bells ringing and cannons firing, William and his protégé Robert Graves, who was now curate of Bowness, led the procession through the village to the site of the new school. There William buried a time capsule, laid the foundation stone and said his piece. 'The stormy day was unlucky,' he later reported to Bolton's family, 'but nevertheless the thing went off in a manner that gratified everyone, and not the less probably for their escape from the long speech I was disposed to inflict upon them.' It was indeed his own speech, not his nephew's, for it was an opportunity to expound all his pet theories on education, as distinct from tuition, and to impress upon the assembled parents the importance of setting an example to their children outside the classroom.

It was 11 May before William finally arrived in London. He had been bombarded with invitations even before he left Rydal Mount and it was an indication of things to come, for there could be no question now that William was leader of the pack where literary lions were concerned. The rarity of his visits to London, his age (he was now sixty-six) and the fact that he was one of the last of his generation combined with his growing poetical reputation to make him the catch of the season. Everyone wanted to meet him. 'I see scores of people that are introduced to me but dont remember the names of one in ten', he admitted in a letter home.

He attended the famous first night at Covent Garden of *Ion*, a play by his friend Talfourd, starring William Macready and Ellen Tree. The play was greeted with huge applause, which gave added zest to the celebratory supper party which followed. William, sitting with the Talfourds, Robinson, Macready and Landor, was placed opposite a twenty-four-year-old poet, Robert Browning. Though this was apparently their first meeting, the conviviality of the occasion prevented any private conversation. 'The happiest day I have spent since I came to London was at Sergeant Talfourd's play and his supper', William told his family. This was ironic, for Landor, in a spiteful satire published soon afterwards, attacked William for remaining unmoved among the general adulation surrounding Talfourd, suggesting that this was because he was incapable of appreciating the merits of his contemporaries. As no one else noted anything of the sort, and Robinson indignantly denied it when he read the satire, Landor's venom can perhaps be attributed to a misunderstanding. Talfourd had sent William a copy of *Ion* in 1835, hoping for endorsement or approval. Arriving, as it did, in the midst of all the Wordsworths' domestic distresses, William had not found heart or time to reply, and Talfourd had taken his silence amiss. When Macready dined with Talfourd in September, he was '*disgusted*' to be told that William had not responded, and this little story he seems to have told to Landor, who was his neighbour at the supper party. What neither man knew was that two months later, in November 1835, William had sent several messages to Talfourd, praising his play liberally. 'If you see Mr Talfourd tell him that we are all delighted with his drama – and which may seem odd – *that* is the very reason why I have put off writing to him – as I wished to do more than merely let him know, with thanks, how much he has pleased us.' And on 28 November, the day after he received a second edition of *Ion*, he wrote immediately to Talfourd, saying he had heard part of it read aloud the night before, and finished it himself that very morning: 'You have most ably fulfilled your own purpose, and your poem is a distinguished contribution to English literature.' A comparatively minor incident in itself, it is scarcely worth the recounting, except for the all-important fact that it is typical of the way so many of the critical stories about William were circulated.

William's visit to London was not entirely recreational. 'I have been run off my legs by business, since I arrived', he complained. His priority was to draw up a final legal release from his responsibilities as executor and guardian of 'Keswick' John; this could only be done through Strickland Cookson, the attorney son of his friends from Kendal, who was now in partnership at Richard Wordsworth's old firm. 'Keswick' John, following in the family tradition, had decided that if he had to earn his living, he would like to join the army, once he had finished his apprenticeship with Gardner. Unlike his cousins, his ambition would be fulfilled, his medical training enabling him to join the Army Medical Service.

Perhaps the most important business of all was to choose the publisher of the next edition of his complete works. William had become increasingly aware that Longman's were old-fashioned in outlook and had been irritated by the way they had casually sought his permission to stereotype *Yarrow Revisited*, without explaining the consequences. He also strongly suspected that he was not getting the best financial deal. The final straw came in the midst of their negotiations when, instead of delivering the statement he had promised, Longman simply sent a note, saying that his partner, Rees, was out of town, nothing could be done in his absence and would William kindly call when Rees had returned.

The contrast with Moxon could not have been more pointed. Moxon was not only an innovative publisher but, being an accomplished poet in his own right, had a natural sympathy with his authors. His first proposal was disappointing, but William stood firm, and his second was liberal. William was to receive £1,000 for an edition of 3,000 copies of his poetical works in six volumes; the books would be printed in stereotype, the copyright and plates remaining in William's hands. Moxon would pay all the expenses of publication, and a further £400 for each future edition. 'So you see dearest Friends there is nothing like standing up for one's self, and one's own legitimate interest', William exulted. His statement of account with Longman showed that the overall profit of his last edition had been £687; the portion he was due to receive at midsummer, with the sum he would also get from the sale of *Yarrow Revisited,* would bring his earnings from poetry this year to £500, 'which may be reckoned as a sort of Godsend'.

The new alliance with Moxon was celebrated with a little excursion to visit Quillinan, at his cottage in Nightingale Vale, in Woolwich. Poet and publisher were accompanied by 'Keswick' John, who had been in regular attendance on his uncle throughout this London visit, and Frank Stone, an artist who had painted Quillinan's daughters. The object of the visit was to persuade Quillinan to assist in preparing the new edition; before the end of June, the two men were both guests at Moxon's house, arranging the distribution of the poems between the six volumes.

Now that all his business was complete, there was nothing to prevent William fulfilling his original intention of accompanying Robinson on a long-dreamt-of tour of Italy. Tentative arrangements had been put in place, but it soon became clear that it was the Wordsworth females who were anxious that he should go, rather than William himself. They thought he needed a change and a rest from 'the worry & agitating feelings which his poor Sister's state kept him in': her presence at home meant that it could never be 'a place of rest for one who feels so keenly for her'. A tour, they thought, was just the thing to provide him with a stock of images and memories to divert his mind throughout the winter.

Within three weeks of his arrival in London, William was already getting cold feet: 'tell me sincerely whether you think I ought to go abroad or not –', he wrote home. 'I like the idea less and less every day, I so long to see you, and I feel so fevered.' The longer he stayed in London, the less appealing the idea became, because he needed at least ten weeks for an Italian tour. He tried blackmail, suggesting he might pop home for a visit, selflessly caring nothing for the expense or fatigue, before setting out. 'I feel decided altogether against going, if you don't approve of my coming down.' This was firmly vetoed from Rydal Mount. He tried to invite pity, confiding that in a fit of absent-mindedness at one of the Earl of Lonsdale's dinners, he had found himself drinking out of a water decanter, instead of a glass. There was no response. In the end, he had to resort to pathetic special pleading.

My heart fails – I am so sad in a morning when I wake and think that more than 4 months will elapse before I see you again, if I go to Italy and after an absence of I believe 7 weeks. I cannot bear to think of it[,] having reached the age that we all have except you dearest Dora – I should have thought nothing of it 20 years ago – but now I sicken at the scheme as I draw near to the appointed time. Do let me put it off, and try the events of another year . . .

Realizing that he was 'heartsick and homesick', Mary and Dora signed his release. William wrote a shamefaced note of apology to Robinson, explaining that after so long an absence from home, he had not the courage to prepare for a Continental tour. Robinson took his disappointment in such good part, cheerfully assuring William that he thought he was right to defer the trip, that Mary felt obliged to write and tell him 'how much we feel your good-tempered bearing towards your vacillating *fellow-traveller that was to have been.* God bless you!'

Pausing only to visit the dentist and have a set of false teeth fitted (his first), William scuttled happily back to Rydal Mount, arriving there on 7 July. Unusually, he embarked almost immediately on what was normally a winter task, the wholesale revision of his complete poetic works for the new Moxon edition. When Quillinan arrived on 2 August for a visit that would last until 16 September, the work began in earnest.

'Here we are *in the Hall* up to the ears in a muddle of counting lines to fill the *2nd vol –*', Mary wrote to Robinson on 28 September,

a body of finished sheets from the first [volume], having arrived along with your letter – and their appearance after many changes gives great satisfaction to the Poet and his Clerk – His *Journeyman* in the Person of Mr Quillinan having left us last week, to my great regret, for he supplied my place, which he filled most admirably, and has quite thrown me into the shade. However the Poet is obliged to be thankful for his old helpmate and a busy house we have – working steadily till dinner time – and in a *disorderly* manner the rest of the day:

It was a trying time for both poet and 'clerk', as day after day, for months on end, 'those everlasting Proofs' arrived 'to blind our eyes'. Mary was not prepared to be the passive secretary her husband expected, and she did not always approve of his corrections. 'I must say that he never makes one that he does not *seem* to convince my understanding and judgment – but . . . not always my *feelings*', she admitted after three months of relentless revision. Half a year later, the work completed and far away from home, William looked back at this time with shame and remorse, and had the grace to make an apology.

Dearest Mary, when I have felt how harshly I often demeaned myself to you, my inestimable fellow-labourer, while correcting the last Edition of my poems, I often pray to God that He would grant us both life, that I may make some amends to you for that, and all my unworthiness. But you know into what an irritable state this timed and overstrained labour often put my nerves. My impatience was ungovernable as I thought *then*, but I now feel that it ought to have been governed. You have forgiven me I know, as you did then, and perhaps that somehow troubles me the more.

It was not surprising that they both looked back wistfully to Quillinan's visit: 'his presence here was a Godsend to me', Mary wrote feelingly at the beginning of November. She would not have felt so kindly towards Quillinan had she known that, while at Rydal Mount, acting on a 'sudden impulse', he had asked her daughter 'a startling question'. 'I had no certain knowledge of what your feelings were and had been for years;' Quillinan later told Dora of this occasion, 'and, when I found that out, I should have been a brute indeed if I had not told you the fact that I had in my heart of hearts held you dearest of all for years too.' This unlikeliest of love affairs, between an ardent, innocent, thirty-two-year-old Anglican and a forty-five-year-old Roman Catholic widower with a reputation as something of a roué, was to remain their secret for some time to come. Though Quillinan wrote to Dora frequently, he knew his letters would be common property at Rydal Mount and he could send her only coded messages. 'Take care of yourself for God's sake, & for many sakes'. Dora's parents suspected nothing, attributing her improved appearance and strength to the kind attentions of Benjamin Brodie, the London physician, who came to Ambleside for a few days in September and advised her to leave off her medicines and 'trust altogether to air, & moderate exercise, and nutritious food'.

'Why is it that I feel a sort of awkwardness in telling the Wordsworths (& with no others do I feel it) that we are suddenly going to Portugal?' Quillinan asked his daughter Jemima. 'Because it is a sudden change of mind; & you think more of their good opinion than of any one else's', was Jemima's 'crude, but shrewd' reply. Reporting this exchange in a letter to Rydal Mount at the end of October was Quillinan's subtle way of apologizing to Dora for what would become a year-long absence from England.

The first two volumes of the new edition were published before Christmas. In his anxiety to gratify Moxon, William had allowed an engraving of his portrait by Pickersgill to appear as the frontispiece. It was a decision he regretted immediately. It was a bad engraving of a bad portrait. By the end of January, William had completed the revision of all his poems and the printing of the sixth and last volume was about to begin. He had only 'another *tug*' at his postscript on the Poor Laws and a few notes to complete, then he would be ready to set off on his deferred journey to Italy.

On 9 February, he wrote a dignified letter to his friend James Stanger, withdrawing his support for the building of a second church at Cockermouth. It was a project dear to his heart and he had been indefatigable in trying to enlist support. In the end, however, the stumbling block was political antipathy. Lord Lonsdale had offered to endow the living to the value of £150 annually, expecting in return that the appointment of the clergyman would rest with him. In a battle that was being repeated up and down the country, many of the other subscribers threatened to withdraw their donations, unless the appointment was in the hands of either the incumbent or the evangelical Simeon Trustees. As all parties would have agreed to vesting the patronage in the bishop, a compromise should have been possible, but feelings were running so high in Cockermouth that no discussion was possible. Lonsdale suggested a breathing space, but William had had enough.

On 10 March William arrived in London, having escorted his wife and daughter as far as Rugby, where Dora would stay with the Arnolds before going on to friends at Leamington, and Mary would travel on to stay with her beleaguered brother's family at Brinsop. Not only was poor Tom completely paralysed, as a result of a fall from his horse, but his oldest daughter, Mary, just twenty years of age, was terminally ill with consumption. The care of Dorothy was delegated to Mary's sister, Joanna, who had been with them since October. They had no qualms about leaving her: she did not notice anyone's absence, had an 'exemplary attendant', another Dorothy, with her constantly and every other member of the household willingly at her beck and call.

For once, this really was to be a short visit to London. William stayed a bare nine days, calling on a few old friends, purchasing a carriage to take them on their tour, getting passports and calling on the printers. At Moxon's, he learned the astonishing news that almost 2,000 copies of the new edition, out of a print run of only 3,000, had already been sold. This exceeded even Moxon's wildest expectations, as he had calculated that the edition would take two years to sell out – an estimate which William had feared was over-optimistic. Another financial windfall came from an unexpected quarter. Isabella Fenwick, with whom he had been staying, now suggested she would like to invest £400 for her godson, John's second son, William, to pay for his future education once he reached the age of fifteen. William persuaded her that it was not a good idea to put the money in John's name, and that it was better for him to remain in ignorance of it, given his extravagant tendencies and small income. The money was therefore invested in the name of three trustees, Dora, William's nephew Chris, and his solicitor, Strickland Cookson, 'a most excellent man, and a tried Friend'. Having completed his business affairs, William wrote a series of farewell letters to family and friends. They were cheerful enough, but the unspoken implication was that he might not live to see them all again.

On 19 March, with Robinson, and Moxon, who was to accompany them as far as Paris, he embarked on a steamboat at the Tower of London and sailed for Calais, on the first stage of the tour of which he had dreamt for so many years. His objective was to get as far as Naples, even Sicily, if possible, but to explore Rome, Florence and Venice, as well as the Roman antiquities in the south of France.

The first thing William did on arriving in Paris was to seek out the Baudouins. 'I have seen the Baudouins all well, a thousand kind enquiries after you', was William's only recorded comment on their several meetings, made in a letter to Dorothy. Having parted with Moxon, whose desire to oblige and good humour had made him an agreeable companion, William and Robinson struck out for the south, passing through Fontainebleau and Nemours, on their way to Avignon. They were unlikely companions, for, despite their long friendship, their interests and habits were diametrically opposed. This became apparent as soon as they reached the south of France, where Robinson proudly showed off the Maison Carrée and the Arena at Nîmes, and was disappointed to find William took more pleasure in the gardens and two pretty little girls near the Arena than in the Roman antiquities. 'I am unable from ignorance to enjoy these sights. I receive an impression, but that is all', was William's rather pompous explanation, confessing, at the same time, that he did not anticipate much pleasure from viewing classical remains on the rest of the tour.

By the third week in April they had reached Rome and took up lodgings in the heart of the 'English Colony' in the Piazza di Spagna, just a few doors away from the house where Keats had died. It was an ideal situation. The square, with its characteristic white marble Bernini fountain, lies at the foot of the elegant Spanish Steps, which lead up to the pale, twin-towered church of Trinità dei Monte. From the balconied piazzetta in front of the church unfolds a magnificent panorama of the city, where Roman theatres and temples jostle for elbow room with the thrusting campaniles of countless churches and, in the distance, the dome of St Peter rises serene and authoritative, like a venerable sage surrounded by quarrelling children.

'This has been a very interesting day', Robinson noted after they had walked round the Coliseum, the Forum and the Pantheon. 'To Wordsworth it must have been unparalleled in the number and importance of new impressions.' 'Nothing can exceed the interest of Rome', William observed, 'but though I have seen the Coliseum the Pantheon and all the other boasted things nothing has in the least approached the impressions I received from the inside of St Peter's.' However, his most memorable moment was watching a sunset over the city from the Pincian Hill. Close to the dome of St Peter's, on the glowing horizon, he noted 'one of those broad-topped pines, looking like a little cloud in the sky, with a slender stalk to connect it with its native earth'. His emotion, on being told that this same tree owed its preservation to Sir George Beaumont, who had paid to secure its natural life against the developer's axe, overwhelmed him. 'Oh, what a gush of tenderness was mine!' he would later write in a sonnet commemorating this moment.

> The rescued Pine-tree, with its sky so bright
> And cloud-like beauty, rich in thoughts of home,
> Death-parted friends, and days too swift in flight,
> Supplanted the whole majesty of Rome ...
> *The Pine of Monte Mario at Rome, ll.8–12*

Trailing about in the baking-hot streets on the seven hills of Rome, which are so unforgiving to the feet, William soon grew weary of playing the dutiful tourist. 'Of churches and pictures and statues in them I am fairly tired ', he confessed to his family on 6 May; 'in fact I am too old in head, limbs and eyesight for such hard work, such toiling and such straining and so many disappointments either in finding the most celebrated picture covered up with curtains, a service going on so that one cannot ask to have a sight, or the church closed when one arrives at the door.' It was a heartfelt complaint, and one in which every modern tourist in Italy will sympathize, as was his final judgement on the Eternal City. 'But after all it is not particular objects ... that make the glory of this City; but it is the boun[d]less variety of combinations of old and new caught in ever varying connection with the surrounding country, when you look down from some one or other of the seven hills'.

William was fortunate in being able to explore much of the countryside round Rome in the more comfortable, lighter carriage of one of Robinson's friends, Frances Mackenzie. She had met his nephews, John and Chris, on their visits to Rome, and was anxious to assist the poet in every way she could. 'You certainly were Wordsworth's good Angel at Rome', Robinson later wrote to her. 'But for you his evenings would have been sad and even his days imperfectly enjoyed.' At her house he had the pleasure of meeting again one of his earliest American visitors, George Ticknor, and many other old friends, including William Collins, the landscape painter, and the two Allen sisters, who had married John and Josiah Wedgwood. He was also reintroduced to the artist Joseph Severn, who had faithfully attended the dying Keats and, after his death, settled in Rome. William sat to Severn for his portrait, which he intended to give to his daughter-in-law, though he feared none of the family would like it. Given the sensitivity with which Severn painted Keats, and the general opinion, even among its critics, that William's portrait was both accurate and 'the most interesting likeness that has been taken', one longs to see it, but it has vanished without trace.

Even before they left Rome, William was beginning to feel his age. The constant sightseeing, however pleasurable, gave him 'never-wanting proof that I am rather too old for such *excessive* exertions'. The tour of Italy, he now realized, could not be completed satisfactorily in less than eight months 'unless a person be young and very strong. The country is inexhaustible for those who are well read in antient story and classical Poetry, and its natural beauty tempts you to exertion in every direction.' The south was to be denied them, however, for cholera in Naples and quarantine restrictions made it impractical. Instead, they turned northwards, tracing the River Tiber towards its birthplace in the Apennines, and visited Assisi. Following the River Arno, they now made their way towards Florence, making detours, on horseback, to three of the most evocative of all Italian monasteries, the Franciscan convents at Laverna and Vallombrosa, and the Benedictine house at Camaldoli. Romantically situated, among 'the sternest solitudes of the Appennines', surrounded by rocks, forests and mountain torrents, they were calculated to appeal to Wordsworth. As they struggled up to Laverna, they heard the 'vagrant Voice' of a cuckoo, sounding like that of John the Baptist, 'the voice of him that crieth in the wilderness'. It was a wonderful image, which William wrought up into the only poem he composed while travelling, *The Cuckoo at Laverna.* The cuckoo's call in such a foreign landscape was deeply poignant, not least because William did not actually hear it until Robinson had drawn his attention to it several times; the poet was forced to accept that age had also dulled his hearing.

William told Robinson that he was not interested in places that merely had a connection with a great man, unless they had also influenced his work. He therefore cared nothing for the Pantheon, the burial place of Tasso, but had a deep interest in Vaucluse. Now he was about to see Vallombrosa, the monastery set in the heart of mountainous woodland which had reputedly given refuge to his hero, Milton. As he wrote in the poem which resulted from this visit,

Vallombrosa! of thee I first heard in the page
Of that holiest of Bards, and the name for my mind
Had a musical charm, which the winter of age
And the changes it brings had no power to unbind.
At Vallombrosa, ll.25–8

He was itching to get to Vallombrosa as soon as possible, so that he could fulfil his dream, but Robinson wanted to defer the visit. They had what Robinson delicately called 'a little quarrel'. William was 'rude' and Robinson, offended, declined to go altogether. It was their first, and only, open disagreement, and as a result William went alone to Vallombrosa, rising at five in the morning and riding up the wooded mountainsides accompanied only by an incompetent guide. This time, his expectations were to be disappointed. The convent stood not in a deep and narrow valley, overshadowed by enclosing hills, but on a shelf on the mountain, surrounded by pines, with chestnut and beech woods above and below. And he did not have time to wander in the monastery grounds to enjoy the views.

Having patched up their quarrel, the two travellers made their way to Florence, but William was already beginning to wish that he was on his way home. 'Of this be assured', he told his daughter, 'that I never shall go from home for any time again, without a female companion.' Robinson was uncomfortably aware that William was not enjoying Florence as he should, confiding to his journal that his fellow traveller was 'never thoroughly happy but in the country'.

After a mere six days at Florence, they took a short nostalgic tour of the Italian Lakes, which brought back painful, as well as pleasing, recollections of his previous tours with Jones, now dead, and Mary and Dorothy, who was no longer the person she had then been. 'I kept much to myself, and very often could I, for my heart's relief, have burst into tears', William confessed to Dora. On 22 June they arrived in Venice, 'with the wonders of which City I shall consider our Italian tour as concluding', William announced unpromisingly. It was a pity that Venice came at the end rather than the beginning of their journey, for William was not in the mood to appreciate its shimmering waters, palatial buildings and the sharp contrast of shadowed alleyways and brilliant sunlit piazzas. St Mark's Square he admitted was 'a splendid spot!', the Venetian architecture 'wonderfully more splendid than Amsterdam . . . quite unique'. But he complained of the heat and that his bedroom was too small, making him very uncomfortable, 'endeavouring to sleep while I was actually in an oven'. He was 'so indifferent to mere sights' that Robinson gave up, and they left after only four days, taking the road north towards Salzburg and Munich.

If Robinson had hoped that the alpine scenery and Austrian lakes would restore William's good humour and persuade him to linger over their homeward journey, he was swiftly disabused. William had seen what he wanted to see and, as he wrote grumpily from Munich on 17 July, 'I consider our *Tour* finished'. Four months of living in each other's pockets had exaggerated the differences in their tastes and habits. Robinson was an ardent Germanophile: 'he takes delight in loitering about towns, gossiping, and attending reading-rooms, and going to coffee-houses; and at *table d'hôtes*, etc., gabbling German, or any other tongue, all which places and practices are my abomination', William complained. In the evenings, William had nothing else to do but go to bed, so he was ready to rise early, which Robinson, who retired at midnight, was not. The one time William had given in to his impulse to compose verse, he had suffered several nights of broken rest, upset his stomach and resolved to refrain in future. 'I have nothing to do,' he fretted, 'and as I cannot speak German my time moves very heavily.'

Robinson was equally frustrated. As they neared Munich Robinson re-read *The Excursion*, to remind himself, one imagines, just why he tolerated its author as a travelling companion. Each man was convinced that he was forgoing his own pleasures for the sake of the other, but they had simply reached the point where they were getting on each other's nerves. The root of the problem, as William acknowledged, was that Robinson, a bachelor, had no incentive to hurry home, whereas he was desperate to see his family again. 'I want the sight of your faces and the sound of your voices', he metaphorically shouted at Mary, when she reproached him for hurrying Robinson home. 'Therefore find no more fault, I undertook this journey as a *duty*, I have gone through with it as such'.

On 7 August they landed back on English soil and parted, Robinson returning to his chambers, William to meet Dora and stay with Moxon. Though they met regularly, with no appearance of animosity, their early return had set tongues wagging, and both men were disconcerted when Rogers made pointed remarks about lost tempers and drew attention to the fact that they sat as far from each other as possible. This was intolerable and, to put the seal on the rumour-mill, they agreed to make 'a sort of supplementary journey' and, in a symbolic gesture, explore the Wye together as far as Tintern Abbey. Dora accompanied them, but they got no further than Brinsop. The excursion was thwarted by bad weather and a sudden recurrence of William's trachoma. With the example of John Monkhouse's patient and cheerful endurance of his blindness daily before him, William could not shame to complain, but his condition deteriorated so rapidly that he had no option but to return home as quickly as possible. On 22 September he and Dora took their places in the Liverpool coach and set off for Rydal Mount.

At sixty-seven years of age, William had fulfilled his long-cherished wish of making a tour of Italy, but the whole experience was marred by an abiding sense that it had come too late. 'I have ... to regret that this journey was not made some years ago, – to regret it, I mean, as a Poet;' he wrote from Salzburg on his way back to England, 'for though we have had a great disappointment in not seeing Naples, etc. ... my mind has been enriched by innumerable images, which I could have turned to account in verse, and vivified by feelings which earlier in my life would have answered noble purposes, in a way they now are little likely to do.' It was a refrain he would repeat again and again, sometimes with uncharacteristic, if understandable, bitterness, suggesting that the blame lay with Jeffrey, and the other reviewers, who had made him a laughing stock and denied him the profits which would have enabled him to go as a vibrant young man.

William returned to Rydal Mount to find his wife well, his sister 'in her better way' but his eldest son's affairs in crisis. On 24 July Isabella had given birth to her fourth child, imaginatively named John Wordsworth. The family were now living at Brigham, John senior having ceded the living of Workington to his brother-in-law, when he came of age. Another child on a restricted income was a problem, but at the beginning of August three of the Curwen coal pits at Workington were swallowed up by the sea. Setting aside the cost in human lives, the financial repercussions on the Curwens were enormous. Isabella's father would lose £3,000 a year by the loss of the pits, but the disaster exposed the fragility of the foundations of the Curwen empire, which was encumbered with debt going back three generations. Isabella's generous allowance, and the expected inheritance, which had made her marriage with John possible, were, quite literally, washed away. The living of Moresby could not support two adults and four children, already indebted beyond their means. In a touching attempt to make ends meet, and in sharp contrast to the younger generation of the Curwen family, who acted as if nothing had happened, John let it be known that he was looking for pupils. His sister suggested that perhaps the Wordsworths too should cut back on unnecessary expenses, but this Mary was not prepared to do. Their only 'extravagance' was a third maid, dedicated to Dorothy's care, who was absolutely necessary to her comfort. 'No, we must not, at this day – and with Father's triumphs sounding in our ears, be called upon to economize', she told Dora, 'not but I could be as happy *personally* upon £100 a year as when we were in the Cottage at Grasmere.' Dora had welcomed the excuse to return home as her father's escort, but her parents were too afraid of the consequences for her health to allow her to remain at Rydal Mount. At the end of October she returned to London. Quillinan, newly returned from Portugal, and ever optimistic that he would be able to persuade her to marry him, was waiting to escort her to Dover, where she was to spend the winter with Isabella Fenwick. Miss Fenwick, whom even the grudging Thomas Carlyle thought 'the wisest person male or female I have fallen in with in London', was now to prove her sterling worth. Under her aegis, Dora and Quillinan were not only allowed, but encouraged, to meet. Quillinan was invited to Dover, and Dora, chaperoned by his sister-in-law, visited Canterbury, where he had taken a cottage. Quillinan, who had brought his own daughters up in the Anglican faith at their mother's request, assiduously escorted her to the cathedral, noting, with quiet irony, that on one occasion the 'fine anthem' was Mozart's 'Plead Thou my cause'.

At the end of November Quillinan went to stay at Rydal Mount, where William was once again 'tinkering' at 'that plaguy poem he has worried so long at'. Quillinan made himself agreeable as only he knew how, talking politics and poetry to the poet, and relieving Mary of the burden of reading the newspapers to him in the evenings. He drove them out to visit their friends, walked with William and accompanied them to church. And all the time he was writing love letters to their daughter. Dora tried hard to keep him at bay, suggesting that her love for him was platonic, but her resistance was half-hearted, and they both knew it.

Mary's suspicions were first aroused when Quillinan flatly refused to let her see a letter from Dora he was reading. 'I felt ashamed', he admitted to Dora, 'as if I was guilty of some I do not know what to call it, for it is not disingenuousness in its culpable sense – my regard for you is not, cannot be a secret in this house – but it is exactly in this house & to its owners that I could not utter a syllable about it'. Quillinan might have been able to half-persuade himself that he was not deceiving the Wordsworths, but he could not screw up the courage to tell them the truth. This was left to Dora, who was incapable of pretence, especially towards her parents. At the first opportunity, and probably in response to probing by her mother, Dora explained how matters stood. It was only then that Quillinan wrote to William, asking permission to marry his daughter.

The Wordsworths' anger was understandable. They felt that their trust had been betrayed. Every aspect of the case put him in a poor light: he was so much older and more worldly than her and he had been neither open nor straightforward in his wooing. They had known him intimately, for almost fifteen years, supported him in his difficulties, indulged and laughed at his flirtations, flippancies and dilettante behaviour. Within the family, he had even been known as Aunt Sara's lover, because they had enjoyed a mutual flirtation. And now he expected them to sanction his marriage to Dora.

William, in particular, was furious. Even his beloved daughter felt his wrath at first, though by 8 February he had calmed down enough to send her a new sonnet 'as a peace-offering, at your dear Mother's request'. With or without her father's consent, the lovers considered themselves engaged. Quillinan even thought they were on the brink of marriage, for on 6 April he bought her a ring which he had engraved with lines of his own composition. When he called to see her, in London, before she left for Brinsop, he was swiftly disillusioned. Dora had just received a vicious letter from her father, which was to prompt a 'really bold speaking-out' response from Dora. Refusing even to allude to Quillinan by name, he had used the analogous situation of thirty-six-year-old Henry Taylor, who had proposed to a girl of seventeen and been rejected, to mount a covert attack on Dora's lover. 'If Men or Women will form engagements so little in accordance with nature and reason, they have no *right* to expect better treatment', he snarled. 'I take no notice of the conclusion of your Letter', he added; '. . . It turns upon a subject which I shall never touch more either by pen or voice. Whether I look back or forward it is depressing and distressing to me, and will for the remainder of my life, continue to be so.'

Both Mary and Miss Fenwick tried to pour oil on troubled waters. Mary assured Dora that her father seemed 'quite a different person' since he had received the assurance that she was on her way home, and he too sent her 'a home-inviting loving message'. 'Well then, what are you to do when you get home?' Quillinan asked.

Nothing at all: be quiet, my dear Dora, and do not attempt to argue the point. Dutiful to Him I know you will be and dutiful to Her, and gentle, and unquerulous in words as you are in truth affectionate to her, I pray you to be for her sake, your sake, & for my sake. –

She has not been very kind to me, but I am sure she has many a heart-ache about you; and who can tell how much kindness even to me is supprest, or how little she really understands, or how much she mistakes, the true nature of this case.

'It is strange', he mused, 'that with all his lucid thought [your father] cannot see that that particular "composition of" your "mind" which has made you so true and tenacious a daughter to <u>him</u>, is the <u>roman</u> cement that also binds you to <u>me</u>.'

William worked off his fury in the garden and when Dora finally returned home, in June, she did not have to face her parents alone. Miss Fenwick accompanied her, and, to all outward appearances, life at Rydal Mount went on as if nothing had occurred. Only Christopher's son John, visiting later in the year, noticed that Dora seemed preoccupied with 'a secret care, which weighs upon the feelings of all here, though they never allude to it in conversation'.

Dora was intimately involved in William's next publication, a single volume containing all his sonnets. In preparing this edition, William was making a public statement about the value he attached to this type of poem. He already had over 400 published sonnets in hand, and would add a further twelve new ones while overseeing the volume through the press. Six of these were composed so late that they could not be included in the main body of the text and had to be added as an appendix. One of these was a remodelling, in sonnet form, of a poem he had written after the death of Mrs Southey, in November 1837. William and Mary had visited her on the day she died, peacefully in her bed, having refused food and water for the previous ten days. Though Southey appeared philosophical about his loss, his poor daughters, who had borne the brunt of nursing her, were tormented by regrets 'for unkind things said & done'. Inevitably, the Wordsworths could not help but make comparisons with Dorothy. 'She is an affecting object', Mary had written after a visit to Mrs Southey in August, '– but what a contrast in regard to beautiful neatness and cleanliness to our poor sufferer.' In mental condition, however, they were much the same. In the first version of his poem, 'Oh! what a Wreck! how changed in mien and speech', William had alluded specifically to Dorothy's condition, as well as Mrs Southey's. The revised sonnet cut out these personal references and the comparison with Dorothy, leaving only the kernel of the poem.

> She is not what she seems, a forlorn wretch,
> But delegated Spirits comfort fetch
> To Her from heights that Reason may not win.
> Like Children, She is privileged to hold
> Divine communion;

By 21 May William had completed all his part of the book, including the notes, table of contents and a short advertisement, making pointed allusion to Milton, the father of the sonnet. The title was honest, if unmemorable, *The Sonnets of William Wordsworth. Collected in One Volume. With a Few Additional Ones.* Complimentary copies were in the hands of friends a month later, but, to give it a chance of attracting attention, the publication was delayed until after the coronation of Queen Victoria on 25 June. Even then, William was still plagued by doubts whether it would succeed or affect the sale of the six-volume edition, and was grateful for a reassurance from Moxon, at the end of July, that both were selling well.

William had more profound reasons for gratitude to Moxon. He alone, out of all the London publishers, had stood out in favour of a bill to extend the term of author's copyright, which was presented to the House of Commons in April. The bill was the work of William's friend Thomas Noon Talfourd, 'an astonishing man – for talents, Genius, and energy of mind', who had entered Parliament at the end of 1835 as member for Reading. Diametrically opposed to William in politics, his election had nevertheless been welcomed by the poet, who offered his sincere congratulations, adding only a single caveat. 'As you so well know my opinions, which differ I believe in fundamentals from your own, I shall only say, respect them so far, as to think a little more about any course you might be inclined to take as a Member of the House, than you otherwise would have done, if you had not been aware that your notions of prudence and mine might be at variance.'

As an author himself, Talfourd had an interest in extending the term of copyright from twenty-eight to sixty years after publication, but he would not have taken up the cause had it not been for William, who had been lobbying for a change in the law for thirty years. As the years had passed, William's own poetic career proved a striking example of the injustice of the copyright laws. By 1835 his rights in *Lyrical Ballads* and *Poems, in Two Volumes* had already lapsed: the moment he died, any publisher could reprint those editions without paying a penny towards his estate. By 1842, the same would be true of *The Excursion* and, the following year, of both the first collected edition of 1815 and *The White Doe of Rylstone*. It had taken thirty years to establish a sale of his works, longer than the term of copyright, and throughout that time he had earned next to nothing. Now, when he was just beginning to reap the financial benefit, his death would mean that his family would be prevented from enjoying the profits of his labours.

Though he still declined to be an individual suppliant for what he considered to be the right of a whole class, and therefore refused to petition, William did write an open letter to Talfourd for him to publish in the *Morning Post*, composed two sonnets pleading the cause for inclusion in the new volume, urged all his literary friends to exert their influence and lobbied indefatigably every Member of Parliament with whom he had even the most tenuous of connections, explaining, cajoling and ultimately asking them to attend the Commons when the bill was reintroduced on 11 April 1838. Three days later he could boast that he had written (or rather dictated, since poor Mary did the writing) scarcely fewer than fifty letters on the subject.

The second reading of the bill was passed by thirty-nine votes to thirty-four – and only then because John Ellis, at the instigation of Sir Robert Inglis and Benjamin D'Israeli, went down in a cab to the Carlton Club during the debate 'where I was fortunate enough to persuade one or two to relinquish their claret and go down for the division'. In the face of mounting opposition from Lord John Russell and

Sir Robert Peel, Talfourd decided on a tactical withdrawal of his bill until the next session, to prevent it being voted out altogether.

William would not admit defeat. He could not afford to do so. All his attempts to find his younger son a new and better-paid post had failed. His elder son's affairs had gone from bad to worse: having lost all his wife's income, he had caught typhus visiting his parishioners. He had been bedridden for a couple of months and recovered very slowly; an excursion to Paris did nothing for him, and when he consulted the doctors in London he was advised to spend the winter in the south of France and be careful of doing duty for two years. France was out of the question financially, but he, his wife and youngest child took up their quarters in Leamington and London for the winter and a substitute had to be found for the interval at Brigham. As Mary lamented, 'truly the expences attending this untoward illness is *to us all* a most serious consideration'. The only bright spot, as far as his doting grandparents were concerned, was that John and Isabella left little Willy, who would be three years old on 27 December, at Rydal Mount. His presence 'brought fresh life to this house', Mary observed, and was an additional incentive to William to continue his labours for copyright reform.

William's position as the grand old man of English letters was now firmly established. Honours showered on him from every side. He politely declined, on the grounds of age and inadequacy, invitations to lecture on poetry in a public institution in London and to contribute 'critical reflections' to the *Transactions* of the Royal Irish Academy. On 21 July 1838 the University of Durham conferred an honorary doctorate on him. It was the first time an honorary graduand had attended the ceremony in person and William was deeply embarrassed that the public oration was not made in Latin, as was customary at Oxford and Cambridge. 'There is . . . some thing very awkward in constraining a Man to hear his own praises, before many listeners, in his Mother tongue', William told Robinson. ' – I object to the practice also as lowering the University.' Nevertheless, he was proud of the honour, and, as it was technically a law degree, it allowed him to tease his barrister friend by urging him 'not [to] scruple when a difficult point of Law occurs, to consult me'. In October he was invited by the Secretary of the Wordsworth Committee to stand for election as Rector of the University of Glasgow, an active role which he felt incapable of fulfilling and declined, though sensible of the honour intended.

With these plaudits ringing in his ears, William now had the confidence to admit publicly that he had failed in the one aspect of his poetic career that mattered most to him. *The Recluse* would never be completed. When Ticknor, William's American friend, called at Rydal Mount in May, 'Mrs Wordsworth asked me to talk to him about finishing the Excursion, or the Recluse; saying, that she could not bear to have him occupied constantly in writing sonnets and other trifles, while this great work lay by him untouched'. William explained that the first part of *The Recluse* was 'partly written in fragments which . . . would be useless and unintelligible in other hands than his own', the second was *The Excursion* and the third was untouched. 'On my asking him why he does not finish it, he turned to me very decidedly, and said, "Why did not Gray finish the long poem he began on a similar subject? Because he found he had undertaken something beyond his powers to accomplish. And that is my case."'

Despite his wife's distaste for such 'trifles', William spent the closing months of the year composing twelve or more new sonnets, some of them arising out of his Italian tour. These he offered to send to Robinson, on condition he did not read them to any '*verse-writers*. We are all in spite of ourselves a parcel of thieves', he told Robinson. 'I had a droll instance of it this morning – for while Mary was writing down for me one of these Sonnets, on coming to a certain line, she cried out somewhat uncourteously "that's a plagiarism" – from whom? "from yourself" was the answer. I believe she is right tho' she could not point out the passage, neither can I.'

The sales of his published work continued to confound all expectations. Only 450 copies remained out of the 3,000 printed for the six-volume edition of 1836–7. A further edition was now necessary and William's nephew 'Cambridge' John, 'the most accurate Man I know', gladly undertook to correct the proofs on his behalf. Evidence that William's reputation was spreading beyond the shore of his native country came from all corners of the globe. The last edition of his poems published in America had a print run of 20,000 copies and the whole of his poetic works were available there in an edition costing less than the modern equivalent of six pence. In a 'highly encomiastic' article in the *New York Review*, written by one of his American editors, Henry Reed, he had been hailed as the successor of Shakespeare, Spenser and Milton. More unexpectedly, an unauthorized edition appeared in Calcutta, giving rise to a controversy about the quality of the poetry in the *Delhi Gazette* of the sort William had thankfully not experienced in twenty years. It too sold for a paltry six rupees.

These successes persuaded William that he would have to overcome his objection to appearing as a petitioner to Parliament on copyright reform. The persistent Talfourd was preparing to try again, and, luckily for William, who was at a loss as to how to proceed, Robinson was paying what had now become almost an annual visit to Rydal. The first version was rejected. 'He is too desirous to express his own impressions and cares, too little about the impressions it will excite in others', Robinson coolly remarked, before amusing himself in rewriting the petition; to his gratification 'a few' of his suggestions were accepted. Adopting a lofty stance, the poet declared that he was on the point of attaining his seventieth year and that his copyrights were now almost all contingent on the duration of his life. He pointed out that he had earned more from his writings in the last four years than in the preceding thirty-four and that this income would have been lost to his family had he died within that period. The main object of the bill, however, was 'to relieve men of letters from the thraldom of being forced to court the living generation, to aid them in rising above degraded taste and slavish prejudice, and to encourage them to rely upon their own impulses, or to leave them with less excuse if they should fail to do so'. Talfourd again got his bill to a second reading, this time with an increased majority, but was thwarted by the unexpected resignation of the ministry in May. Relief for men of letters was not to come for three more years.

25. Real Greatness

'I meant to stay here only a month,' Robinson wrote to his brother on 19 January 1839, 'but the Ws seem so unwilling to let me go that I foresee I shall not get away till the end of five weeks.' He was thoroughly enjoying himself, reading, walking, talking and playing evening games of whist with the Wordsworths, visiting the Arnolds at Fox How, and making the acquaintance of Isabella Fenwick, who was resident for the winter in Ambleside. Like everyone else who came within this remarkable lady's ambit, he fell in love with her. Fifty-six years old, with a deformity of the spine 'but otherwise really rather good-looking', in Carlyle's heartless phrase, Miss Fenwick exuded goodness.

At the beginning of February, she invited Quillinan to stay with her. Afraid to accept, until reassured by William that he had not forfeited his friendship and that his visit would not be considered an 'intrusion', he arrived on 11 February and was invited to call at Rydal Mount. He came to a gloomy house. William was ill with rheumatics, 'a sad nervous derangement', and a cough. Dora was looking ill, and losing her appetite again. Dorothy was Dorothy. For a week, Quillinan spent every day with Dora, returning at night to Miss Fenwick's. He had no private conversation, directly or indirectly, with William on the subject so close to all their hearts, but by the time he left, they had come to an understanding, which Miss Fenwick summarized to Dora as 'a patient waiting for happier circumstances – your father reconciling himself to all objections – & willing to consent – when there could be any reasonable security of your being provided for – and there being no hinderance [*sic*] to your attachment in the mean time'.

As soon as Quillinan had gone, William and Mary went to stay with Miss Fenwick at Ambleside, 'for the sake of her society and change of air'. William was now revising his autobiographical poem, *The Prelude*, so that it would be in a fit state for posthumous publication. Miss Fenwick, observing this process for the first time, was astonished at the labour that went into it. William seldom worked fewer than six or seven hours a day, 'or rather one ought to say the whole day, for it seemed always on his mind – quite a possession'. After one such session, he appeared before Miss Fenwick 'radiant with joy' and bursting to tell her that Mary, in the midst of his dictation, had said, 'Well, William, I declare you are cleverer than ever.' With tears in his eyes, he explained why such an apparent commonplace should mean so much to him. 'It is not often I have had such praise; she has always been sparing of it.' As soon as the revision was complete, William gave the poem to Dora and Elizabeth Cookson to be fair-copied. While the two young women stayed at Rydal Mount to make the new transcript, William and Mary accompanied Miss Fenwick and her niece, Isabella, to Bath. They travelled for the first time by train, on the new line from Preston to Birmingham. 'The rail way is charming travelling, but neither *apparently* so rapid, so smooth or like flying as I expected,' Mary commented. Nor was it cheap, costing the thrifty Wordsworths £1 6s 6d '*each*', plus £4 5d for Miss Fenwick's carriage, and 17s for each of the servants.

Their purpose in going to Bath was twofold, to defer a parting from Miss Fenwick, whose family lived in the city, and to take the waters for their rheumatics. Willy, who had joined them at Lancaster, was also of the party. He was in such a delicate state of health that his appearance quite frightened his mother.

The Wordsworths took lodgings at 101 George Street, halfway between the Pump Rooms and Royal Crescent. They bathed, took the waters, visited assiduously and tried unsuccessfully to avoid the '*terrible* Blue Stocking' and 'perfect pest' Mrs Maltby, who was determined to capture the poet for her salon. They called several times on Mrs de Quincey, who lived nearby at Weston. This was particularly kind, given that the third instalment of her son's revelations about the Wordsworths was published in *Tait's Magazine* that very month. With its unflattering physical descriptions of William, Mary and Dorothy, its gossipy disclosures about their conversation and private lives, and, almost worst of all, its extensive quotation from *The Prelude*, which William himself was deliberately withholding from publication to benefit his children, it was the greatest betrayal of friendship which had yet occurred. In the circumstances, Mary's discretion in reserving the contents of their conversation with Mrs de Quincey 'to be chatted about by Aunty's good fire' seems poignant. William also made contact with another old friend, the seventy-seven-year-old poet William Lisle Bowles, who lived not far away at Chippenham. 'I am truly glad to find <u>your outward Machine</u>, is only a little worse for <u>wear</u>!' Bowles wrote cheerfully to William. 'I am as <u>wizen</u> as a <u>witch</u>, & as <u>Deaf</u> as a Post!', which perhaps explains why he mistook Mary for 'old Dorothy' when they met on 18 April.

The happy atmosphere at Bath was shattered by a letter from Dora, announcing that Quillinan had written to her, demanding a final answer to his proposal. Did she trust him, he asked? Did she dare to run the risk of marrying him, without any assurance of financial security? Did she have any influence over her father, and would she exert it to make their marriage possible? It was a typically impatient Quillinan gesture, but it angered William deeply: 'that calling upon her in so peremptory a manner to act on so important an occasion *during the absence of her parents*, is, to say the least of it, an ill-judged proceeding', he wrote icily to Quillinan. In the time-honoured fashion, he demanded to know what were his would-be son-in-law's prospects, and, in particular, could he provide for Dora after his death?

Everyone waited on tenterhooks, hoping that Quillinan would be able to provide a satisfactory answer. As he well knew, however, this was impossible. Not only were his current finances in disarray, but what little he had was compromised by securities he had foolishly, if generously, given for his brother's business. Powerless to alter the situation, he chose to respond by taking offence at William's letter. His self-justificatory and accusatory reply made a bad situation worse. To Dora herself, caught between them, he declared his conviction that they would never marry; 'now that the hopelessness of the case is manifest, I believe in my soul and conscience that you will be the less unhappy for having arrived at the conviction of its hopelessness'.

It fell to Willy to heal the breach. Having been in the same situation himself, he understood its difficulties better than anyone. He wrote and called on Quillinan, and persuaded his father to write a generous letter to Dora, stating that he believed Quillinan to be 'a most honorable and upright man, and further that he is most strongly and faithfully attached to you – this I must solemnly declare in justice to you both; and to this I add *my blessing upon you and him*, more I cannot do'. A second letter, from Mary, warned Dora, 'my beloved Daughter', not to agitate the matter further, 'or call upon your *tender Father* (for he *does* deserve that epithet if ever Man did) for more than this passive countenance which he is, I feel, ready to give. And may his and your Mother's blessing be upon you both.'

At the end of April William was summoned to London by Thomas Spring-Rice, then Chancellor of the Exchequer, who wrote that 'it had occurred to him' William might appreciate having his office as Distributor of Stamps transferred to his son. It was too good to be true. On 7 May the resignation of the ministry put an end to the transfer.

On 24 May Mary's brother Henry died in Douglas, on the Isle of Man. Seventy years old, he had been in ill-health for many years, so his death was not unexpected. Much more shocking was the death, on 10 May, of the wife of their nephew Charles, Charlotte Wordsworth, who was twenty-two and died giving birth to their only child, a second Charlotte. It was a timely reminder of the perils of marriage and child-bearing to which Dora would be exposed. Having briefly visited the widower and his 'most delightful' baby at Winchester, Mary could not stand being parted from her own daughter any longer and returned early to Rydal Mount, leaving William and Willy to finish business in town. William and Quillinan had several amicable meetings, at which William gave his permission, if not his approval, for the match. 'I cannot think of parting with you with that complacency, that satisfaction, that hopefulness which I could wish to feel', he wrote sadly to Dora. 'But I must submit, and do submit; and God Almighty bless you, my dear child, and him who is the object of your long and long-tried preference and choice.'

On 10 June Quillinan saw William off on the coach from London to Oxford, for what was to be the greatest accolade of his entire poetic career. The university had decided to bestow an honorary doctorate upon him. This was in itself a matter of pride and pleasure, but what turned it into such a triumph was the reception he received from the Oxford men who packed the Sheldonian Theatre to see him become a Doctor of Civil Law. 'He was most enthusiastically received on entering the Theatre yesterday,' Willy wrote to his mother on 13 June, 'such cheering, I never in my life heard, not even at an Election, & I was told by many that, with the exception of the I[n]stallation of the Duke of Wellington, there never was more feeling shown or expressed.' Mary Arnold, who with her husband and daughter, Jane, had come from Rugby to see the ceremony, carried away with her a single striking image:

that of Mr W with his venerable dignified yet humble look as he advanced to receive the University distinction. His grey hair easily distinguished him nor was he less marked by the deafening shouts of applause & approbation w[hi]ch were heard on all sides from the grave looking body of Masters below, as well as from the more vehement undergraduates above.

Everyone there, she went on, must have contrasted this reception with the neglect and contempt with which his earlier works had been treated; 'yet here was the same man his system & principle unchanged, his own dignified simplicity the same both in himself & in his works & yet having conquered that public opinion w[hi]ch he was content to wait for[,] sure that his principle was true & not over anxious about the early acknowledgment of it. In all this there is real greatness'.

The Reverend John Keble, in his public oration (in Latin this time, to William's relief), declared that he stood out uniquely among all the poets, 'because he alone had placed the customs, pursuits and moral observances of the poor not just in a good light, but even in a heavenly one'. Gratifying though this praise was, it could not match the spontaneous acclamation he received from the crowd, which, like the letters he received from ordinary readers, was voluntarily offered and therefore indisputably sincere. In the unpoetic expression of John Peace, the City Librarian of Bristol who travelled to Oxford for the sole purpose of '*joining in the shout*', it was 'a burst from the central heart of the best men of England at the best period of their lives'. So there he stood, the poet who had championed the poor, with the plaudits of the country's intellectual, political and religious leaders, past, present and future, ringing in his ears: living proof of his own dictum that 'we have all of us one human heart'.

Keble gave the oration in his capacity as Professor of Poetry, but he was better known, then as now, as the author of the immensely popular *Christian Year* and founder of the Oxford Movement. His speech therefore had an added significance, for it went beyond mere praise of William's poetry to venerate the spirit in which it was written. For the first time, the poet who had been variously castigated as an atheist, a pantheist and every other kind of theist (but always doctrinally unsound) was now publicly recognized as a *Christian* poet. This was not lost on those present, John Peace included. 'It was a blessed thing', he wrote to Mary afterwards, '. . . that it fell to the lot of the congenial and heavenly-minded John Keble to avouch before fit audience, not few, that the highest praise which Christian life may utter belonged to the Christian Poet who stood before them.' William had always said that he could not write sacred poetry, protesting that he thought it 'a subject too high for him'. His admirers, however, from all walks of life, had always recognized that his poems were instinctively religious. Many a humble admirer had echoed Sir George Beaumont in declaring that they had received more benefit from reading his works than any other book except the Bible. In John Ruskin's beautiful phrase, William had taught them that, 'A snowdrop was to me, as to Wordsworth, part of the Sermon on the mount.' Keble's oration gave the highest possible sanction to this interpretation, which would once have been regarded as blasphemous. It endorsed the crucial shift in critical and popular opinion, which now recognized as William's greatest strengths what had once been seen as his weaknesses. He had succeeded in educating a whole new generation to believe that Cumberland beggars and daffodils were fit subjects for poetry, that philosophical truths could be found in humble subjects and that religion could and should rise above sectarian difference.

What Keble's oration also did was to claim William for the Oxford Movement, which sought to rise above doctrinal squabbles and regenerate the spiritual heart of the Anglican Church. It was no coincidence that, before he left the city, William breakfasted several times with its leading members, including Keble himself, John Henry Newman, Francis Faber (who had written to ask William if he would accept an honorary degree if conferred) and his brother, the charismatic preacher Frederick William Faber. Nor was it a coincidence that all these men had been disciples of his poetry since youth, so that, in influencing them, he might even be said to have laid the foundations for the Oxford Movement. It was a debt which Newman himself identified, saying he had been central to the 'great progress of the religious mind of our Church to something deeper and truer than satisfied the last century.' The poet whose work had once been castigated by Jeffrey as the 'very paragon of silliness and affectation' was now venerated as sage and seer.

William returned to Rydal Mount, and reality, on 15 June, having requested Keble to send him a copy of the oration for him to keep. Pride coming before a fall, he had also sprained his ankle, a troublesome injury which confined him to the grounds and would cause him much future discomfort. He immediately embarked on corrections for the next edition of his *Poetical Works* in six volumes, delegating the task of proofreading *The Excursion* to his nephew 'Cambridge' John. This was the last time William was able to call on the invaluable services of his nephew. John, who had never enjoyed robust health, died, aged thirty-four, on New Year's Eve. His father, who had nursed him devotedly day and night, consoled himself with observing John's patient resignation and Christian fortitude, but admitted to his own brother that 'the loss to me and to his Brothers is, irreparable on this side of the grave.' 'The departed was beloved in this House as he deserved to be . . . his life had been as blameless as a man's could well be', William replied. 'He was a pure Spirit and through the goodness of God, is gone to his reward.'

There was also a parting from another nephew this winter. 'Keswick' John had obtained a commission and posting to the Ionian Islands. Having raised £1,500 by selling part of his estate, he sailed for Gibraltar on 7 November, where he was welcomed by the Chief Justice, William's friend Barron Field, before continuing to his station on Corfu.

At the end of October a new visitor came to Rydal Mount. Margaret Gillies was a professional portrait painter in her mid-thirties. A Scotswoman living in London, she was an enthusiastic Wordsworthian who had asked to paint William's portrait. She came garlanded with recommendations from William's friend Thomas Powell, and Leigh Hunt, who 'guaranteed' that Miss Gillies's portrait would be a good likeness. As usual, the Wordsworths seem to have allowed their affection for the artist to cloud their judgement of the portrait, or rather portraits, as both Mary and Dora also ended up sitting to Miss Gillies before she left. The finished portraits, all watercolour miniatures, painted on ivory, show an amiable-looking William seated in a variety of poses, beside an arch through which a lake and mountains can be seen, in profile, swathed in a monastic-looking cloak, and at a table piled high with books. The third version included Mary, quill pen in hand, gazing up at her husband with the expression of sickly adoration usually reserved for bad religious pictures. Only the portrait of Dora gives any impression of the strength of character which all three possessed. Highly romanticized, with masses of gauzy drapery and her arms folded across her breast, she gazes up in the attitude of a virgin saint, but the deep-shadowed eyes, severely swept back hair and large nose form a striking contrast to the superimposed femininity.

The following year, William stayed quietly at Rydal Mount. Miss Fenwick escorted Dora to London in the middle of February for a series of visits to the Hoares and Sara Coleridge at Hampstead, the Gees at Hendon and the Marshalls in Grosvenor Square. It was an opportunity not just to see old friends, but also to see Quillinan free from the constraints of Rydal Mount. Though not yet official, or public knowledge, her engagement to Quillinan was known and accepted in all these households, enabling him to visit her regularly and accompany her about town. They called together on Moxon and Rogers, and went to Miss Gillies for Dora to have a second sitting 'to have my nose reduced a little'. When she left London, on 24 April, she took Quillinan's elder daughter, Jemima, to spend the summer with her at Rydal Mount.

To celebrate William's seventieth birthday, which fell on 7 April 1840, Miss Fenwick presented him with a cuckoo clock. Surprisingly, the Wordsworths all loved it. 'No children were ever more delighted with a new toy than we are with . . . it', Mary told her. The Great Poet was entranced, hanging it outside his bedroom door so that he could wake to its call and composing a poem in celebration of the gift. The giver herself was more memorably commemorated in a lovely sonnet written just before her departure, which described Miss Fenwick as 'The heart-affianced sister of our love' and compared this late friendship to 'The star which comes at close of day to shine More heavenly bright than when it leads the morn'.

Throughout the spring and summer William produced a crop of poems in a period of more sustained creativity than he had enjoyed in a long time. 'He has been hard at work for the last 3 or 4 months – and tho' he labours in constant fear of his eyes, and complains of discomfort from them – Yet in reality he has had very little suffering', Mary informed her nephew in June; 'and the work that has principally occupied him, you will imagine to have required deep thought and to be delicately treated, when I tell you that he has written 11 Sonnets "On the punishment of Death!"' Almost half a century earlier William had argued the case for transportation, instead of execution, in *The Convict*. Now, as the penal laws were being liberalized and the number of capital crimes reduced by reforming ministries, William argued for the retention of the death penalty on the grounds that it was best for the convict himself. A man condemned to life imprisonment 'needs must eat the heart Out of his own humanity'; a man transported 'In life-long exile on a savage coast' would become hardened to commit more heinous crimes. Hence (by a somewhat obscure logic) William argued that execution was best. The man about to be executed would be sincerely penitent and therefore more likely to earn God's mercy in the Final Judgement. In ending his mortal life, his immortal soul would be saved. 'Strike not from Law's firm hand that awful rod,' he thundered, 'But leave it thence to drop for lack of use'. The *Sonnets Upon the Punishment of Death* are one of William's least appealing productions, but he felt it to be his moral duty to write them and circulate them 'on account of the importance of the subject'.

Summer visitors had poured into the Lakes as usual, more than 300 of them gaining access to Rydal Mount. Among them were some of the most remarkable ones the Wordsworths had ever seen. The Rydal Mount Visitors' Book for July 1840 records among the more familiar names of Faber, Hare, Marshall, Taylor and Southey 'Two Ashan[tee] Princes, Hostages' and 'Adelaide Regina!!'. On 24 July the two African princes, with their tutor, drank tea with the Wordsworths, and were escorted to the waterfalls in Rydal Park by Quillinan. Three days later, they were followed by Queen Adelaide, widow of William IV, her sister, the Duchess of Saxe-Weimar, and a train of grandees. Forewarned by Graves, the curate of Bowness, that she was on her way, William waited to meet her (wearing a new hat) at the lower waterfalls in Rydal Park, and escorted her up to the higher fall. 'The world & his wife were assembled on our front to see the cortege', Dora reported excitedly to Willy. 'If you had seen dear Mammy in Miss Fenwick's white satin bonnet this morning & black lace scarf, you would have been proud of her.' William escorted the dowager Queen to each of the viewpoints in his garden, 'particularly to that, through the summer house, which shows the lake of Rydal to such advantage', then took her into the house, where she was shown Beaumont's drawings and introduced to Mary and Dora. 'Do you think Mammy will be able to sleep tonight after having been shaken by the hand at our own door by a Queen – having talked with the Queen in this very room – & her old husband the old Poet having walked side by side & talked with her Majesty a full hour I am sure[?]'

August passed in the usual social whirl. The house was full of young people and there were picnics, excursions and sailings, culminating, on 31 August, in an ascent of Helvellyn. The seventy-year-old poet led the way, 'mostly poetising by himself', guiding his daughter, on her pony, with Quillinan on foot at her side. 'It was very steep, very hot work, very craggy at times, & in some places worse from being wet

& spongy, but we effected the ascent in about two hours &¼', Quillinan proudly
informed Rotha.

It is a curious fact, that even on that great steep mountain the Poet was followed by strangers
– rather a bore, yet an evidence of the reverence he is held in. – Nobody that is not here
can have the least idea how he is hunted, flattered, puffed, carest &c &c. It is enough to spoil
any human being.

The Wordsworths had a welcome visitor in Rogers, one of the very few living
poets who was older than William himself. He arrived in bad weather and with
gout, but this did not prevent the two friends spending a week together at Lowther
Castle, and making a brief excursion to Drumlanrigg, in Dumfriesshire, at the
invitation of the Duke and Duchess of Buccleuch. As Rogers arrived, Quillinan
and his daughter left Rydal Mount. After six weeks of daily contact with the
Wordsworths, Quillinan's marriage with Dora appeared no closer, but he was
making attempts to raise money by publishing a novel, *The Conspirators*, and was
not entirely without hope.

   Christmas was spent quietly at home, the family circle including both Isabella
Fenwick and Robinson, whose presence at this time of year was now taken for
granted. Much to Robinson's surprise, he found Dorothy 'amazingly' improved.

She can talk for a time rationally enough, but she has no command of herself and has the
habit of blowing with her lips very loudly and disagreeably and sometimes of uttering a
strange scream, something between the noise of a turkey and a partridge but more shrill
than either. She can be withdrawn from this only by being made to repeat verses, which she
does with great feeling, quite pathetically.

   It was while he was at Rydal Mount that Robinson was drawn into the tragedy
which marred Southey's last years and tore apart his family. Less than a year after
his wife's death, Southey had announced to his shocked children that he was going
to marry again. His new wife was Caroline, daughter of the poet William Lisle
Bowles. Twelve years his junior, she had been his admirer and correspondent for
more than twenty years. Initially, the Wordsworths had approved of Southey's
remarrying, and successfully persuaded Bertha and Kate to accept it for their
father's sake. Gradually, however, it became clear that Southey was losing his
mind; he was certainly not in full possession of his mental faculties when he married
in June 1839, and may not have been when he became engaged. This was bad
enough in itself, but worse still was the deteriorating relationship between the new
bride and her stepchildren, especially thirty-one-year-old Kate, who was the only
one still living at Greta Hall, and twenty-one-year-old Cuthbert, who had opposed
the match from the beginning. As Kate was a frequent visitor to Rydal Mount and
Bertha was living at the foot of the hill, the Wordsworths naturally heard more of
their side of the story, but they remained open-minded and counselled patience.
On 28 July 1839 William called on Mrs Southey to see if he could broker a peace

but, realizing that she was implacably hostile to Kate, decided not to intervene, and did not even tell Kate of his visit. Southey himself was in a pitiable state: he did not recognize William. After five minutes William left him as he had found him, 'patting with both hands his books affectionately, like a child'.

When Mrs Southey dismissed Betty, the devoted family servant, who had been with them for many years, refused to allow Kate to see her father for more than a few minutes, once a week, and succeeded in enlisting the support of Edith and her husband, John Warter (who were living far away in the south of England), against her brother and sisters, the Wordsworths could no longer remain neutral. William reluctantly endorsed Cuthbert's demands for a separate establishment within Greta Hall for Kate and for her to have a daily visit to her father. As Cuthbert inadvertently dated his letter from 'Rydal Mount' rather than 'Rydal Lodge', where he was staying with Bertha, Mrs Southey accused William of instigating the demands and denounced him to her clergyman and the Warters. Refusing to be drawn publicly into the mounting cycle of recrimination and bitterness, William wrote a letter to Robinson, setting out his role in the affair, and urged Kate to do the same, in the hope that ultimately these might serve to reconcile the warring siblings to each other, if not to Mrs Southey. A second sealed letter, defending Cuthbert's conduct and character, was entrusted to Robinson, to be used if needed – the unspoken fear being that Mrs Southey's control over her husband, and her open hostility to her stepson, would lead to his being disinherited. William's own position was now clear: 'I have continued, and shall continue to support, and do all in my power to comfort the Children of my afflicted Friend.' Robinson had seen and heard enough to convince him that his first impression in favour of Mrs Southey was wrong; though he refused to take sides, he willingly became the custodian of the written statements of the opposing parties and was given full discretion to show William's open letter wherever, and whenever, necessary.

The dissensions in the Southey family seem to have been a contributory factor in persuading William to withdraw his veto on Dora's marriage. Nothing had changed financially. Quillinan was still as poor as ever, his estate was encumbered and, at fifty years of age, he had no prospect of ever earning a satisfactory living. He had shown willing, however, with his publication of his novel and his insistence that Dora's own money, which would normally have become his on their marriage, should be settled on her to be 'absolutely out of reach of any misfortunes that may occur to me'. By the end of February, it was agreed that the marriage should take place before the summer was out.

After so many years of parental opposition to the match, Quillinan had wanted the ceremony to take place at Rydal and William to give his daughter away. Mary, Dora and Miss Fenwick, however, knew that this might be asking too much and a compromise was reached. The marriage would take place quietly in Bath, but all the Wordsworth family would attend. In an effort to sugar the pill to William, it was arranged that the wedding party would meet at Tintern Abbey before proceeding to Bath, and that the newlyweds would join William, Mary and Miss Fenwick afterwards for a short tour to Alfoxton, before going their separate ways. Herculean efforts were required to persuade both men to submit to these arrangements, but the females got their way.

A few days before the marriage took place, William received a confidential letter from his brother, Christopher, announcing his intention of making a gift to Dora, his goddaughter, of £1,000. It was a munificent present and one which transformed the prospects for the marriage: Dora would have the interest for life, passing to her children after her death; if she died childless, it was to be divided equally between her brothers.

Quillinan arrived at Bath on 8 May and took up residence at the White Hart Inn, on Stall Street. Apart from John's wife, who had just given birth to a sixth child, and 'old aunty', all the immediate Wordsworth family were there; Quillinan's was represented by his half-brother, John, on whose generosity he was largely dependent. Willy organized the marriage licence. John Quillinan insisted on choosing and buying Dora's wedding ring 'for luck'. At nine-thirty a.m. two carriages rolled up at North Parade, the first for the bride, her parents and Miss Fenwick, the second for Ebba and Miss Fenwick's niece, Miss Tudor, who were to be the bridesmaids. At the last minute, William's nerve failed, just as his sister's had at his own wedding, almost forty years before. He was so distressed by having to bid his daughter farewell that he came to Quillinan and said, 'I have told Dora that I would accompany you to church if you wished it, but this interview with my child has already so upset me that I think I can hardly bear it.' 'We all then begged him not to come,' Quillinan told Rotha, '... but he gave us his blessing very affectionately both before & after the wedding: nothing indeed could be kinder than he & all have been.'

At ten o'clock, on Tuesday 11 May 1841, Dora and Edward Quillinan were married in the beautiful Wren-style parish church of St James, at the foot of Stall Street. John Wordsworth conducted the ceremony and Willy gave away the bride, who was dressed in white poplin, with lace collar and cuffs (the latter given by her goddaughter), a silk tippet covered with net and trimmed with lace, and a white silk bonnet, decorated with white orange blossom, and a veil.

After the ceremony, the little party returned to North Parade for a wedding breakfast. William was waiting for them, calm and cheerful, and embraced both his daughter and son-in-law many times before they were allowed to proceed to cut their cake. At two-thirty the newlyweds set off for Piper's Inn, halfway between Wells and Bridgwater, where, next morning, they were joined by William, Mary, Willy and Miss Fenwick. The whole party then made what Mary herself called a '*pilgrimage*' to Alfoxton, where the now-famous poet received a very different reception from that of forty years before: the whole St Albyn family turned out to welcome him and several hours were spent 'most agreeably' in that most exquisite of places. The Friday after the wedding, Dora, Quillinan and Willy returned to the north; Willy left them at Kendal and the bridal pair went to spend the rest of their honeymoon at Rydal Mount. A month later, Dora wrote to Isabella Fenwick, 'I cannot let this last happy day of four happy weeks pass away from me without one word of deep & heartfelt thanks to you to whom I owe it all.' Her gratitude, she said, would be as constant as Miss Fenwick's own kindness, which had never failed for one second 'since my Good Angel first put me under your Angelic protection at Dover'.

William and Mary arrived at Rydal Mount on 22 July, after an absence of four months. Among the sixty-four visitors who called or stayed in August was George Washington Doane, the Bishop of New Jersey. Doane was a supporter of the Oxford Movement, as well as an admirer of William's poetry, and he added his weight to the request of several other American episcopalians that the poet would write on the subject of the daughter church in America for inclusion in his *Ecclesiastical Sonnets*. William bowed to the pressure, composing three sonnets, *Aspects of Christianity in America*, two on the Pilgrim Fathers, and the third celebrating Bishop White, the first Bishop of Pennsylvania, who had been consecrated in England by the Archbishop of Canterbury, and himself consecrated a further twenty-six American bishops. As with most of his poems written out of duty, they are competent, but uninspired.

Far more attractive were the lines he wrote this summer for Owen Lloyd, the curate of Langdale, whom the Wordsworths had known and loved since birth. The sunny, good-humoured youth, who had been a playmate of their own children and lived with them at Rydal Mount, had suffered frequent epileptic fits the previous year, which had left him so physically weak and mentally confused that he had been sent to the Retreat at York. His brother, Edward, and his wife had then taken him into their own home and there, on 18 April 1841, he had died, having just attained his thirty-eighth birthday. At his own request, his body was brought back to Langdale and buried under the shade of a yew he had himself planted in the little churchyard under the towering craggs at Chapel Stile. As the coffin was carried up Langdale, hundreds of people, most of them poor farmers and quarrymen, gathered by the roadside to greet the procession and follow their beloved pastor to his final resting place. The epitaph William wrote was, he thought, too long to serve its purpose, but others thought differently. It was adopted, in its entirety, and, though it clearly proved a challenge to the local stonemason, it can still be seen today, the humble headstone and crude lettering curiously at odds with the graceful cadences of the verse.

The epitaph for 'poor Owen' was one of only a handful of poems William wrote this year, but poetry was never far from his mind. By the end of 1840 *The Excursion* was out of print, and at William's suggestion the new edition, published this year, was printed in double columns stereotyped. He had two motives for this. First, in response to a number of letters he had received from the newly emerging class of educated labourers and mechanics, asking him to put the price of the book within their range; second, to prove to the opponents of the copyright bill that books would sell cheaply even if the term was extended.

More importantly, he had embarked on what was to be his last new publication in his lifetime. This volume was *Poems, Chiefly of Early and Late Years*, and, as its title suggested, it was a gathering together of all his work which had not been included in previous collections. It would see the first publication of his final version of the

Salisbury Plain poem, *Guilt and Sorrow*, and his tragedy *The Borderers*, as well as the hitherto-unseen *Memorials of a Tour in Italy, 1837*, which he was still adding to even as he revised the poems for the press. The decision to publish the early poems was a brave one: he risked drawing attention to, and reviving, all the old controversies about his poetic style and his radical political past.

While William compiled his new book, the correction of the six-volume edition, which was once more being printed this year, was consigned to Carter, his Stamp Office clerk. Six weeks after the corrections had been sent through, William was fretting because the new edition had not yet appeared. When it was finally published, early in the summer, its sale was unexpectedly slow. Only a quarter of the print run of 1,000 copies had been sold by the middle of November, which, in terms of recent sales, was a significant downturn. This was not a reflection on William, but an indication of a general malaise; profits in the whole London book trade were down to a sixth of what they had been only a year before. As he put the finishing touches to the volume over Christmas, William dithered over whether to publish or not. Was there any point if there would be little or no sale?

Christmas at Rydal Mount might have been a sad affair this year, had not Quillinan 'by a special act of generosity', allowed Dora to spend a month there. She arrived on Christmas Eve, escorted by Robinson, after a journey of only sixteen or seventeen hours, compared to the two nights on the road which had been obligatory only a few years earlier. There were the usual dinner and tea parties with the Arnolds, walks in daylight hours, rubbers of whist in the evenings. This Christmas, for the first time, Robinson was introduced to Frederick William Faber, the brilliant young Oxford graduate who was now a tutor in the household of William's cousin Dorothy Harrison. Faber had just returned from a tour of Greece and Turkey with her son, Matthew, during which a Galignani edition of William's poems had been his constant companion. On the Austrian border, as Faber had written to William at the time, the book was taken from him, tied up with string and sealed 'to silence you, till the Censor's verdict at Vienna'. As only the number of sealed books was noted on his passport, he had slipped off the string and seals on the poems and, with delicious irony, transferred them to a novel by Bulwer-Lytton. A customs official found the poems hidden in Faber's nightshirt, but the Viennese censor decided that, because the books were in English, they must be innocuous and returned them; 'Had he opened you among the Sonnets of Liberty, the consequences might have been different.' Robinson took an immediate dislike to this 'ultra-Puseyite High Churchman', but over dinner, and almost against his will, Faber's charm, intelligence and lively manner won him over. Though he still weakly protested his 'utter dissent' from most of Faber's opinions, the sheer power of the young man's personality had cast its spell.

If Robinson was entranced, William and his family were even more in thrall. Faber had taken the Lakes by storm in the summer of 1837, when, aged twenty-three, he was acting curate of Ambleside. Since then, he had been instrumental in securing the honorary doctorate for William at Oxford, paid many visits to Rydal Mount and established himself on intimate terms with the Wordsworths. As with Coleridge and Hamilton, William was dazzled by the younger man's talents. 'He had not only as good an eye for Nature as I have, but even a better one', William freely admitted; 'and he sometimes pointed out to me on the mountains effects which, with all my great experience, I had never detected.' As he walked with the poet, they also conversed, and their talk frequently turned to the subject of religion. The following year, 1842, Faber dedicated his book about his tour, *Sights and Thoughts in Foreign Churches and Among Foreign Peoples*, to William, thanking him not only for personal kindness but also for 'Many Thoughtful Conversations on the Rites, Prerogatives, and Doctrines of the Holy Church'. It was a significant – and double-edged – remark, by which Faber effectively claimed William for the Oxford Movement, just as Keble had done in his oration at Oxford in 1839. It suggested not just the younger man's deference to the older, but also that the poet had impressed *his* views upon the clergyman. This was the opposite of the truth. 'Wordsworth's own religion . . . would not satisfy either a religionist or a sceptic', Robinson had noted in 1836. This was still the case in 1841, and Faber was determined to change it. He wanted to purge all doctrinal unsoundness from William's poetry, particularly the suggestions of pantheism in the early works, and to encourage the poet, in both his life and his work, to become the standard-bearer of the Oxford Movement.

Faber's influence can be detected in a significant alteration to one of William's earliest poems. The old Salisbury Plain poem had ended with the sailor giving himself up to be hanged for the murder he had committed, but in a spirit of bitter defiance. In *Guilt and Sorrow*, the heavily revised version of 1841–2, he welcomes execution for ending the pangs of conscience he had suffered since committing his crime, his last words being, 'My trust, Saviour! is in thy name!' The importance of this change cannot be over-estimated. It is not the sentiment that is new: William had argued in his *Sonnets Upon the Punishment of Death* that remorse and penitence would lead the convicted criminal to welcome death. What is new is that this is the first explicit statement of belief in the redemptive powers of Jesus Christ in all William's poetry – and, indeed, in his prose. Coleridge had always said that William was not a Christian, using the term very precisely to mean that his friend did not believe that it was possible for the death of one man, however virtuous, to satisfy God for the sins of the whole world. Robinson had confirmed that this was still the case in more recent years, even reporting William's comment that 'perhaps' he did not feel the need for a Redeemer himself.

The sailor's declaration of trust in his Saviour's name was a complete reversal of this position and an acceptance of the single most important tenet of Christianity. Was William simply paying lip-service so as not to offend prevailing opinion or his many powerful clergymen friends? This seems unlikely, as he had never felt it necessary to do so before. The inescapable conclusion is that those 'Thoughtful Conversations' with Faber had led to a profound shift in his thinking. It was not a coincidence that, before the year was out, Faber persuaded William to nail a cedarwood cross above his bedroom window, 'where the good old man's pleased eye rests on it first thing when he wakes'. In doing so he claimed not just the poet, but also the man, and not just for the Oxford Movement, but also for Christ.

'W: is become more companionable being more tolerant than he used to be –',
Robinson remarked on 6 January 1842; 'he is now very busy preparing his new
Volume'. To Robinson's great delight, William had decided to dedicate to him the
Memorials of a Tour in Italy, 1837. The problem, as they both acknowledged, was his
unpoetic name. 'W: has confessed to me that he has taken much trouble And
written some half dozen lines but cannot make the ignoble name endurable in
verse – So he has given it up.' Instead, the dedication was titled *To Henry Crabb
Robinson*, and he was referred to as 'Companion!' in the verse. When Moxon
ventured to give him a sneak preview of the nine dedicatory lines, Robinson was
thrilled. 'They do not flatter my vanity,' he explained to Dora, 'but they make me
proud.' Neither extravagant nor fulsome in their praise, the simple lines exude the
one sentiment that really mattered to Robinson: they were sincere. 'They come
from the heart, and the highest praise, after all, that I can receive is that I am an
object of regard to such a man.' What is more, they acknowledged what he himself
thought had passed unnoticed:

> . . . kindnesses that never ceased to flow,
> And prompt self-sacrifice to which I owe
> Far more than any heart but mine can know.

26. Poet Laureate

On 6 April 1842, the eve of William's seventy-second birthday, the Copyright Bill which he had fought so long and hard to obtain was passed. Though watered down by amendments, it became law on 1 July 1842 and transformed the position of authors. The term of copyright was extended from twenty-eight to forty-two years from the date of first publication, or seven years after the author's death, whichever period was longer. The dogged perseverance of Talfourd ensured that the act reached the Statute Books but without William's years of sustained lobbying inside and outside Parliament, his contacts, his persistence, even his sheer longevity, which had proved the need for the legislation, there would have been no act.

It was ironic that it should have been passed at a time when the state of the book trade was so poor. 'Pray tell me what you think is the main cause of the great falling off in the Sale of books?' William asked Moxon. Was it, he wondered, that the frenzy of excitement caused by Charles Dickens's novels, published in serial form in the periodicals, was killing off the classics? This was a matter of some moment to William. His *Poems, Chiefly of Early and Late Years* was published in April 1842, but he was also preparing a new and greatly expanded edition of his *Guide Through the District of the Lakes* for the press.

There was another publication this spring. So insignificant it has been completely ignored by most biographers, even those who have noticed it have misunderstood its importance. The publication was *La Petite Chouannerie, ou Histoire d'un Collège Breton Sous l'Empire*, edited by a Frenchman, Alexis François Rio, and published in Paris by Olivier Fulgence. The book was a celebration of the Breton resistance to Bonaparte, and particularly of the role played by the boys at a college in Brittany who took the lead in the royalist uprising of 1815. It was naturally a subject close to William's heart and, when the author had approached him, the previous summer at a party at the Marshalls' in Grosvenor Square, William had apparently 'promised' to contribute a poem, if provided with sufficient detail. On 11 March 1842 Rio had written to William to call in this 'promise', informing the poet that he had already announced the inclusion of his poem in both England and Brittany 'as the expression of the most honourable sympathy for my countrymen' and hinting darkly that, without it, his favourite chapter on Napoleon and contemporary poets would have to be given up. When William wrote back, as he usually did, saying that he could not write to order, or at such short notice, he received a hysterical and accusatory reply from Rio. The entire book had been printed, except for thirty-two blank pages designated for the chapter 'which I have actually composed as a preface to your poem'. 'I have heard so much about the facility with which those compositions flow from your pen, that I thought it a superfluous precaution to send the materials a long time ago', Rio wailed. Only William and the Italian poet Alessandro Manzoni had let him down and, if necessary, he would have to delay publication till he had received the promised contribution.

William swallowed this story, hook, line and sinker. Tortured by guilt, he sought a way out of his quandary, and found it in the unlikely person of his son-in-law. William had always said that Quillinan knew 'my principles of style better I think than any one else'. Twenty years earlier, he had amended Quillinan's epitaph on his first wife to their mutual satisfaction. Now he did the same thing again, to fulfil an otherwise impossible engagement. Quillinan wrote the first draft of the poem, *The Eagle and the Dove*, and William corrected it so that it could be passed off as his own. '*He* has done the verses for the *Poet* – which are, or will be, satisfactory – when W. has "tinkered" them', Mary wrote on 10 May, adding the next day, 'Poor Q has been drudging at the Frenchman's Verses – which I hope are finished, tho' I hear the Poet humming at his Washing table.' The ominous humming did not indicate more correction, for the poem was dispatched that day to Moxon, with the command to send it off 'without the delay of a single post'.

In the strictest sense of the word, *The Eagle and the Dove* was, of course, a fraud. It is rather delicious to find, therefore, that it was composed in response to a fraud, for Rio had played exactly the same trick on Moore. 'He spoke to me in the midst of a crowded assembly, and I was not well able to make out his wishes or views on the matter', Moore wrote in his journal. 'Have since received a long letter from him . . . pressing me for the verses which they say I promised'. More seriously, however, the solution to this little difficulty was to be a seductive one for future problems which William would find hard to resist. Though he would refuse to include such hybrid productions in future editions of his poems, as he grew older and demands upon him increased, he was not averse to calling on Quillinan for assistance.

Relations with Quillinan had improved dramatically, once William was assured that his daughter was happy in her choice. Characteristically, William had made the first move, writing an unprompted and generous letter to his son-in-law at the beginning of March. If ever there was a moment when Quillinan might have expected William to round on him, it was then, when he was about to be prosecuted for fraud (financial, rather than poetical) in the highest courts of the land. As a trustee of his first wife's property, he had inadvertently become entangled in the complex business dealings of the Brydges family and was now to be tried for his part in defrauding the estate of some £15,000. 'My motive for writing this short letter is merely to assure you of our sympathy in your vexations and distresses,' William wrote,

and still more, very much more, to assure you that you need have no anxiety respecting judgment which we are likely to form of your character on these sad proceedings. We have all an entire confidence in your integrity from the first to the last, in your connection with the Brydges family, and the Barrett property, and furthermore are but too well aware of the generous sacrifices which you have made for them who have proved to be so unworthy of them. The confidence you reposed in them, however chargeable it may be with want of discretion, affords itself a strong presumption of your being incapable of joining in any dishonourable practice.

It was a particularly kind gesture, given Quillinan's notorious sensitivity to slights on his character and the very public nature of the proceedings, in which the Wordsworth name was bound to be invoked. Fortunately, Quillinan's friends were all of the same opinion. In April the Vice-Chancellor gave his judgement, clearing Quillinan of any dishonourable proceedings but holding him legally liable, with the other parties to the crime, for repayment of the missing £15,000. In doing so, he effectively ended any chance of Quillinan ever being able to make financial provision for his wife.

Even when the verdict became known, William avoided all recrimination, and at the beginning of May he, Mary and Willy went to London to give the Quillinans their full support. For the first time also, the Wordsworths stayed with the Quillinans, in their relatively humble lodgings at 7 Upper Spring Street, off Baker Street. William's main objective was to persuade the new Tory administration to appoint Willy to a better-paid government office. The Lowthers were the first port of call. Lord Lonsdale's oldest son, Lord Lowther, was Postmaster General and more than willing to help. He quickly quashed any idea of Willy obtaining a post for which he had not spent years in clerkship, but reverted instead to the old idea of William resigning his distributorship of the Stamp Office in favour of his son. This could be justified on the grounds that Willy was already employed in that department and that savings would be made by transferring the office to him at Carlisle. What no one could guarantee was that William's own loss of income (which he put at £400 a year) would be recompensed by an equivalent government pension.

The letter proposing the transfer to Willy was written and left for the Lowthers to deliver to Peel, the Prime Minister. The pension had to be left to chance. Willy was uncomfortable with the whole arrangement, not wishing to be responsible for his parents losing more than half their income at their time of life, but for William and Mary it was simply a huge relief to have their younger son settled in more suitable and secure employment. They were unconcerned about the prospect of being 'much straitened' and faced the necessity of 'the strictest economy' with perfect equanimity. What they found more difficult to contemplate was the loss of

Carter, who was as much part of the family as indispensable Stamp Office clerk. 'I cannot bear the thought of our ever losing him', Mary wrote in distress. 'Whatever comes of us we must never part with him.'

Despite this being a supposedly low-key visit, William kept up a frenetic pace astonishing in a seventy-two-year-old. 'Every thing here is lost in hurry and distraction', William complained, as he rushed from one gathering to another. Before they left town, William had to find time for several sittings to the artists who were clamouring to take his portrait. Significantly, two of the three were acts of charity. One was for his old friend, Haydon. Unable to get to the Lakes to paint William *in situ*, Haydon had agreed to make do with some sittings in London, supplying the backdrop from his imagination. The first sitting was a disaster. 'Wordsworth sat and looked venerable, but I was tired with the heat and very heavy, and he had an inflamed lid and could only sit in one light, a light I detest, for it hurts my eyes ... We talked of our merry dinner with C. Lamb and John Keats. He then fell asleep, and so did I nearly, it was so hot; but I suppose we are getting dozy.' A couple of days later, they had an altogether livelier session, during which Haydon decided he needed to measure William 'to ascertain his real height'. 'I measured him, and found him, to my wonder, eight heads high, or 5ft 9⅞ inches and of very fine, heroic proportions. He made me write them down, in order, he said, to show Mrs Wordsworth my opinion of his proportions.'

The resulting portrait is unquestionably the most striking and memorable image of William ever painted. It purports to show the poet on Helvellyn, composing his sonnet to Haydon. Though it bears no relation whatsoever to Quillinan's description of that event, it is an extraordinarily powerful portrayal of both the man and the poet. William stands, head slightly bowed, arms folded across his chest, deep in concentrated thought. There are no gimmicks to convey the idea that this is a poet at work, and no attempts to refine the features or the stance to something more gracefully approximating the poetic ideal. Put a flat cap on the head and the face beneath it is instantly recognizable as that of a type still seen today: the northern hill farmer of the Lakes, Dales or Pennines, stubborn, forthright and independent. Yet for all its down-to-earth realism, the portrait also conveys its subject's power of thought. Elizabeth Barrett, in a celebratory sonnet which she sent to William, through Haydon, later in the year, sums it up exactly:

> No portrait this with academic air!
> This is the poet and his poetry.

The second charity portrait was by Mrs Aders, who had played hostess to William, Dora and Coleridge at Godesberg in 1829. Her husband's business and health had failed, and Robinson begged William to sit to her, arguing that a successful portrait might not make her fortune, but it would lead to other commissions. The result was a profile which even the kindly Robinson was forced to admit was not a good likeness – 'A fierce expression and no character'.

With sittings for these two portraits, and to Pickersgill, William had neither time nor inclination to sit for John Lough, Haydon's friend, a sculptor who wanted to take his bust. The Wordsworths had always intended to spend only four or five weeks in town, but the shocking news of the sudden death of their friend Thomas Arnold, on 12 June, sent them hurrying back to Rydal. Arnold was only forty-seven. He had transformed the fortunes of Rugby school, been made Regius Professor of Modern History at Oxford in 1841 and left unfinished his great work, a *History of Rome*, but it was the impact of his death on his large family which everyone feared. 'What a happy house at once broken up!' Robinson exclaimed. William and Mary went over to Fox How to offer what comfort they could to the bereaved family. Always pragmatic at such times, William immediately relieved the afflicted widow of her anxiety about the management of the extensive grounds by offering to undertake it himself. 'We trust that, if we are spared, our society will be of much benefit to her', William wrote before the month was out.

A few days later Mary wrote to Robinson, begging him to come to Rydal Mount to relieve their solitude. He did so, but his departure coincided with that of Willy, Carter and the Stamps, a removal which affected the whole household deeply. Even Anne, the cook, commented that it was 'like a funeral going out of the house, when after so much bustle and pulling down in the Office, they had all passed away'. 'Seeing the last of what has been a nearly 30 years interest, could not but be seriously felt by us, at our age ', Mary told Miss Fenwick, 'and it *was* felt, but with thankfulness that what had been so great a benefit to us (in educating our children, and enabling us to live for so many years in the sort of hospitality we liked best), had passed into the hands of our beloved son – and grateful we are to those who have aided us in this object.' No news of a pension having been granted, Willy was still depressed at his father's sacrifice on his behalf – and more selfishly, dreaded the prospect of being tied to the Office by the presence of the Stamps.

It was not until 15 October that Peel himself wrote to tell William that his name had been placed on the Civil List and he would receive an annual pension of £300 for life. His acceptance of the pension, Peel informed him, would impose no obligations of either a political or a personal nature. 'It will prove a substantial addition to my comforts for the remainder of my life', William replied gratefully; 'and coming as the reward of literary merit from One so eminent in every respect as yourself the gratification is above measure enhanced.'

In fact the granting of the pension cast only one dark shadow. Caroline's husband, Baudouin, reading premature reports in the newspapers, wrote immediately to demand more money. Annette had died eighteen months earlier, on 10 January 1841 (an event which passed unnoticed in, or, more likely, expunged from, the Wordsworth correspondence); with her had also died the government pension which the family had relied on to supplement their income. Despite the supposedly final settlement William had negotiated in 1835, Baudouin was constantly on the look out for opportunities to extract more from his father-in-law. Once again it was left to Robinson, advised by Quillinan, to sort the matter out. Baudouin was given to understand, in no uncertain terms, that William had not the means to do anything further and that his own income had been reduced.

On 4 October 1842, the Wordsworths' fortieth wedding anniversary, Mary looked back with 'heart-felt thankfulness' over the years 'of uninterrupted harmony' they had spent together. 'We, like all mortals, have our sorrows, but these have been endeared to us by perfect sympathy, and only drawn us more closely to each other. Then this beautiful region in which we have been permitted to live – and in such home-society!' Even the loss, in different ways, of Sara, Dorothy and Dora, had been compensated for by the blessing of Isabella Fenwick's friendship. To the newly widowed Mary Arnold, the Wordsworths appeared 'as delightful a picture of old age as you can imagine – happy in themselves & by their loving kindness & benevolence ever contributing to the happiness of others'.

To her parents' undisguised joy, Dora returned to Rydal at the beginning of November, bringing her goddaughter, Rotha, with her. The ostensible reason was that the Quillinans' lodgings were being repaired, but Dora, as Robinson observed, 'looked very poorly' and it was obvious that life in London did not suit her. When Quillinan joined them, a few weeks later, what began as a temporary residence in Rydal lodgings soon became permanent. Though she was not under their own roof, Dora had at least rejoined the family circle. The Quillinans, with the indispensable Miss Fenwick, and Robinson, on his annual Christmas visit, were some compensation for the loss of Arnold, but they all felt his absence. Robinson in particular missed his old ally in his religious and political disputes with William – and was clearly rattled by the presence of Faber, whom he called 'a sad fanatic of an opposite character' and 'a flaming zealot for the new doctrines'. 'This Faber is an agreea[bl]e man,' he informed his brother. 'All the young ladies are in love with him And he has high spirits conversational talent & great facility in writing both polemics & poetry'. They had sparred together on every occasion they met, without either man losing his temper, though they had 'exchanged pretty hard knocks'. What disturbed Robinson was not Faber's avowed dislike of Protestantism and predilection for the Church in Rome ('not *of* Rome *yet*', Robinson predicted), but his apparent hold on William.

Earlier in the year, William had agreed that Samuel Wilkinson, editor of a High Church periodical, the *Christian Miscellany*, could publish a selection of his poetry in an article entitled 'Contributions of W. Wordsworth to the Revival of Catholic Truths'. Unusually, however, he asked to see a copy of the article before it was published, indicating that he had unspoken misgivings about the use that would be made of his poems. He was entirely justified. When the article arrived, he found that it included not just a selection from *Ecclesiastical Sonnets*, as he had expected, but extensive quotation from *The Excursion* and even *The Old Cumberland Beggar*. 'There is little I hope in my poetry that does not breathe more or less in a religious atmosphere; as these verses certainly do,' William protested, 'but if you were to take as wide a range as this Ex[tract] leads to, one scarcely sees why it should be selected in preference to many others.'

What Wilkinson was trying to do was to convince 'any timid Churchman that the doctrines [of the Oxford Movement], which are now branded as Popish, were a few years ago held without persecution, or even without reprehension, by men

whose zeal for the Anglican Church none suspect'. Rightly or wrongly, William
was now seen as the archetypal Anglican and by including, for instance, Faber's
note to *Musings Near Aquapendente* under the heading 'Mr Wordsworth's Opinion
of the Oxford Divines', the article sought to give his specific endorsement to the
Oxford Movement. 'The poet is a *high* churchman,' Robinson stated, 'but luckily
does not go all lengths with the Oxford School – He praises the *reformers* . . . for
inspir[in]g the age with deeper reverence for antiquity – And a more cordial
conformity with ritual observances – As well as a warmer piety – But he goes no
further'. But Wilkinson wanted him to go further and nail his colours to the mast.
'I rather think that I should better serve the cause we have in common, were I to
abstain from what you recommend', was William's careful response. 'It would seem
to enroll me as a partisan'. To the casual reader of 'Contributions of W. Wordsworth
to the Revival of Catholic Truths', that is exactly what William had become. 'He
is claimed by them as *their* poet', Robinson wrote indignantly. 'And they have
published a selection from his works with a dishonest preface from w[hi]ch one
might infer he went all lengths with them'. To Robinson it therefore came as
something of a relief when '*Faber* the ultra-catholic – (not *Roman*)' left Ambleside
for a Midlands curacy early in January 1843.

   With both Faber and Robinson gone, Isabella Fenwick hit on a happy idea for
keeping the poet amused during the long winter evenings which stretched ahead.
She persuaded William to dictate to her a series of notes on his poems, describing
when, where and why they were written. The indispensable tool of all future critics
and biographers, the Fenwick Notes, as they became known, were intended
primarily for the private information of Miss Fenwick and Dora, though, as they
expanded in length and importance, William clearly anticipated that they would
also be circulated among his friends. What makes them so fascinating to the modern
reader is not just the invaluable factual information they contain, but the insights
they give into the poet's mind and character. Miss Fenwick made no attempt to
polish the conversational style of the dictation into something more approaching
a literary essay. The entries range from an abrupt '1799. Germany' for 'A Slumber
did my Spirit Seal' to a five-page discourse prompted by *Epistle to Sir George Beaumont*.
They include, as conversation does, both personal anecdote and impressions of
people and places, together with the occasional digression into diatribe on subjects
which aroused his passion. Most of all what they do is make one realize how much
we have lost through William's hostility to the whole idea of biography.

   The miseries of the extended Southey family affected the Wordsworths deeply
this spring. Sara Coleridge's husband died on 26 January, after a long and painful
illness. His death was not unexpected, but they grieved for his young widow. 'She
is much beloved in this House, as she must be wherever she is half as well known
as we know her'. On 1 February Herbert and Bertha Hill left Rydal for Warwick,
where, thanks in part to a glowing reference from William, Herbert had secured
the headmastership of the Royal Grammar School. 'They will be much missed in
our village,' William wrote sadly, 'and Mr Hill exceedingly both on his own
account, and because there will no doubt be a great falling off in his Successor.'

His daughter had only just left the Lakes when Southey himself had a seizure so violent it left no hope of recovery. He died on 21 March, aged sixty-eight, fought over to the last by his warring wife and children, but passing away 'as gently as a child falling into slumber'. William was pointedly not invited to the funeral by the widow, but he went anyway. Quillinan drove him over early on the dark stormy morning of the funeral and accompanied him to Crosthwaite churchyard, where they were joined by John, and his seven-year-old son William, who was Southey's godson.

Southey was barely cold in his grave before rumours began to circulate about who would replace him as Poet Laureate. The London rumour-mill had it that there were only two possible candidates, the sixty-six-year-old Scottish balladeer Tom Campbell and the thirty-four-year-old Alfred Tennyson. Yet on 30 March the Lord Chamberlain, Earl de la Warr, wrote to William, offering him the position. Like the offer of the Civil List pension, it was put in a way that could not fail to touch William personally. 'May I be allowed to add', the Earl wrote, 'that it is with feelings of very peculiar gratification, that I find myself in a position to propose this mark of distinction to an Individual, whose acceptance of it would shed an additional lustre upon an Office in itself highly honorable.' Instead of instantly and gratefully accepting this final accolade as the triumphant vindication of a career dedicated to changing poetic taste and judgement, William turned it down. 'The Appointment I feel . . . imposes Duties which far advanced in life as I am I cannot venture to undertake and I must therefore beg leave to decline the acceptance of an offer that I shall always remember with no unbecoming pride.' 'Had I been several years younger I should have accepted the office with pride and pleasure', he explained to Lord Lonsdale's daughter, but at his age (one might almost add, at any age) he dreaded the obligation to produce verses to order. 'I hope, therefore, that neither you nor Lord Lonsdale, nor any of my friends, will blame me for what I have done.'

In the end, it was a letter from Peel which persuaded William to change his mind. The Prime Minister assured him that the offer had been made only 'in order to pay you that tribute of Respect which is justly due to the first of living Poets' and that it had both his own and the Queen's entire concurrence. 'Do not be deterred by the fear of any obligation which the appointment may be supposed to imply', Peel urged. 'I will undertake that you shall have nothing <u>required</u> from you. But as the Queen can select for this honorable appointment, no one, whose claims for respect and honor on account of Eminence as a Poet, can be placed in "competition with yours" – I trust you will no longer hesitate to accept it.' How could he do otherwise? On 4 April, three days before his seventy-third birthday, William accepted 'with unalloyed pleasure . . . this high Distinction'.

The appointment was drawn up, William took the oath of allegiance before Thomas Dawson, a local magistrate, and Moxon was given power of attorney to collect the annual salary of £70 a year. Despite the assurances to the contrary, however, William felt the pressure to perform. In July he received an invitation to attend the Queen's Ball, which fortunately arrived only the day before, enabling him to plead 'impossibility for non-obedience', but it was only a matter of time before he would have to make a public appearance. Worse still, through his brother, who had stayed overnight with Earl de la Warr, he received a hefty hint that, though nothing was required of him officially, 'yet ... if your Muse should happen to be in the humour, and could avail herself of any little event which befell the Queen, or any undertaking in which she might happen to engage herself, – he was certain it would be very well taken'. The ever-resourceful Quillinan, disgusted with the idolatrous nature of previous Laureate offerings, suggested that William should compose 'in his own grand way' a hymn invoking 'a blessing on the Queen & Country, or giving thanks for blessings vouchsafed & perils averted'. 'This w[oul]d be a new mode of dealing with the office of laureat[e], & w[oul]d come with dignity & propriety I think, from a Seer of Wordsworth's age & character.' The muse, however, remained stubbornly silent.

William's seventy-third birthday, put off from 7 April to the 20th 'in royal fashion', as Quillinan teased, was celebrated in grand style, as became his new status. Around 130 schoolgirls came to a tea-drinking in Mr North's field and danced to music supplied by a fiddler. The Quillinans organized the event, with the help of the Ambleside Robinsons and Briggses, but it was, of course, Miss Fenwick, who provided the funds for the entertainment.

William's public triumphs were in marked contrast to the private distresses closing in on him. At the beginning of February Willy had surprised and delighted his family by announcing his engagement to Mary Monkhouse, the twenty-one-year-old daughter of his mother's cousin Tom. 'Master Willy might have done worse', was Quillinan's laconic comment. 'She is a nice girl enough – just of age, & has a pretty good fortune – I believe not less than £20,000 besides what she will have from her Uncle Monkhouse. In a worldly point of view it is an excellent match for Willia[m] & in every way we are all inclin[ed to] hope & believe not a bad one for e[ither] party.' Mary's guardians, John Monkhouse and Samuel Horrocks, both gave their joyful consent and everyone welcomed the idea of the Wordsworths and Monkhouses being drawn closer together. Willy's Uncle Christopher offered £100 as a wedding present and his own services to perform the marriage ceremony at Brinsop. Then just as suddenly as the engagement had been announced, it was broken off. Mary Monkhouse broke off a second engagement in 1845 when she decided that her suitor was more interested in her purse than her person (had she suspected this of Willy too?), and ultimately married the Reverend Henry Dew, rector of Whitney in Herefordshire.

While Willy moped at Rydal Mount, his brother's marriage was falling apart. Isabella had been taken seriously ill the previous September: first typhus had been suspected, then it was thought that she was pregnant, and by May, when it was clear she was not, internal inflammation was diagnosed. Clearly, having six children in eight years and the stresses of life on a parson's income were taking their toll on a young woman brought up to expect a life of luxury. The doctors recommended that she should spend the winter in Madeira and on 26 October Isabella, her husband, their daughter, Jane, and penultimate child, Charles, who was almost four, embarked for Madeira, leaving their four other sons, aged between nine and two, in the care of the governess at Brigham. John would eventually return to his old life, but his wife, having developed a taste for the life of the leisured invalid traveller, would not.

It was ironic that, as Isabella went abroad to recover her health, William's nephew 'Keswick' John was trying to return home for the same reason. He had developed the preliminary stages of consumption, and his medical training enabled him to observe the progress of his own disease with a morbid fascination which would lead to frequent bouts of depression. Arriving at Rydal Mount in June, he divided his time between his uncle's family there and 'cousin Dorothy' Harrison, at Green Bank, before settling into his own little cottage at Ambleside to await the inevitable.

William and Mary had intended to visit Brinsop Court in the summer, partly to see Mary's crippled brother, Tom, and partly to avoid the influx of Lakers. Their departure was delayed by concerns about Isabella and visits from John and two of his sons, then by the news that Mary's sister Joanna had suffered a paralytic attack while on a visit to their nephew at Elton, near Stockton. Early reports were favourable, but a month later, she took a sudden turn for the worse and Mary and William set out immediately for Elton, leaving the Quillinans to take charge of Dorothy and Rydal Mount in their absence. It was an uncomfortable and distressing visit, for though they arrived to find Joanna better than they had expected, her nephew, George Sutton, with whom she was staying, was obviously deranged. Instead of simply nursing Joanna, the Wordsworths found themselves arranging lodgings out of his house for her in the village and organizing for Dr Belcombe, who ran a private asylum in York, to send an attendant to confine George within his own home, 'till it shall please God to mitigate the disease of mind under which He is labouring'.

William and Mary arrived at Brinsop on 20 September, having spent six happy hours exploring York in the company of their Robinson relations and attended a service in the Minster, which was (as it always seems to be) in a state of disrepair following a fire in the nave in 1840. Five days after their arrival, on 25 September, Joanna died. She was buried, quietly and simply, as she wished, in the tiny churchyard of the equally tiny church of St John's at Elton, a few hundred yards from the grossly extravagant pile of George Sutton's Elton Hall. The little she possessed in her lifetime had been severely diminished by the decision of the Mississippi State Government to renege on paying interest to its stock-holders, but even that little became a subject of dispute. Her will, written on 5 April 1841, had left the remainder of her personal estate to her brother George, whose misfortunes she had always grieved over, but an improperly executed codicil, dated 27 March 1843, left the money in her savings bank (which was effectively the residue) to her nephew, Jack's son, Henry Hutchinson, who lived in Peel, on the Isle of Man. This was literally a matter of less than £50, but it was an equally important sum to both George and Henry; the latter won, producing inscrutable Manx law as his trump card.

Robinson, who had joined the Wordsworths at Brinsop in the hope of accompanying William on a tour of Wales, observed the stricken silence as Joanna's death was announced and knew that his excursion was doomed. He left the family to their grief, which was soon to be compounded by the death of their old servant, 'dear and good and faithful Jane'. She was buried, next to the Hutchinsons, in the family plot at Brinsop, the Wordsworths testifying to their affection by erecting a headstone in her memory.

Too depressed to pay their visits to friends on the way back to the Lakes, William and Mary decided to face up to family responsibilities and went straight to Rydal Mount. They arrived to find John no better, but no worse, and, for the poet, one of those troublesome tasks of duty which he most disliked, a request to write the epitaph for Southey's monument in Crosthwaite church. There was clearly no one more appropriate, but William had written only a handful of poems over the last twelve months. These did include two significant ones. The first was his beautiful sonnet on Wansfell, whose swelling heights formed the horizon of his own Vale of Rydal, written on Christmas Eve, 1842. This William himself declared to be 'one of his most perfect as a work of art'. In it, he reproached himself for never celebrating the mountain before in his verse, 'For all that thou, as if from heaven, hast brought Of glory lavished on our quiet days'.

> Bountiful Son of Earth! when we are gone
> From every object dear to mortal sight,
> As soon we shall be, may these words attest
> How oft, to elevate our spirits, shone
> Thy visionary majesties of light,
> How in thy pensive glooms our hearts found rest.
>   *['Wansfell! this Household has a favoured lot'], ll.7–14*

The importance of these lines lies not in their beauty, but in the sentiment, which Faber would have deplored, since, despite all his efforts to eradicate such pantheism, it comes as close as anything William had written in his early days to worshipping God in nature. Faber might have imposed the cross upon the poet, but he could not tear out the instinctive heresy in his heart.

The second poem was important for a different reason. *Grace Darling* sang the praises of the daughter of a Farne Island lighthouse-keeper who, in September 1838, with her father, had rowed out to a sinking steamship and rescued nine survivors. Her courage, her sex and her youth (she was only twenty-three at the time of the rescue) had captured the public imagination. For William she was another Lucy, 'Known unto few but prized as far as known'. His tribute came four and a half years after the event – too late for Grace, who had died in 1842 – but it was extraordinary that it came at all, for it cannot have been written without conjuring up visions of the fate of his own brother John.

Like everything connected with poor Southey's last years, the question of a monument was fraught with difficulties and dissensions. 'My verse days are almost over', William had written to Haydon in April. His first impulse then had been to write a prose epitaph, which illustrated perfectly his own dictum that these things were better written after the passage of time. A bare third was devoted to a somewhat anodyne list of Southey's virtues, the rest to the 'slowly-working and inscrutable malady' which had 'prematurely and almost totally obscured' his mind and should serve as a *carpe diem* warning to others. Written less than three months after Southey's death, when the insanity which had afflicted his last five years was painfully uppermost in William's mind, it did not do justice to the vibrant man, poet and scholar of the previous sixty-odd years who was the real Southey. Thankfully, it was rejected, in favour of a far warmer tribute in verse which made only passing allusion to the tragedy of his final years as 'his griefs':

> Ye vales and hills whose beauty hither drew
> The poet's steps, and fixed him here, on you
> His eyes have closed! And ye, loved books, no more
> Shall Southey feed upon your precious lore,
> To works that ne'er shall forfeit their renown,
> Adding immortal labours of his own – ...
> His joys, his griefs, have vanished like a cloud
> From Skiddaw's top; but he to heaven was vowed
> Through his industrious life, and Christian faith
> Calmed in his soul the fear of change and death.
> *Inscription for a Monument in Crosthwaite Church,*
> *in the Vale of Keswick, ll.1–6, 15–18*

Christmas was an altogether more sedentary affair this year. There was no Arnold, or Faber, to walk with, and Robinson disabled himself by falling down the stairs of his lodgings on Christmas Eve. The Wordsworths insisted on transferring him to Rydal Mount, where he was nursed with tender care by their manservant, James Dixon. Brought up in a workhouse, James had been thrown out at the age of nine with 2s in his pocket. On the verge of destitution, he had been taken into service by a farmer and had never been out of a place since. 'He is forty-five years of age, and is really a sort of model servant for a country situation like this,' Robinson admired, 'as he is very religious and moral, as well as an excellent servant ... He is a great favourite with the family, and will, I dare say, never leave them.' Not only could he read and write, but he was a musician and artist, with a talent for wood-carving and painting pace eggs. Such was Robinson's gratitude for his care that, on parting, he presented James with a silver watch, a gift which left him literally speechless.

To the Wordsworths Robinson was equally generous, presenting them with a new set of gilt-rimmed tea and breakfast china. 'Never, since we were housekeepers, did we possess a *Company* Tea Service', Mary wrote in high delight and it made its first appearance on what she proudly called 'The *Laureate's* birth Day'. This year Miss Fenwick extended her invitation to the local schoolboys, as well as girls, so over 300 children came to Rydal Mount to celebrate William's seventy-fourth birthday, accompanied by almost half as many adults of all ages and classes. Tea and currant cake were dispensed to all comers and the children were encouraged to play hide-and-seek through the grounds while the elderly took tea inside the house. Tables were set up on the terrace, covered with moss, laurel leaves and daffodils, and laden with oranges, gingerbread and painted pace eggs, which were presented to the children before they left. Miss Fenwick having provided the feast, she shared the honours with William in getting three cheers from the assembled company. 'I must own I wish that little commemorations of this kind were more common among us', William remarked wistfully. 'One would wish to see the rich mingle with the poor as much as may be upon a footing of fraternal equality. The old feudal dependencies and relations are almost gone from England, and nothing has yet come adequately to supply their place.'

One of the last of those ties had just been broken. On 19 March 'William the Good', Earl of Lonsdale, died in his eighty-seventh year. 'Of my own feelings upon this loss I shall content myself with saying, that as long as I retain consciousness I shall cherish the memory of your father,' William wrote to Lady Mary, 'for his inestimable worth, as one who honoured me with his friendship, and who was to myself and my children the best benefactor.' His son, William, Lord Lowther, for whom William had campaigned in so many elections, succeeded to the Earldom and the Lord Lieutenancy of Cumberland and Westmorland. Fortunately, no epitaph was required or expected of the Poet Laureate, though his advice on an appropriate memorial was sought – and ignored.

The Wordsworths were, as usual, inundated with visitors over the summer, more than 270 of them tramping over the black and white tiles of the entrance porch. One of Robinson's Christmas gifts, they spelt out the appropriate Latin message 'SALVE', or 'Welcome'. The Quillinans, who had spent a few weeks at Flimby, on the Cumberland coast, in a vain effort to instil some better health into Dora, returned in August to spend three months on Belle Isle, the Curwen-owned island near the Windermere ferry. The island was an excellent alternative venue for visitors to Rydal Mount who wanted to picnic or fish on the lake, though getting there had its hazards, as the seventy-year-old Christopher discovered, when he fell into the water at the boathouse.

'We have had swarms of Company since you left us,' William wrote to Moxon on 12 September, 'a great part of whom we would willingly have exchanged for a few days more of your society.' Among the visitors had been not only Moxon himself, and Rogers, but an American artist, Henry Inman, who had been commissioned to paint William's portrait by one of his American editors, Professor Henry Reed, of Philadelphia. To the Wordsworths' astonishment, Inman required only half-hour sittings, and completed the portrait in just nine, but, Dora declared, it was 'by far the best painted likeness yet taken – my Mother even is quite satisfied – the likeness as to features is perfect'. A remarkably candid head-and-shoulders portrait, it is indeed so realistic it could easily be mistaken for a photograph.

Another visitor to Rydal Mount in September was Faber, who had just gained

William's permission to reprint his *Stanzas Suggested in a Steamboat off Saint Bees'*
Heads in his *Life of St Bega*. It was an unexceptionable request – the poem was about
St Bega's life – but what Faber did with it was not. He printed it in Newman's *Lives*
of the English Saints, with a prefatory note, praising the poem as 'a fresh instance of
the remarkable way in which [Wordsworth's] poems ... anticipate the revival of
catholic doctrines among us' and proof of William's own 'affectionate reverence
for the catholic past'. It was clear, when they met now, that William was beginning
to have reservations about Faber. 'He is in the habit of using strong expressions, so
that what he says must be taken with some qualification', William told Miss
Fenwick. 'This practise in so very pious, good and able a man is deeply to be
regretted.' They talked, at length, about Faber's own poetry, which William urged
him to give up. 'A man like him cannot serve two Masters. He has vowed himself
as a Minister of the Gospel to the service of God. He is of that temperament that
if he writes verses the Spirit must *possess* him, and the practise master him, to the
great injury of his work as a Priest.'

Entertaining a party of Quakers on the terrace a few days later, he revealed that,
whatever tinge of disillusionment had crept over his relationship with Faber, his
belief in the central doctrine of redemption, which Faber had brought to him,
remained undiminished. Watching the landscape emerge with perfect clearness
after a wet morning, William commented, 'It is like the human heart emerging
from sorrow, shone on by the grace of God.' When he was asked whether he
thought the scenery had any effect on the minds of poorer people, he replied that
he believed it did, that it dwelt silently within them, though they could not express
it in neat phrases. 'How constantly mountains are mentioned in Scripture as the
scene of extraordinary events', he pondered aloud:

the Law was given on a mountain, Christ was transfigured on a mountain, and on a mountain
the great Act of our Redemption was accomplished, and I cannot believe but that when the
poor read of these things in their Bibles, and the frequent mention of mountains in the
Psalms, their minds glow at the thought of their own mountains, and they realise it all more
clearly than others.

When William spoke of the poor in this way, he meant the rural poor, who were
natives of the Lakes. His view of the urban poor was quite different, as he was
about to make clear, very publicly, to the mortification and embarrassment of his
friends.

In the latter half of September, the Wordsworths learned that a new company,
the Kendal and Windermere Railway, had been formed, with the express intention
of linking Kendal with the Lancaster and Carlisle Railway at Oxenholme and
carrying the line through as far as Lowwood, on Windermere. There could be no
financial justification for extending the line so far merely for the sake of the
inhabitants; it was obvious that the developers expected to recoup their costs and
make their profits from an influx of working-class tourists from the manufacturing
towns of Yorkshire and Lancashire. It was equally obvious to someone as shrewd

as William that the railway would not stop just outside Ambleside. A railway was already under construction between Cockermouth and Keswick, which would ultimately link up the great towns of Whitehaven and Workington to the west, and Penrith to the east. All that would be missing, were the line to Lake Windermere completed, would be a link between Lake Windermere and Keswick – which could only run as the road did, straight through the Vales of Rydal and Grasmere. The view from Rydal Mount, which had been a source of daily pleasure and inspiration to the poet, would never be the same.

William's whole spirit revolted against this desecration of his paradise and, despite his seventy-four years, he flung himself into the campaign with all the vigour of a man half his age. Once again, as he had done when protesting against local enclosures, he would become the voice of the silent hills. 'Is there no nook of English ground secure From rash assault?' he wrote, in a sonnet composed in response to the threat.

> Plead for thy peace, thou beautiful romance
> Of nature; and, if human hearts be dead,
> Speak, passing winds; ye torrents, with your strong
> And constant voice, protest against the wrong.
> *On the Projected Kendal and Windermere Railway,*
> *ll.1–2, 11–14*

The sonnet was published in the *Morning Post* on 12 October and was rapidly reprinted in most of the other national and provincial newspapers. There were many other opponents of the scheme, particularly among the proprietors of land over which the railway would run, but William's name, his status as Poet Laureate and his willingness to stand forward publicly, made it seem as if he alone was barring the way of progress. In the age of railway mania, this appeared to be sheer folly. He was accused of being reactionary, élitist, selfish and even, when his sonnet *Steamboats, Viaducts, and Railways* was quoted, or his reputation as the poet of the poor cited, hypocritical. 'Now that the rail road is coming home to Ambleside, he does not like it. This mere poetical view would equally oppose high-roads', his hitherto loyal disciple Barron Field sneered, in what was the typical response. 'There will always be plenty of nooks for rural retirement.'

William and Mary returned to Rydal Mount early in November after a scant month's absence, to find Dora so unwell that she was again confined to the sofa in her parental home. 'Mr Wordsworth is returned in very good looks, & considerably tranquillized about the Railroad', Mary Arnold observed. The managers of what William called the 'obnoxious' Kendal and Windermere Railway had modified their plans in his absence. The terminus was now to be a mile from Bowness, instead of Lowwood, and it was proposed that a steamer would bring the trippers down Windermere to Ambleside.

Though this decision reduced the immediate threat to the vales of Rydal and Grasmere, it did not remove it altogether and, in any case, the principle remained the same. William was not content to let the matter drop. He wrote two long letters to the *Morning Post* which were published on 11 and 20 December. He did not mince his words, but his turn for the inflammatory phrase now worked against him. His three main arguments against bringing the railway into the heart of the Lakes were simple, effective and, as any visitor today would acknowledge, basically true. The chief attractions of the district were 'its beauty and its character of seclusion and retirement', which a large-scale influx of tourists would destroy. Secondly, anyone who truly wanted to visit the Lakes could already do so easily, whatever his station in life: it cost nothing to walk (as William himself had done many a time) the nine miles from Kendal to Windermere. Thirdly, and more contentiously, he argued that a true appreciation of the scenery was 'neither inherent in mankind, nor a necessary consequence of even a comprehensive education'. Factory hands would gain more benefit from a quiet stroll through the fields near their homes on a Sunday than from being hurtled through the Lakes on cheap railway excursions paid for by their employers. 'Once for all let me declare that it is not against Railways but against the abuse of them that I am contending', he declared towards the end of his second letter. In opposing the undertaking, he spoke not merely for the inhabitants of the Lakes, whose way of life was threatened, but 'for the sake of every one, however humble his condition, who coming hither shall bring with him an eye to perceive, and a heart to feel and worthily enjoy'.

There was nothing new in any of these arguments. William had been making the same points for forty years, complaining about the fashionable Lakers who drove past reading their guidebooks, or falling asleep in their carriages, instead of walking, looking and genuinely appreciating for themselves. In setting himself against the railway, however, he laid himself open to the charge of being what we would call a snob. Comments about the inevitable increase in wrestling matches, horse and boat races, and pot-houses and beer-shops, catering for the taste of these working-class visitors, did not help. Nor did references to the 'Advance, of the Ten thousand ... We should have the whole of Lancashire, and no small part of Yorkshire, pouring in upon us to meet the men of Durham, and the borderers from Cumberland and Northumberland.' Such remarks played into the hands of his opponents, who summed up his view, in the famous opening line of Horace's ode, *Odi profanum vulgus, et arceo*, 'I loathe the common crowd, and drive them from me.'

William attended meetings of Railway Opposition, but he was fighting a lost cause and he knew it. 'I have not the least hope of preventing the Bill being sent to a Committee,' he wrote to Robinson in February, 'but my Letters may prepare an efficient Opposition to another [Bill] which will surely follow this', namely, for a railway from Ambleside to Keswick. In this he was indeed successful. The railway would be carried only as far as Bowness – for which every lover of the Lakes must be forever indebted to him. But it was not without its personal cost. In their recommendation to Parliament, the Board of Trade administered a very public reproof to William.

We must ... state that an argument which goes to deprive the artisan of the offered means of occasionally changing his narrow abode, his crowded streets, his wearisome task and unwholesome toil, for the fresh air, and the healthful holiday which sends him back to his work refreshed and invigorated – simply that individuals who object ... may retain to themselves the exclusive enjoyment of scenes which should be open alike to all ... appears to us to be an argument wholly untenable.

What is more, because his opposition was misunderstood in this way, there is no doubt that his reputation suffered. Barron Field was not alone in asking how the man who had spent almost the last half-century creating a taste for mountains and lakes by extolling them in his poetry could object if the inhabitants of Liverpool and Manchester wanted to see the places he had made famous for themselves? 'I wish he would either complete "The Recluse" or lock up his desk', Field wrote indignantly to Robinson.

27. *Fixed and Irremovable Grief*

The Christmas of 1844–5 was enlivened by the presence of a newcomer to the Lakes, Harriet Martineau, who had overcome deafness to make a name for herself as the authoress of tales of political economy. Robinson was a great admirer of Miss Martineau and was determined to effect a meeting between her and William. This would be difficult. She was staying with another political economist, William Rathbone Greg, who had made his fortune in the cotton trade and retired to Ambleside in 1842 for the sake of his wife's health. The Gregs felt that they had been snubbed by the Wordsworths, who had never called during that time, so it would be awkward to meet there. More importantly, the Wordsworths were appalled by Miss Martineau's widely publicized claims to have recovered from an incurable disease by means of mesmerism, a fashionable form of hypnosis.

The meeting eventually took place on 16 January, on neutral ground, at Dr Davy's new house on the Rydal side of Ambleside. 'By tacit consent the conversation was on purely indifferent matters,' Robinson noted. 'This was better than controversy.' There would have been plenty of opportunity for dispute. Miss Martineau and the Gregs were ardent believers in, and practitioners of, mesmerism; William, Davy and his mother-in-law, Mrs Fletcher, were all scornfully sceptical. William was a High Churchman, a conservative and passionate advocate of the Ten Hours' Bill, which would reduce the daily hours worked by factory hands to a maximum of ten; Greg was a Unitarian, an ultra-radical and, as a cotton-mill owner, opposed any reduction in his workers' hours. The two men were civil, but notably cool, towards each other, though William, meeting and liking Mrs Greg, let it be known that his failure to call had been the fault of old age and distance, rather than a deliberate slight.

William and Miss Martineau both carefully refrained from comment on each other before their mutual friend. Robinson rightly took this to mean that they were both afraid of saying what he would not want to hear. Miss Martineau, though her letters of the time were much more favourably disposed, reserved her venom for a snide account in her *Autobiography*, in which, against all the evidence, she claimed that the Wordsworths sought her opinion as to the possibility of mesmerism curing Dora, mocked William's northern accent, frostily misunderstood his attempts at humour and declared that his 'pieces', as she termed his poems, were not enough to make the man a poet. William was more generous, admitting to Isabella Fenwick that he found Miss Martineau's manners 'a little abrupt and peremptory – But it might be that I was mistaken, I mean in not making sufficient allowance first for her being a Dissenter, and next for being what is somewhat vulgarly called a "BLUE" [-stocking] . . . for everybody else seems to like her without the least drawback.' Miss Martineau was sufficiently enchanted with the scenery to declare her intention of living in the Lakes for six months, eventually settling permanently in her own house at Ambleside. Robinson predicted that she would not 'become cordial' with the Wordsworths, but even she admitted that they were very kind to her.

'The *beauty* of the season with us has exceeded anything –', William enthused early in January, 'such glorious effects of sunshine and shadow, and skies that are quite heavenly in the evenings especially; with moon and mountain-clouds setting each other off in a way that really has transported us to look upon'. The lake was frozen over, so James Dixon, the good-natured 'Skaiting-Master' to all the novices in the vale, and even 'Keswick' John, who was enjoying a brief remission from his consumption, were able to skate several times.

John's fate was inevitable, but Dora's was not. Her family were deeply concerned about her. Throughout the winter and spring she ailed one thing after another, mostly, as her husband and mother suspected, caused by her habit of starving herself. As colds and coughs succeeded one another, each one further wearing down her already fragile frame, Quillinan began to formulate the idea of taking her to Portugal, where the climate and a complete change of lifestyle might restore her. His brother owned a pretty little holiday villa at the mouth of the Douro, three miles from Oporto, and he offered this to the Quillinans for as long as they wished. Apart from the fear of leaving her elderly parents, Dora was 'hopeful & eager to go'. Quillinan began to make travel plans, which were abruptly broken off on 7 April, William's seventy-fifth birthday, when they all gathered at Miss Fenwick's lodgings in Ambleside to hold a celebratory dinner. Everyone talked eagerly of the Oporto plan, but one person, Mary, said nothing '& it was too evident that she was very low on the subject'. Dora was immediately flung into uncertainty as to whether she ought to go and Quillinan, with his usual haste, decided to throw up the scheme: 'if she went it could do her no good to be fretting because she would feel that her Mother was fretting.'

A week after William had informed Moxon that Dora had 'given up the thought of going to Portugal', there was a complete change of heart. The concerted efforts of William, Miss Fenwick and, especially, Dr Davy, convinced Mary that she had to accept this temporary parting. Before she had a chance to have second thoughts, the Quillinans set off for London on 23 April, sailing for Oporto during the first week in May. By a happy coincidence, William had received a second invitation from the Lord Chancellor to attend the Queen's Ball on 25 April, so he could accompany his daughter at least as far as London. After two years as Poet Laureate, it was only 'right & decent' that he should not defer his formal presentation to the Queen any longer.

Rogers, who was now eighty-two and remarkably untouched by age, physically or mentally, coached William through the ceremony, arranging with the Lord Chamberlain that he should not have to pass through the crowds but would be formally noticed, and lending him his own court dress. So, wearing Rogers's bag wig, plum-coloured, high-collared coat with deep cuffs and large silver buttons, shirt with a white jabot falling over a waistcoat, knee breeches, white stockings and flat shoes with silver buckles, and with Sir Humphry Davy's sword buckled to his side, 'science and art being thus fraternally united', William made his way to the Palace. 'The reception given me by the young Queen at her Ball was most gracious', William told everyone. The wife of the American minister Edward Everett was so moved that, as she told Rogers afterwards, she shed tears. 'To see a grey haired Man 75 years of age kneeling down in a large assembly, to kiss the hand of a young Woman is a sight for which institutions essentially democratic do not prepare a spectator of either sex', William intoned to Reed. Less pompously, he admitted in company that the graciousness of the Queen's reception was 'I daresay' to be attributed solely to his years, 'most likely she had not read many of my works'.

Flushed with excitement after this triumph, William, still in the court dress, called on Rogers on his way back to Moxon's. As they walked together, William's attention was arrested by a pretty little girl, sitting alone on the grass, and, as he usually did, he stopped to chat with her. Pleased with her ingenuous answers, he put one hand on her head, delved into his pockets with the other and produced a copy of his *Selections*, which he solemnly presented to her, 'telling her to look well, and note his person; to be sure also to observe well the time of day, and the spot, and to recollect that that little book had been given to her by the author, the celebrated William Wordsworth'.

As the day of Dora's departure approached, William grew steadily more depressed. Perhaps so as not to prolong his agony, the Quillinans left a day earlier than expected. Father and daughter had an emotional parting, neither knowing whether they would ever see the other alive again and, in a final kindly gesture of which Miss Fenwick would have approved, William gave Dora £20, so that she would not be short of money should the need arise.

The day the Quillinans sailed, William was again summoned to court, this time to attend a royal levee. Prompted by Rogers, Lord Northampton took the poet under his wing and escorted him to the reception. It was 'an idle act him going', Robinson reported, 'for he exchanged not a word with the Queen.' Apart from the court events, it was an unusually quiet visit. Both at Moxon's and at Mrs Hoare's, however, he was much gratified by the attentions of Tennyson. The two men were fellow guests at a dinner party at Moxon's, with Aubrey de Vere and a small number of other friends. Before they left, Tennyson approached the old poet and, speaking in a low voice so that he could not be overheard but 'with a perceptible emotion', 'expressed in the strongest terms his gratitude to my writings'. The two poets were aeons apart in their taste and style (Tennyson complained that he 'could not inflame [Wordsworth's] imagination in the least!' with his description of a tropical island where the trees were the colour of blood when they came into leaf), but William had no hesitation in granting the palm to the younger man. 'He is decidedly the first of our living Poets, and I hope will live to give the world still better things.' It was therefore not surprising that William felt 'far from indifferent' to Tennyson's voluntary and obviously sincere compliment.

William did not prolong his stay in London after his daughter's departure, but while staying with Moxon, had much discussion with him about his next publication. A suggestion from Robinson, that Moxon should print a volume containing William's collected prose works, was on the cards, but the need for a new edition of poems was more pressing.

By the beginning of June William and Carter had begun the laborious task of preparation. *Poems, Chiefly of Early and Late Years* would have to be incorporated for the first time and, as always, every poem would have to be 'tinkered'. Optimistically, William hoped it would be ready in time for the Christmas market. A few weeks later, Robinson was alarmed to learn from Moxon that the new edition would contain 'many alterations'. 'I hope they are merely verbal', he muttered gloomily, but he was right in suspecting that they were not. Taking his cue from Reed's American edition of 1837, William had greatly expanded the number of poems included in the classification of imagination. More importantly, his Christianization of his verse had continued. Margaret's death in *The Ruined Cottage*, which had been absorbed into the second book of *The Excursion*, became an explicitly Christian one. In lines added for the first time, the Pedlar declared that Margaret, 'in her worst distress', had often felt

> The unbounded might of prayer; and learned, with soul
> Fixed on the Cross, that consolation springs,
> From sources deeper far than deepest pain,
> For the meek Sufferer.

In place of the suggestion that 'sorrow and despair' could be overcome by the contemplation of tranquillity, the lines were changed to say that such griefs could never obtain

> ....dominion o'er the enlightened spirit
> Whose meditative sympathies repose
> Upon the breast of Faith.
> *The Excursion,* ii, *935–9, 953–6*

Less radical, but important as an indication of Faber's influence, was the introduction of three new poems in the *Ecclesiastical Sonnets* series, written specifically at

Faber's request, to celebrate 'more explicitly our debt to the papacy'. They did not go as far as Faber hoped, but William intended them 'to qualify or mitigate the condemnation which by conscience I am compelled to pass upon the abuses of the Roman See'.

Now, in his seventy-sixth year, William could still surprise even himself by being prompted to write new poems while he was editing the old. 'It was only a few days ago that I was able to put into Verse the Matter of a short Poem which had been in my mind with a determination and a strong desire to write upon it for more than thirty years', William wrote to a friend on 24 June. The poem rightly belonged in the *Poems on the Naming of Places* series and therefore to the opening years of the nineteenth century. It celebrated the 'twin peaks' between White Moss Common and Bainriggs, where the 'two adventurous Sisters', Mary and Sara Hutchinson, had loved to climb for the view over the merging vales of Rydal and Grasmere. Perhaps because of its subject matter, it shows little diminution in power and the casual reader could be forgiven for not realizing the decades that separated its composition from that of its brethren.

The same could not be said of the sonnet *At Furness Abbey*, written about the same time and inspired by a scene witnessed by Miss Fenwick. She and Kate Southey had taken a party of Arnold and Davy children to Furness Abbey, where a new railway line was being built '*profanely* near this holy pile'. The directors had originally demanded that part of the ruins should be demolished and the line run straight through the abbey, but Lord Burlington had persuaded them to deviate their course slightly, so that it was now being built around the ruins, but so close that passengers on the railway could almost touch the great east window. He '*ought* to have insisted on a still *greater distance*', the indignant Miss Fenwick scolded. The navvies building the line appeared to feel the same, for as William observed in his sonnet, they wandered round the ruins in their lunch break with 'grave demeanour' and seemed 'to feel the spirit of the place'. 'Profane Despoilers', he accused those who had planned and permitted the line,

> stand ye not reproved,
> While thus these simple-hearted men are moved?
> *At Furness Abbey, ll.13–14*

'Sacred as that relic of the devotion of our ancestors deserves to be kept,' William wrote of Furness Abbey, 'there are temples of Nature, temples built by the Almighty, which have a still higher claim to be left unviolated.' He meant, of course, the Vale of Rydal, and one can only imagine his feelings when, a few weeks after writing this sonnet, he saw the railway surveyors at work, planning a line that was to run through Rydal Park and immediately behind Rydal Mount.

William could be under no illusions about the seriousness of this threat. The new railway line about to be built between Cockermouth and Workington would run straight through his son's gardens at Brigham. The ill-fated parsonage, whose site had been chosen with such care for its views, which had cost over £1,200 to build and drained so much of John's income, would be uninhabitable – and John, who was still abroad with his wife, knew nothing of what was planned. William immediately demanded compensation from the railway company. He soon realized that this would be inadequate, as it would not reimburse all those, including the Church bodies, who had contributed towards the cost. 'The more I think about the Brigham Vicarage as it will be affected by the Railway, the more am I convinced, that justice to the Church and the present Incumbent, requires the Insertion in the Act of a clause enjoining the Erection of a new Parsonage', he wrote to Lord Lonsdale. With the aid of 'Keswick' John's stepfather, the attorney Mr Lightfoot, and Willy, he organized a petition to Parliament to be drawn up to that effect. This was successful and, before the end of the year, William and Willy were back at Brigham to choose a site for John's new vicarage.

The new edition would simply be called *The Poems of William Wordsworth*, but for the first time the title-page would carry the roll-call of his honours: the DCL, Poet Laureateship and, as of this year, honorary membership of the Royal Society of Edinburgh and the Royal Irish Academy. By the end of November William was happy with the book but gloomy about its prospects. 'We are about to publish this expensive Vol. at a most unfavorable time', he told Moxon. 'Nothing is now thought of but railway shares. The Savings-banks are almost emptied of their old deposits, and scarcely any thing has come into them – all gone to Railway Speculation – a deplorable state of things.'

Robinson, who received one of the first copies, thought it 'A handsome Vol: which makes a beautiful present'. When he came on his annual Christmas visit he suggested to William that it would be an appropriate gesture to have a copy specially got up for presentation to the Queen from her Laureate. Bound in green covers by Westley, the volume was fetched to Rydal Mount by Moxon and inscribed with an unrecognizably Wordsworthian poem, addressed to 'Queen, Wife and Mother', which expressed the hope that it might bring 'Some solace under weight of royal care'. Robinson undertook to convey the book safely back to London, where it was presented to the Queen by the Lord Chamberlain. Her Majesty apparently considered the offering '<u>very gratifying</u>' and the inscription admirable and was pleased to present her Poet Laureate with an engraving of a portrait of the royal children.

Moxon's arrival, on 27 December, for a week's visit, proved a welcome diversion: he 'very much improved our conversations in vivacity, as he brought with him a good deal of book gossip'. Robinson had enjoyed as hearty a welcome as ever when he came, ten days earlier, but he noticed immediately subtle changes which could have been perceived only by an old friend. The house was emptier than he had ever seen it before – the Quillinans being in Portugal and Miss Fenwick in lodgings at Ambleside. Anxiety and grief at Dora's departure and John's troubles had taken their toll on William's appearance, so that he now looked '*very* old'. He had been depressed by the deaths, in quick succession, of Mrs Coleridge, the much-wronged wife of Samuel Taylor; of thirty-four-year-old Julia Myers, only child of his long-dead cousin John Myers; and of his own cousin Sarah Crackanthorpe. 'Link after link is broken,' he wrote to Derwent Coleridge, 'and yet for the most part we do not bear those severings in mind as we ought to do'.

He had also felt deeply the news that Faber had defected from the Church of England and become a Roman Catholic. Faber had not even had the courage to write to him personally but had sent him a single-sentence circular letter, written by a clerk, announcing that he had, that day, been received into 'what he calls the Church', as William bitterly described it. Having had so much influence on the new edition, it was particularly galling that Faber's conversion was unintentionally timed almost exactly to coincide with its publication. It appeared to prove what his critics and those of the Oxford Movement had said all along: that far from aiming at a spiritual revival of the Anglican Church, these High Churchmen were not 'catholics', as they claimed, but closet Roman Catholics who wanted to restore the Papacy in England. Robinson, a die-hard Protestant, took care to remind William that he had not carried out his intention of introducing into the new edition 'a note expressing his regret that he had ever uttered a word favourable to Puseyism'. William's justification for this omission, which Robinson thought 'a very insufficient reason', was 'that he was at last quite tired'. It was a significant admission. After almost fifty years of meticulous, intensive, thoughtful labouring over his poems, William had reached the end of the road. The single-volume edition of 1845 was the last he would revise thoroughly and see personally through the press.

On Christmas Eve, the Wordsworths heard the devastating news that their youngest grandson, four-year-old Edward, had died in Rome. Isabella had not bothered to inform her husband that three of their children were 'in the fever' and her letter informing the Wordsworths of Edward's death on 10 December did not arrive at Rydal Mount until the 24th, by which time the child had been buried in the leafy oasis of the Protestant cemetery in Rome. Terrified for the safety of his remaining children, John decided to return immediately to Italy and bring his family home. His parents doubted his ability to persuade Isabella either to return or to part with her children. Either way, the future for their marriage looked bleak. 'Even if his wife recovers her health, nothing can heal the worse and sorer sicknesses which through her illness have grown up and been fully revealed', Sara Coleridge wrote gloomily to Miss Fenwick; '– nothing, I fear, can turn *her* into a wise woman or *him* into an energetic high-minded man ... A wearisome wasting thing it will be, from year to year, to see that couple wronging each other and mismanaging their children – one pulling this way and the other that.'

The Wordsworths had barely recovered from the shock of Edward's death when their nephew Charles wrote to tell them that his father had died that morning. At seventy-one, he was four years younger than William. Christopher was buried in the churchyard at Buxted, in Sussex, the country parish to which he had retired after resigning the mastership of Trinity College. Charles, who had resigned his post at Winchester school in order to look after his father, was mortified not to be presented to the living, which the Archbishop of Canterbury gave to one of his own relatives. 'I am now quite <u>homeless</u> – & quite uncertain which way to turn.'

Troubles crowded in. 'Keswick' John was now so ill that the doctor expected him to be carried off at any moment. Dreadful reports of Isabella's state prompted her brother and seventy-year-old mother to set off at once for Rome. Mary's niece Margaret Hutchinson, the daughter of her youngest brother, had become a member of the Mormon sect, and secretly fled to America.

John and his sons arrived at Rydal Mount on 5 April. At his parents' suggestion, he had left thirteen-year-old Jane with their friend Mrs Gee, who ran a school for girls at Hendon. A clever, bookish child, she 'requires the discipline of a School, which she has never had'. The two oldest boys, Henry and William, were to be sent to the new Church of England school at Rossall, near Fleetwood, on the Lancashire coast. 'They are a little too fond of their own ways and pursuits', their grandfather noted sternly. Henry was destined to be a civil engineer, his brighter, more attentive sibling for university. Eight-year-old John and the youngest, Charles, who was only six, would stay with their grandparents at Rydal Mount until their mother's return.

In the midst of these griefs William appeared to casual observers, like Harriet Martineau, to be taking everything in his stride, but as he reached and passed his seventy-sixth birthday, what he confided in Isabella Fenwick revealed a very different picture. Doing what she loved best, caring for two young children, Mary had thrown off her depression, which had affected her health as well as her spirits, and was now able to keep herself well by 'marvellous activity of mind and body'.

I wish I could do the same – but many things do not touch her which depress me, public affairs in particular – my contempt for the management of these both in England and Ireland is quite painful ... My pleasures are among Birds and Flowers, and of these enjoyments, thank God, I retain enough; but my interests in Literature and books in general seem to be dying away unreasonably fast – nor do I look or much care for a revival in them ... I ... often think that my life has been in a great measure wasted.

Mary, too, noticed the change in her husband: 'he sits more over the fire in silence etc etc and is sooner tired on his walks – which he is ever unwilling to commence unaccompanied by me'. When he now wrote to Robinson he felt he had nothing of value to say: 'in our course of life one day is just a repetition of its predecessor. Persons we see few except our old Neighbours, and new Books none.' Even his annual day excursion to Hawkshead was depressing: 'how changed!' he lamented. 'In my time we had more than a 100 Boys playing and roaming about the Vale; now not one was to be seen, the School being utterly deserted.'

By the end of June the Wordsworths heard the glad tidings that Dora and her husband were safely back on English soil. Sara Coleridge, who saw them at the Hoares' as they made their way northwards, reported that 'Dora looks like a rose. The improvement in her is marvellous. I have not seen her look so well since her teenish girlhood'. Quillinan, on the other hand, who had suffered a serious attack of pleurisy in Paris, was thin and delicate, though cheerful. They returned to a joyous welcome at Rydal, where, for the first time, they would have a proper home of their own. Carter, who spent most of the year at Carlisle, had built himself a cottage under Loughrigg and offered the tenancy to the Quillinans, with the proviso that he could stay there whenever he was in Rydal. It was the perfect solution for them all, because the cottage, Loughrigg Holme (which Dora poignantly told Carter she would call 'Loughrigg Home'), was within easy walking distance of both Rydal Mount and Ambleside. However, it was William who was to pay the rent of £80 a year, to include servants' wages, which was more than the total income Quillinan and his daughters had to live on.

In Portugal Dora had said she was selfish enough to hope that she would see her 'child', 'Keswick' John, again before he died. Her wish was granted, but with unforeseen and tragic consequences. He was now, aged thirty-one, in the final stages of consumption: when he was removed from his waterbed to a sofa or easy chair, he had to be carried, wrapped in a blanket. The Wordsworths, Dora now among them, took it in turn to visit him daily. On 18 August his long trial ended. 'He expired without any suffering, Nature being quite worn out', William wrote. His mother and his cousin Willy were with him at the end. He was buried in Grasmere churchyard on 22 August with all the ceremony due to the last in the direct line of the Sockbridge Wordsworths. By John's death, William became the owner of the Sockbridge estate, which he had administered during his nephew's minority, and of his own brother John's sword, which had been recovered from the wreck of the *Earl of Abergavenny*. John left Willy his gold watch and chain and his sword and Dora nineteen guineas, but nothing to their brother. Once again, John was excluded from family financial arrangements, though the (non-existent) residue of the estate was to go to his son, John, who was 'Keswick' John's godson.

After such a prolonged period of gloom, Willy's announcement that he was engaged to be married was a ray of sunshine. His fiancée, Fanny Graham, came from a family 'in very moderate circumstances' as Quillinan remarked. She was the twenty-six-year-old daughter of a Cumberland stockbroker who had retired to Brighton. Willy had known her for fourteen years and though William and Mary had never met her, Dora and 'cousin Dorothy' Harrison both knew and liked her well. 'Had I not been prepared to love you from the favourable impression you had made upon my daughter, I must now have loved you for the happiness you have conferred upon my dear Son', Mary wrote in one of the effusive letters of congratulation which were dispatched from Rydal to Sussex, as the Wordsworths looked forward eagerly to the prospect of welcoming their new daughter-in-law.

The flow of visitors through Rydal Mount continued unabated throughout the summer and autumn, despite the Wordsworths' private distresses. John and his family were also there as often as not, for Isabella had taken one look at the bleak parsonage at Plumblands, which was not even properly furnished, and fled, first to Fleetwood, then, for a lengthier period, to Hastings on the south coast, where she was joined by her niece, Clara, and her youngest son. 'He <u>ought</u> to have made the house that is two or three rooms in it really comfortable for his miserable wife', was Dora's forthright opinion, 'not that that would have kept her there – but she would have had no good reason to throw in <u>his face</u> for leaving her home – I pressed this upon him again & again but all in vain'.

In September there were two visitors of particular interest. The first was the Chartist Thomas Cooper, a former apprentice cobbler, who taught himself to read Greek, Latin and Hebrew, and became a schoolmaster and journalist. As editor of a Chartist paper, he had taken part in the strikes of 1842 and been imprisoned for sedition, writing a poem, *The Purgatory of Suicides,* in gaol, which had been published the previous year. A devotee of *The Excursion,* Cooper could not walk past Rydal Mount without at least attempting to see the poet. As a 'forlorn hope', he simply scribbled, 'Thomas Cooper, author of "The Purgatory of Suicides," desires to pay his devout regards to Mr Wordsworth' and handed it in at the door. To his utter astonishment, he was shown in and the poet greeted him with a warmth and friendliness that brought tears to Cooper's eyes. Expecting vanity and egotism, Cooper was confounded by William's liberal praise of other poets (apart from his *bête noire,* Byron). 'Mr Tennyson affords the richest promise', he told Cooper. 'He will do great things yet; and ought to have done greater things by this time.' When the inevitable subject of politics came up, Cooper could not believe his ears to hear a hearty endorsement of Chartism from the 'Tory' Wordsworth. '"You were right," he said; "I have always said the people were right in what they asked; but you went the wrong way to get it ... there is nothing unreasonable in your Charter: it is the foolish attempt at physical force, for which many of you have been blamable."'

As the People's Charter had included demands for universal suffrage, annual ballots and Parliaments, the abolition of the property qualification for, and payment of salaries to, Members of Parliament, Cooper had every right to be amazed. What made the Charter attractive to William, however, was its nostalgic attempt to turn the clock back on the Industrial Revolution. Every working man, it said, should have his own cow and a few acres to cultivate for his family, just like the statesmen of the Lakes, whose virtues William had sung for so long. In an ideal society, where every man was a statesman or Chartist, then democracy was not only possible but desirable. 'I am a Democrat', William had informed Reed three years earlier, and it was as true in the 1840s as it had been in the 1790s. Except that for the last forty years he had also believed that the people had to be capable of exercising power responsibly, which meant having a vested interest in the land. Knowledge was spreading, he told Cooper, and constitutional liberty was sure to follow. '"The people are sure to have the franchise," he said, with emphasis, "as knowledge increases; but you will not get all you seek at once – and you must never seek it again by physical force," he added, turning to me with a smile: "it will only make you longer about it."' Before Cooper took his leave, William introduced him 'as a poet!' to Dorothy, who was being wheeled in her chair along the terrace, walked him to the gate, shook his hand and wished him well. 'I left him', Cooper said, 'with a more intense feeling of having been in the presence of a good and great intelligence, than I had ever felt in any other moments of my life.'

The second visitor of interest was a Quaker, William Bennett, who, with his wife, children and artist friend T. C. Galpin, spent several months in the neighbourhood in the autumn. Like Cooper, he found William kind, attentive and expansive. The particular interest of Bennett's account is not his encounters with

William, fascinating though they are, but that he gives us a rare glimpse of Dorothy. At William's invitation, the Bennett party came regularly into the gardens to draw and sometimes saw Dorothy being wheeled out on fine days or heard her 'shrill voice' reading or reciting aloud. Knowing of her mental imbecility, they always maintained a discreet distance, but one day they unexpectedly encountered her sitting alone in the shade of an oak tree. 'Won't you speak to me?' she shrieked at them. Pretending they had not heard, they moved on, only to hear repeated pleas and a heartbreaking 'Oh! you're too proud.' Mrs Bennett protested that they had not wanted to intrude, to which they received the unanswerable retort, 'You don't intrude, if I invite you.' Unwillingly drawn in, they were enchanted when Dorothy offered to recite some of her own verses and did so 'in the most clear and beautiful accents, and with that modulation and emphasis which only the poet can give to his own productions'. As she recited, she took off her bonnet,

exposing clear and striking features, now furrowed and worn down by suffering, surmounted by a noble intellectual forehead quite bare, except where sprinkled over by a few grey hairs; she closed her eyes, and giving herself up to the full feeling of it, threw her whole soul into the poetry. – Even her loss of teeth, interfering with some of the modulations, seemed to add force and impressiveness. – The impression was most solemn and affecting. She paused at the conclusion; then opened her eyes, and looked towards us, her features gilded up with the smile of expected approbation, which indeed was not withheld, but most genuinely awarded.

In the course of the conversation that followed, she appeared completely lucid, telling them about her own illness and the death of her brother John, whose last words she quoted. She then repeated some more verses and, when her attendant returned 'to our no small relief', they were all touched when she took the hand of each of them, including their little girl, in her own 'shrunk and withered hand'.

Bennett remarked several times on William's 'visibly enfeebled step', but Isabella Fenwick was also privately raising doubts about his mental strength. There is no evidence of this in either his conversations with Bennett or his letters of the time, but he was undoubtedly under severe strain due to the deaths of so many of those closest to him. Two of these were particularly distressing. Haydon, after years of poverty and rejection, committed suicide at the age of sixty: in a final pathetic gesture, the artist sent his unsold portrait, *Wordsworth on Helvellyn*, to Elizabeth Barrett, the poetess who had written in praise of it, 'to protect' after his death. His suicide, in June, was followed in November by that of Lamb's close friend Thomas Alsager, the scholarly music critic, who, at sixty-seven, cut his own throat when he was dismissed from *The Times*. And at the end of September the Wordsworths' beloved old friend Thomas Clarkson, the unsung champion of the abolition of slavery, died. His widow, Catherine, hinted strongly that, as one of the few left alive who had known her husband intimately, William might supply some memorial lines, but, as the poet now freely admitted, his writing days were over.

On 19 January 1847 the Wordsworths held a grand wedding feast to celebrate their youngest son's marriage. Between fifty and sixty of their friends, neighbours and servants were invited to tea at Rydal Mount and the health of the newlyweds was proposed by Thomas Troughton. The Quillinans, including Jemima and Rotha, Mary Hutchinson, who had come from Mathon to help her sister-in-law, and Robinson, who was on his annual visit, were among the guests. As Dora learned afterwards, however, it had all been a little premature. At two o'clock that afternoon Mary had received a letter saying that the wedding had been postponed another day. With only three hours to go before the guests started arriving, she consulted with her sister-in-law and they decided to take a chance and go ahead. No one else, not even William or Dora, was in on the secret, lest it should spoil the occasion for them. Though the two 'wily women' 'felt queer' when Troughton proposed his toast, their boldness was vindicated when Thursday's post brought a letter from Willy and Fanny announcing that they were now man and wife. The wedding had taken place on 20 January, at Brighton, and ten days later the newlyweds arrived at Rydal Mount. The Wordsworths were delighted with their tall, pretty daughter-in-law, with her quiet, gentle manners and sweet voice, who seemed at once 'quietly at ease' with them.

On 19 February William and Mary set out for Bath, on a long-planned visit to Isabella Fenwick. 'How I wish you were here, instead of our being obliged to go to you', William grumbled. They left Dorothy in the care of Dora, who had been 'wonderfully strong and well' since her return from Portugal, but was now suffering her usual winter cough and cold. 'She looks like a witch for thinness', her mother remarked, but Dora was as cheerful and unconcerned as usual. She was busy putting the final touches to her *Journal of a Few Months' Residence in Portugal and Glimpses of the South of Spain*, which Moxon had agreed to publish, generously offering her two-thirds of any profit, yet taking all the risk to himself. 'Women observe many particulars of manners and opinions which are apt to escape the notice of the Lords of the Creation', William remarked drily, but he had reconciled himself to Dora's decision to publish only because she would do so anonymously.

On 3 March they were at last reunited with their beloved Miss Fenwick, who had taken a house at 8 Queen's Square, a large Georgian square overlooking a central garden, on the hill above the Theatre Royal. A few days later they were joined by Robinson, who soon persuaded William to walk with him over the hills to Witcombe, where his mother was buried. 'I was afraid it would be too much for my companion', Robinson noted, 'But he was not so fatigued as I was on our return.' Sara Coleridge, who, with her daughter Edith, had joined them on 18 March, was not so impressed. 'He can walk seven or eight miles very well', she told her cousin, 'but is always losing his way, and making out *he* is obliged to look sharp after his wife, whose eyesight is grown so bad that she is not to be trusted.'

Sara had just finished editing Coleridge's *Biographia Literaria*, which, despite William's private reservations about the nature of the book, he had allowed her to dedicate to him. Sara, who had not seen William for two years and Mary for even longer, found them both looking 'older in the face' and 'slower and feebler in their movements of body and mind'. Mary was, nevertheless, 'wonderfully active'. On the day appointed for fasting and 'National Humiliation' on account of the Irish famine, she went three times to church 'and would have fasted almost wholly, had not Mr W., in a deep, determined voice, said "Oh, *don't* be so *foolish*, Mary!"' Of William she made the perceptive remark that he seemed 'rather to recontinue his former self, and repeat by habit what he used to think and feel, than to think anything new'.

It was while they were in Bath that William received a request which he felt he could not ignore. Prince Albert was about to be installed as Chancellor of the University of Cambridge and he wanted William to write the words for an Installation Ode which would be set to music and performed at the ceremony. 'His Royal Highness would have felt considerable hesitation in thus breaking in upon your retirement', the private secretary wrote, 'were it not that his Royal Highness felt that he thus might bear testimony to His admiration of your Genius, and might be the means of procuring for the University of Cambridge another valuable work of one of her most distinguished Sons.' Who could resist such flattery? Even though he was opposed to Prince Albert's election and said he personally would have voted against him, William agreed to retouch the harp he thought he had laid aside for good. Robinson undertook to locate Wright's *Inaugural Ode*, which was to be the model, but by 9 April the ode was, as Mary described it, 'unbegun yet!'

The Wordsworths had left Miss Fenwick at Bath the previous day and had now taken up residence at Mrs Hoare's, from where they hoped to go to Playford Hall, to visit the widowed Catherine Clarkson. It was to be a quiet visit to Hampstead, without the frenetic socializing which had characterized earlier trips to London. Friends who knew the Wordsworths' whereabouts came to see them. A recently married Anna Ricketts came to introduce her husband and stepdaughter; Charles Wordsworth and his daughter, with his new wife, who was half his age, called to say farewell before departing for Scotland, where he was to found Trinity College at Glenalmond; Robinson brought the book needed for the Installation Ode; Moxon called, with Dora's *Journal of a Few Months' Residence in Portugal*, hot from the press, in two volumes. All the time, however, the Wordsworths were racked with anxiety about their daughter. 'We remain here and in London solely because we think she will do better without than with us', William told Fanny.

On 20 April William and Mary moved to Westminster, to stay with their nephew Chris and his family. William had an engagement to sit to a talented twenty-one-year-old artist, Leonard Wyon, the second engraver at the Royal Mint, who wanted to make a study for a silver medallion. The portrait, in profile, of a dignified but stern-looking William was taken in the cloisters at Westminster, three weeks after his seventy-seventh birthday. As Robinson watched the artist at work, a letter arrived and William was called out of the room. He never returned. The letter was from Quillinan. It said that Dr Fell had examined Dora and, for the first time, 'expressed fears' about her. William and Mary did not hesitate. They left immediately for home and were back at Rydal Mount the next day. The following day, 28 April, they called in the Kendal physician, Dr Gough, for a second opinion. He examined Dora '& gave us no <u>hope</u>', Quillinan bleakly recorded in his diary, '"a question only of time"'.

'You never knew her – perhaps never saw her', Hartley Coleridge wrote on hearing the news.

I have known her from her infancy. But if you had seen her as I have seen her and seen how a beautiful Soul can make a face not beautiful most beautiful, if you had seen how by the mere strength of affection she entered into the recesses of her Father's Mind and drew him out to gambol with her in the childishness that always hung upon her womanhood, you would feel, as we do, what earth is about to lose and Heaven to gain.

'Dearest Dora!' his sister echoed. 'It seems scarce credible that so much life and love, and such a noble heart, – such a bright open mind should be passing away so soon! She is one of those whom it is scarce possible to think of as thus drawn within the vail [*sic*]'.

The diagnosis was pulmonary consumption, or tuberculosis, which the Words-worths, like all their contemporaries, believed was inherent, developing out of neglect of or a tendency to coughs and colds. In fact, it is purely infective. The full extent of the Wordsworths' tragedy becomes clear only with the realization that Dora's death sentence was, unwittingly, the bequest of 'her child', her beloved cousin 'Keswick' John, who had died the previous autumn. Had she not nursed him so devotedly throughout his final weeks, she would not have caught the infection.

Opinion was divided on whether Dora should be informed of the diagnosis but, in the end, it was Dora herself who settled the question, by quietly insisting that she should be told. She was 'not only resign'd but happy', Hartley informed his sister. 'Her parents bear up like Christians, but are quite absorb'd by their sorrow. I have not seen them – (excepting Mr Wordsworth on the road . . .). I would gladly go, if I could be of any use or comfort, but the Doctor advises me not. They wish to see no one.' Dora was, from the first, nursed at Rydal Mount, where she had been taken ill. Apart from her immediate family and the servants, only Hannah Cookson was admitted to her sickroom. 'H.C. is a treasure to us – being an incomparable nurse – so thoughtful – tender and such presence of mind! as under such circumstances is scarcely to be looked for in one whose heart and affections are so deeply interested.'

Dora dealt swiftly with her worldly concerns, jotting down a memo to her father in an unusually untidy hand that she wished to leave £20 to each of her godchildren, Edward Hill, son of Herbert and Bertha, and Priscilla Wordsworth, daughter of Chris and Susan. Her other cash bequests were all to the loyal servants who had been with them so long they seemed part of the family: Mary and Elizabeth, the maids, were to get £5 each, James Dixon £10 and John Carter, who had provided her with her first and only marital home, 'out of gratitude for his affec[tionate] Kindness to my Parents' £100. Her marriage settlement ensured that all her personal property would belong to Quillinan for life and after his death would be divided equally between her brothers. This Dora now varied in a gesture of female solidarity with her goddaughter and only niece, Jane, whose financial prospects did not look promising. After Quillinan's death, she was to receive £300 from Dora's estate.

'She is calm and happy,' Quillinan wrote to Robinson on 19 May,

suffers little or no bodily pain, her mind is clear and cheerful, her affections are as much alive as ever, she does not forget a friend, she is prepared to die & willing to live, resigned to departure at any hour, yet hoping, & I think believing with good reason, that she may live many days perhaps several weeks. But it is a treacherous complaint, & she may be snatched away from us in a moment.

Throughout the long dark days of Dora's final illness, mother and daughter revealed a mutual strength and courage that was humbling to behold. Instead of giving way to bitterness or selfish lamentation, they thanked God simply for the fact that they were able to be together and comfort one another. Dora refused to allow her physical sufferings to cow her spirit: 'How mercifully I am dealt with', she would say repeatedly, even finding time and strength of mind to write a farewell letter to Isabella Fenwick. Her mother, who passed every night till two in the morning alone with her daughter in the sickroom, returning to her vigil five or six hours later, was grateful simply for possessing the strength to carry on. 'For myself how thankful I ought to be that such a blessing has been spared to us so long', Mary wrote on 27 May; '– at 77 the <u>separation</u> cannot be long; & how merciful to me is our heavenly Father, that I am yet able to minister to her earthly comforts while I trust I am profitting by the example of her patience, & chearful resignation of all she so intensely loves – & by the humility of her aspirations towards the home whither she is hastening.' For William there was no such comfort. Lacking Mary's unshakeable faith and unable to assist in nursing his daughter, he was simply helpless.

Throughout the ordeal, William was constantly being harassed by Thomas Walmisley, the Professor of Music at Cambridge who had been commissioned to write the music for the Installation Ode. Incapable of composing anything suitable in time but unable to get out of the engagement, he asked his son-in-law for help. Quillinan wrote a first draft which William then revised and corrected, so that he could legitimately claim some part in its composition. A second, corrected draft had been sent to Walmisley within a couple of days of William's return to Rydal Mount, but that was not the end of it. First of all Walmisley asked for an additional verse to end the ode on a more joyous note, then he rejected the new lines, 'words of four syllables are extremely difficult to put into musical rhythm' and expressed the hope that the next version 'may not commence with the word "Albert"'. Harried beyond endurance, William gave Walmisley *carte blanche* to do what he liked with the poem: 'adopt or reject any alterations as they suit you or not'. Nothing could have more clearly indicated his changed priorities than this surrender of control over a poem which would inevitably be the subject of immense public interest. Weighed in the balance against his dying daughter, poetic reputation no longer mattered.

Despite all Dora's 'humility, her repentance resignation faith & hope which is unbounded', there were still occasions when she suffered what she called 'the pangs of death'. One of them was on 1 June. 'A cloud came over her, a fear & cold trembling as if she had lost the support of her Saviour', Quillinan noted sadly. In these crises, Quillinan acknowledged, Mary was the best spiritual comforter Dora could have, but he could not help regretting that the clergyman who attended his wife was her brother John. 'He has shewn more sensibility ... than I might have given him credit for', Quillinan admitted,

but, between you and me, I could wish that there were some more influential more really spiritual pastor at hand, for though the poor Mother thinks him very superior to what he is, & though Dora loves him truly & faithfully, I cannot but think that a higher toned mind than his would be more competent to minister to any death-bed doubt or trouble; more in accord with a fine & pure Spirit like Her's.

On 1 July, during a temporary respite from the continuous diarrhoea which marked her approaching end, Dora could still joke about her 'fat', the tubercles, or glandular swellings, which were now appearing all over her face and body, though she was so emaciated that she was covered in pressure sores.

Her sufferings ended on 9 July. 'At One o'clock A. M. this morning, my precious Dora, your true friend, breathed her last', Quillinan wrote to Robinson. She died, without fuss, in possession of her faculties and a few weeks short of her forty-fourth birthday.

Joseph Cottle wrote from Bristol to express his shock: 'To lose a Daughter, and an only Daughter, and such a Daughter, must have afflicted you with a poignancy, of which I can but imperfectly conceive.' He alone, out of the many who wrote to congratulate William on the successful performance of his Installation Ode on 6 July, remarked how uncongenial the task of writing it must have been. It was small consolation to the grieving father to learn that it had been greeted with rapturous applause, or to receive a note from Buckingham Palace, written the day Dora died, which, with unconscious irony, declared, 'The force and beauty of the ideas, and the elegance of the Versification fully proved to Her Majesty and the Prince, that Time had been powerless over the Mind or Skill of the Poet.' In other circumstances, one could well imagine that William would have smiled wrily and handed the note to Quillinan.

'We bear up under our affliction as well as God enables us to do,' William wrote to Moxon, 'but O my dear Friend our loss is immeasurable'. He had been quite convinced that Mary's long vigils would wear her out and that she would quickly follow her daughter to the grave, a fear that had been echoed by their friends, but Mary was made of sterner stuff. She looked 'more aged & feeble', Miss Fenwick reported, '– but she is still able to move about with her accustomed activity'. Her husband 'bears up with firmness, but has paroxysms of great suffering'. He found his chief consolation in constant attendance on his sister, adding to the daily duty he had always performed of pushing her in her chair out on the terrace on fine days. Perhaps her grateful dependence on him was a compensation for his inability to do anything for Dora.

The weeks and months of Dora's final illness had seen a change in the balance of her parents' relationship. Mary's strength of character had seemed to grow in direct proportion as her husband's sank and withered away.

When Miss Fenwick left them, Mary tried to divert her husband's grief by focusing his attention on their surviving sons. In September she persuaded him to visit John in his deserted new vicarage, built by the railway company, at Brigham; his wife was now in Paris, with her brother. Mary had hoped that being in a place so strongly connected with his childhood, rather than with Dora, would rekindle her husband's interest, but she was foiled by bad weather that prevented them walking out. When they got to Carlisle, Mary and Willy persuaded him to sit to a local artist, Thomas Carrick, a famous painter of miniatures on marble. The daily sittings occupied his time but not his mind or heart: the resulting portrait, ineffably sad, depicts the poet staring bleakly from sunken eyes, his mouth unnaturally compressed, as if by force of will. It was a 'striking likeness', Robinson admitted. 'But it is too sad . . . it has an expression of fixed and irremovable grief.'

William was anxious to return home, 'but will he be more at ease here?' Quillinan asked. 'Mrs W with as much feeling, & with a <u>mother's</u> feeling to boot, has a happier method of dealing with her sorrows. – Her remaining children, her grand children & her husband occupy her mind & heart usefully.' If William had felt excluded by the closeness of his wife's relationship with their dying daughter, his son-in-law felt equally shut out by both his wife's parents. 'I have never for a moment felt that I was otherwise than alone', he told Miss Fenwick. '<u>It is a horrible desolation</u>, & I cannot yet call it anything else.'

'You kindly express a hope that Mr Quillinan and I walk together –', William wrote at the beginning of December, after his return from Carlisle; 'this has not been so, I cannot bear to cross the Bridge and Field that leads to his Abode; and he does not come hither, so that except once on the highway, and once or twice at Church, and one evening when he dined here with Mr Scott, his friend, I have not seen him at all.' When Robinson arrived for his Christmas visit on 18 December, he was deeply perturbed at what he found. 'Both Mr & Mrs Wordsworth have received a blow, the effects of which I fear they will never be able to counteract –', he confided to his brother five days later.

Neither of them has yet ventured to pronounce the name of their beloved daughter – And very few & slight have been the allusions to their loss – Who feels the most intensely – who shall say? But at least Mrs W is able to mix more with her friends And discharge as she has been accustomed the ordinary functions of her domestic life. Mr W keeps very much alone And whichever room I may happen to be in, he goes into the other . . .

For Robinson, it was a miserable visit. During the three weeks he stayed at Rydal Mount, he noted in his journal almost daily that William was 'very silent' and he had to endure the distressing sight of William sobbing through the church service on Christmas Day. The final evening of his visit was particularly painful. William was 'as moody and silent as on the other evenings', so Robinson read the newspapers, 'which filled up the time'. Rising early the next morning, he had a private conversation with James, lamenting William's inability to submit to the will of providence. 'Ah! Sir And so I took the liberty of saying to Master', James replied. ' – He merely said – "Oh she was such a bright creature["] – And then I said *"But Sir don't you think she is brighter now than she ever was,*["] And then Master burst into a flood of tears.'

When the time came to part with Robinson, William was again so overcome with emotion that he wept uncontrollably and could not speak to take leave of his friend. Despite all the indications to the contrary, Robinson remained optimistic: 'he has a strong nature in body as well as mind   And he may yet rally'. William himself was not so sure. 'I suffer most in head and mind before I leave my bed in a morning –', he wrote to Isabella Fenwick. 'Daily used She to come to my bedside and greet me and her Mother and *now* the blank is terrible. But I must stop. She is ever with me and will be so to the last moment of my life.'

28. Bowed to the Dust

The most unfortunate result of the temporary estrangement between Dora's father and husband was that Quillinan was deprived of the opportunity to become William's biographer. Early in November 1847 the Wordsworths were surprised by a letter from their nephew Chris, announcing that he and his wife, Susan, intended to visit Rydal Mount. That there was a purpose behind the visit soon became clear, when Chris offered to prepare some biographical notices of his uncle, after the latter's death. Written by an official family biographer, he argued, such a work might pre-empt gossipy publications of the sort the Wordsworths felt had done so much to diminish Coleridge's posthumous reputation. William gladly agreed, though Mary was uncomfortably aware that Quillinan would be hurt at being passed over, 'for you know he is easily offended'.

Yet Quillinan had just cause for offence, because no one said a word about the arrangement to him. He dined at Rydal Mount when Chris and Susan were there and entertained them to lunch and dinner at Loughrigg Holme, but the subject was not raised. This cannot have been accidental. On the very morning of the day Chris and Susan spent at Quillinan's, William drew up a formal notice, witnessed by his wife, requiring his family and friends to assist his nephew in preparing the biography. What could have been more natural than to discuss this with Quillinan? When he found out, several months later, from a casual reference by a close friend, he was mortified. 'In Dora's time, it was perfectly understood by her & by myself (& not by us only) that if I should survive my fatherinlaw, the task of writing his Life would, for many reasons, be confided to me. Every thing was changed when I lost my wife . . .'

Why did William change his mind? There was no question that Quillinan would have made a better biographer. Even Mary remarked of Chris that he knew less about William's poetry than almost any person she knew. His appointment over

Quillinan seems inexplicable. Chris might not have been the best man for the job, however, but he had other advantages. He had the Wordsworth name, for a start, held a high and influential position in the Church of England and was an indefatigable author of books and pamphlets on Church affairs. If he undertook the task there would be no question that he would complete it and that his work would carry authority. The same could not be said of poor Quillinan, an impoverished, dilettante author of lightweight novels, poems and journalistic criticism.

Before Chris left Rydal Mount, he 'requested Mr Wordsworth to favour him with a brief sketch of the most prominent circumstances in his life'. William therefore began to dictate a series of biographical memoranda to Susan, but his heart was not in it. They are flat and dull, a duty task rather than a voluntary outpouring of musings to a dear friend. Poignantly, they limp to a halt with the death of his two children. 'They died in 1812,' he dictated, 'and in 1813 we came to Rydal Mount, where we have since lived with no further sorrow till 1836 [*sic*], when my sister became a confirmed invalid, and our sister Sarah Hutchinson died. She lived alternately with her brother and with us.' He could go no further, for he could not yet speak of his newest and greatest grief.

Miss Fenwick's response to the news that Chris was to be the official biographer was characteristic. Feeling that Quillinan had been unjustly snubbed, she quietly put into his hands the most important material for any potential biographer, the notes she had taken at the poet's dictation in 1843. The letter she sent him, forewarning him of their arrival, was marked 'Private' to ensure that, if he received it in William or Mary's presence, he would not read it to them, 'and that on account of these notes – for on Mr W's being reminded of them – he would immediately wish to see them and you might have some difficulty of getting them again not that there would be any design of keeping them from you but because he would intend to add to them'. Without casting aspersions about the conduct of any of the Wordsworths, Miss Fenwick managed to make it clear that this gift was a gesture of practical support, to ensure that Quillinan could not be entirely excluded in the important decisions that would lie ahead. She told him, quite candidly, that Mary had mentioned the notes in one of her letters, but that she had made no answer.

Relations between William and his son-in-law did improve greatly in the spring, thanks to Robinson's kindly intervention. 'Mr Wordsworth & I walk about together a good deal now, & he seems to seek & to take pleasure in my company', Quillinan reported to his benefactor on 1 February.

He talks constantly of my beloved Wife, & this suits my feelings, though it is so sad a theme. He comes to this house too occasionally. This is a great step gained, for I could not endure his absenting himself altogether, though I have learnt to respect the feeling that kept him away, or at least to think charitably of it. – Mrs Wordsworth too comes frequently: & this is very gratifying to me.

In one of the most heartening indications that the two men were finding mutual comfort in sharing their sorrow, they were even thinking of a joint publication of all their poems relating to Dora for private circulation among their friends. To Mary, however, her 'beloved Mourner' still seemed 'bowed to the dust ... His mind and spirits (except for a brief while when, with almost *indifferent* Persons, he can rally a little and appear quite himself) is in the lowest state of *humiliation* and deep sorrow ... May the Almighty in his mercy see fit to send support ere long.'

One of the 'indifferent Persons' who was brought to Rydal Mount in February by Miss Martineau was the American essayist Ralph Waldo Emerson. They found William asleep on the sofa and woke him. Disturbed from his sleep and unaware of who he was even talking to, the poet was, unsurprisingly, 'short & surly'. After spending an hour and a half in conversation, Emerson found all his previous prejudices confirmed. He dismissed William as 'a bitter old Englishman', a view which he toned down only slightly for his published account of the meeting. The article was padded out with a series of anecdotes from the literary circuit to illustrate William's miserly habits; like Chinese whispers, each carried a kernel of truth. Harriet Martineau, for instance, said that in his early days William had offered his guests 'bread & plainest fare', telling them that if they wanted more, they would have to pay for it. Greg, the mill-owner, added that Walter Scott had been compelled to sneak out daily when he was the Wordsworths' guest to satisfy his hunger at the Swan Inn. Barry Cornwall, in a particularly venomous account, quite untruthfully claimed intimacy with William in early life and asserted that the poet 'had no personal friend. He was not amiable, & he was stingy. He would receive anything, but he never gave'. Completely insensitive to William's recent loss, of which he cannot have been unaware, though he makes no mention of it, Emerson had few qualms about repeating such malicious gossip in print. It made for an entertaining read, but it was a gross and hurtful caricature of the man whose hospitality he had abused.

At the beginning of April Mary, anticipating the trauma of celebrating William's seventy-eighth birthday at Rydal Mount without Dora, persuaded her husband to spend a month away from home, dividing their time equally between their sons. 'I faintly hope that my poor husband may *possibly* be benefited by the change,' Mary said. The visit to Brigham was enlivened by the presence of his granddaughter. Jane was in disgrace. The previous autumn her mother had left her with her cousin Clara in a boarding school at Brighton, while she resumed her Continental travels. It was run by a pair of Evangelical sisters who thought Shakespeare immoral and deprived Jane of her copy of Keble's *Lyra Innocentium*, a High Church book of 'Thoughts in Verse on Christian Children', because it was 'improper reading'. The cousins complained of being 'tyrannised over' and sent to bed early for imaginary faults and, with another girl, decided to run away from school. Clara did not get away, but the other two girls escaped and got as far as London, before they were recaptured and hauled before Chris, who sent them back to Brighton.

Jane was astute enough to play off her parents' marital differences, declaring that 'her father's friends had never wanted her to be at that school', and she succeeded in persuading her doting father to remove her. Mary thought it 'almost an unpardonable offence – especially in so sensible a Girl', but John and his father were indulgent and Jane rapidly made herself indispensable by devoting herself to teaching her two youngest brothers. Mary's pleas for Jane to be sent to another school fell on deaf ears. Until Isabella returned to England from Italy, where her doctors said she needed to spend another year to renovate her health, Jane would have to take her mother's place at home.

When they returned home, Mary found it difficult to persuade William to leave the house. Even his once favourite walks had become anathema to him, because of their associations with Dora. Mary almost despaired. 'Where can we find a place or an object on earth to look upon that is not beset with like hauntings! Could but the thoughts be *fixed* upon that blessed Haven where we trust she now is, we should there find comfort.' Mary's unspoken fear was that her husband's excessive grief would eventually turn his brain and that he would end up like his sister. She noted with foreboding that he had already become, like Dorothy, a lover of a large fire, 'by which he sits close, when within doors'. Rumours of his imbecility were even appearing in the newspapers. Though his family and friends did what they could to combat them, there was clearly cause for concern.

As William found it so hard to go from home but company seemed to be essential to force him to maintain at least a show of spirits, Mary tried to encourage a constant flow of visitors. Kate Southey came to stay in June, followed, in July, when the first anniversary of Dora's death had to be faced, by an influx of relatives and friends. The two youngest grandsons were almost a permanent fixture and as they celebrated their tenth and eighth birthdays on 24 and 25 July, all the children in the neighbourhood were invited to a grand party, the highlight of which was the sending up of a balloon made by the deft-fingered James. Mary's cousin John Monkhouse paid a rare visit from the Stow; almost completely blind, he was cheerful as ever, and had just come fresh from his triumph at the York Agricultural Meeting, where one of his bull calves had won the £20 prize. He won the hearts of both the grandsons, promising ten-year-old John that, when he had gone through the proper training, he could come to the Stow 'to finish his education by learning to breed Prize Bulls'.

And this year the Lakers descended in their droves. Few had sought admission the previous summer and fewer still had obtained it. This year, however, Mary discreetly encouraged all the strangers who arrived with introductions or 'just happened' to be visiting friends in the area, wisely foreseeing that it would distract her husband from his sorrows to speak to them. 'It seems to me as if America had broken loose, so many, especially from New York, of that country make their way to the Poet', she marvelled.

In addition to the usual Lakers, however, the Wordsworths were experiencing for the first time the effect of the new railway line from Kendal to Bowness, which had opened on 21 April 1847. Just as William had predicted, hordes of cheap excursionists from the manufacturing towns descended on the Lakes, but instead of demanding beer shops and wrestling, they too wanted to see the poet. 'The Country is strangely changed –', Mary noted; 'think of an Hotel – Omnibus and Carriages running at different hours in the day between Grasmere and the Train!

And of numbers pouring in by Monster trains'. 'Yesterday as I happened to be on
the Terrace at Rydal Mount,' Quillinan told Robinson on 12 August,

no less than 50, or 60 (I counted 48 & then left off) Cheap-trainers invaded the poet's
premises at once. They walked about all over the terraces & garden, without leave asked,
but did no harm; & I was rather pleased at so many humble men & women & lasses having
minds high enough to feel interest in Wordsworth. I retreated into the house; but one young
lady rang the bell, asked for me, & begged me to give her an autograph of Mr W. – I had
none. 'Where could she get one?' I did not know. – Her pretty face looked as sad as if she
had lost a lover.

'At this moment', Mary observed a few days earlier, 'a groupe of young Tourists
are standing before the window (I am writing in the Hall) and Wm reading a
newspaper – and on lifting up his head a profound bow greeted him from each –
they look as if come up from the Steamer for the day. I wish you could have seen
them.'

As Mary and Dora's joint birthday approached, Mary again persuaded the poet
to leave home, taking him on a ten-day nostalgic excursion to their remaining
friends and relatives at Penrith, Newbiggin and Hallsteads.

On 24 September news came from Brigham that Isabella Wordsworth had died
in Italy. This must have come as something of a surprise, for the family had long
since ceased to believe she had any genuine ailment. As Quillinan commented, her
loss could not weigh heavily with the Wordsworths, but it was the cause of
additional anxiety about John and his children. The two oldest boys, Henry and
William, were now at Sedbergh, their father's *alma mater*, but the three younger
ones were effectively being brought up by fifteen-year-old Jane. It had now
become much more difficult for the Wordsworths to leave home because William's
humouring of his sister since Dora's death had made Dorothy more tyrannical than
ever. At the end of November, however, they managed to spend a fortnight at
Brigham, where they found the whole household more than ever dependent on
Jane, and father and daughter equally determined that she should not be sent off
to school again. It was a sign of William's mounting spirits that, on their return
journey, he was able to face not only an overnight visit to Mary Stanger, Dora's
earliest schoolfriend, at Keswick, but also a trip to Applethwaite, the little estate
which Beaumont had given to him and he in turn had passed to Dora.

Robinson had deliberately delayed his annual visit till after Christmas, fearing
a repetition of the emotional scenes of the previous year, but when he arrived on
27 December he was relieved and rejoiced to find the Wordsworths 'far more
cheerful'. 'In the two days I have spent already here I have had more conversation
with the poet than during the whole of my last visit', he crowed to his brother. The
house was further enlivened by the presence of Henry and William, on holiday
from Sedbergh, and, on 28 December, by that of Derwent Coleridge, making his
first visit to the Lakes in many years.

The reason for Derwent's visit was anything but cheerful: he had been summoned to Nab Cottage to attend the deathbed of his fifty-two-year-old brother, Hartley. Derwent's presence relieved Mary of the daily burden of nursing and visiting Hartley, as well as the responsibility for him which she had borne since his mother had left the Lakes in 1829. She had kept an eye on him, paid his bills, organized his clothes and doled out the allowance provided by his family to prevent him spending it all at once on a drunken binge. She had not always been successful and Hartley's fatal illness was the result of his having got drunk and spent five hours in the open air on a wet and windy night trying to find his way home. 'A more worthless life cannot be imagined than his', Robinson wrote disapprovingly, but Hartley was beloved by all in the vales around his home, and by the Wordsworths more than most. As he lay dying, he was tended by four doctors, all of whom gave their services free of charge. When Hartley died, on 6 January 1849, William was 'dreadfully affected', and could not go in to see his body. Appropriately, it was left to Mary to perform the final rites for the eccentric man to whom she had been a second mother since childhood.

Two days later Robinson accompanied William and Derwent to Grasmere churchyard, to choose where Hartley should lie. As far as William was concerned, there was only one appropriate place. 'When I turned from my daughter's grave', he said of Dora's funeral, 'the first face that met me was Hartley's standing there!' On 11 January Hartley was buried on a bitter cold day, when the mountains were capped with snow and showers of sleet were interspersed with gleams of sunshine. William and Quillinan attended the funeral, without ill-effect on the poet's mind. Robinson returned to London later that day with the 'comfortable assurance' that his old friend's grief was now 'softened down to an endurable sadness'. Even his long-suffering wife was cautiously optimistic: 'I think I may say, with much thankfulness, that y[ou]r dear Uncle's spirits begin to revive, <u>even</u> when he is <u>not</u> in company.'

The day after Hartley's funeral William walked through snow and sleet to Loughrigg Holme and sat for an hour 'in his most cheerful mood', talk about his grandchildren leading him to reminisce about his own boyhood and then to talk of Coleridge. 'If I had been inclined to Boswellise, this would have been one of my days for it. He was particularly interesting', Quillinan noted. Visiting Willy at Carlisle a few weeks later, with Mary and their sister-in-law Mary Hutchinson, William was so far his old self as to be drawn into Willy's protest against the latest proposed changes at the Stamp Office, which threatened a further reduction in his income, weighing in with so many letters to the Prime Minister, Sir Robert Peel, and the Chancellor of the Exchequer, Sir Charles Wood, that he clearly tried their patience.

In June the Wordsworths had a reunion with Miss Fenwick, who had taken lodgings at Malvern while they were on a visit to the Hutchinsons at Mathon. On the 21st they were joined by Robinson and Moxon and the visit confirmed all Robinson's hopes about William. 'Wordsworth was in good *health*, but the *strength* of his mind has declined – There is no want of intelligence, but of vigour – No delusions but little power – happy but not active. Is not this a comfortable old age?'

The day after their arrival, Robinson and Moxon joined the Wordsworths and Hutchinsons on a picnic party at the top of the Camp, a hill about five miles from Malvern. William was soon forced to mount one of the carriages, but he explored the hilltop entrenchments with the best of them and, two days later, aged seventy-nine, 'crossed the Malvern Hill *twice* without suffering any inconvenience'.

At the end of the month they arrived at Rydal Mount to find Elizabeth and Hannah Cookson waiting to welcome them. 'My dearest Brother,' Mary wrote to Tom that evening, 'I trust to hear a good account of you – and I must hope we may meet again – even in this world – but our prayers must be offered for a heavenly Union that may not be severed. That the Almighty may award us all this blessing is what we now yearn after – satisfied as we ought to be with our earthly blessings – and grateful to be supported under its trials.' For once, William echoed her. 'A mournful return it is to this place, but upon that sorrow I must not dwell. May God give us strength to support our grievous and irreparable loss with resignation to his Will. It is not long that Persons in their 80th year can have to bear these trials.'

The Wordsworths had left Mathon on Saturday morning and reached their home that same evening. At ten o'clock on Monday evening, they were startled by the unexpected arrival of their nephew Tom Hutchinson. He had come, at his mother's request, to break to them, in person and as gently as possible, the news that his father, whom they had left fit and well, had died suddenly and peacefully in the early hours of that morning. 'What a shock for those old people –', Quillinan exclaimed. 'Mrs Wordsworth's favourite brother!' 'He was a beloved friend & Brother to me', Mary mourned. Apart from her youngest brother, George, with whom she had never been very intimate, she was the only one of the ten Hutchinson siblings left alive.

The day after Thomas's arrival, the Wordsworths were to have been guests at the wedding of 'Cousin Dorothy' Harrison's daughter, another Dora. James was dispatched to Green Bank to break the news that they could not come, but, on the morning of the wedding, William had a change of heart. Though he declined to attend the festivities afterwards, he did go to church and gave away the bride, as he had promised to do. 'Mr & Mrs Wordsworth are wonderfully well, and *he* is even cheerful, or seems so, to his neighbours & other visitors', Quillinan observed on 12 July. 'I believe it is true "that one great grief makes every other less"'.

Visitors there were a-plenty, including John and all five of his children. Fifteen-year-old Henry had just been removed from Sedbergh and was belatedly swotting for his entrance examinations to the Royal Naval College at Woolwich. Having observed him at work, or rather not at work, his grandfather realized that he was unlikely to pass and wrote to Lord Grey, the Secretary for War, candidly blaming Henry's 'own slackness' for the need to seek a deferral from November to the following May. His place at Sedbergh was to be taken by his ten-year-old brother, Charles, but none of the brothers showed the academic ability of William the third, who was destined for a first-class honours degree at Balliol College, Oxford, and to become a pioneer of Indian education. With the departure of Charles, Jane, too, was about to be sent to school in Edinburgh, to acquire those ladylike refinements her grandmother thought she needed.

Mary and Dora's joint birthday, 16 August, passed unmarked. 'Nothing was said about it,' Quillinan told Robinson, 'though they & I well knew that the day was not forgotten.' The Wordsworths did not accompany Quillinan, a month later, to Grasmere churchyard to see the erection of a headstone on Dora's grave. More elaborate than any of the other Wordsworth graves, it was carved with a pattern of ivy leaves round the edge and depicted a lamb, bearing the Cross, at the top. The inscription was simple enough, 'Dora Quillinan 9th Day of July 1847. Him that cometh to me I will in no wise cast out', for Quillinan's original choice of verse had been vetoed by Chris Wordsworth as being 'expressive of, and identified with, a dangerous System of Theology'.

On 1 November, the first two volumes of the six-volume *Poetical Works of William Wordsworth* were published. This was the last edition to appear in the poet's lifetime, but he had played little more than a consultative role in its preparation. Minor corrections of punctuation and proofreading could safely be delegated to Quillinan and Carter who had also been responsible for this year's new edition of the cheap single-volume, double-columned *Poems of William Wordsworth*. Even excluding this latter edition, William estimated that the sale of his poems was running at about 1,000 copies a year, 'which is remarkable as it is upwards of half a century since I began to publish'.

Accolades continued to flow in upon him from every direction. He was invited as a guest of honour to attend the public dinner in Edinburgh to mark the unveiling of the monument to Scott and to the inaugural meeting of a Shakespeare Anniversary festival at Stratford-upon-Avon. To his great pride, he was again proposed as a candidate for the Lord Rectorship of the University of Glasgow, winning a majority of the student votes but, owing to the form of the election, losing to Lord John Russell at the final stage by the casting vote of the then Lord Rector. What was particularly gratifying was that the candidates were almost always drawn from the field of politics, but the students had nominated him 'from a high admiration of your Genius & literary greatness'. The defeat came as a relief, for he feared to cause offence by declining a post which he felt himself too old to accept. Had he known Russell's own sentiments, he would probably have felt the honour even more. 'I should be very sorry to be the cause of preventing the election of Mr Wordsworth', Russell wrote during the contest. '. . . Cannot you represent to the students that I think this would be a good opportunity of making the distinction purely literary? It is a great honour to be thought of for the honour, but I should greatly prefer seeing it conferred on Mr Wordsworth, whose genius has performed so much in which men of all political parties find delight.'

'The time is drawing on for our good friend Mr Robinson's annual visit to us, which we always look forward to with much pleasure', Mary wrote on 29 October. 'You will find your old and faithful friend the poet pretty much as he was on y[ou]r last visit', Quillinan wrote reassuringly. 'The same social cheerfulness – company cheerfulness – the same fixed despondency (uncorrected) I esteem him for both: I love him best for the latter.' For the first time in many years, however, Robinson did not come, being reluctant to face the journey as he had just had a large carbuncle on his back lanced under the new anaesthetic, chloroform. 'Mrs Arnold said, Why, it will be hardly Xmas here without him! – & so we all think', Quillinan replied. 'But what must be must.' It was a decision Robinson was to regret ever after.

Despite Robinson's absence, a large party gathered at Rydal Mount for the double celebration of Christmas Day and Dorothy's seventy-eighth birthday: Quillinan and his two daughters, Hannah Cookson, who had been staying for some time with the Wordsworths, Rolleston, the curate, and three of John's sons. Dorothy herself came down in the evening to join them, as was now her custom. On 2 January William and Mary were invited to Loughrigg Holme. 'Today we are to dine at Mr Quillinans', William told Miss Fenwick, 'a trial which I feel that I am unable to bear as with due submission to God's Will I ought to do. May He have mercy upon me, and upon the Mother of Her whom we have lost.'

The winter of 1850 was long, severe and changeable, alternating between snow and rain, then harsh frosts. The Quillinans were snowed up for several days under Loughrigg and walking was difficult with the snow and slush. William amused himself by the fireside, correcting a memoir of his old friend Westall, written by the artist's son, and regretting that he could not recollect anything further to add to it. On 10 March he attended the morning service at Rydal chapel, as usual, and then in the evening insisted on accompanying Quillinan on his walk to Grasmere churchyard. It was 'very keen cold weather' but he refused to be mollycoddled into wrapping up well. 'I remonstrated with him on being so thinly clad', Quillinan protested, but William simply said, '"I care nothing about it" . . . as if poor man he was invulnerable'. With his niece Ebba Hutchinson, he walked as far as Town End, leaving Quillinan to visit Dora's grave alone. The next day, with Mary, Ebba and her sister, Sarah, he called at Loughrigg Holme to say goodbye to his son-in-law, who was going on a week-long visit to Armathwaite and Carlisle. It was, as Quillinan noted in his diary with a certain grim satisfaction, 'the last house he was ever in except his own'.

On 13 March he went to bed early, complaining of a cold. A week later Mary told Moxon that her husband had suffered a 'severe attack' in consequence of catching cold, but he was much better and they hoped he would be quite well again in a few days' time. On 22 March, Quillinan had every reason to hope that the crisis had passed and there was no longer any danger. William had enjoyed an excellent night and Mary had 'shared the good & sound sleep that has been so beneficial to him'; neither of them had heard Miss Fenwick's cuckoo clock outside their bedroom door between three and seven in the morning. At this stage, Quillinan was more concerned about Mary's 'indefatigable nursing'; 'she is very unwilling to accept help, thinking, no doubt quite justly, that her services are more acceptable to her husband than those of anyone else'.

'This vile bright keen half-snowy cutting north-easterly weather is not good for any age, least of all for old age', Quillinan complained. It was unfortunate, they all felt, that William's trusted friend Dr Davy was absent. 'It is impossible for any medical assistance to be more kindly & anxiously given than that which Mr W receives', Quillinan admitted. 'But unluckily (<u>entre nous</u>) he says he does not like the <u>dolorous</u> face of Green, whom we all understand to be a very able man. I ventured to tell Fell to-day to ask his partner not to look so <u>very</u> solemn.' By the end of the month, William was free from fever, 'but without appetite & very low and weak and inert', and Quillinan was sick of writing bulletins on his father-in-law's health. Mary had wisely tried to keep William's illness a secret from all but their closest friends, knowing that they would be inundated with inquiries, but too many people in Ambleside had too many contacts in London for such news to be suppressed for long. The harassing duty of answering them all devolved on Quillinan. 'I rather submit to the infliction than offend well-meaning though not always considerate, enquirers', he said. 'I answer them *all*! You may suppose I have enough to do, though to some I am very *curt*.' Very few of them even deserved a reply, he thought; two-thirds, he estimated, 'only value Wordsworth for his fame, not from any appreciation of the sterling quality of his mind, nor from even any thing like apprehension of his genius'.

On Easter Sunday, 31 March, Fell assured them all that William was improving. His pulse was steady and his breathing 'free & strong'. Mary was so cheered that she left her husband to attend church and take the sacrament. 'You will be glad to hear that dear William is better', she wrote to Mary Hutchinson,

yet I dare say it will be some time before he *thinks* himself as well as he was previous to this ugly attack – which any one who did not know him as I do, would have thought a *frightful* one: to me it has brought back his old habit of exaggerating his *bodily* ailments, which for nearly 3 years he has never seemed conscious of having *one* to complain of, so completely has his mind been engrossed by his sorrows.

William was not better, however. The pleurisy or pneumonia that had threatened his lungs seemed to have been kept at bay by blistering and the application of leeches, but almost all his strength had gone with the fever. He was growing progressively weaker and more lethargic: he would not eat, move nor speak. On 6 April Dr Davy returned from town. Quillinan called on him immediately and Davy went straight up to Rydal Mount. His verdict was hopeful: the patient was in 'a precarious state but <u>not</u> a <u>hopeless</u> one' and he needed strengthening. The next day, William's eightieth birthday, prayers were said for him in Rydal chapel and Davy thought him already improved. 'Since tea he has awaked and so sweetly!' Mary told Miss Fenwick two days later, 'asking me "if I thought he would ever get well?" and upon my expressing my thoughts and explaining why he was so weak and what was to be done to regain lost strength, he jocosely observed – "You preach very nicely" – "Now read to me." This office I turned over to [Ebba], to whom he said "You must excuse me if I fall asleep" – And truly it is even so'. Despite Davy's continuing optimism, Mary was wiser. 'The hopes beloved Friend which lingered about my heart when last Evening I wrote so far,' she continued in a shaking hand, '*have* after a quiet night, passed away, and I feel I must – and I feel

I must [*sic*] no longer [no longer: deleted] rest them *here*. I have your prayers and your invaluable love.'

Her unperceptive son John was almost brutal in his assessment of the situation. 'What we have now, I think, most cause to apprehend, is his falling into a condition in some respects similar to our dear Aunt's', he informed his cousin. 'Habitual somnolence, apathy, or paralytic affection is I think to be apprehended.' To prevent it, William was removed from bed and forced to sit in an armchair for an hour every day. 'This is a most painful operation, to all the parties concerned,' John admitted, 'though on his part it arises in a great measure from extreme sensitiveness & nervous apprehension. From the lusty manner in which he screams out when touched he cannot be as weak as he appears to be'. John tried to rally his father with bracing advice, holding up the example of Scott, who had preferred to die of the remedies rather than the disease. '<u>He</u> on the contrary gives way to the disease in every way – but this <u>in fact</u> is mainly <u>the disease</u> – there is no organic mischief going on.'

John and Willy came as often as they could to Rydal Mount, but the constant daily attendance devolved on Mary, with the devoted assistance of Quillinan, the Hutchinson girls, James, and Hannah Holmes, one of the servants, who all took turns at the bedside vigil. Mary, as usual, was a tower of strength. Dorothy, amazingly, seemed 'as much herself as she ever was in her life, & has an absolute *command* of her own will! does not make noises; is not all self; thinks of the feelings of others (Mrs W's for example), is tenderly anxious about her brother; &, in short, but for age & bodily infirmity, is almost *the* Miss Wordsworth we knew in past days.'

By 20 April even John had realized that there was no hope. He gave his father the sacrament for the last time and decreed that he should be left in peace. William lay tranquil and undisturbed in a small bed at the foot of the one he had shared with Mary for almost half a century. 'Poor dear Mother was sadly overcome last night', Willy wrote to his wife and baby daughter at eleven o'clock on the morning of 23 April:

she went to bed at eleven, & she only got out of her bed once during my stretch to have a look at poor dear Father, & try to wrap up his poor cold feet in a warm flannel shawl, to w[hi]ch he was as averse as ever the moment he felt the clothes being moved – Dear Mother did however gain snatches of sleep & pleased I was whenever I heard her poor sobs subdued by them . . . Dear Aunt Hutchinson much to dearest Mother's comfort arrived by mail this morning . . . I wish you were both here this lovely day & could hear the glorious thrush that has been singing on the mount ever since day break . . .

Before he could sign his name to his letter, Willy was called back to his parents' bedroom and within ten minutes all was over. William had passed away so calmly and so 'very very quietly' that his beloved Miss Fenwick's cuckoo clock could be heard distinctly, shouting the midday hour outside the bedroom door. Across the Vale of Rydal, high up on Loughrigg Fell, Fanny Arnold and her sister watched as the blinds were slowly drawn down at Rydal Mount and they knew that William Wordsworth was dead.

The funeral was held on 27 April. Mary had hoped to keep it as private as possible, so, apart from the immediate family, only Davy was invited. Few were asked, but many came. It was a day, Quillinan said, 'which will long be remembered in these vales, for almost all their population was in the Church & Church-yard of Grasmere'. When the family arrived at the church, they found it filled with ladies and gentlemen, all dressed in the deepest mourning. 'When Mrs Wordsworth, supported by her two sons, followed the coffin into the church, I should not have recognized her figure, it was so bowed down with grief', Mrs Fletcher said; 'but she bore it calmly, and I stood opposite to her when she bent over the grave.' William was buried, as he wished to be, beside the daughter he had loved so much. When Mary got into the carriage to go home she almost fainted, but the courage that had borne her through so many trials did not fail her now. By the time she returned to Rydal Mount she had regained her composure so completely that she was able to make tea for all the assembled mourners.

Mrs Fletcher, only a few months older than William herself, who had arrived in the Lakes imbued with the Edinburgh disdain for the poet and the man but, through years of intimacy, had learned to respect both, and owed her home at Lancrigg and its beautiful grounds to his taste and judgement, wrote a touching poem after the funeral. *Thoughts on leaving Grasmere Churchyard, April 27, 1850, after the Funeral of William Wordsworth* is moving on two levels: first, because it is a sincere, if amateur, expression of feeling, but second, and more important, because it could not have been written had there not been a William Wordsworth. Even to its use of blank verse, it is imbued with his spirit, his style, his message, despite the fact that Mrs Fletcher was his diametric opposite in faith and politics. It is a fitting tribute, of the kind William himself would have most appreciated, because it was unsolicited and spoke from the heart.

> We saw him laid within the quiet grave,
> Near to the yew he had planted. 'Twas a day
> Of most rare brightness, and the little birds
> Sang no sad requiem o'er the hallowed spot:
> 'Twas as they welcomed him to his last home.
> All Nature glowed instinct with tender love
> For him, her fervent worshipper, no more
> To chant her praises 'mid her mountain wilds,
> Her streams and valleys, 'vocal thro' his song.'
> There lives not one whose pilgrimage on earth
> Has been more blest, by God's especial grace,
> In stirring Heaven-ward thoughts in fellow-men.
> His was no narrow creed; he loved mankind
> Because God's law is love; and many hearts
> In loneliness and grief have felt his power

Work like a charm within them, lifting high
Their thoughts from earthly aims and sordid cares
To life's great purpose for the world to come.
Sweet was the privilege of those who shared
His daily converse, marked his blameless course,
And learned the true philosophy of life
Under his teaching, simple, but sublime.
Peace to his honoured memory; peace to those
Who cherish fervently within their souls
The beautiful realities he taught.

The headstone that was eventually erected over William's grave was, as he wished, stark in its simplicity. A plain piece of Lakeland stone, it simply stated to the curious passer-by, 'William Wordsworth 1850'. As neither of his sons had a grain of poetry in them, it was left to Quillinan, the son-in-law who had so often felt excluded, to pronounce his elegy.

It is said that Shak[e]speare died, on his birthday, April 23, if that be the real date. This great man, Wordsworth, was no Shak[e]speare, and the dramatic power perhaps was not in him. But he had a grand and tender genius of his own that will live in the heart of his country; and these mountains will be his noblest monument. His life was a long & prosperous life, and he was rewarded in the latter part of it at least, for the virtuous use he had made of the great power entrusted to him, with 'honour, love, obedience, troops of friends, & all that should accompany old age.' He has, no doubt, now a higher reward: he is gone to Dora.

Epilogue

Mary Wordsworth remained quietly at Rydal Mount, outliving many of those she cared most about. Edward Quillinan died of pleurisy on 8 July 1851, a day short of the fourth anniversary of Dora's death. Dorothy, whose newly regained self-possession deserted her as soon as her brother died, survived him by almost five years. Mary remained devoted to her, despite the increasing difficulty of managing her as she became more restless and violent. Dorothy died, aged eighty-four, on 25 January 1855 and was buried in Grasmere churchyard, next to 'her loved Companion' Sara Hutchinson.

Mary found consolation in her family, as she had always done, becoming the much-loved confidante of her grandchildren, whose fortunes in Australia and in the Crimean War she followed with pride, anxiety and simple empathy. 'My belongings', as she referred to them, were the business of her life. Though her eyesight gradually failed until she became totally blind, she remained calm, cheerful and uncomplaining. When she died, aged eighty-eight, in January 1859, her son John declared he had never seen a happier deathbed. She died, as she had lived, contented with her lot, thankful for the kindness shown her, and trusting implicitly in the faith which had upheld her through so many and such long trials. And being the competent organizer that she was, she had quietly arranged the precise spot where she was to be buried. William had wanted to be buried next to Dora. In the crowded Wordsworth corner of Grasmere churchyard there was not enough room between her grave and that of Sara Hutchinson to allow for two separate graves. When William was buried Mary had therefore ordered the grave to be dug deep enough to contain her own coffin as well as her husband's. That way, she said, she had 'the heartfelt satisfaction' of knowing 'that She, as well as the Father, would lie beside their beloved daughter'.

Index